Low-Band DXing

by John Devoldere, ON4UN

Published by the
American Radio Relay League
225 Main Street
Newington, CT 06111

Preface

In 1961, when I received my Amateur Radio license at the age of 19, low-band DXing was quite different from what it is today. It was then an occasional activity for a small elite group of amateurs. Little, if anything, was written about low-frequency DXing in the Amateur Radio magazines. The receivers in use in those days were quickly saturated by the many strong commercial signals present on the low-frequency ham bands after dark (especially 80 meters), so most amateurs used the low bands only for local contacts.

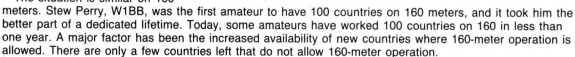

It took me five years to work my first 100 countries on 80 meters. Now, well-equipped stations have done it in one contest weekend. It is also obvious that the 5-band DXCC, 5-band WAS and 5-band WAZ awards have greatly promoted low-band DXing.

The situation is similar on 160 meters. Stew Perry, W1BB, was the first amateur to have 100 countries on 160 meters, and it took him the better part of a dedicated lifetime. Today, some amateurs have worked 100 countries on 160 in less than one year. A major factor has been the increased availability of new countries where 160-meter operation is allowed. There are only a few countries left that do not allow 160-meter operation.

After 26 years of 80 meter DXing (with ups and downs, yielding over 110,000 QSOs in my 70 logbooks), I have now come to the point where I need only eight countries in order to have all ARRL DXCC countries confirmed.

Besides holding the 5-band DXCC and 5-band WAS, I am also the proud holder of the USA-CA (United States County Award) for having worked and confirmed all 3086 US counties, all SSB (Cliff Corne award #417).

On January 1, 1987, we were given 160 meters in Belgium. In just over three months I have worked 140 countries, 47 states and 38 zones on 160. The knowledge I had accumulated on 80 meters was certainly the major reason for this success on the top band.

I have always considered that the CQ World Wide and the ARRL DX contests were excellent opportunities for evaluating my station performance. In 1965 I set a world record for 80-meters in the CQ World-Wide DX phone contest; in 1966 I was second worldwide in the same category; and in 1969 I helped set another world record in the multi-operator/single station category. In 1977, I made third worldwide on 14-MHz in the CQ World-Wide DX phone contest, and first worldwide on 14 MHz in the 1978 CQ WPX contest.

When I wrote my first book, *80-meter DX Handbook,* in 1976, there was a very limited amount of material available for the low-band DXer. I hope the book (which sold some 14,000 copies worldwide) was instrumental in helping some operators achieve greater success in 80-meter DXing. In the past five years, an abundance of articles on topics related to low-band DXing have appeared in Amateur Radio magazines. There is still a lack of well-organized material in the field, however. In addition, I have had many requests from readers of the first book (and from newer hams who could not find the original book) for a further edition.

The major part of this new book deals with antennas, related to low band DXing. Some theoretical aspects are addressed in more detail than is usual for amateur literature, only because of their particular importance. Vertical antenna design and vertical array design are two such topics.

In this era of personal computers, I have included a number of BASIC computer programs which will be of help to the serious DXer. The programs related to array network design are essential for the design of a properly working array system. Theoretical analysis as well as the design of antennas has always been complicated because of the amount of number crunching involved. The advent of personal computers has now made this all fast and easy. I sincerely hope some readers will also discover this aspect of Amateur Radio.

I hope this new book, including a systematically organized list of reference works, will fill a gap. If you find the book useful, please let me know.

I dedicate this book to Marlene.

John Devoldere, ON4UN/AA4OI
215 Poelstraat
B9220 Merelbeke
Belgium
May 1987

Acknowledgments

Collecting all the material used in this book would not have been possible without help received from many friends. This assistance is much appreciated. Wilfried, ON4HW, was of invaluable help in providing the astronomical equations for sunrise and sunset times. Sincere thanks to Guenter, DL1BU, Forest, K2BT and Jim, AC3J for their stimulating help. Many thanks to my proofreaders: Ghis, ON5NT, Ben, OZ8BV and my colleague at work, Bob Bland. Additional thanks go to all my 80-meter DX friends who participated in the survey and sent me information on their stations, antennas and DX status, as well as photographs; all this was welcome material for the book.

I would also like to thank all those who have published articles related to low-band DXing (especially antenna articles). Such articles make Amateur Radio progress. I have tried to include a complete bibliography in this book. Forgive me if I have omitted a few articles. My special thanks go to those who allowed me to quote from their work.

Finally, I know I neglected my family during the many months it took to write this book. Without the understanding and encouragement of Frida and Marlene I would never have finished the book. Thank you both.

Trademark Notices

Apple is a registered trademark of Apple Computer, Inc.
Commodore 64 is a registered trademark of Commodore Business Machines, Inc.
Commodore 128 is a registered trademark of Commodore Business Machines, Inc.
CP/M is a registered trademark of Digital Reasearch, Inc.
IBM is a registered trademark of International Business Machines Corp.
MS-DOS is a registered trademark of Microsoft Corporation
PRO-DOS is a registered trademark of Apple Computer, Inc.

Table of Contents

Chapter III Transmitters

Chapter IV Receivers

Chapter V Transceivers

Chapter VI Low-Band DX Operating

Chapter VII Computer Programs

Chapter VIII Literature Review

Index

Chapter I
Low-Band Propagation

Most professional literature on radio propagation describes graphical methods for determining optimum HF propagation for a given path at a given time of day. While these methods are considered quite reliable for relatively short distances (up to 5000 km or 3000 miles typically), studying these methods will give the interested radio amateur very little insight into propagation mechanisms. The use of graphical methods in amateur radio is indeed very limited, as is the degree of applicability (not all frequencies can be used, there are certain power restrictions etc). We will start from some very basic observations and mechanisms to explain particular aspects of radio propagation on 80 meters. Basic principles of radio propagation by ionospheric refraction are described in great

detail in many handbooks (Ref 101, 103, 104 and 105), and will not be dealt with here.

Basically there are two parameters which determine and influence 80-meter propagation: *Time* and *Location*.

1.1 Time

With regard to propagation, time is considered not only for short durations but also long durations. We will consider time in three aspects: the *year*, the *season* and the *time of day*.

1.1.1 THE YEAR

It is well known that radio propagation by ionospheric

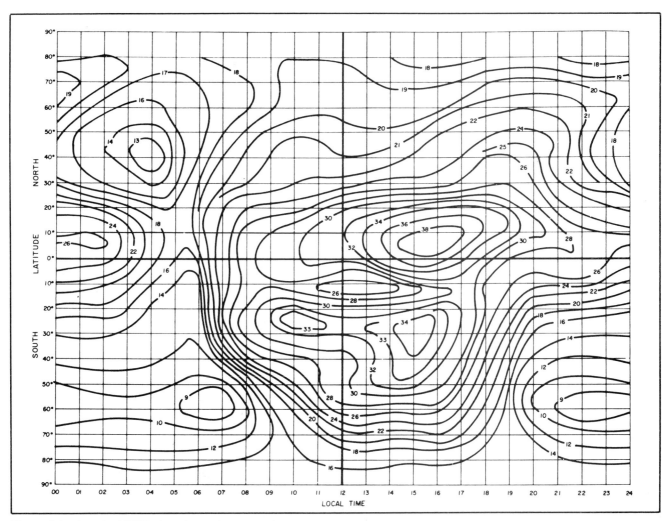

Figure 1.1—A typical MUF chart for a given month (June 1968). Note the lower MUF regions in the southern hemisphere where it is winter.

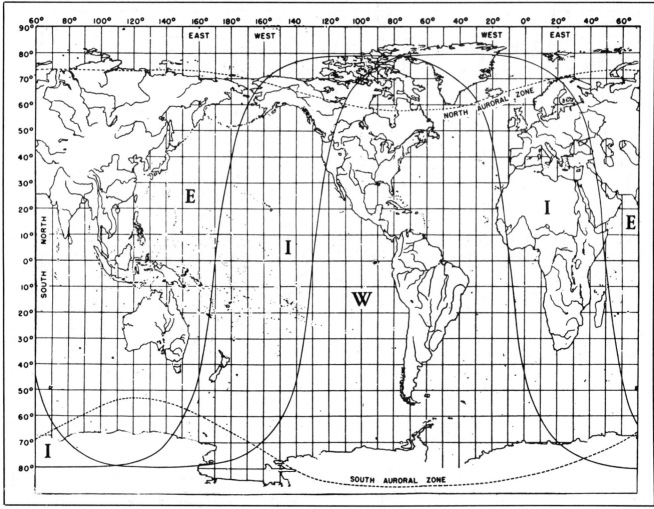

Figure 1.2—A world map made by the conform or Mercator projection. If a transparent copy of the MUF chart (Figure 1.1) is made, it can be used as an overlay on this and shifted horizontally (to adjust local times) to find the actual location of MUF boundaries.

refraction is greatly influenced by the sunspot cycle, simply because ionization is caused mainly by ultraviolet radiation from the sun, which in turn is highly dependent on solar activity. Sunspot activity will influence 80-meter propagation in three major areas: MUF (maximum usable frequency), D-layer activity (absorption) and the frequency of magnetic disturbances.

1.1.1.1 Maximum Usable Frequency (MUF) and Optimum Communication Frequency (FOT)

The MUF is the highest frequency at which reliable radio communications via ionospheric propagation can be maintained over a given path. The MUF changes with time and your specific location on the earth, or to be more exact, with the geographic location of the ionospheric refraction points. The MUF for a given path with multiple refraction points will be equal to the lowest MUF along the path. Figure 1.1 shows a typical MUF chart. From this chart we can see that the MUF is lower during local winter and much lower at night than during the daytime. This is a typical overlay chart that can be used in conjunction with a conform or Mercator projection map of the Earth (Figure 1.2), in methods for predicting propagation paths. With the aid of a great-circle overlay chart (Figure 1.3) we can identify the MUF along a given great-circle path between two points. It is generally

accepted that the optimum communication frequency (FOT) is about 80 percent of the MUF. On much lower frequencies, the situation is less than optimum as the absorption in the ionosphere increases. We now have computer programs available that will accurately predict MUF and FOT for a given path (see Section 1.4.6).

We have all experienced that a high sunspot number means a high MUF and good conditions on 10 and 15 meters. Higher absorption on the low-frequency bands can also be expected during sunspot maxima.

The *critical frequency* is the highest frequency at which a signal transmitted straight up at a 90 degree elevation angle is returned to Earth. The critical frequency is continuously measured in several hundred places on Earth by devices called ionosondes. At frequencies higher than the critical frequency all energy will travel through the ionosphere and be lost in space (Figure 1.4). The critical frequency varies with sunspot cycle, time of year and day, as well as geographical location. Typical values are 9 MHz at noon and 5 MHz at night.

During periods with low sunspot activity the critical frequency can be as low as 2 MHz. During those times we can witness dead zones on 80 meters at night.

At frequencies slightly higher than the critical frequency, refraction will occur for a relatively high wave angle and all lower angles. As we increase the frequency, the maximum

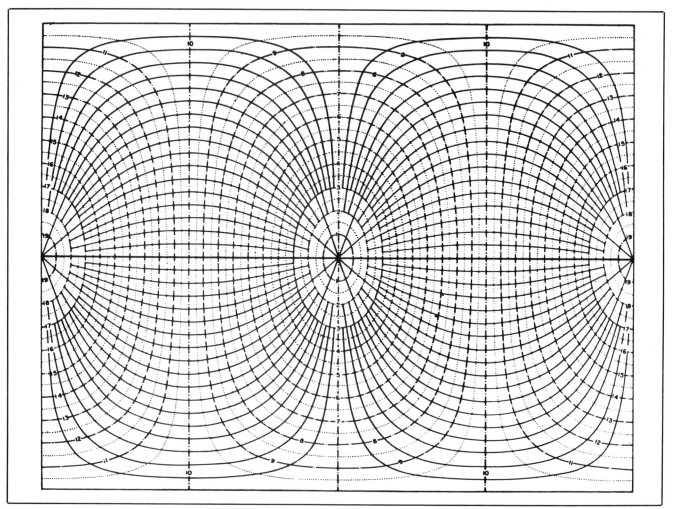

Figure 1.3—This great-circle chart is used with the Mercator projection of the world (Figure 1.2). Each of the solid lines represents a great circle (the radial lines on a great-circle or azimuthal projection map). The dashed lines give great-circle distances in thousand kilometers. This chart is also to be used as an "overlay" on the world map from Figure 1.2.

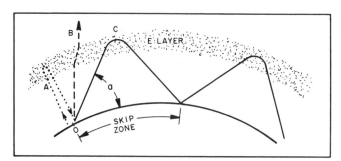

Figure 1.4—Ionospheric Propagation. In case A we witness refraction of a vertically transmitted wave. This means that the frequency is below the critical frequency. In case B the angle is too high or the frequency too high and the refraction is not sufficient to return the wave to earth. In case C we have the highest angle at which the refracted wave will return to earth. The higher the frequency the lower the angle A will become. Note the "skip zone."

elevation angle at which we have ionospheric refraction will become lower and lower. At 30 MHz during periods of active sunspots, such angles can be on the order of 10 degrees.

The relation between MUF and critical frequency is the wave elevation angle, where:

$$MUF = F_{CRIT} \times \left(\frac{1}{\sin (a)} \right)$$

where a = angle of elevation.

Table 1 gives an overview of the multiplication factor ($1/\sin(a)$) for a number of take-off angles (a). For the situation where the critical frequency is as low as 2 MHz it can be seen that any 3.8-MHz energy radiated at angles higher than 30 degrees will be lost in space. This is one reason for using an antenna with a low radiation angle for the low bands.

Several researchers have performed long series of measurements to ascertain the radiation angles of HF signals for a given path. Most of the work has been done between Europe and the US, and the figures obtained must be handled

Table 1

Multiplication Factor for Varying Take-Off Angle

a (degrees)	10	20	30	40	50	60	70	80	90
$\dfrac{1}{\sin(a)}$	5.8	2.3	2.0	1.6	1.3	1.2	1.1	1.0	1.0

with care before extrapolating them to different paths and different path lengths. For a path between New Jersey and Germany, angles between 10 and 45 degrees are quoted for 80 meters by Schwarzbeck (Ref 111). This subject will be further addressed in Chapter 2.

1.1.1.2 D-Layer Activity

During the day, the lowest ionospheric layer in existence is the D layer, at an altitude of 40 to 60 miles (60 to 100 km). Figure 1.5 shows how low-angle, low-frequency signals are absorbed by the D layer. The D layer absorbs signals rather than refracting them because it is much denser than the other ionospheric layers. The density of neutral, non-ionized particles, which make up the bulk of the mass in this region, is 1000 times greater in the D layer than in the E layer. For a layer to refract, the number of neutral atoms must be small enough so that they do not frequently collide with free electrons. In the D layer however, a given electron will collide with an atom about 10 million times per second, and so the electrons are not given the chance to refract signals, and absorption occurs instead. The absorption level is inversely proportional to the arrival angle of the signal, so high-angle signals pass through relatively unattenuated. This is why our high angle (low to the ground) dipoles work so well for local traffic on 80 meters. Around sunset, the D layer begins to dissipate; it disappears completely at night and is reformed around sunrise.

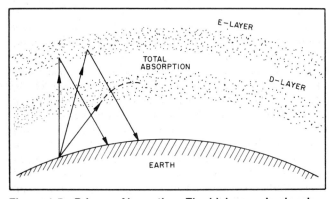

Figure 1.5—D-Layer Absorption. The higher-angle signals pass through the D layer and are reflected by the E layer. Low-angle signals are absorbed. This explains the need for a high-angle radiator to work short-range stations during daytime.

How does the sunspot cycle affect this phenomenon? When sunspot activity is low, the formation of the D layer is slower; D-layer build-up before noon is less pronounced, while the evening disintegration of the layer occurs faster. This is because there is less ultraviolet energy from the sun to create and sustain the high ionization level of the D layer. This means, in turn, that at sunspot minimum, absorption in the D layer will be less than at sunspot maximum, especially around dusk and dawn.

The absorption mechanism of the D layer has been studied repeatedly during solar eclipses. Reports (Ref 121 and 125) show that during an eclipse, D-layer attenuation is greatly reduced and signals similar to nighttime signals are produced on short-range paths.

1.1.1.3 Frequency of Magnetic Disturbances

Auroral activity is one of the great 80-meter propagation

anomalies and still largely a field of research for scientists. Amateurs living within a radius of a few thousand miles around the magnetic poles know all about the consequences of the phenomenon. The aurora phenomenon will be covered in detail in Section 1.2.2.

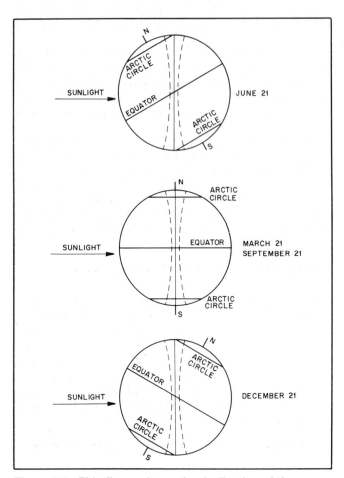

Figure 1.6—This figure shows the declination of the sun and the different position of the terminator (solid line) at different times of the year. The gray line is represented as a zone of variable width to emphasize that its behavior near the poles differs from its behavior near the equator.

1.1.2 THE SEASON

We all know the mechanism that originates our seasons: the declination of the sun against the equator. The inclination reaches a maximum of 23.5 degrees around December 21 and June 21 (see Figure 1.6). This coincides with the middle of the winter and the middle of the summer. At those times the days are longest or shortest and the sun rises to the highest or lowest point at local noon in the non-equatorial zones.

On the equator, the sun will rise to its highest point at local noon twice a year, at equinox around September 21 and March 21. These are the times of the year when the sun-earth axis is perpendicular to the earth-axis proper (sun declination is zero), and when nights and days are equally long at any place on earth (equi = equal, nox = night). On December 21 and June 21, the sun is still very high at the equator (90 − 23.5 = 66.5 degrees). The maximum height of the sun at any latitude on Earth is given by the expression

height = 90 degrees + 23.5 degrees − north latitude

with a maximum of 90 degrees. In other words, the sun never

rises higher than 23.5 degrees at the Poles, and never higher than 53.5 degrees where the latitude is 60 degrees.

Because of this mechanism, it is clear that the seasonal influence of the sun on 80-meter propagation will be complementary in the northern and southern hemispheres. Any influence will be most prominent near the poles, and less pronounced in the equatorial zones (± 23.5 degrees of the equator). But how do the changing seasons influence 80-meter propagation?

1) The longer the sun's rays can create and activate the D-layer, the more absorption there will be during the dusk and dawn periods. During local winter the sun will rise to a much lower apex and the rate of sunrise will be much smaller, and accordingly D-layer ionization will build up much more slowly.

2) Many thunderstorms are generated in the summer. Electrical noise (QRN) will easily mask weaker DX signals and discourage even the most arduous DX operator.

3) When the nights are longest in winter, you will have the greatest possible time for DX openings. Indeed, you have to be in darkness or twilight not to suffer from excessive D-layer absorption and have acceptable conditions for long distance propagation on 80 meters.

1.1.2.1 Winter (15 October to 15 February in the Northern Hemisphere)

Low MUF, short days, lots of darkness, sun rising slowly, reduced D-layer activity at dusk and dawn, and no QRN from thunderstorms. This period is ideal for all stations located in the northern hemisphere during the winter. Conversely, this condition will not exist in the southern hemisphere. Therefore the winter period in the northern hemisphere is ideal for east-to-west and west-to-east propagation between two stations both located in the northern hemisphere. Typical paths are: US-Europe, US-Japan, US-Asia etc.

1.1.2.2 Summer (15 April to 15 August in the Northern Hemisphere)

Higher MUF, long days, faster rising sun, increased D-layer activity at dusk and dawn, and much QRN due to local thunderstorms. These factors create the worst conditions one can expect for east-to-west or west-to-east propagation in the northern hemisphere. What we should realize, however, is that while the large majority of amateurs may be fighting the local QRN in the northern hemisphere in summertime, our friends down under are enjoying ideal winter conditions.

1.1.2.3 Equinox Period (15 August to 15 October and 15 February to 15 April)

During these periods the ionospheric conditions are fairly similar in both the northern and the southern hemisphere: similar MUF values, days and nights approximately 12 hours long on both sides of the equator, reduced QRN etc. Clearly this is the ideal season for transequatorial propagation, especially the NE-SW and NW-SE paths. Typical examples are Europe to New Zealand and west coast US to Indian Ocean.

1.1.2.4 Propagation into the Equatorial Zones

In principle, all seasons can produce good conditions for propagation from the northern or southern hemisphere into but not across the equatorial zone. The only real limiting factor is the MUF distribution along the path and more so the amount of QRN in the equatorial zone itself. Unfortunately, there is no rule of thumb to tell us everything

about the electrical storm activities in these zones.

We must conclude that it is not true that DX on 80 meters can only be worked during the local winter. The equinox period is excellent for long-haul transequatorial propagation, while in the middle of the summer (QRN being acceptably low for us) rare DX stations from down under or from the equatorial zones are commonplace.

1.1.3 THE TIME OF DAY

We know how the Earth's rotation around its axis creates the mechanism of day and night. The transition from day to night is very abrupt in equatorial zones. The sun rises and sets very quickly; the opposite is true in the polar zones.

Let us, for convenience, subdivide the day into four periods:
1) Daytime (from after sunrise-dawn until before sunset-dusk)
2) Sunset-dusk (period around sunset)
3) Nighttime (from after sunset-dusk until before sunrise-dawn)
4) Sunrise-dawn (period around sunrise)

1.1.3.1 Daytime

After local sunrise, the D layer is slowly building up under the influence of ultraviolet radiation from the sun. Maximum D-layer ionization and activity is reached shortly after local noon. This means that from zero absorption (due to the D-layer) before sunrise, the absorption will gradually increase until a maximum is reached just after local noon. The degree of absorption will in the first instance depend on the height of the sun at any given time.

For example, near the poles, such as in northern Scandinavia, the sun rises late and sets early in local winter. The consequence will be a late and slow build-up of the D layer. In the middle of the winter the sun may be just above the horizon (for regions just below the north-pole circle, situated at $90 - 23.5 = 66.5$ degrees above the Equator), or actually below the horizon all day long for locations above the Arctic Circle. It can consequently be understood that absorption due to D-layer ionization will be minimal or nonexistent under these circumstances. This is why stations located in the polar regions can actually work 80-meter DX almost 24 hours a day in winter. Contacts between Finland or Sweden and the Pacific or the west coast of the US are not uncommon around local noon in northern Sweden and northern Finland at that time of year.

It is obvious that this is not a good example of typical daytime conditions, as in those polar regions we never actually have typical daytime conditions in midwinter but remain in dusk and dawn periods all day long.

It has been mentioned that during typical daytime conditions, when the D-layer ionization is very intense, low-angle signals will be totally absorbed while high-angle signals will get through and be refracted in the E-layer. Only at peak ionization, just after noon, may the absorption be noticeable on high-angle signals. The signal strength of local stations, received via ionospheric refraction, will dip to a minimum just after local noon. As stated before, in order to have good local coverage on 80 meters during daytime, it is essential to have an antenna with a high vertical angle of radiation. We will later see that this can very easily be obtained (for example with a low dipole).

1.1.3.2 Nighttime

After sunset, the D layer gradually dissolves and disappears. Consequently, good propagation conditions can be expected if both ends of the path, plus the area in between, are in darkness. The greatest distances can be covered if both ends of the path are at the opposite ends of the darkness zone (both located near the terminator, which is the dividing line between day and night). During nighttime, and with low sunspot activity, the critical frequency may descend to values below 3.7 MHz and dead zones (skip zones) will show up regularly.

1.3.3 DUSK AND DAWN; TWILIGHT PERIODS

The terminator, mentioned before, is only an imaginary dividing line between one half of the earth in daylight and the other half in darkness. Visual transition from day to night and vice versa happens quite abruptly in the equatorial zones, and very slowly in the polar zones (see Section 1.1.3.1). The so-called *gray line* is a gray band between day and night, usually referred to as the twilight zone. Dusk and dawn periods produce very interesting propagation conditions which are not limited to the lower HF frequencies.

Long before sunrise there is no D-layer activity above or in the western direction from a particular station location. Hence, there is no absorption at all (situation A in Figure 1.7). Later, as the earth rotates, we come to situation B, where the gradual build-up of the D layer commences at the transmitter site. Initially the density of ionization is rather low, and arriving signals will be refracted rather than absorbed. This phenomenon can lower the effective angle of radiation as seen from the reflecting E layer. This results in a longer single-hop distance or in a greater signal strength for a given number of hops. This is one of the reasons why DX signals always peak during the dusk and dawn periods over all E-W, NE-SW and NW-SE paths. This does not apply to N-S paths.

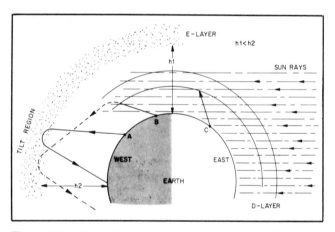

Figure 1.7—At sunrise signals are refracted slightly by the D layer which is only marginally ionized, and then refracted back to earth in the E layer. Due to the tilt in the E layer in the region where night changes into day, a further lowering of the effective radiation angle occurs.

In addition, the ionosphere, responsible for the refraction of the low-band signals, is changing abruptly in height at sunrise/sunset time. This effective ionospheric tilt helps to create the necessary conditions for trapped-wave or chordal-hop propagation (see further in this Section).

There is another reason why we seem to be able to work DX much better during these twilight periods. When the sun is rising in the morning, all signals coming from the east (which can often cause a great deal of QRM during the night) are greatly attenuated by the D layer existing in the east. The net result is often a much quieter band from one direction

(east in the morning and west in the evening), resulting in a much better signal-to-noise ratio on weak signals.

It is also of utmost importance to know how long these special propagation conditions exist; in other words how long the effects of the radio-twilight periods last. To understand the mechanism, it should be clear that the rate of D-layer build-up depends upon the rate of sunrise, or in other words the height of the sun at local noon. There are two factors that determine this rate: The season (the sun rises faster in summer than in winter) and the latitude of your location (the sun rises very high near the equator, and culminates in low angles near the poles).

The effect of advantageous propagation conditions at sunrise and sunset has been recognized since the early days of low-band DXing. It was Dale Hoppe, K6UA and Peter Dalton, W6NLZ who called the zone in which the special propagation conditions exist the *gray line* (Ref 108). The gray line is a zone centered around the geographical terminator. It should be clear from the above explanation that the effective width of the zone is certainly not constant over its total circumference, and will actually depend on the speed of sunrise. This means we have a narrow gray line near the equator, and a wide gray line near the poles. The time span during which we will benefit from typical gray-line conditions will accordingly be short near the equator and long in the polar regions. This means that the gray-line phenomenon is much less important to the low-band DXer living in equatorial regions than to his colleague close to the polar circles. We should not forget, however, that a total propagation path consists of two terminal points and a long stretch in between. Propagation is not only determined by circumstances at the two terminal points.

It is not clear whether propagation proper inside the gray line along the terminator benefits from its existence. It is clear, however, that signal launching at the transmit and receive end does benefit greatly from the mechanism.

Some authors (Ref 108 and 118) have mentioned that gray-line propagation always happens along the terminator. On the low bands there has been occasional proof of such propagation although most of the gray-line situation benefits have been noticed on paths typically perpendicular to the terminator. One of the few really long-distance propagation paths along the gray-line zone is mentioned in Section 1.3.2.2. Excellent propagation was observed for a path between Europe and Alaska both on long path via the south pole at sunrise in Europe and via short path via the north pole at sunset in Europe.

Some authors have shown the gray-line zone as a zone of equal width all along the terminator. This is incorrect as far as the related radio propagation phenomenon is concerned. R. Linkous, W7OM, recognizes this varying zone width and accordingly emphasizes its importance in his excellent article "Navigating To 80 Meter DX" (Ref 109).

The author has developed an algorithm that calculates the effective width of the gray line as a function of the location as well as the time of year. The total width of the gray line can be calculated as follows:

1) Calculate the sun declination:

$$A = -23.5 \times \sin\left(360 \times \frac{D - 80}{365}\right)$$

where D is the day of the year (1 to 365).

2) Calculate the height of the sun at local noon:

$$H = 90 - (L + A)$$

where L is the latitude. If H is less than zero then add 90 degrees to H. If H = 0 then the width of the gray line (W) = 12 (if no sunrise, the width of the gray line is 12 hours).

3) Calculate the effective window:

$$W = \frac{1}{4 \tan (A \times 0.95)}$$

If W is greater than 12 then W = 12, and if W is less than 0.33 then W = 0.33. This algorithm is used in the computer program "GRAYLINE" mentioned in Chapter VII.

This algorithm gives a good approximation of the effective width of the gray line as far as low band propagation is concerned. The correction to the formula makes the gray line no narrower than 20 minutes in the equatorial zones, and no larger than 24 hours in the polar regions during midwinter.

A gray-line short path exists when the station on the western end of the path is having sunset about the same time that the station on the eastern end of the path is having sunrise. A long-path condition exists when the station at the eastern side of the path is having sunset at approximately the same time as the station at the western end of the path is experiencing sunrise.

Multi-hop propagation with intermediate ground reflections has long been the only way to explain propagation of radio waves by ionospheric refraction. In the last ten years a great deal of scientific work has been done enabling us to calculate exact path losses due to ionospheric absorption (deviative and non-deviative losses), free-space attenuation (path distance related) and earth (ground or water) reflection losses. While the theory of propagation with ground reflections is satisfactory to explain short- and medium-range contacts, the additional losses through ground reflections can no longer be accepted to explain some of the very high signal levels obtained over very long distances, especially when gray-line propagation and genuine long-path situations are involved. Recent work, based on experimental observations (Ref 100) and theoretical studies (Ref 131) have firmly established the existence of a specific propagation mode, called *whispering gallery* or *chordal hop* propagation. This form of ionospheric propagation without intermediate ground reflections appears to offer a good explanation for long-distance propagation.

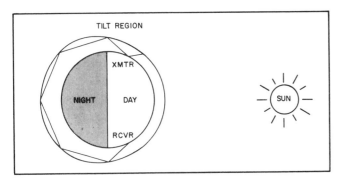

Figure 1.8—Signal Ducting. The deformation of the ionospheric layer (the changing altitude and ionization density of the E layer) at sunrise and sunset can produce circumstances where total internal reflection on the bottom side of ionosphere sustains very low-loss propagation.

Right around sunrise or sunset, low-band signals will be refracted in the E-layer in a tilted region (Figure 1.8), resulting in a condition which will make the waves enter the ionosphere again without having an intermediate ground reflection. This type of propagation is called chordal-hop propagation. With decreasing chordal-hop length this propagation turns into whispering-gallery mode which means that the waves are guided along the concave bottom of the ionospheric layer acting as a single-walled duct. The flat angles of incidence necessary for chordal-hop propagation are possible through refraction in the building-up D layer, and because of the tilt in the E layer at both ends of the path. Chordal-hop propagation modes over long distances can easily account for up to 12 dB of gain due to the omission of the ground reflection losses. Y. Blanarovich, VE3BMV, described a very similar theory (Ref 110). Long-delayed-echoes, or "round the world echoes" witnessed by several amateurs on frequencies as low as 80 meters, can only be explained by propagation mechanisms excluding intermediate ground reflections.

Every low-band DXer undoubtedly knows that it is relatively easy to work into regions near the antipodes (points directly opposite one's QTH on the globe), although those are the longest distances that one can encounter, and as such one would expect weak signals as a rule. The phenomenon of ray-focusing in near-antipodal regions must be used to explain the high field strengths encountered at those long distances (often in addition to the gray-line phenomenon and chordal hops). Antipodal focusing is based on the fact that all great circles passing through a given QTH intersect at the antipode of that QTH (see Section 1.3.1). Therefore, radio waves radiated by an antenna in a range of azimuthal directions and propagating around the earth along great-circle paths are being focused at the antipodal point. Exact focusing can occur only under ideal conditions, i.e. if the refracting properties of the ionosphere are ideal and perfectly homogeneous all over the globe. As these conditions do not exist (patchy clouds, MUF variation, etc), antipodal focusing will only exist over a limited range of propagation paths (great circle directions) at a given time.

The smaller the section of the shell involved in the focusing (i.e. the narrower the beam width), the closer the actual properties will approximate the ideal conditions. This means that in order to benefit to the maximum from antipodal focusing, the optimum azimuth (yielding the lowest average MUF) has to be known. Fixed, highly directive antennas (fixed on the geographical great-circle direction) may not be ideal, however, as the optimum azimuth is changing all the time (see Section 1.3.2.1). Rotatable or switchable arrays are the ideal answer, but omnidirectional antennas perform very well for paths near the antipodes, at least for transmitting. The focusing gain can be as high as 30 dB at the antipodes, and will range in the order of 15 dB at distances a few thousand kilometers away from the exact antipode.

1.2 Location

In the previous material the author has referred a number of times to the geographical location of the station. There is of course a close relationship between the time and the location when considering the influence of solar activity. Location is the determining factor in three different aspects of low-band propagation:

1) Latitude of your station vs. rate of sunrise
2) Magnetic disturbances
3) Local atmospheric noise (QRN)

1.2.1 LATITUDE OF YOUR QTH VS. SOLAR ACTIVITY

This aspect has already been dealt with in detail. The

latitude of the QTH will influence the MUF, the best season for a particular path, and the width of the gray-line zone.

1.2.2 MAGNETIC DISTURBANCES (AURORA)

This is a very important factor in the long-distance propagation mechanism on the low bands, and certainly the most important one for those living at latitudes of 60 degrees or more and within a few thousand miles of the magnetic poles.

During a solar storm, clouds of charged particles are thrown off by the sun; these clouds can reach the earth approximately 26 hours after the storm. The particles, when approaching the earth, are trapped by the earth's magnetic field. Hence, they follow the magnetic field lines and travel towards the magnetic north and south poles. As they approach the poles, the particles collide with atoms of the upper atmosphere and create violent ionization. This collision forms a ring of extremely dense ionization, which can be seen as a fluorescent ring around the magnetic poles, called Aurora Borealis near the North Pole and Aurora Australis near the South Pole. As far as low-band propagation is concerned, this heavily ionized belt, at a height of approximately 65 miles (100 km) as a rule acts much like the D layer in existence during the day; it totally absorbs all low-band signals trying to go through the belt.

On at least one occasion, it has been noted that on 160 meters, propagation conditions have occurred similar to those well known on VHF during an extremely heavy aurora. Around 1600 to 1800 UTC on February 8th, 1986, at the same time that auroral reflection was very predominant on VHF and 28 MHz, as witnessed by the author, KL7 and KH6 stations were heard and worked in Europe on a path straight across the North Pole, with the buzzy sound typical for auroral reflection. At the same time this phenomenon was not noticed on 80 meters. This proves that under exceptional conditions (the aurora was extremely intensive), aurora can be beneficial to low-band DXing. The aurora mentioned above generated an alpha equal to 238 units. K values were reported between 8 and 9. This was one of the largest geomagnetic storms since 1960.

Enhanced propagation conditions shortly after a major aurora appear quite regularly. One striking example was witnessed by the author on November 12, 1986, when only nine hours after a major disturbance during the morning hours, N7AU produced S9 signals via the long path for more than 30 minutes, just before sunset in Belgium. Normally long-path openings occur to the US West Coast from Belgium only between the middle of December and the middle of January, and even then the openings are extremely rare. During the November opening, the author witnessed N7UA calling CQ Europe with signals between S6 and S9 for almost ½ hour. The propagation was very selective, as only Belgian stations were returning his calls! A few days earlier DJ4AX was heard working the West Coast and giving 57 reports while the W6/W7 stations were completely inaudible in Belgium, only 200 miles to the northwest! It is more than likely that an ionospheric ducting phenomenon is responsible for such propagation. This means that very specific launching conditions have to be present at both sides of the path. It now appears that duct "exit" conditions are very critical and thus area selective, and more so as the path length is increased. It also seems that aurora disturbances can create and enhance such critical conditions.

As the aurora phenomenon is linked to solar storms and hence to Sudden Ionospheric Disturbances (SIDs), it is clear

that the frequency of aurora will be greatest at the sunspot maximum. There is *some* degree of aurora, however, about 200 days a year!

The magnetic North Pole lies about 11 degrees south of the geographic North Pole and 71 degrees west of Greenwich. The magnetic South Pole is situated 12 degrees north of the geographic South Pole and 111 degrees east of Greenwich. The intensity of the aurora phenomenon determines the diameter of the aurora belt. In cases of heavy aurora the belt can split into several smaller belts.

Generally we can say that in most cases of auroral activity the absorption will exist in a zone delimited by the outer aurora belt. For typical aurora densities the radius of the zone will be approximately 2000 miles (3250 km). Figure 1.9 shows the outline of this zone on great-circle maps centered on Washington DC, Central United States, San Francisco and Europe.

The great-circle distances from Washington, DC to Tokyo and Yemen are equal. For a signal to travel in a straight line to Tokyo, however, it has to go through the aurora zone. In the Yemen case, the straight-line path stays well clear of the aurora belt region. This means that when there is any degree of aurora activity, the Washington, DC to Tokyo path will be greatly affected, while the Yemen path will remain unattenuated by the aurora phenomenon. Looking at a globe, on which are drawn some aurora circles centered on the magnetic poles, it becomes clear why stations located near the equator will suffer much less from auroral absorption than stations located near or inside the aurora belt zones.

Radio waves propagate in a semi-scattering fashion due to refraction and reflection in a cloudy type of ionized environment. Therefore the Washington-Tokyo example case will often be subject to a large degree of path bending resulting in a valid propagation path bent round the outer aurora belt. This means that for stations located away from the outer aurora belt these crooked paths can often bring relief (see also Section 1.3.2.2). For those of us living very near or in the actual aurora belt zones, there is no compensating mechanism to alleviate the consequences of aurora.

1.2.3 LOCAL ATMOSPHERIC NOISE

Most local atmospheric noise (static or QRN) is generated by electrical storms or thunderstorms. We know that during the summer, QRN is the major limiting factor in copying weak signals on the low bands, at least for those regions where thunderstorm activities are serious. To give you an idea of the frightening power involved, a thunderstorm has up to 50 times more potential energy than an atomic bomb! There are an estimated 1800 thunderstorms in progress over the earth's surface at any given time throughout the year. The map in Figure 1.10 shows the high degree of variation in frequency of thunderstorms in the US. On the average lightning strikes somewhere on the earth 100 times a second, generating a tremendous amount of radio-frequency energy.

In the northern hemisphere, above 35 degrees latitude, QRN is almost nonexistent from November until March. In the middle of the summer, when an electrical storm is near, static crashes can produce signals up to 40 dB over S9, and make even local QSOs impossible (and dangerous). It is obvious that in equatorial zones, where electrical storms are very common all year long, this phenomenon will be the limiting factor in low-band DXing. This is why, as stated earlier, we cannot generally speak of an ideal season for DXing into the equatorial zones since QRN is a random possibility all year long.

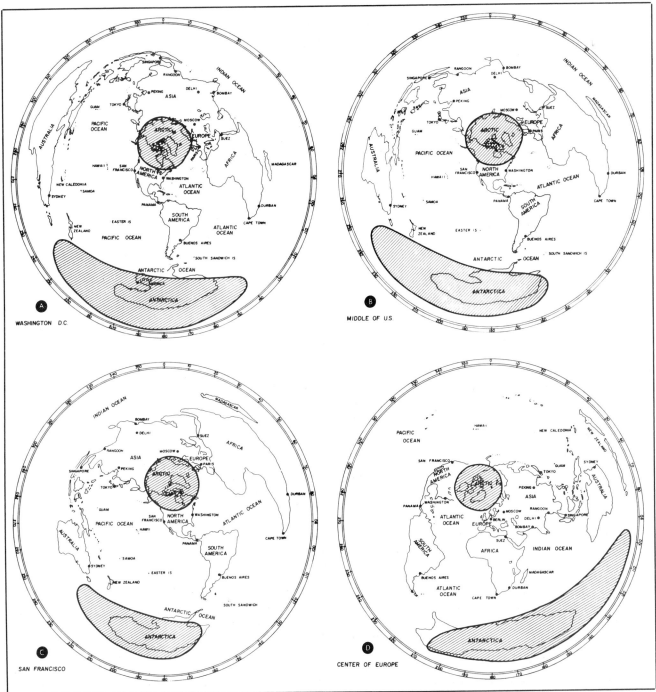

Figure 1.9—Azimuthal projection world maps, or great-circle maps that have been centered on different locations in the world. The aurora belt zones have been included in each example. A is centered on Washington DC, B on the middle of the US, C on San Francisco, and D on the center of Europe.

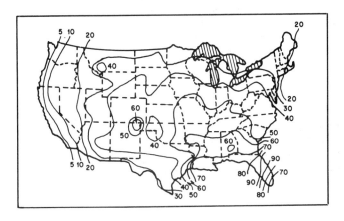

Using highly directive receiving antennas, such as Beverage antennas or small loop antennas (Section 2.13.2) can be of great help in reducing QRN from electrical storms by producing a null in the direction of the storm. Unless directly overhead, electrical storms in general have quite a sharp directivity pattern.

Rain, hail or snow are often electrically charged and can cause a continuous QRN hash when they come into contact

Figure 1.10—This map shows the mean number of thunderstorm days in the US. The figure is related to both mountainous terrain and seasonal weather patterns.

with antennas. Some antennas are more susceptible to this precipitation noise than others; vertical antennas seem to be worst in this respect. Closed-loop antennas generally behave better than open-ended antennas (e.g. dipoles), while Beverage receiving antennas are almost totally insensitive to this phenomenon.

1.3 Propagation Paths

In this section we will discuss the following items to help our understanding of low-band propagation paths:
1) Great-circle paths
2) Particular non-great-circle paths
3) The gray-line globe
4) The DX EDGE
5) Calculating sunrise and sunset times
6) The sunrise-sunset tables
7) Personal computer programs

1.3.1 GREAT-CIRCLE PATHS

Great circles are all circles obtained by cutting the globe with any plane going through the center of the earth. All great circles are 40,000 km long. The equator is a particular great circle, the cutting plane being perpendicular to the earth's axis. Meridians are other great circles, going through both poles.

A great-circle map is an azimuthal projection, centered on one location. For that reason it is often called an azimuthal-equidistant projection. This map has the unique property of showing the great circles as straight lines, as well as showing distances to any point in the map from the center point. On such a projection, the antipodes of the center location will be represented by the outer circle of the map. Great-circle maps are specific to a particular location. They are most commonly used for determining rotary beam headings for DX work.

Chapter VII lists a computer program (DIRECTIONS/ DISTANCES), written by the author, which calculates the great-circle direction and distance from your own QTH to any target QTH. The coordinates of the target QTH can be entered from the keyboard, or alternatively one can specify the target by merely entering the name (or the first few letters of the name) of the country or a major city. The coordinates of nearly 600 locations worldwide are contained in the related data base.

Another program (LISTING DIRECTIONS/ DISTANCES) prints out the great circle directions and distances to nearly 600 locations all over the world in tabular form on paper. All you have to do is to enter the coordinates of your own QTH.

1.3.2 OTHER NON-GREAT-CIRCLE PATHS

Most, but not all, 80-meter paths are great-circle paths. It is obvious that paths over relatively short distances are more or less straight-line great-circle paths. Let us assume that paths are basically always of the great-circle type, unless there is a good reason for them not to be. Consider some specific cases.

1.3.2.1 The Heterogeneous Ionosphere

We often think of radio waves as a single ray of energy sent in a specific direction, refracted in the ionosphere and reflected from a perfectly flat reflecting surface on the earth. This has been the standard method of visualizing radio propagation in a simplified way. HF energy is, however, in most practical cases, radiated in a range of azimuths and over a range of elevation angles.

The ionosphere is not a perfect mirror, but should rather be thought of as a cloudy and patchy heterogeneous region. Travelling ionospheric disturbances are wave-like disturbances, or variations in ionization density, usually moving between one and ten km per minute, producing well-known effects such as marked variations in signal strength and a shift in the direction of arrival of received signals.

The non-homogeneous nature of the ionosphere also accounts for the MUF being different at different places on the earth at a given time. Power is radiated by the transmitter in a whole range of directions, and radio waves will propagate in all those directions. D-layer absorption at the launching site and the state of the higher ionized layers all over the world have a large effect on the direction of propagation. Radio waves will be more heavily attenuated by travelling through regions with high MUFs. Where the MUF is below the operating frequency all power will be lost in space. The lowest degree of attenuation will result from travelling through zones where the MUF is near (and above) the operating frequency.

For relatively short-distance paths (less than 10,000 km or 6000 miles), low-band radio waves will propagate almost in straight lines. This is also true for north-south transequatorial paths (e.g. Europe-Africa, North America-South America). Deviations from great-circle headings will not often be observed. Since the introduction of switchable or rotatable arrays for 80 meters, it has been possible to observe and analyze the phenomena of non-great-circle paths in greater detail.

The most typical example of non-great-circle propagation is caused by the unequal MUF distribution over the world. As stated earlier there is an indefinite number of great-circle paths to the antipodes. As low-band signals travel only over the dark side of the globe, however, the usable number of great-circle paths is limited to 180 degrees (assuming there is no aurora activity screening off part of the aperture). This very seldom means that signals will arrive with equal strength over 180 degrees, however. The principle is that signals will be received with the greatest signal strengths from those directions where the ionization is optimal along the entire length of the path. In general this means areas with low MUF. Indeed, the attenuation will be lower through these zones with low MUF than through ionosphere regions with higher MUF. Prediction can be done with the help of a MUF map or with the aid of computer programs such as MINIMUF (see Section 1.4.7.2).

New Zealand is about 19,000 km (11,800 miles) short path from Belgium, or about 21,000 km (13,000 miles) long path. The theoretical great-circle headings are 25 to 75 degrees east of north on short path and 25 to 75 degrees west of south on long path (205 to 255 degrees). When working ZLs on long path during winter (in the northern hemisphere), signals always arrive via North America, which is 90 degrees off from the great-circle direction. Indeed, at that time, it is summer in South America, and the MUF is much higher in the southern hemisphere than in the north. The path is not a great-circle path, but inclined in order to leave the southern hemisphere as fast as possible (both the ZLs and the Europeans will beam across North America in the winter). As we continue towards spring, the optimum path between western Europe and New Zealand will move from across North America to across Central America (February-March), and eventually beaming across South America will yield the best signals even later in the year (April onwards). Somewhere around equinox it happens that all three paths produce equally good signals, in which case abnormally strong signal strengths can be recorded (see the discussion of antipodal focusing). It needs no further explanation that these are examples of gray-line propagation. It can also be seen that none of those favored propagation paths ever coincide with the gray line proper. The actual path happens to be more or less perpendicular to the terminator at all times of the year! To summarize, one can say that for long paths and paths to areas near the antipodes, the signal paths will as a rule be bent in such a way that the signals will travel the longest possible distance in the hemisphere where it is winter.

A similar phenomenon is also seen over shorter paths. During the winter, signals from Argentina and Chile regularly arrive in Belgium at beam headings pointed directly at North America, 90 degrees from the expected great-circle direction. This shows again that signals travel along areas of lowest MUF; the signals from South America travel straight north in order to ''escape'' the summer conditions in the southern hemisphere, and are then propagated towards Europe.

1.3.2.2 Avoiding Auroral Zones

A similar phenomena will occur when signals travel around the auroral belts or zones. In the northern hemisphere signals will travel more southerly than one would expect from great-circle information.

Practical examples. The short path between the west coast of the US and western Europe has always been a difficult path, because of the interference of the aurora-belt with the great-circle path. For the same reason the short path is almost non-existent between the west coast and northern Scandinavia (Scandinavia being inside the aurora-belt zone). The writer has experienced several cases where the path was generally believed to be dead, and where nevertheless a good QSO could be made with W6NLZ. Pete was using a 4 element KLM Yagi and the author was using his Beverage (for reception), both beaming across South America which is 90 degrees off the great-circle heading. Similar experiences of southerly bent paths have been confirmed by several west coast stations.

An even more striking example was a contact the writer had with KL7U in early 1985. The path between western Europe and Alaska is considered one of the worst, again because of the aurora phenomena. Looking at the globe, there is a great-circle path, only about 7,500 km long, but beaming right across the magnetic north pole. The distance is similar to the distance between western Europe and Florida. Straight short-path openings are a rare exception, happening at most a few days every year. There are other more exotic paths that sometimes can bring relief, however. One possible path is a so-called long path, where we would work Alaska at their sunrise and around our sunset. Looking at the globe and the dark side at about 1600 UTC in the middle of the winter, we can see that the short-path great-circle path (beaming approx 350 degrees) is following the terminator (gray line). The geographical long path follows the gray line in a southerly direction (170 degrees). In addition we have a whole range of darkness between 350 and 170 degrees.

The writer has made contacts with KL7U at about 1600 UTC, with excellent signal strengths, hearing him only when listening at 350 degrees. By the classic definitions of short and long path this would have been a long-path QSO (see Section 1.3.3.3); however, it was not. It is obvious that this can only happen when there is no auroral absorption at

all. An equally extraordinary path was experienced again with KL7U in the morning around my sunrise. I was called by VE3CDP/W9 informing me that Lon, KL7U was calling me. As nothing could be heard from him beaming north-west or north I switched the Beverages, and finally got him Q5 and made a perfect QSO beaming due *south*. These kinds of propagation paths are quite common, and their existence should be noted, and the mechanism understood in order to be able to work the DX on the other end of the path.

1.3.2.3 Crooked Polar Paths In Midwinter

By the classic definition of long path (Section 1.3.3), a long path exists between western Europe and Japan in midwinter, centered around 0745 UTC on January 1. It has been observed by several European stations that the so-called long-path opening from Europe to Japan in midwinter sometimes (not frequently) starts with signals arriving west of north through the aurora zones, obviously when there is no auroral activity. The reason for the signals coming in across North America instead of South America (which is the genuine long-path direction) has been given when explaining why the ZLs come in across North America in the winter also (Section 1.3.2.1). Signals are usually quite weak at that time. A short time later signals will come in from a direction east of north.

More frequently, such openings will not show an early opening to the west of north, however. If we look at the darkness/daylight distribution across the world at that time, we see that we have indeed more than just the genuine long path possibility (the real long path being 180 degrees opposite to the short path). A range of crooked paths bent east of the north pole across northern Siberia are all the way in darkness. They are of much shorter distance (approx 10,000 km vs 30,000 km for the genuine long path) and are better candidates. Note that these paths more or less follow the terminator, and could be considered as typical gray-line propagation as defined by Hoppe and others (Ref 108 and Ref 118).

Often such openings are very area-selective, probably because of the ducting phenomena involved, occurring only when the required specific signal-launching conditions exist. This is only so for very specific locations where D-layer ionization is partial and the F-layer tilt is optimal (see Section 1.1.3.3). In several cases JA stations were worked by the author with signals up to S9, while signals were reported to be undetectable in Germany only 300 miles away. In all cases the signals were peaking about 10 degrees east of north. In Japan the openings seem to be very selective as well, as can be judged from the call areas worked. Northern Japan (JA7 and JA8) obviously leads the opening, central Japan follows 30 minutes later, and southern Japan often comes too late for this kind of opening.

In midwinter there is a 1.5 hour spread in sunset time between northern and southern Japan. Similar paths exist in midwinter between California and Central Asia (Mongolia) around 0030 UTC, between eastern Europe (Moscow) and the northern Pacific (Wake island) around 0615 UTC, and between the east coast and midwest of the US and northern Scandinavia around 1230 UTC. All of those polar-region paths are east of the pole and should not be influenced by aurora as much as paths going west of the north pole. The gray-line globe is a tremendous help in finding those paths.

A geographically similar condition exists in midwinter between Scandinavia and the west coast of the US. In this particular case however, the alternative crooked path (at the time of the long path) goes right across the magnetic north pole with the well-known consequences of high probability of auroral absorption. Although both cases seem alike from a geographical point of view, they are quite dissimilar from a geomagnetic point of view.

The so-called long-path propagation around sunset in Scandinavia and sunrise on the US west coast looks like a genuine long path from an azimuthal launching angle point of view. In Scandinavia the beam headings generally indicate an optimum launching angle of approximately 100 degrees. However, along their way, the signals will be least attenuated in those areas of the ionosphere where the MUF is lowest. This phenomenon will make the signals follow a crooked path, whereby areas of high MUF will be avoided.

D. Riggs, N7AM, who is using a rotary quad for 80 meters, writes:

"We have learned that the 80-meter long path between the Pacific Northwest and Scandinavia is following the LUF (lowest usable frequency). I have always believed that the long path to Europe was not across the equator but leaves us at 240 degrees and since the MUF is highest at the equator it cannot continue at 240 degrees but it bends westerly going under the Hawaiian islands, across the Philippines under Japan and across the Asian continent to Scandinavia. The MUF charts prove this fact. The fact that the long path to Europe lies north of the equator is proven by the northern Europeans working JAs and Southeast Asia before and after the west coast peak."

1.4 DXing Tools

1.4.1 THE GRAY-LINE GLOBE

The now famous and exclusive gray-line globe forms an integral part of many a dedicated low-band DXer's shack. Columbus Verlag (D7056, Weinstadt-Beutelsbach, B.R.D.) has been selling the gray-line globe for over 10 years now (Figure 1.11). The globes are not locally distributed in the US. Overseas customers can order globes directly from the manufacturer in single quantities (order number 42 34 59). In 1979 an amateur version was added to the collection. This version has the great-circle lines printed, centered on central Europe (order number 43 34 52-9). The gray-line globe was the first tool available to the dedicated low-band DXer giving a whole range of accurate information on sunrise/sunset plus the visual three-dimensional information that cannot be replaced by two-dimensional maps.

The amateur version of the globe measures more than 13 inches (33 cm) in diameter, has very detailed printing (all DXCC prefixes, plus the call areas in the larger countries and WAZ zones), and clearly shows the daylight and darkness zones. The inclination of the earth's axis (vs. the sun) can be changed and set in increments of 1 day or as little as 0.1 degree! There is a scale on the base of the globe that allows you to set the inclination with the aid of a simple day-by-day calendar (Figure 1.12). In addition to setting the inclination of the terminator, there is also a time-graduated ring along the equator so that you can set the position (rotation) of the globe for any given time, in increments of 15 minutes. Interpolation can easily be done down to a few minutes (15-minute markings being about ½ inch or 12 mm apart on the ring). This allows exact local time and UTC to be accurately read off the scale for any spot on the globe. Inversely, for a given location the sunset and sunrise times (local time or UTC) can be found with an accuracy of a few

Figure 1.11—The Columbus Verlag gray-line globe. Note the large ring over the equator which is imprinted with the time of day scale.

Figure 1.12—The day by day calendar on the globe stand must be used to set the right inclination of the terminator.

minutes. As explained in Section 1.4.6.4, the globe mechanism does not take into account the deviations caused by the slightly elliptical orbit of the earth around the sun. The times found with the globe correspond wonderfully well with those obtained with the non-corrected formulas shown in Section 1.4.6.1. The possible deviations from the astronomically correct sunrise/sunset times are listed in a table in Section 1.4.6.4, and can be as much as 23 minutes for the author's QTH at one time of the year (Oct 1).

To summarize, here is what one can do with this superb tool:

1) Convert local time (sun time) to UTC or your standard time (and vice versa).

2) Find out where the sun is rising or setting for a given day and any time of that day.

3) Find out the exact sunrise and sunset time for any spot on earth, for any day of the year.

4) Determine if there is a time of the year when your QTH and any other location both lay on the terminator (gray line).

5) Have an overall and detailed view of the total globe illumination pattern at any particular time (of year and of day).

6) Visualize and understand on a large-sized globe, carrying all necessary information, what the possible "non-standard" propagation paths could be.

7) Decorate your shack.

8) Know what to ask the XYL (OM) for on your next birthday.

1.4.2 THE DX EDGE

The DX EDGE (Figure 1.13) is a slide-rule type calculator that gives you roughly the same information as the gray-line globe. It consists of a plastic carrier and a set of 12 slides (one for each month). The carrier is 11¾ by 4¾ inches and imprinted with a double (side by side) conform-projection map of the world. Because of its small size it only shows the 40 zones and a few prefixes for some large countries. The plastic slides are 6½ by 4¾ inches and are imprinted with the terminator (gray line) and the darkness/daylight zones. By sliding the inserts through the carrier you can find out the relevant information regarding the darkness/daylight zones

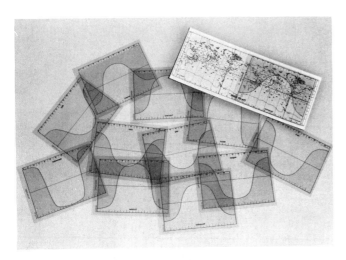

Figure 1.13—The DX EDGE provides a good visual impression of what happens at whatever time of the year and the day.

and the terminator. The time information is printed on the slide inserts, and therefore is local sun time. The author's DX EDGE has the time scale identified with "local Standard Time," which is not correct. It should read "local sun time."

Conversion to local standard time and UTC is not always as straightforward as one thinks. This problem does not occur with the gray-line globe. The fact that one has only 12 slide inserts limits the accuracy of the tool, as interpolation is necessary for more accurate outputs. The DX EDGE is manufactured by DX EDGE, PO Box 834, Madison Square Station, New York, NY 10159. The DX EDGE is also available through distributors (see advertisements in Amateur Radio magazines.)

There is also a computer version of the DX EDGE. For detailed description see Section 1.4.8.4.

1.4.3 SM6BGG MAPS

Wiksten, SM6BGG produces an impressive set of 7 maps, 12 × 16 inches (30 × 40 cm), each custom computer-plotted in four colors. Two of these can be used with two four-color transparencies as overlays for showing the sunrise and sunset gray lines in intervals of 1 month (See Figure 1.14). The sunrise and sunset maps are Mercator (or conform) projections of the world. The maps show the continent and

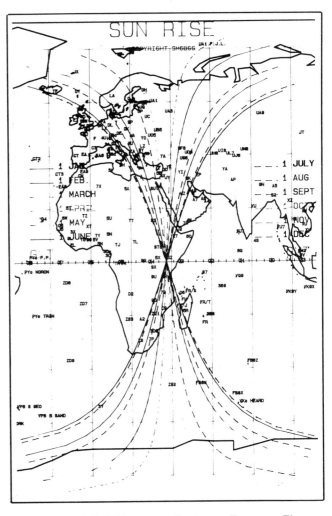

Figure 1.14—SM6BGG personalized gray-line map. The sunrise overlay is positioned onto the sunrise map with the July 1st gray-line over the author's QTH. The gray line crosses the equator with the UTC time scale at 0335 UTC.

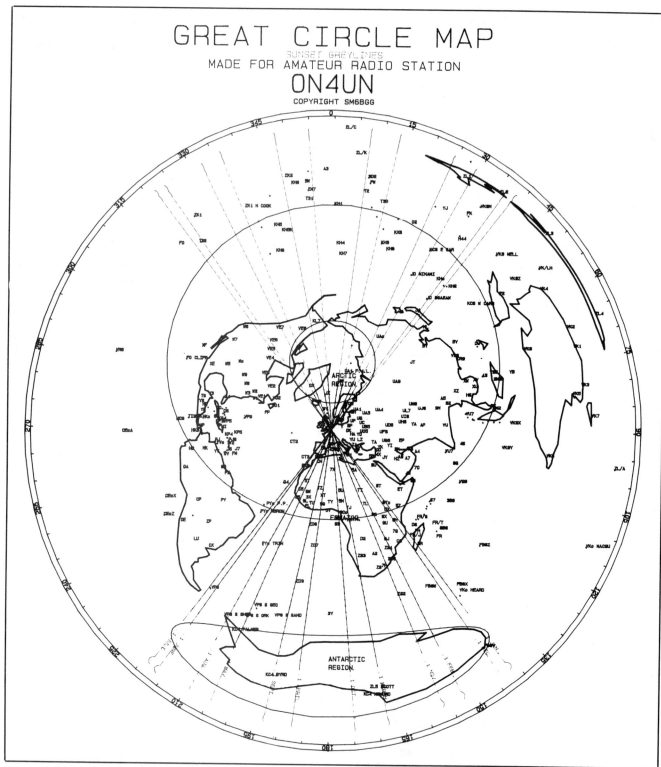

Figure 1.15—SM6BGG personalized great-circle map. This custom great-circle map shows the gray lines as straight lines. A table indicating the customer's sunrise/sunset at ½ month increments is also included.

major island boundaries as well as the major radio prefixes. A time scale is printed on the equator and enables the user to establish sunrise or sunset time for any location in the world, together with transparent overlays showing the gray lines. The package includes another set of two customized azimuthal or great-circle projections, one showing the sunrise gray lines, the other the sunset gray lines, both as straight lines (Figure 1.15). These maps also carry a printout of the sunrise and sunset times of the customer's QTH (in ½ month

intervals). A fifth map is a standard great-circle projection map (12 inch or 30 cm diameter) showing all major prefixes, the arctic circles and the equator. Two more maps complete the set, one being a conform-projection prefix map, while the last one is a perspective projection of the world, from right above your QTH as seen from an altitude of 250,000 km (160,000 miles). The direct application of this projection is not so obvious but the least one can say is that it is an interesting view from above!

As if this was not enough, the package includes a 12-page printout listing 645 geographical locations throughout the world, with the prefixes (in alphabetical order), DXCC country name, city name, continent name, CQ zone, ITU zone, distance (from your QTH) in km and bearing (including long path if distance is greater than 10,000 km). This excellent package is obtainable from K. Wiksten, SM6BGG, Hillingsseter, 45800 Fargelanda, Sweden.

This product differs from the DX EDGE in that it is completely customized. There are two gray-line transparencies, one for the sunrise gray line and one for the sunset gray line, and each carries 12 curves (one per month). The combination of these transparencies with the appropriate conform projection map gives less of a total visual impression of the daylight/darkness distribution across the world than the DX EDGE or the gray-line globe. This is mainly because the DX EDGE uses both an "extended" gray-line overlay as well as conformal world-projection map. In addition, the accuracy in determining sunset and sunrise times is limited by the possibility to read a QTH from the map and the interpolation using the overlays. As the size of the map and the overlay is substantially larger than with the DX EDGE, the accuracy should accordingly be better. As with the DX EDGE, it is doubtful if enough accuracy can be obtained for 160-meter work.

1.4.4 THE K6UA GRAYLINER

Hoppe, K6UA, who was the first to write about gray-line propagation (Ref 108) has introduced an improved version of the gray-line map system. The K6UA system is similar to the DX EDGE, but larger in size (effectively four times the size or 7.5 × 10 inches). There are 12 transparent overlays, each carrying the gray lines for two months, dated on the 15th of the month. The multi-color map is mounted on a double drum transport system, enabling the user to move the map under the overlay. The whole system is enclosed in a hand-finished wood enclosure measuring 8.5 × 10.6 × 1.5 inches.

The tool, which is really a deluxe version of the DX EDGE, has the same drawbacks as any similar system: limited accuracy. When tested for accuracy, the Grayliner showed deviations from the correct sunrise/sunset times ranging from − 10 to +15 minutes for a QTH of latitude 50 degrees. This evaluation was done at the 15th of each month, where the terminator is drawn on the plastic overlays. For other dates, where visual interpolation must be made, the accuracy may be further limited. The big advantage over the DX EDGE is that the Grayliner uses an excellent world map showing the boundaries of all countries and the locations of major cities. This helps to accurately locate the target QTH. The Grayliner can be obtained from D. Hoppe, PO Box 693, Fallbrook, CA 92098.

1.4.5 THE GEOCHRON GRAY-LINE MAP

Geochron Enterprises (899 Arguello St, Unit A, Redwood City, CA 94063), manufactures a wonderful gray-line map, which measures 33 × 22.5 × 4.5 inches. The Geochron, shown in Figure 1.16, has a fixed time scale across the top of the map. A continuous-loop mylar map is rotated by a motor on two drums, and moves linearly across the Geochron under a pane of glass, illuminated by fluorescent bulbs. As the map moves across the Geochron, the darkness/daylight zones are projected onto the map, and the shape is adjusted continuously. The Geochron also carries a calendar, which is moved with the same precision as the map. Manual setting

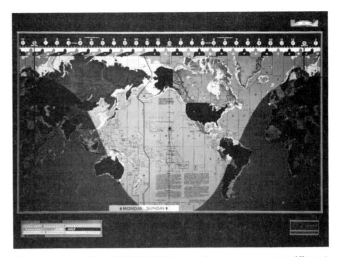

Figure 1.16—The GEOCHRON gray-line map; a magnificent motorized luxury model of the DX EDGE, measuring 33 × 22.5 inches.

of the date and time can be easily accomplished as well. The Geochron is available in 50 and 60 Hz versions. It is a truly magnificent gray-line map, the only drawback being its high price (approximately $1000).

1.4.6 CALCULATING SUNRISE AND SUNSET TIMES

1.4.6.1 Basic Formulas

Instead of using the gray-line globe or the DX EDGE, a calculator or personal computer can be used to calculate sunrise and sunset times. There is only one correct way to calculate sunrise and sunset times, and the algorithms involved are quite complex (see Section 1.4.6.2). They take into account a range of mechanisms which disturb the ideal, almost circular, orbit of the earth around the sun. However, if we can live with a certain inaccuracy (which is certainly not recommended for 160 meter operation), there are very simple formulas which can be used. If we assume that the orbit of the earth around the sun is indeed circular (it is not to a rather small degree), we can apply the following set of formulas:

$$\text{Sunrise Time} = \frac{LO}{15} + \frac{\cos^{-1}[\tan(A) \times \tan(LA)]}{15} \quad \text{[a]}$$

$$\text{Sunset Time} = \frac{LO}{15} - \frac{\cos^{-1}[\tan(A) \times \tan(LA)]}{15} \quad \text{[b]}$$

where
    LA = latitude north of QTH in decimal degrees (south uses − sign)
    LO = longitude west of QTH in decimal degrees (east uses − sign)
    A = declination of the sun (− 23.5 to + 23.5 deg)

Both formulas give time as decimal UTC, where minutes are represented as tenths and hundredths of hours. For example, 2.5 decimal UTC is 2:30 in the normal representation.

If we assume the sun inclination varies following a sine law, we can use the following formula to determine the day by day value of the inclination:

$$A = 23.5 \times \sin\left[\frac{360 \times (D - 80)}{365}\right] \quad \text{[c]}$$

where D is the Julian day number (1 to 365)

For example, to find the sunrise time in Botswana on February 1:

Botswana: Longitude W = − 24 degrees
Latitude N = − 22 degrees

February 1: D = 32

$$A = 23.5 \times \sin\left[\frac{360 \times (32 - 80)}{365}\right] = -17.3 \text{ degrees}$$

$$\text{Sunrise time} = \frac{-24}{15} + \frac{\cos^{-1}[\tan(-17.3) \times \tan(-22)]}{15}$$

$$= 3.86 \text{ decimal UTC}$$
$$= 3:52 \text{ UTC}$$

In some cases it is possible that the result will be greater than 2400 or smaller than 0000 (negative). In the first case, subtract 2400 and in the second case, add 2400 to the result to get the exact time (for example 2615 becomes 0215).

For locations with latitudes above 67 degrees (north or south) the product (tan A × tan Lon N) can sometimes become greater than 1 or smaller than − 1. In this case the arc cosine of the product does not exist, and the formula cannot be used. When the product becomes greater than 1 or smaller than − 1, it means that the sun does not rise (polar night in the winter above the polar circle) or does not set (in the summer).

1.4.6.2 Corrections

As the earth moves in an elliptical orbit around the sun, it moves at varying speeds. As a result, the actual time (sun time) can be as much as 16 minutes ahead or 14 minutes behind our clocks depending on the months of the year. The correction times shown in Table 2 must be added to the times obtained by formulas [a] and [b].

The correction times in Table 2 must be used to determine true north by the sun. At exactly local noon the sun is due south. The following expression can be used to determine exact local noon time (expressed in UTC):

$$N = 12 + \frac{L}{15} + \frac{C}{60}$$

where
  N = local noon time expressed in UTC time (hours plus decimal fraction)
  L = Longitude in degrees west of Greenwich
  C = correction factor in minutes (from table above)

Table 2

Correction Factor for Sunrise and Sunset Times

Month/Day	Minutes	Month/Day	Minutes
Jan/1	3	Jul/1	4
Jan/16	9	Jul/15	6
Feb/1	14	Aug/1	6
Feb/15	14	Aug/16	4
Mar/1	13	Sep/1	0
Mar/15	9	Sep/16	−5
Apr/1	4	Oct/1	−10
Apr/16	0	Oct/16	−14
May/1	−3	Nov/1	−16
May/16	−4	Nov/16	−15
Jun/1	−2	Dec/1	−11
Jun/16	0	Dec/16	−5

For example, to calculate true noon for Newington, CT on November 1:

L (Newington) = 72.75 degrees

$$N = 12 + \frac{72.75}{15} + \frac{-16}{60} = 16.5833$$

Conversion to minutes: 0.5833 × 60 = 35 minutes. Local noon occurs at 1635 UTC.

1.4.6.3 Other Formulas

Other authors have published or used different formulas to calculate sunrise and sunset times:

1) Frenaye, K1KI (Ref 128) uses the same algorithms [a] and [b] as described in Section 1.4.6.1, but calculates the inclination by:

$$A = -23.5 \cos(10 + 0.988D)$$

where D = Julian day number (1 to 365)

2) Overbeck and Steffen, N6NB and KC6A (Ref 107) use the following Fourier Transforms in their computer program "sunrise chart":

$$A = 0.456 - 22.915 \cos(D) - 0.43 \cos(2D) - 0.156 \cos(3D)$$
$$+ 3.83 \sin(D) + 0.06 \sin(2D) + 0.082 \sin(3D)$$

$$C = -(0.008 + 0.51 \cos(D) - 3.197 \cos(2D)$$
$$- 0.106 \cos(3D) + 0.15 \cos(4D) - 7.137 \sin(D)$$
$$- 9.471 \sin(2D) - 0.391 \sin(3D) - 0.242 \sin(4D))$$

where

  D = Julian day number (1 to 365)
  A = sun declination
  C = correction factor (in minutes)

Formulas [a] and [b] still apply, and C is to be added to both.

3) Brollini, NS6N (Ref 119) uses still another algorithm:

$$A = (0.379 - 23.267 \cos(P + 0.1793)$$
$$- 0.381 \cos(2P + 0.1292) - 0.171 \cos(3P + 0.5184)$$
$$- 0.008 \cos(4P + 0.4538) - 0.003 \cos(5P + 1.658))$$
$$\times \frac{\pi}{180}$$

where
  P = 0.017202 × (D − 1.5)
  D = Julian day number (1 to 365)
  A = sun declination

The rest of the algorithm is slightly different from Formula [a] described in Section 1.4.6.1. Additional correction factors have been included by the author.

$$B = 0.017202 \times (D - 1.5)$$

$$E = (-1.842 \sin(B - 0.05952) - 2.482 \sin(2B + 0.3557)$$
$$- 0.79 \sin(3B + 0.2967) - 0.055 \sin(4B + 0.6981)$$
$$- 0.003 \sin(5B + 0.7156)) \times 1/15$$

$$C = 12 - E + \frac{LO \times 180}{15\pi}$$

$$F = \cos^{-1}\left[\frac{-0.01454 - (\sin(LA) \times \sin(A))}{\cos(LA) \times \cos(A)}\right] \times \frac{180}{15\pi}$$

where
  D = Julian day number (1 to 365)

A = earth axis inclination in radians
E = correction factor in hours
LO = west longitude of QTH in radians
LA = north latitude of QTH in radians
π = 3.14159
Sunrise Time = C − F
Sunset Time = C + F
Both in decimal UTC.

4) Van Heddeghem (ON4HW) developed a method based on classical astronomy to calculate sunrise and sunset times. The equations are given in Figure 1.17 in the form of a BASIC program. This program can be enhanced by incorporating lines 150 though 350 in a for-next loop in order to have the sunrise/sunset times for a number of days throughout the year.

It should also be fairly simple to adapt this APPLESOFT program to other popular dialects of BASIC language. The program does not use any arc sin or arc cos functions as they are not available in all BASIC dialects. A full-fledged sunrise-sunset program (SUNRISE) developed by the author is referred to in Chapter VII (computer programs). It calculates sunrise and sunset times for your own QTH and displays these times side by side with those for any other place on earth. The tables list the times in ½ month intervals.

The program uses a data base containing the coordinates of almost 600 locations all over the world. All the user has to do is to enter the name (or the first few letters of the name) of a country or city, and the program will look up the coordinates. Alternatively one may also enter the coordinates from the keyboard. Another program prints out the sunrise and sunset tables for a given day, for all 600 locations in the database. This program (LISTING SUNSET) can be very useful when preparing for contests.

```
10 CLEAR
20 PI = 3.1415927
30 SW = -.97599592
40 CW = .21778881
50 SE = .39777961
60 CE = .9174811
70 K1 = -.014834754
80 PRINT "ENTER WEST LONGITUDE IN DECIMAL DEGREES"
90 INPUT LO
100 PRINT "ENTER NORTH LATITUDE IN DECIMAL DEGREES"
110 INPUT LA
120 LO = LO * PI/180
130 LA = LA * PI/180
140 PRINT "ENTER DAY NUMBER ( 1 TO 365)"
150 INPUT D
160 M = (2 * PI * D + LO) / 365.24219 - .052708
170 L = M - 1.351248
180 C1 = 1 - .03343 * COS (M)
190 C2 = .99944 * SIN (M) / C1
200 C3 = (COS (M) - .03343) / C1
210 C4 = SW * C3 + CW * C2
220 C5 = CW * C3 - SW * C2
230 C6 = SE * C4 : REM SINE OF SUN DECLINATION
240 B1 = K1 - C6 * SIN (LA)
250 B2 = (COS (LA))^2 * (1 - C6^2) - B1^2
260 IF B2 <= 0 THEN R$ = "NO.SR": S$ = "NO.SS" : GOTO 340
270 B3 = ATN (B1 / SQR (B2)) - PI/2
280 B4 = ATN((COS(L)*CE*C4-SIN(L)*C5)/(SIN(L)*CE*C4+COS(L)*C5))
290 GOSUB 370
300 R$ = STR$ (B6)
310 B3 = -B3
320 GOSUB 370
330 S$ = STR$ (B6)
340 PRINT "SUNRISE : ";R$
350 PRINT "SUNSET  : ";S$
360 GOTO 140
370 B5 = B4 + B3 + LO + PI
380 IF B5 < 0 THEN B5 = B5 + 2*PI
390 B5 = INT (B5 * 720 / PI + .5) : REM MINUTES PAST 0000 UTC
400 IF B5 > 1439 THEN B5 = B5 - 1440
410 B6 = .4 * INT (B5/60) + B5/100 : REM TIME IN HH.MM
420 RETURN
```

Figure 1-17—BASIC program to calculate sunrise and sunset times by the Van Heddeghem equations, as explained in the text.

1.4.6.4 Comparing Sunrise Times

Table 3 lists results from the following formula combinations:

[T1] = according to formula [a] and [c] (Section 1.4.6.1.)
[T2] = [a] + Overbeck and Steffen algorithm (Section 1.4.6.3B)
[T3] = using the Brollini procedure (Section 1.4.6.3C)
[T4] = using the Van Heddeghem procedure (Section 1.4.6.3D)

Table 3
Comparison of Sunrise Times Calculated by Different Methods

Month/Day	[T1]	[T2]	[T3]	[T4]
Jan/1	7.51	7.55	7.48	7.48
Feb/1	7.15	7.28	7.23	7.22
Mar/1	6.24	6.34	6.32	6.30
Apr/1	5.22	5.23	5.23	5.21
May/1	4.26	4.21	4.20	4.19
Jun/1	3.43	3.41	3.36	3.36
Jul/1	3.38	3.43	3.34	3.34
Aug/1	4.12	4.21	4.09	4.09
Sep/1	5.07	5.09	4.56	4.57
Oct/1	6.07	5.56	5.43	5.44
Nov/1	7.06	6.49	6.35	6.36
Dec/1	7.46	7.37	7.24	7.25

The sunrise times given below were calculated for the writer's QTH in Belgium. The coordinates are 51 degrees 0 minutes north (+51.00 degrees) and 3 degrees 45 minutes east (−3.75 degrees).

The results obtained from the gray-line globe were noted accurately and compared with the results obtained mathematically. The results are within a few minutes (reading tolerance) of those obtained by the uncorrected formulas ([T1]). The times obtained with the different formulas were compared with publications from Nautical Almanacs from different parts of the world. The sunrise/sunset times obtained by the Brollini and the Van Heddeghem procedures matched the published figures typically within 1 to 2 minutes. The reason for this slight deviation is that the formulas do not take into account the leap year (every fourth year) and the correction of 1 day (in the reverse direction) every 128 years.

Strictly speaking, the sunrise and sunset times vary from year to year, but this variance should be no more than 0.5 minutes. Constants in the Van Heddeghem procedure (Section 1.4.6.3D) are given for the year 1979. This means that D = 1 for 1 Jan 1979. For 1 Jan 1980, D = 366, for 1 Jan 1981 D = 732 etc.

It is not possible to evaluate the accuracy of the DX EDGE slide rule. Due to the nature of the tool, accuracy is limited to the order of magnitude of 15/30 minutes. Consequently its usefulness may be questionable, especially for dedicated 160-meter operators who know that their sunrise/sunset openings are much shorter on 160 than on 80 meters. Accuracy is certainly an important requirement for 160 meter operations!

1.4.7 THE SUNRISE/SUNSET TABLES

The sunrise/sunset tables booklet designed by the author shows sunrise and sunset times for over 500 different locations

```
                    -ON-
BELGIUM                              (BRUSSELS)

========================================================
50.60 DEG N                          - 4.35 DEG W

  DATE          SUNRISE          SUNSET
  ----          -------          ------
  JAN  1        07.48            15.48
  JAN 15        07.38            16.06
  FEB  1        07.20            16.32
  FEB 15        06.55            16.58
  MAR  1        06.30            17.21
  MAR 15        05.57            17.46
  APR  1        05.22            18.12
  APR 15        04.49            18.36
  MAY  1        04.20            19.00
  MAY 15        03.55            19.23
  JUN  1        03.36            19.44
  JUN 15        03.30            19.56
  JUL  1        03.33            19.59
  JUL 15        03.47            19.50
  AUG  1        04.07            19.30
  AUG 15        04.30            19.04
  SEP  1        04.54            18.32
  SEP 15        05.17            17.59
  OCT  1        05.40            17.25
  OCT 15        06.04            16.53
  NOV  1        06.31            16.21
  NOV 15        06.57            15.58
  DEC  1        07.20            15.42
  DEC 15        07.37            15.38
```

Figure 1.18—A typical printout from the SUNRISE/SUNSET tables computer program, published by the author.

in the world (including 100 different locations in the US) in tabular form. Increments are given per half month. Figure 1.18 shows an example of a printout for one location.

The third edition of this booklet, using the astronomically correct algorithms, is now available from the author, ON4UN. For delivery outside the US, contact the author directly (John Devoldere, ON4UN, Poelstraat 215, B9220 Merelbeke, Belgium). US residents, should contact W. R. Jorden, K7KI, 6861 Kenana Place, Tucson AZ 85704.

1.4.7.1 General Rules For Using Sunrise/Sunset Times

For all E-W, W-E, NW-SE and NE-SW paths there are two propagation peaks to be expected (short path):

1) The first peak will be around the sunrise at the station at the eastern end of the path.

2) The second peak is about sunset at the station at the western end of the path.

For N-S paths there are no pronounced peaks around either sunset or sunrise. Often the peak seems to occur near midnight.

The use of the tables can best be explained with a few examples:

Example 1. What are the peak propagation times between Belgium and Japan on February 15? From the tables can be found:

Belgium 15 Feb SRW = 0656 SSW = 1659
Japan   15 Feb SRE = 2130 SSE = 0824

where

SRE = Sunrise, eastern end
SRW = Sunrise, western end
SSE = Sunset, eastern end
SSW = Sunset, western end

The first peak is around sunrise in Japan or SRE = 2130 UTC. This is after sunset in Belgium (SSW = 1659), so the path is in darkness. Always check this.

The second peak is around sunset in Belgium or SSW = 1659 UTC. This too is after sunset in Japan (0824) so the path is in darkness.

Is there a possibility for a long-path opening? The definition of a long-path opening (see Section 1.1.3.1) says we must have sunset at the eastern end before sunrise at the western end of the path. In the example this is not true, because SRW = 0656 is not earlier than SSE = 0824.

Example 2. Is there a long-path opening from Japan to Belgium on January 1?

Belgium 1 Jan SRW = 0744 SSW = 1549
Japan   1 Jan SRE = 2152 SSE = 0740

Here, SRW (0744) is later than SSE (0740). There is indeed a valid condition for a long path opening. It will be of short duration and will be centered around 0746 UTC (see Section 1.3.2.3).

1.4.7.2 Remarks

In practice, long-path openings are possible even when the paths are partially in daylight. Near the terminator we are in the so-called gray-line zone and can take advantage of the enhanced propagation in these zones. The width of the gray line has been discussed earlier (Section 1.1.3.3). A striking example of such an excellent genuine long-path QSO was a contact made between the author and Arie, VK2AVA on March 19, 1976 at 0700 UTC. The long-path distance is 22,500 km. Note that the QSO was made almost right at equinox (March 21), and the path is a textbook example of a NE-SW path. On that day we had the following conditions:

Sunrise West (Belgium)   = 0555 UTC
Sunset East (Sydney, Australia) = 0812 UTC

This means that the long path was in daylight for more than two hours. The QSO was made one hour after sunrise in Belgium and more than one hour before sunset in Australia.

Another similar example was a QSO with VKØGC from Kermadec Island (long-path distance 21,500 km). On Jan 21, 1985 a long-path contact was made on 80 meters that lasted from 0800 until 0830 UTC, with excellent signals. This was more than one hour before sunset on Macquarie (0950) and almost one hour after sunrise in Belgium (0731).

Because the locations of these stations (VK2 and VKØ) are fairly close to the antipodes from Belgium, the long paths can safely be considered genuine long paths. Indeed there are no crooked paths which could provide an alternative to the genuine long paths. The gray-line globe is a unique tool to help you visualize a particular path like this.

1.4.8 PERSONAL COMPUTER PROGRAMS

With the advent of the home computer and its introduction in the shack, computer programs have been developed as aids for the serious minded DXer. Most of the software available is supported either by the Radio Shack TRS-80, Apple,

Commodore 64 or the IBM PC and IBM PC compatible machines. It leaves no doubt that during the coming years more refined software will become available, all running on 16- and 32-bit processors and making use of the larger data storage capacity. On the older 8-bit machines development of complex systems accessing large data banks is difficult and needs extra memory bank switching (to access more than 64 kbytes of memory).

Many amateurs develop their own programs, and share the public domain software with friends, while other interesting software is made commercially available. Some of it is reviewed below.

1.4.8.1 *Computer Programs For Amateur Radio*

Computer Programs For Amateur Radio is a book written by Wayne Overbeck (N6NB) and James Steffen (KC6A) (see Ref 107). The publisher is Hayden Book Company, in Hasbrouck Heights, NJ. The book can be bought with a 5¼-inch diskette listing a range of well-conceived programs for the active DXer and contester. There are versions available for the Apple computer, Radio Shack TRS-80 and the Commodore 64. Most of the book is taken up by the printouts of all the programs (three versions of each program). There is practically no information given about the concept of the programs to help with simple modifications, although anyone

```
          GRAY LINE CALCULATION PROGRAM

FOR ON4UN AT 51 N LAT  3.75 E LONG


YOUR SUNRISE OCCURS AT 7:49 GMT
YOUR SUNSET OCCURS AT  16:0 GMT
ON 1/15

  - PLACES ON YOUR GRAY LINE TODAY -

AT YOUR SUNRISE...

TIME (GMT)                LOCATION


7:20       (RISE) - HB       SWITZERLAND
7:20       (RISE) - 4U       GENEVA (ITU)
7:20       (RISE) - OH       FINLAND,HELSINKI
7:21       (SET)  - JA       JAPAN,SAPPORO
7:22       (SET)  - ZL       CHATHAM IS
7:26       (SET)  - YJ       NEW HEBRIDES
7:27       (RISE) - C3       ANDORRA
7:27       (SET)  - UA0      AS.USSR,KHABAROV
7:28       (RISE) - J5       GUINEA-BISSAU
7:30       (RISE) - LX       LUXEMBOURG
7:33       (SET)  - KC6      E CAROLINE IS
7:35       (RISE) - C5       THE GAMBIA
7:38       (RISE) - ZB       GIBRALTAR
7:38       (RISE) - OZ       DENMARK,COPENHAG
7:38       (SET)  - ZL1      NEW ZEALAND,AUCK
7:38       (RISE) - EA9      MELILLA & CEUTA
7:40       (RISE) - CN       MOROCCO,CASABLAN
7:40       (RISE) - DA-DL    WEST GERMANY,BON
7:40       (SET)  - FK       NEW CALEDONIA
7:40       (RISE) - SM       SWEDEN,STOCKHOLM
7:41       (RISE) - OH0      ALAND IS
7:41       (RISE) - EA       SPAIN,MADRID
7:42       (RISE) - 5T       MAURITANIA
7:45       (RISE) - OJ0      MARKET REEF
7:45       (RISE) - 6W       SENEGAL,DAKAR
7:45       (SET)  - JA       JAPAN,TOKYO
7:46       (RISE) - F        FRANCE,PARIS
7:46       (RISE) - ON       BELGIUM,BRUSSELS
7:47       (SET)  - VK9      NORFOLK IS
7:49       (SET)  - H4,VR4   SOLOMON IS
7:50       (SET)  - ZL2      NZ,WELLINGTON
```

Figure 1.19—An example of the gray-line tables for Belgium on January 15, produced with the programs developed by Overbeck (N6NB) and Steffen (KC6A). The width of the zone was arbitrarily taken as 30 minutes. Notice that close-by countries are also listed although those are generally of no interest to the DXer.

with a certain degree of experience in basic programming should be able to read the programs which are written fairly straightforward BASIC language.

The majority of the programs are of interest to the contester, but the diskette also includes a sunrise chart program using the algorithm described in Section 1.4.6.3D, and a gray-line program allowing you to print out any of over 400 locations of the world that are on your own QTH gray line for a given day of the year (an example is shown in Figure 1.19). It would be nice if the user could enter a minimum distance range, under which he is not interested in gray-line information. This would prevent printing out information for local countries (e.g. European countries in Figure 1.19). The width of the gray line has to be entered by the user, but is constant for any QTH (same width near the poles as near the Equator). The program uses the same algorithm as in the sunrise chart. The gray-line program prints out the list of countries on the gray line, with prefixes and exact sunrise/sunset times.

1.4.8.2 MINIMUF

In the last 10 years, specially developed MUF-predicting programs have appeared that run on large mainframe computers (Ioncap, ITS-78, Skywave). MINIMUF is a simplified MUF-prediction program for microcomputers. The MINIMUF program has been extensively described in the literature (Ref 127). The total BASIC program is very short and can easily be entered via keyboard. Figure 1.20 shows

```
DATE: 25 DEC
TRANSMITTER LOCATION:
   LAT 36   LONG 120
RECEIVER LOCATION:
   LAT 51   LONG -3.75
SOLAR FLUX NR: = 70
SUNSPOT NUMBER = 6


HOUR          MUF (MHZ)


0               7.5
1               7.4
2               7.3
3               7.2
4               7.2
5               7.1
6               7.1
7               7.1
8               7.1
9               7.4
10              7.3
11              7.2
12              7.2
13              7.1
14              12.2
15              13.5
16              13
17              12.1
18              10.9
19              8.5
20              8.2
21              7.9
22              7.7
23              7.6
```

Figure 1.20—This printout from MINIMUF shows the MUF at 1 hour intervals for inputs specified by the user (path coordinates plus solar flux number and sunspot number).

a printout from the MINIMUF program. A listing is available in the reference article. MINIMUF is also used as part of the DX-1 and DX-2 system.

1.4.8.3 DX-1 and DX-2

Brollini, NS6N describes an excellent system in "DXing by Computer" (Ref 119). The system has since been commercialized and copyrighted under the name DX-1 and DX-2. The DX-1 system includes the gray-line feature (including the QTH data bank, all on one diskette), while DX-2 retains all other features of the system without the gray-line option. In addition to giving sunrise and sunset times the DX-1 system will give the user great-circle distances, beam headings, MUF (Maximum Usable Frequency), FOT (Frequency of Optimum Transmission) and Quality Factor for a given path. Figure 1.21 shows a sample printout of DX-1. For FOT and MUF the MINIMUF program as described in Section 1.4.8.2 is used. A definition of MUF was given in Section 1.1.1.1.

```
DEC 25
                                        PATH
        LAT     LONG              SHORT   LONG
BASE: 51:00  -003:45   DIST:      4717  16883
TARGET NAME: CALIFORNIA
TARGET EPREFIX: W6-CA

          SUNRISE   SUNSET
BASE      07:47     15:42    GEO-MAG   1
TGT-AVE   15:06     00:43    10.7cm    70
TGT-MIN   14:39     00:32    SUNSPOT   8
TGT-MAX   15:42     01:00    Q-FACT    4.2

      MAXIMUM USEABLE FREQUENCY
00  7.5 05  7.1 10   7.3 15 13.5 20   8.2
01  7.4 06  7.1 11   7.2 16 13.0 21   7.9
02  7.3 07  7.1 12   7.2 17 12.3 22   7.7
03  7.2 08  7.1 13   7.1 18 10.9 23   7.6
04  7.2 09  7.3 14  12.4 19  8.5 24   7.5

    FREQUENCY OF OPTIMUM TRANSMISSION
00  6.3 05  6.2 10   6.2 15 11.5 20   6.9
01  6.3 06  6.0 11   6.1 16 11.1 21   6.6
02  6.2 07  6.0 12   6.1 17 10.4 22   6.6
03  6.1 08  6.0 13   6.1 18  9.3 23   6.4
04  6.1 09  6.2 14  10.5 19  7.2 24   6.3
--------------------------------------------
```

Figure 1.21—A sample printout from the DX-1 program produced by V. Brollini, NS6N. Note that the printout gives geographical information (great-circle direction and distance, sunrise and sunset at both ends, with minimum and maximum figures for large areas), as well as propagation information (path Q factor and the MUF or FOT table).

Above the MUF radio signals will penetrate the F layer and no longer be reflected. By definition the MUFs as generated by this program support reliable communication for 50 percent of the days of the month. The FOT means that communication is being supported at the FOT frequencies for 90 percent of the days of the month. The quality factor is a number from 0 to 9 representing radio quality. J. Harris (Ref 117) developed the analytical mathematical formulation. The quality factor is based on the daily solar flux (F) and the daily geomagnetic A value (A). The formula is:

$$Q = 10 \times \left[\log(F \cdot 4)^a\right] \times \left[e^{-0.01A}\right] + 0.82$$

where

$e = 2.718$

A = geomagnetic A index

F = 2800 MHz (10.7 cm) solar flux, and

$a = 1 + 0.2625 \sin^2 (0.49315 \, D)$, where D = Julian day number

The value of the geomagnetic A index and the solar-flux number are transmitted every hour at 18 minutes past the hour by WWV. WWV transmits on 2.5, 5, 10, 15 and 20 MHz from Boulder, Colorado. Detailed information on WWV broadcasts is available in ARRL Handbooks (Ref 101). An alternative for US hams is to use the National Bureau of Standards hotline 303-497-3235. Forecasts for the solar-flux number are published monthly in most Amateur Radio magazines, and are regularly broadcast by many amateur organizations. The ARRL bulletins are a good example. The bulletin schedule is announced in *QST*, the monthly ARRL journal.

The DX-1 and DX-2 programs also allow the printout of a gray-line chart (listing all countries on the gray line for a given day of year and hour of day). The listing prints the name of the country, the prefix, and distances in miles and beam heading for both short and long paths. The listing does not show the exact sunrise/sunset time for each of the countries or areas on the gray line, however. The user is requested to enter the width of the gray line (in degrees). This means that the gray line remains constant in width all along its circumference. A refinement where the width of the zone would automatically be adjusted to the latitude and the date (earth axis inclination) would be a welcome improvement. This correction is applied in the gray-line program developed by the author (Section 1.3.3.3) and mentioned in Chapter VII. It is obvious of course that this addition requires extra memory space.

The DX-1 and DX-2 computer programs on diskette can be obtained from DX Enterprises, Van Brollini NS6N, 5861 Bridle Way, San Jose CA 95123; tel 408-578-3708. The very precise algorithm (described in Section 1.4.6.3C) is used to calculate sunrise/sunset times. The program is written in Pascal and runs on an Apple II computer. For both the DX-1 and the DX-2 program an Apple II with 64 kbytes of memory and one disk drive is required. The software and documentation are excellent. The method of calculating minimum and maximum sunrise and sunset times for large countries and areas is very original and well thought out. It is described in detail by its author in "DXing By Computer" (Ref 119).

1.4.8.4 DX EDGE Computer Version

The DX EDGE slide rule (Section 1.4.2) is also available in a computerized version for use on a Commodore 64. Although the second edition of the software is substantially faster than the original one, it still is a very slow tool. It is doubtful that, in the midst of a DX session, any DX operator would take the time to use the computer version of the DX EDGE to look for sunrise/sunset information. The DX EDGE slide rule is much more appropriate for such applications, and in a matter of seconds one can have the information. The program, on a diskette, is available from The DX Edge, PO Box 834, Madison Square Stn, New York, NY 10159. It is also obtainable through distributors (see advertisements in Amateur Radio magazines).

1.4.8.5 MUFPLOT

MUFPLOT is a computer program showing in graphical format the MUF, FOT and LUF for any given path. The program is available for the Commodore C64 computer, for the Apple computer and the IBM PC. The program includes a data base of 400 targets, listed by prefix or by state

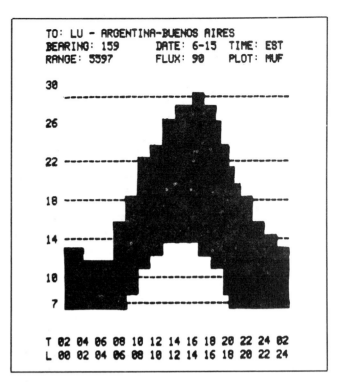

Figure 1.22—Typical video display produced on the Commodore C64 by the MUFPLOT program. The MUF is plotted as the upper limit, and the LUF as the lower limit. The upper limit is user selected (MUF, HPF or FOT). The time scale shows both local and target time.

abbreviation (US). The data base can be changed and customer entries can be added. The software is based on the MINIMUF program (see Section 1.4.8.2), with enhancements to improve accuracy over so-called multi-hop paths. The MUF is printed on the screen in graph form. The C64 version has a lower frequency limit of 7 MHz and the Apple version's low limit is 4 MHz. The graph shows either MUF, FOT or HPF (highest possible frequency, at 10 percent probability), as selected by the user, and the LUF (lowest usable frequency). The program is very user-friendly. The documentation is well written, and includes a short explanation on propagation mechanisms and the methods used in the program. Figure 1.22 shows the typical screen display available on a Commodore C64 computer. The programs can be obtained from Base (2) Systems, 2534 Nebraska Street, Saginaw MI 48601.

1.4.8.6 ON4UN Propagation Programs

While writing this book, the author developed a number of computer programs as aids for the active DXer. More information on these programs can be found in Chapter VII.

•SUNRISE-SUNSET TIMES. This program lists the sunrise and sunset times in half-month increments for the user's QTH. In addition, you can list the same times for any other QTH side by side with your own times. The target QTH can be specified either by coordinates or by name. When specified by name, the coordinates are looked up in a data base containing over 500 locations worldwide. Figure 1.23 shows a practical run.

•LISTING SUNRISE SUNSET TIMES. This program provides a paper printout of the sunrise and sunset times of a collection of over 500 locations worldwide for a user-specified day. This can be very useful when preparing for a contest or a DXpedition. Figure 1.24 shows a partial printout.

	12.41	22.40	JAN 1	17.07	07.44			
	12.41	22.52	JAN 15	17.20	07.43			
	12.34	22.52	FEB 1	17.37	07.34			
ATLANTA	12.21	23.21	FEB 15	17.53	07.20		NEW ZEALAND	
GEORGIA	12.07	23.32	MAR 1	18.06	07.04		AUCKLAND	
------	11.48	23.44	MAR 15	18.20	06.43		------------	
LONG=84.23	11.26	23.56	APR 1	18.34	06.20		LONG=-174.45	
LAT =33.45	11.07	00.07	APR 15	18.47	05.58		LAT =-36.53	
===========>>>	10.50	00.19	MAY 1	18.59	05.40		<<<==============	
	10.37	00.30	MAY 15	19.12	05.35			
	10.28	00.41	JUN 1	19.24	05.15			
	10.26	00.48	JUN 15	19.32	05.13			
	10.30	00.51	JUL 1	19.35	05.13			
	10.38	00.48	JUL 15	19.32	05.24			
	10.48	00.38	AUG 1	19.21	05.36			
UTC TIMES	10.59	00.24	AUG 15	19.06	05.48			
	11.10	00.05	SEP 1	18.45	06.00			
	11.20	23.44	SEP 15	18.23	06.12			
	11.30	23.24	OCT 1	18.01	06.24			
	11.41	23.04	OCT 15	17.39	06.37			
	11.54	22.47	NOV 1	17.19	06.52			
	12.08	22.35	NOV 15	17.05	07.08			
MORE > M	12.22	22.29	DEC 1	16.58	07.23			
EXIT > E	12 33	22.31	DEC 15	16.58	07.36			

Figure 1.23—The author's sunrise and sunset program shows the sunrise and sunset times for the user's QTH and the target QTH side by side for easy interpretation.

MONTH = 1 / DAY = 5

PREFIX	COUNTRY	CITY	SUNRISE	SUNSET
1A	ORDER OF MALTA	ROME	06.38	15.55
1S1	SPRATLEY		22.29	10.29
3A	MONACO		07.04	16.09
3B6-7	AGALEGA, ST BRANDON		01.59	14.41
3B8	MAURITIUS		01.37	14.55
3C	EQUATORIAL GUINEA	MALABO	05.33	17.29
3C0	PAGALU		05.38	17.50
3D2	FIJI ISL		17.38	06.48
3D6	SWAZILAND	MBABANE	03.09	16.53
3V	TUNESIA	TUNIS	06.32	16.18
3X	REP OF GUINEA	CONAKRY	07.11	18.47
3Y	BOUVET		03.23	20.22
3Y	PETER 1ST ISL		NO SR	NO SS
4S	SRI LANKA	COLOMBO	00.54	12.40

etc...

Figure 1.24—A sunrise/sunset listing can be a very useful tool when preparing for a contest or a DXpedition. This partial example is for January 5th (ON4UN program).

•SUNRISE CALENDAR. When you need a sunset-sunrise calendar for a given QTH, this program will provide a printout. The start date and end date, as well as the days increment can be user specified. The maximum calendar will print sunrise and sunset times for every day of the year. Figure 1.25 shows an example.

•GREAT CIRCLE DIRECTIONS/DISTANCES. This program will calculate and display the great circle direction and distance between the user's QTH and any other target QTH which can be specified by coordinates or by name. The user can specify kilometers or miles for the distance.

•LISTING GREAT CIRCLE DIRECTIONS/ DISTANCES. This program provides a printout of the directions and distances to over 500 target locations worldwide. Figure 1.26 shows a partial printout.

•GRAYLINE PROGRAM. This program uses a unique algorithm which adapts the radio effective width of the gray-

Figure 1.25—This user defined sunrise/sunset calendar shows the times for San Diego on a weekly basis (ON4UN program).

COUNTRY: USA
CITY: SAN DIEGO
CALL: W6YA
LATITUDE NORTH: 32.43
LONGITUDE WEST: 117.09

MONTH/DAY	SUNRISE	SUNSET
JAN/1	14.50	00.54
JAN/8	14.51	00.59
JAN/15	14.50	01.05
JAN/22	14.48	01.12
JAN/29	14.45	01.18
FEB/5	14.40	01.25
FEB/12	14.34	01.31
FEB/19	14.27	01.37
FEB/26	14.20	01.43
MAR/5	14.11	01.49
MAR/12	14.03	01.54
MAR/19	13.54	01.59
MAR/26	13.44	02.04
APR/2	13.35	02.09
APR/9	13.27	02.13

etc...

```
STATION COORDINATES: 37.47 DEG NORTH, 122.25 DEG WEST.

PREFIX     COUNTRY              CITY         DIR     (KM) DIST. (MILES)
------     -------              ----         ---     ------------------
()         ABU AIL                           18      14058       8737
1A         ORDER OF MALTA       ROME         32      10084       6267
1S1        SPRATLEY                          300     12448       7736
3A         MONACO                            34      9671        6010
3B6-7      AGALEGA, ST BRANDON               2       16971       10547
3B8        MAURITIUS                         1       18077       11234
3B9        RODRIGUEZ                         343     17925       11140
3C         EQUATORIAL GUINEA    MALABO       59      13189       8197
3C0        PAGALU                            65      13315       8275
3D2        FIJI ISL                          236     8768        5449
3D6        SWAZILAND            MBABANE      71      17199       10689
3V         TUNESIA             TUNIS        36      10435       6485
3X         REP OF GUINEA       CONAKRY      70      10986       6827
3Y         BOUVET                            132     15525       9648
3Y         PETER 1ST ISL                     168     12064       7497
etc...
```

Figure 1.26—Partial printout of the great-circle distance and directions listing as provided by the author's program (centered on San Francisco).

```
YOUR LATITUDE IS 37.47 DEG. NORTH    YOUR LONGITUDE IS 122.25 DEG. WEST
TIME OF YEAR (MONTH/DAY) = 1/15
YOUR SUNRISE IS AT 15.22 UTC         YOUR SUNSET IS AT 01.14 UTC
GRAY LINE WIDTH IS 52 MINUTES        MINIMUM TARGET DISTANCE IS 2000 MILES.
----------------------------------------------------------------------
PREFIX     COUNTRY         CITY         MILES    START    END     MIN/TARG
------     -------         ----         -----    -----    ---     --------
.
.
OH         FINLAND         HELSINKI     5433     14.56    15.34   205
OHO        ALAND ISL                    5335     14.56    15.48   215
OJ0        MARKET REEF                  5351     14.56    15.48   207
OK         CZECHOSLOVAKIA  PRAHA        5832     14.56    15.48   99
ON         BELGIUM         BRUSSELS     5541     15.19    15.48   95
OX         GREENLAND       GODTHAB      3356     15.07    15.48   380
OX         GREENLAND       THULE        3136     14.56    15.48   1440
OY         FAROE ISL                    4680     14.56    15.48   262
OZ         DENMARK         COPENHAGEN   5481     14.56    15.48   132
PA         NETHERLANDS     AMSTERDAM    5460     15 05    15.48   105
S7         SEYCHELLES      MAHE         8673     15.35    15.48   21
SM         SWEDEN          STOCKHOLM    5378     14.56    15.48   185
SP         POLAND          WARSCHAU     5857     14.56    15.45   105
ST         SUDAN           KHARTOUM     8425     15.27    15.48   24
SU         EGYPT           CAIRO        7461     14.57    15.37   39
SV         GREECE          ATHENS       6804     15.05    15.48   52
SV         CRETE                        6970     15.09    15.48   48
SV         DODECANESE                   6982     14.56    15.45   49
SV         MOUNT ATHOS                  6667     14.56    15.48   58
T5         SOMALI          MOGADISHU    9587     14.59    15.19   20
TA         TURKEY          ANKARA       6875     14.56    15.17   56
TF         ICELAND         REYKJAVIK    4222     14.56    15.09   378
UA         EUR. USSR       LENINGRAD    5547     14.56    15.09   192
UA1        FRANZ JOSEF LAND             4248     14.56    15.48   1440
UA2        KALININGRADSK                5705     14.56    15.45   122
UB5        UKRAINE         KJEV         6145     14.56    15.10   94
UB5        UKRAINE         ODESSA       6403     14.56    15.16   76
UB5        UKRAINE         LVOV         6080     14.56    15.37   90
UC2        WHITE RUSSIA    MINSK        5888     14.56    15.18   115
UO5        MOLDAVIA        KISNOV       6323     14.56    15.23   79
etc...
```

Figure 1.27—Partial gray-line printout for San Francisco on January 15, with a minimum distance input of 2000 miles. MIN/TARG is the width of the gray line at the target QTH in minutes. The program uses an exclusive algorithm to calculate the effective radio-width of this zone.

line zone to the location and the time of the year. In addition the user can specify a minimum distance under which he is not interested in gray-line information. The printout (on screen or paper) lists the distance to the target QTH, the beginning and ending time of the gray-line window, as well as the effective width of the gray line at the target QTH. Figure 1.27 shows a printout of a gray-line run.

1.5 Future Work

Many active low-band DXers all over the world do their daily bit of low band propagation observation and try to correlate it with known mechanisms and past experiences. It would be advantageous, however, if a number of highly interested and active low-band DXers could get involved in a common program where all locally made observations, data on sunspot activity (number, flux etc), and magnetic activity would be entered in a large data base system for more systematic and better-structured analysis and interpretation.

Some active low-band DXers have claimed that usually after a good long-path opening, the short-path opening (½ day later) will be below average. The writer is in no position to confirm this, but would rather deny it based on some limited personal observations. Enhanced propagation has been witnessed along certain paths just prior and subsequent to a major aurora activity. Enough data should enable us to more precisely understand this phenomenon and take advantage of it. Many other similar non-standard propagation situations are excellent subjects for more systematic observation and subsequent analysis. A high enough number of observations from different areas around the world, together with day-by-day MUF maps, and data on sunspot and magnetic activity would make a systematic analysis of these observations more meaningful, and would help to further explain and maybe even predict some of the less usual propagation phenomena. Anyone interested in cooperating in such a program is welcome to contact the author.

Figure 1.28—Propagation conditions on the low bands present a real challenge, but one that can be overcome by a dedicated operator. Bob, ZL2BT, has 307 countries confirmed on 80 meters.

Chapter II

Antennas

The ARRL Antenna Book (Ref 600) contains a wealth of excellent and accurate information on antennas. The antenna chapter of this book will emphasize typical aspects of low-band antennas, and will explain how and why some of the popular antennas work.

2.1 Purpose of an Antenna

2.1.1 TRANSMITTING ANTENNAS

We expect our transmitting antenna to radiate all the RF energy supplied to it in the desired direction with the required elevation angle (directivity).

2.1.1.1 Wanted Direction

Horizontal Directivity

The chapter on propagation shows that most of the propagation paths are rectilinear paths (great circle, short path, and so on) for short and medium distances (up to 10,000 km or 6000 miles). We also know that for areas near the antipodes the propagation path can vary almost over a 180° angle with season (Section 1.3.3.1). All this must be taken into account when designing an antenna system. Rotary systems will provide a great deal of flexibility as far as horizontal directivity is concerned. Here it must be emphasized that the term horizontal directivity is really meaningless without further definition. Zero angle (perfectly parallel to the horizon) wave directivity is of very little use, as practical antennas produce no signal at zero wave angle over real ground. Horizontal directivity should always be specified at a given elevation angle. An antenna can have quite different azimuthal directional properties at different elevation angles.

Vertical Directivity

Very little has been published in amateur literature on optimum wave angle for given paths on the lower bands. Results of tests between England and North America have been extrapolated and are given in Table 1.

Most of the professional literature deals with research near the MUF. For commercial links it is most advantageous to operate near the MUF. In our hobby, working DX on the low bands, we are certainly not operating near the MUF under most circumstances. We operate far below the MUF and FOT and in many cases near the LUF (lowest usable frequency).

From experience, the author has learned a few things about the optimum angle of radiation. There are many factors that influence the optimum wave angle, such as:

- Time of day.
- MUF situation at the path ends.
- Time of year.
- Propagation near, through or into aurora zones.
- Propagation into equatorial zones.

It is not always true that the lower the angle, the better. I have found that there are optimum radiation angles on 80 meters for certain kinds of communications. They are listed below.

- East-west propagation during the night for distances shorter than 6000 km or 3700 miles: 35 to 45°.
- Same paths at dusk and dawn: 20 to 40°.
- Long distances at dusk or dawn (6000 to 20,000 km (3700 to 12,400 miles)): 15 to 25°.
- Paths into or near the (active) aurora zone: 15 to 25° (also for distances as short as 1600 km (1000 miles)).
- Paths into the equatorial zone: 35 to 60°.

It should be clear that in no case is an angle higher than 50° required for an effective DX antenna.

2.1.1.2 Efficiency

The efficiency of a transmitting antenna is simply the ratio of power radiated from an antenna to the power applied to it. Any energy that is not radiated will be converted into heat in the lossy parts of the antenna.

2.1.2 RECEIVING ANTENNAS

For a receiving antenna, the requirements are slightly different. Here we expect the antenna to receive only signals from a given direction and at a given wave angle (directivity), and we expect the antenna to produce signals which are substantially stronger than the internally generated noise of the receiver, taking into account losses in matching networks and feeders. This means that the efficiency of a receiving antenna is not the main requirement. An important asset of a good receiving antenna system is the ability to change directions very rapidly. In practice, this can only be obtained by switching among a number of unidirectional antennas or by using an array of phased verticals, where the directions can be changed by merely changing the delays in the feed lines.

In most amateur applications, the transmitting antenna is used as the receiving antenna, and the transmitting requirements of the antenna outweigh the typical receiving requirements.

Table 1

Angle of Arrival of Signals Between England and North America

Freq (MHz)	Probability >99%	Probability >99%	Probability >50%
7.0	<37°	>11°	>22°
3.5	<53°	>13°	>33°

2.2 Definitions

We will introduce antenna theory by examining a number of classic antennas. The antennas to be dealt with are:
- Horizontal dipole
- Vertical monopole
- Inverted V dipole
- Sloping dipole
- Vertical dipole
- Loop antenna
- Half-loop and half-sloper
- Arrays made of omnidirectional antennas
- Arrays made of directional antennas
- Antennas with parasitic elements
- Beverage antenna
- Receiving loop

2.2.1 RADIATION PATTERNS

The radiation pattern of an antenna is defined as the collection of all points around the antenna with the same field intensity. The radiation pattern is always a three-dimensional body. In most cases, however, we will deal with the pattern in a plane. If we cut the three-dimensional pattern through a plane (often defined as perpendicular to the antenna wire), we obtain several planar radiation patterns. These patterns are often identified as vertical (cutting plane perpendicular to the ground) or horizontal (cutting plane parallel to the ground). The latter is of very little use as practical antennas over real ground produce no signal at zero wave angle. The so-called horizontal directivity should in all practical cases be specified as directivity in a plane making a given angle with the horizon (usually the main wave angle).

2.2.2 THE ISOTROPIC ANTENNA

An isotropic antenna is a theoretical antenna of infinitely small dimensions that radiates an equal signal in all directions. The isotropic antenna is often used as a reference antenna for gain comparison, expressed in decibels over isotropic (dBi). The radiation pattern of an isotropic antenna is a sphere by definition.

2.2.3 FREE SPACE CONDITION

Free space is a condition where no ground or any other conductor interacts with the radiation from the antenna. In practice, such conditions are approached only at VHF and UHF, where very high antennas (in wavelengths) are common.

2.2.4 GROUND CONDITIONS

Low-band antennas always involve real ground. For evaluation purposes, we often use a perfect ground—a ground consisting of an infinitely large, perfect reflector. Real grounds have varying properties, in both conductivity and dielectric constant. In this chapter, frequent reference will be made to different qualities of real grounds, as shown in Table 2.

Table 2

Qualities of Various Types of Real Ground

Ground Type	Conductivity (mS/m)	Dielectric Constant
Desert	1	7
Average ground	5	15
Swamp	20	30
Salt Water	5000	80

2.2.5 RADIATION RESISTANCE

Radiation resistance (referred to a certain point in an antenna system) is the resistance which, inserted at that point, would dissipate the same energy as is actually radiated from the antenna. This definition does not state where the antenna is being fed, however. There are two common ways of specifying radiation resistance:
- The antenna being fed at the current maximum ($R_{rad}[1]$).
- The antenna being fed at the base between the antenna lower end and ground ($R_{rad}[2]$).

The latter definition is applicable to monopole antennas, or to dipoles when considering their half-size monopole equivalents. $R_{rad}[1]$ will be primarily used for determining the weight factor in calculating absolute field strength figures, while $R_{rad}[2]$ will be used in efficiency calculations (Section 2.2.6).

2.2.6 ANTENNA EFFICIENCY

The efficiency of an antenna is expressed as follows:

$$\eta = \frac{R_{rad}[2]}{R_{rad}[2] + R_{loss}}$$

where $R_{rad}[2]$ is the radiation resistance of the antenna as defined in Section 2.2.5, and R_{loss} is the total equivalent loss resistance of all elements of the antenna (R-losses, dielectric losses, equivalent R-losses, ground losses, etc).

2.2.7 BANDWIDTH

The bandwidth of an antenna is the difference between the highest and the lowest frequency on which a given property exceeds or meets a given performance mark. This can be gain, front-to-back ratio or SWR. In this book, "bandwidth" refers to SWR bandwidth unless otherwise specified. In most cases the SWR bandwidth is determined by the 2:1 or 3:1 SWR points on the SWR curve. In this text the SWR limits will be specified when dealing with antenna bandwidths.

2.3 Horizontal Dipole

Although we often think of dipoles as ½ λ-long, center-fed antennas, this is not always the case. The definition used here is a center-fed radiator with a symmetrical sinusoidal standing-wave current distribution.

2.3.1 RADIATION PATTERN OF THE ½ λ DIPOLE IN FREE SPACE

The pattern in the plane of the wire has the shape of a figure-8. The pattern in a plane perpendicular to the wire is a circle (Figure 2.1). The three dimensional representation of the radiation pattern is shown in the same figure. The gain of this dipole over an isotropic radiator is 2.14 dB.

2.3.2 THE DIPOLE OVER GROUND

In any antenna system, the ground acts more or less as an imperfect or lossy mirror that reflects energy. Simplifying, and assuming a perfect ground, we can apply the Fresnel reflection laws, whereby the angles of incident and reflected rays are identical.

2.3.2.1 Vertical Radiation Pattern of the Horizontal Dipole

The vertical radiation pattern determines the wave angle of the antenna. Since obtaining a low angle of radiation is one of the main considerations when building low-band antennas, we will usually consider only the lowest lobe in case

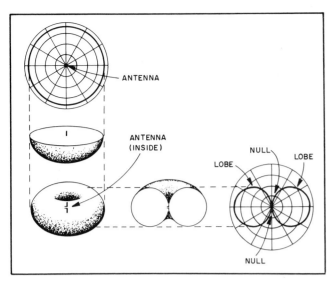

Figure 2.1—Vertical (left) and horizontal (right) radiation patterns as developed from the three-dimensional pattern of a horizontal dipole.

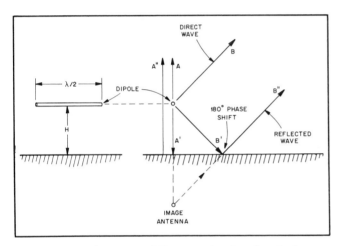

Figure 2.2—Reflection of RF energy by the electrical "ground mirror." The eventual phase relationship between the direct and the reflected horizontally-polarized wave will only depend on the height of the dipole over the reflecting ground.

the antenna produces more than one vertical lobe. In free space, the radiation pattern of the isotropic antenna is a sphere. As a consequence, any plane pattern of the isotropic antenna in free space is a circle. In free space, the pattern of a dipole in a plane perpendicular to the antenna wire is also a circle. Therefore, if we analyze the vertical radiation pattern of the horizontal dipole over ground, its behavior is similar to an isotropic radiator over ground.

Ray Analysis

Refer to Figure 2.2. In the vertical plane (perpendicular to the ground), an isotropic radiator radiates energy equally in all directions (by definition). Let us now examine a few typical rays. A and A' radiate in opposite directions. A' is reflected by the ground (A'') in the same direction as A. B'', the reflected ray of B', is reflected in the same direction as B.

The important issue is now the phase difference between A and A'', B and B'', etc. Phase difference can also be called path difference (length is directly proportional to time, as speed of propagation is constant).

If at a very distant point (in terms of wavelengths), the rays at points A and A'' are in phase (the path difference is equal to a number of half wavelengths), then their combined field strength will be at a maximum and will be equal to the sum of the magnitudes of the two rays. If they are out of phase, the resulting field strength will be less than the sum of the individual rays. If A and A'' are identical in magnitude and 180° out of phase (path-length difference is equal to an odd number of quarter wavelengths) total cancellation will occur.

If the dipole antenna is at very low height (less than a quarter wavelength), A and A'' will reinforce each other. Low-angle rays (B and B'') will be almost completely out of phase, resulting in cancellation and thus very little radiation at low angles. At increased heights, A and A'' may be 180° out of phase (no vertical radiation) and lower angles such as B and B'' may reinforce each other. In other words, the vertical radiation pattern of a dipole depends only on the height of the antenna above the ground.

Vertical Radiation Pattern Equations

The radiation pattern can be calculated with the following equation:

$$F(a) = \sin(h \sin a)$$

where

F(a) = field intensity at vertical angle a
h = height of antenna in degrees
a = vertical angle of radiation.

One wavelength height is 360°. The equation is valid only for perfectly reflecting grounds. For imperfect grounds, the angles at which maxima and minima occur will be slightly lower, while the total pattern, especially the nulls, will be less pronounced.

The above equation can be rewritten as follows:

$$H(1) = \frac{90}{0.366 \, f \sin a}$$

where

H(1) = height in feet for first lobe
f = frequency
a = vertical angle for which the antenna height is sought.

If height in meters is required, multiply the result by 0.3048 (1 foot = 0.3048 meters). When more lobes are of interest, replace 90 with 270 for the second lobe, with 450 for third lobe, etc. If the nulls are sought, replace 90 with 180 for first null, with 360 for second null, etc. A simple computer program written in Applesoft BASIC for determining wave angles for a given antenna height is given in Chapter VII. Table 3 gives the major lobe angles as well as reflection-point distances for heights ranging from 80 to 200 feet for 40, 80 and 160 meters.

Sloping Ground Locations

In many cases, an antenna cannot be erected above perfectly flat ground. A ground slope (Ref 630) can greatly influence the wave angle of the antenna. A BASIC program allowing us to assess the influence of the slope angle on the required antenna height to achieve a required wave angle is listed in Chapter VII. Table 4 shows the influence of the slope angle on the required antenna height for a given wave angle on 80 meters.

The results from Table 4 can easily be extrapolated to 40 or 160 meters by simply dividing or multiplying all of the results by 2. All heights and distances are in feet.

Table 3

Major Lobe Angles and Reflection Point for Various Antenna Heights

Antenna Height		40 Meters			80 Meters			160 Meters		
(ft)	(m)	Angle (deg)	Distance (ft)	(m)	Angle (deg)	Distance (ft)	(m)	Angle (deg)	Distance (ft)	(m)
60	18	36	83	25	90	0	0	90	0	0
80	24	26	163	50	54	58	18	90	0	0
100	30	20	266	81	40	118	36	90	0	0
120	36	17	391	119	33	187	57	90	0	0
140	42	15	540	148	28	268	82	77	31	9
160	48	13	710	217	24	362	110	59	97	30
180	54	—	—	—	21	467	142	49	154	47
200	60	—	—	—	18	584	178	43	213	66

Table 4

Slope Angle Versus Antenna Height at 3.5 MHz

Slope Angle (deg)	20° Wave Angle		30° Wave Angle		40° Wave Angle	
	Height (ft)	Distance (ft)	Height (ft)	Distance (ft)	Height (ft)	Distance (ft)
35	—	—	—	—	906	10,364
30	—	—	—	—	430	2441
25	—	—	819	9367	275	1029
20	—	—	396	2249	201	553
15	768	8789	258	966	158	340
10	378	2146	192	528	131	227
5	251	937	153	329	113	161
0	189	520	129	224	100	120
−5	153	329	113	161	91	91
−10	131	227	102	121	85	72
−15	116	166	94	94	81	57
−20	107	127	89	75	79	45
−25	101	101	87	61	78	36
−30	97	91	86	49	78	28

Antennas Over Real Ground

Up until this point, a perfect ground has been assumed. Perfect ground does not exist in practical installations, however. Perfect ground conditions are approached only when an antenna is erected over salt water. Real ground produces the following effects (Ref 618, 637):

• The height of the antenna over the "virtual" ground is slightly higher than the physical height above ground.

• Because of the poor conductivity of the reflecting plane, part of the RF energy will be absorbed.

• As already explained, it is the quality of the ground at the point of reflection which is important (Table 3).

Note that the point of reflection can be quite a distance from the antenna if the antenna is producing a low wave angle. This is the main reason why it is also important to erect a horizontally polarized antenna well clear of surrounding obstacles.

Figure 2.3 shows vertical patterns of a horizontal dipole over both near-perfect ground (salt water) and desert, the two extremes. The decibel figures are referenced to a half-wave dipole in free space. With a perfect ground (reflector) a maximum gain of 6 dB is possible (direct and reflected wave in phase with no absorption at ground level). Note that the scale is at +6 dB on the outer ring (with respect to the dipole in free space). When comparing the dipoles at ¼ λ height (66 feet for 3.8 MHz) notice that for a 90° wave angle, the antenna over real ground shows a loss of almost 3 dB, due

to absorption in the imperfect reflector. This loss for the main low-angle lobe decreases for heights greater than 1 λ. Notice that for a height of ½ λ (132 feet for 3.8 MHz), the sharp null at 90° elevation angle has been degraded to a mere 12 dB attenuation over desert-type ground. The wave angle of the major lobe is also slightly lower, due to the effective antenna height being higher than the physical height. This effect is marginal at ½ λ, but very pronounced at ¼ λ height. See also Table 6.

From this we can conclude that the effects of absorption over poor ground are quite pronounced with low antennas and become less pronounced as the antenna height is increased. Artificial improvement of the ground conditions by the installation of ground wires is only practical if one wants maximum gain at 90° wave angle (zenith) from a low dipole (1/8 to ¼ λ height). This can be done by burying a number of wires (½ to 1 λ long), spaced about 2 feet (60 cm) below the dipole, or by installing a parasitic reflector wire (½ λ long plus 5%) between one foot and several feet above ground, about 1/8 to ¼ λ under the dipole. Improving the efficiency of the reflecting ground for low-angle signals produced by high dipoles is impractical and yields very little benefit (see Figure 2.3). The active reflection area can be as far as 10 λ away from the antenna!

2.3.2.2 Horizontal Pattern of Horizontal Half-Wave Dipole

The horizontal radiation pattern of a dipole has the shape

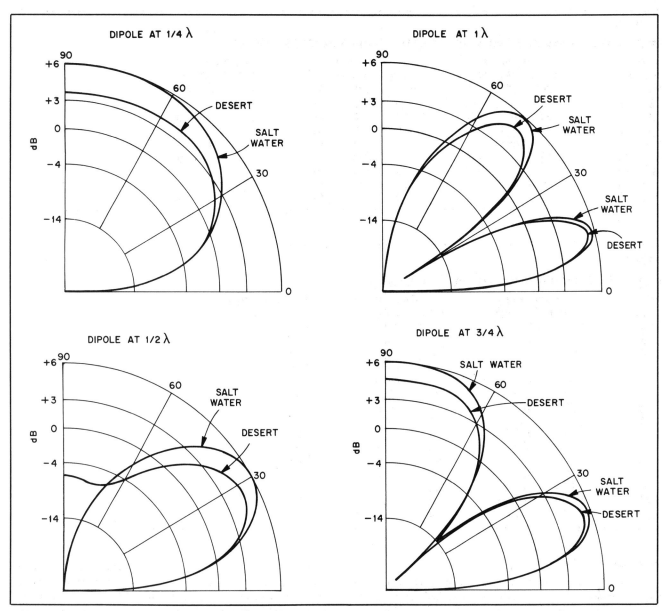

Figure 2.3—Vertical radiation patterns of dipoles at ¼, ½, ¾ and 1 λ over excellent (salt water) and poor (desert) ground. Note that the gain difference is much more noticeable at low heights. With high antennas, the gain difference at low wave angles is quite small.

of a figure-8, and its sharpness depends on the height of the antenna and the vertical radiation angle at which one measures the horizontal patterns.

The horizontal directivity of a dipole depends on two factors:

1) Antenna height.

2) The wave angle at which we measure the directivity.

Figure 2.4 shows the horizontal directivity of half-wave horizontal dipoles at heights of ¼, ½ and ¾ λ over average ground. Directivity patterns are included for wave angles of 15 through 60° in increments of 15°.

Notice that a low dipole has practically no directivity at high angles. At low angles, where it has more directivity, it hardly radiates at all. Therefore it is quite useless to put two dipoles at right angles for better overall coverage if those dipoles are at low heights. At heights of ½ λ and higher there is discernible directivity, especially at low angles. Figure 2.5 gives a visual representation of the three-dimensional radiation pattern of a half-wave dipole at ½ λ above average ground.

2.3.3 HALF-WAVE DIPOLE EFFICIENCY

Dipole efficiency is given by the equation:

$$\eta = \frac{R_{rad}[2]}{R_{rad}[2] + R_{loss}}$$

The relationship of the radiation resistance and impedance of a half-wave dipole to its height above ground is shown later in this chapter in Figure 2.44. Radiation resistance varies between 60 and 90 ohms for all practical heights on the low bands.

The losses in a half-wave dipole are caused by:
- RF resistance of antenna conductor (wire).
- Dielectric losses of insulators.
- Ground losses.

Table 5 gives the effective RF resistance for common conductor materials, taking skin effect into consideration. The resistances are given in ohms/km. For ohms/1000 feet, divide values by 3.28 (1 km = 3281 feet). The RF resistance values

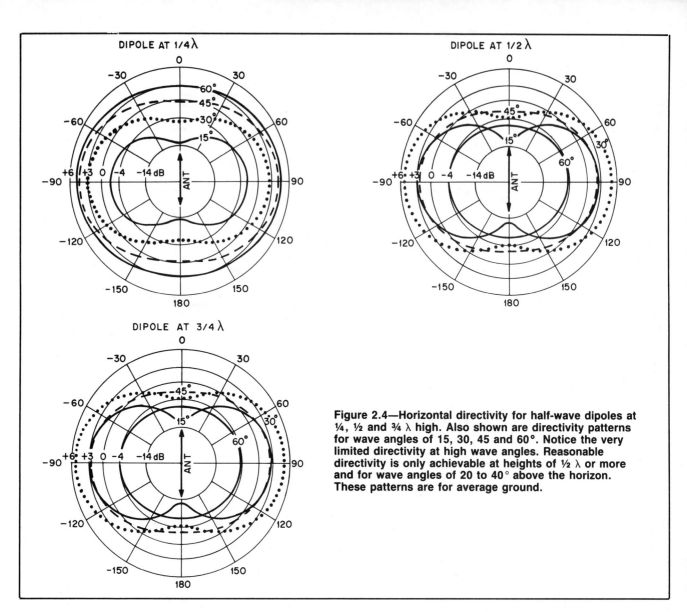

DIPOLE AT 1/4 λ

DIPOLE AT 1/2 λ

DIPOLE AT 3/4 λ

Figure 2.4—Horizontal directivity for half-wave dipoles at ¼, ½ and ¾ λ high. Also shown are directivity patterns for wave angles of 15, 30, 45 and 60°. Notice the very limited directivity at high wave angles. Reasonable directivity is only achievable at heights of ½ λ or more and for wave angles of 20 to 40° above the horizon. These patterns are for average ground.

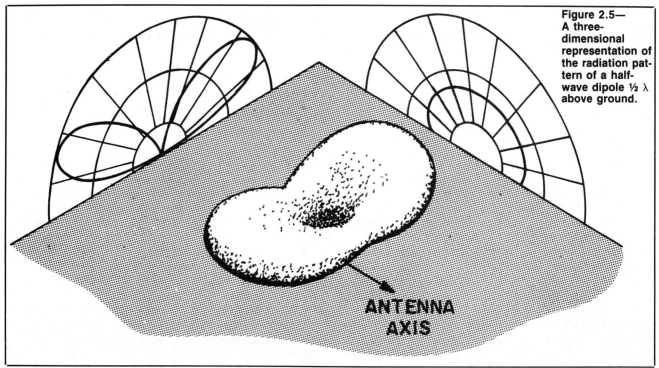

Figure 2.5—A three-dimensional representation of the radiation pattern of a half-wave dipole ½ λ above ground.

ANTENNA AXIS

Table 5
Resistance of Various Wire Types

Wire Diameter	Copper dc (Ω/km)	Copper 3.8 MHz (Ω/km)	Copper-clad dc (Ω/km)	Copper-clad 3.8 MHz (Ω/km)	Bronze dc (Ω/km)	Bronze 3.8 MHz (Ω/km)
2.5 mm (AWG10)	3.4	61	8.7	61	4.5	81
2.0 mm (AWG12)	5.4	97	13.8	97	7.2	130
1.6 mm (AWG14)	8.6	154	22.0	154	11.4	206
1.3 mm (AWG16)	13.6	246	35.0	246	18.2	328
1.0 mm (AWG18)	21.7	391	55.6	391	29.0	521

in Table 5 are valid at 3.8 MHz. For 1.8 MHz the values must be divided by 1.4, while for 7.1 MHz the values must be multiplied by the same factor. The RF resistance of copper-clad steel is the same as for solid copper, as the steel core does not conduct any RF at HF. The dc resistance is higher by 3 to 4 times, depending on the copper/steel diameter ratio. The RF resistance at 3.8 MHz is 18 times higher than for dc (25 times for 7 MHz, and 13 times for 1.8 MHz).

Dielectric Losses in Insulators

Dielectric losses are difficult to assess quantitatively. Care should be taken to use good quality insulators, especially at the high-impedance ends of the dipole. Several insulators can be connected in series to improve both quality and reliability.

Ground Losses

Reflection of RF at ground level coincides with absorption in the case of non-ideal ground. With a perfect reflector, the gain of a dipole above ground is 6 dB over a dipole in free space (the field intensity doubles). Table 6 lists the relative losses of dipoles at heights of ¼ and ½ λ as well as the maximum angle of vertical radiation. Note that the angle is lowered as the quality of the ground deteriorates, due to the increased effective antenna height.

Attempting to improve ground conductivity for improved performance is a common practice with ground-mounted vertical antennas. One can also improve the ground conductivity with dipoles, although it is not quite as easy, especially if one is interested in low-angle radiation and if the antenna is physically high. From Table 3 we can find the distance from the antenna to the ground reflection point. For the major low angle lobe this is 118 feet (36 m) for an 80 meter dipole at 100 feet (30 m). Consequently, this is the place where the ground conductivity must be improved. Because of the horizontal polarization of the dipole, any wires that are laid on the ground (or buried in the ground) should be laid out parallel to the dipole and should be 1 λ long. In view of the small gains that can be realized, especially with high antennas and for low wave angles, however, it is very doubtful that any such improvement of the ground is worth all the effort. The efficiency of low dipoles (¼ λ high and less), which essentially radiate at the zenith angle (90°), can be improved by placing wires under the antenna in the same direction as the antenna. A variation on this approach is to put a parasitic reflector wire (½ λ plus 5%) under the dipole, spaced at 1/8 to ¼ λ. Note that radiation resistance varies slightly with the effective electrical height of the dipoles over grounds of varying qualities.

Table 7 gives the efficiencies of ½ λ 80-meter dipoles made of different conductor materials. The table lists the R_{rad}, the R_{loss}, the resulting efficiency and equivalent power loss (= 20 × log (Eff)), and the ground losses. The last column

Table 6
Characteristics of Dipole Antennas at 0.25 and 0.5 λ

Ground Quality	Antenna Height (λ)	Gain Over Dipole in Free Space (dB)	Relative Loss (dB)	Angle of Max Radiation (deg)
Perfect	0.25	6.0	0.0	90
Reflector	0.50	6.0	0.0	30
Salt Water	0.25	5.7	0.3	77
	0.50	5.9	0.1	30
Swamp	0.25	5.4	0.6	69
	0.50	5.7	0.6	69
Average	0.25	4.8	1.2	64
Ground	0.50	5.4	0.6	28
Desert	0.25	3.8	2.2	57
	0.50	4.8	1.2	27

yields the total loss for the system (in dB referenced to a perfect, lossless system). One item in this table can be controlled rather easily: the dipole conductor. Do not use very thin wire. Never use steel wire—its conductivity is extremely poor, especially at high frequencies.

2.3.4 SHORT DIPOLES

On the low bands, it is often impossible to use full size radiators. This section describes the characteristics of short dipoles.

2.3.4.1 Radiation Resistance

The radiation resistance of a vertical monopole (shorter than or equal to a quarter wavelength) can be calculated as follows:

$$R_{rad} = 1450 \times \frac{H^2}{\lambda^2}$$

where
  H = effective antenna height (in meters)
  λ = wavelength of operation (300 / f in MHz).

In this case both definitions of radiation resistance (Section 2.2.5) apply, as the monopole will have a current maximum at the base, and will be fed at that point ($R_{rad}[1] = R_{rad}[2]$). The effective height of the antenna is the height of a theoretical antenna having a constant current distribution all along its length, the area under this current distribution line being equal to the area under the current distribution line of the "real" antenna. See Figure 2.6 for a graphic representation of the areas discussed. The formula is valid for antennas with a ratio of antenna length to conductor diameter greater than 500:1 (typical of wire antennas). The

Table 7

Characteristics of Dipole Antennas over Various Types of Ground

	Conductor	R_{rad} (Ω)	R_{loss} (Ω)	Efficiency (%)	(dB)	Ground Loss (dB)	Total Loss (dB)
Dipole for 3.8 MHz							
Desert Ground	1.3 mm copper	74	9.33	89	1.0	2.2	3.2
Average Ground		74	9.33	89	1.0	1.2	2.2
Swamp		74	9.33	89	1.0	0.6	1.6
Salt Water		74	9.33	89	1.0	0.3	1.3
Desert Ground	2.0 mm copper	74	3.69	95	0.4	2.2	2.6
Average Ground		74	3.69	95	0.4	1.2	1.6
Swamp		74	3.69	95	0.4	0.6	1.0
Salt Water		74	3.69	95	0.4	0.3	0.7
Dipole for 1.8 MHz							
Desert Ground	1.6 mm copper-clad	74	8.89	89	1.0	2.2	3.2
Average Ground		74	8.89	89	1.0	1.2	2.2
Swamp		74	8.89	89	1.0	0.6	1.6
Salt Water		74	8.89	89	1.0	0.3	1.3
Desert Ground	2.0 mm copper-clad	74	5.61	93	0.6	2.2	2.8
Average Ground		74	5.61	93	0.6	1.2	1.8
Swamp		74	5.61	93	0.6	0.6	1.2
Salt Water		74	5.61	93	0.6	0.3	0.9

Table 8

Current Distribution for a Shortened Dipole

Length (degrees)	180	160	140	120	110	100	90	80	70	60
R_{rad} (ohms)	73.3	51.6	35.9	24.4	19.9	15.9	12.6	9.7	7.2	5.3

radiation resistance of a dipole in free space will be twice the value of the equivalent monopole.

Table 8 shows the radiation resistance (in ohms) of a dipole as a function of its electrical length in degrees ($360° = 1 \lambda$). The table is valid only for a dipole with sinusoidal current distribution and without loading elements at the dipole tips or along its length, other than at the center where the feed point is located. Figure 2.6B shows the current distribution for such a shortened dipole. Only half of the dipole—the equivalent monopole—is shown. The value of the radiation resistance of a dipole loaded along the two half-elements is higher than the figure given in Table 8.

We can use the same procedure we followed for the full-size half-wave dipole for calculating the radiation resistance of any form of loaded monopole or dipole. We can analyze the following dipoles by adding the mirror images of the monopoles. The dipoles shown in Figure 2.6 are:

A) Full-size half-wave dipole.
B) Center-loaded dipole.
C) End-loaded dipole.
D) Dipole loaded along the element.
E) Continuously-loaded dipole (helically wound).
F) Dipole loaded at the end and the center.

We will also consider the linear-loaded dipole shown in Figure 2.8.

For each case, the analysis will be done for the equivalent half-size monopole. Multiply the radiation resistance by 2 to obtain the correct value for the dipole (double the size of the monopole).

Full-Size Half-Wave Dipole

For a full-size, quarter-wave antenna (Figure 2.6A) the radiation resistance can be calculated as follows:

Current at the base of the antenna = 1 Amp (given)
Area under sinusoidal current distribution curve = 1 A $\times$ 1 radian = 1 A $\times$ 180/π degrees/radian = 57.3 A-deg
Equivalent length = 57.3° (1 radian)
Electrical length = 300 / 3.8 = 78.95 m

$$\text{Effective height} = \frac{78.95 \times 57.3}{360} = 12.57 \text{ m}$$

$$R_{rad} = \frac{1450 \times 12.57^2}{78.97^2} = 36.7 \text{ ohms}$$

For a half-wave dipole the R_{rad} value must be multiplied by 2.

R_{rad} (dipole) = 73.4 ohms.

Center Loading (Base Loading with Monopoles)

Center loading for a dipole means loading at the maximum current point (equivalent to base loading with verticals). Monopole B (Figure 2.6) is physically 50% shorter than the full-size, quarter-wave monopole and has base loading.

Current at the base of the antenna =
1 A $\times$ (cos 45) = 0.707 A
Area under sinusoidal current distribution curve =
$$\int_{45}^{90} \cos L \, dL = \sin 90 - \sin 45 = 0.293$$

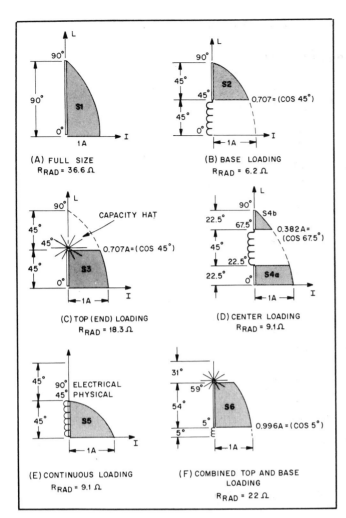

Figure 2.6—Graphical representation of the area under the current distribution curve for the quarter-wave monopole and various forms of loaded short monopoles. For dipoles, add the mirror-image pattern below the baseline and double the radiation resistance.

0.293×57.3 degrees/radian $= 16.78$ A-deg

Equivalent length $= 16.78 / 0.707 = 23.73°$

Electrical length $= 300 / 3.8 = 78.95$ m

Effective height $= \dfrac{78.95 \times 23.73}{360} = 5.2$ m

$R_{rad} = \dfrac{1450 \times 5.2^2}{78.95^2} = 6.3$ ohms

For a half-wave dipole, the R_{rad} value must be multiplied by 2.

R_{rad} (dipole) $= 12.6$ ohms.

Figure 2.8—The linear-loading device at A is merely a part of the antenna folded back on itself in order to shorten the physical length of the antenna. At B is the graphical representation of the area under the current distribution curve for a linear-loaded dipole. The shaded area in C represents the increase in radiation resistance over the base-loaded equivalent. Since no coils are used in this form of loading, linear loading can be done almost without loss.

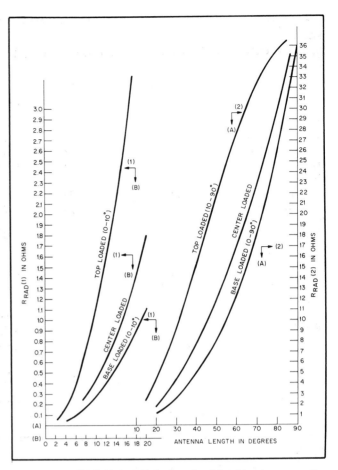

Figure 2.7—Radiation resistance chart for short monopoles (up to 90° long). For lengths up to 20°, the radiation resistance can be read from the scale on the left side of the diagram. For larger antennas, the right-hand scale should be used. For equivalent double-size dipoles, the radiation resistance should be multiplied by 2.

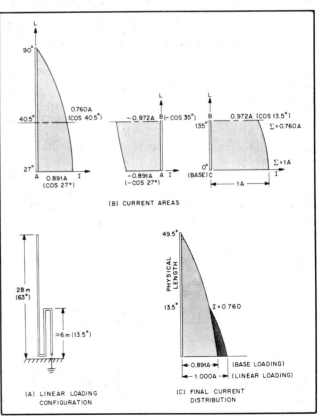

Byron, W7DHD, uses another formula for base-loaded monopoles (Ref 742):

$$R_{rad} = \frac{36 \times (1 - \cos L)^2}{\sin^2 L}$$

where L = the length of the monopole in degrees (or length of half of the shortened dipole in degrees). According to this formula, the radiation resistance of the half-size dipole is $2 \times 6.18 = 12.36$ ohms, which is very close to the above calculated value.

Hall, K1TD, derived another equation (Ref 1008):

$$R_{rad} = \frac{L^{2.736}}{6096}$$

where L = electrical length of the equivalent monopole (half of the dipole length). This very simple formula yields accurate results for monopole antenna lengths between 70 and 100°, but should be avoided for shorter antennas.

End (Top) Loading

End loading is loading at the extreme ends of the dipole. It is equivalent to top loading with verticals. Monopole C (Figure 2.6) is physically 50% shorter than the reference full-size, half-wave dipole and uses top loading.

Current at the base of the antenna = 1 A
Area under sinusoidal current distribution curve =

$$\int_0^{45} \cos L \, dL = \sin 45 - \sin 0 = 0.707$$

0.707×57.3 degrees/radian = 40.51 A-deg

Equivalent length = 40.51°
Electrical length = 300 / 3.8 = 78.95 m

$$\text{Effective height} = \frac{78.95 \times 40.51}{360} = 8.88 \text{ m}$$

$R_{rad} = 18.36$ ohms

For a half-wave dipole the R_{rad} value must be multiplied by 2.

R_{rad} (dipole) = 36.72 ohms.

Byron, W7DHD also provided a simplified formula applicable only to top loaded monopoles (Ref 742):

$$R_{rad} = 36 \times \sin^2 L$$

where L is the length of the monopole in degrees (the length of half of the shortened dipole in degrees). The 50% shortened dipole with pure end loading has a radiation resistance of: $R_{rad} = 2 \times 36 \times \sin^2 (45°) = 36.0$ ohms, which again compares very well with the 36.72 ohms found earlier.

Figure 2.7 gives the radiation resistance for both base-loaded and top-loaded short monopoles ranging from 2 to 90° in electrical length. For center-loaded dipoles the results must be multiplied by 2.

Loading Along the Elements

Loading along the elements of a dipole is equivalent to center loading with verticals. Monopole D (Figure 2.6) is loaded along the elements.

A practical approximation of the radiation resistance can be found as follows:

1) Calculate the radiation resistance for top loading (R_t).
2) Calculate the radiation resistance for base loading (R_b).
3) Calculate the difference: $D = R_t - R_b$.
4) Calculate the physical length of antenna in degrees (L).
5) Calculate the radiation resistance at any point between bottom and top of antenna using following approximation:

$$R(x) = ((1 - \cos (x \times 90/L)) \times D) + R$$

where x = height of the loading coil in degrees.

Example (monopole):
L = 45°
R_b = 6.27 ohms
R_t = 18.34 ohms
D = 18.34 − 6.27 = 12.07
For x = 20°:
R(20) = ((1 − cos 40) × 12.07) + 6.27
= 9.09 ohms

For a half-wave dipole the R_{rad} value must be multiplied by 2.

R_{rad} (dipole) = 18.18 ohms.

Continuous Loading (Helical Loading)

Continuous loading of a dipole can be done by helically winding the entire radiator. Monopole E from Figure 2.6 uses such continuous loading.

Current at the base of the antenna = 1 A
Area under sinusoidal current distribution curve =

$$0.5 \times \int_0^{90} \cos L \, dL = \sin 90 - \sin 0$$

$$= 0.5 \times 1 \times 57.3 \text{ degrees/radian} = 28.65 \text{ A-deg}$$

Equivalent length = 28.65°
Electrical length = 300 / 3.8 = 78.95 m

$$\text{Effective height} = \frac{78.95 \times 28.65}{360} = 6.28 \text{ m}$$

$$R_{rad} \text{ (monopole)} = \frac{1450 \times 6.28^2}{78.95^2} = 9.18 \text{ ohms}$$

For a half-wave dipole the R_{rad} value must be multiplied by 2.

R_{rad} (dipole) = 18.36 ohms.

Combined Top (End) and Base (Center) Loading

Top and base loading are frequently used together. Top loading is often done by capacitive-hat loading, but is often limited by the practical size of the capacity hat. In such cases the remaining loading may be done by base loading. The same mathematical approach can be used to calculate the radiation resistance, and one example is given below (Figure 2.6F). Assume a vertical 0.15 λ long (54°), with 31° of top loading and 5° of base loading.

Area calculation:

$$S = \int_5^{59} \cos L \, dL = \sin 59 - \sin 5$$

$$= 0.77 \times 57.3 \text{ degrees/radian} = 44.12 \text{ A-deg}$$

Equivalent length = 44.12 / 0.996 = 44.29°
Electrical length = 300 / 3.8 = 78.95 m

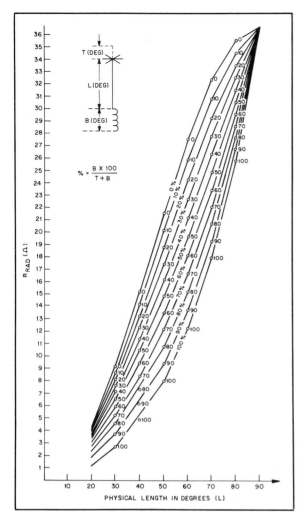

Figure 2.9—Radiation resistance of a monopole with combined top and base loading. This chart is applicable for monopoles with physical lengths from 20 to 90°. For equivalent dipoles (twice the physical size), multiply the radiation resistance by 2.

$$\text{Effective height} = \frac{78.95 \times 44.29}{360} = 9.71 \text{ m}$$

$$R_{rad} = \frac{1450 \times 9.71^2}{78.95^2} = 21.95 \text{ ohms}$$

Figures 2.9 and 2.10 show the radiation resistance for monopoles with combined top and base loading. The physical length of the antenna (L) + Top loading (T) + Base loading (B) must total 90°. The calculation of the required capacitance and the dimensions of the capacity hat are explained further in the Section 2.3.4.2.

Linear Loading

Designing linear-loaded elements can best be done graphically as shown in Figure 2.8. Let us use an example of a vertical monopole, 28 meters (92 feet) long, and linearly loaded for 1.8 MHz. A quarter-wave (90°) vertical for 160 meters measures:

$$\frac{300}{1.8 \times 4 \times 1.04} = 40 \text{ m}$$

28 meters represents: $\frac{90 \times 28}{40} = 63°$

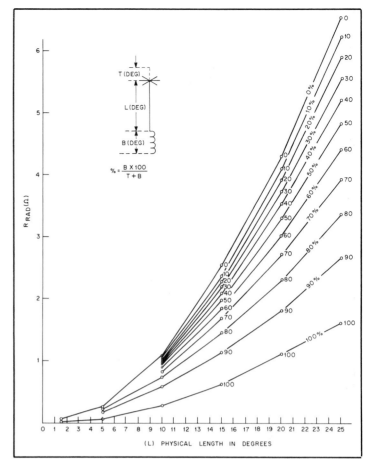

Figure 2.10—Extension of the radiation resistance chart from Figure 2.9 for shorter monopoles (2 to 25° long).

The remaining 27° is made up by a linear loading device, which is simply a folded length of radiator.

Figure 2.8B shows the current distribution for the antenna. The physical length of the linear loading device is typically 10 to 20% longer than the missing electrical length (see Section 2.3.4.2). Assuming an antenna current of 1 A at the feed point, the current can be calculated at key points:

At 13.5°: I(a) = cos 13.5 = 0.972 A
At 27.0°: I(b) = cos 27 = 0.891 A
At 40.5°: I(c) = cos 40.5 = 0.760 A

Summing the currents at these points: I(tot) at 49.5° from the top = 0.760 − 0.972 + 0.972 = 0.760 A
I(tot) at base of antenna = 0.891 − 0.891 + 1.0 = 1.0 A

Figure 2.8C shows the resulting total current distribution.

Area of the top section =

$$\int_{40.5}^{90} \cos L \, dL = \sin 90 - \sin 40.5$$
$$= 0.35 \times 57.3 \text{ degrees/radian} = 20.1 \text{ A-deg}$$

Equivalent length of the top section = 20.1 / 0.76 = 26.44°

Area of the bottom section:

$$\text{Average width of the trapezoid} = \frac{1.0 + 0.76}{2} = 0.880$$

S2 = 13.5° × 0.880 = 11.88 A-deg
Equivalent length of the bottom section = 11.88°
Total effective height = 26.44 + 11.88 = 38.33°

Electrical length $= 300 / 3.8 = 78.95$ m

Effective height $= \dfrac{78.95 \times 38.33}{360} = 8.41$ m

$R_{rad} = \dfrac{1450 \times 8.41^2}{78.95^2} = 16.43$ ohms

Let us quickly compare linear loading with base loading for the same antenna structure. Figure 2.8C shows the resulting total current distribution.

$\text{Area} = \int_{27}^{90} \cos L \, dl = \sin 90 - \sin 27$

$\qquad = 0.546 \times 57.3$ degrees/radian $= 31.3$ A-deg

Equivalent length $= 31.3 / 0.89 = 35.11°$
Electrical length $= 300 / 3.8 = 78.95$ m

Effective height $= \dfrac{78.95 \times 35.11}{360} = 7.7$ m

$R_{rad} = \dfrac{1450 \times 7.7^2}{78.95^2} = 13.8$ ohms

These R_{rad} values are for monopoles. For equivalent dipoles, multiply the values by two.

Thus it is clear that linear loading has two advantages over base loading:

1) The radiation resistance is slightly higher with linear loading.

2) Linear loading can be done with much lower loss than a (large) base-loading coil.

The linear-loading technique described above is used with great success on the Telex/Hy-Gain 402BA shortened 40 meter beam, where linear loading is used at the center of the dipoles. It is also used successfully on the KLM 40 and 80 meter shortened Yagis and dipoles, where linear loading is applied a certain distance from the center of the elements (Figure 2.11).

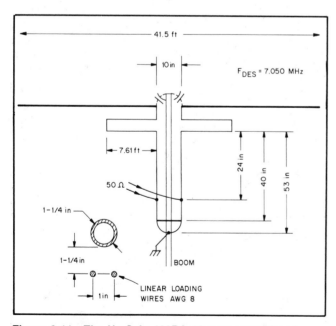

Figure 2.11—The Hy-Gain 402BA 40-meter monoband antenna uses the linear-loading principle to reduce element size. KLM use the same principle for their 40- and 80-meter shortened Yagis, but the loading devices are incorporated some distance out from the center of the elements for increased radiation resistance.

2.3.4.2 Tuning or Loading the Short Dipole

There are a few ways to tune the short dipole system:
- Tuned feeders.
- Lumped-constant elements to tune out the capacitive reactance.
- Linear loading.
- Capacitive end loading.

Tuned Feeders

Tuned feeders were common in the days before the arrival of coaxial feed lines. Very low-loss open-wire feeders can be made. The Levy antenna is an example of a short dipole fed with open-wire line. If we take the example of a dipole ¼ λ long (R_{rad} = approximately 13 ohms and X_C = approximately 1350 ohms), it can be fed with open-wire feeders (400-600 ohms) of any length into the shack, where we will match it to 50 ohms via an antenna tuner. An outstanding feature of this approach is that the system can be "tuned" from the shack via the antenna tuner, and is not narrow-banded as in the case of loaded elements. Let us calculate the losses in such a system.

The losses of the antenna proper can be assumed to be zero (provided wire elements of the proper size and composition are used). The loss in a flat open-wire feeder is typically 0.01 dB per 100 feet at 3.5 MHz. The SWR on the line will be an unreal value of 280:1 (this value was calculated using the program "SWR RATIO," listed in Chapter VII). The additional line loss due to SWR for a 100-foot line will be on the order of 1.5 dB (Ref 600, 602). Let us assume the feeder length has been adjusted to a value that allows a reasonable match with the antenna tuner (on a line with standing waves, the impedance is different at every point), an impedance which gives a better match to the tuner can be found. This can be done with the programs "FEEDLINE VOLTAGE" or "COAX TRANSFORMER" listed in Chapter VII). A good antenna tuner should be able to handle this matching task with a loss of less than 0.2 dB. The total system loss depends essentially on the efficiency with which the tuner can handle the impedance transformation. The typical total loss in the system should be under 2.0 dB.

Lumped Constants (Coils)

Another method of tuning the antenna is to load the elements by lumped constants (coils) to make them resonant at the operating frequency. The inductive reactance required to resonate the quarter-wave dipole from the previous example is approximately 1350 ohms. To effect this, two 675-ohm (reactance) coils will need to be installed at the feed point. We should be able to realize a coil Q (quality factor) of 300.

$R_{loss} = \dfrac{X_L}{Q} = \dfrac{675}{300} = 2.25$ ohms

The total equivalent loss resistance of the coils is 4.5 ohms. The antenna efficiency will be:

$\eta = \dfrac{R_{rad}}{R_{rad} + R_{loss}} = \dfrac{13}{13 + 4.5} \times 100\% = 74\%$

The equivalent power loss is: $10 \times \log (0.74) = 1.3$ dB
The feed-point impedance of the antenna is 20 ohms (resistive) at resonance.

If the use of coaxial feed lines is desired, an additional matching system will be needed to adapt the 20-ohm balanced feed-point impedance to the 50- or 75-ohm unbalanced coaxial

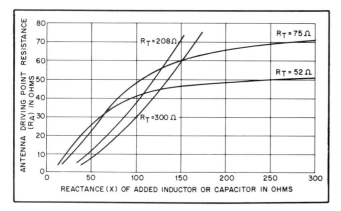

Figure 2.12—Hairpin (or stub) reactance required to match various antenna resistances to four commonly used transmission-line impedances.

cable impedance. A hairpin matching system is a practical way to raise the impedance to 50 ohms. Figure 2.12 shows the hairpin reactance required to match a range of low impedances to higher-impedance feed lines. In the case of a 20-ohm radiation resistance, a reactance of approximately 40 ohms is needed to achieve a 50-ohm feed-point impedance. This capacitive reactance can be obtained by shortening the dipole slightly.

The required amount of shortening can be calculated by the method described below. First calculate the surge impedance, and then calculate the length as follows:

$$t = \arctan \frac{Z_s}{X_C}$$

where

Z_s = surge impedance in ohms
X_C = required capacitive reactance in ohms
t = shortening length in degrees.

For the given example (using Z_s = 1200 ohms and X_C = 40 ohms), the result is 2°, which for a design frequency of 3.8 MHz means a shortening (on each side of center) of 0.43 m (1.4 feet).

The same result can also be obtained by tuning the shortened dipole slightly higher in frequency. An approximation formula is:

$$f = \frac{3.8 \times (90 + x)}{90}$$

where x = 2° shortening on each 90° long side, which results in a frequency of 3.88 MHz. The required hairpin coil has an inductance of:

$$L = \frac{40}{2\pi \times 3.8} = 1.7 \ \mu H$$

(Ref 1417). Such a matching system can account for another 0.1 dB loss. The total system loss is now around 1.63 dB, assuming a feed-line length of 100 feet (0.23 dB). The resulting efficiency is very close to the result obtained with open-wire feeders. However, there are certain advantages and disadvantages to this concept. An advantage is the fact that coaxial cable is easier to handle than open-wire line, especially when dealing with rotary systems. One disadvantage is that the system bandwidth is very narrow, and it uses high-Q coils at the antenna, which are critical as far as power-handling, weather degradation and so on.

The following procedure can be followed to calculate the required inductance for inductive loading of the shortened dipole:

1) Calculate the dipole surge impedance, Z_s:

$$Z_s = 276 \log \left(\frac{S}{d \sqrt{1 + \frac{S}{4h}}} \right)$$

Z_s = antenna surge impedance
S = electrical length of antenna
d = antenna conductor diameter
h = antenna height above the ground.

S, d, and h should be in the same units (inches, mm or whatever). Note: This formula is valid only for dipoles. The formula for monopoles is given in Section 2.4.3.3.

2) Calculate the capacitive reactance of the shortened dipole, X_C:

$$X_C = -Z_s \times \cotan (t)$$

where t is half of the electrical length of the shortened dipole. A total inductive reactance (for both halves of the dipole) equal (but opposite in phase) to the calculated capacitive reactance will be needed to resonate the dipole.

Figure 2.13 gives the reactance for short dipoles ranging from 60° (0.17 λ) to 180° (½ λ), as well as the required values for central loading for 160, 80 and 40 meters. The design frequencies are 1.8, 3.8 and 7.1 MHz, the wire diameter is 2 mm (AWG 12), and the antenna height is 20 meters (66 feet).

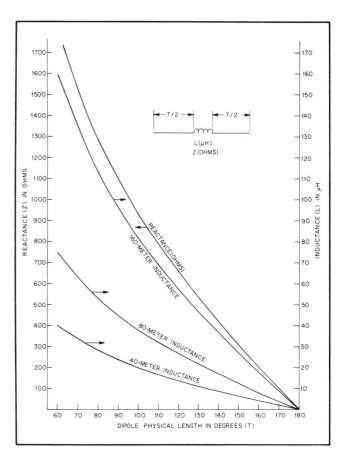

Figure 2.13—Loading-coil reactance required for center-loaded short dipoles. The required inductance is also shown for 40, 80 and 160 meters. The chart is valid for wire dipoles made of 2-mm OD wire (AWG12). For larger diameters, the coil values can vary greatly.

The required values can also be calculated, as in the following example.

S = 2250 cm
d = 0.2 cm
h = 2000 cm

(S = 2250 cm represents an electrical length of 108° as opposed to the full half-wave length of 3750 cm).

Z_0 = 1099 ohms (for d = 2 mm and h = 2000 cm or 20 m)

$$t = \frac{180 \times 0.6}{2} = 54°$$

X_L = 1099 × cotan 54 = 798 ohms

The required inductance is:

$$L = \frac{X_L}{2\pi f}$$

where L is in μH and f is in MHz. For 3.8 MHz,

$$L = \frac{798}{6.28 \times 3.8} = 33 \ \mu H$$

There are two ways of loading and feeding the shortened dipole with a centrally located loading coil:

1) Use a single 33 μH loading coil and link-couple the feed line to the coil. This method is used by both Mosley and Cushcraft for their shortened 40-meter antennas.

2) Split the required loading coil of 33 μH into two identical coils of 16.5 μH each, to be installed in each half of the shortened dipole at the center. Since two coils in close proximity will heavily couple with one another (resulting in a much higher total inductance than required), the coils may need to be moved slightly away from the center on the two half-elements without changing the required values, but avoiding the mutual coupling between the two coils. A practical value is 5% of the physical length of the shortened dipole (1.125 meters for this example). The feed line can be connected (via an appropriate balun) to the center of the dipole.

The influence of the placement of the loading devices on the elements on radiation resistance was explained above. It is clear that it is advantageous to put loading coils away from the center, provided the benefit of higher radiation resistance is not counteracted by higher losses in the loading device.

As loading coils are placed farther out on the elements, the required coil inductance increases. With increasing values of inductance, the Q factor is likely to decrease, and the equivalent series losses will increase. A practical rule of thumb is to place the loading coils half way out on the elements.

The reactance of the coil can be calculated as follows:

1) Calculate the coil reactance, X_{L1}, as for a center loaded dipole (base-loaded monopole).

2) Calculate the new X_{L2} using the following formula:

$$X_{L2} = X_{L1} \left(\frac{1}{\sin \left(90 \times \left(\frac{L-H}{H} \right) \right)} \right)$$

where

L = physical length of the dipole (or monopole)
H = separation between coils (dipole) or height of loading coil above ground (monopole).
(Note: H and L must be expressed in the same units.)

Example:

Assume the antenna length is 22.5 meters (108°) and coil

separation is 10 meters. The center-loaded coil inductance was calculated above as 33 μH, or 2 × 16.5 μH (per side). The inductance value for a coil separation of 10 meters is:

$$L = \frac{16.5}{\sin \left(90 \times \frac{22.5 - 10}{22.5} \right)} = 21.5 \ \mu H$$

The reactance is

$$X_L = \frac{798}{\sin \left(90 \times \frac{22.5 - 10}{22.5} \right)} = 1041 \ \Omega$$

1041 / 2 = 520 ohms per coil.

Assuming a Q-factor of 200, the equivalent series resistance of each loading coil is: R_{loss} = X_L / Q = 520 / 200 = 2.6 ohms. The radiation resistance of this antenna can be calculated as explained in Section 2.3.4.1, or from the chart in Figure 2.7.

Spacing (center of dipole to coil): 5 meters (24°)
Element length beyond coil: 54° − 24° = 30°
Electrical length of the coil = 36°
R_{rad} (top loaded) = 24 ohms
R_{rad} (base loaded) = 9.5 ohms

$$R(x) = \left(\left[1 - \cos \left(\frac{90x}{L} \right) \right] \times D \right) + R$$

(Section 2.3.4.1)

$$R_{rad} = \left(\left[1 - \cos \left(\frac{90 \times 24}{54} \right) \right] \times 14.5 \right) + 9.5 = 12.9 \ \Omega$$

For a dipole, the value must be doubled, so R_{rad} (dipole) = 25.8 ohms.

The total antenna efficiency is:

$$\eta = \frac{25.8}{25.8 + (2 \times 2.6)} \times 100\% = 83.2\%$$

which represents an equivalent power loss of 10 × log (0.832) = 0.8 dB. The impedance of the shortened dipole will be 31 ohms, which will require a matching system to be fed with 50-ohm coax.

Linear Loading

In the commercial world, we have seen linear loading used on shortened dipoles and Yagis for 40 and 80 meters, but not very frequently on monopole antennas. Linear-loading devices can be installed anywhere in the antenna. The required length of the loading device (in each half dipole or in the monopole) will be somewhat longer than the difference between the quarter-wave length and the physical length of the half-dipole (monopole).

Example: A dipole for 3.8 MHz is physically 28 meters (91.86 feet) long. The full half-wavelength is 39 meters, (127.95 feet). The missing electrical length is 11.0 meters (32.80 feet). It is recommended that the linear loading device be constructed approximately 30% longer than half of this length:

$$\ell = 11 \ / \ 2 + 30\% = 7 \ m \ (23 \ feet)$$

Trim the length of the loading device until resonance on the desired frequency is reached. When constructing an antenna with linear-loading devices, make sure the separation between the element and the folded linear-loading device is large enough, and that you use high-quality insulators to prevent arc-over and insulator breakdown when running high power.

Capacitive End (Top) Loading

In order to calculate the required top-loading capacitive reactance, the following procedure can be followed:

1) Calculate the antenna surge impedance as for inductive loading (as explained before).

2) Calculate the required top capacitance.

Assume we want to replace a length equal to $t°$ (outer ends) by capacitance hats. Applying the open transmission line equation:

$$\cot an (t) = \frac{X_C}{Z_0}$$

We can calculate the multiplication factor $\cot an (t)$ by which we must multiply the surge impedance to obtain the required capacitive loading reactance.

Example: A shortened dipole will be loaded for 80 meters. The physical length of the dipole is 18.75 meters (approx 40% shortening factor).

S = 18.75 m
d = 0.2 cm
h = 20 m
Z_0 = 1196 ohms
t = 36°.

This means we must replace the top 36° of each side of the dipole with a capacitive hat (a half-wave dipole is 180°). Cotan (t) = 1.38. The required capacitive reactance (X_C) is X_C = 1196 × 1.38 = 1646 ohms.

The capacitance (f = 3.8 MHz) is:

$$\frac{1}{2\pi f X_C} = 25.4 \text{ pF}$$

The required diameter of the hat disk is given by

D = 1.12 C

where
    D = hat diameter in inches
    C = the required capacitance in pF.

In our example, D = 1.12 × 25.4 = 28.5 inches (72.4 cm).

A capacity hat can be made in the shape of a wheel with at least four spokes. This design will approach the performance of a solid disk. For ease in construction, the spokes can be made of four radial wires, joined at the rim by another wire in the shape of a circle. Capacitive loading has the advantage of physically shortening the element length at the end of the dipole where the current is lowest (least radiation), and without introducing noticeable losses (as inductors do). End-loaded short dipoles have the highest radiation resistance, and coupled with the negligible intrinsic losses of the loading device, end or top-loading is highly recommended.

Combined Methods

Any of the loading methods already discussed can be employed in combination. It is essential to develop a system which will give you the highest possible radiation resistance and which employs a loading technique with the lowest possible inherent losses. Gorski, W9KYZ (Ref 641) has described an efficient way of loading short dipole elements by using a combination of linear and helical loading. He quotes a total efficiency of 98% for a two-element Yagi. This

very high percentage can be obtained by using a wide copper strap for the helically-wound element, which results in a very low RF resistance. Some years ago, Kirk electronics (W8FYR) built Yagis for the HF bands, including 40 meters, using this approach (fiberglass elements wound with copper tape).

2.3.4.3 Bandwidth

The bandwidth of a dipole is determined by the Q factor of the antenna. The antenna Q factor is defined by:

$$Q = \frac{Z_0}{R_{rad} + R_{loss}}$$

where
    Z_0 = surge impedance of the antenna
    R_{rad} = radiation resistance
    R_{loss} = total loss resistance.

The bandwidth can be calculated from:

BW (3:1 SWR) = f (MHz)/ Q factor.

The Q factor (and consequently the bandwidth) will depend on:
• The conductor-to-wavelength ratio (influences Z_0).
• The physical length of the antenna (influences R_{rad}).
• The type, quality, and placement of the loading devices (influences R_{rad}).
• The Q factor of the loading device(s) (influences R_{loss}).
• The height of the dipole above ground (influences R_{rad}).

For a given conductor length-to-diameter ratio and a given antenna height, the loaded antenna with the narrowest bandwidth will be the antenna with the highest efficiency. Indeed, large bandwidths can easily be achieved by incorporating pure resistors in the loading devices like the Maxcom "dummy" dipole (Ref 663). The worst-radiating antenna one can imagine is a dummy load, where the resistor can be seen as the ohmic loading device while the radiating component does not exist. Judging by bandwidth this "antenna" is a wonderful performer, as a good dummy load can have an almost flat SWR curve over thousands of megahertz!

2.3.4.4 The Efficiency of the Shortened Dipole

Besides the radiation resistance (which was extensively studied in Section 2.3.4.2), the RF resistance of the shortened-dipole conductor is an important factor in the antenna efficiency. Refer to Table 5 for the RF resistances of common wire conductors used for antennas. For self-supporting elements, aluminum tubing is usually used. Both the dc and RF resistances are quite low, but special care should be taken to ensure that the best possible electrical RF contact between parts of the antenna is made. Some makers of military-specification antennas go as far as gold plating the contact surfaces for low RF resistance! As a general rule, loading coils are the lossy elements, and capacitive end-loading should always be employed if at all possible. Linear loading is also a better choice than inductive loading.

2.3.5 LONG DIPOLES

Long dipoles can give added advantages over the standard half-wave variety. The "long" antennas discussed in this paragraph are not strictly dipoles, but arrays of dipoles. The following antennas will be covered:
• Two half waves in phase.
• Double-extended Zepp.

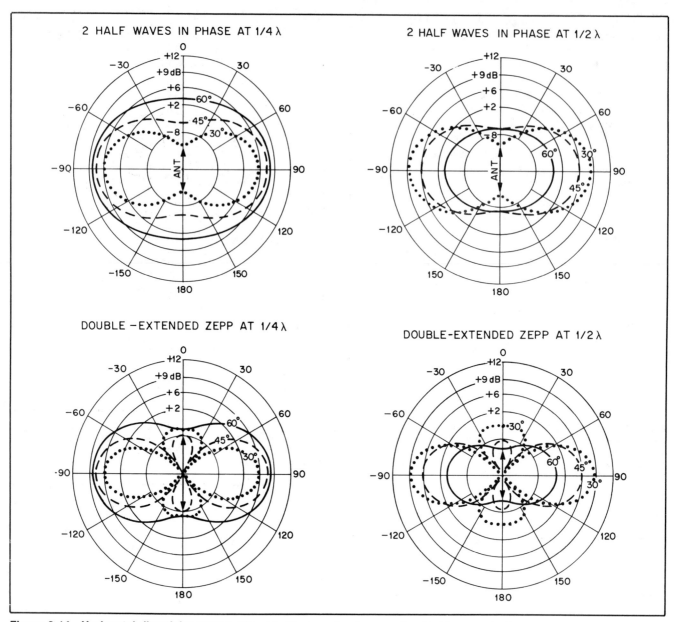

Figure 2.14—Horizontal directivity pattern of two half-waves in phase and a double-extended Zepp (two legs each 5/8 λ long), at wave angles of 30, 45 and 60°, for antenna heights of ¼ and ½ λ (over good ground). R_{rad} [1] was measured as 140 and 104 ohms respectively, with a resulting weight factor of 0.5 and 0.7 for relative field-strength comparison. The gains listed are with respect to a half-wave dipole in free space.

2.3.5.1 Radiation Patterns

Center-fed antennas can be lengthened to approximately 1.125 λ in order to achieve increased directivity without introducing objectionable side lobes. Figure 2.14 shows horizontal radiation patterns for 2 × ½ λ and 2 × 5/8 λ (double-extended Zepp) long dipoles, at heights of ¼ and ½ λ and for wave angles of 30, 45 and 60°. Further lengthening of the dipole will introduce major secondary lobes in the horizontal pattern unless phasing stubs are inserted to achieve the correct phasing between the half-wave elements. Figure 2.15 shows the pattern for four half waves in phase at ½ λ height with the horizontal radiation patterns for wave angles of 20, 30 and 40°. Figure 2.16 shows what the pattern would be if the phasing stubs were omitted.

The phasing stubs are ¼ λ long and shorted at the end. The easiest way to dimension the stubs correctly is to couple a dip oscillator to the end of the stub and prune the length

until the desired resonant frequency is reached. The phasing lines are usually made of 400-600 ohm open-wire line.

As with the half-wave dipole, the vertical wave angle depends only on the height of the antenna above ground (see Section 2.3.2.1).

2.3.5.2 Radiation Resistance

The radiation resistance of a long dipole is twice that of the equivalent half-size monopole. The chart in Figure 2.17 shows the radiation resistance of monopoles, according to definition A from Section 2.2.5, (antenna fed at current maximum). This $R_{rad}[1]$ will mainly be used as a weight factor for calculating radiation patterns (Section 2.4.1.2). The radiation resistance ($R_{rad}[2]$) for the equivalent half-size monopole is given in Figures 2.21 and 2.22. This is also known as monopole feed resistance. $R_{rad}[2]$ will be used in all calculations regarding antenna efficiency.

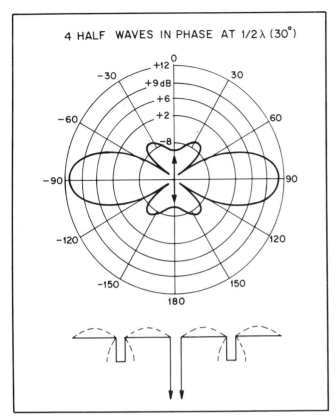

Figure 2.15—Four half-waves in phase at ½ λ height over average ground, using phasing stubs to achieve symmetrical current distribution. The R_rad [1] was measured as 124 ohms, resulting in a weight factor of 0.6 for relative field-strength calculation.

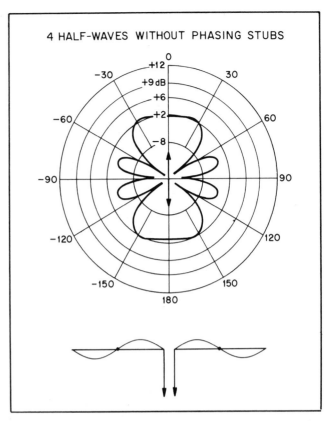

Figure 2.16—The omission of the phasing stubs results in a different current distribution than the four half-waves in phase and the antenna now has an almost useless radiation pattern.

Since the center-fed long antennas will not be loaded with lossy elements which will reduce their efficiency, long dipoles can have efficiencies very close to 100% if care is taken to use the best material for the antenna conductor.

The list below shows some common monopole and dipole equivalents.

Dipole	*Monopole*
Half-wave dipole	Quarter-wave vertical
Double Zepp (two half-waves in phase)	Half-wave vertical
Double-extended Zepp	5/8-wave vertical

2.3.5.3 Feeding Long Dipoles

Figures 2.21 through 2.24 represent the radiation resistances and reactances of monopoles, and can be used (with some caution) to evaluate long dipoles. The charts are valid only for rather thick conductors (like towers), and do not list any values for wire sizes (typically 0.01 ° in diameter, or antenna height/diameter ratios of 10,000:1 to 20,000:1). Only near the half-wave points does it become difficult to assess the exact resistances and reactances, because of the very high Q of antennas with thin conductors.

Long dipoles are normally fed with open-wire line, and the feeders usually terminate in an antenna tuner. An alternative feed method is shown in Figure 2.18, where the open-wire feeder is short-circuited and designed to resonate the whole system. A point can be found on the feeder near the short-

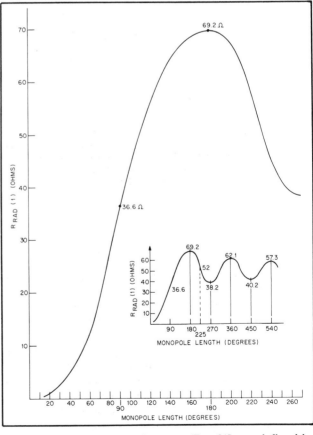

Figure 2.17—Radiation resistances (R_rad [1]—as defined in Section 2.2.5) of monopoles with sinusoidal current distribution. The chart is also usable for dipoles, but all radiation resistance values must be doubled.

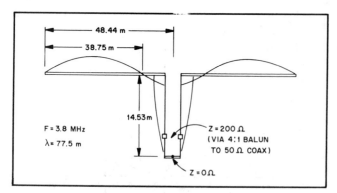

Figure 2.18—The double-extended Zepp antenna is fed with 600-ohm open-wire line 3/8 λ long and shorted at the end. The 200-ohm impedance point is best found experimentally, and a 4:1 balun can be attached for use with 50-ohm coaxial feed line.

circuited end where the impedance is 200 ohms, and where a coaxial cable can be connected via a 4:1 balun. The dimensions given are for 3.8 MHz.

2.4 Vertical Monopole

Vertical monopoles are often called ground-mounted verticals or simply verticals. They are by definition mounted perpendicular to the surface on which they are erected, and fed at the ground end.

2.4.1 RADIATION PATTERNS

2.4.1.1 Vertical Pattern of Monopoles Over Ideal Ground

The radiation pattern produced by a ground-mounted vertical antenna is basically half of the radiation pattern of a half-wave antenna in free space (with twice the physical size of the vertical and symmetrical current distribution). As such, the radiation pattern of a quarter-wave vertical over perfect ground is half of the figure-8 we have shown for the half-wave dipole in free space (see Section 2.3.1). The representation is shown in Figure 2.19.

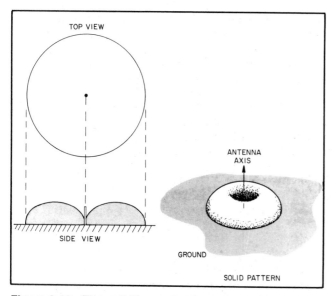

Figure 2.19—The radiation patterns produced by a vertical monopole. The top view is the horizontal pattern, the side view is the vertical pattern.

The relative field strength of a vertical antenna with sinusoidal current distribution and a current node at the top is given by:

$$E_f = kI \left[\frac{\cos (L \cos a) - \cos L}{\cos a} \right]$$

where

E_f = relative field strength
a = angle above the horizon
L = electrical height of the antenna
k = constant
I = antenna current, (proportional to $\sqrt{(P/R)}$).

This simplified formula does not take into account imperfect ground conditions and is valid for antenna heights between 0 and 180° (0 to ½ λ). The "form factor" containing the trigonometric functions is often published by itself for use in calculating the field strength of a vertical antenna. If used in this way, however, it appears that "short" verticals are vastly inferior to tall ones, as the antenna length appears only in the numerator of the fraction. Replacing I in the equation with the term

$$\sqrt{P/(R_{rad} + R_{loss})}$$

gives a better picture of the actual situation. For short verticals, the value of the radiation resistance is small, and this term largely compensates for the decrease in the form factor. This means that for a constant power input, the current into a small vertical will be greater than for a larger monopole. In practice, however, the current is not only determined by the radiation resistance (R_{rad}[1]), but also by the sum of the radiation resistance and the loss resistance(s). This is why, with a less-than-perfect ground system and less-than-perfect loading elements (lossy coils in case of lumped-constant-loaded verticals), the total radiation at low angles can be significantly less than in the case of a larger vertical (where R_{rad} is large in comparison to the ground loss and where there are no lossy loading devices).

Interestingly, short verticals are almost as efficient low-angle radiators as are longer verticals, provided the ground system is good and there are no lossy loading devices. When calculating radiation patterns of vertical antennas, the weight factor must precede the form factor in the formula (Refs 656-658 and Refs 660, 661 and 729).

Table 9 shows the relative field strength for verticals from 10 to 90° long at wave angles between 0 and 45°. The intrinsic radiation properties of verticals substantially shorter than a quarter wavelength are very good. When the losses of the ground system and the loading devices are brought into the picture, however, the sum ($R_{rad} + R_{loss}$) will get larger, and as a result, part of the supplied power will be lost in the form of heat in these elements. For instance, if $R_{rad} = R_{loss}$, half of the power will be lost. Note that with very short verticals, these losses can be much higher (see Section 2.4.2). Great care should be taken when interpreting the figures from Table 9. They do not show that a 50° vertical is 2.3 dB better than a 90° vertical! It can easily be proven, however, that very short monopoles radiate only 5 percent (0.44 dB) less power than their full quarter-wave counterparts, provided there are no associated losses and that the power can be efficiently fed to the short antenna. These figures only show that the shape of the three-dimensional pattern is slightly different, and that the taller verticals radiate slightly better at low angles.

Table 9

Vertical Radiation Patterns of Short Monopoles (Relative dB Values)

Antenna deg	R_{rad}	Wave Angle 0	5	10	15	20	25	30	35	40	45
90	36.5	0.0	0.0	0.1	0.4	0.7	1.2	1.7	2.4	3.1	4.0
85	30.7	0.0	0.0	0.2	0.4	0.7	1.2	1.7	2.3	3.0	3.9
80	25.7	0.1	0.1	0.3	0.5	0.8	1.2	1.7	2.3	3.1	3.9
75	21.5	0.3	0.3	0.4	0.6	1.0	1.3	1.8	2.4	3.1	3.9
70	17.9	0.5	0.5	0.7	0.9	1.2	1.6	2.0	2.6	3.3	4.1
65	14.8	0.8	0.8	1.0	1.2	1.5	1.8	2.3	2.9	3.5	4.3
60	12.1	1.2	1.2	1.4	1.6	1.8	2.2	2.7	3.2	3.9	4.6
55	9.9	1.7	1.7	1.8	2.0	2.3	2.7	3.1	3.7	4.3	5.0
50	7.9	2.3	2.3	2.4	2.6	2.9	3.2	3.7	4.2	4.8	5.6
45	6.2	3.0	3.0	3.1	3.3	3.6	3.9	4.3	4.9	5.5	6.2
40	4.8	3.8	3.8	3.9	4.1	4.4	4.7	5.1	5.6	6.3	7.0
35	3.6	4.8	4.8	4.9	5.1	5.4	5.7	6.1	6.6	7.2	7.9
30	2.6	6.0	6.0	6.1	6.3	6.5	6.9	7.3	7.8	8.4	9.1
25	1.7	7.4	7.5	7.6	7.8	8.0	8.3	8.7	9.2	9.8	10.5
20	1.1	9.3	9.3	9.4	9.6	9.8	10.2	10.6	11.0	11.6	12.3
15	0.6	11.7	11.7	11.8	12.0	12.2	12.6	13.0	13.0	14.0	14.7
10	0.2	15.2	15.2	15.3	15.5	15.7	16.0	16.4	16.9	17.5	18.2

2.4.1.2 Vertical Pattern of Monopoles Over Real Ground

For evaluating patterns over real ground, more complex tools must be used. Rautio, AJ3K has developed an excellent computer program, ANNIE, which has been described in literature (Ref 656, 657, 658, 660 and 661). The program runs on Apple II computers, on the Commodore 64, and on the IBM PC and is available from the author (4397 Luna Course, Liverpool, NY 13088). The program allows the user to create tabular printouts or to plot radiation angles of dipole/monopole antennas; antennas constructed by assembly of dipoles and/or monopoles; and arrays of both (including inverted Vs and sloping dipoles). Data can be obtained for these antennas operating over perfect ground as well as over poorly conducting ground. Both conductivity and dielectric constant can be specified by the user. This program is highly recommended to anyone who has more than just a casual interest in antennas.

Another very good antenna design and evaluation program is MININEC (Mini-Numerical Electromagnetics Code) a personal computer version of the NEC antenna modeling program developed by the Naval Ocean Systems Center (NOSC) in San Diego, CA 92152. Technical Document 516 describes the system and gives a source listing of the basic program. Copies of the document or a diskette containing an Apple-compatible version of the software can be obtained from Rautio. This program is very slow and much less user friendly than ANNIE, but it can yield very accurate results.

All patterns in this chapter were developed using ANNIE. The patterns shown in Figure 2.20 represent the vertical radiation patterns for monopoles of different lengths over four types of ground. The weighting (antenna current adjustment) was done in accordance with the radiation resistance ($R_{rad}[1]$) as in Section 2.2.5.

Table 10 shows the radiation resistance (see Section 2.4.2) values for six different verticals between 30 and 125° long. If it is desired to compare the gains of these antennas to a dipole in free space (R_{rad} = 73.2 ohms), we have to adjust the weight in Rautio's program according to the ratios of the radiation resistances. For this purpose, one must always use the radiation resistance for the base-loaded version of the antenna (lowest value), regardless of the loading method to

be used on the actual antenna. The different values of radiation resistance for different methods of loading must be used for calculating antenna efficiency. For the quarter-wave vertical (R_{rad} = 36.6 ohms), the weight factor is: 73.2/36.6 = 2. For 30° long monopoles, the weight factor is: 73.2/2.5 = 29. Using these weight factors allows direct comparison of decibel figures and the quoting of gains with respect to the half-wave dipole in free space. Most patterns in this book show 0 dB as the maximum radiation of a half-wave dipole in free space. With this definition, a dipole over perfectly reflecting ground will show 6 dB of gain in a given direction (at a given wave angle).

2.4.1.3 Horizontal Pattern of a Vertical Antenna

The horizontal radiation pattern of both the ground-mounted monopole and the vertical dipole is a circle.

2.4.2 RADIATION RESISTANCE OF MONOPOLES

The definition of $R_{rad}[1]$ and $R_{rad}[2]$ was given in Section 2.2.5. The radiation resistance of monopoles (equal to or shorter than ¼ λ) has been covered in the Section on dipoles (Section 2.3.4.1). The formula used for calculating the radiation resistance was developed for dipoles where the antenna length-to-diameter ratio is large (wire radiator). For monopoles up to ¼ λ long where $R_{rad}[1]$ = $R_{rad}[2]$, the formula from Section 2.3.4.1 and the charts in Figures 2.7, 2.9 and 2.10 can be applied. Longer monopoles are usually not fed at the current maximum, but at the antenna base, so that $R_{rad}[1]$ is no longer the same as $R_{rad}[2]$. $R_{rad}[2]$ for long verticals is given in Figures 2.21 and 2.22 (Source: Henney, *Radio Engineering Handbook*, McGraw-Hill, NY, 1959, used by permission) while $R_{rad}[1]$ is given in Figure 2.17. The value can be calculated from the following formula (Ref 722):

$$R_{rad}[1] = e^{-0.7L + 0.1}[20 \sin (12.56637L - 4.08407)] + 45$$

where L = antenna length in radians (radians = degrees/57.3). The length must be greater than $\pi/2$ (90°).

Figure 2.25 shows the difference between $R_{rad}[1]$ and $R_{rad}[2]$ for four types of monopoles. For the short monopole (less than ¼ λ) and the quarter-wave antenna, I_{max} is at the antenna base. P1 is the power radiated by the antenna, P2

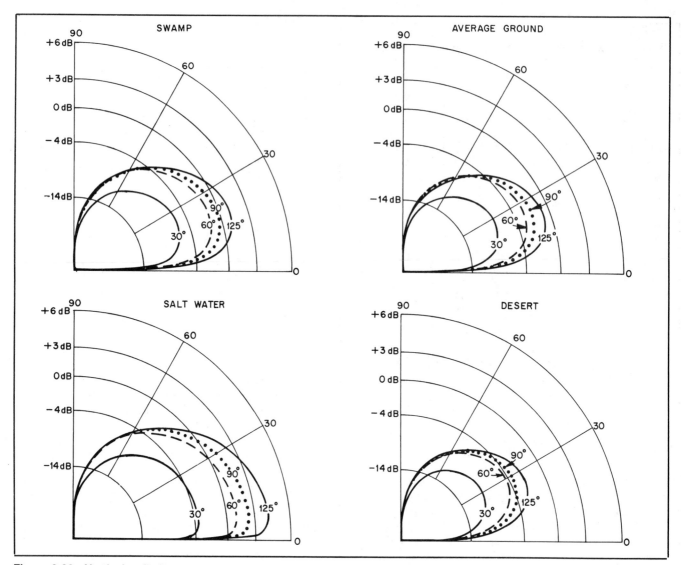

Figure 2.20—Vertical radiation patterns of 30, 60, 90 and 125°-long monopoles over poor, average, swamp and salt-water grounds. The design parameters are:
R_{rad} of 30° antenna: 2.5 ohms, weight factor: 29
R_{rad} of 60° antenna: 12 ohms, weight factor: 6
R_{rad} of 90° antenna: 36 ohms, weight factor: 2
R_{rad} of 125° antenna: 125 ohms, weight factor: 1.22.

Table 10

Radiation Resistance for Shortened Verticals

Antenna Length (deg)	——Radiation Resistance in Ohms——			
	Top-Loaded	Center-Loaded	Base-Loaded	Unloaded
30	8.6	5.8	2.5	
60	26.8	16.3	12.0	
90				36
125				57

is the power dissipated by resistor R. If P1 = P2 then by definition $R_{rad}[1] = R_{rad}[2] = R$. The values of R_{rad} given in Figures 2.7, 2.9 and 2.10 can be used for antennas with diameters ranging from 0.1 to 1°. Sevick, W2FMI (Ref 818) obtained very similar results experimentally, while the values in the figures mentioned above were derived mathematically (see Section 2.3.4.1). For antennas made of thicker elements, the charts from Figures 2.21 and 2.22 can be used. For

monopoles longer than ¼ λ, I_{max} is not at the base. For a 135° antenna (3/8 λ), $R_{rad}[2] = R_{feed} \approx 300$ ohms, but the value of 2R, inserted in the theoretical antenna at the maximum current point will be lower (57 ohms). If P1 (radiated power) = P2 (dissipated power in 2R), then $R_{rad}[1] = 2R$. These values of $R_{rad}[1]$ are given in Figure 2.17, while $R_{rad}[2]$ can be found in Figures 2.21 and 2.22. Figures 2.23 and 2.24 show the reactance of monopoles (at the base feed point) for varying antenna lengths and antenna diameter (Source: E. A. Laport, *Radio Antenna Engineering*, McGraw-Hill, NY, 1952, used by permission). For antennas with thin elements the values from Figure 2.13 can be applied (divide reactance by 2).

2.4.3 EFFICIENCY OF THE MONOPOLE ANTENNA

The same formula given before,

$$\eta = \frac{R_{rad}[2]}{R_{rad}[2] + R_{loss}}$$

applies for vertical monopoles as well as dipoles. However, the equivalent series circuit of the monopole differs in one

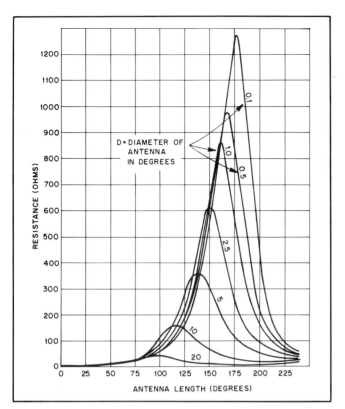

Figure 2.21—Feed-point resistances (R_{rad} [2]) of monopoles with varying diameters. These values were computed for perfect ground. (360° = 1 λ.)

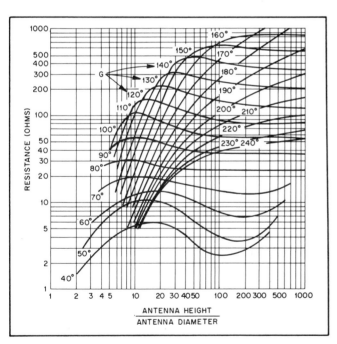

Figure 2.22—Feed-point resistances (R_{rad} [2]) of monopoles with different antenna height/diameter ratios over perfect ground.

respect from the dipole, in that it includes the RF loss resistance of the ground.

The constituents of the total loss in a monopole system are:
- Conductor RF resistance.
- Parallel losses from insulators.
- Equivalent series losses from any loading elements.
- Ground losses.

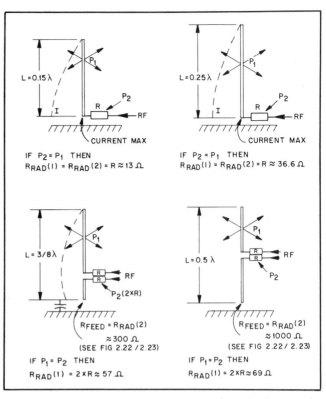

Figure 2.25—Radiation resistance definitions for long and short verticals. See text for details.

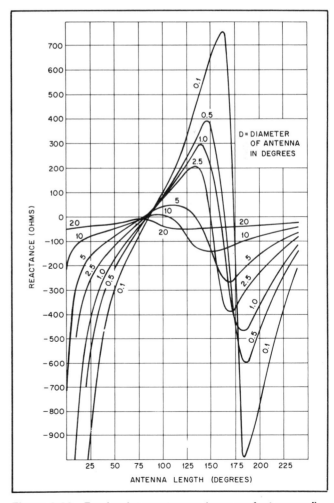

Figure 2.23—Feed-point reactances (over perfect ground) of monopoles with varying diameters.

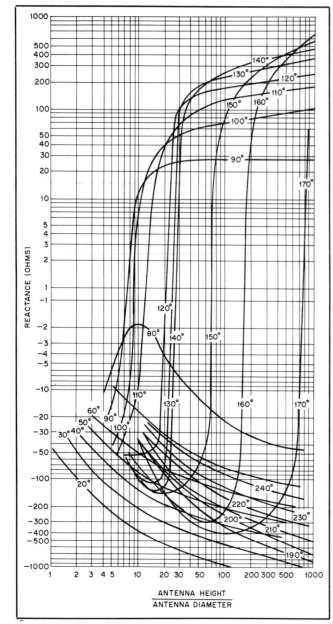

Figure 2.24—Feed-point reactances (over perfect ground) of monopoles with different antenna height/diameter ratios.

2.4.3.1 Conductor RF Resistance

When multisection towers are used for a vertical antenna, care should be taken to ensure proper electrical contact between the sections. If necessary, a copper braid strap should interconnect the sections. Rohrbacher, DJ2NN provided a formula to calculate the effective RF resistance of conductors of copper, aluminum and bronze:

$$R_{loss} = (1 + 0.1L) \left(f^{0.125} \right) \left(0.5 + \frac{1.5}{D} \right) \times m$$

where

L = length of the vertical in meters
f = frequency of operation in MHz
D = conductor diameter in mm (1 inch = 25.4 mm)
M = material constant (M = 0.945 for copper, 1.0 for bronze and 1.16 for aluminum).

2.4.3.2 Parallel Losses in Insulators

Base insulators often operate at low-impedance points. For monopoles near a half-wavelength long however, care should be taken to use good quality insulators as very high voltages can be present. There are many military surplus insulators available for this purpose. For medium and low impedance applications, insulators made of nylon stock (turned down to the appropriate diameter) are excellent. An inverted plastic bottle can be used as a cover to keep the insulator dry (Figure 2.26).

2.4.3.3 Equivalent Series Losses in Loading Devices

If the vertical is shorter than 90°, some form of loading will be needed to resonate the antenna. Linear loading and top-capacity loading are the preferred methods because these systems can be made virtually loss-free. Linear loading does not have to be implemented at the bottom end of the vertical. Applying it higher up on the vertical does, however, make it necessary to electrically open up the vertical at the point of loading.

When applying top-capacity loading, especially on 160 meters, the practical limitation is likely to be the size (diameter) of the top hat. Therefore, when designing a short vertical, it is wise to start by dimensioning the top hat.

Consider the design of an 80-foot (24.38 m) vertical with a 10-foot (3.048 m) diameter capacity hat for 1.8 MHz.

The capacitance of a disk hat is given by

C = D/1.12

where

C = hat capacitance in pF
D = hat diameter in inches (1 inch = 2.54 cm).

In this example, C = 120 inches/1.12 = 107 pF.
The capacitive reactance of the hat is 825 ohms at 1.8 MHz.

For loading the short vertical (Section 2.3.4.2), the surge impedance of the vertical must be calculated first. The formula is different from the one used for dipoles:

$$Z_0 = 60 \times (2.31 \log (h/d) - 1)$$

where

h = antenna height
d = antenna diameter (both in the same units).

Let us assume the radiator diameter is 10 inches (tower sections) and the height is 720 inches:

$$Z_0 = 60 \times (2.31 \log (720/10) - 1) = 197 \text{ ohms}$$

Notice that the conductor diameter has a great influence on the result. The same vertical made of 2-inch tubing has a surge impedance of 293 ohms.

The electrical length of the capacitive top-hat is calculated as follows:

tan(t) = 197/825 or, t = arc tan (197/825) = 13.4°

For the thinner radiator, the electrical length of the hat would be higher (19.55° for d = 2 inches).
Radiator electrical length = 52.66°.
Top capacity hat = 13.43°. Since the sum of the two is 66.09°, another 23.91° of loading are required to make a full 90°.

Let us assume that it is mechanically difficult to electrically open the vertical along its length for inserting a loading coil or a linear-loading device. Therefore, we will calculate the two remaining alternatives:

1) Coil base loading.

2) Linear loading at the antenna base.

Only the coil loading will be examined in detail as it will become clear that the required inductance for the remaining base loading will be quite small and as such the equivalent losses can be made small also.

Coil base loading:
Calculation of radiation resistance:

$$S = \int_{23.91}^{76.57} \cos L \ dL = \sin 76.57 - \sin 23.92$$

$$= 0.567 \ A\text{-radians}$$

Equivalent area $= 0.567/\cos 23.91 = 0.62$
Total equivalent area: 0.62 radians $= 0.62 \times 57.3 = 35.54°$
Electrical length $= 300/1.8 = 166.67$ m

$$\text{Effective height} = \frac{35.54 \times 166.67}{360} = 16.45 \text{ m}$$

$$R_{rad} = \frac{1450 \times 16.45^2}{166.67^2} = 15 \text{ ohms}$$

Calculation for the loading coil:
The surge impedance was calculated above as 197 ohms. The capacitive reactance is

$$X_C = \frac{Z_0}{\tan t}$$

where t is the electrical length of the vertical (tower + top loading). In this example, $X_C = 197/\tan 66.09 = 87.33$ ohms. Since X_L must equal X_C,

$$L = \frac{X_C}{2\pi f} = \frac{87.33}{2 \times 3.14 \times 1.8} = 7.72 \ \mu H$$

Calculation of equivalent series resistance:
For a Q factor of 200, $R_{loss} = 87.3/200 = 0.43$ ohms

2.4.3.4 Ground Losses

In the preceding sections, we have carefully examined the importance of achieving a high radiation resistance by (1) choosing the greatest possible physical length (up to 225° or 5/8 λ), (2) choosing the most appropriate place for the required loading devices and (3) choosing the loading devices with the lowest inherent losses. The ground system is of at least equal importance with monopoles or ground-mounted vertical antennas. There have been a number of good articles (Refs 806 to 822) which are recommended as reading material.

The influence of the reflecting ground has been emphasized already when dealing with two different antenna performance parameters: efficiency of monopoles and wave angle (vertical angle of radiation of horizontal and vertical antennas).

The quality of the reflecting ground system in the immediate vicinity of the monopole (up to approximately ½ λ from the base) is important for the efficiency of the antenna. The radials serve to collect the return currents from the vertical antenna.

The ground quality at greater distances will play an important role in the Brewster angle for the location (Ref 750). A good ground for a long distance out from the antenna will allow for a low Brewster angle, which also means that the tip of the (lowest) wave angle lobe will be closer to the horizon. Those fortunate enough to be situated right near the ocean know how well vertical antennas can perform. Hawker, G3VA (Ref 779) writes: "ground conductivity right out to about 100 λ in the target direction affects radiation angle."

With the advent of powerful analytical computer-aided tools for antenna evaluation, theoretical analysis has become a reality. Edward, N2MF, used NEC (Numerical Electromagnetic Code, method of moments) to reach very similar results as obtained by experimental methods (Ref 816).

Edward discovered that for a given number of radial wires, there is a corresponding length beyond which there is no appreciable signal improvement. This length is, surprisingly enough, independent of earth conditions. Table 11 shows the optimum radial length as a function of the number of radials (within 0.1 dB of maximum gain).

Over poor ground (desert), going from 4 to 96 radials yields a signal improvement of 3.9 dB. With average ground, the signal improvement is 3.5 dB, while for very good ground, the improvement is only a little over 1 dB.

Table 11
Optimum Length versus Number of Radials

Number of Radials	Optimum Length (λ)
4	0.10
12	0.15
24	0.25
48	0.35
96	0.45
120	0.50

Short radials (up to ¼ λ long) do not influence the wave angle of the vertical. The wave angle is dramatically influenced by the ground conditions, however. The wave angle is 30° for a quarter-wave monopole over poor earth with ¼ λ radials, 26° under the same conditions with average ground, and 20° with a very good ground. Adding many long radials will significantly reduce the wave angle over poor and average ground (a lowering of the wave angle of up to 10° can be achieved with 120 radials each 0.5 to 0.6 λ long). This confirms the earlier remark that good earth conductivity plays a dual role: (1) as a path acting as the return circuit for the antenna current where the ground loss influences the efficiency of the antenna, and (2) as an electrical mirror at further distances from the monopole, creating reflection conditions for the low-angle "rays," and as such lowering the Brewster angle and the wave angle (Ref 821).

Sectorized radial systems with very long radials (up to 10 λ long) have been evaluated and found to be very effective for lowering the wave angle in certain directions. A similar situation occurs when verticals are mounted right at the salt-water line.

It has been the author's experience, and has been confirmed by others, that using a solid metal plate of reasonable size (4 to 10 feet square) right under the antenna can result in a notable decrease in ground resistance, and consequently ground loss. Another possible improvement to an existing radial system has been reported by Sherwood (Ref 809) and is also used by the author. Installing strips of chicken wire (2 to 3 feet wide) in different directions from the antenna base can significantly reduce the losses of the ground system.

Figure 2.26 shows the base of the author's vertical antenna and the solid aluminum plate (4 feet square) from which

Figure 2.26—The author's 88-foot (26.8-m) vertical is made of 10-inch (25-cm) wide steel lattice tower. It rests on a 3-inch nylon insulator covered by an inverted plastic bottle to protect it from the elements. Eighty radials are connected to the outer edges of the large aluminum plate under the antenna by stainless-steel hardware. Remember that corrosion will occur when dissimilar metals are joined; copper with aluminum is a particularly corrosive combination. It is best to protect such joints from humidity by covering them with silicone rubber or petroleum jelly.

80 radials between 50 and 120 feet long extend in all directions. During winter, six 40-foot long, 2-foot wide strips of galvanized chicken wire are added on top of the lawn. This has been found to reduce the resistance of the ground system on 160 meters from 9 to 6 ohms, which is a vast improvement on an 85-foot linear-loaded vertical with a radiation resistance of approximately 13 ohms.

When only a few (fewer than 6) radials are used, the gauge of the wires is important for maximum efficiency—the heavier the better. With many radials, the wire size becomes unimportant since the return current is divided over a large number of conductors.

DXpeditions using temporary antennas just have to take a small spool with, say, 10,000 feet of no. 24 or 26 (0.5 or 0.4 mm diameter) enameled magnet wire. This is inexpensive, and can be used to establish a very efficient RF ground system.

Only a few of the more fortunate among us have the ability to run any number of radials of good length in all directions because of the real estate required. In practice, the rule of thumb for designing a good ground system is to use as many radials as possible, including as many really long ones as possible. The addition of a ground screen is definitely to be

advocated where space for an elaborate radial system is not available.

Ground rods are important for achieving a good dc ground, but contribute very little to the RF ground. Ground rods can constitute an acceptable minimum RF ground when a rich soil is predominant, or when the ground requirements are minimal, such as for use in terminating a Beverage antenna.

Evaluating the Ground System

The classic way to evaluate the losses of a ground system is to measure the feed-point resistance of the vertical while steadily increasing the number of radials. The feed-point resistance will drop consistently and will approach a lower limit when a very good ground system has been installed. Be aware, however, that the intrinsic ground conductivity can vary greatly with time and weather, so it is recommended that you do such a test in a very short time frame in order to minimize the effects of varying environmental factors on your tests (Ref 818, 819).

Radiation resistance can be measured with a noise bridge or an antennascope with an appropriately expanded scale (Ref 105, 1600, 1601, 1607). Antennas shorter or longer than a quarter wavelength are first resonated (loaded) to the operating frequency if an antennascope is used. With a noise bridge, direct resistance and reactance measurement can be made on any frequency within the range of the receiver used.

The figures from Table 12 can be used to get an idea of the equivalent ohmic losses of radial systems over good ground. For poor ground, higher resistances can be expected, especially with only a few radials.

Table 12
Equivalent Resistance of Radial System in Ohms

Radial Length (λ)	Number of Radials				
	2	15	30	60	120
0.15	28.6	15.3	14.8	11.6	11.6
0.20	28.4	15.3	13.4	9.1	9.1
0.25	28.1	15.1	12.2	7.9	6.9
0.30	27.7	14.5	10.7	6.6	5.2
0.35	27.5	13.9	9.8	5.6	2.8
0.40	27.0	13.1	7.2	5.2	0.1

Other Ground Systems

There are basically two different types of ground systems: buried radial systems and elevated counterpoise systems. Most ground systems used on 80 and 160 meters are buried radial systems, consisting of buried wires extending radially from the antenna base. Brown (Ref 801) described the buried radial system extensively in 1937 and his work led to the now-common requirement that broadcast antennas use at least 120 radials, each at least ¼ λ long.

Doty, K8CFU, concluded from his experimental work (Ref 807 and 820) that elevated radial wires make a more efficient ground system than buried bare radials. The reasoning is that in the case of an elevated radial or counterpoise system, the return currents do not have to travel for a considerable distance through high-resistance earth, as is the case when buried radials are used. Frey, W3ESU, uses the same counterpoise system with his MINIPOISE short low-band vertical (Ref 824). He reports that connecting the elevated and insulated radials wires together at the periphery definitely yields improved performance. If an elevated radial system cannot be used, Doty recommends using insulated radials lying right on the ground, or buried as close as possible to the surface. Leo, W7LR, (Ref 808) on the other hand writes that burying the radials a few inches below the surface does not detract from their performance.

The required number of radials in an elevated radial/counterpoise system depends on the height of the system above the poorly conducting ground. A rule of thumb is to make the number of radials as large as required so that the tips of two adjacent radials are separated by a distance no greater than half the height of the radial system above ground.

Sherwood, WBØJGP, has described and compared ground systems consisting of wide strips of ground screens (Ref 809). Anyone tempted to try the ''screen'' approach should be warned of one thing: never use steel wire for a buried ground system, whether it be single wire or chicken wire. Steel is a very poor conductor at RF. The steel wire will also corrode in a very short time, although a thick layer of galvanization may improve the resistance to corrosion.

Most hams will be forced to use a buried radial system. Installing radials can be quite a chore. Hyder, W7IV (Ref 815) and Mosser, K3ZAP (Ref 812) have described systems and tools for easy installation of radials. Radials can also be laid on the ground in areas that are suitable. Another neat way of installing radials in a lawn-covered area is to cut the grass really short at the end of the season (October), and lay the radials flat on the ground, anchored here and there with metal hooks. By the next spring, the grass will have covered up most of the wires, and by the end of the following year the wires will be completely covered by the grass. This method also meets the recommendation by Doty, K8CFU, to bury the radials as close as possible to the surface of the ground.

2.4.4 SHORT VERTICALS

All the remarks given in the chapter on short dipoles apply to short verticals. To summarize, if verticals shorter than a quarter wavelength long must be used, it is essential to:
- Make the short vertical physically as long as possible.
- Make use of capacitive top (hat) loading to achieve the highest radiation resistance possible, if necessary in combination with a small amount of base loading.
- Use linear loading instead of coil loading whenever possible to reduce losses.
- Use the best possible ground system.

Efficient verticals that are quite small can be constructed, but the wavelength involved cannot be made smaller than it is. The ground around the antenna (to a great distance away from it) is almost as important as the antenna itself, even more than with horizontally polarized antennas such as dipoles. There is no way to get around this unless you can drastically raise the radiation resistance of the vertical by making it very long—a half wavelength for instance. Even then, a good ground is essential in order to obtain the lowest possible wave angle.

It is a widespread misconception that vertical antennas don't require much space. Nothing is farther from the truth. Verticals take much more space than dipoles! A good ground system for a short vertical (less than 7/16 λ long) takes much more space than a dipole, unless you live right at the coast, over salt water (see Section 2.4.10).

Another common misconception is that folded elements increase the radiation resistance of an antenna, and thus increase the system efficiency. However, the radiation resistance of a folded element is not the same as its feed-point impedance. The folding of the element transforms the feed-point impedance to a higher value, which may be advantageous from an ease-of-feeding standpoint. A folded monopole with two equal diameter legs will show a feed-point impedance with the resistive part equal to $4 R_{rad}$. The higher feed-point impedance does not help to reduce the losses due to low radiation resistance, however, since with the folded element the lower feed current now flows in one more conductor, totaling the same loss. In a folded monopole, the same current ends up flowing through the lossy ground system, resulting in the same loss—whether a folded element is used or not.

One way to improve the radiation efficiency of a vertical over a poor ground is to replace the single radiating element with several close-spaced verticals, all fed in phase. The design of such a system is described in Section 2.11.1.5.

2.4.5 BANDWIDTH

As with dipoles, the bandwidth of verticals primarily depends on the length of the radiator. Figure 2.27 shows the typical 2:1 SWR bandwidth of ground-mounted verticals from 10 to 90° long, assuming a perfect ground and a standard L-network to match the antenna to 50 ohms (Ref 728). This shows that we can expect to cover up to 400 kHz on 80 meters with a ''full-size'' quarter-wave vertical.

The bandwidth of a vertical can be determined by calculating the antenna Q factor (3:1 SWR points, see Section 2.2.7). Q factor = surge impedance/$(R_{rad} + R_{loss})$. The bandwidth (in MHz) = f (MHz)/Q factor.

Example: Assuming a linear-loaded vertical for 160 meters with a physical length of 88 feet (26.8 m) and a diameter of 10 inches, the following inputs apply:
Z_{surge} = 197 ohms
R_{rad} = 13.00 ohms

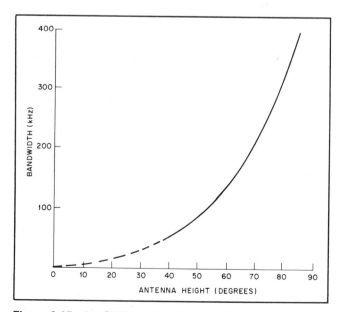

Figure 2.27—2:1 SWR bandwidths of a shortened 80-meter vertical antenna matched by an L-network. The short antennas do not have any separate loading devices. The figures were obtained experimentally using a very good ground system (100 ¼-λ radials).

$R_{loading}$ = 0.25 ohms (loss of the linear loading system)
R_{ground} = 6 ohms (good ground system)
R_{loss} = 6.25 ohms (sum of $R_{loading}$ and R_{ground})
f = 1.8 MHz

$$BW\ (3{:}1\ SWR) = \frac{1.8}{\dfrac{197}{13\ +\ 0.25\ +\ 6}}$$

$$= 0.175\ MHz = 175\ kHz$$

The 2:1 SWR bandwidth for the same antenna as measured experimentally by the author is approximately 70 kHz using an elaborate ground system with an equivalent loss resistance of approximately 6 ohms, and an L-network to achieve a 50-ohm input impedance. Running one of the design computer programs mentioned in Section 2.4.6 will show that, for a given antenna diameter (as the antenna is shortened and the missing part being partly or totally replaced by a loading coil), the bandwidth will decrease up to a point, and will then begin to increase again as the influence of the equivalent resistive loss in the large coil begins to positively influence the bandwidth of the antenna. If an unusually broad bandwidth is measured for a given vertical design, one should suspect a poor-quality loading coil or some other lossy element in the system.

2.4.6 DESIGN COMPUTER PROGRAMS FOR SHORT VERTICALS

The author has developed two programs for the design and evaluation of short verticals. The programs use only formulas explained in this chapter. The first program deals with coil or lumped-constant loaded short verticals, where the coil can be positioned anywhere from the feed point to the top of the monopole. At the top, the coil should be replaced with capacitive top hat. The second program is for combined top capacity-hat loading and base-coil loading (base loading can be replaced with linear loading), whereby a slight increase in radiation resistance will occur, while the associated loading coil losses will be negligible. The listings of the programs are given in Chapter VII (Computer Programs). The programs are written in Applesoft BASIC and will run on an Apple IIe or IIc computer equipped with an 80-column card. The programs are written in a very straightforward way and can be easily adapted to other dialects of BASIC.

2.4.6.1 Design of Lumped-Constant Loaded Verticals

User inputs:
A) Design frequency (MHz).
B) Total equivalent RF loss resistance (ground plus element, in ohms).
C) Diameter of the antenna, in centimeters or inches, as defined by the user.
Outputs:
The program will print the following data in tabular form, for a range of antenna heights (5 to 90° long in 5° increments) and loading coil heights (0° to top of antenna, in 5° steps):
A) The length of the vertical antenna in both electrical degrees and in meters or feet.
B) Loading-coil height in degrees.
C) Loading-coil height in meters or feet.
D) Radiation resistance in ohms.
E) Surge impedance in ohms.
F) Required inductive reactance for base-loading coil (ohms).

G) Required inductance for the coil (μH).
H) Equivalent series resistance of the coil.
I) Q-factor of the antenna.
J) Bandwidth at 3:1 SWR points.
K) Efficiency of the antenna in percent.
L) Equivalent loss in dB.
M) Antenna impedance at resonance (ohms).

The zero-degree loading coil height corresponds to base loading. Loading at the top of the antenna means capacity hat loading. The second program (Section 2.4.6.2) has been specially developed for verticals with capacity-hat top loading. Two partial runs (for design frequencies of 3.775 and 1.825 MHz) are listed in Chapter VII.

Required lengths for quarter-wave radiators can be calculated with the "ELEMENT TAPER" program listed in Chapter VII. The same program can be used for dipoles or Yagi elements.

2.4.6.2 Design of Combined Top/Base-Loaded Verticals

The computer program listing for design of combined top/base-loaded verticals as well as a sample printout is shown in Chapter VII (Computer Programs). The concept of the program is similar to the one above.

User inputs:
A) Design frequency in MHz.
B) Equivalent total loss resistance (ground plane plus element losses in ohms).
C) Electrical length of the capacity hat in degrees (90° minus the length of the vertical radiator).
D) Diameter of the antenna in centimeters or inches.

Outputs:
With the given inputs, a listing is produced for a range of antenna heights from 2° to 90° (minus the equivalent length of the capacity hat). The outputs are the same as for the previous program, with two exceptions:
B) Capacitance of top hat in pF.
C) Diameter of capacity hat (disk) in centimeters or inches.

A sample printout is given in Chapter VII for a practical example: 20° of capacitive loading on a vertical for 1.83 MHz. The other inputs used are: loading coil Q: 300, total loss resistance = 12 ohms, antenna element diameter = 10 inches.

2.4.7 TALL VERTICALS

Short verticals have been dealt with in detail, mostly with 160 meters in mind. On higher frequencies, taller verticals are quite feasible. A full-size quarter-wave radiator on 80 meters is only 64 feet high (19.4 m). On 40 meters, more than ¼ λ (32 feet) should be easily obtainable. The lowest angle of radiation from a single vertical structure without phasing stubs can be achieved with a 5/8 λ vertical (see Section 2.3.5). The author has been using a single 5/8 λ vertical for 40 meters for more than 20 years with good success. It does not compete with the big Yagis at 150 feet, but using separate receiving antennas (Beverages), it has been a good performer. Some of the advantages of using verticals longer than ¼ λ are higher radiation resistance and slightly lower angle of radiation.

The base resistance (R_{rad}[2]) and feed-point reactance for monopoles is given in Figures 2.21 and 2.23 as a function of the conductor diameter in degrees, and in Figure 2.22 and 2.24 as a function of the antenna length/diameter ratio. The graphs are accurate only for structures with rather large diameters (not for single-wire structures). A conductor diameter of 1° equals 833/f(MHz) in mm or 32.8/f(MHz) in inches. The

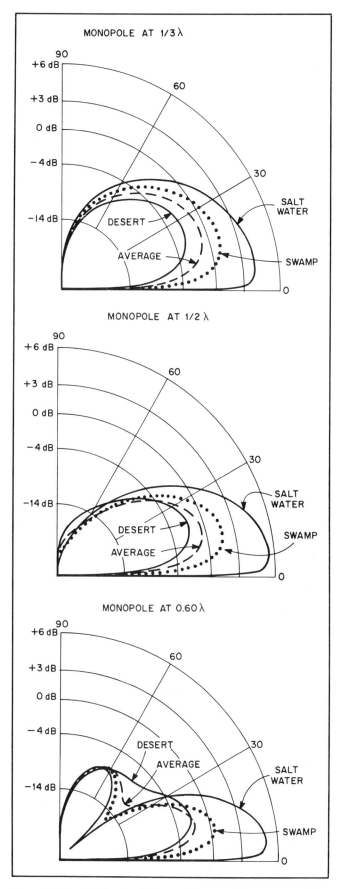

Figure 2.28—Vertical radiation patterns of long monopoles (⅓, ½ and 0.6 λ long) over poor, average and excellent ground. The design parameters used were:
R_{rad} **of ⅓ λ antenna: 55.5 ohms, weight factor: 1.29**
R_{rad} **of ½ λ antenna: 69.5 ohms, weight factor: 1.05**
R_{rad} **of 0.6 λ antenna: 60.5 ohms, weight factor: 1.2.**

higher radiation resistance (R_{rad}[2]) of a long vertical can be used advantageously where poor ground is encountered, because it contributes to increased efficiency.

Figure 2.28 shows the vertical radiation patterns of long verticals (⅓, ½ and 5/8 λ long) over desert, average, swamp and excellent (salt water) grounds. Compare the patterns and gain figures with the small verticals of Figure 2.20.

2.4.8 FEEDING THE VERTICAL

Quarter-wave verticals will usually give a very reasonable match to a 50-ohm coaxial feed line ($Z_k = R_{rad} + R_{loss}$ at resonance). Shorter verticals will end up with low characteristic impedances at resonance, including the losses, and a matching network will then be required.

2.4.8.1 Matching Real Impedances

The L-network is the simplest network that will match almost any impedance to the coaxial cable impedance. Many amateur handbooks only publish the formulas for calculating L-networks for matching non-complex antenna impedances to a coaxial line. These formulas can be used after first tuning out any reactance from the antenna (with some L or C). If the resistive component of the antenna impedance is higher than the characteristic impedance of the coax, the following formulas apply:

$$X_L = \sqrt{(Z_{coax} \times R_{ant}) - Z_{coax}^2}$$

$$X_C = \frac{Z_{coax} \times R_{ant}}{X_L}$$

The capacitor value is found as follows:

$$C = \frac{1}{2\pi f X_L}$$

The capacitor is connected between the antenna terminal and ground. The coil goes between the antenna terminal and the center conductor of the coax. The coil inductance is:

$$L = \frac{X_L}{2\pi f}$$

This type of L-network is called a series-input L-network.

If the resistive part of the antenna impedance is lower than the characteristic impedance of the coax, the following formulas apply:

$$X_C = Z_{coax} \times \sqrt{\frac{R_{ant}}{Z_{coax} - R_{ant}}}$$

$$X_L = \frac{Z_{coax} \times R_{ant}}{X_C}$$

In this case, the capacitor is connected between the center conductor of the coax and ground, and the coil goes from the antenna terminal to the coax. This is the shunt-input L-network.

Figure 2.29 shows how this approach for matching can be used for antennas that show either inductive or capacitive reactance at the design frequency. In both cases, tuning can be done in two ways:

1) Use an antennascope and an RF generator tuned to the design frequency, or a noise bridge and a receiver. You can use a dip oscillator or a low-power transmitter (appropriately attenuated) as an RF generator (see Figure 2.37). Vary the

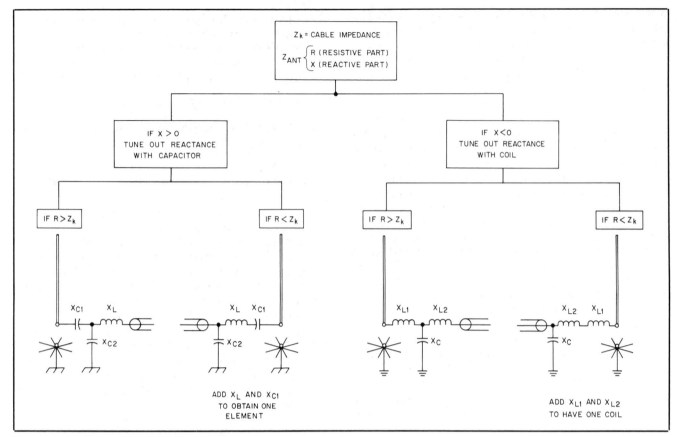

Figure 2.29—Two-step matching of non-resonant verticals using series reactances (L or C) and L-networks. See text for calculation and adjustment procedures.

value of the series reactance (vary the L if the antenna is shorter than a quarter wavelength or longer than a half wavelength, and vary the C if the antenna is between a quarter wave and a half wave long) until resonance is found at the design frequency. Note the resistance of the bridge at resonance. That is the feed resistance and also the value that will have to be matched to the impedance of the coaxial line.

2) Use a dip meter coupled with a one- or two-turn link between the series reactance and the ground. Tune the C or L until a dip is found right at the design frequency. Use the lightest possible coupling between the link and the dip meter. This method does not allow you to actually measure radiation resistance, so it will have to be calculated using the formulas or charts from Section 2.4.2 or the computer program mentioned in Section 2.4.6.

Tuning the L-network using either set of formulas described above is fairly simple. Cut the coil for the calculated value and provide two extra taps, one at +10% and one at -10%. Use these three taps with different settings of the loading capacitor until a 1:1 SWR is found at the design frequency.

2.4.8.2 Matching Complex Impedances

L-networks can also match complex impedances to the coax line, but the formulas are slightly more complex. Leo, W7LR (Ref 1404 and 1411) and Franke, WA2EWT (Ref 1410) have covered the design of L-networks for such applications. Gehrke, K2BT, uses matrix algebra for calculating a range for the networks he uses in his array designs (Section 2.11.1.4). The author has developed a computer program (L-NETWORK DESIGN) that will compute all possible L-network solutions for a given transformation ratio. The listing of the program is given in Chapter VII (Computer

Programs). In all cases, there are at least two alternatives to choose from.

So-called shunt-input L-networks are used when the resistive part of the output impedance is lower than the required input impedance of the network. The series-input L-network is used when the opposite condition exists. In some cases, a series-input L-network can also be used when the output resistance is smaller than the input resistance. All possible alternatives (at least two, but four at the most) will be given by the program. The choice will be up to the user, but in many cases, component values will determine which choice is more practical. In other instances, performance may be the most important consideration: Low-pass networks will give some additional harmonic suppression of the radiated signal, while a high-pass filter may help to reduce the strength of strong medium-wave broadcast signals from local stations.

Some solutions provide a direct dc ground path for the antenna through the coil. If dc grounding is required, such as in areas with frequent thunderstorms, this can be achieved by placing an appropriate RF choke at the base of the antenna (between the driven element and ground). L-networks are preferred for use with transformation ratios up to 5. If higher ratios are used, the bandwidth of the system will suffer. One may alternatively use two series-connected L-networks to cover higher ratios to improve system bandwidth. This configuration results in a so-called Pi-L network. For example, a 50- to 600-ohm transformation could be done in two steps, from 50 to 150 ohms and from 150 to 600 ohms. The "L-NETWORK" program also calculates the input and output voltages and currents of the network. These can be used to determine the required component ratings. Capacitor current ratings are especially important when the capacitor is the series element in a network. The voltage rating is most important when the capacitor is the shunt element in the network. Consideration regarding component ratings and the construction of toroidal coils are covered in Section 2.9.4.3, while a practical network adjustment procedure is discussed in Section 2.9.4.5.

For those who do not use a home computer to solve their engineering problems, Tables 13 and 14 list a range of L and C values computed for a design frequency of 3.65 MHz. The resistive and reactive values for the load impedance listed in the tables are those most commonly encountered with vertical antennas. The nominal feed-line impedance is 50 ohms. For 1.825 MHz, multiply all figures by 2. In every case, the coil is connected between the bottom end of the vertical and the coaxial cable inner conductor. For resistance values below 50 ohms, the capacitor is connected between the inner conductor of the feed line and ground (shunt-input L-network). If the resistive part of the antenna impedance is greater than 50 ohms, the capacitor goes between the antenna feed point and ground (series-input L-network).

The tables do not give all the solutions, and the antenna designer is strongly advised to use the "L-NETWORK" program for a more complete analysis. If the output load impedance is both high and essentially resistive (such as for a half-wavelength vertical fed at the bottom), one may also use a broadband transformer, such as is used in transistor power amplifier output stages. Figure 2.30 shows one transformer design. Two turns of AWG 12 Teflon-insulated wire are fed through two stacks each of fifteen ½-inch (OD) powdered-iron toroidal cores (Amidon T50-2) as the primary low impedance winding. The secondary consists of 8 turns. The turns ratio is 4:1; the impedance ratio is 16:1.

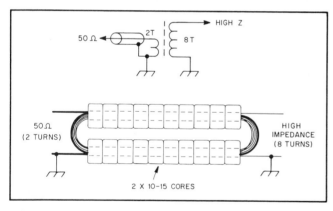

Figure 2.30—A wide-bandwidth high-power transformer for large transformation ratios, such as for feeding a half-wave vertical antenna at its base (R_{rad} [2] = 600-1000 ohms, depending on the diameter of the element). The transformer uses two stacks of 10-15 ½-inch OD powdered-iron cores (Amidon T50-2). The primary is 2 turns, the secondary is 8 turns (for a 50-800-ohm transformer). See text for details.

The efficiency of the transformer can be checked by terminating it with a high-power 800-ohm dummy load (or the antenna, if no suitable load is available), and running full power to the transformer for a couple of minutes. Start with low power—better safe than sorry. If there are signs of heating of the cores, add more cores to the stack. Such a transformer has the advantage of introducing no phase shift between input and output, and therefore can easily be incorporated into phased arrays (see Section 2.11.1.3).

There are other networks that can be used to match complex impedances to a resistive value. The stub approach and derived methods are described in detail in Section 2.12.3.

2.4.9 PRACTICAL VERTICAL ANTENNAS

2.4.9.1 Single-Band Quarter-Wave Vertical for 40, 80 or 160

The length of a full-size quarter-wave vertical is given by:

$$H = \frac{234}{f \text{ (MHz)}}$$

where H is in feet. The formula incorporates a 95% shortening factor, which makes it suitable for large-diameter structures. Quarter-wave verticals are easy to match to 50-ohm coaxial feed lines. The radiation resistance plus the usual earth losses will produce a feed-point resistance close to 50 ohms. Quarter-wave verticals are also popular elements for arrays, as they do not require any matching networks which introduce additional phase shift (Section 2.4.8.2).

If you don't mind using a matching network at the antenna base, and if you can manage a few more meters of antenna height, extra height will give you increased radiation resistance (see Figure 2.17), higher efficiency and a lower radiation angle (see Figure 2.28). The feed-point impedance can be found in the charts of Figures 2.21 through 2.24. The matching networks can be designed using the program from Section 2.4.8.2.

Consider the following example:

Tower height = 27 meters (90 ft)
Tower diameter = 25 centimeters (10 in)
Design frequency = 3.8 MHz

Assuming a shortening factor of 0.95, 27 meters represents 123° length. The tower diameter is 1°, so the height/diameter ratio is 123:1. From the charts of Figures 2.21 through 2.24, we find:

R = 200 ohms
X = + j240 ohms

Using the L-network design program, we calculate a high-pass network with the following values:

C = 283 pF (connected between the coax center conductor and the antenna)
L = 11.6 μH (connected between antenna and ground)

We could have alternately chosen a low-pass filter network (if a little additional harmonic suppression is more important than dc grounding of the antenna and the rejection of broadcast signals). In that case, the capacitance (between the antenna and ground) would be 357 pF, and the inductance (between the antenna and the feed line) would be 6.19 μH.

2.4.9.2 Top-Loaded Vertical

Capacitively top-loaded short verticals can be made quite efficient. The computer design program from Chapter VII will produce all design parameters for capacitively top-loaded verticals. Table 15 gives the dimensions for such antennas for different element lengths and capacity hat diameters on 80 and 160 meters. The table shows an interesting characteristic of short verticals: radiation resistance remains quite high right down to a physical radiator length of 60° (with a 30° capacity hat). On 160 meters, this represents an antenna 27 meters long

Table 13
L-Network Values for F_{design} = 3.65 MHz

R/X	−25	−50	−75	−100	−125	−150	−175	−200	−225	−250	−275
2.5	1.5/3801	2.6/3801	3.7/3801	4.8/3801	5.9/3801	7/3801	8.1/3801	9.1/3801	10.2/3801	11.3/3801	12.4/3801
5	1.7/2616	2.8/2616	3.9/2616	5/2616	6.1/2616	7.1/2616	8.2/2616	9.3/2616	10.4/2616	11.5/2616	12.6/2616
7.5	1.8/2075	2.9/2075	4/2075	5.1/2075	6.2/2075	7.3/2075	8.4/2075	9.4/2075	10.5/2075	11.6/2075	12.7/2075
10	1.9/1744	3/1744	4.1/1744	5.2/1744	6.3/1744	7.4/1744	8.5/1744	9.5/1744	10.6/1744	11.7/1744	12.8/1744
12.5	2/1510	3.1/1510	4.2/1510	5.3/1510	6.3/1510	7.4/1510	8.5/1510	9.6/1510	10.7/1510	11.8/1510	12.9/1510
15	2/1332	3.1/1332	4.2/1332	5.3/1332	6.4/1332	7.5/1332	8.6/1332	9.7/1332	10.8/1332	11.9/1332	12.9/1332
17.5	2.1/1188	3.2/1188	4.3/1188	5.4/1188	6.4/1188	7.5/1188	8.6/1188	9.7/1188	10.8/1188	11.9/1188	13/1188
20	2.1/1068	3.2/1068	4.3/1068	5.4/1068	6.5/1068	7.6/1068	8.6/1068	9.7/1068	10.8/1068	11.9/1068	13/1068
22.5	2.1/964	3.2/964	4.3/964	5.4/964	6.5/964	7.6/964	8.7/964	9.8/964	10.8/964	11.9/964	13/964
25	2.1/872	3.2/872	4.3/872	5.4/872	6.5/872	7.6/872	8.7/872	9.8/872	10.9/872	11.9/872	13/872
27.5	2.1/788	3.2/788	4.3/788	5.4/788	6.5/788	7.6/788	8.7/788	9.8/788	10.8/788	11.9/788	13/788
30	2.1/712	3.2/712	4.3/712	5.4/712	6.5/712	7.6/712	8.6/712	9.7/712	10.8/712	11.9/712	13/712
32.5	2.1/639	3.2/639	4.3/639	5.4/639	6.4/639	7.5/639	8.6/639	9.7/639	10.8/639	11.9/639	13/639
35	2/570	3.1/570	4.2/570	5.3/570	6.4/570	7.5/570	8.6/570	9.7/570	10.8/570	11.9/570	12.9/570
37.5	2/503	3.1/503	4.2/503	5.3/503	6.3/503	7.4/503	8.5/503	9.6/503	10.7/503	11.8/503	12.9/503
40	1.9/436	3/436	4.1/436	5.2/436	6.3/436	7.4/436	8.5/436	9.5/436	10.7/436	11.8/436	12.8/436
42.5	1.8/366	2.9/366	4/366	5.1/366	6.2/366	7.3/366	8.4/366	9.4/366	10.5/366	11.6/366	12.7/366
45	1.7/290	2.8/290	3.9/290	5/290	6.1/290	7.1/290	8.2/290	9.3/290	10.4/290	11.5/290	12.6/290
47.5	1.5/200	2.6/200	3.7/200	4.8/200	5.9/200	7/200	8.1/200	9.1/200	10.2/200	11.3/200	12.4/200
52.5	1.1/40	2.1/21	3.2/14	4.2/10	5.3/8	6.4/7	7.4/6	8.5/5	9.5/4	10.6/4	11.7/3
55	1.2/77	2.1/41	3.1/28	4.2/21	5.2/16	6.2/14	7.3/12	8.3/10	9.3/9	10.4/8	11.4/7
57.5	1.3/109	2.2/60	3.1/41	4.1/31	5.1/25	6.1/20	7.1/17	8.1/15	9.1/13	10.2/12	11.2/11
60	1.3/137	2.2/78	3.1/54	4/40	5/32	6/27	7/23	8/20	9/18	9.9/16	10.9/15
62.5	1.4/162	2.2/95	3.1/66	4/50	4.9/40	5.9/34	6.9/29	7.8/25	8.8/22	9.8/20	10.7/18
65	1.5/185	2.2/111	3.1/78	4/59	4.9/48	5.8/40	6.7/34	7.7/30	8.6/27	9.6/24	10.5/22
67.5	1.5/205	2.2/126	3/89	3.9/68	4.8/55	5.7/46	6.6/39	7.6/35	8.5/31	9.4/28	10.4/25
70	1.6/222	2.3/140	3/100	3.9/77	4.8/62	5.6/52	6.5/45	7.4/39	8.4/35	9.3/31	10.2/28
72.5	1.7/238	2.3/154	3/110	3.9/85	4.7/69	5.6/58	6.5/50	7.3/44	8.2/39	9.1/35	10/32
75	1.7/252	2.3/166	3/120	3.8/93	4.7/75	5.5/63	6.4/55	7.2/48	8.1/43	9/38	9.9/35
77.5	1.8/265	2.3/178	3/129	3.8/101	4.6/82	5.4/69	6.3/59	7.1/52	8/46	8.9/42	9.7/38
80	1.8/276	2.4/188	3/138	3.8/108	4.6/88	5.4/74	6.2/64	7/56	7.9/50	8.7/45	9.6/41
82.5	1.9/286	2.4/198	3/147	3.8/115	4.5/94	5.3/80	6.1/69	7/60	7.8/54	8.6/49	9.4/44
85	2/295	2.4/208	3.1/155	3.8/122	4.5/100	5.3/85	6.1/73	6.9/64	7.7/57	8.5/52	9.3/47
87.5	2/303	2.5/217	3.1/163	3.7/129	4.5/106	5.2/90	6/78	6.8/68	7.6/61	8.4/55	9.2/50
90	2.1/310	2.5/225	3.1/171	3.7/136	4.5/112	5.2/95	6/82	6.7/72	7.5/64	8.3/58	9.1/53
92.5	2.1/317	2.5/232	3.1/178	3.7/142	4.4/117	5.2/99	5.9/86	6.7/76	7.4/68	8.2/61	9/56
95	2.2/323	2.6/240	3.1/184	3.7/148	4.4/122	5.1/104	5.9/90	6.6/80	7.4/71	8.1/64	8.9/59
97.5	2.2/328	2.6/246	3.1/191	3.7/154	4.4/127	5.1/109	5.8/94	6.5/83	7.3/74	8/67	8.8/61
100	2.3/332	2.6/252	3.1/197	3.7/159	4.4/132	5.1/113	5.8/98	6.5/87	7.2/78	8/70	8.7/64

(90 feet) and a capacity hat just under 5 meters (16.7 feet) in diameter. This seems quite a reasonable height and is still mechanically feasible, although the capacity hat is sizeable. This antenna would be the next choice after its full-size, 135-foot counterpart.

2.4.9.3 Duobanders for 40/80

A 5/8 λ vertical for 40 meters is probably the best all-around DX transmitting antenna next to a Yagi or a quad. The length of a 5/8 λ (225°) long vertical made of 25-cm diameter mast (assuming a 0.95 shortening factor) on 7.1 MHz is 25.1 meters (83.5 feet). On 3.65 MHz, this length represents 116° (3.65 MHz was chosen because this antenna will easily cover 3.5-3.8 MHz with less than 2:1 SWR).

The feed-point impedances can again be found in the charts of Figures 2.21 through 2.24. The diameter is 1° on 80 meters and 2° on 40 meters.

The matching networks (calculated with the L-network design program in Chapter VII) and a two-band switching arrangement are shown in Figure 2.31. Several switching configurations are possible. The required inductances and capacitances will help the user choose the network. Air-wound coils are preferred for values up to 5 μH, and powdered-iron toroidal cores can be used for higher values. Ferrite cores are not suitable for this application, as these cores are much less stable and are easily saturated. The larger-size powdered-iron toroidal cores, which can be used for such applications, are listed in Table 16.

The required number of turns for a certain coil can be determined as follows:

$$N = 100 \sqrt{\frac{L}{AL}}$$

where L is the required inductance in microhenrys. The AL value is taken from Table 16. The amount of transmitter power will determine the core size. It is a good idea to choose a core a little on the large side, just in case. One may also stack two identical cores to increase power-handling capability, as well as the AL factor. The power limitations of powdered-iron cores are usually determined by the temperature increase of the core. Use large-gauge enameled copper wire for the minimum resistive loss, and wrap the core with glass-cloth electrical tape before winding the inductor. This will prevent arcing at high power levels.

Consider this example: The 14.4 μH coil from Figure 2.31 would require 20 turns on a T400A2 core. AWG 4 or AWG 6 wire can be used with equally spaced turns around the core. This core will easily handle well over 1500 watts. The required working voltages of the capacitors used in the

−300	−325	−350	−375	−400	−425	−450	−475	−500	−525	−550
1.5/3801	14.6/3801	15.7/3801	16.8/3801	17.9/3801	19/3801	20/3801	21.1/3801	22.2/3801	23.3/3801	24.4/3801
13.7/2616	14.8/2616	15.9/2616	17/2616	18/2616	19.1/2616	20.2/2616	21.3/2616	22.4/2616	23.5/2616	24.6/2616
13.8/2075	14.9/2075	16/2075	17.1/2075	18.2/2075	19.3/2075	20.4/2075	21.4/2075	22.5/2075	23.6/2075	24.7/2075
13.9/1744	15/1744	16.1/1744	17.2/1744	18.3/1744	19.4/1744	20.4/1744	21.5/1744	22.6/1744	23.7/1744	24.8/1744
14/1510	15.1/1510	16.2/1510	17.2/1510	18.3/1510	19.4/1510	20.5/1510	21.6/1510	22.7/1510	23.8/1510	24.9/1510
14/1332	15.1/1332	16.2/1332	17.3/1332	18.4/1332	19.5/1332	20.6/1332	21.7/1332	22.8/1332	23.8/1332	29.9/1332
14.1/1188	15.2/1188	16.3/1188	17.3/1188	18.4/1188	19.5/1188	20.6/1188	21.7/1188	22.8/1188	23.9/1188	25/1188
14.1/1068	15.2/1068	16.3/1068	17.4/1068	18.5/1068	19.5/1068	20.6/1068	21.7/1068	22.8/1068	23.9/1068	25/1068
14.1/964	15.2/964	16.3/964	17.4/964	18.5/964	19.6/964	20.7/964	21.7/964	22.8/964	23.9/964	25/964
14.1/872	15.2/872	16.3/872	17.4/872	18.5/872	19.6/872	20.7/872	21.8/872	22.8/872	23.9/872	25/872
14.1/788	15.2/788	16.3/788	17.4/788	18.5/788	19.6/788	20.7/788	21.7/788	22.8/788	23.9/788	25/788
14.1/712	15.2/712	16.3/712	17.4/712	18.5/712	19.5/712	20.6/712	21.7/712	22.8/712	23.9/712	25/712
14.1/639	15.2/639	16.3/639	17.3/639	18.4/639	19.5/639	20.6/639	21.7/639	22.8/639	23.9/639	25/639
14/570	15.1/570	16.2/570	17.3/570	18.4/570	19.5/570	20.6/570	21.7/570	22.8/570	23.9/570	24.9/570
14/503	15.1/503	16.2/503	17.2/503	18.3/503	19.4/503	20.5/503	21.6/503	22.7/503	23.8/503	24.9/503
13.9/436	15/436	16.1/436	17.2/436	18.3/436	19.4/436	20.4/436	21.5/436	22.6/436	23.7/436	24.8/436
13.8/366	14.9/366	16/366	17.1/366	18.2/366	19.3/366	20.4/366	21.4/366	22.5/366	23.6/366	24.7/366
13.7/290	14.8/290	15.9/290	17/290	18/290	19.1/290	20.2/290	21.3/290	22.4/290	23.5/290	24.6/290
13.5/200	14.6/200	15.7/200	16.8/200	17.9/200	19/200	20/200	21.1/200	22.2/200	23.3/200	24.4/200
12.7/3	13.8/3	14.9/3	15.9/2	17/2	18/2	19.1/2	20.2/2	21.2/2	22.3/2	23.4/1
12.4/7	13.5/6	14.6/6	15.6/5	16.6/5	17.6/5	18.7/4	19.7/4	20.7/4	21.8/4	22.8/3
12.2/10	13.2/9	14.2/9	15.2/8	16.2/7	17.3/7	18.3/7	19.3/6	20.3/6	21.3/6	22.3/5
11.9/13	12.9/12	13.9/11	14.9/11	15.9/10	16.9/9	17.9/9	18.9/8	19.9/8	20.9/7	21.9/7
11.7/17	12.7/15	13.6/14	14.6/13	15.6/12	16.6/12	17.5/11	18.5/10	19.5/10	20.5/9	21.4/9
11.5/20	12.4/18	13.4/17	14.3/16	15.3/15	16.2/14	17.2/13	18.2/12	19.1/12	20.1/11	21/11
11.3/23	12.2/21	13.1/20	14.1/18	15/17	16/16	16.9/15	17.8/14	18.8/14	19.7/13	20.6/12
11.1/26	12/24	12.9/22	13.8/21	14.8/19	15.7/18	16.6/17	17.5/16	18.4/15	19.3/15	20.3/14
10.9/29	11.8/27	12.7/25	13.6/23	14.5/22	15.4/20	16.3/19	17.2/18	18.1/17	19/16	19.9/16
10.7/32	11.6/30	12.5/27	13.4/26	14.3/24	15.2/22	16/21	16.9/20	17.8/19	18.7/18	19.6/17
10.6/35	11.4/32	12.3/30	13.2/28	14.1/26	14.9/25	15.8/23	16.7/22	17.5/21	18.4/20	19.3/19
10.4/38	11.3/35	12.1/32	13/30	13.8/28	14.7/27	15.6/25	16.4/24	17.3/23	18.1/21	19/20
10.3/41	11.1/37	12/35	12.8/32	13.6/30	14.5/29	15.3/27	16.2/26	17/24	17.9/23	18.7/22
10.1/43	11/40	11.8/37	12.6/35	13.5/32	14.3/31	15.1/29	15.9/27	16.8/26	17.6/25	18.4/24
10/46	10.8/42	11.6/39	12.5/37	13.3/34	14.1/32	14.9/31	15.7/29	16.5/28	17.4/26	18.2/25
9.9/49	10.7/45	11.5/42	12.3/39	13.1/37	13.9/34	14.7/32	15.5/31	16.3/29	17.1/28	17.9/26
9.8/51	10.6/47	11.3/44	12.1/41	12.9/38	13.7/36	14.5/34	15.3/32	16.1/31	16.9/29	17.7/28
9.7/54	10.4/50	11.2/46	12/43	12.8/40	13.6/38	14.3/36	15.1/34	15.9/32	16.7/31	17.5/29
9.6/56	10.3/52	11.1/48	11.9/45	12.6/42	13.4/40	14.2/38	14.9/36	15.7/34	16.5/32	17.3/31
9.5/59	10.2/54	11/51	11.7/47	12.5/44	13.2/42	14/39	14.8/37	15.5/35	16.3/34	17/32

networks are determined by the transmitter power level and the impedance of the capacitor on the operating frequency. Table 17 can be used as a guideline for determining the working voltage of capacitors used as shunt elements in L-networks. It is advisable to use a safety factor of 2 when determining the capacitor voltage rating. This safety factor is *not* included in the figures in the table. Broadcast-type multi-gang tuning capacitors can be used for the large-value capacitors.

After tuning, it may often be possible or desirable to replace the tunable capacitors with fixed-value types. Use only high-quality mica capacitors, wired in series or in parallel to obtain the required value. These capacitors carry a large amount of RF current, so when they are used as series elements in the network, the current rating of the capacitors is important. One way to find out if there are any losses in the capacitor resulting from large RF currents is to measure or feel the temperature of the components (*not* with power applied!) in question after having stressed them with a solid carrier for a few minutes. This is a valid test for both coils and capacitors in a network. If excessive heating is apparent, consider using heavier-duty components.

2.4.9.4 Duobanders for 80/160 Meters

Full-size, quarter-wave verticals (40 m or 132 feet on 160 m) are out of reach for all but a few amateurs. Often an 80/160-meter duoband vertical will be limited to a height of around 100 feet (30.5 meters). This represents an electrical length of 140° at 3.65 MHz. We can determine R and X from Figures 2.21-2.24. Given a radiator diameter of 1°, R = 550 ohms and X = +j250 ohms. To base-load this vertical for 1825 kHz (electrical length is 68°), R = 14 ohms (Figure 2.7) and X = −j125 ohms. Figure 2.32 shows several of the alternative methods of matching this antenna. All of these solutions were calculated using the "L-NETWORK" program from Chapter VII. Again, the choice of the network will be dictated by the component values. The two-step solution is preferred if reasonable network bandwidth is required. Notice that for 160 meters, there are four different L-network choices available.

Linear loading (as explained in Section 2.4.3.1) provides a higher radiation resistance and ensures low coil loss, as no large-value inductors are required in the matching network. The exact length of the linear loading device must be found experimentally, but a good starting point is to make the loading device as long as the antenna would have to be extended to make it a full quarter wavelength long. If the linear-loaded vertical for a given length of the loading device is still shorter than an electrical quarter wavelength, the still-missing length can be compensated for with a capacitor

Table 14

L-Network Values for F_{design} = 3.65 MHz

R/X	25	50	75	100	125	150	175	200	225	250	275
60	1.4/662	2.2/804	3.1/773	4.1/691	5.1/608	6.1/536	7.1/476	8.1/426	9.1/385	10.1/351	11.1/322
70	1.6/626	2.3/740	3.1/731	3.9/671	4.8/601	5.7/537	6.6/481	7.6/433	8.5/394	9.4/360	10.3/331
80	1.9/595	2.4/688	3.1/692	3.8/649	4.6/591	5.5/534	6.3/483	7.1/438	8/400	8.9/367	9.7/338
90	2.1/568	2.5/645	3.1/656	3.8/626	4.5/579	5.3/529	6/483	6.8/441	7.6/404	8.4/372	9.2/344
100	2.3/545	2.7/610	3.2/624	3.8/603	4.4/566	5.1/523	5.9/480	6.6/442	7.3/407	8.1/376	8.8/349
110	2.5/524	2.8/579	3.2/596	3.8/582	4.4/551	5/514	5.7/477	6.4/441	7.1/408	7.8/379	8.5/352
120	2.7/506	2.9/553	3.3/570	3.8/561	4.4/537	5/505	5.6/472	6.2/439	6.9/408	7.5/380	8.2/355
130	2.8/490	3.1/531	3.4/547	3.9/542	4.4/523	4.9/496	5.5/466	6.1/436	6.7/408	7.4/381	8/357
140	3/475	3.2/511	3.5/527	3.9/525	4.4/509	4.9/486	5.4/460	6/433	6.6/406	7.2/381	7.8/358
150	3.1/461	3.3/493	3.6/508	4/508	4.4/496	4.9/476	5.4/453	5.9/428	6.5/404	7.1/380	7.6/358
160	3.3/449	3.5/477	3.7/492	4.1/493	4.5/483	4.9/467	5.4/446	5.9/424	6.4/401	6.9/379	7.5/358
170	3.4/437	3.6/463	3.8/476	4.1/479	4.5/471	4.9/457	5.4/439	5.8/419	6.3/399	6.9/377	7.4/357
180	3.6/427	3.7/450	3.9/463	4.2/465	4.6/460	4.9/448	5.4/432	5.8/413	6.3/394	6.8/375	7.3/356
190	3.7/417	3.8/438	4/450	4.3/453	4.6/449	5/439	5.4/424	5.8/408	6.3/390	6.7/372	7.2/355
200	3.8/408	3.9/427	4.1/438	4.4/442	4.7/438	5/430	5.4/417	5.8/402	6.2/386	6.7/370	7.1/353
210	3.9/399	4/416	4.2/427	4.5/431	4.7/429	5.1/421	5.4/410	5.8/397	6.2/382	6.6/367	7.1/351
220	4.1/391	4.2/407	4.3/417	4.5/421	4.8/419	5.1/413	5.4/403	5.8/391	6.2/378	6.6/363	7/349
230	4.2/383	4.3/398	4.4/407	4.6/412	4.9/411	5.2/405	5.5/397	5.8/386	6.2/373	6.6/360	7/346
240	4.3/376	4.4/390	4.5/399	4.7/403	4.9/402	5.2/398	5.5/390	5.9/380	6.2/369	6.6/357	7/344
250	4.4/369	4.5/382	4.6/390	4.8/394	5/394	5.3/391	5.6/384	5.9/375	6.2/365	6.6/353	7/341
260	4.5/363	4.6/375	4.7/383	4.9/387	5.1/387	5.3/384	5.6/378	5.9/370	6.2/360	6.6/350	6.9/338
270	4.6/357	4.7/368	4.8/375	5/379	5.2/380	5.4/377	5.7/372	5.9/365	6.3/356	6.6/346	6.9/336
280	4.7/351	4.8/361	4.9/368	5/372	5.2/373	5.5/371	5.7/366	6/360	6.3/352	6.6/342	6.9/333
290	4.8/346	4.9/355	5/362	5.1/366	5.3/367	5.5/365	5.8/361	6/355	6.3/347	6.6/339	6.9/330
300	4.9/340	5/349	5.1/356	5.2/359	5.4/360	5.6/359	5.8/355	6.1/350	6.3/343	6.6/335	7/327
310	5/335	5.1/344	5.2/350	5.3/353	5.5/355	5.7/353	5.9/350	6.1/345	6.4/339	6.7/332	7/324
320	5.1/330	5.2/338	5.3/344	5.4/348	5.5/349	5.7/348	5.9/345	6.2/341	6.4/335	6.7/328	7/321
330	5.2/326	5.3/333	5.3/339	5.5/342	5.6/344	5.8/343	6/340	6.2/336	6.5/331	6.7/325	7/318
340	5.3/321	5.3/329	5.4/334	5.5/337	5.7/339	5.8/338	6/336	6.3/332	6.5/327	6.8/321	7/315
350	5.4/317	5.4/324	5.5/329	5.6/332	5.8/334	5.9/333	6.1/331	6.3/328	6.5/323	6.8/318	7.1/312
360	5.5/313	5.5/320	5.6/324	5.7/327	5.8/329	6/329	6.2/327	6.4/324	6.6/320	6.8/315	7.1/309
370	5.6/309	5.6/315	5.7/320	5.8/323	5.9/324	6.1/324	6.2/323	6.4/320	6.6/316	6.9/311	7.1/306
380	5.6/305	5.7/311	5.8/316	5.9/319	6/320	6.1/320	6.3/319	6.5/516	6.7/313	6.9/308	7.1/303
390	5.7/302	5.8/307	5.8/312	5.9/314	6/316	6.2/316	6.3/315	6.5/313	6.7/309	6.9/305	7.2/300
400	5.8/298	5.9/304	5.9/308	6/310	6.1/312	6.3/312	6.4/311	6.6/309	6.8/306	7/302	7.2/298
410	5.9/295	5.9/300	6/304	6.1/307	6.2/307	6.3/308	6.5/307	6.6/305	6.8/303	7/299	7.2/295
420	6/292	6/296	6.1/300	6.2/303	6.3/304	6.4/305	6.5/304	6.7/302	6.9/299	7.1/296	7.3/292
430	6.1/288	6.1/293	6.1/297	6.2/299	6.3/301	6.4/301	6.6/300	6.7/299	6.9/296	7.1/293	7.3/289
440	6.1/285	6.2/290	6.2/293	6.3/296	6.4/297	6.5/298	6.7/297	6.8/296	7/293	7.2/290	7.4/287
450	6.2/282	6.2/287	6.3/290	6.4/292	6.5/294	6.6/294	6.7/294	6.9/292	7/290	7.2/288	7.4/284
460	6.3/280	6.3/284	6.4/287	6.4/289	6.5/291	6.6/291	6.8/291	6.9/289	7.1/288	7.3/285	7.4/282
470	6.4/277	6.4/281	6.4/284	6.5/286	6.6/287	6.7/288	6.8/288	7/287	7.1/285	7.3/282	7.5/279
480	6.4/274	6.5/278	6.5/281	6.6/283	6.7/284	6.8/285	6.9/285	7/284	7.2/282	7.3/280	7.5/277
490	6.5/271	6.5/275	6.6/278	6.7/280	6.7/281	6.8/282	7/282	7.1/281	7.2/279	7.4/277	7.6/275
500	6.6/269	6.6/272	6.7/275	6.7/277	6.8/278	6.9/279	7/279	7.1/278	7.3/277	7.4/275	7.6/272
510	6.7/266	6.7/270	6.7/272	6.8/274	6.9/276	7/276	7.1/276	7.2/276	7.3/274	7.5/272	7.7/270
520	6.7/264	6.8/267	6.8/270	6.9/272	6.9/273	7/274	7.1/274	7.3/273	7.4/272	7.5/270	7.7/268
530	6.8/262	6.8/265	6.9/267	6.9/269	7/270	7.1/271	7.2/271	7.3/270	7.4/269	7.6/268	7.8/266
540	6.9/259	6.9/262	6.9/265	7/267	7.1/268	7.2/268	7.3/268	7.4/268	7.5/267	7.6/265	7.8/263
550	6.9/257	7/260	7/262	7.1/264	7.1/265	7.2/266	7.3/266	7.4/266	7.6/265	7.7/263	7.8/261
560	7/255	7/258	7.1/260	7.1/262	7.2/263	7.3/264	7.4/264	7.5/263	7.6/262	7.7/261	7.9/259
570	7.1/253	7.1/256	7.1/258	7.2/259	7.3/261	7.3/261	7.4/261	7.5/261	7.7/260	7.8/259	7.9/257
580	7.2/251	7.2/253	7.2/256	7.3/257	7.3/258	7.4/259	7.5/259	7.6/259	7.7/258	7.8/257	8/255
590	7.2/249	7.2/251	7.3/253	7.3/255	7.4/256	7.5/257	7.6/257	7.7/257	7.8/256	7.9/255	8/253
600	7.3/247	7.3/249	7.3/251	7.4/253	7.5/254	7.5/255	7.6/255	7.7/254	7.8/254	7.9/253	8.1/251

between the bottom of the tower (where the linear-loading device is connected) and ground. If you choose to make the capacitor motor-driven, you will find that this is a neat way of adjusting the resonant frequency of the antenna from the shack. The Hy-Gain 402BA 40-meter linear-loaded Yagi has an effective capacity between the element ends and the boom (caused by the element mounting and insulating technique) which lowers the element resonant frequency by about 600 kHz. This method of tuning the linear-loaded 160-meter vertical is shown in Figure 2.38.

If the vertical is made from lattice-type tower sections, the linear loading device can be made of two 1-inch aluminum tubes spaced about 12 inches (30 cm) apart and about the same distance from the tower. Figure 2.33 shows the installation of the linear loading device on the author's tower. The antenna is an 85-foot (25.5 meter) tower which is matched for 40 and 80 meters and linear-loaded on 160 meters.

2.4.9.5 Using the Beam Tower as a Low-band Vertical

The approximate electrical length (in degrees) of a tower loaded with a Yagi or Yagis is given by:

$$L = 0.38f \times \left(H + \sqrt{\frac{S\,(1000 - H)}{500}} \right)$$

300	325	350	375	400	425	450	475	500	525	550
12.1/297	13.1/276	14.1/257	15.1/241	16.1/226	17.1/213	18.1/202	19.1/192	20.2/182	21.2/174	22.2/166
11.2/306	12.2/284	13.1/265	14/249	15/234	15.9/221	16.8/209	17.8/199	18.7/189	19.6/180	20.5/172
10.6/313	11.4/292	12.3/273	13.2/256	14/241	14.9/228	15.8/216	16.6/205	17.5/195	18.4/186	19.2/178
10/320	10.8/298	11.7/279	12.5/262	13.3/247	14.1/234	14.9/222	15.7/211	16.5/201	17.4/192	18.2/183
9.6/325	10.3/304	11.1/285	11.9/268	12.6/253	13.4/239	14.2/227	15/216	15.7/206	16.5/197	17.3/188
9.2/329	9.9/308	10.7/290	11.4/273	12.1/258	12.8/244	13.6/232	14.3/221	15/211	15.8/201	16.5/193
8.9/332	9.6/312	10.3/294	11/277	11.7/262	12.4/249	13.1/236	13.8/225	14.5/215	15.2/205	15.9/197
8.6/335	9.3/315	9.9/297	10.6/281	11.3/266	11.9/252	12.6/240	13.3/229	13.9/219	14.6/209	15.3/200
8.4/337	9/317	9.7/300	10.3/284	10.9/269	11.6/256	12.2/244	12.8/232	13.5/222	14.1/213	14.8/204
8.2/338	8.8/319	9.4/302	10/286	10.6/272	11.2/259	11.9/247	12.5/236	13.1/225	13.7/216	14.3/207
8.1/339	8.6/321	9.2/304	9.8/288	10.4/274	11/261	11.5/249	12.1/238	12.7/228	13.3/219	13.9/210
7.9/339	8.5/321	9/305	9.6/290	10.1/276	10.7/264	11.3/252	11.8/241	12.4/231	13/221	13.6/213
7.8/339	8.3/322	8.9/306	9.4/292	9.9/278	10.5/266	11/254	11.6/243	12.1/233	12.7/224	13.3/215
7.7/338	8.2/322	8.7/307	9.2/293	9.7/280	10.3/267	10.8/256	11.3/245	11.9/235	12.4/226	13/217
7.6/337	8.1/322	8.6/307	9.1/293	9.6/281	10.1/269	10.6/257	11.1/247	11.6/237	12.2/228	12.7/219
7.5/336	8/321	8.5/307	9/294	9.4/281	9.9/270	10.4/259	10.9/248	11.4/239	11.9/230	12.5/221
7.5/334	7.9/320	8.4/307	8.8/294	9.3/282	9.8/271	10.3/260	10.8/250	11.2/240	11.7/231	12.2/223
7.4/333	7.9/319	8.3/307	8.7/294	9.2/282	9.7/271	10.1/261	10.6/251	11.1/241	11.6/233	12/224
7.4/331	7.8/318	8.2/306	8.7/294	9.1/283	9.5/272	10/261	10.5/252	10.9/243	11.4/234	11.9/226
7.3/329	7.7/317	8.2/305	8.6/294	9/283	9.4/272	9.9/262	10.3/253	10.8/244	11.2/235	11.7/227
7.3/327	7.7/315	8.1/304	8.5/293	8.9/282	9.4/272	9.8/262	10.2/253	10.6/244	11.1/236	11.5/228
7.3/325	7.7/314	8.1/303	8.5/292	8.9/282	9.3/272	9.7/263	10.1/254	10.5/245	11/237	11.4/229
7.3/322	7.7/312	8/302	8.4/291	8.8/282	9.2/272	9.6/263	10/254	10.4/245	10.8/237	11.3/230
7.3/320	7.6/310	8/300	8.4/291	8.7/281	9.1/272	9.5/263	9.9/254	10.3/246	10.7/238	11.1/230
7.3/318	7.6/308	8/299	8.3/289	8.7/280	9.1/271	9.5/263	9.8/254	10.2/246	10.6/238	11/231
7.3/315	7.6/306	8/297	8.3/288	8.7/279	9/271	9.4/262	9.8/254	10.2/246	10.5/239	10.9/231
7.3/313	7.6/304	7.9/296	8.3/287	8.6/278	9/270	9.3/262	9.7/254	10.1/246	10.5/239	10.8/232
7.3/310	7.6/302	7.9/294	8.3/286	8.6/277	8.9/269	9.3/261	9.7/254	10/246	10.4/239	10.8/232
7.3/308	7.6/300	7.9/292	8.2/284	8.6/276	8.9/269	9.3/261	9.6/253	10/246	10.3/239	10.7/232
7.3/305	7.6/298	7.9/290	8.2/283	8.6/275	8.9/268	9.2/260	9.6/253	9.9/246	10.3/239	10.6/232
7.3/302	7.6/296	7.9/289	8.2/281	8.5/274	8.9/267	9.2/260	9.5/253	9.9/246	10.2/239	10.6/232
7.4/300	7.6/293	7.9/287	8.2/280	8.5/273	8.8/266	9.2/259	9.5/252	9.8/245	10.2/239	10.5/232
7.4/297	7.7/291	7.9/285	8.2/278	8.5/271	8.8/265	9.1/258	9.5/251	9.8/245	10.1/239	10.4/232
7.4/295	7.7/289	7.9/283	8.2/277	8.5/270	8.8/264	9.1/257	9.4/251	9.7/244	10.1/238	10.4/232
7.4/292	7.7/287	8/281	8.2/275	8.5/269	8.8/263	9.1/256	9.4/250	9.7/244	10/238	10.3/232
7.5/290	7.7/285	8/279	8.2/273	8.5/267	8.8/261	9.1/255	9.4/249	9.7/243	10/237	10.3/232
7.5/288	7.7/283	8/277	8.2/272	8.5/266	8.8/260	9.1/254	9.4/248	9.7/243	10/237	10.3/231
7.5/285	7.8/280	8/275	8.3/270	8.5/265	8.8/259	9.1/253	9.4/248	9.6/242	9.9/236	10.2/231
7.6/283	7.8/278	8/273	8.3/268	8.5/263	8.8/258	9.1/252	9.3/247	9.6/241	9.9/236	10.2/231
7.6/280	7.8/276	8.1/2782	8.3/267	8.5/262	8.8/256	9.1/251	9.3/246	9.6/241	9.9/235	10.2/230
7.6/278	7.9/274	8.1/270	8.3/265	8.6/260	8.8/255	9.1/250	9.3/245	9.6/240	9.9/235	10.2/230
7.7/276	7.9/272	8.1/268	8.3/263	8.6/259	8.8/254	9.1/249	9.3/244	9.6/239	9.9/234	10.1/229
7.7/274	7.9/270	8.1/266	8.4/262	8.6/257	8.8/253	9.1/248	9.3/243	9.6/238	9.9/233	10.1/228
7.8/271	8/268	8.2/264	8.4/260	8.6/256	8.8/251	9.1/247	9.3/242	9.6/237	9.8/233	10.1/228
7.8/269	8/266	8.2/262	8.4/258	8.9/254	8.9/250	9.1/245	9.3/241	9.6/236	9.8/232	10.1/227
7.8/267	8/264	8.2/260	8.4/257	8.6/253	8.9/249	9.1/244	9.3/240	9.6/236	9.8/231	10.1/227
7.9/265	8.1/262	8.3/259	8.5/255	8.7/251	8.9/247	9.1/243	9.3/239	9.6/235	9.8/230	10.1/226
7.9/263	8.1/260	8.3/257	8.5/253	8.7/250	8.9/246	9.1/242	9.4/238	9.6/234	9.8/229	10.1/225
8/261	8.1/258	8.3/255	8.5/252	8.7/248	8.9/245	9.1/241	9.4/237	9.6/233	9.8/229	10.1/225
8/259	8.2/256	8.4/253	8.5/250	8.7/247	8.9/243	9.2/240	9.4/236	9.6/232	9.8/228	10.1/224
8/257	8.2/255	8.4/252	8.6/249	8.8/245	9/242	9.2/238	9.4/235	9.6/231	9.8/227	10.1/223
8.1/255	8.3/253	8.4/250	8.6/247	8.8/244	9/241	9.2/237	9.4/234	9.6/230	9.9/226	10.1/222
8.1/253	8.3/251	8.5/248	8.6/246	8.8/243	9/239	9.2/236	9.4/232	9.6/229	9.9/225	10.1/222
8.2/251	8.3/249	8.5/247	8.7/244	8.9/241	9/238	9.2/235	9.4/231	9.7/228	9.9/224	10.1/221
8.2/250	8.4/247	8.5/245	8.7/242	8.9/240	9.1/237	9.3/234	9.5/230	9.7/227	9.9/224	10.1/220

where

L = electrical length of the loaded tower in degrees
f = frequency of operation in MHz
H = the height of the tower under the Yagi in feet
S = the area of the Yagi in square feet.

This formula was derived by experimentation. To convert feet to meters, divide feet by 3.28. To convert square feet to square meters, divide square feet by 10.77.

Consider the following example:

Tower height = 80 feet.

Yagi: 5-el 20 meter Yagi on 46-foot boom, area = 1250 square feet.
f = 1.825 MHz.

The formula yields an L of 100°, which means that the tower/beam is a little longer than a quarter wavelength on 160 meters. This should be an excellent starting point for an efficient DX antenna for 160 meters.

A second method of finding the resonant length of a tower was given by DeMaw, W1FB (Ref 774). A shunt-fed wire is dropped from the top of the tower to ground level, and a small 2 or 3 turn loop between the end of the wire and ground is

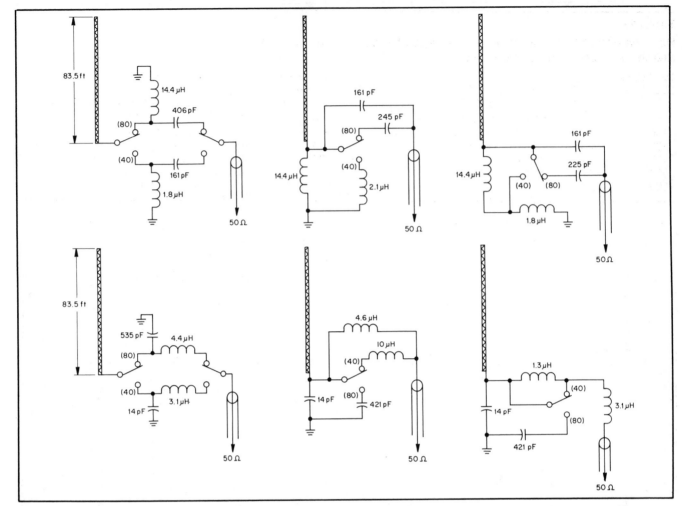

Figure 2.31—Examples of L-network matching solutions for an 83.5-foot (25.1-m) vertical for 40 and 80 meters. The schematics show how components can be used in parallel or series if two-band operation is desired. Whenever coils are wired in series or in parallel, care must be taken to keep the coils at right angles from each other and to maintain as much separation as possible.

Table 15

Capacity Hat Characteristics

Hat Size (deg)	3.5/3.8 MHz			1.8/1.9 MHz		
	Hat Diam (cm)	Length (m)	R_{rad} (Ω)	Hat Diam (cm)	Length (m)	R_{rad} (Ω)
0	0/0	20.95/19.3	37	0/0	40.95/38.8	37
5	38/35	19.8/18.2	36	70/67	38.7/36.6	36
10	77/72	18.6/17.1	35	143/136	36.3/34.4	35
15	119/115	17.4/16.0	34	221/210	34.1/32.2	34
20	164/154	16.2/14.9	32	303/290	32.5/30.0	32
25	213/200	15.0/13.8	30	394/377	29.4/27.8	30
30	269/252	13.8/12.7	27	496/475	27.1/25.6	27
35	332/312	12.6/11.6	24	612/586	24.8/23.4	24
40	407/382	11.5/10.5	21	748/716	22.5/21.2	21

used to grid-dip the tower (Figure 2.38). The lowest dip found is then the resonant frequency of the tower/beam. The electrical length at the design frequency is then given by:

$$L = \frac{90\ f_{design}}{f_{resonant}}$$

Therefore, if $f_{resonant}$ = 1.6 MHz and f_{design} = 1.8 MHz, then L = 101 degrees.

There is no reason why the tower must be resonant at the

Table 16

Toroid Cores Suitable for Matching Networks

Supplier	Code	Permeability	OD (in)	ID (in)	Height (in)	AL
Amidon	T-400-A2	10	4.00	2.25	1.30	360
Amidon	T-400-2	10	4.00	2.25	0.65	185
Amidon	T-300-2	10	3.05	1.92	0.50	115
Amidon	T-225-A2	10	2.25	1.41	1.00	215
Amidon	T-225-2	10	2.25	1.41	0.55	120

Table 17

Recommended Minimum Working Voltages for Capacitors Used as Shunt Elements in L Matching Networks

80 Meters

Cap Value (pF)	Power Level		
	500 W	1000 W	2000 W
50	670 V	940 V	1330 V
100	470 V	670 V	940 V
200	330 V	470 V	670 V
400	240 V	330 V	470 V
800	170 V	240 V	330 V
1600	120 V	170 V	240 V

160 Meters

Cap Value (pF)	Power Level		
	500 W	1000 W	2000 W
50	940 V	1330 V	1880 V
100	670 V	940 V	1330 V
200	470 V	670 V	940 V
400	330 V	470 V	670 V
800	240 V	330 V	470 V
1600	170 V	240 V	330 V

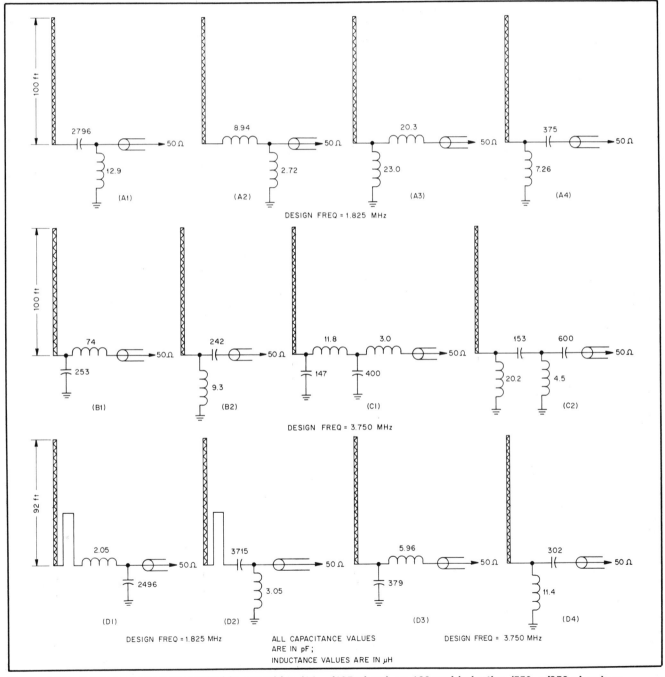

Figure 2.32—A 100-foot (30.5-m) vertical is capacitive (14 −j125 ohms) on 160 and inductive (550 +j250 ohms) on 80 meters. On 160 meters, there are four different L-network solutions (A1 through A4). On 80 meters, a single-stage L-network will show a limited bandwidth (B1 and B2). A two-stage matching system is recommended (C1 and C2). The author's 92-foot (28-m) vertical (D1 through D4) is linear loaded and matched with low-pass L-networks to the transmission line.

Figure 2.33—The author's 88-foot vertical is loaded for 160 meters by two 17-foot-long linear loading tubes that run along the lower section of the tower. For 80 and 40 meters, the tower is matched by an L-network.

Figure 2.34—The linear-loading device is made of two 1-inch OD lengths of aluminum tubing spaced 12 inches apart, and is mounted 12 inches away from the tower. A U-shaped aluminum crossbar at the top can be used for fine adjustment of the loading device.

operating frequency, but it is important to know the electrical length of the antenna structure to be able to design a shunt-matching system. It is also important to have a knowledge of the antenna radiation resistance to assess the radiation efficiency. The builder must also make sure that the antenna is not over 0.6 λ long on the design frequency, in the interest of maintaining optimum low-angle radiation.

There are many approaches to matching the loaded tower. DeMaw uses the shunt-fed wire and matches the bottom end via a T-network. An L-network should work just as well. The impedance at the bottom of the shunt-fed wire can be measured with a noise bridge. The L-network design program may be useful once again in this situation.

Gamma and Omega Matching

Gamma and omega matching techniques are most widely used on loaded towers. The design of gamma matches has been described in the literature (Ref 1401, 1414, 1421, 1426 and 1441). In many design cases, the physical length of the gamma rod comes out to be longer than the top-loaded vertical. In this case, the omega match comes to the rescue. In general, it is advisable to use the omega match configuration, as the shunt capacitor effectively changes the length of the gamma rod, and thus allows a wider matching range. Table 18 shows data for designing omega matching networks for 80 and 160 meters. The value of the shunt capacitor is approximately

Table 18
Values for Omega Matching Networks

Electrical Length (deg)	80 Meters Length (m)	Cap (pF)	160 Meters Length (m)	Cap (pF)
60	10.0	100	18.3	200
70	7.3	175	12.8	420
80	5.0	350	8.5	800
90	4.5	450	12.5	700
100	7.6	270	17.0	450
110	9.2	195	19.2	330
120	10.0	150	20.7	280
130	10.7	130	22.5	240
140	11.3	120	23.5	220
150	11.7	105	23.9	210
160	12.0	100		
170	12.2	95		
180	12.2	90		

Shunt Capacitance: 500-750 pF for 80 m, 1000-1500 pF for 160 m

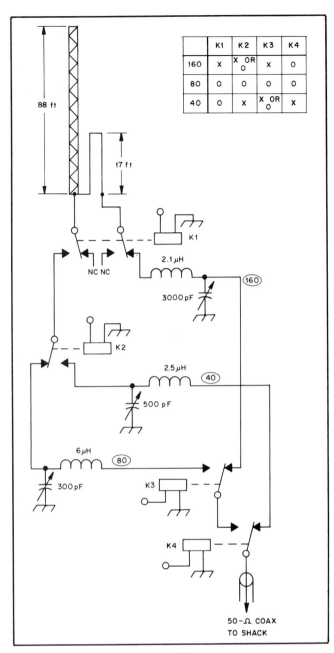

	K1	K2	K3	K4
160	x	x OR o	x	o
80	o	o	o	o
40	o	x	x OR o	x

Figure 2.35—Schematic diagram of the wiring of the three L-networks for the triband vertical tuner. The relays switching the 50-ohm sides of the network can be any type of relays suitable for use in power amplifiers. For the relays switching the antenna side of the networks, relays with large contact spacing (or vacuum relays) are recommended.

500-750 pF on 80 meters, and 1000-1500 pF on 160.

Consider the following example. As above, we have an 80-foot (24.38-meter) tower, which is loaded with a 5-element 20-meter Yagi. This configuration is 100° long at 1.8 MHz. The table tells us to attach the gamma rod to the tower approximately 17 meters above the ground. The figures from Table 18 are for a typical gamma rod with a diameter of 1 inch (2.54 cm), spaced 10 to 15 inches (25 to 38 cm) out from a tower with a cross section of 10 to 15 inches.

Figure 2.39 shows the correct wiring of both the gamma and omega matching networks on a loaded tower. Notice the correct connection of the shunt capacitor in the case of the omega match.

Figure 2.36—The three-band tuner used by the author uses overrated parts and a huge relay intended for open-wire transmission-line switching (Army surplus) for K1. The tuner is contained in a concrete housing at the base of the antenna. Even with the extreme humidity changes of the Belgian climate, the tuner has been extremely reliable for over 10 years.

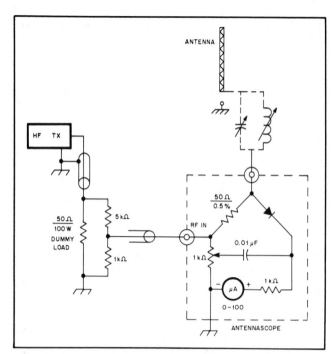

Figure 2.37—Test setup for measuring antenna impedance. Some RF (8 V max) is used to drive the antennascope. The schematic of the antennascope is also shown. The capacitor or the inductor connected between the antenna and the antennascope output is adjusted together with the antennascope potentiometer for a null reading on the bridge. The bridge resistance reading will be equal to the resistive part of the antenna impedance, while the reactive part of the impedance can be derived by measuring the value of the series element and then calculating its impedance at the operating frequency.

Tuning Procedure

When using the design procedure outlined above, a good 1:1 match should be obtainable in almost all cases. If no match can be obtained and the capacitor is at minimum capacitance, then the gamma rod is too long or it is too far away from the tower. If the shunt capacitor is fully meshed and no match is found, then the gamma rod is too close to the tower or the shunt feed point must be moved higher on the tower.

Bandwidth

If wide frequency excursions are planned, it is advisable to make the gamma rod of large-diameter material. Gamma or omega networks using a wire as a shunt-feeding element are very narrow-banded (5 kHz on 160 meters). The bandwidth can be increased by using the cage approach (Ref 1007 and 1426), or by motorizing the series and shunt capacitors of the omega match, and then controlling the values from the shack.

Practical Hints

All cables leading to the tower and up to the rotator and antennas should be firmly secured to a tower leg, preferably on the inside of the tower. All leads from the shack to the tower base should be buried underground, in order to provide sufficient RF decoupling. If there is still RF on some of the cables, one may wish to coil up a length of the cable where it enters the shack. Care should be taken to ensure good electrical continuity between the tower sections, and between the rotator, the mast and the tower. Large braid (such as the

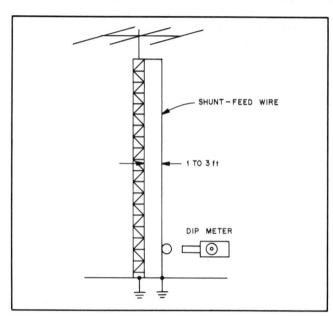

Figure 2.38—A method of dipping a tower with a shunt-feed wire connected at the top.

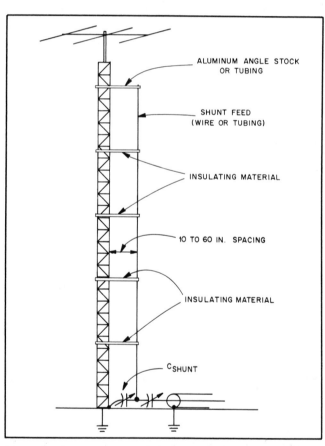

Figure 2.39—An omega-matching scheme (with the shunt capacitor) adds a great deal of flexibility to the system. If a gamma match is used, the shunt capacitor can be omitted. Refer to the text for design procedure.

flattened braid from old coax or a piece of car-battery cable) can provide the necessary electrical contact and physical flexibility. The gamma rod can be supported with sections of plastic pipe attached to the tower with U-bolts or stainless steel radiator hose clamps. If the tower is a crank-up type, heavy, insulated copper wire can be used for the gamma element, but the trade-off is the much decreased bandwidth mentioned earlier. As with any vertical, this system requires the best possible ground system for optimum low-angle radiation (Section 2.4.3.4).

2.4.9.6 Inverted-L Antenna

Inverted-L antennas (and to a lesser degree, T antennas) are quite popular, especially on 160 meters. These antennas are top-loaded verticals, where the loading device produces a horizontal component of radiation, as a result of its structure. Most inverted-Ls are of the quarter-wave variety, although this does not necessarily need to be the case. The vertical portion of an inverted-L is most frequently put up alongside a tower supporting HF antennas. The longer the vertical part of the antenna, the better the low-angle radiation characteristics of the antenna. The horizontal part of the antenna accounts for the high-angle radiation that the antenna produces. If you are looking for an antenna that radiates reasonably well at both low and high angles, an inverted-L may be an excellent choice for you. Since it is a loaded monopole, an inverted-L requires a good ground system for optimum low-angle radiation. A resonant inverted-L can be fed directly with 50-ohm coax in most cases.

Figure 2.40 shows the vertical and horizontal radiation patterns for an inverted-L antenna with 1/8 λ vertical and 1/8 λ horizontal. Notice how the vertical part of the antenna takes care of the low-angle radiation, while the horizontal part assures high-angle output. The pattern shown is for the direction perpendicular to the plane of the inverted-L. At right angles to this plane, horizontally polarized (high-angle) radiation will be minimal.

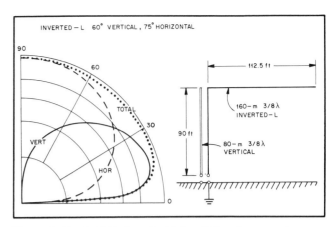

Figure 2.41—A 3/8 λ inverted-L for 160 meters can be placed near a 3/8 λ 80-meter vertical. Using 3/8 λ antennas reduces mutual coupling. The horizontally polarized radiation component will be minimal in the plane containing the L.

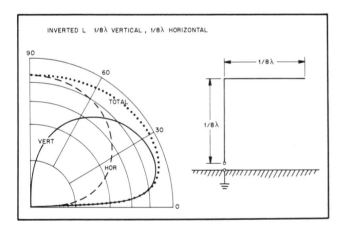

Figure 2.40—Inverted-L antenna configuration with 1/8 λ vertical and 1/8 λ horizontal, plus associated vertical radiation patterns in the plane perpendicular to the antenna. Notice the vertical and horizontal polarization components.

An inverted-L is also an attractive solution for the operator who needs to use an 80-meter vertical antenna as a support for a 160-meter antenna. Some precautions need to be taken, however, as the placement of an 80-meter vertical in close proximity to a 160-meter vertical will result in very heavy coupling, degrading the performance of the 80-meter antenna. This situation can be prevented by using an inverted-L which is not resonant on 160 meters.

Consider the following example. Assume a 90-foot (3/8-wave) vertical for 80 meters. If the 160-meter inverted-L is made 3/8 λ long (60.4 m or 198.2 feet), then its half-wave resonant frequency will be 2.48 MHz, which is far

enough from the resonant frequency of the 80-meter antenna to cause only minor interaction. For the L-antenna made of wire (such as AWG 12), the impedance of the 3/8-wave vertical can be quite high, both resistively and reactively (about $600 + j400$ ohms). Probably the most elegant solution is to feed the antenna with 600-ohm open-wire line to an antenna tuner in the shack (Ref 775). An L-network would also be a good solution, but the bandwidth of the network may restrict the total bandwidth of the system. In any case, one should make sure that the 160-meter antenna does not resonate near 80 meters. If it does, steps must be taken to move its resonant frequency, such as decoupling the feed line from the antenna at the base of the antenna. The radiation patterns of this antenna, calculated in the plane containing the inverted-L, are shown in Figure 2.41. Note that, in this case, the total directivity (vertical + horizontal) is almost constant from 90° (zenith) all the way down to 25°.

2.4.9.7 T-antennas

In general, T-antennas are loaded vertical antennas with a current minimum at ground level. T-shaped loading can, however, be applied to verticals of any length. the high-impedance T-antenna consists of a quarter-wave vertical section loaded by a half-wave horizontal flat-top wire. The advantage of such a quarter-wave inverted vertical is the same as with a half-wave vertical: it does not require an elaborate ground system from a return current point of view (for high radiation efficiency). As far as low-angle radiation is concerned, the same reasoning applies as with half-wave verticals (see Section 2.7). To obtain maximum low-angle radiation (low Brewster angle), the ground should be of very good quality (conductivity) for a long distance away from the antenna.

The T-antenna can also be seen as a bobtail antenna (see Section 2.12.2.4) with the two vertical end sections missing. As such, this antenna is a poor performer with respect to the bobtail antenna, where the directivity and gain is obtained through the use of the three vertical elements.

Hille, DL1VU, dramatically improved the T-antenna by folding the half-wave flat top section in such a way that the radiation from the flat top section is effectively suppressed. Figure 2.42 shows the configuration of this antenna. It can easily be proven that the area under the current distribution line for the central part (which is 1/12 λ long) is the same as

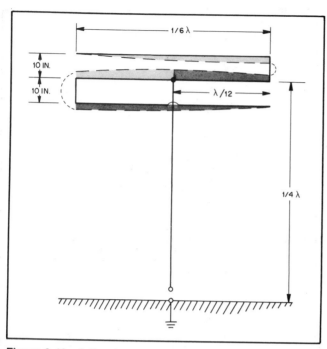

Figure 2.42—A T antenna with half-wave flat-top that is folded back on itself in order to minimize horizontally polarized radiation.

the area for the remaining part of the loading device (which is 1/6 λ long). Because of the way the wires are folded, the radiation from the horizontal loading device is effectively canceled.

2.4.10 LOCATION OF THE VERTICAL ANTENNA

Many low-band DXers have wondered why some verticals don't work well at all, while others work like gangbusters. The poor performers generally have the poor locations. A vertical is not a space-saving antenna! A good vertical takes a lot of real estate. If you really want good low-angle radiation, long radials (at least ½ λ long) are a must. This means that for 80 meters, you need about a 240-foot square lot (1.5 acres) in which to place all the radials (preferably 80-120 of them!). The area beyond the ends of the radials is also important. Figure 2.43 shows how much clearance a vertical antenna should have for optimum performance.

Assuming a quarter-wave vertical with an excellent ground

system, the wave angle can be as low as 20 to 25°. RF radiated from the top of the 62-foot vertical will hit the ground about 135 feet away from the base, arriving at an angle (the main wave angle) of approximately 25°. That is one way to say that long radials are absolutely necessary for optimum low-angle performance. The RF will be reflected from this point (Fresnel reflection law) at an angle of 25°. Therefore, beyond this point, a clear path should be provided for these low-angle rays in order to obtain maximum low-angle radiation. From Figure 2.43 it can be seen that this means that no structures taller than the antenna should be closer than 270 feet away from it. Smaller interfering and absorbing obstacles can be a little closer, as long as the size remains small enough to refrain from interfering with the low-angle energy reflected from ground level 135 feet from the antenna base.

The maximum height of a neighboring obstacle can be calculated with the following formula:

$$H_{max} = \left(D - \frac{468}{f}\right) \times \tan a$$

where

D = distance in feet of the obstacle from the antenna base
f = frequency in MHz
a = the wave angle in degrees (25° is a good rule of thumb).

This means, for instance, that at a point 200 feet from a 3.5-MHz antenna, the maximum height of a structure should be limited to 30 feet. What about trees closer in? Trees are reasonably good conductors and can be very lossy elements in the near field of a radiator. A case has been reported in the literature where a quarter-wave vertical with an excellent ground system showed a much lower radiation resistance than expected. It was found that trees in the immediate area were coupling heavily with the vertical and were causing the radiation resistance of the vertical to be very low. Under such circumstances of uncontrolled coupling into very lossy elements, far from optimum performance can be expected. Of course if the trees are short in relation to the (quarter) wavelength, it is reasonable to assume that the danger of such coupling is minimal.

Even though neighboring structures such as trees may not be resonant, they will always absorb some RF to an unknown degree. Objects that are very likely to affect the performance of a vertical are nearby antennas and towers. Mutual coupling can be considered the culprit if the radiation resistance of the vertical is lower than expected. Another way of checking for

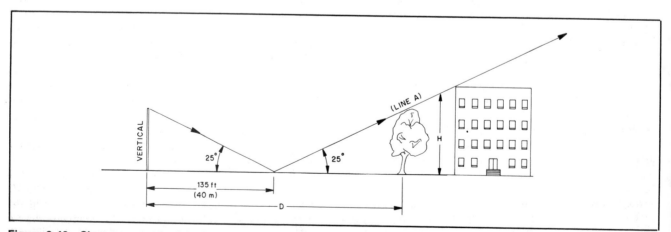

Figure 2.43—Clearance required for ideal layout of a vertical antenna. Any neighboring structures should fall below line A. See text for discussion.

coupling with other antennas is to alternately open- and short-circuit the suspect antenna's feed line while watching the SWR or the radiation resistance of the vertical antenna. If there is any change, you are in trouble.

It may come as a surprise that a vertical is so demanding of space. Again, most amateur verticals are not anywhere near ideal, and good performance can still be obtained from practical setups, but the builder of a vertical should understand what factors are important for optimum performance, and why.

2.5 Inverted V Dipole

In the past, the inverted V-shaped dipole has often been credited with almost magical properties. The most common property claimed of it has been excellent low-angle radiation characteristics. Others have more correctly called it a poor-man's dipole, as it only requires one high support. Let's find out what the truth is.

2.5.1 RADIATION RESISTANCE

The radiation resistance of the inverted V dipole changes with height above ground (as with a regular dipole) and with the apex angle (angle between the legs of the dipole). Consider the two extremes. When the apex angle is 180°, the inverted V is a flat-top dipole, and the radiation resistance (in free space) is 73 ohms. Now take the case where the apex angle is 0°, and the inverted V dipole is an open-wire transmission line, a quarter-wavelength long, open at the end. This configuration will not radiate at all (current will cancel completely, as it should in a well-balanced feed line) and the input impedance of the line is zero ohms (a quarter-wave stub open at the end reflects a dead short at the input). This zero-angle inverted V will have a radiation resistance of 0 ohms and consequently will not radiate at all. Figure 2.44 shows the radiation resistances of a straight vertical and horizontal half-wave dipole and a 90° apex inverted V, as a function of antenna height (apex height in the case of the inverted V). Values of radiation resistance for inverted Vs with different apex angles and at different heights are given in Table 19. The equations given earlier (Section 2.4.1.2) can be used for calculation of absolute field strength patterns, allowing direct comparison between antennas (Section 2.5.2).

2.5.2 RADIATION PATTERNS OVER REAL GROUND

2.5.2.1 Vertical Radiation Angles (Wave Angle)

The behavior of the inverted V dipole has been extensively examined using ANNIE (see Section 2.4.1.2). The weight figures needed to calculate absolute field intensities (enabling comparison with a dipole in free space) were derived from the radiation resistance values in Figure 2.44. For an inverted

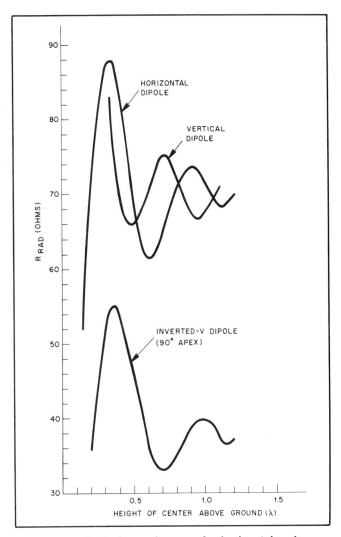

Figure 2.44—Radiation resistances for horizontal and vertical half-wave dipoles, as well as for a half-wave inverted V with a 90° apex angle.

V with a 120° apex angle, the weight figure is 1.29. All other weight factors can be found in Table 13. The weight for the straight dipole is taken as 1.00, although the radiation resistance is not constant (it depends on the height of the dipole).

What Does the Analysis Show?

1) *Antenna at ¼ λ height.* Over average ground, broadside to the antenna (Figure 2.45A), the dipole is better by about 3 dB than the three inverted Vs. Off the end of the antenna (Figure 2.45B) the dipole is still better at high angles, but the inverted Vs take over at low angles. This shows that there is a significant amount of vertically polarized radiation in this configuration. It also means that the low inverted V has less directivity at low angles, and more at high angles when compared to the straight dipole.

2) *Antenna at 3/8 λ height.* Over average ground, the picture is quite similar. Figure 2.45C shows the radiation pattern broadside to the antennas. At wave angles between 15° and 45°, the dipole is 1 to 3 dB better than any of the inverted Vs. The inverted Vs, however, show a little more high-angle radiation (approximately 2 dB at the zenith angle). Off the end of the

Table 19
Radiation Resistance of Inverted V Dipoles

| Apex Angle (deg) | 0.25 λ Apex | | 0.375 λ Apex | | 0.50 λ Apex | |
	R_{rad} (ohms)	Weight Factor	R_{rad} (ohms)	Weight Factor	R_{rad} (ohms)	Weight Factor
180	80	1.00	85	1.00	69	1.00
120	62	1.29	76	1.13	64	1.07
90	45	1.78	55	1.56	46.5	1.48
60	24.5	3.27	30	2.85	25.5	2.69

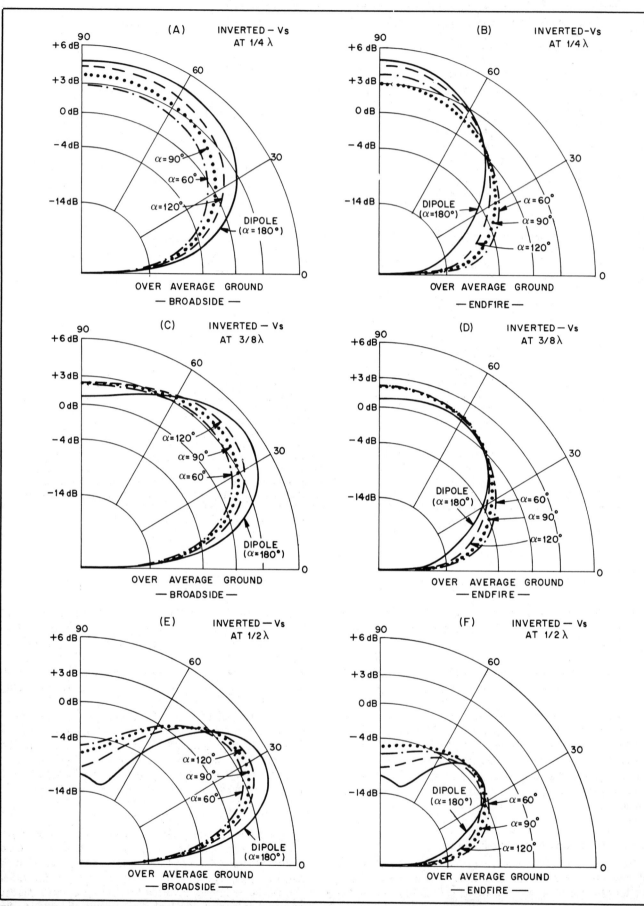

Figure 2.45—Vertical radiation patterns of dipoles and inverted Vs with 120, 90 and 60° apex angles at 1/4, 3/8 and 1/2 λ above ground. All patterns are for average ground, and for each height both the broadside direction and end-fire (at right angles) are given. The pattern for a dipole at the same height is also shown for reference. The weight figures for the analysis were taken from Table 2.13.

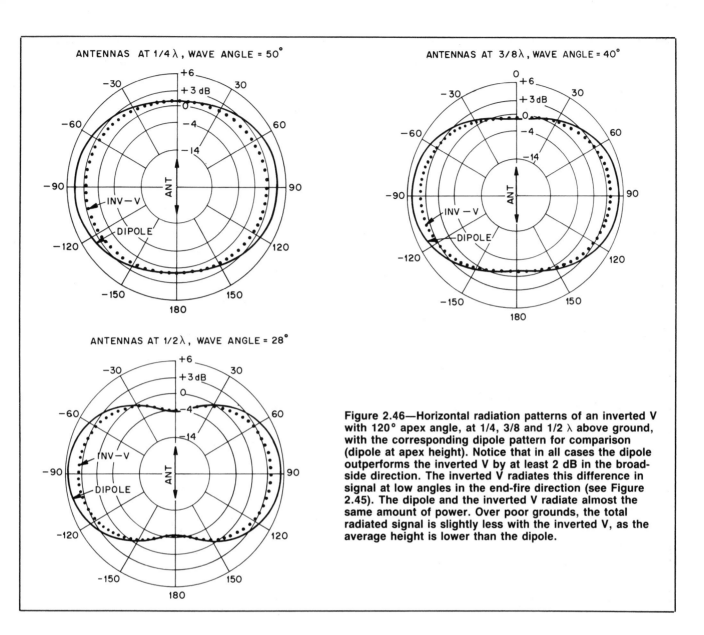

Figure 2.46—Horizontal radiation patterns of an inverted V with 120° apex angle, at 1/4, 3/8 and 1/2 λ above ground, with the corresponding dipole pattern for comparison (dipole at apex height). Notice that in all cases the dipole outperforms the inverted V by at least 2 dB in the broadside direction. The inverted V radiates this difference in signal at low angles in the end-fire direction (see Figure 2.45). The dipole and the inverted V radiate almost the same amount of power. Over poor grounds, the total radiated signal is slightly less with the inverted V, as the average height is lower than the dipole.

antenna, the inverted Vs again show more low-angle signal as a result of the vertically polarized component of the signal (Figure 2.45D).

3) *Antenna at ½ λ height.* At this height, the inverted V shows a 1 to 2 dB loss with respect to the straight dipole at the main wave angle of the inverted V (approximately 30°). At high angles, the inverted Vs are superior radiators (or inferior in rejection, whichever way you look at it). See Figure 2.45E. Off the end, the same remarks apply as for the 0.38-wave high antennas, (Figure 2.45F).

To summarize, it can be said that the inverted V is a fairly good compromise antenna. At the major wave angles, inverted Vs give up about 1 to 3 dB to the horizontal dipole. The high-angle nulls are much less pronounced than with the straight dipole.

2.5.2.2 Horizontal Radiation Pattern

Between ¼ and ½ λ height, both the dipole and inverted V show very similar horizontal directivity at their major wave angles (28° for ½ λ, 40° for 3/8 λ, and 50° for ¼ λ). The dipole does, however, show approximately 2 dB gain over the inverted V in the broadside direction (Figure 2.46).

One might say that it is not accurate to compare the apex height of an inverted V to the flat-top height of a dipole. In many cases it will indeed be possible to erect an inverted V much higher (at the apex) than would be possible with a dipole, which would need two supports at the same height. Let's examine one possible situation. An inverted V can be suspended from a single available support at 3/8 λ. For a 90° apex angle, that brings the ends down to 0.2 λ. The average height of the dipole is $(0.375 + 0.2)/2 = 0.2875$ λ. Now compare the inverted V with a horizontal dipole at 0.2875 λ. Figure 2.47 shows that the lower dipole still outperforms the inverted V at all angles in the broadside direction. The difference is minimal however, ranging from only 0.5 dB at 30° to 2.5 dB at 90°. This confirms that the inverted V really is a poor man's dipole, but the trade-off is minimal.

2.5.3 LENGTH OF THE INVERTED V

The usual formulas for calculating the length of the straight dipole cannot be applied to the inverted V. The length depends on both the apex angle of the antenna and the height of the antenna above ground. These effects counteract each other. Closing the legs of the inverted V in free space will increase the resonant frequency. On the other hand, the antenna will become electrically longer when closer to the ground due to the end-capacity effect of the ground on the inverted V ends. There is no single formula that is always accurate for

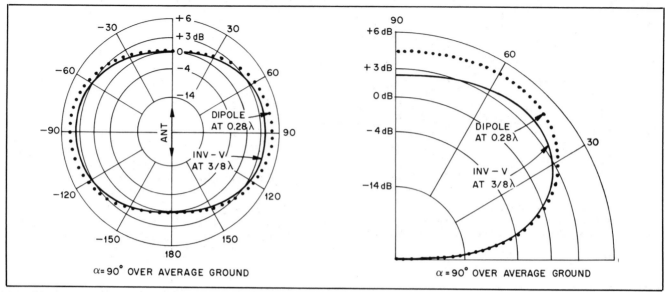

Figure 2.47—Vertical and horizontal radiation patterns of a dipole at 0.28 λ height and an inverted V (90° apex angle) at 3/8 λ. See text for details.

calculating the length of an inverted V. The solution is to use the straight dipole formula, find the resonant frequency by determining the point of minimum SWR, and then calculate the length to be cut off the dipole to arrive at the desired frequency. It is unlikely that wire will have to be added because of the end-capacity effect of the ground on the antenna.

2.5.4 BANDWIDTH

The bandwidth of an inverted V dipole decreases with decreasing apex angle and decreasing height above ground. When fed with 50-ohm coax, the 2:1 SWR bandwidth of an inverted V with a 120° apex angle will be approximately f(MHz)/30 at ¼ λ, f(MHz)/20 at ½ λ and f(MHz)/15 at ¾ λ (this represents 120, 170 and 240 kHz, respectively, for 80 meters). Inverted V dipoles with narrow apex angles will have narrower bandwidths.

2.6 Sloping Dipole

Sloping half-wave dipoles have been used occasionally on the low bands to achieve some degree of front-to-back ratio. Let us examine how they perform in comparison to other classic antennas that can be put up using the same supports.

2.6.1 PHYSICAL DIMENSIONS

In order to be able to erect a sloping half-wave dipole one must have a support equal to or higher than:

$$H (\lambda) = 0.5 \times \sin (90 - A)$$

where A represents the slope angle (the angle between the vertical support and the sloping dipole). The center height (feed point height and average height of the sloping dipole) is:

$$h (\lambda) = H - (0.25 \times \sin (90 - A))$$

where H is the support height in wavelengths. The radiation patterns of four different antennas are compared in Section 2.6.3:

1) Inverted V dipole at height H with 90° apex angle.
2) Horizontal dipole at average height (h).
3) Vertical half-wave dipole with center at average height (h).

4) Sloping dipole (top at height H).

2.6.2 RADIATION RESISTANCE

The radiation resistance of horizontal and vertical half-wave dipoles (and inverted Vs with 90° apex angles) is shown in Figure 2.44. The radiation resistances of slopers can be compared with the radiation resistances of half-wave vertical and horizontal dipoles at the same average height (h) to assess their radiation resistance. Knowledge of the radiation resistance is required to be able to calculate field strength patterns and compare absolute patterns.

Example: Assume the support is ½ λ high (H). The average height of a sloper with a 40° angle between it and the support is 0.31 λ (Section 2.6.1). The radiation resistance of the horizontal dipole at 0.31 λ is 87.5 ohms. The radiation resistance of the vertical dipole at the same height is 79 ohms. By assuming a linear relationship (an approximation), we can calculate the radiation resistance for the sloper as:

$$R_{rad} = 79 + \left[(87.5 - 79) \times \frac{40}{90} \right] = 82.78 \ \Omega$$

The radiation resistance of an inverted V dipole (90° apex at ½ λ) is 68 ohms.

2.6.3 RADIATION PATTERN

The radiation patterns of sloping dipoles at various slope angles and over various grounds have been covered extensively by Rautio, AJ3K (Ref 656).

2.6.3.1 Vertical Radiation Pattern

The vertical radiation patterns of the sloping dipole and the three comparison antennas are given in Figure 2.48. The computed results are for average ground conditions.

Pattern 2.48A is the vertical radiation in the broadside directions of the dipole and inverted V and in the plane containing the sloper. Notice the relatively small front-to-back ratio of the sloper. The front-to-back ratio depends on the slope angle and ground quality. Note that the sloper exhibits no front-to-back over perfect ground. Notice also that the sloper pattern is more than 4 dB down from the inverted V and the horizontal dipole at wave angles of 30 to 40°, which

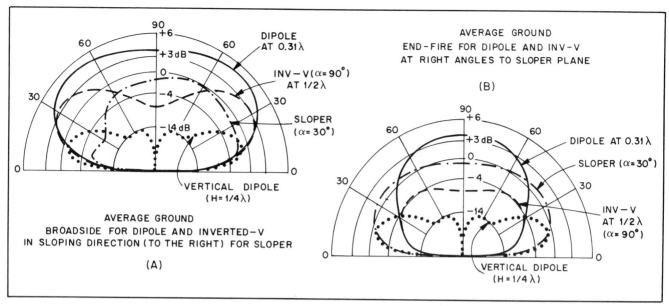

Figure 2.48—Vertical broadside and end-fire radiation patterns for the sloping dipole (apex at ½ λ, 40° slope angle), and the comparison antennas, the dipole at 0.31 λ (height of the sloper feed point), an inverted V with a 90° apex angle at ½ λ and a vertical dipole at ½ λ. For the sloping dipole, the broadside direction is defined as the direction of the sloping wire. The slope angle is the angle between the vertical support and the dipole. See text for discussion.

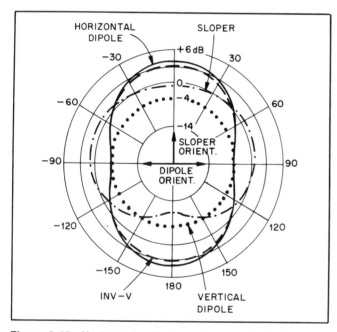

Figure 2.49—Horizontal radiation pattern of the half-wave sloping dipole at ½ λ (40° slope angle), compared to a dipole at 0.31 λ (average sloper height), an inverted V (90° apex angle) at ½ λ and a half-wave dipole at ½ λ. Note that the sloper exhibits more gain off the sides than in the slope direction. See text for discussion.

are quite important wave angles for low-band DX work.

Pattern 2.48B holds a surprise. This pattern shows the radiation at right angles to pattern 2.48A. For the sloper, it is in the direction perpendicular to the plane containing the sloper and the support. The sloper is 2 to 3 dB better off both sides than in the forward direction for angles between 15 and 60°. The maximum radiation from a sloper is actually 70 to 80° away from the "front" of the antenna.

2.6.3.2 Horizontal Radiation Pattern

Figure 2.49 shows the horizontal radiation pattern of all four antennas for a wave angle of 30°, which is the angle of main interest for a support ½ λ high. The horizontal dipole (at 0.31 λ) and the inverted V (apex at ½ λ) yield almost identical results, which are more than 4 dB better than the sloper in its "forward" direction. Off the sides, the sloper is about 5 dB better than the dipole and the inverted V.

Conclusion: Although the half-wave sloper has some front-to-back, it has no forward gain. It radiates better off the sides than off the front. Unless you are looking for an antenna with some front-to-back (about 12 dB) at about a 30° wave angle off the back of the antenna, the half-wave sloper should not be your choice. The author would prefer an inverted V or a delta loop on that ½ λ high support.

Note: In calculating the patterns in Figures 2.48 and 2.49, the following inputs were used:

- Horizontal dipole at H = 0.31 λ: R_{rad} = 87.5 ohms, weight factor = 1.
- Vertical dipole at 0.31 λ: R_{rad} = 79 ohms, weight factor = 1.11.
- Sloping dipole (top at ½ λ): R_{rad} = 82.7 ohms, weight factor = 1.06.
- Inverted V (top at ½ λ): R_{rad} = 68 ohms, weight factor = 1.26.

2.7 Vertical Dipole

Vertical dipoles can be excellent low-angle radiators, provided the ground quality is very good. On the low bands, vertical dipoles are rather difficult to erect, as they are very tall. An 80-meter quarter-wave vertical can be base-loaded on 40 meters for good low-angle radiation. From a return current point of view, the very high base impedance of the vertical does not necessitate an extensive radial system. In most cases, however, this will already be available for proper operation on 80 meters. In order to have optimum low-angle radiation, a good ground up to many wavelengths away is essential. As far as low-angle radiation is concerned, vertical half-wave dipoles are extremely effective when erected over excellent grounds (such as salt water).

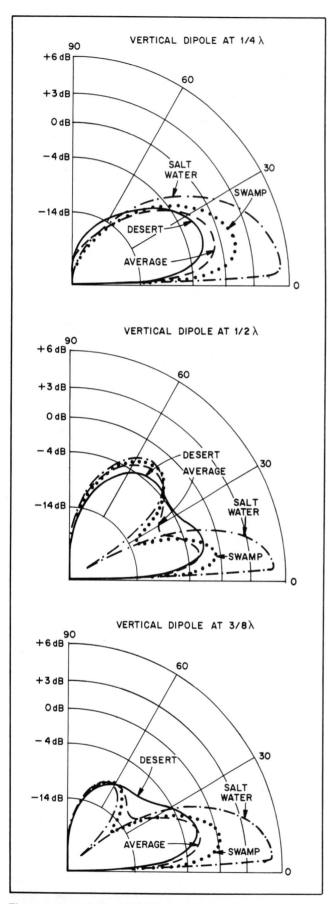

Figure 2.50—Vertical radiation patterns of half-wave vertical dipoles with centers at 1/4, 3/8 and 1/2 λ above ground, for four types of ground (desert, average, swamp and salt water). Notice what an excellent performer this antenna is over good ground.

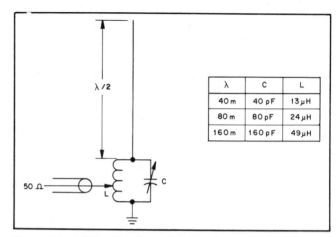

λ	C	L
40 m	40 pF	13 μH
80 m	80 pF	24 μH
160 m	160 pF	49 μH

Figure 2.51—Base feeding of a thin-conductor half-wave vertical can be done by loading a parallel-tuned circuit with the antenna. The table lists values for L and C which ensure adequate bandwidth. For antennas with diameters larger than 2.5 electrical degrees (360° = 1 λ), an L-network can also be used (if the resistive part of the antenna impedance is less than 500 ohms).

2.7.1 RADIATION PATTERNS

The horizontal radiation pattern of a vertical dipole is the same as for a horizontal dipole, but revolved 90°. Vertical patterns for excellent ground (salt water), swampy ground, average and poor grounds are given for heights of ¼, 3/8 and ½ λ (Figure 2.50). Notice what an excellent performer the half-wave vertical dipole is over salt water. Over anything else but this near-perfect reflector, the vertical dipole does not score very well. Mostly because of its physical height, the vertical dipole is not used extensively on the low bands, except as the slightly different sloping dipole (see Section 2.6).

2.7.2 RADIATION RESISTANCE

The radiation resistance of a vertical half-wave dipole is given in Figure 2.44 as a function of its height above ground.

2.7.3 FEEDING THE VERTICAL

Vertical dipoles can be practically fed in at least two ways: they can be center-fed like the horizontal dipole, or since in most cases a vertical dipole will have one end at ground level (center at ¼ λ), the dipole can be fed between the base end and ground. One way of feeding this high-impedance point of the antenna is to install a parallel-tuned network between the antenna end and ground. The L/C ratio should be high to ensure adequate bandwidth. A good starting point is to make the capacitor as large (in pF) as the wavelength involved (80 pF for 80 meters). The coaxial cable can be tapped on the coil, or a link could alternatively be used (Figure 2.51). The impedance will only be *very* high (greater than 800 ohms) in the case of a thin-conductor half-wave dipole. Consult Figures 2.21 and 2.22 for listings of the feed point resistances of bottom-fed half-wave vertical dipoles. For a conductor one degree in diameter (25 cm or 10 inches on 80 meters), the feed resistance is approximately 500-600 ohms. This impedance can also be matched with an L-network—preferably in two steps, to ensure adequate bandwidth (see Section 2.4.8.2). Another alternative is to use a broad-band matching network as used by Collins, W1FC, and described in Section 2.4.8.2.

2.8 Loop Antennas

Loop antennas have been very popular with 80-meter DXers

for the last 20 years or so. The exact shape of the loop is not particularly important. The loop with the highest gain, however, is the loop with the shape that covers the largest area for a given circumference. This is a circular loop, which is difficult to construct. Second-best is the square loop (quad), and the equilateral triangle (delta) comes third in line (Ref 677).

The maximum gain of a full-wave loop over a half-wave dipole in free space is approximately 1.35 dB. In the presence of ground, however, loops can show a respectable gain over a half-wave dipole at a correspondingly low apex height (depending on the chosen polarization). Delta loops are used extensively on the low bands at apex heights of 1/4 to 3/8 λ above ground. At such heights, the vertically polarized loops far outperform dipoles or inverted Vs, assuming that reasonably good ground conditions prevail in the area.

2.8.1 QUAD LOOPS

Belcher, WA4JVE, and Casper, K4HKX (Ref 1128), and Dietrich, WAØRDX (Ref 677), have published studies comparing the horizontally polarized quad loop with a dipole. A horizontally polarized quad-loop antenna (Figure 2.52A) can be seen as two short, end-loaded dipoles, stacked 1/4 λ apart with the top antenna at 1/4 λ and the bottom one just above ground level. There is no broadside radiation from the vertical wires of the quad because of the current opposition in the vertical members. In a similar manner, the vertically polarized quad loop (Figure 2.52B) consists of two top-loaded, quarter-wave vertical dipoles, spaced 1/4 λ apart.

Figure 2.52 shows how the current distribution along the elements produces cancellation of radiation from certain parts of the antenna, while radiation from other parts (the horizontally or vertically stacked short dipoles) is reinforced.

The square quad can be fed either for horizontal or vertical polarization by merely changing the feed point from the center of a horizontal arm to the center of a vertical arm. At the higher HF bands, where the quads are typically 1/2 to 2 λ high, quad loops are usually fed to obtain horizontal polarization. Polarization by itself is of little importance, because it becomes random after ionospheric refraction. For low-band DX work however, vertical polarization has great advantages as far as wave angle is concerned, at least on 80 and 40 meters (see Figure 2.53). The radiation resistance of an equilateral quad loop in free space is approximately 100 ohms. This figure may be as low as 70 ohms at very low heights.

Quad Loop Patterns

A horizontally polarized quad-loop antenna (two stacked short dipoles) produces a wave angle which is dependent on the height of the *top* horizontal wire. For a quad loop with the top wire about 1/4 λ above the ground, the wave angle will be 90°.

The vertically polarized quad loop (Figure 2.52B) can be considered as two shortened top loaded vertical dipoles, spaced 1/4 λ apart. Broadside radiation from the horizontal elements of the quad is minimal, because of the opposition of currents. The wave angle in the broadside direction will essentially be the same as either of the vertical members. The total radiation angle will depend on the quality of the ground up to several wavelengths away from the antenna, as is the case with all vertically polarized antennas. The typical wave angle is under 30° for a top height just over 1/4 λ, which is attractive for low-band DX work.

Figure 2.53 shows both the horizontal and vertical radiation patterns of quad loops at an apex height of 0.27 λ, which puts the bottom end of the loop at 0.02 λ. This is a very realistic situation on the low bands. The vertically polarized quad loop radiates an excellent low-angle wave (at approximately 20°) when operated over ideal ground. Under less ideal conditions, the wave angle would be closer to 30°. The horizontal directivity is very poor, and amounts to less than 3 dB of side rejection at any wave angle. As expected, the horizontally polarized quad radiates most of its energy right at zenith angle. The horizontal pattern of Figure 2.53 is plotted for a wave angle of 60°. At lower angles, the practical gain of this antenna over a dipole can be as high as 7 dB.

2.8.2 DELTA LOOPS

Just as the inverted V has been described as the poor-man's dipole, the delta loop can be called the poor-man's quad loop. Because of their shape, delta loops with the apex on top are very popular antennas for the low bands, as they need only one support.

The equilateral triangle produces the highest gain and the highest radiation resistance for a three-sided loop configuration. As we deviate from an equilateral triangle towards a triangle with a long baseline, the effective gain and the radiation resistance of the loop will decrease (bottom-corner-fed delta loop). In the extreme case (where the height of the triangle is reduced to zero), the loop has become a half-wavelength long transmission line shorted at the end, which

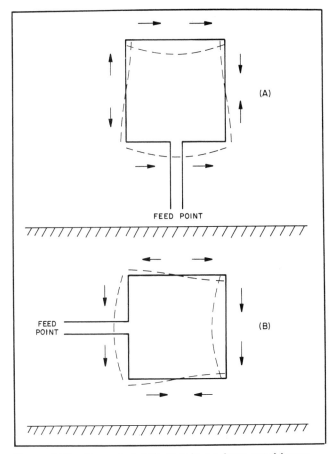

Figure 2.52—Current distribution in 1 λ-long quad loops, fed for horizontal (A) and vertical (B) polarization. Note how the opposing currents in two legs results in cancellation of the radiation in the plane of those legs, while the currents in the other legs are in phase and will reinforce radiation.

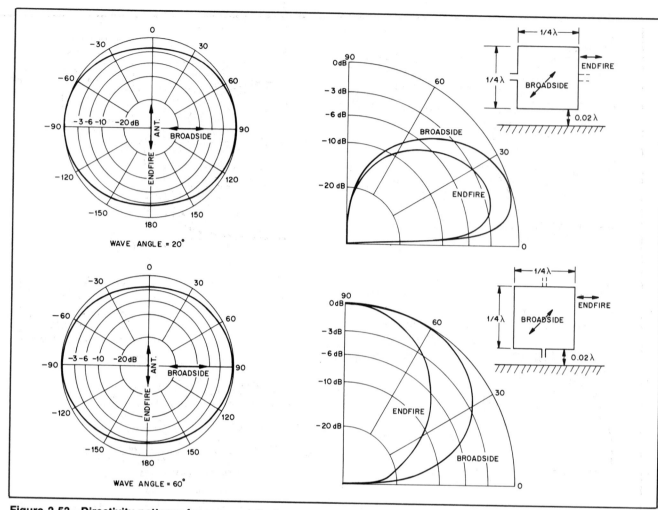

Figure 2.53—Directivity patterns for square delta loops with the top leg at 0.27 λ above the ground. The vertical patterns are in the broadside and in the end-fire directions (calculated over excellent ground). Notice the dramatic difference in favored wave angle between the vertically and horizontally polarized loops.

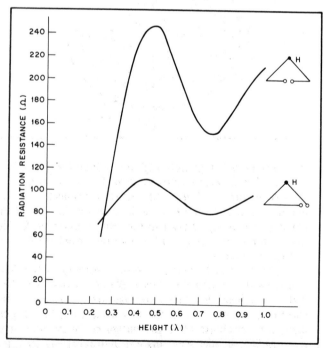

Figure 2.54—Radiation resistances of equilateral delta loops, fed at the center of the baseline (for horizontal polarization) and at one corner of the bottom leg (for vertical polarization), both for apex heights of ¼ to 1 λ.

shows a zero-ohm input impedance (radiation resistance), and thus zero radiation (well-balanced open-wire line does not radiate).

2.8.2.1 Radiation Resistance

Figure 2.54 shows the radiation resistance of equilateral delta loop antennas fed in different places and for different heights. The loops with the longest baseline will show the lowest radiation resistance. For a baseline length of 3/8 λ and an apex height of ¼ λ, the radiation resistance of a corner-fed delta loop is 50 ohms, which makes a perfect match for RG-8, RG-213, or any similar 50-ohm coax.

2.8.2.2 Radiation Pattern

Mayhead, G3AQC, investigated the radiation patterns of loops at low height (¼ λ), as measured on scale models (Ref 1136). Nitschke, DJ5DW, and Wanderer, DF3LW, produced a whole range of vertical radiation patterns for delta loops with different feeding arrangements (Ref 1109). The following discussion of the vertical and horizontal radiation patterns of loops takes into consideration the low height at which the average loop will be erected on the low bands. At high elevations, which is normally the case on the higher HF bands, the clear distinction in performance between vertically and horizontally polarized loops no longer exists.

By virtue of its shape and its current distribution (which depends on the location of the feed point on the loop), the

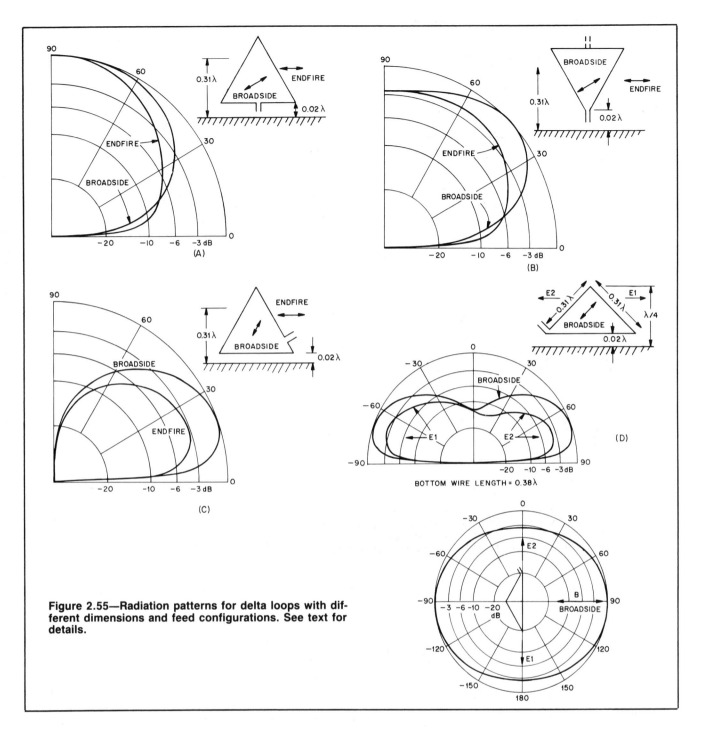

Figure 2.55—Radiation patterns for delta loops with different dimensions and feed configurations. See text for details.

delta loop will often transmit a partially vertically polarized signal. Where the horizontal component is largest, the delta loop will act as any horizontally polarized antenna over real ground; its wave angle will depend only on the height of the antenna over the ground, which means that the wave angle will be high for typical low-band antenna installations. Figure 2.55 shows the major radiation lobes for a range of popular triangular-loop antennas.

Complete cancellation of the horizontal or vertical component only occurs with perfectly equilateral triangles fed to achieve fully symmetrical current distribution. Most delta loops at low heights are not equilateral, however, and are often fed to produce unbalanced current distribution (Figure 2.55D). In those cases, both horizontally and vertically polarized radiation components will exist. The delta loops in Figure 2.55A and B are fed for horizontal polarization, and

the wave angle is high (although lower than for a dipole or inverted V at the same height). Antenna B shows a lower angle than A because the horizontal section (responsible for the major part of the horizontal radiation) is at the top of the antenna, much higher than in the case of antenna A. The radiation patterns are given for both the broadside and the end-fire directions.

Notice the very limited degree of directivity of the delta loops (less than 3 dB at any wave angle). At angles below 15°, delta loops A and B actually produce stronger signals in the end-fire direction than in the broadside direction. Figure 2.55C is the equilateral triangle configured for optimum low-angle radiation. The wave angle is approximately 20°, and the side rejection is just over 3 dB at those low angles. All patterns shown in Figure 2.55 were computed for excellent ground conditions. Figure 2.55D shows the popular

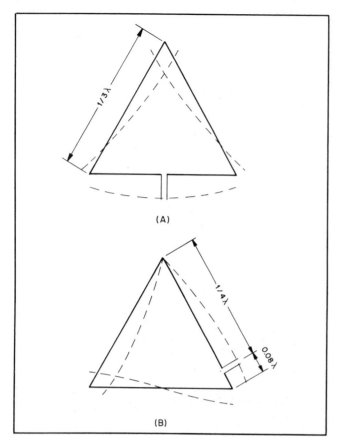

Figure 2.56—Current distribution for equilateral delta loops fed for horizontal (A) and vertical (B) polarization.

configuration of a non-equilateral delta loop, with an apex height of ¼ λ and the bottom wire 0.02 λ above ground. The triangle is fed at a bottom corner. This yields an asymmetrical current distribution, which in turn results in a slightly asymmetrical end-fire pattern (pattern in the plane of the antenna). The difference, however, is under 2 dB at low angles.

For DX work, the delta loop should be fed in such a way that vertical radiation is emphasized to the highest possible degree. Antenna C is fed to achieve maximum vertically polarized radiation. For an equilateral triangle (each side ⅓ λ), the optimum feed point is ¼ λ from either bottom corner. For the inverted, equilateral delta loop (horizontal wire at the top), the feed point is still at ¼ λ, but now from either top corner.

If the triangle has a longer horizontal leg (such as 0.28 λ), which is often the case, the feed point should remain ¼ λ from the top or bottom corner, regardless of the length of the baseline, in order to obtain maximum low-angle radiation.

Figure 2.56 shows the current distribution of a delta loop fed for horizontal and another fed for vertical polarization.

2.8.2.3 Loop Dimensions

The total loop length should be close to a full electrical wavelength. It is best not to use any shortening factor, and if the antenna is too long, a few inches may be more easily removed than added. The loop length (in feet) is: L = 1005/f(MHz). A loop designed for 3.775 MHz uses 266.2 feet of wire, while at 3.510 MHz it requires 286.3 feet.

2.8.2.4 Bandwidth

A typical 80-meter delta loop with the apex at 70 feet

(21 m) and fed at the bottom corner (about 64 feet from the apex), will have a 2:1 SWR bandwidth of approximately 170 kHz. This figure will decrease as the baseline of the delta is lengthened. For an 80-meter loop with a baseline of 100 feet (30 m), the bandwidth will drop to approximately 125 kHz.

2.8.2.5 Practical Loops

Loops are often suspended from the tower that supports high-band beams. Because of their outstanding properties for low-angle radiation at low heights, delta loops have become quite popular. The problem of restricted bandwidth can be overcome by either feeding the loop via open-wire feeders and an antenna tuner, or by installing a stub, coil or length of wire which can be switched in and out of the antenna circuit by a relay or a switch (Figure 2.57).

It is fairly common knowledge that dipoles at right angles can be mounted in very close proximity and still show a great deal of isolation (very little mutual coupling). This is not true with inverted Vs and is even less so with delta loops. For that reason, it is not advisable to mount two delta loops at right angles on the same support. Reduced-size loops have been described in amateur literature (Ref 1115, 1116, 1121, 1129).

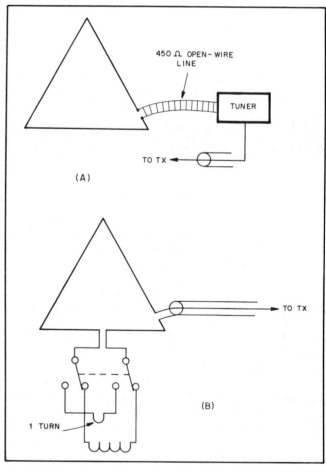

Figure 2.57—Alternative arrangements for wideband (CW and phone) operation with a delta or quad loop. If arrangement B is used, switching can be done from the shack. In the highest-frequency position, you may keep a one-turn loop in the circuit in order to dip the antenna. Dipping is not essential, as the antenna can be cut for the highest operating frequency and then adjusted for minimum SWR (this will be the resonant frequency of the antenna), the coil or loop can be adjusted for minimum SWR in the CW subband.

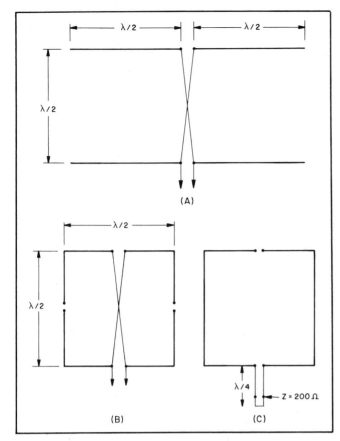

Figure 2.58—The bi-square antenna is a lazy-H antenna (two collinear dipoles, stacked ½ λ high and fed in phase). The tips of the elements are bent down (or up), and connected to each other (voltages are in phase). The top half of the antenna does not have to be driven, because it is excited by the connection of the tips. Feed impedance is very high (3000 ohms) and feeding can best be done via a quarter-wave stub arrangement.

2.8.3 BI-SQUARE

The bi-square antenna is not really a loop antenna, as the total wire length of 2 λ is opened at a point opposite the feed point. A quad antenna can be considered as a pair of shortened dipoles with ¼ λ spacing. In a similar way, the bi-square can be considered a lazy-H antenna with the dipole ends folded vertically, as shown in Figure 2.58. Not many people are able to erect a bi-square antenna, as the dimensions involved on the low bands are quite large. This antenna has excellent gain, however (as much as 5 dB over a dipole).

The horizontal and vertical radiation patterns of the bi-square are shown in Figure 2.59. The feed-point impedance is high (a few thousand ohms), and the recommended feed system consists of a quarter-wave stub, shorted at the end. A point on the stub can be found where Z = 200 ohms, and where the coaxial cable can be attached via a 4:1 balun (Figure 2.58).

2.9 Half-Loop

The half-loop was first described by Belrose (Ref 1120 and 1130). This antenna, unlike the half-sloper (see Section 2.10) cannot be mounted on a tall tower supporting a quad or Yagi. If this was done, the half loop would shunt-feed RF to the tower and the radiation pattern would be upset.

A half-delta loop was analyzed using ANNIE. The tower height was 0.1666 λ, which results in a 60° angle between the

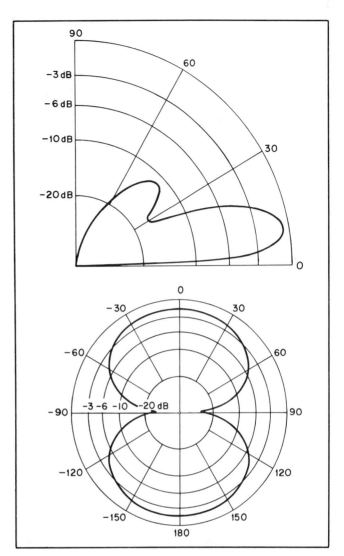

Figure 2.59—Horizontal and vertical radiation patterns of a bi-square antenna with the top at 5/8 λ. This pattern was calculated for good ground (the dB values are relative). The horizontal pattern was calculated for a wave angle of 15°.

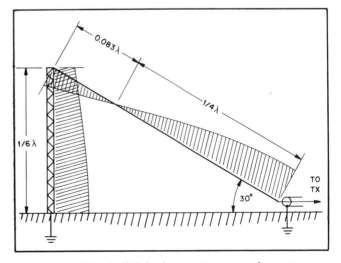

Figure 2.60—The half-delta loop antenna can be seen as a top-fed equilateral delta loop laid on its side. A good ground system (radials) must be provided at both the tower base and the feed point. The tower cannot extend beyond the sloping wire attachment point and cannot be used to support other antennas (such as Yagis).

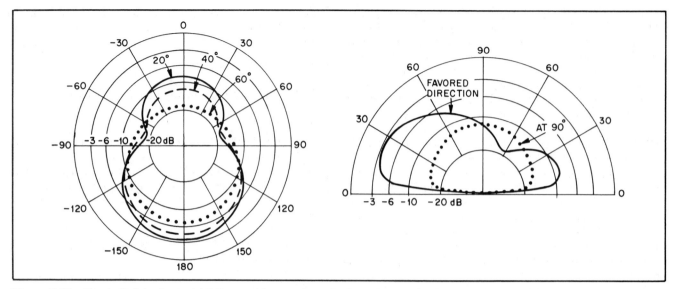

Figure 2.61—The half-delta loop exhibits good low-angle radiation when a good ground system is provided. The front-to-back ratio is 5 dB at low angles and rises to about 10 dB at 60°. The side rejection (100° off center) is 15 dB.

tower and the slope wire for a total radiator length of ½ λ (Figure 2.60).

The horizontal and vertical radiation patterns are given in Figure 2.61. The directivity is in the direction of the slanting wire, and for low-angle signals, about a 12 dB front-to-side ratio and a 7 dB front-to-back ratio can be achieved. High-angle radiation from the half-loop is minimal. Belrose reports an input impedance of 74 ohms for the antenna on its resonant frequency. The antenna can be fed either at the end of the sloping wire or at the base of the tower (if insulated from ground) via an L-network. This antenna is not yet very popular with the low-band DX fraternity, but it is worth experimenting with where large and high antennas are not allowed or are impractical.

2.10 Half-Slopers

Unlike the half-delta loop, the half-sloper is a very difficult antenna to analyze, as the nature of the tower on which the sloper is mounted will influence the performance of the antenna to a great extent. Quarter-wave slopers are a new breed of low-band antennas. They are the typical result of ingenuity and inventiveness. Many DXers, short of space for putting up large, proven, low-angle radiators have found their half-slopers to be good performers. Others have reported that they could not get their half-sloper to resonate on the desired frequency. To make a long story short, half-slopers seem to be very unpredictable, and are difficult to analyze because of the vastly different environments in which they are erected (different tower heights, different tower loading, different slope angles, and so forth).

Belrose, VE2CV, thoroughly analyzed the half-sloper using scale models on a professional test range (Ref 647). His findings were confirmed by DeMaw, W1FB (Ref 650). Earlier, Atchley, W1CF, reported outstanding performance from his half-sloper on 160 meters (Ref 645).

From the papers mentioned here, the following can be extracted:

• The vertical antenna support (antenna tower) is an active part of the antenna. The tower should be adequately grounded to a ground rod and radial system. The tower sections should be checked for good electrical continuity.

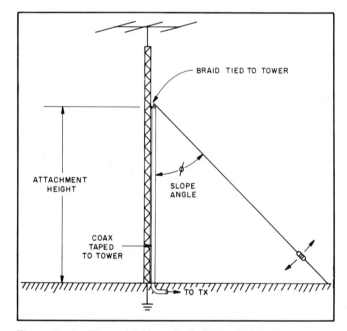

Figure 2.62—The mysterious half sloper: It has been a successful antenna for some and a disappointment for others. Changing the height of the attachment point, the slope angle, and the length of the wire will bring the SWR to a reasonable value in most cases.

• Slopers seem to work best when attached about a quarter wavelength above ground (Figure 2.62).

• Both the slope angle and the wire length have a great influence on the SWR at resonance.

• Loading of the tower above the sloper attachment point greatly influences the resonant frequency of the system.

• Running multiple half-slopers off the same tower seems to be impossible because of excessive coupling between the systems.

• Quarter-wave slopers have good low-angle radiation, but very little directivity (Ref 647).

• The quarter-wave sloper has been reported by several reliable sources to have outperformed half-wave slopers in the same location.

Together with the fact that the lowest system SWR is most often obtained with sloper lengths vastly different from an electrical quarter-wavelength, this seems to indicate that the system is working as a top-fed, top-loaded vertical (Ref 647).

Wermager, KØEOU, describes a variation on the true half-sloper. The sloping element, which is fed at the tower in the case of a classic half-sloper, is connected to the tower without a feed. For 80-meter operation, the length is 74 to 78 feet, and the height of the attachment point to the tower is 46 to 60 feet. A second fed element is attached approximately 15 feet up the tower and consists of 2 parallel wires (52 to 53 feet long) sloping to a height of approximately 8 to 12 feet at the far end. The SWR curve of this antenna is practically flat from 3.5 to 4 MHz. The antenna was modeled by Hall, K1TD, using MININEC and found to have little front-to-back at low angles (just a few dB). This antenna requires a good ground system for optimum performance.

To summarize the performance of half-slopers, it is worthwhile to note Belrose's comment, "If I had a single quarter-wave tower, I'd employ a full-wave delta loop, apex up, lower corner fed, the best DX-type antenna I have modeled." Of course, a delta loop still has a baseline of approximately 100 feet (on 80 meters), which is not the case with the half-sloper. The half-sloper does have a space advantage over many other low-band antennas, even though in many cases success is only realized after much experimentation.

2.11 Arrays

Dipoles, monopoles and other antennas can be combined to form an array in order to obtain increased directivity in either the horizontal or the vertical plane (or both). Horizontal directivity is commonly sought on the HF bands, while at VHF, vertical directivity is often needed to concentrate RF energy close to the horizon (as with repeater antennas).

2.11.1 ARRAYS OF MONOPOLES

2.11.1.1 Horizontal Radiation Pattern of Arrays

Ray Analysis

Let us consider two verticals with spacing D and fed with a phase difference of $\alpha°$. Figure 2.63 shows two vertical antennas (A and B). The paper is the ground and both radiators are omnidirectional by definition. Rays a and a′ from antenna A and B have a phase difference which depends on four factors:

1) Spacing S.
2) The phase difference with which RF is applied at the feed point of the antennas.
3) Angle of ray a and a′ with respect to the line AB.
4) The current in each antenna.

Consider the specific case where the spacing is ¼ λ and phase difference is 90°, as shown in Figure 2.63. Rays b and b′ are clearly in phase (¼ wave due to spacing minus ¼ wave due to phase difference of 90°). Similarly, d and d′ are 180° out of phase. Rays a and a′ will reinforce one another, but c and c′ will complement each other to a much lesser degree. The resulting radiation pattern is called a cardioid.

Directivity Over Perfect Ground

McGuire, WB5HGR, developed a BASIC program for calculating the horizontal directivity of an array of vertical antennas (Ref 920), which runs on a Radio Shack TRS-80 computer. The program was reworked and extended by the author for the Apple computer. The program allows the evaluation of arrays with up to 10 elements, and the listing can be found in Chapter VII (Computer Programs).

A sample printout can be found with the program listing. The example is for two verticals, spaced 90° and fed 90° out of phase (the cardioid pattern). The first table gives the field strength in absolute values for the total azimuthal range (0 to 360° in 10° steps), and for wave angles ranging from 0 to 90° (also in 10° steps). The values are for a perfect ground. The second table lists values in decibels versus the peak response of the array.

Figure 2.64 shows a range of radiation patterns obtained by different combinations of two monopoles over perfect ground and at zero wave angle. These directivity patterns are classics in every good antenna handbook.

Directivity Over Real Ground

As stated earlier, we don't live in a perfect world with a perfect ground, and normally we are not interested in the array performance at zero wave angle. Here again, ANNIE comes to our rescue (see Section 2.4.1.2).

2.11.1.2 Vertical Radiation Pattern

For an array made of a number of identical vertical antennas, the beamwidth will decrease with the number of antennas in the array. Depending on the quality of the ground around the antenna, this can result in an effective gain of several decibels, in addition to the gain caused by horizontal pattern.

2.11.1.3 Vertical Radiator Length

In principle, the whole range of verticals described in

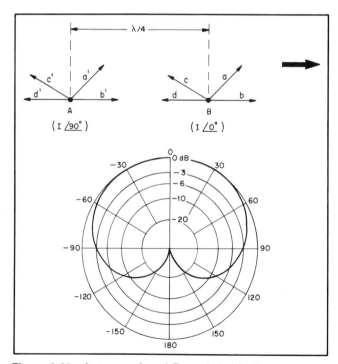

Figure 2.63—Antennas A and B are fed with the same current, but antenna A leads in phase by 90°. Graphic analysis of a few rays shows that the array will radiate most power in the direction of rays B and B′ where these rays, because of the physical separation and phase relationship between the elements, will show maximum reinforcement. The resultant radiation pattern is calculated at a 0° wave angle over ideal ground.

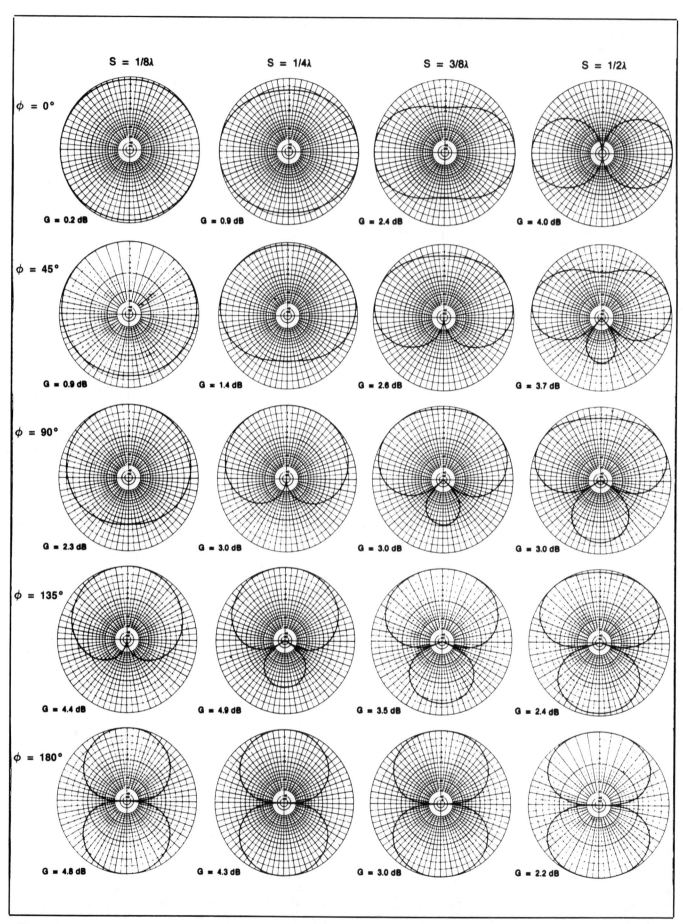

	S = 1/8λ	S = 1/4λ	S = 3/8λ	S = 1/2λ
φ = 0°	G = 0.2 dB	G = 0.9 dB	G = 2.4 dB	G = 4.0 dB
φ = 45°	G = 0.9 dB	G = 1.4 dB	G = 2.6 dB	G = 3.7 dB
φ = 90°	G = 2.3 dB	G = 3.0 dB	G = 3.0 dB	G = 3.0 dB
φ = 135°	G = 4.4 dB	G = 4.9 dB	G = 3.5 dB	G = 2.4 dB
φ = 180°	G = 4.8 dB	G = 4.3 dB	G = 3.0 dB	G = 2.2 dB

Figure 2.64—Horizontal radiation patterns for two-element vertical arrays (both elements fed with the same current magnitude). The elements are in line with the vertical axis, and the top element is the one with the lagging phase angle. Patterns are for zero wave angle over ideal ground.

Section 2.4 can be used as elements for arrays. Quarter-wave elements have gained a reputation of giving a reasonable match to a 50-ohm line, which is certainly true for single vertical antennas. Section 2.11.1.4 covers the reasons that quarter-wave resonant verticals do not have a resistive 36-ohm feed point impedance when operated in arrays. Quarter-wave elements still remain a good choice, however, as they have a reasonably high radiation resistance, which ensures good overall efficiency. On 160 meters, the elements could be top-loaded verticals using a 25° long capacitive top hat. Each vertical will then be 93 feet long, with a 17-foot diameter capacity hat. The self impedance will be approximately 45 ohms assuming an equivalent return ground-loss resistance of 10 ohms. Nonresonant lengths can also be used, and have no intrinsic disadvantages with the feed methods described below (Section 2.11.1.4 and 2.11.1.5). Collins, W1FC, has been successful in using bottom-fed half-wave vertical elements. Using tubular aluminum elements, he found the resonant-frequency impedance to be on the order of 800 ohms. A matching system that does not introduce phase shift consists of a very tightly coupled broadband transformer as described in Section 2.4.8.2.

2.11.1.4 Getting the Right Current and the Right Phase

Few articles in Amateur Radio publications have addressed the problems associated with mutual coupling in designing a phased array and in making it work as it should. Gehrke, K2BT, wrote an outstanding series of articles on the design of phased arrays (Ref 921-925, 927). These are highly recommended for anyone who is considering putting up phased arrays of verticals. Another excellent article by Christman, KB8I (Ref 929), covers the same subject.

Mutual Coupling

If we bring two resonant circuits into the vicinity of each other, mutual coupling will occur. This is the reason that antennas with parasitic elements work as they do.

Horizontally polarized antennas with parasitically excited elements are widely used on the higher bands, but not on the low bands because of the disturbing influence of the ground, which is usually very close to the antenna in terms of wavelengths. This frequently makes it impossible to obtain the right amount of current with the correct phase in the parasitic element. Therefore, we usually use arrays where all elements are physically excited by applying power to the elements via individual feed lines. Each feed line supplies current of the correct magnitude and phase.

There is one frequently overlooked major problem with arrays. As we have made up our minds to feed all elements, we too often assume (incorrectly) there is no mutual coupling or that it is so small that we can ignore it. Taking mutual coupling into account complicates life, as we now have two sources of applied power to the elements of the array (parasitic coupling plus direct feeding).

If a single quarter-wave vertical is erected, we know that the self impedance will be $36 + j0$ ohms, assuming resonance and a perfect ground system. This is not true if other elements are closely coupled to the original element. Each of the other elements will couple energy into the original element and vice versa. This results in drive impedances being totally different from the self impedance in most cases. Mutual impedance is a term that relates to the interaction of closely spaced elements in an array, causing the driving impedances of the elements to be different from the self impedance.

The calculated mutual impedances and driving impedances

have been extensively covered by Gehrke, K2BT (Ref 923). Mutual impedances are calculated from measured self and driven impedances. Here is an example: We are constructing an array with three quarter-wave elements in a triangle, spaced ¼ λ apart. We erect the three elements and install the ground system. Then the following steps are followed:

1) Open-circuit elements 2 and 3 (opening the element will effectively isolate it from the other elements in the case of quarter-wave elements, when using half-wave elements the elements must be grounded for maximum isolation, and open-circuited for maximum coupling).

2) Measure the self impedance of element 1 (= Z11).

3) Ground element 2.

4) Measure the driven impedance of element 1 with element 2 coupled (= Z1,2).

5) Open-circuit element 2.

6) Ground element 3.

7) Measure the driven impedance of element 1 with element 3 coupled (= Z1,3).

8) Open-circuit element 3.

9) Open-circuit element 1.

10) Measure the self impedance of element 2 (= Z22).

11) Ground element 3.

12) Measure the driven impedance of element 2 with element 3 coupled (= Z2,3).

13) Open-circuit element 3.

14) Ground element 1.

15) Measure the driven impedance of element 2 with element 1 coupled (= Z2,1).

16) Open-circuit element 1.

17) Open-circuit element 2.

18) Measure the self impedance of element 3 (= Z33).

19) Ground element 2.

20) Measure the driven impedance of element 3 with element 2 coupled (= Z3,2).

21) Open-circuit element 2.

22) Ground element 1.

23) Measure the driven impedance of element 3 with element 1 coupled (= Z3,1).

This is the procedure for an array with three elements. The procedures for two- and four-element arrays can be derived from the above.

As one can see, measurement of coupling is done by pairs of elements. At step 15, we are measuring the effect of mutual coupling between elements 2 and 1, and it may be argued that this has already been done in step 4. It is useful, however, to make these measurements again in order to recheck the previous measurements and calculations. Mutual couplings Z12 and Z21 calculated (see below) using the Z1,2 and Z2,1 inputs should in theory be identical, and in practice should be within an ohm or so.

The self impedances and the driving impedances of the different elements should match closely if the array is to be made switchable.

The mutual impedances can be calculated as follows:

$$Z12 = \pm \sqrt{Z22 \times (Z11 - Z1,2)}$$

$$Z21 = \pm \sqrt{Z11 \times (Z22 - Z2,1)}$$

$$Z13 = \pm \sqrt{Z33 \times (Z11 - Z1,1)}$$

$$Z31 = \pm \sqrt{Z11 \times (Z33 - Z3,1)}$$

$$Z23 = \pm \sqrt{Z33 \times (Z22 - Z2,1)}$$

$$Z32 = \pm \sqrt{Z22 \times (Z33 - Z3,2)}$$

It should be obvious that if Z11 = Z22 and Z1,2 = Z2,1, then Z12 = Z21. If the array is perfectly symmetrical (such as in a 2-element array or in a 3-element array with the elements in an equilateral triangle) all self impedances will be identical (Z11 = Z22 = Z33), and all driving impedances as well (Z2,1 = Z1,2 = Z3,1 = Z1,3 = Z2,3 = Z3,2). Consequently, all mutual impedances will be identical as well (Z12 = Z21 = Z31 = Z13 = Z23 = Z32). In practice, the values of the mutual impedances will vary slightly, even when good care is taken to obtain maximum symmetry.

Because all impedances are complex values (having real and imaginary components), the mathematics involved are rather complex. Chapter VII lists a computer program written in BASIC language, which performs the mutual impedance calculation in seconds ("MUTUAL IMPEDANCE").

Table 20 shows the mutual impedance to be expected for quarter-wave elements at spacings from 0 to 1.0 λ. The resistance and reactance values vary with element separation as a damped sine wave, starting at zero separation with both signs positive. At about 0.10 to 0.15 λ spacing, the reactance sign changes from + to −. This is important to know in order to assign the correct sign to the reactive value (obtained via a square root).

Gehrke, K2BT, feels it is important to actually measure the element self and drive impedances, and to calculate the mutual impedances, rather than to go by published values such as those listed in Table 20. The table shows "ballpark" figures, enabling you to verify your calculated results.

After calculating the mutual impedances, the driving point impedances can be calculated, taking into account the drive current (amplitude and phase). The driving point impedances are given by:

$$Zn = \frac{I1}{In}Zn1 + \frac{I2}{In}Zn2 + \frac{I3}{In}Zn3 + \ldots + \frac{In}{In}Znn$$

where n is the total number of elements. The number of equations is n, this one is for the nth element. Note also that Z12 = Z21 and Z13 = Z31 etc.

The BASIC program called "DRIVING IMPEDANCE" in Chapter VII performs the rather complex driving point impedance calculations for arrays with up to 4 elements. The required inputs are 1) the number of elements and 2) the driving current and phase for each element. The outputs are the driving point impedances Z1 through Zn.

As we work through the theory of array feed-system design, we will use the example of an array consisting of two quarter-wave long verticals, spaced a quarter wavelength apart and fed with equal magnitude currents, with the current in element 2 lagging the current in element 1 by 90°. This is the most common end-fire configuration with a cardioid pattern.

The elements of such an array have a self impedance of 36.4 ohms over a perfect ground. A nearly perfect ground system consists of at least 120 half-wave radials (see Section 2.4.3.4). For example, a system with 60 radials may show a self impedance on the order of 40 ohms. The mutual impedances were calculated (with the BASIC program "MUTUAL IMPEDANCE") to be: Z12 = Z21 = 15 − j15 ohms. With the BASIC program "DRIVING IMPEDANCE" we calculate the driving point impedances of the two elements and find: Z1 = 21.4 − j15 ohms for the zero-degree element and Z2 = 51.4 + j15 ohms for the −90° element.

This means that if we feed these elements with 50-ohm coaxial cable, we cannot simply use lengths of feed line as delay lines by making the line length in degrees equal to the

Table 20
Mutual Impedance for ¼ λ Elements for Spacings of 0 to 1.0 λ

Spacing (λ)	Mutual Impedance (ohms)
0.00	36.3 + j21.3
0.05	35.8 + j12.1
0.10	33.7 + j3.8
0.15	30.2 − j3.6
0.20	25.7 − j9.6
0.25	20.4 − j14.2
0.30	14.6 − j17.2
0.35	8.7 − j18.7
0.40	3.1 − j18.7
0.45	−2.0 − j17.4
0.50	−6.3 − j15.0
0.55	−9.5 − j11.7
0.60	−11.7 − j7.9
0.65	−12.6 − j4.0
0.70	−12.4 − j0.1
0.75	−11.3 + j3.3
0.80	−9.3 + j6.1
0.85	−6.7 + j8.2
0.90	−3.8 + j9.3
0.95	−0.8 + j9.5
1.00	+2.0 + j8.9

desired delay in degrees. The electrical length of a feed line is equal to its delay only under specific circumstances, such as when the lines are terminated in their characteristic impedance, when the delay lines are a half-wavelength (or multiple half-wavelengths) long, or when the phasing lines are an odd number of quarter wavelengths long and terminated in resistive loads of any value (Ref 921).

Feed Systems

All array configurations assume defined currents being fed to all elements. In many arrays, the current amplitudes to the elements are the same. If we feed 1 A of current into the two elements of the cardioid array described above, the first element will take 21.4 W, and the second one 51.4 W. Wilkinson power dividers have been widely used for supplying equal power to two terminations having the same impedances. The power divider is not the correct device for feeding elements in an array where equal drive power is generally not the objective (see Section 2.12.4).

Gehrke Method

Gehrke, K2BT, has developed a technique where the elements of the array are fed with randomly selected lengths of feed line, and where he accomplishes the required impedance transformation through the use of L-networks, and adjusts the delay in one or more element feeds through the use of constant impedance delay networks (Pi- or T-networks). The detailed description of the procedure is given in Ref 924 and further in this section.

The Gehrke method consists of selecting equal lengths for the feed lines running from the elements to a common point (where the array switching and matching will be done). Using this method, the length of the feed lines can be chosen by the designer to suit any physical requirements of the particular installation. The cables should be long enough to reach a common point, such as the middle of the triangle in the case of a triangle-shaped array. Figure 2.65 shows a typical

```
 _____
|                               |                                           |
| ARRAY: (2 El 1/4 wave spacing | CABLE VELOCITY FACTOR:                    |
|        (ENDFIRE, CARDIOID     | MIN FEEDER LENGTH:                         |
|        (90 DEG PHASE          |                                           |
|-------------------------------|-------------------------------------------|
|A|            ELEM 1.      | ELEM.2      |    ELEM.3      |    ELEM.4       |
|N|----------------------------|------------|---------------|-----------------|
|T|   Z(1,2)= 15-j15       |Z(2,3)=     |Z(3,4)=        |                 |
|E|   Z(1,3)=              |Z(2.4)=     |               |                 |
|N|   Z(1,4)=              |            |               |                 |
|N|                        |            |               |                 |
|A|Z (ohm)  =| 21.4-j15    | 51.4 + j15 |               |                 |
|S|E (V, deg)=| 26.13 / -35.03 | 53.5 / -73.73 |          |                 |
| |I (A, deg)=| 1 / 0      | 1 / -90    |               |                 |
|=|========================|============|===============|=================|
| |                        |            |               |                 |
|N|Z(series)               |            |               |                 |
|E|Z(parallel)             |            |               |                 |
|T|Value. ser              |            |               |                 |
|W|Value. par.             |            |               |                 |
|O|    Z(ohm)=             |            |               |                 |
|R|   E(E,deg)=            |            |               |                 |
|K|   I(A,deg)=            |            |               |                 |
| |1                       |            |               |                 |
|=|========================|============|===============|=================|
| |                        |            |               |                 |
|N|Z(series)               |            |               |                 |
|E|Z(parallel)             |            |               |                 |
|T|Value. ser              |            |               |                 |
|W|Value. par.             |            |               |                 |
|O|    Z(ohm)=             |            |               |                 |
|R|   E(E,deg)=            |            |               |                 |
|K|   I(A,deg)=            |            |               |                 |
| |2                       |            |               |                 |
|=|========================|============|===============|=================|
| |                        |            |               |                 |
|N|Z(series)               |            |               |                 |
|E|Z(parallel)             |            |               |                 |
|T|Value. ser              |            |               |                 |
|W|Value. par.             |            |               |                 |
|O|    Z(ohm)=             |            |               |                 |
|R|   E(E,deg)=            |            |               |                 |
|K|   I(A,deg)=            |            |               |                 |
| |3                       |            |               |                 |
|=|========================|============|===============|=================|
| |                        |            |               |                 |
|N|Z(series)               |            |               |                 |
|E|Z(parallel)             |            |               |                 |
|T|Value. ser              |            |               |                 |
|W|Value. par.             |            |               |                 |
|O|    Z(ohm)=             |            |               |                 |
|R|   E(E,deg)=            |            |               |                 |
|K|   I(A,deg)=            |            |               |                 |
| |4                       |            |               |                 |
|_____|
```

Figure 2.65—The array network-design worksheet is laid out for a maximum of four array elements. This example has only the element parameters filled in. The fields on the worksheet provide room for noting the relevant information about each network used.

worksheet that can be used when designing a feed system. The example shows the inputs for the two-element end-fire array with a cardioid pattern.

Next, the required impedances at the T junction must be determined. Continuing with the above example, the element feed-point impedances are:

$Z1 = 21.4 - j15$ ohms
$Z2 = 51.4 + j15$ ohms

As the current in both antennas is 1 A, (arbitrarily chosen), the power levels are:

$P_1 = 21.4 \times 1 \times 1 = 21.4$ W
$P_2 = 51.4 \times 1 \times 1 = 51.4$ W
$P_{tot} = 21.4 + 51.4 = 72.8$ W.

If you want to work with real powers, voltages, and currents, divide the transmitter output power by P_{tot}, and replace the 1 A of current with the square root of the output power divided by the total power. Example: If $P_{out} = 1500$ W, then

$$I = \sqrt{\frac{1500}{72.8}} = 4.54 \text{ A}$$

Now you can read real voltages and real currents, which can be an advantage when sizing components for the circuit.

At the T junction, (assuming we want an SWR of 1:1 on the 50-ohm line to the shack) the voltage will be:

$$E = \sqrt{RP} = \sqrt{50 \times 72.8} = 60.3 \text{ V}$$

Looking toward element 1, the impedance at the T junction must be:

$$Z = \frac{E^2}{P} = \frac{60.3^2}{21.4} = 170 \ \Omega$$

For element 2, the impedance at the T point must be 70.8 ohms. A simple check can be made to verify that the resulting impedance will be 50 ohms:

$$\frac{1}{170} + \frac{1}{70.8} = \frac{1}{50}$$

Gehrke then proceeds to convert the currents at the element feed points and the element driving-point impedances to their voltage equivalents in a 50-ohm system. This can be done as follows:

$Z1 = 21.4 - j15$ ohms
$I = 1$ A $\underline{/0°}$

$$E \text{ (magnitude)} = \sqrt{21.4^2 + (-15)^2} = 26.13 \text{ V}$$

$$E \text{ (angle)} = \text{arc tan}\left(\frac{-15}{21.4}\right) = -35.02°$$

Or, $E = 26.13$ V $\underline{/-35.02°}$
In a similar way, the voltage at point 2 is found to be:
$E = 53.54$ V $\underline{/16.27°}$
The program "COAX TRANSFORMER," listed in Chapter VII, can do all of these calculations in seconds.

E1 and E2 are the voltages (magnitude and phase) that must be present at the feed points of the elements in order to produce the pattern resulting from quarter-wave spacing, equal current magnitude, and 90° phase delay. Figure 2.66 shows the impedance, current and voltage values, and where they are present in the array.

The values of I, E and Z must now be transformed to the

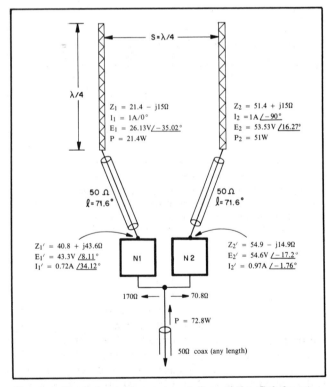

Figure 2.66—Schematic representation of the Gehrke approach to matching the elements of an array. Note the required (resistive) impedances at the T junction, which will ensure the correct power distribution and the correct antenna currents. Networks N1 and N2 will transform the complex impedances at the ends of the feed lines to these resistive values at the T junction, and at the same time provide voltages that are identical in magnitude and phase.

ends of the coaxial feed lines. If we decide to make the direction of the array switchable, it is recommended that all feed lines be cut to the same electrical length, unless one element remains in the same position (such as the center element in a three-element in-line array), because the direction-switching harness will be easier to construct. Otherwise, there is no reason why the feed lines must be of equal length. Gehrke's design example (Ref 925) uses two 71.6° long 50-ohm cables.

Transforming impedance, voltage and current values with a coaxial cable can be done with a Smith chart, or more accurately by matrix algebra (Ref 925). The program "COAX TRANSFORMER" can also be used for this purpose.

The result of the transformation via the 71.6° long 50-ohm lines is:

$Z1' = 40.8 + j43.6$ ohms
$E1' = 43.3$ V $\underline{/80.1°}$
$I1' = 0.72$ A $\underline{/34.12°}$
$Z2' = 54.9 - j14.9$ ohms
$E2' = 54.6$ V $\underline{/-17.2°}$
$I2' = 0.97$ A $\underline{/-1.81°}$

These are the values of Z, I and E that must be present at the end of the coaxial cables in order for the array to perform as it was designed to.

Next, Gehrke calculates the lumped-constant networks. Figure 2.67 shows a completed worksheet for this array. The network must be designed to transform the impedances at the end of the cables to the resistive values (determined above as 170 and 70.8 ohms). This transformation can be done with a shunt-input L-network, as the output impedance is lower than the input impedance. The only requirement for the network is the impedance transformation. L-networks have a phase delay which is inherently coupled to the transformation ratio, which means that we have no separate control over the phase delay. The phase delays in current and voltage can be calculated using matrix algebra (Ref 925). The BASIC program "L-NETWORK" can also be used to perform these calculations. Each L-network design yields at least two solutions, where the input voltage magnitudes are the same, but the phase angles are different.

Solution 1
$Z2'' = 70.8$ ohms (design objective)
$E2'' = 60.3$ V $\underline{/27.5°}$
$I2'' = 0.85$ A $\underline{/27.5°}$

Solution 2
$Z2'' = 70.8$ ohms
$E2'' = 60.3$ V $\underline{/-30.9°}$
$I2'' = 0.85$ A $\underline{/-30.9°}$

A similar L-network can now be inserted in the feed line to element 1 (Figure 2.66). This network must transform $Z1'$ ($40.8 + j43.6$ ohms) to 170 ohms resistive. Choosing a series-input L-network, the transformed values of $Z1'$, $E1'$ and $I1'$ are:

Solution 3
$Z1'' = 170$ ohms (design objective)
$E1'' = 60.3$ V $\underline{/-26.6°}$
$I1'' = 0.35$ A $\underline{/-26.6°}$

Solution 4
$Z1'' = 170$ ohms
$E1'' = 60.3$ V $\underline{/94.86°}$
$I1'' = 0.35$ A $\underline{/94.86°}$

```
|           (2 El 1/4 wave spacing      |      CABLE VELOCITY FACTOR: 0.66
| ARRAY: (ENDFIRE, CARDIOID             |      MIN FEEDER LENGTH: 71.6 DEG
|           (90 DEG PHASE               |      F = 3.75 MHz
```

A N T E N N	ELEM 1.	ELEM.2	ELEM.3	ELEM.4
I	Z(1,2)= 15-j15	Z(2,3)=	Z(3,4)=	
	Z(1,3)=	Z(2,4)=		
	Z(1,4)=			

A S I		ELEM 1.	ELEM.2
	Z (ohm) =	21.4 - j 15	51.4 + j15
	E (V, deg)=	26.13 /-35.03	53.5 /-73.73
	I (A, deg)=	1 /0	1 /-90

	CABLES -->	50 OHM, 71.6 deg	50 ohm, 71.6 deg
N E T W O R K 1	Z(series)		
	Z(parallel)	SWR = 2.59/1	SWR=1.34/1
	Value. ser		
	Value. par.		
	Z(ohm)=	40.8+j43.6	53.9-j14.9
	E(E,deg)=	43.3 /+80.1	54.6 /-17.2
	I(A,deg)=	0.72 /+34.12	0.97 /-1.81

N E T W O R K 2	SHUNT INPU L NETW ----(1)----	SHUNT INPUT L NETW ----(2)----	SHUNT INPUT L NETW ----(3)----	SHUNT IN L NETW ----(4)----
Z(series)	-116	+29	+45.1	-15.3
Z(parallel)	+95.5	-95.5	-126.4	+126.4
Value. ser	365 pF	1.23 uH	1.91 uH	2777 pF
Value. par.	4.05 uH	444 pF	336 pF	5.37 uH
Z(ohm)=	170	170	70.8	70.8
E(E,deg)=	60.3 /-26.6	60.3 /+94.86	60.3 /+27.5	60.3 /-30.9
I(A,deg)=	0.35 /-26.6	0.35 /+94.86	0.85 /+27.5	0.85 /-30.9

N E T W O R K 3	IN(1) --> OUT(3) --(5)---	---(6)---	IN(3) --> OUT(1) --(7)---	---(8)--	IN(4) --> OUT(1) --(9)--	---(10)--	IN(1) --> OUT(4) --(11)--	--(12)-
Z(series)	-57 (PI)	-36.1 (T)	+138 (PI)	+87 (T)	-13 (PI)	-6.4 (T)	+5.3 (PI)	+2.7 (T)
Z(parallel)	+138	+57.3	-333	-137	+4528	+12.8	-1883	-5.30
Value. ser	740 pF	1174 pF	5.87 uH	4.10 uH	3330 pF	6650 pF	0.22 uH	0.11uH
Value. par.	5.9 uH	2.4 uH	127 pF	342 pF	192 uH	10.54 uH	23 pF	7995 pF
Z(ohm)=	70.8	70.8	170	170	170	170	70.8	70.8
E(E,deg)=								
I(A,deg)=								

N E T W O R K 3	IN(3) --> OUT(2) --(13)--	--(14)--	IN(2) --> OUT(3) --(15)--	--(16)--	IN(4) --> OUT(2) --(17)-	--(18)---	IN(2) --> OUT(4) --(19)--	--(20)-
Z(series)	-157 (PI)	-113 (T)	+65 (PI)	+47 (T)	-138(PI)	-332 (T)	+57 (PI)	+138 (T)
Z(parallel)	+255	+157	-106	-65	+87	+138	-36.2	-57.4
Value. ser	270 pF	374 pFH	2.77 uH	2.0 uH	308 pF	128 pF	2.4 uH	5.9 uH
Value. par.	10.8 uH	6.7 uH	399 pF	650 pF	3.7 uH	5.9 uH	1170 pF	739 pF
Z(ohm)=	170	170	70.8	70.8	170	170	70.8	70.8
E(E,deg)=								
I(A,deg)=								

Figure 2.67—At the level of network 1, we find the two 50-ohm coaxial feed lines. At the network 2 level, we have the choice between two L-networks in each leg. Next we can provide the required phase shift in either leg 1 or leg 2. For each of the four L-network inputs, we have two different line stretcher solutions (Pi or T). Since the two L-network solutions in each leg have different phase outputs, we have even more choices. There are 16 different network possibilities for matching this simple array.

Again, voltage and current are in phase, as the impedance is 170 ohms resistive. Now we can decide which L-networks to use. Our choice will depend on the values of the components involved, as well as on the phase difference that will have to be compensated for with the line stretcher network. Let's assume we have chosen solutions 1 and 3.

Looking at the voltage inputs to the above two networks, we can see that the magnitudes are the same, but the phase relationships are different (+26.6° in element 2 and -26.6° in element 1, as one example). In this case, an additional phase delay will have to be accomplished in a line stretcher in order to make up for the 26.6 + 26.6 = 53.2°. This is done with a symmetrical Pi- or T-network designed around an input (and output) impedance of 170 ohms and delivering a phase shift of 53.2°. This network can be designed using the programs

"PI-FILTER LINE STRETCHER," or "T-FILTER LINE STRETCHER" listed in Chapter VII.

There are a total of 16 different L-network/line stretcher combinations which will fulfill the system requirements. Eight of them would be installed in the feed line to element 1, and the other eight in the feed line to element 2. Keep in mind that this is only a two-element array, and yet there are 16 different combinations! Just for illustrative purposes, all of those solutions are shown in Figure 2.68. Not all are equally manageable as far as component values are concerned, as one can see. In the original Gehrke article (Ref 925), the first solution was selected, which seems to be the one with the most readily available component values.

Beyond the line stretcher, the voltages are identical in both amplitude and phase, and the terminals of networks N1 and

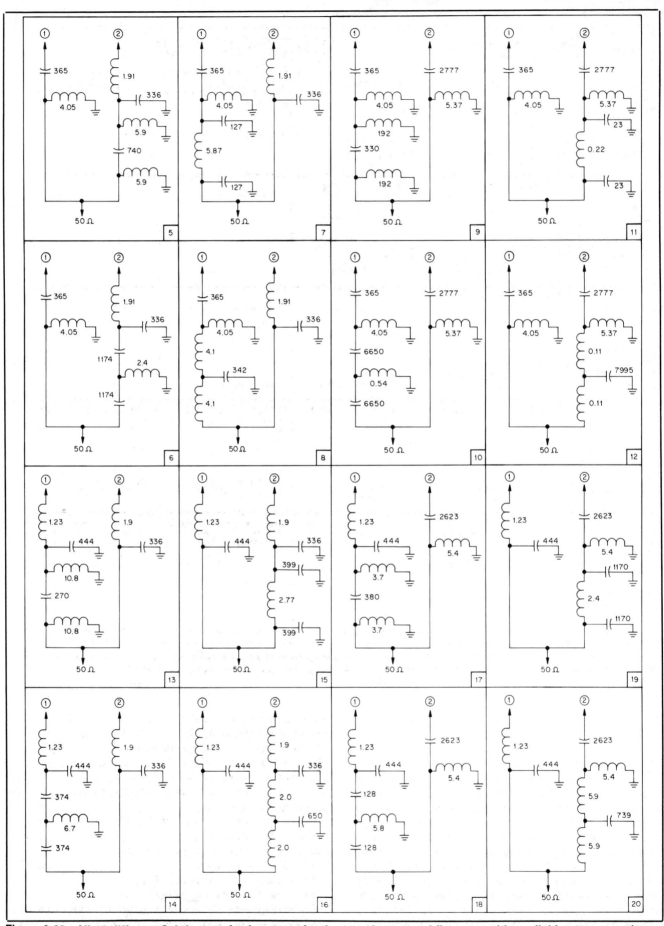

Figure 2.68—All 16 different Gehrke type feed systems for the two-element end-fire array with cardioid pattern are shown. All solutions were worked out by way of examples on the worksheet in Figure 2.67. Note that some of the networks do not have ''convenient'' component values. All inductances are in microhenrys; all capacitance values are in picofarads.

ARRAY: (2 El 1/4 wave spacing (ENDFIRE, CARDIOID (90 DEG PHASE		CABLE VELOCITY FACTOR: 0.66 MIN FEEDER LENGTH: 71.6 DEG F = 3.75 Mhz		
A N T E N N A		ELEM 1.	ELEM.2	ELEM.3	ELEM.4
	Z(1,2)= 15-J15 Z(1,3)= Z(1,4)=		Z(2,3)= Z(2,4)=	Z(3,4)=	
Z (ohm) =	21.4-J15	51.4 + J15		
E (V, deg)=	26.13 /-35.03	53.4 /-73.7		
I (A, deg)=	1 /0	1 /-90		
CABLES	50 ohm, 84 deg	50 ohm, 161 deg		
NETWORK 1 Z(series) Z(parallel) Value. ser Value. par	SWR = 2.59/1	SWR = 1.34/1		
Z(ohm)=	62.3 + j 53.7	48.22 + j 11.73		
E(E,deg)=	48.21 /+87.34	48.64 /+87.53		
I(A,deg)=	0.587 /+46.57	1.09 /+72.21		
PARALLELLING BOTH IMPEDANCES				
NETWORK 2 Z(series) Z(parallel) Value. ser Value. par				
Z(ohm)=	26.9 + j 12.1			
E(E,deg)=	48.3 /+87.4			
I(A,deg)=	1.64 /+63.18			
	SHUNT INPUT L NETW ——(1)——	SHUNT INPUT L NETW ——(2)——	SERIES REACTANCE ——(3)——	PARALLEL REACTANCE ——(4)——
NETWORK 3 Z(series)	12.83	-37.03	-12.1	-79.9
Z(parallel)	-53.96	53.96	-	-
Value. ser	0.54 UH	1146 pF	3507 pF	590 pF
Value. par	786 pF	2.29 uH	-	-
Z(ohm)=	50 + j0	50 + j0	26.9 + j0	32.3 +j0
E(E,deg)=	60.1 /+106.0	60.5 /+20.4	44.04 /+63.18	48.3 /+87.4
I(A,deg)=	1.20 /+106.6	1.21 /+20.4	1.64 /+63.18	1.49 /+87.4
			QUARTER WAVE TRANSF ——(5)——	QUARTER WAVE TRF. ——(6)——
NETWORK 4 Z(series) Z(parallel) Value. ser Value. par			Z COAX = 50 ohm	Z COAX = 37 ohm (=2 x 75 ohm in parallel
Z(ohm)= E(E,deg)= I(A,deg)=			50 + j0	50 + j0

Figure 2.69—Worksheet for the Christman feed system for the two-element end-fire cardioid array. The only lumped-constant networks used are listed in the row "network 3." The four possible solutions are discussed in the text.

N2 can be paralleled to obtain the required feed-system impedance.

Christman Method

Christman, KB8I, developed an alternative method. His approach is based on feeding the elements with the proper current magnitude and phase for points where equal voltage is present (Ref 929). At those points, the feed lines are simply connected in parallel. This ensures proper distribution of power and correct current and phase in the elements. Where the feed lines are joined at points showing identical voltages, the resulting impedance is not likely to be exactly 50 ohms. Therefore, an appropriate matching network will have to be installed at this point to ensure a properly matched line to the shack. Figure 2.69 shows the worksheet for the Christman feed method.

The difference between the Christman and Gehrke methods is Christman's use of calculated lengths of feed line to perform a given transformation, while Gehrke uses lumped-constant networks exclusively for this purpose.

It must be said, however, that we cannot apply the Christman method in all cases. The author has encountered situations where identical voltage points along any of the feed lines could not be found.

The BASIC program "FEEDLINE VOLTAGE," listed in Chapter VII, calculates the voltages along the feed lines in one-degree increments. The inputs are:
- Feed-line impedance.
- Driving-point impedances (R and X).
- Current magnitude and phase.

Continuing with the above example of a two-element configuration (90° spacing, 90° phase, equal currents, cardioid pattern), we find E1 = 48.21 + j87.34 V at a point 84° from element 1, and E2 = 48.64 + j87.53 V at a point

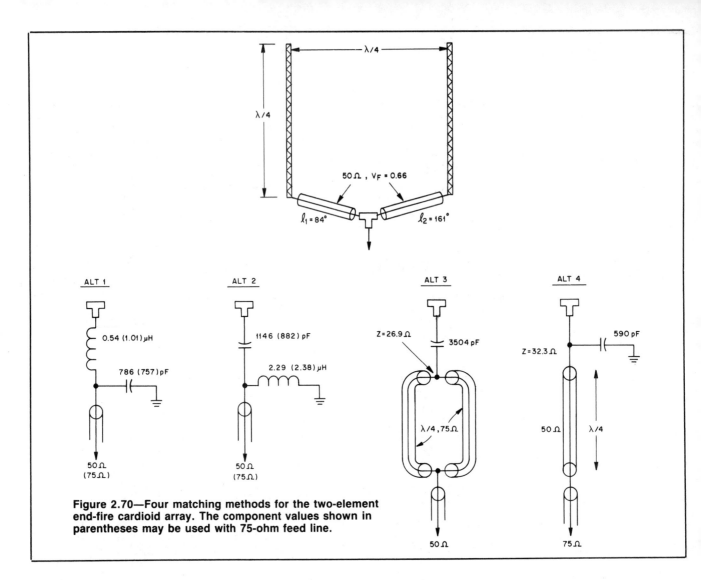

Figure 2.70—Four matching methods for the two-element end-fire cardioid array. The component values shown in parentheses may be used with 75-ohm feed line.

161° from element 2. A full printout of this case is given in Chapter VII. Figure 2.70 shows the feed system for this array as designed with the Christman procedure.

If element 1 is fed with a ¼ λ feed line and element 2 is fed with the same ¼ λ length plus an additional ¼ λ delay line (as is advocated in most amateur literature), one can see from the printout in Chapter VII that the voltages at 90° on line 1 and at 180° on line 2 are not identical. Nearly identical voltages can be found at the 90° point on line 1 and the 163° point on line 2. This is only so if the quarter-wave lines as well as the delay line are made of 50-ohm line. With 75-ohm coax, this statement no longer holds true, as can be verified by running the "FEEDLINE VOLTAGE" program in Chapter VII. This means that a 73° phasing line produces almost exactly 90° of delay in the two-element cardioid array using quarter-wave spacing, but only when using 50-ohm feed lines to the elements. The impedance in the T junction is $25 + j45$ ohms, which can easily be matched to 50 ohms by an L-network. This can be designed with the program "L-NETWORK" listed in Chapter VII.

To design an appropriate L-network, we must calculate the impedances in both cables at the T junction point in order to find the resulting parallel impedance at the junction. This can be done with the BASIC program "T-JUNCTION" listed in Chapter VII, or by using the Smith Chart. Best accuracy can be obtained by the numerical method.

Connecting the two impedances ($62.3 + j53.7$ ohms and

$42.82 + j11.73$ ohms) in parallel yields a total impedance of $26.9 + j12.1$ ohms.

The BASIC program "L-NETWORK" can help us to quickly design the proper L-network to transform $26.9 + j12.1$ ohms to 50 ohms. From the two available solutions, we have chosen the network which, for 3.8 MHz, consists of a 0.54-μH coil and a 786-pF capacitor connected as shown in Figure 2.70.

In this particular case, an alternative solution would be to tune out the inductive reactance (12.1 ohms) with a series capacitor, and then use a quarter-wave coaxial transformer, which must have an impedance of:

$$Z = \sqrt{26.9 \times 50} = 36.7 \text{ ohms}$$

This value can be approached by putting two 75-ohm feed lines (RG-59, RG-11, or 75-ohm CATV cable) in parallel. Make sure both lines have identical electrical lengths (both ¼ λ). Figure 2.70 shows the alternative matching methods for this two-element array. The value of the series capacitor is given by:

$$C = \frac{10^6}{2\pi f X_C}$$

The required value for a frequency of 3.75 MHz is 3504 pF. If we use a parallel reactance, a 590-pF capacitor will tune

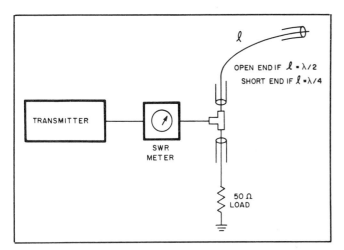

OPEN END IF $\ell = \lambda/2$
SHORT END IF $\ell = \lambda/4$

TRANSMITTER

SWR METER

50 Ω LOAD

Figure 2.71—Very precise trimming of ¼ λ and ½ λ lines can be done by connecting the line under test in parallel with a 50-ohm dummy load and watching the SWR meter while the feed line length or the transmit frequency is changed. See text for details.

out the reactance. This seems to be the better choice from a component value point of view. The final impedance will be 32.2 ohms however, and either a direct feed with two parallel 60-ohm cables, or a 50-ohm quarter-wave transformer will provide a good match to a 75-ohm feed line. (60-ohm cable is mentioned frequently in this chapter because it is commonly available in Europe.)

One way to adjust quarter- or half-wavelength cables exactly for a given frequency is shown in Figure 2.71. Connect the transmitter through a good SWR meter (the author uses a Bird model 43) to a 50-ohm dummy load. Insert a coaxial "T" connector at the output of the SWR bridge. The length of coax to be adjusted will be connected to this point and the reading of the SWR bridge will indicate where the length is resonant. Quarter-wave lines should be short-circuited at the end. On the resonant frequency, the quarter-wave cable represents an infinite impedance (assuming lossless cable) to the T junction. At the resonant frequency, the SWR will not change when the quarter-wave shorted stub is connected in parallel with the dummy load. At slightly different frequencies, the stub will present small values of inductance or capacitance across the dummy load, and these will influence the SWR reading accordingly. The author has found this method very accurate, and the lengths can be trimmed precisely (to within a few kHz).

When adjusting half-wave lengths, the far end should remain open-circuited. Odd lengths can also be trimmed this way if one first calculates the required length difference between a quarter (or half) wavelength on the desired frequency and the actual length of the line on the desired frequency. For example, if you need a 73° length of feed line on 3.8 MHz, that cable would be 90° long on (3.8 × 90/73) = 4.685 MHz. The cable can now be cut to a quarter wavelength on 4.685 MHz using the method described above. The dip oscillator method isn't the most accurate way to cut a 90° length of feed line, and it often accounts for length variations of 2 or 3° (for a quarter-wavelength). One can also use a noise bridge and use the line under test to effectively short-circuit the output of the noise bridge to the receiver.

When all the directional switching of an array has to be done with the same feeding and phasing network, it is of great importance to provide maximum symmetry between the elements. Gehrke trims the radiator length and uses extra radials to equalize the self impedances of the elements (all other elements decoupled).

In the discussion of some popular array designs, we will list mutual and feed impedances. These can be used for designing the feed network, but Gehrke emphasizes that the designer should actually measure the impedances. Some methods of doing this are described in Ref 923.

Commercially available noise bridges will almost certainly not give the required degree of accuracy, as rather small deviations in resistance and reactance must be accurately recorded. A genuine impedance bridge is more suitable, but with care, a well-constructed and carefully calibrated noise bridge may be used. Two excellent articles covering noise bridge design and construction were published: one written by Hubbs, W6BXI, and Doting, W6NKU (Ref 1607), and the other by Gehrke, K2BT (Ref 1610). These articles are recommended reading for anyone considering using a noise bridge in array design and measurement work. The computer program "RC/RL TRANSFORMATION," listed in Chapter VII is very handy for transforming the value of the noise bridge capacitor, connected in parallel with either the variable resistor or the unknown impedance, first to a parallel reactance value and then to an equivalent reactance value for a series LC circuit. This enables the immediate computation of the real and imaginary parts of the series impedance equivalent, expressed in "a $+jb$" form.

Collins Method

After an unsuccessful attempt to use Wilkinson power dividers (see Section 2.12.4) in array feed systems, Collins, W1FC, developed a broadband phasing/feed system which is applicable to all quadrature-fed arrays. (Quadrature-fed arrays are arrays where the element feed current delays are multiples of 90°.) Actual arrays using a feeding/phasing system with Wilkinson power dividers were measured to have a current amplitude unbalance of 6:1, while the phase was as much as 40° away from the desired value.

Collins makes use of a very specific property of ¼ λ long feed lines: The magnitude of the input current of a quarter-wavelength transmission line is equal to the output voltage divided by the characteristic impedance of the line, and is independent of the load impedance. In addition, the input current phase lags the output voltage by 90°, and is also independent of the load impedance.

Let us work out the example of the two-element end-fire array (¼-wave spacing, 90° out of phase, cardioid pattern). We already know the element driving impedances (21.4 $-j15$ ohms for the zero-degree element and 51.4 $+j15$ ohms for the $-90°$ element).

We can run the "COAX TRANSFORMER" program, and will find the following values at the input end of the quarter-wave feed lines:

Feed line to the 0° element
$I_{out} = 1A \angle 0°$
$Z_{out} = 21.4 -j15$ ohms
$Z_{in} = 87.33 +j54.91$ ohms
$I_{in} = 0.52$ A $\angle +54.97°$
$E_{in} = 50$ V $\angle +90°$
SWR = 2.59:1

Feed line to the $-90°$ element
$I_{out} = 1A \angle -90°$ $E_{in} = 50$ V $\angle 0.0°$
$Z_{out} = 51.4 +j15$ ohms   SWR = 1.34:1
$Z_{in} = 44.82 -j13.08$ ohms
$I_{in} = 1.07$ A $\angle 16.27°$

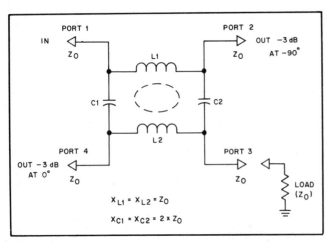

Figure 2.72—Hybrid coupler providing two −3-dB outputs with a phase difference of 90°. Coils L1 and L2 are closely coupled. See text for construction details.

Collins, W1FC, now uses a quadrature hybrid coupler, shown in Figure 2.72. The coupler divides the input power (at port 1) equally between ports 2 and 4, with no power output at port 3, if all 4 port impedances are the same. When the impedances are not the same, however, power will be dissipated in the load resistor connected to port 4, but the phase shift will remain essentially unchanged. Such hybrid couplers can provide a high degree of directivity, and reflected power at any of the two main output ports will only show up at port 4. Collins reports 25 dB of directivity with his designs.

Hybrid Coupler Construction

The values of the hybrid coupler components are:

$X_{L1} = X_{L2} = 50$ ohms ($=$ system impedance)
$X_{C1} = X_{C2} = 2 \times 50$ ohms

For 3.65 MHz, the component values are:

$$L1 = L2 = \frac{50}{2\pi \times 3.65} = 2.18\ \mu H$$

$$C1 = C2 = \frac{10^6}{2\pi \times 3.65 \times 2 \times 50} = 436\ pF$$

When constructing the coupler, one should take into account the capacitance between the wires of coils L1 and L2—which can be as high as 10% of the required total value for C1 and C2. The correct procedure is to first wind the tightly coupled coils L1 and L2, then measure the inter-winding capacitance and deduct that value from the theoretical value of C1 and C2 to determine the required capacitor value. For best coupling, the coils should be wound on powdered-iron toroidal cores. The T225-2 ($\mu = 10$) cores from Amidon are a good choice for power levels well in excess of 2 kW. The larger the core, the higher the power-handling capability. Consult Table 16 for core data. The T225-2 core has an AL factor of 120, which results in a required number of turns of:

$$N = 100 \sqrt{\frac{2.18}{120}} = 13.5\ turns$$

The coils should be wound with AWG 14 or AWG 16 multi-strand Teflon-covered wire. The two coils can be wound with the turns of both coils wound adjacent to one another, or the

two wires of the two coils can be twisted together at a rate of 5 to 7 turns per inch before winding them (equally spaced) onto the core.

At this point, the inductance of the coils must be measured (using an impedance bridge or an LC meter) and trimmed as closely as possible to the required value of 2.18 μH for each coil. Moving the windings on the core can help you fine tune the inductance of the coil. Now the inter-winding capacitance can be measured. This is the value that must be subtracted from the value calculated above (436 pF). A final check of the hybrid coupler can be made using a vector analyzer or a dual-trace oscilloscope. Terminating ports 2, 3 and 4 with 50-ohm resistors, one can now fine tune the hybrid for perfect 90° phase shift between ports 2 and 4. The output voltage amplitudes should be equal.

The SWR on the quarter-wave feed lines to the two elements (in the cardioid pattern configuration) is not 1:1. Therefore, the impedance at the end of the quarter-wave feed lines will depend on the element impedance and the characteristic impedance of the feed lines. We want to choose the feed-line impedance such that a minimum amount of power is dissipated in the port 3 terminating resistor.

We can also design the hybrid coupler with an impedance which is different from the quarter-wave feed line impedance in order to realize a lower SWR at ports 2 and 4 of the coupler. The load resistor at port 3 must of course have the same ohmic value as the hybrid design impedance. With the aid of the program "SWR ITERATION" listed in Chapter VII, one can scan the SWR values at ports 2 and 4 for a range of design impedances. The results can be cross-checked by measuring the power in the terminating resistor by alternately connecting 50- and 75-ohm quarter-wave feed lines to the elements.

Table 21 shows the performance of a 3-dB hybrid coupler made for a design frequency of 3.7 MHz, and measured from 3.5 through 4.0 MHz. The isolation of the coupler was measured as 23 dB with the unused ports terminated.

Table 21

Performance of a 3-dB Hybrid Coupler, Design Freq = 3.7 MHz

Frequency (MHz)	Output 1		Output 2	
		Ref Port		90° Port
	Power (dB)	Phase (deg)	Power (dB)	Phase (deg)
3.5	−3.15	0	−2.85	92.5
3.6	−3.05	0	−2.95	91.5
3.7	−3.05	0	−3.05	90.0
3.8	−2.85	0	−3.15	88.5
3.9	−2.75	0	−3.25	87.5
4.0	−2.65	0	−3.35	87.0

Lewallen Method

Lewallen, W7EL, uses a method which, like the Collins method, takes advantage of the specific properties of quarter-wave feed lines (Lewallen calls it "current forcing"). The required phase shift is obtained by a different method, however. Figures 2.73 and 2.74 show the Lewallen method applied to the two-element end-fire array with quarter-wave spacing and fed 90° out of phase. Refer to the Collins method described above for the voltage and impedance values at the ends of the quarter-wave feed lines.

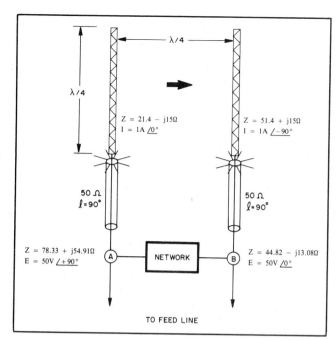

Figure 2.73—The elements in the Lewallen-type feed system are fed with quarter-wave feed lines. An appropriate network is installed between the ends of both feed lines in order to ensure identical voltages at the point where the feed lines are joined. The feed point can be either A or B.

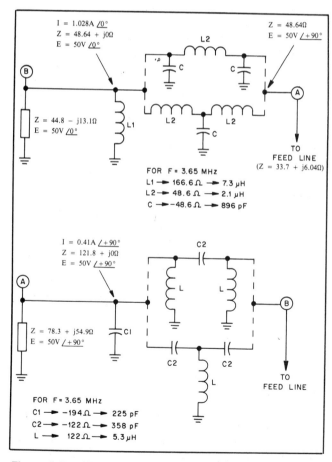

Figure 2.74—The Lewallen method of network design is straightforward and is explained in the text. This figure shows both the Pi- and T-network alternatives for either A or B as the network feed point. A suitable matching network must be added at the feed point to match the array to a 50-ohm line.

A network must be installed between points A and B that will provide the correct voltage transformation. The array can be fed at either point A or point B, but the same impedance transformation network cannot be used at both points.

If the array is to be fed at point A, the impedance at point B (44.82 −j13.08 ohms) is the output impedance of the network. The standard procedure is to calculate a shunt impedance to be placed across the above output impedance that will make this impedance resistive. This can be done with the program "SHUNT IMPEDANCE NETWORK." In this case, a parallel reactance of 166.66 ohms will produce a resistive impedance of 48.64 ohms. The voltage across this impedance is still 50V $\angle 0°$.

Now we can provide the required 90° phase shift by connecting either a Pi- or T-network line stretcher between points A and B. These networks can easily be designed using the "PI-FILTER LINE STRETCHER" or "T-FILTER LINE STRETCHER" programs. Make sure you specify the correct input and output phase angles. In a case where 90 or 270° of phase shift is required, the values of the parallel and series elements of the networks have a straightforward relationship with the characteristic impedance of the filter, as can be seen from Figure 2.74. The figure shows both the Pi- and T-network alternatives and component values for a design frequency of 3.65 MHz. In this particular example, tuning out the reactance of the 44.82 −j13.08-ohm impedance with a 166.6-ohm reactance results in an impedance which is very close to the impedance of a standard 50-ohm cable. Phase shifts other than 90° can also be obtained, so this method is not limited to use with quadrature-fed arrays.

The feed-point impedance at point A is the result of paralleling 48.46 +j0 ohms and 87.33 +j54.9 ohms. The result is 33.68 +j6.04 ohms. This value will require a matching network (an L-network or a stub) to present a low SWR to a 50-ohm feed line.

If the feed point is to be at the B element, the approach is the same as for the A element. The designer must choose the alternative that is most appropriate based on component values and so on. In either case, the correctness of the calculations can be checked by comparing the power at the radiating elements to the power in the branches of the T junction (A or B) of the feed system. For the example above, the power in the "back" element is 21.4 W. The "front" element power is 51.4 W. The power levels at the junction point A are: 21.4 W and 51.4 W, which are identical to those at the antenna elements, as all elements are considered to be lossless.

2.11.1.5 Popular Vertical Arrays

End-Fire Two-Element Array Producing a Cardioid Pattern

Two verticals spaced ¼ λ apart and fed 90° out of phase is a popular configuration on the low bands. The gain is 3 dB over a single vertical and the forward lobe is very wide (3 dB forward beamwidth = 170°). The pattern is shown in Figure 2.63, and element data is given in Table 22. Mutual impedances and driving impedances shown here are typical values, and the builder of such an array should measure and calculate all relevant values as explained in Section 2.11.1.4. The BASIC computer programs in Chapter VII were developed so that no high-level algebra knowledge is required to use and understand them.

The design of the Gehrke, Christman, Collins, and Lewallen feed systems for this particular array was explained in detail in Section 2.11.1.4. Figure 2.75 shows a possible final

Table 22
Element Data for 2-el Vertical Array (Cardioid Pattern)

Element	Current Ratio	Phase Angle (deg)	Mutual Impedance (ohms)	Driving Impedance (ohms)
1	1	0	$Z(12) = 15 - j15$	$Z(1) = 21.4 - j15$
2	1	-90		$Z(2) = 51.4 + j15$

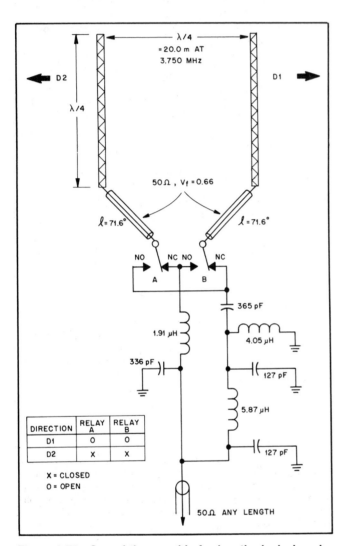

Figure 2.75—One of the possible feed methods designed according to the Gehrke method. The values were calculated on the worksheet in Figure 2.67.

arrangement for the Gehrke method as suggested in the original Gehrke article (Ref 924 and 925). The Christman feed method (using an L-network to match the system to a 50-ohm feed line) is shown in Figure 2.79. The worksheets used for designing both feed systems are shown in Figures 2.67 and 2.69. The feed method shown in Figure 2.80 is the "almost correct" method, which uses a 73° long phasing line to produce a 90° delay. This method is shown because it is very easy to convert the incorrect but commonly used feed system using a 90° phasing line into an almost perfect feed system by simply shortening the delay line from 90 to 73°, and by removing any Wilkinson power divider present. Directivity switching arrangements are also shown in their respective figures.

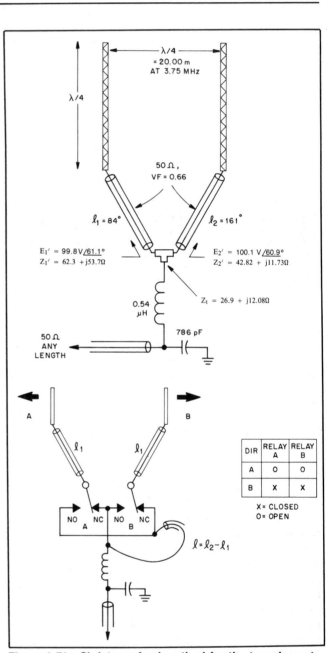

Figure 2.79—Christman feed method for the two-element end-fire array. Directivity switching can be done easily, as shown. Note that the actual electrical length of the delay line ($\ell = \ell2 - \ell1$) is only 77° to produce a 90° phase delay.

Figure 2.76 shows the wiring of the array with the Collins feed system, including the switching harness. Positions 1 and 2 are for the two end-fire cardioid patterns. In position 3, both elements are fed in phase, and an L-network can be used to match the paralleled quarter-wave lines to the feed line.

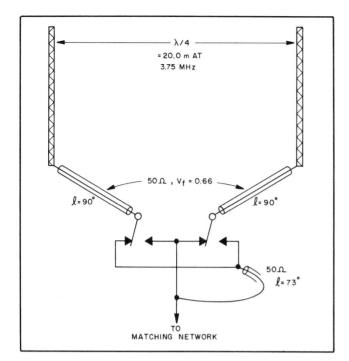

**Figure 2.80—Two-element end-fire arrays that use 90°
long phasing lines to achieve the additional 90° phase lag
can be improved by shortening the delay line from 90 to
73°. The results are almost ideal. The impedance at the
T junction is not 50 ohms, so an additional L-network may
be required to obtain a low SWR on the feed line to the
shack.**

In this configuration, the array will have a bidirectional
broadside pattern with a gain of 0.9 dB over a single vertical.
The front to side ratio is only 3 dB. The feed impedance of
two quarter-wave spaced elements fed in phase is
$51.4 -j14$ ohms (computed with program "DRIVING
IMPEDANCE." At the end of quarter-wave, 50-ohm feed
lines, this impedance is $44.8 +j13.1$ ohms (as computed with
the "COAX TRANSFORMER" program). Paralleling the
two feed lines yields an impedance of $22.41 +j6.54$ ohms.
The "L-NETWORK" program allows the design of an
L-network with a series inductance of 0.8 μH and a parallel
capacitance of 967 pF for a design frequency of 3.65 MHz.

Two-Element End-Fire Array, 1/8-wave Spacing, 135 Degrees
Out of Phase, Equal Current Magnitudes

This array is known as the ZL-special or the HB9CV array.
The gain of this array is 4.4 dB, with a −3 dB beamwidth
of 135°. The element data is as follows: *Element 1*: Current
Ratio = 1, Phase Angle = 0°, Mutual Impedance Z12 =
$30 -j3$ ohms, Driving Impedance $Z(1) = 13.1 -j19.1$ ohms.
Element 2: Current Ratio = 1, Phase Angle = −135°,
Mutual Impedance Z21 = $30 -j3$ ohms, Driving Impedance
$Z(2) = 17.3 +j23.3$ ohms. Because the elements are not fed
in quadrature in this array, the Collins feed method cannot
be used; the Gehrke, Christman, or Lewallen methods can
be used, however.

Lewallen Method

Using the "COAX TRANSFORMER" program listed in
Chapter VII, we first calculate Z, I, and E at the ends of the
four quarter-wave feed lines.

At the end of the feed line to the back element:

$Z = 61.1 +j81.0$ ohms

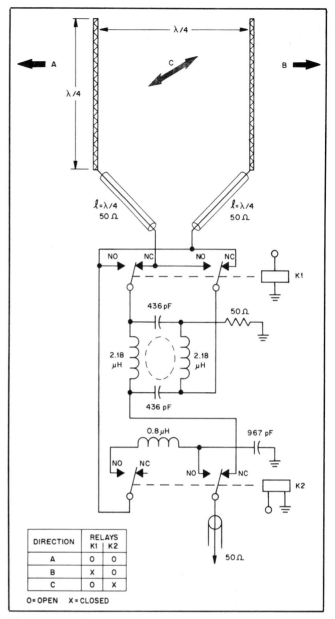

**Figure 2.76—Collins-type feed system for a two-element
array with elements spaced ¼ λ apart. In directions A and
B, the array produces the end-fire cardioid pattern. A gain
of 0.9 dB is achieved in the bidirectional (broadside)
directions (C).**

$E = 50\ V\ \underline{/90°}$
$I = 0.463\ A\ \underline{/23.33°}$

At the end of the feed line to the front element:

$Z = 51.35 -j69.2$ ohms
$E = 50\ V\ \underline{/-45°}$
$I = 0.58\ A\ \underline{/4.8°}$
$SWR = 3.58:1$

We can choose either A or B as the array feed point (see
Figure 2.77). If we choose point A, point B becomes the
network output, and the network output impedance is
$51.35 -j69.2$ ohms. The shunt impedance (calculated with
the "SHUNT IMPEDANCE NETWORK" program)
required to achieve a resistive impedance is 107.3 ohms. At
this point, we need to insert either a Pi- or T-network line
stretcher between A and B to take care of the 135° phase shift.

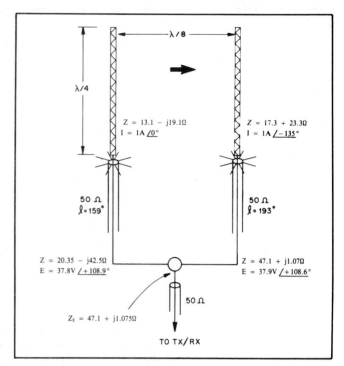

Figure 2.78—When the elements in the array are fed as shown, the impedance at the T junction is very close to 50 ohms, so no additional matching for the coaxial line will be required. Notice that an extra 135° of phase shift between the elements is achieved with only a 34° difference in feed-line length.

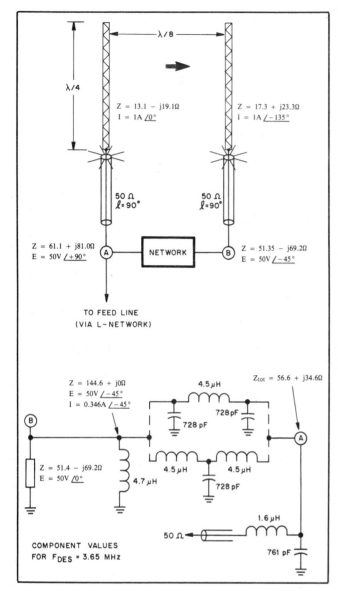

Figure 2.77—If the Lewallen-type feed system is used in the ZL-special end-fire array, the array may be fed at either point A or point B. The matching network will be different depending on the feed point chosen.

These networks can be designed with the help of the corresponding programs in Chapter VII.

The impedance at point A (which can be calculated with the "T-JUNCTION" program) is 56.6 + j34.6 ohms. An L-network can provide a good match to a 50-ohm feed line.

Christman Method

Figure 2.78 shows the Christman feed method for this array. Using the program "FEEDLINE VOLTAGE," one can scan both 50-ohm feed lines for points where the voltages are the same on both lines. Two such points are found in this case, one 159° from the back element and at 193° from the front element, and the other at 34° from the back element and at 156° from the front element. There is a clear choice here because the second set of points occurs at areas of high variation of feed line voltage for small variations in distance, making these points a poor choice. Using the second set of points would also decrease the bandwidth of the array. Neither of these problems are encountered with the first set of

points—even though more feed line will be required to reach them, they are still the best choice.

The feed lines can now simply be paralleled at these points. The impedances can be calculated using the "COAX TRANSFORMER" program, and the combined impedance can then be calculated with the "T-JUNCTION" program. The impedance for this array comes out to 47.1 + j1.07 ohms, which yields an SWR of 1.07:1 when connected to a 50-ohm cable, and will require no further matching. This system looks like the best choice, with the only minor drawback being the slightly greater amount of feed line required to perform the matching and phasing.

Two-Element Broadside Array with Half-Wave Spacing, Fed In Phase

Bidirectional broadside radiation can be obtained with verticals spaced ½ λ apart and fed in phase. The theoretical gain of a two-element array is 4.0 dB over a single vertical. One can also design a system with more verticals. Swank, W8HXR (Ref 906), describes a four-element array consisting of two side-by-side end-fire arrays with a cardioid pattern. The groups are spaced ½ λ apart, placed side-by-side, and fed in phase. The original four-element 80-meter vertical array by Atchley, W1HKK (now W1CF) (Ref 930), used four quarter-wave verticals all spaced ¼ λ apart with a switchable phasing arrangement. This allowed all four verticals to be fed in phase for broadside radiation, or with 90° of phase shift between each vertical to achieve end-fire radiation (a four-element cardioid array). The element data for the two-element broadside array is given in Table 23.

Because this arrangement shows driving point impedances which are (theoretically) equal for both elements, we can use

Table 23

Element Data for 2-el Vertical Array (Broadside Pattern)
Spacing = ½ λ, Fed in Phase

Element	Current Ratio	Phase Angle (deg)	Mutual Impedance (ohms)	Driving Impedance (ohms)
1	1	0	Z(12) = −9 −j13	Z(1) = 27.4 −j13
2	1	0		Z(2) = 27.4 −j13

Note: Z(21) = Z(12)

```
|                                                                                      |
|  ARRAY: (2 El 1/2 wave spacing      |     CABLE VELOCITY FACTOR: 0.66                |
|         (BROADSIDE, BIDIRECTIONAL   |     MIN FEEDER LENGTH: 132 DEG                 |
|         (IN PHASE                   |     F = 3.75 MHz                               |
|----------------------------------------------------------------------------------------
|A|            |      ELEM 1.       |     ELEM.2      |      ELEM.3     |     ELEM.4    |
|N|------------|--------------------|----------------|----------------|--------------|
|T|            | Z(1,2)= -9 -j13    | Z(2,3)=        | Z(3,4)=        |              |
|E|            | Z(1,3)=            | Z(2,4)=        |                |              |
|N|            | Z(1,4)=            |                |                |              |
|N|------------|--------------------|----------------|----------------|--------------|
|A|Z (ohm)   = | 27.4-j13           | 27.4 -j13      |                |              |
|S|E (V, deg)= | 30.33 / -25.38     | 30.33 / -25.38 |                |              |
| |I (A, deg)= | 1 / 0              | 1 / 0          |                |              |
|=|===========================================================================|
| | CABLE --> | 50 ohm, 138 deg    | 50 ohm, 138 deg|                |              |
|N|Z(series)  |                    |                |                |              |
|E|Z(parallel)|   SWR = 1.99/1     |  SWR = 1.99/1  |                |              |
|T|Value. ser |                    |                |                |              |
|W|Value. par.|                    |                |                |              |
|O|   Z(ohm)= | 59.77-j37.25       | 59.77-j37.25   |                |              |
|R|E(E,deg)=  | 47.68 / +115.27    | 47.68 / +115.27|                |              |
|K|I(A,deg)=  | 0.677 / +147.2     | 0.677 / +147.2 |                |              |
|1|===========================================================================|
| | PARALLEL BOTH COAX. CABLES                                                  |
|N|Z(series)  |                                                                |
|E|Z(parallel)|                                                                |
|T|Value. ser |                                                                |
|W|Value. par.|                                                                |
|O|   Z(ohm)= | 29.88 -j18.62                                                  |
|R|E(E,deg)=  | 47.68 / +115.27                                                |
|K|I(A,deg)=  | 1.35 / +147.2                                                  |
|2|===========================================================================|
| |           |SHUNT INPUT L NETW |SHUNT INPUT L NETW| SERIES REACTANCE  | PARALLEL REACT. |
| |           |-------(3)-------  |-------(4)------- | ------(1)-------  | ------(2)------- |
|N|Z(series)  |+43.14             |-5.9              | 18.62             | -               |
|E|Z(parallel)|-60.93             |+60.93            | -                 | 66.57           |
|T|Value. ser |1.83 uH            |7195 pF           | 0.79 uH           | -               |
|W|Value. par.|696 pF             |2.59 uH           | -                 | 2.83 uH         |
|O|   Z(ohm)= |50 + j0            |50 + j0           | 29.88 + j0        | 41.5+j0         |
|R|E(E,deg)=  |52.34 / -173.4     |52.34 / +107.8    | 40.50 / +147.2    | 47.68 / +115.3  |
|K|I(A,deg)=  |1.05 / -173.4      |1.05 / +107.8     | 1.35 / +147.2     | 1.15 / +115.3   |
|3|===========================================================================|
| |           |                   |                  | QUARTER WAVE TRANSF|                |
| |           |                   |                  | ------(1')------- |                |
|N|Z(series)  |                   |                  | Z = 38 ohm        | SWR is 1.2/1    |
|E|Z(parallel)|                   |                  | (=2x75 ohm in     | without further |
|T|Value. ser |                   |                  | parallel)         | matching        |
|W|Value. par.|                   |                  |                   |                |
|O|   Z(ohm)= |                   |                  | 50 + j0           |                |
|R|E(E,deg)=  |                   |                  |                   |                |
|K|I(A,deg)=  |                   |                  |                   |                |
|4|                                                                            |
```

Figure 2.81—The feed system for the two-element half-wave-spaced broadside array is very simple. The only lumped-constant networks are at the network 3 level. There are two options for matching: We can use one of two L-networks to match to a 50-ohm line, or we can work with series or parallel reactances at the T junction to tune out the reactance, and transform the remaining resistive impedances with quarter-wave transformers.

a simple feed system, consisting of two equal-length feed lines, which are paralleled for equal power/current division. The design worksheet is shown in Figure 2.81.

One approach to designing this feed system is to first determine the required physical length of both feed lines. When the elements are ½ λ apart (39.5 m at 3.8 MHz) we need two feed lines, each 20 meters long, to reach the midpoint between the elements. Next we need to calculate the electrical

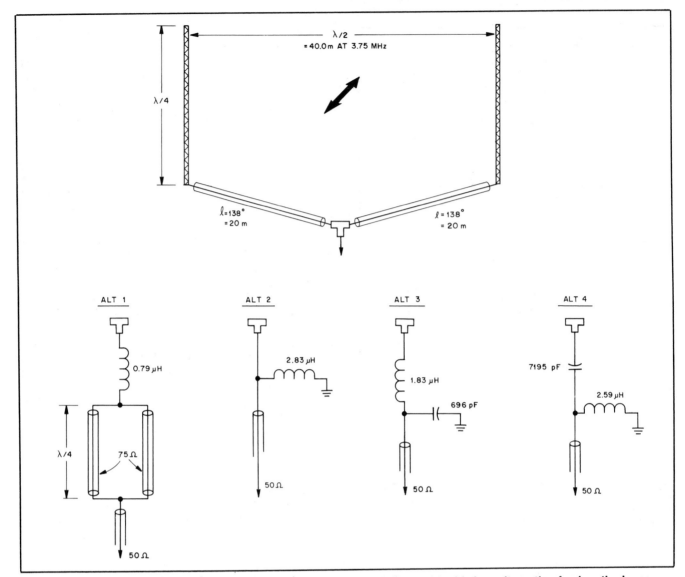

Figure 2.82—Two-element ½ λ-spaced broadside array (elements fed in phase) with four alternative feed methods, as calculated on the worksheet in Figure 2.81.

length (in degrees) of these 20-meter cables on 3.8 MHz. One wavelength on 3.8 MHz is:

$$\lambda = \frac{c}{f}$$

where λ = wavelength, c = 3 × 10⁸ (the speed of light) and f is the frequency in hertz. Using this equation:

$$\lambda = \frac{3 \times 10^8}{3.8 \times 10^6} = 78.9 \text{ meters}$$

The length of a one-wavelength solid polyethylene insulated cable (such as RG-8, RG-213, RG-11 or RG-58) with a velocity factor of 0.66 is 78.9 × 0.66 = 52.1 meters. Since one electrical wavelength is 360 degrees, to find the electrical length of a 20-meter-long cable we can write:

$$\frac{\ell}{360} = \frac{20}{52.1}$$

And solving for ℓ, we have

$$\ell = \frac{360 \times 20}{52.1} = 138.2°$$

With the "COAX TRANSFORMER" program, we will determine the impedance on the 50-ohm feed lines at 138° from the load (element). The impedance at this point is 59.77 −j37.25 ohms. At the point where the coaxial cables are connected in parallel, the impedance will be halved, so Z = 29.88 −j18.62 ohms. This is the impedance we will have to match to the feed line to the shack.

Assuming the feed line is of the 50-ohm variety, we can use a quarter-wave transformer (after having tuned out the 18.62 ohms of capacitive reactance with a coil having the conjugate reactance). The coil value needed is:

$$L = \frac{18.63}{2\pi \times 3.8} = 0.79 \ \mu H$$

The required value for the quarter-wave feed line transformer is:

$$Z = \sqrt{29 \times 50} = 38.7 \text{ ohms}$$

Two paralleled 75-ohm quarter-wave transmission lines can be used in this case. Figure 2.82 shows the feed system.

Another possible solution uses a parallel inductance of

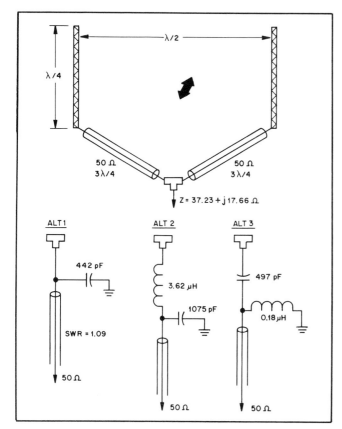

Figure 2.83—In order to achieve proper matching and phasing (even when the feed impedances of the two elements are not identical), ¾ λ-long feed lines are used. The resulting impedance at the T junction can be matched to a 50-ohm line with one of two L-networks, or an almost perfect match can be obtained by merely connecting a capacitor across the T junction.

better to use a ¼ λ or ¾ λ-long feed lines. These odd quarter-wavelength long feeders have unique properties described in Section 2.11.1.4 and provide the correct in-phase current feed even if the element impedances are different. This is not the case with random (equal) lengths.

Because two quarter-wave line lengths would not reach the mid-point between the two radiators, we will have to use ¾ λ long feed lines (270°). Using the "COAX TRANSFORMER" program we can calculate the impedances at the end of two ¾ λ-long 50-ohm feed lines feeding the elements, which both have a $27.4 - j13$ ohm impedance. The values are $74.47 + j35.33$ ohms. The SWR on both element feed lines is 1.99:1. The SWR for reactive loads can be calculated with the "SWR VALUE" program listed in Chapter VII. When connected in parallel, the impedance becomes $37.33 + j17.66$ ohms, which represents an SWR of 1.65:1 when connected to a 50-ohm line at the T-junction. We must include an L-network in this line to provide a 1:1 SWR. An alternative is to connect a shunt capacitor at the T-junction, which would provide a 1.09:1 SWR on a 50-ohm line. The calculation can be done with the "SHUNT IMPEDANCE NETWORK" program. The feed system schematic is shown in Figure 2.83.

A similar feed system can also be designed using 75-ohm cables feeding the antennas. Using two ¾ λ-long feed lines (yielding a physical length of 40.68 m at 3.65 MHz with cable with a velocity factor of 0.66, such as RG-11), the impedance at the T-point is $83.78 + j39.75$ ohms. The SWR on a 75-ohm feed line is 1.66:1, which requires an L-network to impedance-match the line to the shack on either a 75- or 50-ohm line.

If we want to use 75-ohm cable with expanded polyethylene insulation, the velocity factor is usually about 0.80. In any case, the velocity factor must be measured before using foam type coaxial cable in array feed systems. This can be done by the method described in Section 2.11.1.4, where the electrical quarter-wave length is compared to the physical length of the sample under test.

2.83 μH across the T junction. The value can be computed with the BASIC program "SHUNT IMPEDANCE NET-WORK." Alternatively, we could use an L-network right at the T junction. The resulting SWR on a 50 ohm line is 1.2:1, which is acceptable. The values can be computed with the BASIC program "L-NETWORK." The computed values are 1.83 μH for the series coil and 696 pF for the shunt capacitor, or 7195 pF for the series capacitor and 2.59 μH for the shunt inductor. (The latter solution seems less attractive because of the 7195 pF capacitor value.) See Figure 2.82 for the correct wiring of these networks.

In practice, we often see that both the self impedances and the driving impedances of the two in-phase verticals will be slightly different because of differences in such things as ground systems and surrounding objects. In such a case it is

Two-Element Bidirectional End-Fire Array, ½-wave Spacing, Fed 180 Degrees Out of Phase

Bidirectional end-fire radiation can be obtained with verticals spaced ½ λ and fed currents that are equal in amplitude and 180° out of phase. The gain for this two-element array is about 4 dB over a single-element vertical.

The element data for the two-element broadside array is given in Table 24. In this arrangement, the driving-point impedances are also theoretically equal for both elements. Here again, the feed system will be rather simple. Provided both impedances are really identical, the feed system can consist of two equal-length feeders with another feeder (an extra 180° long) in one line to obtain the required phase shift.

Table 24

Element Data for 2-el Vertical Array (Broadside Pattern)
Spacing = ½ λ, Fed 180° Out of Phase

Element	Current Ratio	Phase Angle (deg)	Mutual Impedance (ohms)	Driving Impedance (ohms)
1	1	0	$Z(12) = -9 - j13$	$Z(1) = 45.4 + j13$
2	1	−180		$Z(2) = 45.4 + j13$

Note: $Z(21) = Z(12)$

ARRAY:	(2 El 1/2 wave spacing (ENDFIRE, BIDIRECTIONAL (180 DEG PHASE		CABLE VELOCITY FACTOR: 0.66 F = 3.75 MHz		
		ELEM 1.	ELEM.2	ELEM.3	ELEM.4
A N T E N N A		Z(1,2)= -9-j13 Z(1,3)= Z(1,4)=	Z(2,3)= Z(2,4)=	Z(3,4)=	
A S I =	Z (ohm) = E (V, deg)= I (A, deg)=	45.4 + j13 47.22 / +15.97 1 / 0	45.4 + j 13 47.22 / -164.02 1 / -180		
	CABLES -->	50 ohm, 138 deg	50 ohm, 318 deg		
N E T W O R K 1	Z(series) Z(parallel) Value. ser Value. par. Z(ohm)= E(E,deg)= I(A,deg)=	SWR = 1.33/1 37.51 - j1.09 41.28 / +144.8 1.1 / +146.5	SWR = 1.33/1 37.51 -j1.09 41.28 / +144.8 1.1 / +146.5		
N E T W O R K 2	PARALLEL BOTH COAXIAL CABLES Z(series) Z(parallel) Value. ser Value. par. Z(ohm)= E(E,deg)= I(A,deg)=	18.75 -j0.545 41.28 / +144.8 2.20 / +146.5			
N E T W O R K 3	Z(series) Z(parallel) Value. ser Value. par. Z(ohm)= E(E,deg)= I(A,deg)=	SHUNT INPUT L NETW ------(1)------- +24.75 -38.73 1.05 uH 1095 pF 50 + j0	SHUNT INPUT L NETW -------(2)------- -23.66 +38.73 1784 pF 1.64 uH 50 + j0	SERIES REACTANCE ------(3)-------- +0.545 - 0.02 uH - 18.75 + j0 41.26 / +146.5 2.19 / +148.1	SHUNT REACTANCE ------(4)------- - 644 - 27.37 uH 18.75 + j0 41.28 /+144.8 2.199 /+144.8
N E T W O R K 4	Z(series) Z(parallel) Value. ser Value. par. Z(ohm)= E(E,deg)= I(A,deg)=			QUARTER WAVE TRANSF -------- Z = 30 ohm (2x60 Ohm coax in parallel)	

Figure 2.84—Four possible feed arrangements for the end-fire, bidirectional, two-element (½-wave spacing, 180° out of phase) array, as covered by the worksheet in Figure 2.85.

If the two element impedances are not absolutely identical, one element should be fed via a line consisting of an odd number of quarter wavelengths and the other one via the same length of line plus 180°. Further impedance matching at the T junction can be done by using an L-network or quarter-wave coaxial transformers.

Let us examine a few feeding alternatives. Assume the feed-point impedances are strictly identical and we are using 20-meter long feed lines to reach the switching point located halfway between the elements, which are physically separated by 39.5 meters. Reaching the center is only required if one wants to feed both elements in phase to obtain broadside radiation. Using 50-ohm feed lines, the impedance on line 1 at 138° (which is the electrical equivalent of 20 meters of solid polyethylene coax) from the element will be Z1 = 37.51 −j1.09 ohms. The voltage at that point will be V = 41.3 V /144.8°.

On line 2, the same voltage (magnitude and phase) is found 318° from the load (138 + 180). At this point, the impedance is also the same (Z2 = 37.51 −j1.09 ohms). Paralleling the impedances results in a total impedance of 18.75 −j0.55 ohms. One way to match this to a 50-ohm line is to tune out the capacitive reactance with a small series coil having an inductive reactance of 0.55 ohms at the design frequency (0.02 µH at 3.8 MHz, which is a very small coil), and then to route the 50-ohm line to the shack via a 30-ohm quarter-wave transformer. (This can be made by paralleling two 60-ohm cables.) If a parallel inductance was to be used to tune out the reactance, the value of the required inductance would be high (27.73 µH), and the resulting resistive impedance would remain close to 18.75 ohms. In practice, we do not need the 27.37 µH inductance (the reactance is negligible). The feed arrangements are shown in Figure 2.84. Alternatively, one of two L-network solutions could be used. Figure 2.85 shows a typical worksheet for this antenna.

Similar designs can be worked out for 75-ohm feed lines

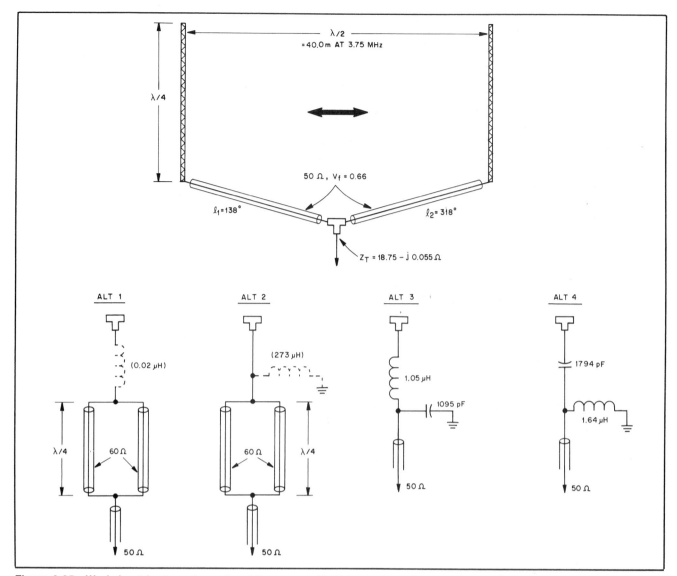

Figure 2.85—Worksheet for two-element end-fire array with ½ λ spacing, elements fed 180° out of phase. Note that in this special case, the extra 180° of phase shift comes from an extra 180° length of feed line. If the L-network solution is used, the whole feed system requires only two discrete components.

with either solid or expanded polyethylene dielectric (velocity factor = 0.66 or 0.80 nominal).

The recommended feed system uses a 90° line to one element and a 270° line to the other element. Figure 2.86 shows the final feed arrangement. Using 50-ohm feed lines, the 45.4 +j13 ohm element feed point impedances are transformed into 50.89 −j14.57 ohms at the end of the 90- and 270° long lines (calculated with the ''COAX TRANSFORMER'' program). The SWR on the feed lines to the elements is 1.33:1. The paralleled impedance is 25.45 −j7.28 ohms, which is really too low for a direct connection to a 50-ohm feed line (SWR = 2.02:1). An L-network using a 1.41-μH series inductor and a 856-pF shunt capacitor (at 3.65 MHz design frequency) yield a perfect 1:1 SWR on the 50-ohm feed line.

Using 75-ohm cable, the SWR on the feed lines is now 1.73:1 and the total parallel impedance at the T junction becomes 57.25 −j16.40 ohms. This impedance results in a 1.44:1 SWR without further adaptation, or an SWR of 1.40:1 on a 50-ohm feed line. Both require an L-network for a good match to the feed line to the shack.

Figure 2.87 shows a switchable half-wavelength spaced array that covers both end-fire and broadside directions.

Three-Element End-Fire Array

A very effective three-element end-fire array uses quarter-wave spacing and 90° of phase shift between adjacent elements. The center element is supplied with twice as much current as the outer ones. This array has a gain of 5 dB over a single vertical with the same dimensions; front-to-back ratio is better than 20 dB over more than 90°, and the 3-dB forward beamwidth is 140°. The horizontal directivity pattern is given in Figure 2.88. (All the numbers in Figure 2.88 were calculated for a wave angle of 30° over excellent ground.) The element data for this array is given in Table 25.

We now need to design a feed system for this array. The first step is to run the ''FEEDLINE VOLTAGE'' program, which after close examination shows that we can easily find points on the feed lines to elements 1 and 3 that have the same voltage. The only requirement we have as to the location of these points is that they are at least 138° from the antenna, in order to reach the central element (element 2) where the switching harness will be located. We then find a point at 147° on line 1 where V = 43.45 /107.29°, and at 280° on line 3

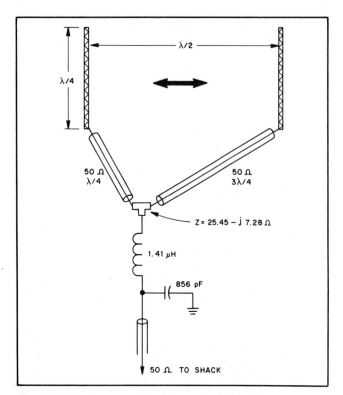

Figure 2.86—Recommended feed system for the two-element, bidirectional, end-fire array. Choosing feed lines that are multiple quarter wavelengths guarantees proper operation, even if both elements have slightly different feed impedances.

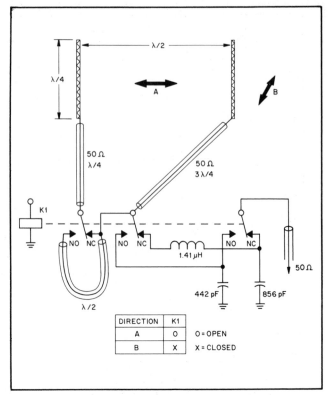

Figure 2.87—Switchable bidirectional end-fire/broadside two-element array, with ½ λ spacing. Note that the switch box will be located off-center between the two elements, because of unequal feed-line lengths.

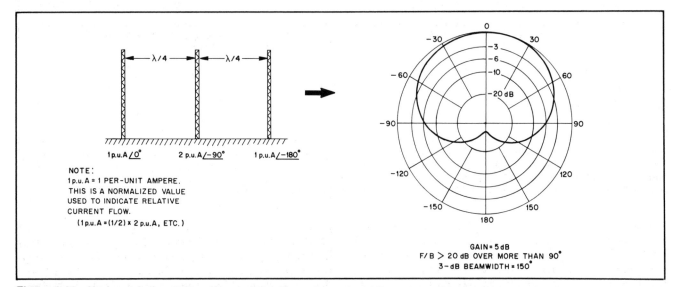

Figure 2.88—Horizontal directivity pattern of the three-element end-fire array, with the elements spaced ¼ λ apart and fed with 90° of phase shift between adjacent elements. Notice that the center element is fed with twice the current of the outer elements. The pattern shown was computed for a 30° wave angle over excellent ground.

Table 25

Element Data for 3-el Vertical Array (Endfire Pattern)

Element	Current Ratio	Phase Angle (deg)	Mutual Impedance (ohms)	Driving Impedance (ohms)
1	1	0	Z(12) = 15 −j15	Z(1) = 15.4 −j17
2	2	−90	Z(23) = Z(12)	Z(2) = 36.2 +j0
3	1	−180	Z(13) = −9 −j13	Z(3) = 75.4 +j43

```
+-------------------------------------------------------------------------------------------------------------+
|            | (3 El in line, 0.25 wave  |          CABLE VELOCITY FACTOR: 0.66                                |
|  ARRAY:    | (spacing, fed in 90 deg   |                                                                     |
|            | (steps, center el 2 x I   |          F = 3.75 MHz                                                |
+------------+---------------------------+-----------------------------------------------------------------------+
|A |         |        ELEM 1.            |      ELEM.2          |        ELEM.3          |        ELEM.4         |
|IN|         |                           |                     |                       |                      |
+--+---------+---------------------------+---------------------+-----------------------+----------------------+
|T |         | Z(1,2)= 15-j15            | Z(2,3)=15-j15       | Z(3,4)=               |                      |
|E |         | Z(1,3)= -9-j13           | Z(2,4)=             |                       |                      |
|N |         | Z(1,4)=                  |                     |                       |                      |
+==+=========+===========================+=====================+=======================+======================+
|A |Z (ohm) =| 15.4 - j17               | 36.4 + j0           | 75.4 + j43            |                      |
|S |E (V,deg)=| 22.94 / -47.83          | 72.8 / -90          | 86.8 / -150.3         |                      |
|  |I (A,deg)=| 1 / 0                   | 2 / -90             | 1 / -180              |                      |
+==+=========+===========================+=====================+=======================+======================+
|  | CABLES -->| 50 ohm, 147 deg         | 50 ohm, 7 deg       | 50 ohm, 280 deg       |                      |
|  |         | -------(A)-------         | -------(B)-------   | -------(C)-------     |                      |
|N |Z(series)|                           |                     |                       |                      |
|E |Z(parallel)|     SWR = 3.66/1        |   SWR = 1.37/1      |   SWR = 2.21/1        |                      |
|T |Value.ser|                           |                     |                       |                      |
|W |Value.par|                           |                     |                       |                      |
|O |  Z(ohm)=| 33.83 - j54.8            | 36.66 + j2.86       | 23.22 - j7.14         |                      |
|R |E(E,deg)=| 43.45 / +107.29          | 73.28 / -80.43      | 43.78 / +107.4        |                      |
|K |I(A,deg)=| 0.675 / +165.6           | 1.99 / -84.9        | 1.80 / +124.5         |                      |
|1 |         |                           |                     |                       |                      |
+==+=========+===========================+=====================+=======================+======================+
|  |         | SER. INPUT L NETW        | <------->            | SER. INPUT L NETW.    |                      |
|  |         | -------(1)-------         |                     | -------(2)--------    |                      |
|N |Z(series)| -17.65                   |                     | +17.65                |                      |
|E |Z(parallel)| +29.06                 |                     | -25.87                |                      |
|T |Value.ser| 2404 PF                  |                     | 0.75 uH               |                      |
|W |Value.par| 1.23 uH                  |                     | 1640 pF               |                      |
|O |  Z(ohm)=| 13.1 + j0                |                     | 13.1 + j0             |                      |
|R |E(E,deg)=| 43.6 / -133.8            |                     | 43.6 / -27.01         |                      |
|K |I(A,deg)=| 3.33 / -133.8            |                     | 3.33 / -27.01         |                      |
|2 |         |                           |                     |                       |                      |
+==+=========+===========================+=====================+=======================+======================+
|  |         | PI STRETCHER             | T STRETCHER         | PI STRETCHER          | T STRETCHER          |
|  |         | -------(3)-------         | -------(4)-------   | -------(5)--------    | -------(6)-------    |
|N |Z(series)| -11.48                   | +22.2               | +9.37                 | +31.17               |
|E |Z(parallel)| +7.75                  | -11.48              | -5.52                 | -9.36                |
|T |Value.ser| 3697 pF                  | 0.94 uH             | 0.4 uH                | 1.32 uH              |
|W |Value.par| 0.33 uH                  | 3697 pF             | 7709 pF               | 4535 pF              |
|O |  Z(ohm)=| 13.1 + j0                | 13.1 + j0           | 13.1 + j0             | 13.1 + j0            |
|R |E(E,deg)=| Phi in =+107.29deg       | Phi in =+107.29deg  | Phi in =+107.4deg     | Phi in =+107.4deg    |
|K |I(A,deg)=| Phi out=-133.8deg        | Phi out=-133.8deg   | Phi out=-27.01 deg    | Phi out=-27.01deg    |
|3 |         |                           |                     |                       |                      |
+==+=========+===========================+=====================+=======================+======================+
|  |         | PARALLELED INPUTS        |                     | SHUNT INPUT L NETW    | SHUNT INPUT L NETW   |
|  |         | -------                   |                     |                       |                      |
|N |Z(series)| (A)+(C)+(3) or (4)       |                     | +19.68                | -16.52               |
|E |Z(parallel)| or (5) or (6)          |                     | -21.41                | 21.41                |
|T |Value.ser|                           |                     | 0.84 uH               | 2570 pF              |
|W |Value.par|                           |                     | 1982 pF               | 0.91 uH              |
|O |  Z(ohm)=| 7.75 - j1.58             |                     | 50 + j0               | 50 + j0              |
|R |E(E,deg)=|                           |                     |                       |                      |
|K |I(A,deg)=|                           |                     |                       |                      |
|4 |         |                           |                     |                       |                      |
+-------------------------------------------------------------------------------------------------------------+
```

Figure 2.89—Worksheet for the feed network for the three-in-line end-fire array designed according to the Christman method. Two alternative L-networks are shown at the network 2 level; T- and Pi-network line stretcher alternatives are shown at the network 3 level, and another two L networks appear at the network 4 level.

where V = 43.77 $\underline{/107.4°}$. The impedances at those points can now be calculated with the "IMPEDANCE ITERATION" program. They are: Z1 = 33.83 $-j54.80$ ohms and Z3 = 23.22 $-j7.14$ ohms. We decide to keep the feed line to element 2 short (1 m or 7°). At that point, the voltage is: V2 = 73.28 $\underline{/-80.43°}$ and Z2 = 36.66 $-j2.86$ ohms.

Now a matching network must be designed. It must provide a given phase delay for the given output voltage (magnitude and phase) and the given output impedance. Because the phase delay is related to the transformation ratio, we cannot impose any impedance transformation. This is not really a problem, as we are paralleling different and random impedances at the T-junction point. Because we look for an input voltage which is lower than the output voltage, it is likely that a series-input L-network will be needed. Such an L-network can be designed with the "SERIES-INPUT L-NETWORK ITERATION" program listed in Chapter VII. For Z_{out} = 36.4 $-j2.86$

ohms, V_{out} = 73.28 $\underline{/-80.43°}$, and V_{in} = 43.7 $\underline{/107.3°}$, the program will scan through a range of input impedances, each time showing the input voltage. By a simple iteration technique, the value of Z_{in} can be found for which the required voltage magnitude is obtained at the input. In our example, this value is 13.1 ohms. The two alternative solutions are:

1) A series capacitor of 2404 pF and shunt inductor of 1.23 μH.

2) A series capacitor of 1640 pF and shunt inductor of 0.75 μH.

Both solutions are equally attractive from a component value point of view. Next, we have to add a line stretcher in one of the legs. The worksheet in Figure 2.89 shows the four alternatives (Pi and T in both the leading or lagging feed line). The T-network with the 0.40 μH coil and two 1361-pF capacitors seems to have the most comfortable component values. At this point, the resulting parallel impedance of the

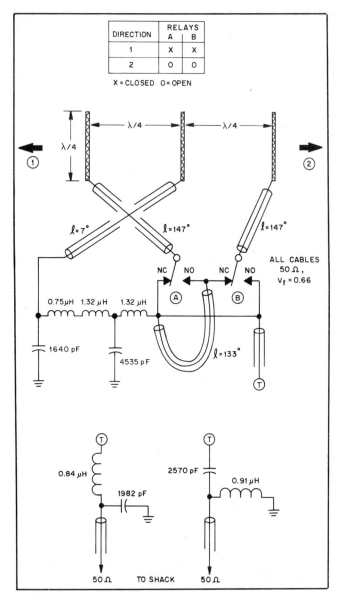

Figure 2.90—The feed system for the three-in-line array designed according to the modified Christman method. The two relays, the two capacitors and the two coils should be housed in a cabinet 1 meter (7°) from the feed point of the middle antenna.

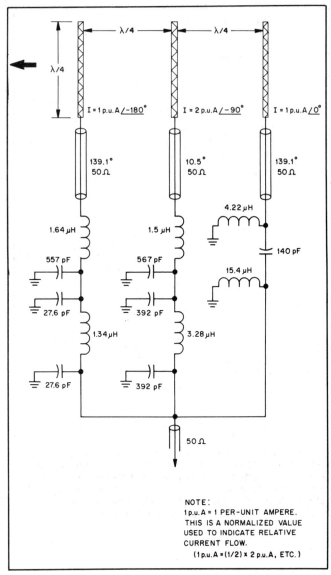

Figure 2.91—The Gehrke feed system for the three-in-line array as published in the original article (Ref 924). Notice that this system uses six coils and seven capacitors, as compared to two coils and two capacitors in the system described in Figure 2.90. The direction switching can be done as shown in Figure 2.90.

three feed systems can be calculated using the program "T-JUNCTION." The resulting impedance is: $7.75 - j1.58$ ohms, which can be matched to a 50-ohm feed line with an L-network where, again, two solutions are available. A series inductance of 0.84 μH and a parallel capacitor of 1982 pF are the logical choice. The feed system that we have just designed is shown in Figure 2.90 with its directivity switching arrangement.

With the computer programs listed in Chapter VII, it takes only a few minutes to design the whole feed system. Many alternatives are possible, and going through the design iterations in great detail is done to familiarize the potential user with the design procedures.

Figure 2.91 shows the feed network designed for this antenna by Gehrke. Detailed analysis of the design can be found in Ref 924.

Since the array elements are fed in quadrature (90° out of phase), the Collins feeding/phasing method can be used. The center element requires twice the current magnitude as the two

outer elements. This requirement can be satisfied by feeding the center element with a feed line having half the characteristic impedance of the feed lines to the outer elements. This can be verified by computing impedances, voltages and currents on the lines using the "COAX TRANSFORMER" program.

As explained in Section 2.11.4.1, it is desirable to make use of the properties of quarter-wave feed lines. Quarter-wave feed lines can only be used to feed the elements if the array is not to be made switchable. (The same conditions also apply to ¾ λ-long feed lines.) The "COAX TRANSFORMER" program yields the following values for 50-ohm feed lines.

1) For a 90° long feed line to the 0° element
($I_{out} = 1$ A $\angle 0°$, $Z_{el} = 15.4 - j17$ ohms):

$Z_{in} = 73.17 + j80.77$ ohms
$I_{in} = 0.46$ A $\angle +42.2°$
$E_{in} = 50$ V $\angle +90°$
SWR = 3.66:1

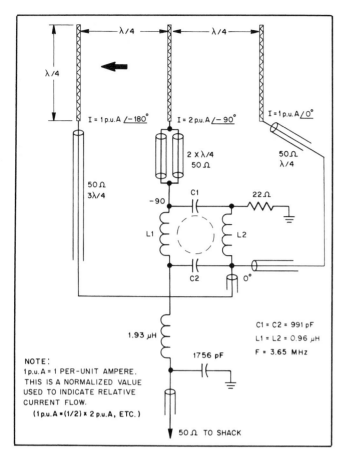

Figure 2.92—Collins-designed feed system for the three-in-line array. Note the use of parallel-connected coaxial cables to the center element, which ensures the right current amplitude (twice that of the outer elements). The hybrid coupler was designed for an impedance of 22 ohms; this yields the lowest SWR at the output ports.

2) For two parallel 90° long feed lines to the −90° elements (I_{out} = 1 A $\angle -90°$, Z_{el} = 36.29 +j0 ohms):

Z_{in} = 17.26 +j0 ohms
I_{in} = 2.9 A $\angle 0°$
E_{in} = 50 V $\angle 0°$
SWR = 1.38:1

3) For a 270° long feed line to the −180° element (I_{out} = 1 A $\angle -180°$, Z_{el} = 75.4 +j43 ohms):
Z_{in} = 25.02 −j14.30 ohms
I_{in} = 1.74 A $\angle +119.7°$
E_{in} = 50 V $\angle +90°$
SWR = 2.21:1

Paralleling the feed lines to the 0° and −180° elements yields a total impedance of 25.45 −j7.31 ohms. Through a 50-ohm hybrid coupler port, this would represent a 2.01:1 SWR, which would upset the performance of the coupler. We can, however, design a more appropriate coupler for the design impedance. If a coupler impedance of 22 ohms is selected, the SWR will be 1.40:1 for the combined 0 and −180° feed lines, and 1.27:1 for the −90° feed line. Those values are quite acceptable. The best coupler impedance can be calculated using the program "SWR ITERATION." The 22-ohm hybrid coupler can be constructed as described in Section 2.11.1.4, but with X_{L1} = X_{L2} = 22 ohms and X_{C1} = X_{C2} = 44 ohms. For a design frequency of 3.65 MHz, the component values are: L = 0.96 μH and C (nominal) = 991

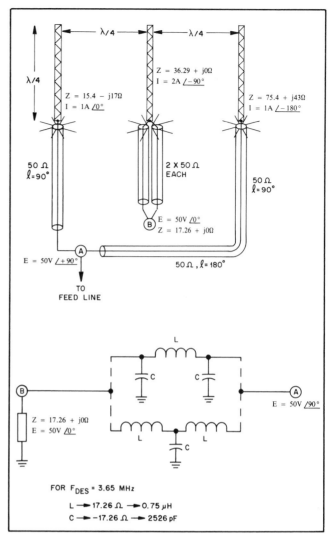

Figure 2.93—In the Lewallen-designed feed system for the three-element array, the shunt reactance normally found at point B is missing, as the impedance at the end of the quarter-wave feed lines to the center element is purely resistive.

pF. For a T225-2 core (AL = 120) the required number of turns is 8.9. For construction and test details, refer to Section 2.11.1.4.

One could experiment with different feed line impedances (50, 60 or 75 ohms) and different hybrid coupler design impedances in order to find a combination that results in the lowest possible SWR to the coupler ports, as well as the minimum amount of power loss in the port 3 load resistor. On the input side of the coupler, the nominal line impedance can be restored via quarter-wave impedance transformers or an L-network. In this case, a quarter-wave transformer made of two 75-ohm cables in parallel (Z = 37.5 ohms) would result in a feed-line SWR of 1.27:1. A better match can be obtained with an L-network. Figure 2.92 shows the arrangement with its directivity switching harness.

The Lewallen method is shown in Figure 2.93. The impedance, voltage and current values at the end of the feed lines are the same as in the Collins feed method. The 90° long feed line to the back element and the 270° long feed line to the front element are connected in parallel at point A (the voltage at the end of both feed lines is 50 V $\angle +90°$. The voltage at the end of the two parallel feed lines connected to the center element (point B) is 50 V ∠0°. The network connected between points A and B consists of a shunt impedance and a Pi or T line stretcher as explained in Section 2.11.1.4. In this case, no shunt impedance is required as the load impedance is purely resistive (17.26 + j0 ohms). The Pi and T filter line stretchers are shown in Figure 2.93.

The resultant parallel impedance of the array (as calculated by the program "T-JUNCTION" in Chapter VII) is 10.5 − j1.2 ohms. An appropriate L-network or stub matching system can provide a 1:1 SWR with a 50-ohm feed line.

Four-Square Array

Atchley, W1CF, described two arrays which were computer-modeled, and later built and tested with good success (Ref 930, 941).

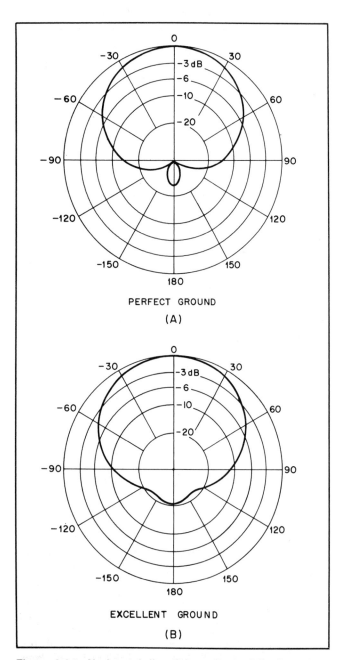

PERFECT GROUND

(A)

EXCELLENT GROUND

(B)

Figure 2.94—Horizontal directivity pattern of the four-square array with ¼ λ spacing between the elements. Pattern A is for zero wave angle over perfect ground (ideal case), and B shows a typical 30° wave angle pattern over excellent ground.

Directivity patterns for the four-element diamond array are shown in Figure 2.94, for cases over ideal ground with a 0° wave angle, and for a more practical 30° wave angle over excellent ground. The four elements of the antenna are positioned in a square, with quarter-wave spacing between adjacent elements. All elements are fed with equal current. The rear element is fed at 0° (reference element), the two side elements are fed at −90°, and the front element is fed at 180°. The direction of maximum signal is along the diagonal from the rear to the front element. In a real situation over excellent ground, the array gain is approximately 7 dB over a single vertical, the 3-dB beamwidth is 97°, and the theoretical front-to-back ratio is 20 dB or more over a 120° beamwidth.

Atchley later developed an improved feeding and switching arrangement where it was possible to switch the array directivity in increments of 45°. In this configuration, two front elements are fed at −90° and two back elements at 0° (two cardioids side-by-side, spaced ¼ λ apart). The directivity pattern of the array fed in this way is shown in Figure 2.95 (over excellent ground at a 30° wave angle). The practical advantage of the extra directivity steps does not seem to be worth the effort required to design the much-more-complicated feeding and switching system, as the forward lobe is so broad that switching in 45° steps makes very little difference. It is also important to keep in mind that the more complicated a system is, the more failure-prone it is. The element data for both configurations are given in Table 26.

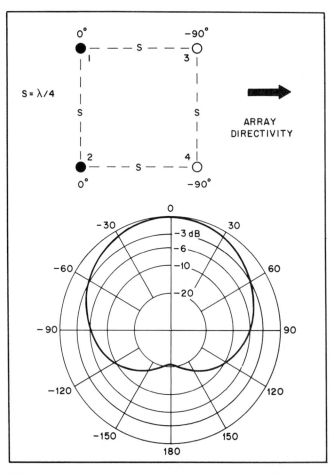

Figure 2.95—Horizontal directivity pattern of the four-square array excited as two quarter-wave spaced, side-by-side end-fire arrays (90° spacing, 90° phase delay—resulting in a cardioid pattern). The pattern was calculated for a 30° wave angle over excellent ground.

Table 26

Element Data for 4-el Vertical Array

Configuration 1: ¼ λ Spacing, Diamond Square

Element	Current Ratio	Phase Angle (deg)	Mutual Impedance (ohms)	Driving Impedance (ohms)
1	1	0	Z(12) = 15 −j15	Z(1) = 3.4 −j12.5
2	1	−90		Z(2) = 39.4 −j17.5
3	1	−90	Z(14) = −3 −j17.5	Z(3) = 39.4 −j17.5
4	1	−180		Z(4) = 63.4 +j47.5

Note: Z(12) = Z(13) = Z(24) = Z(34)
      Z(23) = Z(14)

Configuration 2: ¼ λ Spacing, Side-by-Side Cardioid

Element	Current Ratio	Phase Angle (deg)	Mutual Impedance (ohms)	Driving Impedance (ohms)
1	1	0	Z(12) = 15 −j15	Z(1) = 18.9 −j33
2	1	0		Z(2) = 18.9 −j33
3	1	−90	Z(14) = 3 −j17.5	Z(3) = 83.9 +j3
4	1	−90		Z(4) = 83.9 +j3

Note: Z(12) = Z(13) = Z(24) = Z(34)
      Z(23) = Z(14)

Configuration 3: 1/8 λ Spacing

Element	Current Ratio	Phase Angle (deg)	Mutual Impedance (ohms)	Driving Impedance (ohms)
1	1	0	Z(12) = 30 −j3	Z(1) = −1.27 −j13.2
2	1	−135		Z(2) = 18.9 −j33
3	1	−135	Z(14) = 25 −j9	Z(3) = 18.9 −j33
4	1	−270		Z(4) = −10.8 +j21.7

Note: Z(12) = Z(13) = Z(24) = Z(34)
      Z(23) = Z(14)

Table 26 lists the element data for the square array with 1/8 λ spacing, which is an attractive configuration, especially on 160 meters. Gehrke investigated the square array with 1/8 λ spacing, with all elements fed with the same current magnitude, but with the center two elements lagging in phase by 135°, and the rear element lagging by 270°. The gain of this array is slightly better than the quarter-wave-spaced array, and the front-to-back ratio increases to nearly infinity at 135° off both sides of the favored direction. The 3-dB forward beamwidth is slightly less than for the quarter-wave-spaced array (90° versus 97°), but the F/B ratio is 25 dB or more over about 90°. Table 26 also lists the impedance data for this design. Note that, especially with close-spaced designs, driving-point impedances with a negative resistive part can be found. This means that the parasitic coupling supplies too much current (power) to this element, and that the element is then supplying this power back into the feed network. Figure 2.96 shows the radiation pattern of this array. The operating bandwidth over which this array shows a usable front-to-back ratio is expected to be rather narrow, which is not a great handicap on 160 meters.

Quarter-Wave-Spaced Square

The following feed system design is done according to the Christman method. The voltage at any point along the 360° long 50-ohm coaxial lines feeding the three elements can be found using the "FEEDLINE VOLTAGE" program listed in Chapter VII (elements 2 and 3 are identical in all respects in this array). First we must determine what the minimum feed-line length should be in order to reach to a common point where the matching and switching can take place. (This will be in the middle of the square.) In the case of coaxial cable with a solid polyethylene dielectric (velocity factor = 0.66), the minimum electrical length is 100° (which is 14.5 m for 3.75 MHz).

It now becomes necessary to find points of identical voltage on the feed lines. We find these on the feed lines to elements 2 and 3 at 109° from the antenna, and to element 4 at 147° from the antenna. We then take a point on the feed line to element 1 (more than 100° from the load) where we will insert an L-network and a line stretcher to obtain the same input voltage as is on the combination point of elements 2, 3 and 4. Theoretically, there is an infinite number of solutions. We choose a length of 120° on our worksheet in Figure 2.97. Using the BASIC program "COAX TRANSFORMER," voltages, currents and impedances at the end of the four lengths of coaxial cable can be calculated. At the same time, the program calculates the SWR of the line, which is necessary information for evaluation of losses and the power-handling requirements of the feed lines. The voltage at 120° from element 1 (49.58 V /91.96°) will now have to be transformed to an input voltage of 54.5 volts (the voltage at the ends of the other three feed lines). Because the input voltage is higher than the output voltage, we use the BASIC program

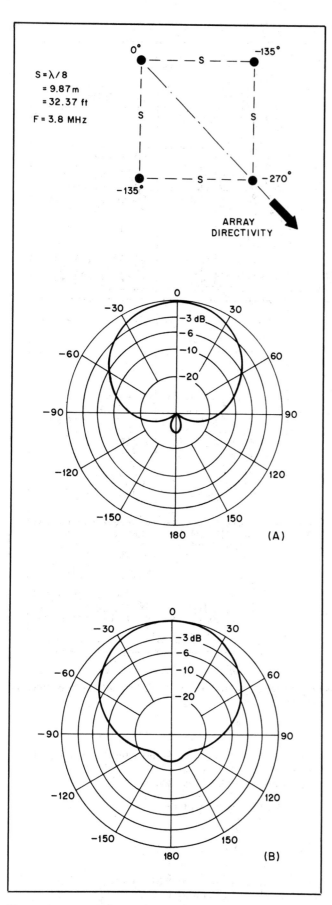

Figure 2.96—Horizontal directivity pattern of a four-square array with 1/8 λ spacing between elements. Pattern A is for 0° wave angle over perfect ground, B shows the pattern at a wave angle of 30° over excellent ground. Notice the relative phase between the antenna elements.

"SHUNT-INPUT L-NETWORK ITERATION" to look for an input impedance that will give the required voltage transformation. Again, two solutions are found, in both cases, for an input impedance of 864 ohms (purely resistive).

There is little reason to favor one solution over the other as far as component values are concerned. All that remains is to add the necessary phase delay so that the voltages on all four feed lines are identical. Pi- or T-network line stretchers can be designed with the "PI-FILTER LINE STRETCHER" and "T-FILTER LINE STRETCHER" programs in Chapter VII. All four possible alternatives are shown on the work sheet in Figure 2.97. Alternative 3 is clearly the most convenient one, as it requires the least inductance. Now the parallel impedance can be calculated using the "T-JUNCTION" program. The value of $16.285 + j8.206$ ohms must now be transformed to $50 + j0$ ohms. There is no clear choice between solutions (7) and (8) from the worksheet. Both use similar component values. The remaining alternative is to tune out the reactance in the $26.285 + j8.206$-ohm impedance with either a series or a parallel network (reactive). These solutions are shown under (9) and (10) on the worksheet.

In the last cases, the remaining resistive impedance (16.285 ohms and 20.42 ohms respectively) can be matched to a 50-ohm line by using a 30-ohm quarter-wave transformer (two 60-ohm lines in parallel). Figure 2.98 shows the final feed system including the direction switching scheme.

Figures 2.99 and 2.100 show the worksheet and feed-network schematics for the Gehrke design method (Ref 925) of the four-square array with ¼ λ element spacing.

Collins, W1FC, designed a feed system for the four-square array based on the principles explained in Section 2.11.1.4. The elements must be fed with quarter-wave feed lines to a common point at the center of the array. We cannot reach the center of a square measuring ¼ λ on each side (20.54 m at 3.65 MHz) using solid polyethylene insulated coaxial cables. With a velocity factor of 0.66, a quarter-wave would be only 13.65 m, while 14.95 m is needed to reach the center. Instead, we must use expanded polyethylene insulated coaxial cable, which has a velocity factor of 0.73.

As mentioned earlier, we cannot rely on the manufacturer's published figures for velocity factor. Each quarter-wave line must be electrically measured using one of the methods described in Section 2.11.4.1. Alternatively, ¾ λ long lines made of solid polyethylene insulated coaxial cable (VF = 0.66) could be used for all four feed lines, but this would be a waste of cable. Figure 2.101 shows the diagram without directivity switching. Note that the particular properties of the quarter-wavelength feed lines described in Section 2.11.1.4 also apply for ¾ λ feed lines. The following values can be computed with the program "COAX TRANSFORMER" for 50-ohm feed lines.

1) For a 90°-long feed line to the 0° element
($I_{out} = 1$ A $\angle \underline{0°}$, $Z_{el} = 3.4 - j12.5$ ohms):

$Z_{in} = 50.65 + j186.22$ ohms
$I_{in} = 0.26$ A $\angle \underline{+15.21°}$
$E_{in} = 50$ V $\angle \underline{+90°}$.
SWR $= 15.63:1$

2) For 90°-long feed lines to the $-90°$ elements
($I_{out} = 1$ A $\angle \underline{-90°}$, $Z_{el} = 39.4 - j17.5$ ohms):

$Z_{in} = 52.99 + j23.53$ ohms
$I_{in} = 0.86$ A $\angle \underline{-23.95°}$
$E_{in} = 50$ V $\angle \underline{0°}$
SWR $= 1.58:1$

```
|-----------------------------------------------------------------------------------------------------|
| ARRAY:  (4 SQUARE ARRAY        |      CABLE VELOCITY FACTOR: 0.66                                    |
|         (1/4 WAVE SPACING      |      MIN FEEDER LENGTH: 100 DEG                                     |
|         (QUADRATURE FED        |      F = 3.80 MHz                                                   |
|-----------------------------------------------------------------------------------------------------|
```

A I N I T E N N		ELEM 1.	ELEM.2	ELEM.3	ELEM.4
A I N		Z(1,2)= 15-j15 Z(1,3)= 15-j15 Z(1,4)= 3-j17.5	Z(2,3)= 3-j17.5 Z(2,4)= 15-j15	Z(3,4)= 15-j15	
A S I E	Z (ohm) = E (V, deg)= I (A, deg)=	3.4 -j12.5 12.95 ∠ -74.29 1 ∠ 0	39.4-j17.5 43.11 ∠ -113.95 1 ∠ -90	39.4-j17.5 43.11 ∠ -113.95 1 ∠ -90	63.4+j47.5 79.22 ∠ -143.16 1 ∠ -180
	CABLES -->	50 ohm, 120 deg	50 ohm, 109 deg ------(A)------	50 ohm, 109 deg ------(B)------	50 ohm, 147 deg ------(C)------
N I E I T I W I O I R I K I 1	Z(series) Z(parallel) Value. ser Value. par. Z(ohm)= E(E,deg)= I(A,deg)=	SWR = 15.6/1 40.55 - j166.36 49.58 ∠ +91.96 0.298 ∠ +168.26	SWR = 1.58/1 70.97 + j17.73 54.5 ∠ +13.61 0.745 ∠ -0.412	SWR = 1.58/1 70.97 + j17.73 54.5 ∠ +13.61 0.745 ∠ -0.412	SWR = 2.34/1 27.38 + j23.24 54.6 ∠ +13.33 1.521 ∠ -26.99
		SHUNT IN L NETW. ------(1)------	SHUNT IN L NETW. ------(2)------		
N I E I T I W I O I R I K I 2	Z(series) Z(parallel) Value. ser Value. par. Z(ohm)= E(E,deg)= I(A,deg)=	+349 -192 14.6 uH 217 pF 864 + j0 54.5 ∠ -114.4 0.0627 ∠ -114.4	-17.7 +192 3267 pF 8.08 uH 864 + j0 54.5 ∠ +90.7 0.0627 ∠ +90.7		
		PI STRETCHER ------(3)--------	T STRETCHER ------(4)--------	PI STRETCHER ------(5)--------	T STRETCHER ------(6)--------
N I E I T I W I O I R I K I 3	Z(series) Z(parallel) Value. ser Value. par. Z(ohm)= E(E,deg)= I(A,deg)=	+683 -424 29 uH 100 pF 864 + j0 54.5 ∠ +13.3	+1760 -684 75 uH 62 pF 864 + j0 54.5 ∠ +13.3	-843 +1078 50 pF 46 uH 864 + j0 54.5 ∠ +13.3	-648 +840 62 pF 36 uH 864 + j0 54.4 ∠ +13.3
		PARALLEL IMPED	SHUNT IN L NETW. ------(7)-------	SHUNT IN L NETW. ------(8)-------	SER Z | PAR Z --(9)---|--(10)-
N I E I T I W I O I R I K I 4	Z(series) Z(parallel) Value. ser Value. par. Z(ohm)= E(E,deg)= I(A,deg)=	parallelling (A)+ (B)+(C)+(3) or (4) or (5) or (6) 16.285 + j8.206 54.5 ∠ +13.3 2.98 ∠ -13.44	+15.23 -34.75 0.65 uH 1221 pF 50 + j0 85.28 ∠ +41.76 1.71 ∠ +41.76	-31.64 34.75 1341 pF 1.47 uH 50 + j0 85.28 ∠ -68.64 1.71 ∠ -68.64	-8.206 | - - | -40.4 5172pF | 1047pF - | - 16.28+j0 | 20.42+j0 48.6/+13 | 54.5/+13 3.0/+13 | 2.7/+13

Figure 2.97—Worksheet for the four-square array with ¼ λ spacing designed according to the Christman method. Several alternative network sections are shown at the different levels. See text for details.

3) For a 270°-long feed line to the −180° element ($I_{out} = 1$ A $\angle -180°$, $Z_{el} = 63.4 + j47.5$ ohms):

$Z_{in} = 25.26 - j28.92$ ohms
$I_{in} = 1.58$ A $\angle +126.8°$
$E_{in} = 50$ V $\angle +90°$
SWR = 2.34:1

Paralleling the two −90° feed lines yields a total impedance of $26.5 + j11.76$ ohms, which represents an SWR of 2.03:1 for the 50-ohm port (port 2) of the hybrid coupler. Paralleling the feed lines to the 0- and −180° elements results in a total impedance (calculated with the "T-JUNCTION" program) of $29.37 - j15.38$ ohms, which corresponds to an SWR of 1.93:1 at the 50-ohm port (port 4) of the hybrid coupler. These values are not very good.

The same calculations for 75-ohm cable yielded the following results.

1) Feed line to the 0° element:

$Z_{in} = 113.97 - j418.99$ ohms
$I_{in} = 0.17$ A $\angle +15.22°$
$E_{in} = 75$ V $\angle +90°$
SWR = 22.67:1

2) Feed lines to the −90° elements ($I_{out} = 1$ A $\angle -90°$, $Z_{el} = 52.99 + j23.53$ ohms):

$Z_{in} = 119.24 + j52.96$ ohms
$I_{in} = 0.58$ A $\angle -23.95°$
$E_{in} = 75$ V $\angle 0°$
SWR = 2.04:1

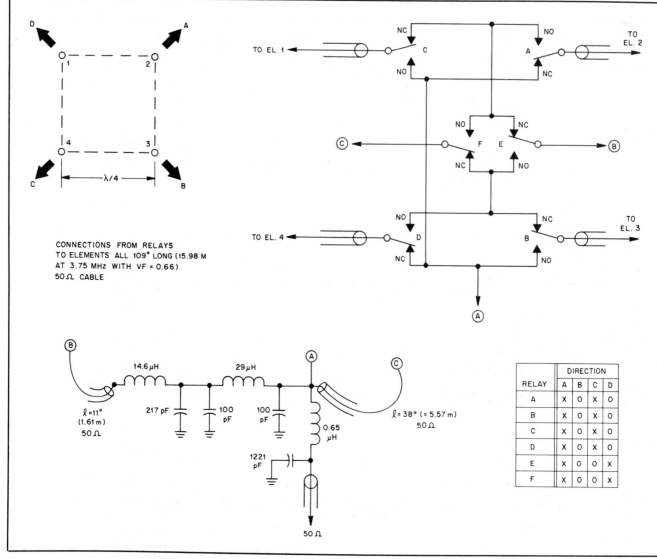

Figure 2.98—Final modified Christman feed method for the four-square array with ¼ λ spacing. Note the simplicity of the network compared to the other alternatives. The 1.61- and 5.57-meter long coaxial cables can be coiled up inside the matching/switching equipment housing. The minimum bending radius is approximately 10 inches.

3) Feed line to the −180° element:

Z_{in} = 56.82 −j42.57 ohms
I_{in} = 1.06 A $\angle +126.84°$
E_{in} = 75 V $\angle +90°$
SWR = 2.00:1

Paralleling the two −90° feed lines yields a total impedance of 59.62 +j26.48 ohms, which represents an SWR of 1.57:1 for the 75-ohm port (port 2) of the hybrid coupler. Paralleling the feed lines to the 0° and −180° elements results in a total impedance of 66.06 −j34.61 ohms, which in turn results in an SWR of 1.65:1 at the 75-ohm port (port 4) of the hybrid coupler. The program "SWR ITERATION" can be used to select a hybrid coupler design impedance which would result in compromised low SWR values at ports 2 and 4.

It appears that the 75-ohm feed system is the better choice. This value will result in the smallest amount of power dissipation in the terminating resistor at port 3. The required power rating of the 75-ohm terminating resistor at port 3 can best be determined experimentally. Feed the array at the frequencies farthest away from the design frequency (the band edges) and measure the dissipated power into a 75-ohm dummy load using a wattmeter. A 50-ohm wattmeter such as the Bird 43 can be used, as only relative power measurements are required. Later one can substitute a high-power dummy load with the appropriate power rating.

Collins measured the power in the terminating resistor for a range of frequencies. The measurements were done using a hybrid coupler having a design impedance of 50 ohms. With a 75-ohm hybrid coupler, the results should be a little better (less power will be dissipated in the load), as explained above. The results of Collins' measurements are listed in Table 27. This table shows that a 200-W dummy load should be sufficient for transmitter output power well in excess of 1500 W, if the array is designed for a nominal frequency of 3.65 MHz and operated between 3.5 MHz (CW band) and 3.8 MHz (SSB DX band). If the array will be used over a much more restricted spectrum, a 100-W load may be substituted.

The higher SWR on the individual feed lines to the array elements is of little importance, as the losses at the low frequencies are minimal. CATV-type 75-ohm Hardline makes excellent feed line for this array. The 75-ohm hybrid coupler

ARRAY: (4 SQUARE ARRAY (1/4 WAVE SPACING (QUADRATURE FED		CABLE VELOCITY FACTOR: 0.66 MIN FEEDER LENGTH: 100 DEG F = 3.80 MHz		
ANTENNA	ELEM 1.	ELEM.2	ELEM.3	ELEM.4
	$Z(1,2)= 15-j15$ $Z(1,3)= 15-j15$ $Z(1,4)= 3-j17.5$	$Z(2,3)= 3-j17.5$ $Z(2,4)= 15-j15$	$Z(3,4)= 15-j15$	
Z (ohm) = E (V, deg)= I (A, deg)=	$3.4 -j12.5$ $12.95 \; \underline{/-74.29}$ $1 \; \underline{/0}$	$39.4-j17.5$ $43.11 \; \underline{/-113.95}$ $1 \; \underline{/-90}$	$39.4-j17.5$ $43.11 \; \underline{/-113.95}$ $1 \; \underline{/-90}$	$63.4+j47.5$ $79.22 \; \underline{/-143.16}$ $1 \; \underline{/-180}$
CABLES -->	50 ohm, 100 deg ------(A)------	50 ohm, 100 deg ------(B)------	50 ohm, 100 deg ------(C)------	50 ohm, 100 deg ------(D)------
NETWORK 1 Z(series) Z(parallel) Value. ser Value. par. Z(ohm)= E(E,deg)= I(A,deg)=	SWR = 15.6/1 $348.8 + j386.7$ $51.40 \; \underline{/+90.66}$ $0.099 \; \underline{/+42.71}$	SWR = 1.58/1 $62.40 + j22.57$ $52.7 \; \underline{/+7.45}$ $0.79 \; \underline{/-12.43}$	SWR = 1.58/1 $62.40 + j22.57$ $52.7 \; \underline{/+7.45}$ $0.79 \; \underline{/-12.43}$	SWR = 2.34/1 $22.73 - j11.37$ $42.44 \; \underline{/-74.97}$ $1.67 \; \underline{/-48.39}$
NETWORK 2 Z(series) Z(parallel) Value. ser Value. par. Z(ohm)= E(E,deg)= I(A,deg)=	SHUNT IN L NETW. ------(1)------ -1177 $+944$ 36 PF 40.1 uH $2141+ j0$ $85.3 \; \underline{/-23.5}$ $0.0398 \; \underline{/-23.5}$	(B)+(C) IN PARALL. ------(2)------ $31.2 + j11.28$ $52.7 \; \underline{/+7.45}$ $1.59 \; \underline{/-12.43}$	SHUNT IN L NETW. ------(3)------ $+32.4$ -66 1.38 uH 643 pF $92.4 +j0$ $85.3 \; \underline{/+42.05}$ $0.923 \; \underline{/+42.05}$	SHUNT IN L NETW. ------(4)------ $+57.1$ -57.1 2.42 uH 744 pF $114.8 + j0$ $85.3 \; \underline{/+15.18}$ $0.743 \; \underline{/+15.18}$
NETWORK 3 Z(series) Z(parallel) Value. ser Value. par. Z(ohm)= E(E,deg)= I(A,deg)=	PI NETWORK ------(7)------ $+1949$ -3325 82.7 uH 13 pF $2141 + j0$ $85.3 \; \underline{/+42.05}$ $0.0398 \; \underline{/+42.05}$			PI NETWORK ------(8)------ $+51.9$ -481 2.2 uH 88.3 pF $114.8 + j0$ $85.3 \; \underline{/+42.05}$ $0.743 \; \underline{/+42.05}$
NETWORK 4 Z(series) Z(parallel) Value. ser Value. par. Z(ohm)= E(E,deg)= I(A,deg)=		(3)+(7)+(8) PARAL. ------(9)------ $50 + j0$ $85.30 \; \underline{/+42.05}$ $1.71 \; \underline{/+42.05}$		

Figure 2.99—Worksheet for the Gehrke feed method for the four-square array with ¼ λ spacing. Only the networks with the most attractive component values are shown.

can be constructed as described in Section 2.11.1.4, but with $X_{L1} = X_{L2} = 75$ ohms and $X_{C1} = X_{C2} = 150$ ohms. For a design frequency of 3.65 MHz, the component values are: $L = 3.27$ μH and $C = 291$ pF (nominal). For a T225-2 core $(AL = 120)$ the required number of turns is 16.5. For construction and test details refer to Section 2.11.1.4. The hybrid coupler can be fed with a 75-ohm feed line, via an L-network to a 50-ohm line, or via a non-synchronous transformer (as described in Section 2.12.3) into a 50-ohm feed line.

The front-to-back ratio can be fine-tuned for ultimate rejection by inserting a variable length of feed line between port 2 and the paralleled feed lines to the $-90°$ elements. This line should be between 1 and 9 electrical degrees long (1 to 6 feet). Using a vertically polarized test antenna several wavelengths away from the array, one can achieve infinite F/B ratio by adjusting the length of this short phase corrector. The practical usefulness of such a corrector is doubtful, however, as actual signals will not be arriving at zero wave angle, and the optimum length of the phase corrector will depend on the arrival angle of the (interfering) signal off the back of the array. Figure 2.102 shows the final configuration of the Collins feed system for the four-square diamond array. Table 28 shows the measured phase and current balance at the output ports of the hybrid coupler.

The Lewallen (W7EL) design method can also be applied to this array. This method also takes advantage of the special properties of ¼ λ long transmission lines. Let's design the required network into a 50-ohm system. The voltage at the end of the 90° feed line to the back element (reference point)

Table 27
Power Reflected Into Dummy Load

Frequency (MHz)	Power Reflected into Load (dB)
3.5	−7.2
3.6	−10.0
3.7	−12.2
3.8	−18.0
3.9	−13.5
4.0	−10.5

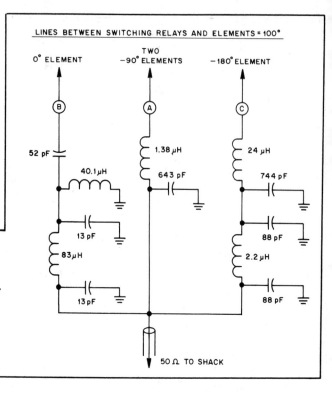

Figure 2.100—Gehrke feed method for the four-square array with ¼ λ spacing. Refer to Figure 2.82 for further details on the connections of points A, B and C.

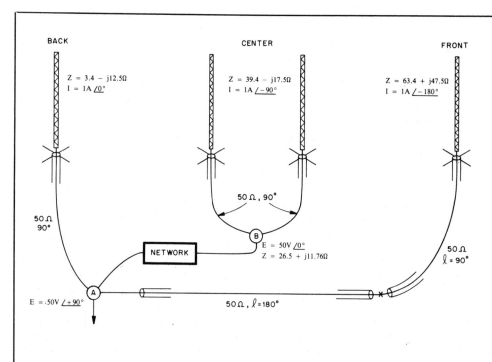

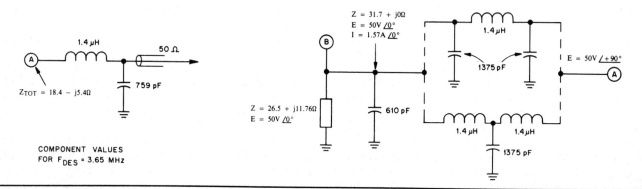

Figure 2.101—In the Lewallen feed system for this array, the voltages at the end of the ¼ λ feed line to the rear element and the ¾ λ feed line to the front element are identical. The center elements are fed with the same voltage amplitude, but not the same phase. The network is designed to shift the phase between A and B by 90°. See text for details.

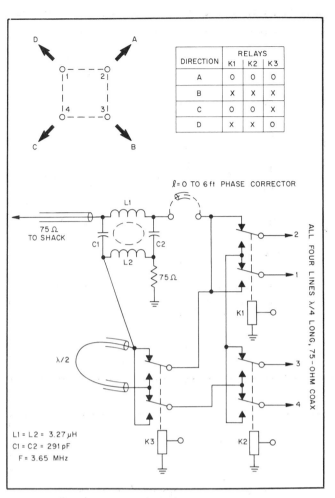

DIRECTION	RELAYS		
	K1	K2	K3
A	O	O	O
B	X	X	X
C	O	O	X
D	X	X	O

ℓ = 0 TO 6 ft PHASE CORRECTOR

L1

75 Ω
TO SHACK

C1   C2

L2

75 Ω

λ/2

K1

2

1

ALL FOUR LINES λ/4 LONG, 75-OHM COAX

3

4

K3   K2

L1 = L2 = 3.27 μH
C1 = C2 = 291 pF
F = 3.65 MHz

Figure 2.102—Collins feeding and switching method for the four-square diamond array. The coaxial phase corrector can be replaced by a short circuit. See text for details.

and at the end of the 270° feed line to the front element (−180° element) is: 50 V $\angle 90°$. As with the Collins feed systems, these feed lines can simply be paralleled. The two 90° feed lines to the two center elements (both fed at −90°) have a voltage of: 50 V $\angle 0°$. Therefore, we will need a network that will transform 50 V $\angle 90°$ at the T-junction to 50 V $\angle 0°$ at the junctions of the feed lines to the two center elements.

The complete design can be done in minutes with the computer programs listed in Chapter VII. Refer to Figure 2.101 for the following discussion. In order to achieve a resistive impedance at point B, we need to connect a shunt impedance across that point. The impedance at point B was 26.5 +j11.76 ohms. Using the "SHUNT IMPEDANCE NETWORK" program, we can calculate the impedance (and subsequently the capacitance or inductance) required to tune out the reactance at that point. The shunt impedance turns out to be −160.72 ohms, which corresponds to 610 pF of capacitance at 3.65 MHz. Since the capacitor is to be wired in parallel with the impedance at point B, the voltage remains 50 V $\angle 0°$. The impedance (now purely resistive) at this point is 31.7 ohms.

The only thing left to do now is to add a line stretcher between A and B to take care of the required phase shift. The "PI-FILTER LINE STRETCHER" program calculates the component values for a symmetrical Pi network. For 3.65 MHz, the series inductor is 1.38 μH and the parallel

Table 28
Hybrid Coupler Measurements

Frequency (MHz)	Back Element Current (amps)	Angle (deg)	Side Elements Current (amps)	Angle (deg)	Front Element Current (amps)	Angle (deg)
3.5	7.7	0	7.5	83	7.8	173
3.8	7.9	0	8.5	90	7.9	180
4.0	6.3	0	8.2	90	6.5	185

capacitors are 1375 pF. Another alternative would be a T-network line stretcher (see Figure 2.54).

We can check the results of our calculations for accuracy by the method described in Section 2.11.1.4. Assuming 1-A current magnitude in all four elements, the power in the rear element is 3.4 W, while each of the two center elements take 39.4 W, and the front element takes 63.4 W. Assuming lossless feed lines and networks, the same power ratios should be found at the T-junction of point B.

The current at the end of the 90° feed line to the back element is 0.17 A $\angle 15.22°$, while the impedance looking towards the antenna is 113.97 −j418.99 ohms. For the front element, the values at the end of the 270° line are: I = 1.06 A $\angle 128.84°$, and Z = 56.82 −j42.57 ohms. At the input of the network, the current is 1.57 A $\angle 0°$, and the impedance is 31.7 +j0 ohms. The power levels in the three branches coming together at point A are 3.4 W, 63.4 W and 78.4 W, the sum of which is the total power going to the two center elements. The power ratios are the same as those calculated at the antenna elements, proving that our design calculations are valid. This network has a relatively narrow bandwidth, so if operation on both the SSB and CW portions of the band is desired, separate networks will be required.

1/8-Wavelength-Spaced Square

As this array shows very low (and negative) feed-point impedances for both the director and reflector elements, the impedances and component values are more difficult to handle. One possible network design (according to the Gehrke method) is shown in Figure 2.103. The first thing to do is to determine the required impedances at the junction points, which are: −1013 ohms, 68.1 ohms, 68.1 ohms, and −119 ohms. This example was worked out with feed lines 50° long. This is enough to reach the center of the square, and it is half of the 100° length needed in case we want to use the same feed lines in a duoband array. The impedances at the end of the 50° long lines are calculated with the program "COAX TRANSFORMER." Because the lines to elements 2 and 3 are to be paralleled at this point (in the center of the array), we must calculate the circuit parameters present here. The voltage will remain the same, but the impedance will be halved, so the current will double.

Now we need to design three L-networks: one to transform −1.78 +j35.24 ohms to −1013 +j0 ohms, one to transform 6.61 +j5.8 ohms to 34.05 +j0 ohms (half of the 68.1 ohms determined above) and one to transform −87.32 +j121.81 ohms to −119 +j0 ohms. The choice of the L-network alternatives is influenced by the component values and the voltage phase angle. In the example, after many iterations it was decided that the line stretchers should be put in the feed line to elements 2 and 3 and the feed line to element 4. Despite the extreme impedance ratios, the component values are very reasonable. Note, however, that due to these extreme ratios

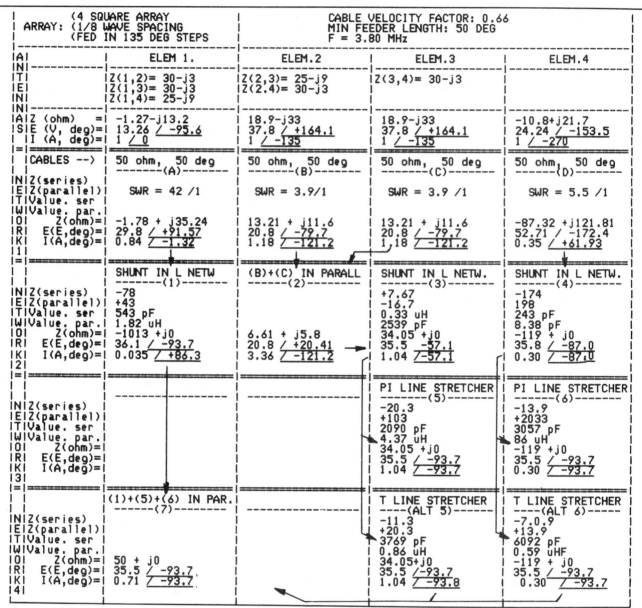

```
| (4 SQUARE ARRAY          |               CABLE VELOCITY FACTOR: 0.66
ARRAY: (1/8 WAVE SPACING   |               MIN FEEDER LENGTH: 50 DEG
      (FED IN 135 DEG STEPS |              F = 3.80 MHz
----------------------------------------------------------------------------------
|A|            |     ELEM 1.     |     ELEM.2     |     ELEM.3     |     ELEM.4
|N|------------
|T|            |Z(1,2)= 30-j3    |Z(2,3)= 25-j9   |Z(3,4)= 30-j3
|E|            |Z(1,3)= 30-j3    |Z(2,4)= 30-j3   |
|N|            |Z(1,4)= 25-j9    |                |
|N|
|A|Z (ohm)  = |-1.27-j13.2      | 18.9-j33       | 18.9-j33       | -10.8+j21.7
|S|E (V, deg)=| 13.26 /-95.6    | 37.8 /+164.1   | 37.8 /+164.1   | 24.24 /-153.5
| |I (A, deg)=| 1 /0            | 1 /-135        | 1 /-135        | 1 /-270
|=
| |CABLES --> | 50 ohm, 50 deg  | 50 ohm, 50 deg | 50 ohm, 50 deg | 50 ohm, 50 deg
| |           |-----(A)-----    |-----(B)-----   |-----(C)-----   |-----(D)-----
|N|Z(series)  |                 |                |                |
|E|Z(parallel)|   SWR = 42 /1   |  SWR = 3.9/1   |  SWR = 3.9 /1  |  SWR = 5.5 /1
|T|Value. ser |                 |                |                |
|W|Value. par.|                 |                |                |
|O|   Z(ohm)= |-1.78 + j35.24   | 13.21 + j11.6  | 13.21 + j11.6  | -87.32 +j121.81
|R|E(E,deg)=  | 29.8 /+91.57    | 20.8 /-79.7    | 20.8 /-79.7    | 52.71 /-172.4
|K|I(A,deg)=  | 0.84 /-1.32     | 1.18 /-121.2   | 1.18 /-121.2   | 0.35 /+61.93
|1|
|=
| |           |SHUNT IN L NETW  |(B)+(C) IN PARALL|SHUNT IN L NETW.|SHUNT IN L NETW.
| |           |-----(1)-----    |-----(2)-----   |-----(3)-----   |-----(4)-----
|N|Z(series)  |-78              |                |+7.67           |-174
|E|Z(parallel)|+43              |                |-16.7           |198
|T|Value. ser |543 pF           |                |0.33 uH         |243 pF
|W|Value. par.|1.82 uH          |                |2539 pF         |8.38 pF
|O|   Z(ohm)= |-1013 +j0        | 6.61 + j5.8    |34.05 +j0       |-119 + j0
|R|E(E,deg)=  | 36.1 /-93.7     | 20.8 /+20.41   |35.5 -57.1      |35.8 /-87.0
|K|I(A,deg)=  | 0.035 /+86.3    | 3.36 /-121.2   |1.04 /-57.1     |0.30 /-87.0
|2|
|=
| |           |                 |                |PI LINE STRETCHER|PI LINE STRETCHER
| |           |                 |                |-----(5)-----   |-----(6)-----
|N|Z(series)  |                 |                |-20.3           |-13.9
|E|Z(parallel)|                 |                |+103            |+2033
|T|Value. ser |                 |                |2090 pF         |3057 pF
|W|Value. par.|                 |                |4.37 uH         |86 uH
|O|   Z(ohm)= |                 |                |34.05 +j0       |-119 +j0
|R|E(E,deg)=  |                 |                |35.5 /-93.7     |35.5 /-93.7
|K|I(A,deg)=  |                 |                |1.04 /-93.7     |0.30 /-93.7
|3|
|=
| |           |(1)+(5)+(6) IN PAR.|              |T LINE STRETCHER|T LINE STRETCHER
| |           |-----(7)-----    |                |----(ALT 5)----- |----(ALT 6)-----
|N|Z(series)  |                 |                |-11.3           |-7.0.9
|E|Z(parallel)|                 |                |+20.3           |+13.9
|T|Value. ser |                 |                |3769 pF         |6092 pF
|W|Value. par.|                 |                |0.86 uH         |0.59 uHF
|O|   Z(ohm)= | 50 + j0         |                |34.05+j0        |-119 + j0
|R|E(E,deg)=  | 35.5 /-93.7     |                |35.5 /-93.7     |35.5 /-93.7
|K|I(A,deg)=  | 0.71 /-93.7     |                |1.04 /-93.8     |0.30 /-93.7
|4|
```

Figure 2.103—Worksheet for the four-square array with 1/8 λ spacing designed according to the Gehrke method. This close-spaced array is attractive for 160 meters; 3/16 λ-long elements with either capacitive top loading or linear loading should be used. The drawback is very low and negative feed-point impedances, which result in narrow-banded feed networks. See text for details.

Figure 2.104—Gehrke-designed four-square array with 1/8 λ spacing. The direction switching arrangement shown in Figure 2.98 can be used.

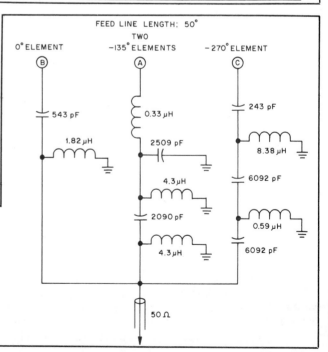

FEED LINE LENGTH: 50°
TWO
0° ELEMENT   −135° ELEMENTS   −270° ELEMENT

```
|================================================================================================================|
| ARRAY: (4 SQUARE ARRAY        |                      CABLE VELOCITY FACTOR: 0.66                                 |
|        (1/8 WAVE SPACING      |                      MIN FEEDER LENGTH: 50 DEG                                   |
|        (FED IN 135 DEG STEPS  |                      F = 3.80 MHz                                                |
|----------------------------------------------------------------------------------------------------------------|
|A|          ELEM 1.           |      ELEM.2         |      ELEM.3          |      ELEM.4             |
|N|---------------------------------------------------------------------------------------------------|
|T|            |Z(1,2)= 30-j3  | Z(2,3)= 25-j9      | Z(3,4)= 30-j3        |                          |
|E|            |Z(1,3)= 30-j3  | Z(2,4)= 30-j3      |                     |                          |
|N|            |Z(1,4)= 25-j9  |                   |                     |                          |
|N|---------------------------------------------------------------------------------------------------|
|A|Z (ohm)  = | -1.27-j13.2   | 18.9-j33          | 18.9-j33            | -10.8+j21.7              |
|S|E (V, deg)=| 13.26 / -95.6 | 37.8 / +164.1     | 37.8 / +164.1       | 24.24 / -153.5           |
| |I (A, deg)=| 1 / 0         | 1 / -135          | 1 / -135            | 1 / -270                 |
|=|===================================================================================================|
| |CABLES -->| 50 ohm,  50 deg | 50 ohm, 187 deg  | 50 ohm, 187 deg     | 50 ohm, 300.5 deg       |
| |           -----(1)-----   | ------(2)-------  | -------(3)-------    | ------(4)------          |
|N|Z(series) |               |                   |                     |                          |
|E|Z(parallel)| SWR = 42 /1   | SWR = 3.9/1       | SWR = 3.9 /1        | SWR = 5.5 /1             |
|T|Value. ser |               |                   |                     |                          |
|W|Value. par.|               |                   |                     |                          |
|O|    Z(ohm)=| -1.78 + j35.24 | 16.38 - j25.55   | 16.38 + j25.55      | -13.32 -j33.6            |
|R|   E(E,deg)=| 29.8 / +91.57 | 32.6 / -9.87    | 32.6 / -9.87        | 32.5 / -9.7              |
|K|   I(A,deg)=| 0.84 / -1.32  | 1.07 / +47.46    | 1.07 / +47.46       | 0.9 / +101.9             |
|1|                         3 |                   |                     |                          |
|=|===================================================================================================|
| |          SHUNT IN L NETW   |                   |                     |                          |
| |          -----(5)------   | ---------------   | ---------------     | ---------------          |
|N|Z(series) | +39           |                   |                     |                          |
|E|Z(parallel)| -74           |                   |                     |                          |
|T|Value. ser | 1.62 uH       |                   |                     |                          |
|W|Value. par.| 567 pF        |                   |                     |                          |
|O|    Z(ohm)=| -840 + j0     |                   |                     |                          |
|R|   E(E,deg)=| 32.6  -93.6  |                   |                     |                          |
|K|   I(A,deg)=| 0.039 / +86.1 |                   |                     |                          |
|4|                           |                   |                     |                          |
|=|===================================================================================================|
| |          PI LINE STRETCHER |                   |                     |                          |
| |          ------(6)-------  | ---------------   | ---------------     | ---------------          |
|N|Z(series) | +836          |                   |                     |                          |
|E|Z(parallel)| -930          |                   |                     |                          |
|T|Value. ser | 35 uH         |                   |                     |                          |
|W|Value. par.| 45 pF         |                   |                     |                          |
|O|    Z(ohm)=| -840 + j0     |                   |                     |                          |
|R|   E(E,deg)=| 32.6 / -9.7  |                   |                     |                          |
|K|   I(A,deg)=| 0.038 / -9.7  |                   |                     |                          |
|2|                           |                   |                     |                          |
|=|===================================================================================================|
| |     (2)+(3)+(4)+(6) PAR   |                   | SUNT IN L NETW      |                          |
| |     ------(7)------       | ---------------   | ------(8)--------   | ---------------          |
|N|Z(series) |               |                   | +23.8               |                          |
|E|Z(parallel)|              |                   | -13.5               |                          |
|T|Value. ser |              |                   | 1.00 uH             |                          |
|W|Value. par.|              |                   | 3101 pF             |                          |
|O|    Z(ohm)=| 3.4 - j11.3   |                   | 50 + j0             |                          |
|R|   E(E,deg)=| 32.5 / -9.7  |        ------->    | 36.0 /+138.4        |                          |
|K|   I(A,deg)=| 2.75 /63.5    |                   | 0.72 / +138.4       |                          |
|3|                           |                   |                     |                          |
|================================================================================================================|
```

Figure 2.105—Worksheet for the Christman-type feed system design for the four-square array with 1/8 λ spacing.

(as in leg 1, where we transform $-1.78 + j35.25$ ohms to $-1013 + j0$ ohms), the operational bandwidth will be very narrow. If more bandwidth is desired, the single L-network must be replaced by cascaded L-networks, each doing part of the transformation. The schematic of the feed network is shown in Figure 2.104.

The Christman approach worksheet is shown in Figure 2.105. After running the "FEEDLINE VOLTAGE" program, it was discovered that identical voltages (32.6 V $/ -9.8°$) were found on the feed lines to elements 2, 3 and 4 at 187, 187 and 301° from the loads. Using the "SHUNT-INPUT L-NETWORK ITERATION" program, an input impedance value was computed for the network that would yield a voltage of 32.6 volts (magnitude). This value is -840 ohms. Notice again the high impedance transformation ratio (-1.78 to -840 ohms), which will seriously limit the bandwidth of the system. Next, the phase-correcting line

stretchers were evaluated, and it was found that the Pi filter yielded reasonable values.

After combining the input of the line stretcher with the junction of the feed lines to elements 2, 3 and 4, the impedance at this point is calculated using the "T-JUNCTION" program. The result is $3.4 - j11.3$ ohms. This value can be transformed to 50 ohms with an L-network. The complete feed system schematic is shown in Figure 2.106.

The Lewallen method can be used as well, making use of two networks, as shown in Figure 2.107. Assume we chose the two center elements as the elements to be fed directly with quarter-wave feed lines. (This is the logical choice, as these are the only two elements that take power from the feed line; the other two supply power to the feed system by virtue of mutual coupling.) The networks between A and B and between A and C are designed as explained above (see Figure 2.107).

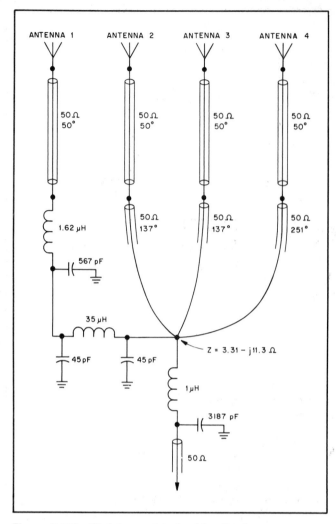

Figure 2.106—Christman-style feed for the four-square array with 1/8 λ spacing between the elements.

As the 1/8 λ-spaced square array does not use quadrature feed angles, the Collins feed method using the quadrature hybrid coupler cannot be used.

Side-by-Side End-fire Arrays with Cardioid Patterns

When attempting to make a Christman-style feed system, we must first run the "FEEDLINE VOLTAGE" program. In our previous attempts to design such a feed system, we have looked for points of equal voltage on the feed lines. With the side-by-side square, we will not use this method. Therefore, the author has developed another feed system which really is a combination of the Gehrke and Christman methods. This method has no advantages over the Gehrke method, but is explained to illustrate the design possibilities the user has with the computer programs listed in Chapter VII.

The feed lines from the elements to the central point are 100° long. At that point we parallel the feed lines to elements 1 and 2, and parallel the feed lines to elements 3 and 4. The worksheet is shown in Figure 2.108. The voltages at the junction points are 55.07 V $\angle +93.42°$ and 50.85 V $\angle +16.65°$. The impedances at the junction points are 25.85 $+j37.49$ ohms and 15.06 $+j2.28$ ohms, respectively. We will now design networks for the leg going to elements 3 and 4, which will provide the voltage at the junction point of elements 1 and 2 (55.07 V $\angle +93.42°$) at its end.

With the "SHUNT-INPUT L-NETWORK ITERATION"

program, we can find the required input impedance for the L-network (18.1 ohms). The low-pass network was chosen and it produces an input voltage of 55.1 V $\angle +32.21°$. Now we need a line stretcher to bridge the angular gap between the 32.21° at the output and the required 93.42° at the input. After evaluation of the Pi- and T-networks, the Pi-network was chosen. Now the input of the line stretcher can be paralleled with the feed line T junction of elements 1 and 2, but we still do not have a 50-ohm impedance. We must now calculate the resulting impedance at the combination point using the "T-JUNCTION" program; 25.85 $+j37.49$ ohms and 18.1 $+j0.0$ ohms in parallel give a total impedance of 13.78 $+j3.68$ ohms. We now need another L-network at the junction point to produce a 50-ohm impedance at the input. Both the low- and the high-pass alternatives yield reasonable component values. The complete schematic is shown in Figure 2.109.

With the Gehrke method, we would have had the last L-network between the junction point of feed lines 1 and 2 and the final T junction, where the required 50-ohm impedance would have been reached without the need for another L-network. The total number of components would have been the same.

The side-by-side array with a cardioid pattern can also be fed with a feed system designed by the Collins method, as described in Section 2.11.1.4. As for the four-square diamond array, the four elements must be fed with quarter-wave lengths of feed line to the point in the center of the square array. Only expanded-polyethylene dielectric cable will allow this. Going through the design procedure for 50-ohm cable gives the following results.

1) For the 90° long feed lines to the 0° elements ($I_{out} = 1$ A $\angle 0°$, $Z_{el} = 18.9 - j33$ ohms):

$Z_{in} = 32.67 + j57.04$ ohms
$I_{in} = 0.76$ A $\angle +29.8°$
$E_{in} = 50$ V $\angle +90°$
SWR = 3.92:1

Paralleling the two feed lines results in Z = 16.34 $+j28.52$ ohms.

2) For the 90° long feed lines to the −90° elements ($I_{out} = 1$ A $\angle -90°$, $Z_{el} = 83.9 + j3$ ohms):

$Z_{in} = 29.76 - j1.06$ ohms
$I_{in} = 1.68$ A $\angle 2.04°$
$E_{in} = 50$ V $\angle 0°$
SWR = 1.68:1

Paralleling the two feed lines results in Z = 14.88 $-j0.53$ ohms.

Using the program "SWR ITERATION," we can calculate an optimum value for the hybrid coupler impedance. For the parallel feed lines to the 0° elements, the SWR in a 50-ohm system is 3.36:1. In a 28.12-ohm system, the SWR is 1.89:1. For the parallel feed lines to the other elements, the SWR is 4.14:1 in a 50-ohm system and 3.81:1 in a 28.12-ohm system. The value of 28.12 ohms was determined as being the transformed impedance of 50 ohms using a quarter-wave feed-line transformer section consisting of two paralleled 75-ohm cables ($Z_{tot} = 37.5$ ohms) and seems to be the best compromise impedance for this system. However, the SWR for this array is not good, and less than optimal performance must be expected from this feeding/phasing approach.

The input port (port 1) of the coupler will be fed via a quarter-wave 37.5-ohm cable to the 50-ohm feed line going

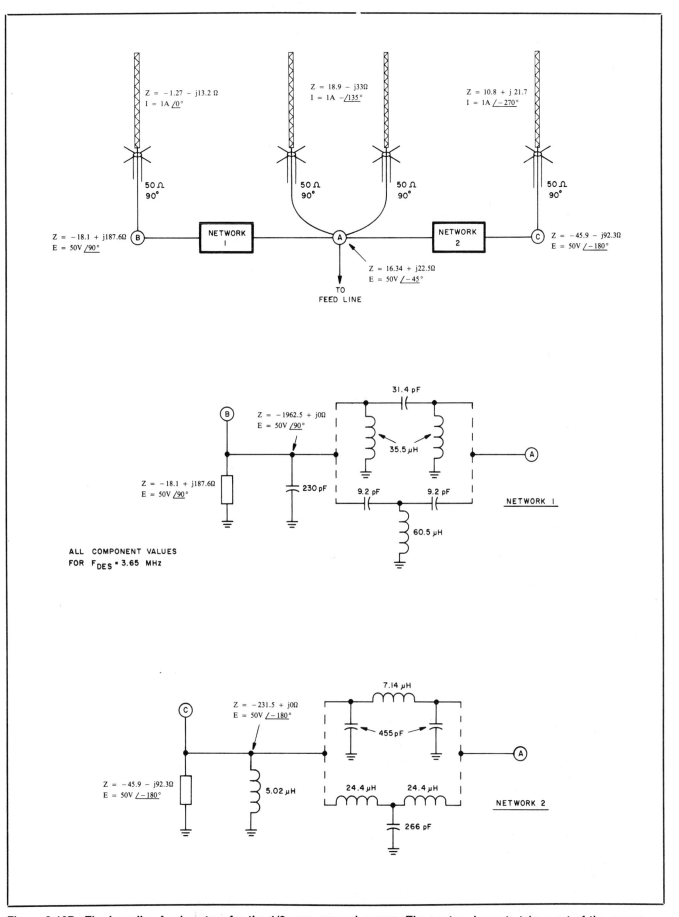

Figure 2.107—The Lewallen feed system for the 1/8-wave-spaced square. The center elements take most of the power, while the front and rear elements feed some power back into the system. Because of this, the array is fed at point A. Two networks take care of the necessary phase shifting.

```
ARRAY: (4 SQUARE, SIDE BY SIDE        CABLE VELOCITY FACTOR: 0.66
       (ENDFIRE, CARDIOD              MIN FEEDER LENGTH: 100 DEG
       (90 DEG PHASE                  F = 3.8 MHz
```

	ELEM 1.	ELEM.2	ELEM.3	ELEM.4
ANTENNA IN	Z(1,2)= 15-j15 Z(1,3)= 15-j15 Z(1,4)= 3-j17.5	Z(2,3)= 3-j17.5 Z(2,4)= 15-j15	Z(3,4)= 15-j15	
A SIDE Z (ohm) = E (V, deg)= I (A, deg)=	18.9 -j33 38.03 / -60.2 1 / 0	18.9 -j33 38.03 / -60.2 1 / 0	30.13 +j4.57 50.85 / +16.65 1 / -90	30.13 +j4.57 50.85 / +16.65 1 / -90
CABLES -->	50 ohm, 100 deg ------(A)-------	50 ohm, 100 deg ------(B)-------	50 ohm, 100 deg ------(C)-------	50 ohm, 100 deg ------(D)-------
NETWORK 1 Z(series) Z(parallel) Value. ser Value. par.	SWR = 3.91/1	SWR 3.92/1	SWR = 1.68/1	SWR = 1.68/1
Z(ohm)= E(E,deg)= I(A,deg)=	51.71 +j74.99 55.07 / +93.42 0.605 / +38.0	51.71 +j74.9 55.07 / +93.42 0.605 / +38.0	30.13 + j4.57 50.85 / +16.65 1.67 / +8.02	30.12 + j4.57 50.85 / +16.65 1.67 / +8.02
NETWORK 2 Z(series) Z(parallel) Value. ser Value. par.	(A)+(B) IN PARAL. ------(1)-------		(C)+(D) IN PARAL. ------(2)-------	SHUNT IN L NETW. ------(3)------ +4.49 -40.3 0.19 uH 1039 pF
Z(ohm)= E(E,deg)= I(A,deg)=	25.85 + j37.49 55.07 / +93.42 1.21 / +38.8		15.06 + j2.28 50.25 / +16.65 3.3 / +8.04	18.1 + j0 55.1 / +32.2 3.04 / +32.2
NETWORK 3 Z(series) Z(parallel) Value. ser Value. par.		(1)+(5) IN PARAL. ------(4)-------		PI LINE STRETCHER ------(5)------ +15.9 -30.6 0.66 uH 1369 pF
Z(ohm)= E(E,deg)= I(A,deg)=		13.78 + j3.68 55.1 / +93.42 3.86 / +78.5		18.1 + j0 55.1 / +93.42 3.04 / +93.42
NETWORK 4 Z(series) Z(parallel) Value. ser Value. par.		SHUNT IN L NETW. ------(7)------ +18.7 -30.8 0.78 uH 1358 pF		
Z(ohm)= E(E,deg)= I(A,deg)=		50 + j0 101.4 / +136.8 2.02 / +136.8		

Figure 2.108—Worksheet for the side-by-side square cardioid array. A combination of the Gehrke and Christman principles was used in this design. See text for details.

into the shack. The quarter-wave line consists of two paralleled 75-ohm lines.

The design parameters for the coupler are: $X_{L1} = X_{L2} = 28.12$ ohms, and $X_{C1} = X_{C2} = 56.24$ ohms. For a design frequency of 3.65 MHz, this represents component values of 1.23 μH for the coils, and 775 pF for the capacitors. Using a T225-2 core, L1 and L2 require 10.1 turns each. The terminating resistor value at port 3 will be 28.12 ohms. See Section 2.11.1.4 for further details. The feed system is illustrated in Figure 2.110A.

The Lewallen feed method can also be applied to this array. (Figure 2.110B shows all the possible configurations.) The two feed lines running to the back elements are paralleled at point A, and the feed lines to the front elements at point B. The matching network will be connected between points A and B, and considering that we can use either a Pi- or T-network line stretcher, there are four possible feed configurations. If point A is to be the array feed point, the output impedance of the array will be found at point B, and it is this value that must be made resistive with a shunt-input network. All four possible feed networks are shown in Figure 2.110B.

Triangular Array

Atchley, W1CF, described a three-element array where the verticals are positioned in an equilateral triangle with sides measuring 0.29 λ (Ref 939 and 941). The lead element is fed at 0° and the two side elements at −90°. The gain of this array is 5.5 dB over a single vertical, and the F/B ratio is better than 10 dB over a beamwidth of 120°. Using one leading element and two lagging elements, only three directions can be selected with this configuration. Because the 3-dB beamwidth is 140°, this is not a problem. By using two elements with leading phase and one element with lagging phase, another three directions can be obtained which are

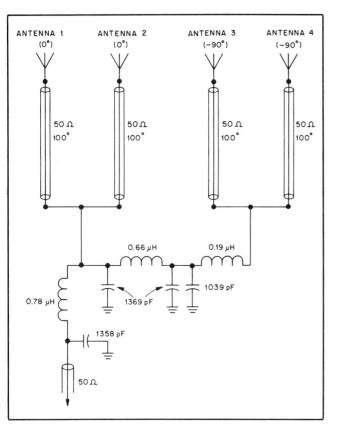

Figure 2.109—Modified Christman/Gehrke feed method as developed on the worksheet in Figure 2.108 for the four-square array (side-by-side end-fire arrays). The direction switching method as shown in Figure 2.98 can be used.

offset by 60° from the first three directions. The directivity pattern and gain is very similar to the former configuration.

Gehrke, K2BT, improved the same array by feeding the two back elements with half the current of the front element. This improved the zero-angle front-to-back ratio to almost infinity with a back rejection of 20 dB or better over a beamwidth of 60°. In real conditions (computed at a wave angle of 30°), the forward lobe 3-dB beamwidth is 150°, and the F/B ratio is reduced to 20 dB (with a rejection of only 10 dB over an 80°-wide lobe). This shows how important it is to calculate patterns over real ground, and how much the figures can differ from those calculated for ideal conditions.

Figure 2.111 shows the patterns for the triangular arrays for ideal as well as for real conditions. In view of the beamwidth of the arrays (150°), there is no real need to have more than three directions to cover 360°. Nevertheless, the pattern of the array feeding the two side elements with the leading current and the third element with the lagging current was also evaluated, and produced exactly the same pattern as in the former configuration. The element data for this array is given in Table 29.

Figure 2.112 shows the worksheet for the triangular array. Because two of the three elements have identical feed point voltages, the solution methodology is very similar to the one adopted for the two element cardioid array. The only lumped-constant elements needed in the feed system are one inductor and one capacitor which constitute the L-network for matching the impedance at the T junction $(13.81 - j9.1$ ohms) to the 50-ohm line to the shack. The 1.32 μH series inductance and the 1356-pF parallel capacitance seems the logical choice. We can use one less discrete component by using a quarter-

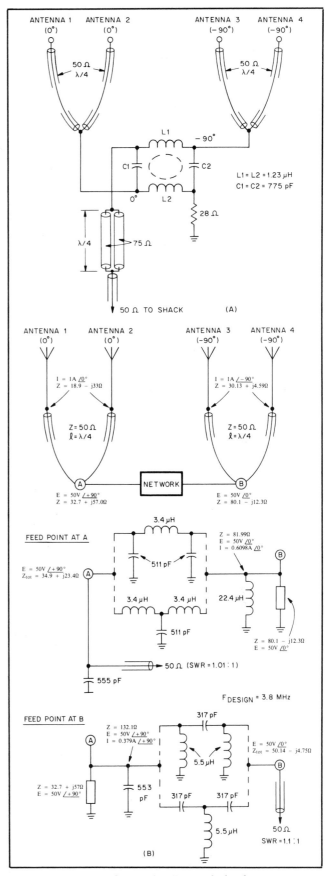

Figure 2.110—The Collins feeding and phasing arrangement for the side-by-side four-element cardioid array is shown at A. The hybrid coupler was designed for a system impedance of 28 ohms to provide the best possible coupling efficiency. Part B shows the feed systems for this array designed using the Lewallen method.

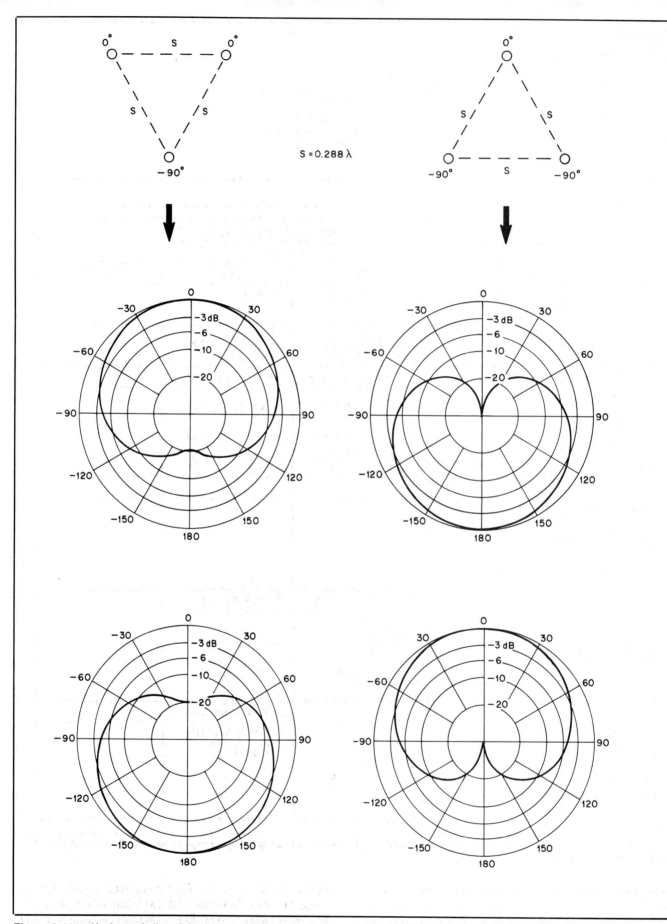

Figure 2.111—Horizontal directivity patterns for triangular arrays using 0.288 λ spacing between elements. Notice the two feed alternatives for the array, which result in identical patterns. The two elements that are fed with the same phase are fed with ½ the current of the third element.

Table 29

Element Data for 3-el Triangular Array

Element	Current Ratio	Phase Angle (deg)	Mutual Impedance (ohms)	Driving Impedance (ohms)
1	1.0	0	Z(12) = 10 −*j*16	Z(1) = 20.4 −*j*10
2	0.5	−90		Z(2) = 78.4 +*j*4
3	0.5	−90		Z(3) = 78.4 +*j*4

Note: Z(12) = Z(23) = Z(13)

ARRAY: (3 El TRIANGULAR ARRAY (0.289 WAVE SPACING (90 DEG PHASE SHIFT		CABLE VELOCITY FACTOR: 0.66 MIN FEEDER LENGTH: 72 DEG F = 3.8 MHz		
	ELEM 1.	ELEM.2	ELEM.3	ELEM.4
ANTENNAS	Z(1,2)= 10-j16 Z(1,3)= 10-j16 Z(1,4)=	Z(2,3)= 10-j16 Z(2.4)=	Z(3,4)=	
Z (ohm) =	20.4 - j10	78.4 +j4	78.4 + j4	
E (V, deg)=	22.72 / -26.11	39.25 / -87.08	39.25 / -87.08	
I (A, deg)=	1 / 0	0.5 / -90	0.5 / -90	
CABELE -->	50 ohm, 157 deg --------(A)--------	50 ohm, 222 deg --------(B)--------	50 ohm, 222 deg --------(C)--------	
NETWORK 1 Z(series) Z(parallel) Value. ser Value. par.	SWR = 2.57/1	SWR = 1.57/1	SWR = 1.57/1	
Z(ohm)=	27.75 - j28.87	49.73 - j 22.84	49.73 - j 22.84	
E(E,deg)=	34.3 / +123	34.1 / +122	34.1 / +122	
I(A,deg)=	0.857 / +169.28	0.628 / +146.68	0.628 / +146.68	
NETWORK 2	(A)+(B)+(C) IN PAR. --------(1)--------			
Z(series)				
Z(parallel)				
Value. ser				
Value. par.				
Z(ohm)=	13.81 - j 9.1			
E(E,deg)=	34.2 / +123			
I(A,deg)=	2.07 / +156.3			
NETWORK 3	SHUNT IN L NETW. --------(2)--------	SHUNT IN L NETW. --------(3)--------	SERIES NETWORK --------(4)--------	
Z(series)	+31.65	-31.16	+9.1	
Z(parallel)	-30.89	+30.89	-	
Value. ser	1.32 uH	3183 pF	0.38 uH	
Value. par.	1356 pF	1.29 uH	-	
Z(ohm)=	50 + j0	50 + j0	13.81 + j0	
E(E,deg)=	54.3 / +145	54.3 / +98.4	2.07 / +156.4	
I(A,deg)=	1.09 / +145	1.09 / +98.4		
NETWORK 4			QUARTER WAVE TRANSF	
Z(series) Z(parallel) Value. ser			25 OHM SECTION (2 x 50 ohm in parallel)	
Value. par.				
Z(ohm)=				
E(E,deg)=				
I(A,deg)=				

Figure 2.112—Worksheet for the triangular array with one leading- and two lagging-current elements. The Christman method was used to design this system.

wave transformer. A quarter-wave line with a 25-ohm impedance (two 50-ohm lines in parallel) provides an excellent match between 13.81 ohms and 50 ohms. The required series inductance is 0.38 μH. Alternatively, one may use an L-network (network 2 and 3 in Figure 2.112).

Figure 2.113 shows the Gehrke feed system (Ref 924) and Figure 2.114 shows the Christman feed system for the triangular array. Note that while the Gehrke method requires only three relays for switching directivity, it requires a total of three coils and three capacitors. The Christman approach requires six relays, but only one coil and one capacitor.

The Collins feed method can also be used to design a feed

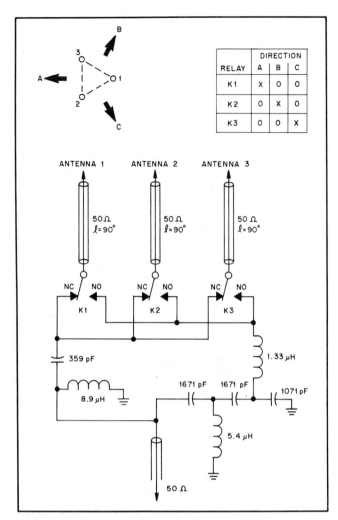

RELAY	DIRECTION		
	A	B	C
K1	X	O	O
K2	O	X	O
K3	O	O	X

Figure 2.113—Feed system for the triangular array designed according to the Gehrke method (Ref 924). Note that three SPDT relays are required for direction switching.

system for this array. However, the two elements fed in phase require half the current amplitude of the third element. (This can be accommodated by feeding the element requiring the higher current with a quarter-wave feed line having half the characteristic impedance of the feed line to the two lower-current elements.) Consider the following example. The $0°$ element is fed with unity (amplitude) current, while the two $-90°$ elements are fed with half the current magnitude.

1) For a $90°$ long feed line with a 37.5-ohm impedance (paralleled 75-ohm lines) to the $0°$ elements ($I_{out} = 1$ A $\angle 0°$, $Z_{el} = 20 - j10$ ohms):

$Z_{in} = 56.24 + j28.13$ ohms
$I_{in} = 0.59$ A $\angle +63.4°$
$E_{in} = 37.5$ V $\angle +90°$
SWR $= 3.82:1$ on each of the 75-ohm lines.

2) For $90°$ long 75-ohm feed lines to the $-90°$ elements ($I_{out} = 0.5$ A $\angle -90°$, $Z_{el} = 78.4 + j4$ ohms):

$Z_{in} = 71.56 - j3.65$ ohms
$I_{in} = 0.52$ A $\angle 2.9°$
$E_{in} = 37.5$ V $\angle 0.0°$
SWR on each line $= 1.04:1$.

Paralleling the two feed lines results in
$Z = 35.78 - j1.83$ ohms.

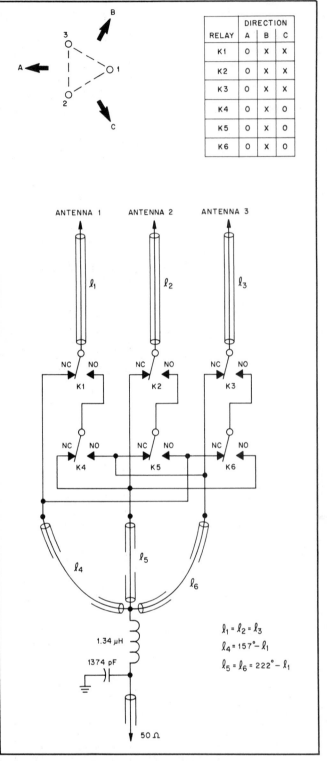

RELAY	DIRECTION		
	A	B	C
K1	O	X	X
K2	O	X	X
K3	O	X	X
K4	O	X	O
K5	O	X	O
K6	O	X	O

$\ell_1 = \ell_2 = \ell_3$
$\ell_4 = 157° - \ell_1$
$\ell_5 = \ell_6 = 222° - \ell_1$

Figure 2.114—Feed method for the triangular array according to the Christman method, as calculated on the worksheet in Figure 2.112. This arrangement uses only two discrete components, but it does require six relays.

We can use the program "SWR ITERATION" to select the best hybrid coupler design impedance for low input SWRs at ports 2 and 4. A 50-ohm impedance value yields an SWR of 1.71:1 at port 2 and 1.4:1 at port 4. It is rather difficult to make this array switchable, because the feed lines are not of the same impedance. One could consider running two 75-ohm feed lines in parallel to all three elements, and using them as parallel elements when a 37.5-ohm impedance is

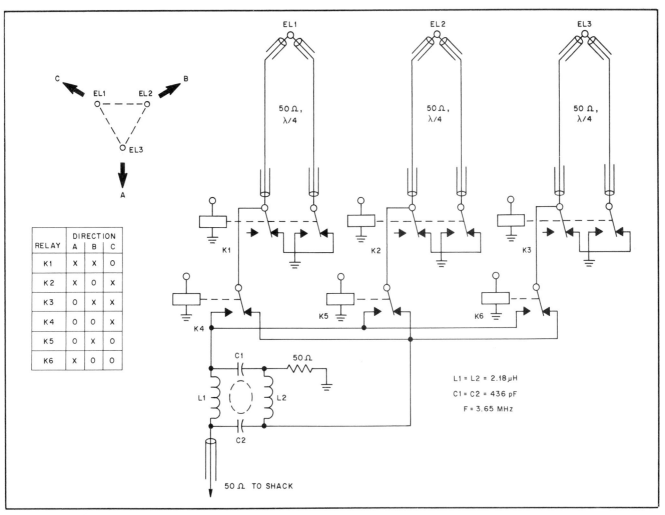

Figure 2.115—Collins feed method for the triangular array. Notice that two 75-ohm feed lines run to each element. The element requiring twice as much current as the other two is fed via the two paralleled coaxial cables. At the other two elements, the end of one of the two quarter-wave lines will be shorted to ground, effectively disconnecting it from the element at the other end. See text for further details.

required, and shorting the center conductor to ground (at the switching box) when 75 ohms is required. This would decouple the second feed line from the element. (Its length is a quarter wavelength, so the short circuit at one end is transformed into an open circuit at the element feed point.) This approach is shown in Figure 2.115

The Lewallen-type feed-system design is similar to the Collins-type feed-system design for this array. Figure 2.116 shows the four possible Lewallen-type networks that can be designed using the procedure described in Section 2.11.1.4. The array can be fed at either point A or point B. The network will be installed between points A and B. Depending on the position of the array feed point, either point A or point B can be the output of the network. First we need to calculate the shunt reactance to be placed across the output impedance in order to make this impedance resistive by use of the "SHUNT IMPEDANCE NETWORK" program. When designing the line stretcher required to provide the 90° phase shift, make sure to specify the input and output phase angles correctly. Directivity switching can be done in the same way as it is done for the Collins-type array design.

Close-Spaced Multi-Element Array with Elements Fed in Phase

Arrays with several close-spaced elements (typically spaced

0.05 λ apart) and fed in phase do not exhibit any appreciable gain in any direction, but they have another valuable property. When installed over a poor ground, the system efficiency can be improved substantially by using two or more close-spaced in-phase elements.

Using the "DRIVING IMPEDANCE" program listed in Chapter VII, we can calculate the individual element impedances, given the mutual impedances and feed current amplitude and phase. For quarter-wave elements, we can take the mutual impedances from Table 19. In practice, however, the mutual impedances must be calculated by the designer. This can be done with the "MUTUAL IMPEDANCE" program.

Consider the examples of quarter-wave elements over two vastly different ground systems, one with an equivalent resistance of 10 ohms (good ground) and one with an equivalent resistance of 50 ohms (poor ground). The efficiencies in both cases are calculated by dividing the radiation resistance by the sum of the radiation resistance and the loss resistance.

Table 30 shows the mutual impedances, taken from Table 19, for four systems (single vertical, two in line, three in a triangle and four in a square). The feed-point impedances are calculated with the "MUTUAL IMPEDANCE" program for a spacing (between adjacent elements) of 0.05 λ. The

Table 30

Ground Loss Characteristics for Vertical Systems

System	Mutual Impedance* (ohms)	10-Ohm Ground Loss				50-Ohm Ground Loss			
		Z_{feed} (ohms)	R_{rad} (ohms)	Efficiency (%)	(dB)	Z_{feed} (ohms)	R_{rad} (ohms)	Efficiency (%)	(dB)
1 el		46 +j0	36.0	78	1.0	86 +j0	36.0	42	3.8
2 el	Z(12) = 36 +j12	82 +j12	71.8	88	0.6	122 +j12	71.8	59	2.3
3 el	Z(12) = 36 +j12	118 +j24	107.6	91	0.4	158 +j24	107.6	68	1.7
4 el	Z(12) = 36 +j12	152 +j56	142.4	93	0.3	192 +j56	142.4	74	1.3
	Z(14) = 35 +j32								

*Note: For 2 el, Z(12) = Z(21).
For 3 el Z(12) = Z(13) = Z(23) = Z(32).
For 4 el, Z(12) = Z(13) = Z(24) = Z(34) and Z(14) = Z(23).

radiation resistances are listed and the resulting efficiencies are expressed in percentages and in dB values for both the 10-ohm and the 50-ohm ground. Because all of the vertical elements have the same driving impedance, they can all be fed with equal lengths of feed line to a point in the center of the element feed points.

Note that the efficiency improvement is only worthwhile for the poor ground system, where 2.5 dB of gain can be achieved by replacing the single element with four elements, as evidenced by Table 30. With eight elements, the gain would be 3 dB. Although this approach is not frequently used by hams, it is an attractive way of realizing high efficiency in a vertical over a poor ground (such as desert).

A feed system for a four-square array can consist of four 93-ohm coaxial lines connected to a common point at the center of the system. For an 80-meter array with 0.05 λ spacing between adjacent elements, the distance from each element to the center is 0.03036 λ, or 10.9°. With the "COAX TRANSFORMER" program, we can calculate the impedance at the end of the feed lines. In the case of the 50-ohm ground, the 152.4 +j56-ohm element feed impedance is transformed to 209.6 − j24.04 ohms. The SWR on each 93-ohm feed line is 2.3:1. No current, voltage or power-handling problems should be encountered, even with 1500 W applied to the array, as only ¼ of the total power is carried by each feed line. At this power level, the current amplitude at each element is only 1.39 A, with a voltage of 281 V. At the point where the four feed lines are combined, the impedance is 52.4 − j6.51 ohms, which is an near-perfect match for a 50-ohm line (SWR = 1.15:1).

The same approach can be used for calculating the radiation efficiency gains and feed systems for shorter elements. In many circumstances, this may be an attractive solution for 160-meter work, where short elements are often used in combination with rather poor ground systems. Another application is for mobile operation, where two or four close-spaced whip antennas fed in phase can produce worthwhile omnidirectional gain. Directional gain will be negligible, as the elements are fed in phase and closely spaced.

Choosing the Best System

Until Gehrke published his series on vertical arrays, it was general practice to simply use feed lines as delay lines, and to equal electrical line length to phase delay under all circumstances. We now know that there are better ways of accomplishing the same goal. Fortunately, as Gehrke states, these vertical arrays are relatively easy to get working. It can be seen from the plots in Figure 2.64 that from a forward gain point of view, the phase delays are not always critical. From a rejection (front-to-back) point of view, however, phasing accuracy is much more critical. This is one reason why many arrays with reasonable gain but only mediocre front-to-back ratios are in use.

The Christman method makes maximum use of the transformation characteristics of coaxial feed lines, thus minimizing the number of discrete components required in the feed networks. This is an attractive solution, and should not scare off potential array builders. The Collins approach has two advantages over the Gehrke and Christman methods: it requires very few discrete components and has a better bandwidth than the other two systems. The disadvantage is that power is lost in the terminating resistor. Collins claims that essentially the same front-to-back ratio can be achieved from 3.5 to 3.8 MHz, which makes this approach very attractive for those who want broadband performance. The Gehrke and Christman feed methods yield maximum F/B ratio over a rather limited bandwidth, although the gain will remain nearly constant over large frequency spans. The front-to-back deteriorates faster as the frequency is lowered than as it is raised.

The Collins and Lewallen system of "current forcing" have the advantage that they are not as sensitive to less-than-perfect symmetry in the array in the case of direction switching as the other systems. This can be seen in the more-constant front-to-back ratios in different directions with these systems.

The Lewallen method resembles the Collins method in some respects, and has all the same advantages, except for the Lewallen system's lack of broadbandedness. The design methodology used in this chapter to calculate component values for the Lewallen networks is believed to be original, and is very easy to use if the computer programs are available.

Typically, a Gehrke system designed for 3.8 MHz would show very little F/B ratio on 3.5 MHz although the gain would remain essentially unchanged. When we consider 160 meters, where the required bandwidth may be very narrow, the Christman method (using very few discrete components) is certainly a good choice for several array designs, especially for the popular two-element end-fire, quarter-wave-spaced array with a cardioid pattern.

All of the computer programs discussed in this chapter can be used for many other RF applications, and are listed in Chapter VII. All programs are written in APPLESOFT BASIC. Compiled versions, which run very quickly on an Apple IIe or IIc computer (with an 80-column card), are available from ARRL on diskette. The same diskette also contains all the other programs discussed in this book. This

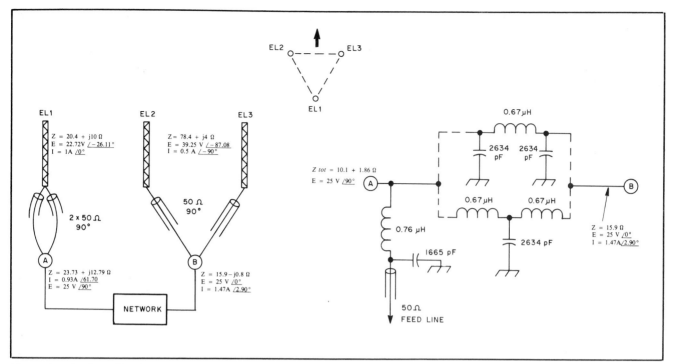

Figure 2.116—Lewallen feed system for the triangular array.

software is also available in other computer formats. See Chapter VII for more details.

Network Component Ratings

When designing array feed networks using the computer programs listed in Chapter VII, one can use absolute currents instead of relative currents as is most commonly done in the design phase. The procedure is explained under the Section called *Feed Systems*. The computer programs will then give the user real current and voltage information at all points in a network, and the choice of the components can be made accordingly. Table 31 shows the multiplication factors for all

currents and voltages shown in the previous worksheets for a given range of transmitter power levels.

If there is any question as to the voltage rating of any of the feed lines that are used as transformers in our designs (all have a SWR greater than 1), the program ''FEEDLINE VOLTAGE,'' with the real current as an input, can be used to calculate what the highest voltage is at any point on the line. We find that for the two-element array with a cardioid pattern (fed according to the Christman method), the highest voltage on a feed line of any length on the line to element 1 (which has a 2.89:1 SWR) is only 338 V with 3 kW applied. For feed line 2, the maximum voltage is 378 V. For the four-square diamond array with ¼ λ spacing, the feed-line-voltage

Table 31
Multiplication Factor for Component Ratings Based on Power Level

Array Type	Transmit Power			
	100 W	800 W	1500 W	3000 W
Two-el End-Fire, ¼ λ Spacing (Cardioid Pattern)	1.17	3.31	4.54	6.42
Two-el End-Fire Bidirectional ½ λ Spacing	1.04	2.97	4.06	5.75
Two-el Broadside Bidirectional ½ λ Spacing	1.35	3.82	5.25	7.39
Three-in-line, ¼ λ Spacing	0.89	2.51	3.43	4.86
Four-Square Array, ¼ λ Wave Spacing	0.83	2.34	3.21	4.54
Four-Square Array, 1/8 λ Spacing	1.96	5.56	7.61	10.76
Four-Square Array, Side-by-Side Cardioids	0.70	1.97	2.70	3.82
Triangular Array, 0.289 λ Spacing	0.73	2.08	2.85	4.02

values are 234 V, 253 V, 253 V and 391 V. This should not represent any problem with good quality RG-213 cable. In a similar fashion the voltages across capacitors or currents through capacitors in the lumped-constant networks can be determined. When evaluating coils, use the following guidelines: For up to 5 μH, it is advisable to use air-wound coils. The best Q factors are achieved with coils having a length/diameter ratio of 1. For higher values, use powdered-iron toroidal cores if necessary. Information on this subject is given in Section 2.4.9.3. The BASIC computer program "COIL CALCULATION" may be helpful in designing the coils.

Tuning and Measuring Vertical Arrays

Measurement of gain is something which is out of reach for all but a few of those lucky enough to have access to an antenna test range. Front-to-back ratio, however, can be measured fairly easily with the help of a second antenna mounted several wavelengths away from the antenna under test. The problem with this approach is that in order for the measurements taken this way to be accurate, the second antenna must be elevated at 20-30° with respect to the antenna under test, since that is the range of wave angles in which the antenna will be primarily used. Careful attention to the construction of an antenna is the one thing that the builder can do to ensure the proper functioning of the antenna.

Impedance Measurement

If one wishes to construct an array using either the Gehrke or Christman feed methods, access to an accurate impedance bridge is essential. The bridge will be needed for measurement of element impedances and, in the case of a Gehrke-type feed system, measurement of the reactances of the components that make up the networks.

Commonly available noise bridges are generally not accurate enough for this kind of thing. Greater success can be obtained with a home-built bridge of the type discussed by Hubbs (W6XU) and Doting (W6NKU) in Ref 1607, and Gehrke (K2BT) in Ref 1610. In order to obtain maximum directivity from an array, it is essential that the self impedances of the elements be identical. Measurement of this also requires a good impedance or noise bridge. Equalizing the resonant frequency can be done by changing the radiator lengths, while equalizing the self impedance can be done by changing the number of radials used.

Network Measurements

Constructing a Gehrke-type feed system requires quite a bit of network designing. Off-site measurement and adjustment of the networks is required also. To do this, first make dummy antennas that have the same impedance as the feed impedance of the array elements (such as 21.4 − j15 ohms

---

Radial Systems for the Array

Radial systems for simple vertical arrays were detailed in Section 2.4.3.4. The same basic rules apply for radial systems for arrays. There are a few specific details that should be noted for arrays, however.

In order to make the self-impedance of all the array elements equal, the number of radials under each element (the quality of the reflecting ground system) may be varied. Having the self-impedances equal is a great advantage when direction-switching the array. See Section 2.11.1.4.

It is inevitable that some of the radials from one element in an array will intersect radials from another element. The accompanying figure shows how the radials might be laid out for a 4-element diamond array with ¼ λ spacing between elements. In a buried radial system one can first install the intersecting wires from A to B and from C to D. Then many radials (about 40) can be installed under each of the four verticals. Where the radials intersect the wires running from A to B and C to D, the radials are soldered to the AB/CD wires. The self impedances of the verticals should then be checked. Make sure that you are only measuring the impedance of the element you wish to measure; all the other elements must be completely decoupled from the system. The length of the elements can be carefully trimmed to make them all resonate on exactly the same frequency. The number of radials may also be varied to achieve identical feed-point impedances.

A similar approach can be used with an elevated radial system where the tips of all the radials are soldered to an outer ring. The area of the radial system shown in Figure A is approximately 3600 square meters (roughly 1 acre) for a 3.65-MHz array. The antenna system requires 21 support poles; 4 at the base of the verticals, 9 for guy wires (if the antennas are not self-supporting) and radials, and 8 for the outer ring of the radial system. One approach would be to connect all 21 support poles with a heavy conductor, such as no. 12 or no. 14 copper-clad steel or bronze wire. Approximately 1000 m (3300 ft) would be required for the 80-meter array shown. This makes the whole system very stable, and the radial wires can then be added. The wire used for the radials can be much smaller (no. 20 or so). If one radial wire is used every 5 degrees (72 radials per element) a total of 5000 m (17,000 ft) of wire will be used

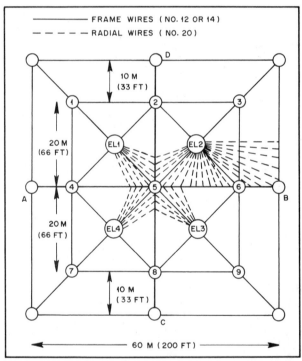

Figure 2.117—Radial system layout for the four-square array. Support poles 1 through 9 are also used as anchors for the antenna guy wires. For an elevated ground system, all the support poles are connected with no. 12 or 14 copper-clad steel or bronze wire. The box containing the switching relays can be mounted on pole number 5 under the radial wires.

for radials. The distance between the tips of ¼ λ radials should not be less than twice the height of the radial system above ground. Radials spaced every 5 degrees should be approximately 3.5 m (12 ft) above ground.

and 51.4 $+j15$ ohms in the case of the two-element end-fire array with cardioid pattern). The former is a series connection of a 21.4-ohm resistor and 2792 pF of capacitance (at 3.75 MHz); the latter is a series connection of a 51.4-ohm resistor with a 0.628 μH inductor. Inductors can be measured precisely by dipping the resonant circuit made by the coil and a standard-value capacitor. Alternatively, one may measure air-wound or toroidal coils using an impedance bridge or an LC meter. The various sub-units of the feed system can now be tested in the lab. Voltages can be measured using a high-quality oscilloscope. If a dual-trace scope is used, the phase difference between two points of interest can also be measured.

Suitable current amplitude and phase probes have been described by Gehrke (Ref 927). When measuring the impedances of the building blocks of a total feed system, make sure you know exactly what you are measuring. All impedances mentioned during the design were impedances looking from the generator toward the load. If a network is measured in the reverse direction (terminating the input of the network with a resistive impedance to measure the output impedance), we will measure the conjugate value. (A conjugate value has the opposite reactance sign; the conjugate of A $+j$B is A $-j$B). All tuning and measurement procedures were adequately covered by Gehrke in Ref 927. The correct coaxial cable lengths can be cut using methods shown in Figure 2.71.

On-site, the builder must make use of an RF ammeter for element-current amplitude measurements and a good dual-trace oscilloscope to measure the phase difference. The two inputs to the oscilloscope will have to be fed via identical lengths of coaxial cable. Figure 2.118 shows the schematic of the RF current probes for current amplitude and phase angle measurement. Details of the devices can be found in Ref 927.

The Christman feed system requires the same initial element impedance measurements, although no network designing will be necessary. L-networks used for the sole purpose of transforming 50 ohms to 75 ohms generally do not need to be checked any other way than by measurement of the transmission line SWR and, if necessary, adjustment of the component values in the network for a perfect match.

The Lewallen method of feed system design makes it necessary to know the exact impedances of the elements in the array. The necessary matching networks can then be designed and tested off-site using dummy antennas with the same impedances as the array elements.

Quadrature-Fed Arrays

If you are designing an array with quadrature-fed elements, it is possible to check the element current magnitudes and phase relationships by using the simple piece of test equipment described below.

The heart of the circuit is a wideband, single-ended, push-pull transformer. When fed as shown in Figure 2.119, the secondary (C/D) should be completely out of phase. To test this, you can rectify the RF and measure the sum of the two voltages. If you connect points A and B to the end of the quarter-wave feed lines (feeding the elements with a current phase difference of 90°), the voltages at C and D will be 180° out of phase if the voltages at A and B are 90° out of phase. The transformer can be wound on a ferrite core, such as an Indiana General BBR-7731 (also used for feeding Beverage antennas, see Sections 2.13.1.2, 2.13.1.6, and 2.13.1.13) The

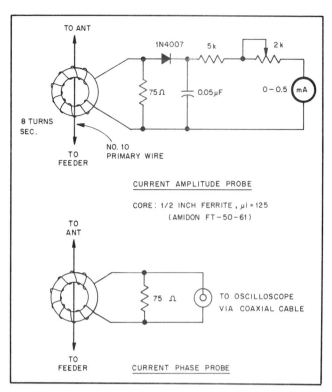

Figure 2.118—Current amplitude and phase probes used for measuring the exact current at the feed point of each array element. See text for details.

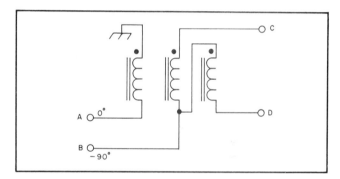

Figure 2.119—This quadrature transformer has a trifilar winding. Notice the phasing dots; the windings must be correctly phased. If voltages A and B are 90° out of phase, the voltage from B to C will be 180° out of phase.

winding consists of four turns, of AWG 20-26 enameled copper wire, trifilar wound. Make sure the phasing is as shown in Figure 2.119.

Where quarter-wave feed lines are used (current forcing method), measuring identical voltage magnitudes at the ends of those lines guarantees identical element feed current magnitudes (if all the feed lines have the same impedance).

Figure 2.120 shows the schematic diagram of this piece of equipment. It can be built in a small, well-shielded box. The circuit contains four voltage-doubling rectifier arrangements with separate sensitivity adjustment potentiometers. All modules should be adjusted for the same sensitivity with the output potentiometers.

The measuring circuit is a straightforward differential FET voltmeter that is fed with a small 9-V battery. The ganged potentiometers in the source circuit of the FETs can be used

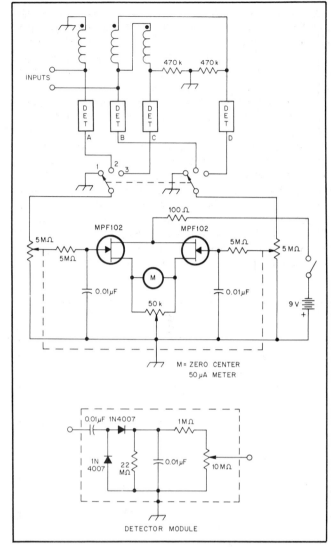

Figure 2.120—This quadrature tester consists of a transformer, four detector modules, a mode switch and a differential voltmeter.

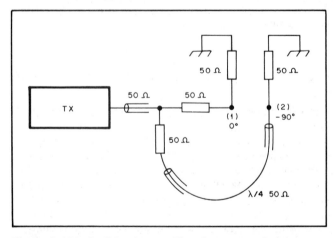

Figure 2.121—In this phase-calibration system for the quadrature tester, RF from the transmitter is divided by two 50-ohm series resistors (to ensure a 1:1 SWR), routed directly to a 50-ohm load, and through a 90° long 50-ohm line (RG-58) to the second 50-ohm load. For a frequency of 3.65 MHz, the cable has a nominal length of 44.49 feet (13.56 m). The cable length should be tuned using the method described in Section 2.11.1.4.

to adjust the overall circuit sensitivity. The three-position input switch has a balancing position (position 1) for adjustment of the 50-kilohm balance potentiometer. With the switch in position 2, the circuit measures the difference between the magnitudes of the voltages at the two inputs. Identical voltage inputs are indicated by a zero meter reading.

With the switch in position 3, the circuit checks for a 90° phase difference between the two inputs. In order to make a non-zero phase shift reading more meaningful, the meter can be calibrated with the setup shown in Figure 2.121. The phase calibrator consists of a quarter-wavelength 50-ohm delay line. At the frequency where the delay line is exactly ¼ λ long, the voltages at A and B will be equal in magnitude but 90° out of phase. The meter can be calibrated by varying the transmit frequency by 5% down and noting the meter reading, then moving the transmit frequency 5% up and making sure that the meter reading is the same. The test circuit can be checked for symmetry by inverting the inputs. The meter should read the same value for the normal or inverted mode. Note that for actual testing in an array, the device must be installed at the ends of the quarter-wave feed lines to the elements (where the direction switching is done).

This device is a very handy tool for making fine adjustments in a Lewallen-type feed system. The meter could be mounted in the shack for convenience. If you are building a Collins-type feed system, you can use this device to check the performance of the hybrid coupler by terminating all three output ports of the coupler with resistors equal to the design impedance of the coupler and then connecting the quadrature checker between the ports that have a 90° phase shift between them. If the coupler is working properly, the meter should read zero.

2.11.2 PHASED ARRAYS MADE WITH DIRECTIONAL ANTENNAS

The horizontal directivity pattern of an antenna is the product of the horizontal patterns of the individual elements and the array directivity pattern. The array directivity pattern is that of an array made with individual elements having an omnidirectional horizontal radiation pattern (such as monopoles). Figure 2.64 shows the array directivity patterns for two-element arrays.

Let us examine two cases.

1) *Two horizontal dipoles with ¼ wave parallel spacing, fed 90° out of phase.* The combination of such elements is done in such a way that the main lobe of the elements is in line with the main lobe of the array directivity pattern. This means in our example that the two dipoles will have to be parallel to one another (and spaced ¼ λ apart). The resulting cardioid pattern will be very similar to the cardioid from the array directivity pattern.

Figure 2.122 shows the horizontal directivity patterns of two arrays: 1) two verticals fed 90° out of phase, spaced 90° (cardioid pattern), and 2) two dipoles in the same configuration. Note the much sharper beam of the second configuration. Two vertical antennas have a 3-dB beamwidth of approximately 150°, while the dipole array yields a beamwidth of only 90°. The narrower beamwidth also accounts for the extra gain, in this case due to the directivity of the dipole elements themselves.

2) *Two dipoles spaced 5/8 λ apart, fed in phase.* In this case, we must put the two dipoles in line, as the array will have an end-fire directivity pattern (radiation perpendicular to the axis between the elements). If we put the dipoles parallel

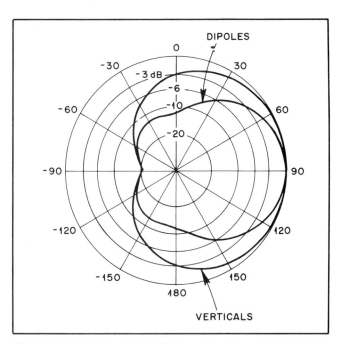

Figure 2.122—Horizontal radiation patterns measured at a 30° wave angle over excellent ground for two quarter-wave verticals and two horizontal dipoles at ½ λ. In both cases, the elements are spaced ¼ λ apart and fed 90° out of phase. Notice the narrower beamwidth of the dipole array, which is a result of the directivity of the individual dipoles.

to one another, a figure-8 pattern would result, and its main lobe would be perpendicular to the broadside pattern associated with the 5/8 λ spacing and in-phase feeding arrangement. As such, no reinforcement of the pattern would occur.

The computer program ANNIE by Rautio, AJ3K, can serve as a very valuable tool for designing your own array, whether it consists of dipoles, monopoles, or sub-arrays.

2.11.2.1 Horizontal Radiation Pattern

The horizontal pattern will depend to a great extent on the quality of the ground. When analyzing an array, it is interesting to first determine the wave angle in several directions, and then analyze the horizontal directivity at one or more main wave angles. As already stated in Section 2.1.1.1, there is no horizontal directivity at zero wave angle under less-than-perfect conditions.

2.11.2.2 Vertical Radiation Pattern

The vertical radiation angle of arrays made of horizontal elements is determined by the height of the elements.

2.11.2.3 Popular Arrays

The ZL Special

The ZL special consists of two dipoles, spaced 1/8 λ apart and driven approximately 135° out of phase. This produces a broadside unidirectional pattern with a gain of approximately 4 dB over a dipole at the same height. When erected horizontally, the radiation angle of the vertically polarized component of the signal will depend only on the height of the array. Good low-angle radiation will only be produced when the antenna is at a height of 3/8 λ or higher.

Different dimensions for this array have been printed in various publications. Correct dimensions for optimum

performance will depend on the material used for the elements and the phasing lines. Jordan, WA6TKT, who designed the ZL special entirely with 300-ohm twin-lead (Ref 908), recommends that the director be 447.3/f (MHz) and the reflector be 475.7/f (MHz), with an element spacing of approximately 0.12 λ. The phasing line, which is electrically 135° long, is made of a 45° long line, in which the connections are reversed to produce 180° of phase shift, resulting in a total delay of 180 − 45 = 135°. Using air-spaced phasing line with a velocity factor of 0.97, the phasing line length is 119.3/f(MHz). The configuration of the ZL special with practical dimensions for a design frequency of 3.8 MHz is given in Figure 2.123. As it is rather unlikely that this antenna will be made rotatable on the low bands, the author recommends the use of open-wire feeders to an antenna tuner. Alternatively, a coaxial feed line can be used via a balun. All formulas here give dimensions in feet. If lengths in meters are required, divide the results by 3.28.

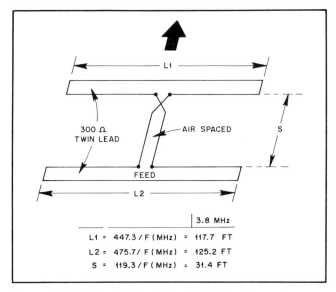

Figure 2.123—The ZL-special (or HB9CV) antenna is a popular design that gives reasonable gain for close element spacing. As with all horizontally polarized antennas, the wave angle will be determined by the height above ground.

Two Half-Waves in Phase, Spaced 0.2 λ, Fed 135° Out of Phase

The array shown in Figure 2.124 has been successfully used by famous low band DXers such as K6UA and N6JL. It is recommended that each element be fed via a ¼ or ¾ λ open-ended, open-wire feeder, on which one looks for the 50-ohm point (which will be quite near the end of the feeders). At this point, 50-ohm coaxial feed lines can be connected via 1:1 baluns. With the proper polarity crossing (180° phase shift), an extra 45° long length of coaxial cable gives the required phase shift for bidirectional broadside radiation. Short-circuited, open-wire feeders of ¼ or ¾ λ are reported to produce very narrowband matching. The array should be at least 120 feet above ground for good low-angle performance.

If the two elements are spaced ¼ λ apart, the arrays can be fed with the two elements 90° out of phase. The elements can be fed via a hybrid coupler as described in the Collins feed method (2.11.1.4).

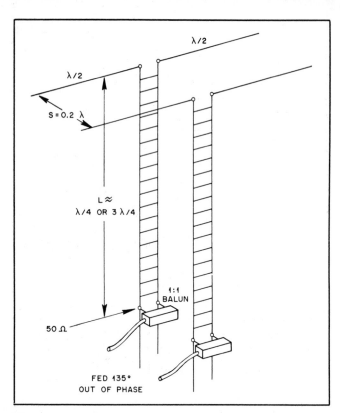

Figure 2.124—The popular two-element, two half-waves in phase. 45° phasing lines plus phase reversal in the coaxial feed line combine to give simple direction switching.

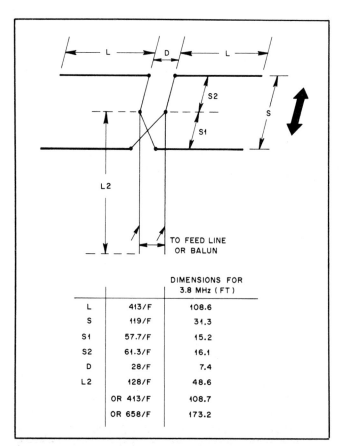

		DIMENSIONS FOR 3.8 MHz (FT)
L	413/F	108.6
S	119/F	31.3
S1	57.7/F	15.2
S2	61.3/F	16.1
D	28/F	7.4
L2	128/F	48.6
	OR 413/F	108.7
	OR 658/F	173.2

Figure 2.125—The W8JK flat-top array produces a bidirectional pattern. To use the antenna on harmonic frequencies, replace the stub-feeding system with open-wire line and an antenna tuner.

W8JK Flat-Top Array

Just as with the ZL special, the W8JK antennas are attractive on the low bands because of the close spacing of the elements (1/8 λ). The W8JK antenna is bidirectional, and has about 6 dB gain over a dipole. A two-section, center-fed, flat-top W8JK array is shown in Figure 2.125. As with all horizontally polarized antennas, the wave angle will depend on the height of the antenna above ground. The antenna is best fed via a stub (Zepp match). The closed stub length can be adjusted for resonance of the array with a grid-dip meter. A low-impedance point can be found near the stub end where we can connect either open-wire line or a coaxial cable (via a balun).

End-fed, flat-top arrays are best in vertical configurations, because the feed points of the elements are close to the ground and readily accessible. Schellenbach, W1JF, described a switchable, vertical W8JK array with reduced total element lengths (Ref 928). His design for 40 and 30 meters could be scaled for 80-meter operation.

Delta Loops and Quads with Cardioid Patterns

Two delta loops in a configuration producing a cardioid pattern are a popular directive array for 80 meters. The systems described in the literature (Ref 1111 and Ref 1132) use a length of transmission line to produce the required phase shift. As explained in Section 2.11.1.4, this will produce exact results only if the feed impedance of the elements is the same as the characteristic impedance of the coaxial cable. Ideally, one should measure the self impedance and the mutual impedance of each element (Ref 923), calculate the element feed impedance and design the proper feed system. The Christman method is recommended for application of the correct current magnitudes and phase angles (see Section 2.11.1.4 and Ref 929).

Fisher, DL6WD, describes an array of two delta loops using 135° phase shift with 1/8 λ spacing (ZL special configuration). He measured self and mutual impedances, and found the feed impedance to be close to 50 ohms. The feed system uses a Wilkinson power divider and an extra 135° length of cable in one of the feed lines (Figure 2.126).

This design uses baluns at both elements. Care should be taken to connect the baluns correctly to provide a 180° phase reversal at the element feed points. This must be done in order to obtain the correct 45° phase shift with the 135° delay line (180 − 135 = 45). The reported bandwidth for a 2:1 SWR is approximately 150 kHz. Anyone tempted to erect this array is cautioned to go to the trouble of measuring impedances and to design the proper matching/phasing/feed-line system for optimum performance, especially when close spacing (such as 1/8 λ) is involved.

The quarter-wave-spaced version (using 90° of phase shift) is less critical in this regard, and simply feeding one element with an extra 90° of feed line may yield acceptable results (Ref 1132). The configuration of this array is the same as shown in Figure 2.126, whereby the 90° phasing line is used with quarter-wave spacing. The balun can be omitted when both feed lines are to be connected to the coax inner conductor going to the sloping quarter-wave section of the deltas.

One can also use the Collins feed method described in Section 2.11.1.4. In this case, two quarter-wave transmission lines run to the quadrature hybrid coupler. The procedure for calculating feed impedances and selecting the most appropriate feed-line and hybrid-coupler design frequency is identical to the one outlined in Section 2.11.1.4. Decoupling

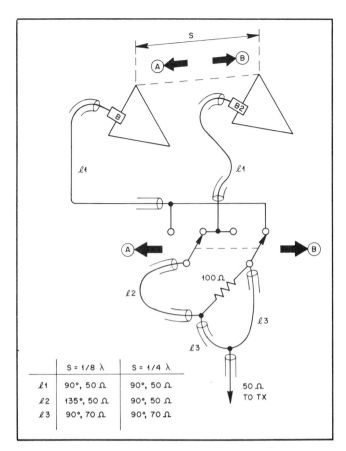

	S = 1/8 λ	S = 1/4 λ
$\ell 1$	90°, 50 Ω	90°, 50 Ω
$\ell 2$	135°, 50 Ω	90°, 50 Ω
$\ell 3$	90°, 70 Ω	90°, 70 Ω

Figure 2.126—Two delta loops can be used in an array. If 1/8 λ spacing is used with 135° of phase shift, baluns must be used at both delta loops, and feed-point connections must be inverted to introduce the required 180° phase shift at that point. With 1/4 λ spacing and 90° phase shift, the coaxial feed lines can be directly connected to the delta loops.

the second element is done by opening the loop (with no feed line connected). Coupling is done by short-circuiting the loop. Collins reports that several amateurs are successfully using his quadrature hybrid coupler for other arrays.

Another feed system for quarter-wave-spaced arrays with 90° of phase shift consists of connecting the feed points of the two elements in parallel via open-wire line with the same impedance as the feed point of the elements. This is quite impractical in most cases, as the typical element feed-point impedances range from 50 to 120 ohms. Open-wire lines with such low impedances are impractical to construct, and air dielectric is required to ensure a velocity factor as close to unity as possible. Figure 2.127 shows this configuration. Each element has a ½ λ-long feed line which can be selected for switching directivity. Quarter-wave lines can also be used provided the unused line is short-circuited. Dvoracek, OK1ATP described a two-element 160-meter array consisting of dipoles, where he uses T-matching systems on both elements to obtain a high enough impedance for an open-wire phasing/feed line with reasonable dimensions (Ref 938).

Delta Loops in Phase (Collinear)

When elements are fed in phase, there are no problems with supplying different amounts of phase shift to each element. All loops are erected in one plane, and spacing between loops will largely influence the array gain. When using close spacing (where the corners of the deltas touch), the feed method must be modified as shown in Figure 2.128. If equilateral triangles

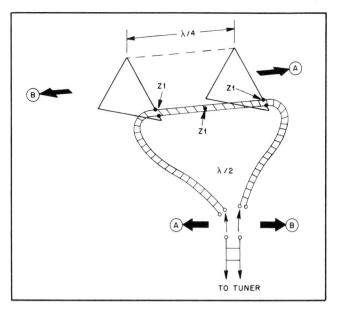

Figure 2.127—This feed method can only be used if an air-dielectric phasing line can be constructed with an impedance that matches the feed impedance of the two array elements. See text for details.

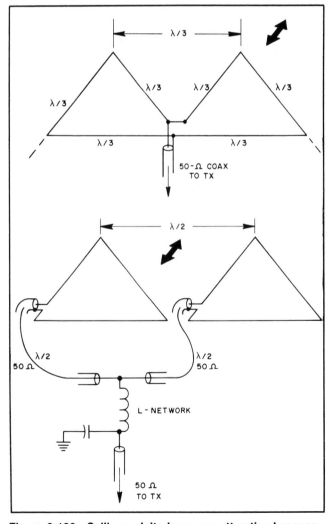

Figure 2.128—Collinear delta loops are attractive because they do not present phasing difficulties. The feed system is very simple for the close-spaced array, but the gain is 1.5 dB less than with ½ λ spacing. The wider spacing also provides better side rejection.

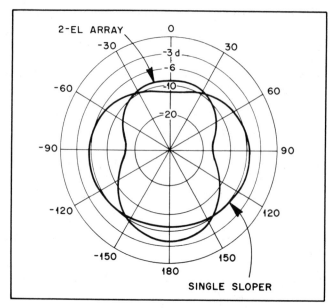

Figure 2.129—The horizontal radiation pattern of the two-element sloper array, calculated at a 30° wave angle over good ground, is not very impressive. Front-to-side ratio is 12 dB, and front-to-back ratio is a mere 5 dB.

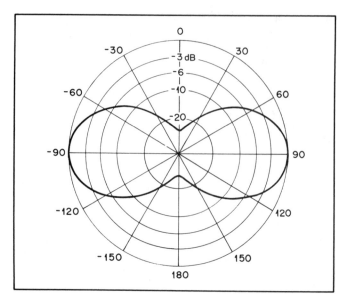

Figure 2.131—Radiation pattern of the Bobtail array at a wave angle of 30°. The directivity is perpendicular to the plane containing the antenna.

are used, the feed-point impedance will be close to 50 ohms. The gain of this array is approximately 3.9 dB over a dipole in free space (Ref 1118), and roughly 2 dB over a single loop. Increasing the spacing from ⅓ λ to ½ λ will increase the gain by approximately 1.5 dB. The front-to-side ratio will also improve markedly. In such a case, the elements should (preferably) be fed via ¾ λ feed lines to a common point where the lines will be connected in parallel. At this point, a simple L-network can provide a good match to a 50-ohm line. (See Section 2.11.1.5.)

Sloping Dipoles in Phase

Half-wave in-phase slopers have been used with great success by Collins, W1FC. Side-lobe performance and gain are both influenced by element spacing. The elements should be fed with feed lines ½ λ long or multiple half wavelengths, as explained above for delta loops in phase. Figure 2.129 shows the horizontal radiation pattern for a two-element sloper array.

Bobtail Curtain

The Bobtail curtain consists of three top-fed quarter-wave verticals, spaced ¼ λ apart and fed via a horizontal wire section. Through this feeding arrangement, the current in the outer verticals is half of the current in the center vertical. The current distribution in the top wire is such that in the favored (broadside) direction, all radiation from this horizontal section is effectively canceled (Figure 2.130).

The gain of this array over a single vertical is close to 5 dB, and the main wave angle is about 30° for operation over average ground. As with all verticals, the effective radiation angle can be lowered if a good RF ground system is used. (A seaside location will give very good results.)

The feed-point impedance (at the center element) is high—a

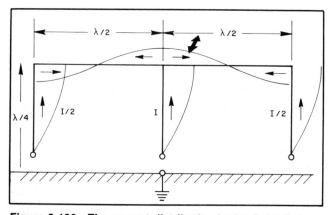

Figure 2.130—The current distribution in the Bobtail array shows how the three vertical elements contribute to the low-angle bidirectional broadside radiation of the array. The horizontal section acts as a phasing and feed line and has very little influence on the broadside radiation of the antenna.

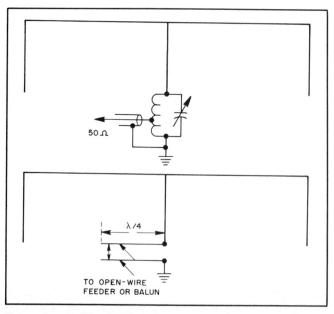

Figure 2.132—The Bobtail curtain can be fed via a parallel-tuned circuit with a high L/C ratio, (as a bottom-fed half-wave vertical). A quarter-wave Zepp match can also be used where the proper impedance can be located for attachment of an open-wire feeder or a balun.

few thousand ohms—which means that no extensive radial system is required from a return current point of view. As explained above, the better the radial system, the better the low-angle radiation will be. The ends of the vertical sections near the ground are at very high voltages, and safety measures must be taken to avoid accidental contact.

Figure 2.131 shows the horizontal radiation pattern for the Bobtail curtain. Maximum radiation is in the broadside direction (perpendicular to the plane containing the three verticals).

Matching can be done by loading a parallel tuned circuit with the antenna. Some experimentation with the L/C ratio and the tap point may be necessary to obtain a good SWR. In order to obtain a reasonable bandwidth, a high L/C ratio is required. A good starting point is to make the resonating capacitor as large as the wavelength involved (80 pF for 3.8 MHz, 160 pF for the 160 meter band). Schiers, NØAN, has described a neat way to use a capacitor made from coaxial cable to resonate the circuit (Ref 1119). If sufficient room is available, one can use a quarter-wave stub into which the coax can be connected via a balun at the 200-ohm point, or alternatively, a 600- or 450-ohm line can be attached to the same Zepp match (Figure 2.132).

Half-Square Antenna

The half-square antenna was first described by Venster, K3BC (Ref 1125). As its name implies, the half-square is half of a bi-square antenna (on its side), with the ground making up the other half of the antenna (see Section 2.8.3). It can also be seen as a Bobtail with half of the antenna missing. Figure 2.133 shows the antenna configuration and the current

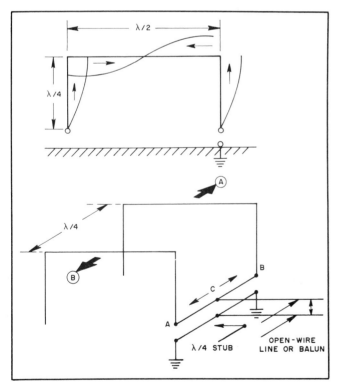

Figure 2.133—The single-element half-square antenna shows a gain of almost 3 dB in the direction perpendicular to the plane of the antenna. The two-element array uses ¼ λ spacing. When the quarter-wave stub is connected to point C, the pattern will be bidirectional. If the stub is attached at point A or B, the array will have a cardioid pattern. If quarter-wave stubs are connected to both A and B, the proper feed line may be selected with a relay.

distribution. The feed-point impedance is very high (several thousand ohms), and the antenna is fed like the Bobtail (Figure 2.132). The gain is expected to be somewhat less than 3 dB over a single quarter-wave vertical. As far as the required ground system is concerned, the same remarks apply as for the Bobtail antenna.

Venster extended the half-square by adding a second (and eventually a third) element, fed as shown in Figure 2.133. For a two-element design, ¼ λ spacing will yield the highest gain (approximately 5 dB over a single quarter-wave vertical), but the trade-off at 0.15 λ spacing is very small, (less than 0.5 dB). The exact placement of the stub on the feed line connecting the squares determines the phase relationship and the power ratio between the elements, and consequently the directivity. Figure 2.134 shows the horizontal directivity of the half-square antenna and a two-element half-square with quarter-wave spacing and a 90° phase delay. If the stub is placed halfway between the elements, a bidirectional pattern will result. Moving the stub to either side will introduce some front-to-back into the array pattern.

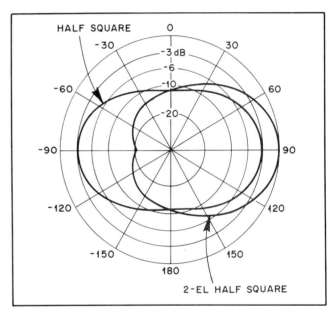

Figure 2.134—Horizontal directivity pattern for the single-element half-square and a two-element array with quarter-wave spacing, fed 90° out of phase.

2.11.3 ANTENNAS WITH PARASITIC ELEMENTS

Antennas with parasitic elements operated in close proximity to the ground (less than a half wavelength) often do not work well. This should not surprise you. In a parasitic array, part of the power applied to the driven element is coupled into the parasitic element(s) through the effect of mutual coupling. When the driven element and the parasitic element(s) are both close to the ground, the image created by the ground will couple heavily with both the driven element and the parasitic element(s). For a single dipole this can be proven by watching the radiation resistance decrease at low heights. This decrease in radiation resistance is the effect of the mutual coupling between the element and its image.

In the case of an array with parasitic elements close to ground, the unwanted interference of the image antenna will make it practically impossible to obtain the desired phase relationship and make it impossible to induce the right current

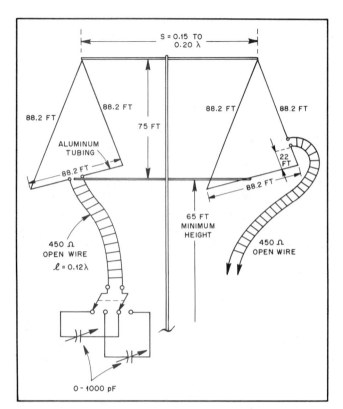

Figure 2.135—Rotatable two-element delta loops are feasible on some large towers. Quick direction reversal can be accomplished by using a switchable 450-ohm open-wire system with a capacitor in the parasitic element. Fine tuning can be done using a dip meter. Another approach for those who want 3.5 and 3.8 MHz coverage is to adjust the parasitic element for resonance at 3.65 MHz, and use this element as director or reflector depending on the frequency of operation (3.5 or 3.8 MHz).

(amplitude and phase) into the parasitic element(s). This is why driven arrays have generally been much more successful on the low bands. It has been shown experimentally that this effect is somewhat less with loop antennas than with dipoles.

2.11.3.1 Multi-Element Quad

Full-size cubical quad antennas have been successfully used on large "Big Bertha" towers by a number of hams. The design rules normally used for HF beams can be used. Figure 2.135 shows how such an arrangement can be applied on a large self-supporting tower. For proper operation, the apex height of the quad should be at least 130 feet (40 m).

Fast front-to-back switching can be accomplished by bringing the parasitic element to a switching arrangement where the necessary capacitance or inductance can be inserted to tune the element to either 5% above or 5% below the design frequency (Ref 1126). Physically both the driven element and the parasitic element are made the same circumference (length in feet = 1005/f (MHz)).

The reactance required to tune such an element as a reflector or director is ±150 ohms (Ref 603). An easy way to accomplish this is to use a capacitor to tune the parasitic element alternatively as a reflector and a director. Using the "COAX TRANSFORMER" program, one can calculate a combination of terminating capacitances (C1 and C2), which will show up as either +150 or −150 ohms at the end of the line. When using the program, enter 0.0001 for the resistive part of the impedance (0 will crash the program), and enter the reactance with the opposite sign. If a 150-ohm impedance

is required for the loop to be a reflector, then the impedance at the end of the 450-ohm line should be −150 ohms (conjugate value). For a given line length, the impedance at the end of the line will be calculated. The reactance to be connected at this point will again have the opposite sign (conjugate reactance).

Example:
Line impedance = 450 ohms, line length = 0.12 λ (43.2°).
Reflector:
Required loop impedance = 150 ohms
Conjugate value = −150 ohms
End-of-line Z = 207 ohms
Element impedance = −207 ohms

$$Required\ capacitance:\ C = \frac{10^6}{2\pi \times 3.8 \times 207} = 202\ pF$$

Director:
Required loop impedance = −150 ohms
Conjugate impedance = 150 ohms
End-of-line Z = 833 ohms
Element impedance = −833 ohms
Required capacitance = 50 pF

The line length has to be selected experimentally. It should produce a negative reactance so that variable capacitors of a value that is readily available can be used. Variable capacitors are easier to use than variable inductors. If fine tuning is required, you can add multiple half wavelengths to the feed lines and bring the tuning end right into the shack.

2.11.3.2 Reduced-Size Two-Element Quad

Courtier-Dutton, G3FPQ, built a reasonably sized two-element rotatable quad that performs extremely well. The quad side dimensions are 50 feet, and the elements are loaded as shown in Figure 2.136. The single loop showed a radiation resistance of 50 ohms. Adding a reflector 40 feet away from the driven element (0.15 λ) dropped the radiation resistance to approximately 30 ohms. The loading wires are spaced 3.5 feet from the vertical loop wires, and are almost as long as the vertical loop wires. The loading wires are trimmed to

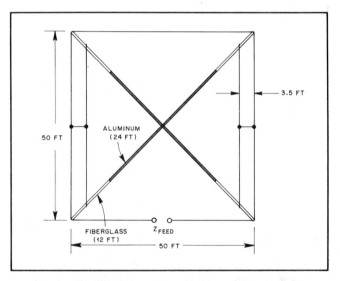

Figure 2.136—Reduced-size two-element quad designed by Courtier-Dutton, G3FPQ. The elements are loaded by a single wire which runs parallel to the vertical wires of the elements, and is connected to the center of those sides. See text for details.

adjust the resonant frequency of the element. G3FPQ reports a 90-kHz bandwidth from the two-element quad with the apex at 135 feet. The middle 24 feet of the spreaders are made of aluminum tubing, and the tips (12 feet) are made of fiberglass. A front-to-back ratio of up to 30 dB has been reported.

2.11.3.3 Shortened Multi-Element Yagis for 80 Meters

In the last 10 years, multi-element rotatable Yagis with shortened elements have made their appearance. KLM Electronics Inc. (P.O. Box 816, Morgan Hill, CA 95037) is marketing two-, three- and four-element Yagis, using 70%-length elements and employing the linear-loading principle (see Section 2.3.4.1 and Section 2.3.4.2). When erected at least 100 feet up (preferably 150 to 180 feet), these antennas are really excellent performers.

The four-element version has a 76-foot (23 m) boom and 90-foot (27.5 m) elements. The linear-loading devices are inserted on the elements approximately 15.8 feet (4.8 m) away from the boom. The loading stubs also serve as mechanical support wires from which to rig the elements. The stub lengths are adjustable to tune the Yagi, and can be varied from 130 inches (3.3 m) to 180 inches (4.6 m), depending on the element and the design frequency. W6NLZ, W6RJ, AA6AA, W2HCW, WA1EKV, W7IVX, KQ5G, W6RR and others have been proving daily that this antenna can be a real winner.

KLM now has a phone/CW switching option which overcomes the relatively narrow bandwidth (100 to 150 kHz) of this antenna by installing relays which effectively change the length of the linear-loading sections when changing from the SSB band (3.750 MHz) to the CW band (3.510 MHz). Figure 2.137A shows the 3-element KLM 80-meter Yagi installed at AA6AA. The detailed picture in Figure 2.137B shows the linear-loading wires, which also serve as horizontal support wires for the elements. Notice the support a few feet from the end of the loading lines. This is a small printed circuit board carrying the relay to shorten the loading lines for operating on the phone portion of the band, while the full length of the loading lines are used for 3.5 MHz.

One of the major problems with antennas of such large dimensions is ice loading. One possible solution would involve inserting a lightweight electrical cable made of resistance wire into the elements and feeding it from a low voltage source at the top of the tower (via the necessary RF chokes).

Creative Design Co., Ltd (4-8 Asanocho Kawasakiku, Kawasaki City, Japan) is producing a two-element reduced-size Yagi for 3.8 MHz (model AFA75-2). Both elements are driven and the spacing is 9 meters (0.113 λ). Taking into account the velocity factor of the phasing line, the array elements appear to be fed 135° out of phase (like a ZL special). The elements are 24 meters (88 feet) long (or approximately 62% of full size), and the loading is done with high-Q coils and a small capacity hat about two-thirds out on the elements. The elements are also loaded at the center with hairpin loading coils (see Section 2.3.4.2), which allows precise matching to the phasing line and the coaxial feed line. The array is fed with 50-ohm coax via a 1:1 balun. The claimed gain is 4-6 dB, with an average front-to-back ratio of 18 dB. Power rating is 4 kW (8 kW PEP), and the total weight is 67 kg. The 2:1 VSWR bandwidth is slightly over 100 kHz. Wind load area is 21.5 square feet.

2.11.3.4 Full-Size Three-Element Yagi for 80 Meters

To the author's knowledge, the first full-size multi-element rotatable Yagi for 80 meters was built and erected in Finland at OH1RY. Peter based his design on the experience he gained

(A)

(B)

Figure 2.137—The 3-element KLM 80-meter Yagi at AA6AA is shown at A. The detail view at B shows the linear-loading wires.

from building a 40-meter Yagi with heavily tapered elements. The 80-meter beam uses elements that taper from 150 mm (6 inches) at the center to 10 mm (0.4 inches) at the tips. By the way, the 6-inch center sections are the bases of aluminum light poles used for street lighting!

Here are Peter's recommendations for anyone wanting to build his own full-size Yagi for 80 meters:

• Use a split driven element. This allows easy measurement of element impedance and resonant frequency. Figure 2.138A shows how the driven elements are mounted to the boom on Peter's antenna. The boom is made of 20-inch steel-lattice tower to which steel plates have been welded to support the element halves at the boom. Two one-inch-thick pieces of epoxy fiberglass (a very strong type of insulator) are mounted on the steel plates. The elements are mounted to these plates on hinges so that they may be lowered into the vertical position for making element-length adjustments while the antenna is on the tower. Figure 2.138B shows a close-up of the antenna with Peter, OH1RY, sitting on the driven element. This should give you an idea how massive this antenna really is!

• Adjust the driven element length for resonance at the desired frequency. The element resonant frequency can be measured by installing a 1-turn link between the two halves of the element, and using a dip meter to measure for resonance. After carefully measuring the length of the driven element (now resonant at the design frequency), mount the director and the reflector (which are 5% shorter and 5% longer than the driven element, respectively). Measure the resonant frequency of the driven element again and adjust

(A)

(B)

Figure 2.138—A close-up of the element-to-boom mounting technique used in the three-element Yagi at OH1RY is shown at A. The boom diameter is 6 inches. The element halves are mounted on a hinged plate which allows them to be lowered into a vertical position for adjustments and maintenance. At B, Peter, OH1RY, is standing on the driven element of the antenna. Note the support directly above the feed point; cables from the boom and the elements are connected to this support. The elements have both lateral and vertical bracing.

the length of the element halves to re-establish resonance at the design frequency. Adjust the parasitic element lengths to −5% (director) and +5% (reflector) of the driven element length.

• Measure the radiation resistance (using an antennascope or noise bridge). This should be between 15 and 25 ohms.

• Fine-tuning of the parasitic elements can be done for either maximum forward gain or maximum front-to-back ratio. Peter tuned his antenna for best F/B ratio with the help

Table 32
Element Section Sizes for OH1RY 80-Meter Yagi

Section	Outer Diameter		Length	
	(in)	(cm)	(in)	(cm)
1	5.91	15.0	98.43	250
2	4.72	12.0	165.35	420
3	2.95	7.5	118.11	300
4	1.97	5.0	236.22	600
5-Dir	0.98	2.5	39.37	100
5-Driven	0.98	2.5	39.37	100
5-Ref	0.98	2.5	59.06	150
6-Dir	0.79	2.0	39.37	100
6-Driven	0.79	2.0	39.37	100
6-Ref	0.79	2.0	59.06	100
7-Dir	0.59	1.5	39.37	100
7-Driven	0.59	1.5	59.06	150
7-Ref	0.59	1.5	78.74	200
8-Dir	0.39	1.0	23.62	60
8-Driven	0.39	1.0	57.09	145
8-Ref	0.39	1.0	47.24	120

of a local ham giving him a steady carrier, and by fine-adjusting both the reflector and director lengths. This means that the Yagi was optimized for front-to-back at zero wave angle. This can be slightly different for actual wave angles, which, for DX signals, range from 15 to 45° in elevation. The best front-to-back ratio was obtained with a reflector 6% longer than the driven element and a director 6.5% shorter than the driven element.

• The final dimensions are:
Boom length: 22 m (72 feet)
Driven element: 41.3 m (135.5 feet)
Director: 38.6 m (126.6 feet)
Reflector: 43.8 m (143.7 feet)

Table 32 lists the dimensions used by Peter for this three-element Yagi. Notice that the elements are much longer than expected, because of the high degree of element taper.

The electrical length of the elements as computed with the W2PV-based "ELEMENT TAPER" program (listed in Chapter VII) for an analysis frequency of 3.775 MHz are director, 0.4575 λ; driven element, 0.4845 λ; and reflector, 0.5123 λ.

The driven element is split-fed via a quarter-wave transformer made of two paralleled 60-ohm coaxial cables (30 ohms total), which yielded a perfect match for the 18-ohm radiation resistance of the Yagi.

Figure 2.139 shows the monster being raised on the tower with a 150-foot hydraulic crane. How does it work? Very well! So well, in fact, that in western Europe, one often has difficulty hearing Peter through all the QRM when he has his beam pointing east. The front-to-back ratio is most impressive, and the radiation angle must be low, because of the antenna height (although the tower itself is only 100 feet (30 meters) high, it sits on a steep slope to the east, which adds another 50 feet (15 meters) to the height). 9U5JB, operated by ON5NT in early 1985, confirmed OH1RY's signal to be at least 15 dB stronger than any other European signal. The reputation of this antenna has long been established on the West Coast of the USA.

Another three-element full-size Yagi was built by Chris, I5NPH, using OH1RY's guidelines. The boom of Chris' Yagi is 24 meters long and the elements have less taper than Peter's (90 mm at the center and 10 mm at the element ends). The driven element is matched to the 50-ohm line with a hairpin

Figure 2.139—The three-element full-size 80-meter beam is lifted to the top of the 100-foot tower by a 150-foot hydraulic crane. Notice the small hill on which the tower is mounted; this hill increases the effective antenna height by 40 feet.

Figure 2.140—The elements of the three-element Yagi at I5NPH. The elements are thinner than those of the OH1RY Yagi—Chris was able to lighten the antenna without sacrificing structural strength by using aircraft-type aluminum tubing.

Table 33

Element Section Sizes for I5NPH 80-Meter Yagi

	Diameter		Length	
Section	OD/ID (in)	OD/ID (cm)	(in)	(cm)
1	3.54/3.15	9.0/8.0	87.79	223
2	3.54/2.76	8.0/7.0	110.24	280
3	2.76/1.97	6.0/5.0	110.24	280
4	1.97/1.57	5.0/4.0	127.95	325
5	1.57/1.18	4.0/3.0	165.35	420
6	1.18/0.79	3.0/2.0	66.93	170
7	0.79/0.39	1.8/1.0	66.93	170
8-Dir	0.39/0.31	1.0/0.8	95.26	68
8-Driven	0.39/0.31	1.0/0.8	39.37	100
8-Ref	0.39/0.31	1.0/0.8	26.77	242

at I5NPH, topped by a 6-element 20-meter Yagi. Table 33 shows the element section sizes and diameters that Chris used.

The hairpin is 130 cm (51.2 inches) long, and the 50-ohm transmission line is attached via a 1:1 balun to a point on the hairpin located 50 cm (19.7 inches) from the driven element and 80 cm (31.5 inches) from the end of the hairpin, which is connected to the boom.

The electrical length of the elements as computed with the W2PV-based "ELEMENT TAPER" program are (at 3.775 MHz) director, 0.4662 λ; driven element, 0.4726 λ; and reflector 0.5018 λ.

matching system, which allows the driven element to be slightly shorter than a half wavelength. Chris reports 27 dB front-to-back ratio on ground wave, as measured with a local station about 2 miles away. Figure 2.140 shows the antenna

Figure 2.141—The 80-meter Yagi at W6MKB. The boom of this Yagi is 80 feet long. The dimensional design of the Yagi was done by J. Forgione, WB6FZC, who uses MININEC and the W2PV element-taper formulas to design Yagis for any band. The gain was calculated as 7.2 dB with a front-to-back ratio of 42 dB at the design frequency. The 2:1 SWR bandwidth is 225 kHz. To minimize the wind load, relatively small-diameter elements with extensive structural bracing were used.

Yet another full-size, three-element rotatable 75-meter Yagi has been put up by W6MKB near San Diego (see Figure 2.141). Note the substantial guying of the elements, which are of relatively small diameter to reduce wind loading. The lesser degree of tapering also results in slightly shorter elements than is the case with the OH1RY design.

Proven Yagi designs are described in Lawson's book *Yagi Antenna Design* (Ref 957). It should be pointed out, however, that Yagis built according to free-space designs do not perform well when used at heights below one wavelength. A Yagi modeled at a lower height (0.6 wavelengths, for example) seems to be short (approximately one percent) as compared to a free-space environment. In all cases modeling the Yagi at the height at which it will be used is recommended. The computer program MININEC is an excellent tool for this purpose.

One can use the computer program "ELEMENT TAPER" to design Yagi elements with any degree of element tapering to match the required electrical element length. This program is based on the work by W2PV as explained in Ref 956 and 957. The program calculates the length of the tapered element back to a theoretical element having a constant diameter of 7/8 inch, and then calculates the electrical length of the element at the given design frequency. A few iterations result in a perfectly designed Yagi which will show optimum gain and front-to-back right at the design frequency.

JRF Engineering (6326 Mt Ackerman Drive, San Diego, CA 92111) provides a computer-assisted Yagi design service, which will deliver optimum performance given the customer's input specification. MININEC and the W2PV taper formulas are part of the design software used by JRF Engineering.

Wire Yagis

Yagis require a lot of space and electrical height in order to perform well. Excellent results have been obtained with fixed-wire Yagis strung between high apartment buildings. There are few circumstances, however, where supports at the right height and in a favorable direction are available. When using wire elements, it is easy to determine the correct length of the elements. The classic dipole formula can be used (with a shortening factor of 0.98), making the director 4 to 6% shorter and the reflector 4 to 6% longer than the driven element. If a folded dipole is used for the driven element, the impedance will probably be between 75 and 100 ohms. In the first case a 75-ohm feed line can be used; in the second case, a 75-ohm quarter-wave transformer will transform the 100 ohms to 50 ohms.

2.11.3.5 LARAE

Clement, W6KPC, describes the "Line Array Rotary Antenna in Echelon" in his article (Ref 603). Vertical stacking of rotary Yagis or horizontal (side-by-side) stacking of Yagis on a common rotating support is not feasible at and below 3.8 MHz. Clement devised a feed system which would allow him to use three 80-meter Yagis, each on a 180-foot tower, installed in-line, to obtain substantial gain in all azimuth directions. Delay lines would have to be switched in the feed lines to the outer Yagis in order to feed these "elements" with the proper phase for a given direction and make the system work. This means that the length of those delay lines would have to be changed incrementally at the same time the three Yagis are rotated. Letho, OH8OS, ran the computer calculations, and as a result, a separation of 1.05 λ between towers would result in a gain of almost 6 dB over a single Yagi (over 12 dB gain over a dipole at 180 feet!) for the LARAE, with virtually no side lobes. Each quadrant would be stepped in eight increments (by delay lines in the outer elements). The design was done for a wave angle of 18°, which is the wave angle of a single Yagi at 180 feet. It is obvious that the gain will be less than the quoted figure at higher angles. At the time of this writing there are no operational LARAEs, but both W6KPC and OH8OS are planning to install LARAE systems. Figure 2.142 shows the in-line configuration of the three Yagis in the proposed LARAE system.

2.11.4 SELECTING THE RIGHT ANTENNA

Those using rotary Yagis for 80 meters (shortened or full-size) claim that Yagis "separate the men from the boys." There is certainly no point in denying that these antennas are putting out outstanding signals worldwide. Well engineered and constructed vertical arrays have one distinct advantage over rotary Yagis: instant direction switching. This can be very important during contest operating. Beverage antennas for receiving (Section 2.13) have the same advantage of instantaneous direction switching.

Antennas with vertical polarization will often perform better into areas of auroral activity during an aurora. This is caused by a phenomenon called *polarization discrimination*, which is prevalent on 160 meters and often on 80 meters. On 160 and 80 meters, the frequencies involved are close to the gyro-frequency of the free electrons in the ionosphere. A wave entering the ionosphere is split into two components. The magneto-ionic component will typically be generated by vertically polarized antennas, while the electro-ionic component will be generated by horizontally polarized antennas. Both components of the wave will show different attenuation while traveling in the ionosphere. The vertically polarized component will typically show 8 dB less attenuation.

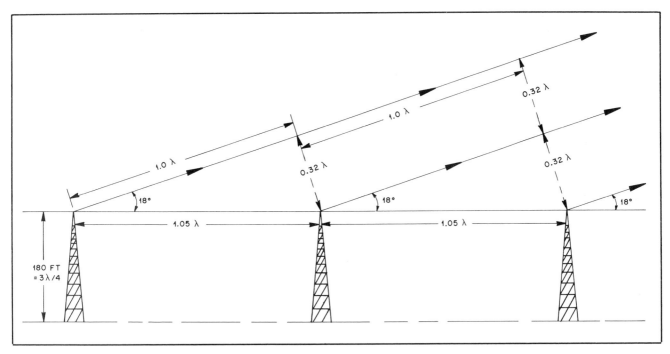

Figure 2.142—The future LARAE array, as designed by Clement, W6KPC and Letho, OH8OS. This array would use three 80-meter Yagis on three in-line 180-foot towers, yielding a net gain of more than 12 dB over a dipole at the same height.

This phenomenon only exists when there is (auroral) absorption and then only for waves traveling more or less along the magnetic field of the earth; for example, south-north when considering the Northern Hemisphere. The mechanism is *not* applicable to north-south paths in the Northern Hemisphere. This theory confirms the practical experience by the author that vertical antennas always outperform horizontal antennas for paths into or across auroral zones. It does not seem to be only a matter of angle of radiation.

Rotatable Yagi antennas and other horizontally polarized arrays (such as half-waves in phase and W8JKs) are definitely preferred in mountainous areas, where ground reflection is usually very poor (or at best random) and uncontrollable. Horizontally polarized antennas on hilltop locations are hard to beat. Terrain slope will give improved low-angle radiation, even if the array itself is at modest height (90-100 feet). Over flat terrain, however, and especially in those areas which are blessed with good ground conductivity, vertical antennas and arrays made of vertical antennas can be quite competitive with horizontal antennas and rotary Yagis, with the distinct advantage of instantaneous direction switching previously mentioned. Over the same flat terrain, Yagis would need to be up around 180 feet to achieve a reasonably low wave angle.

Using half-wavelength-long elements for a vertical antenna (or in arrays) will only be worthwhile if 1) ground conductivity is poor, and one is looking for reduced ground losses resulting from return currents, or 2) when the antenna is located over ground with exceptional conductivity (like salt water) so that the Brewster angle will be lowered, and increased low-angle performance will result. In the first case, however, the half-wave elements will not produce any lower wave angle as compared with the shorter ¼-wave vertical. The same is true for the 5/8-wave vertical. Long elements (half-wave or 5/8-wave) are only advantageous in either locations with *extremely* good ground conductivity or in locations with extremely bad reflecting ground in the immediate vicinity of the antenna (to improve the antenna efficiency).

The author has very often been asked to recommend what would be the best antenna system for an individual. Consulting in a matter like this is almost impossible unless one has seen the location and the area where the antenna system will be erected. The author would probably rate the quality of the reflecting ground as the most important parameter for all low-band antennas with the exception of horizontally polarized antennas at a height of at least 150 feet (45 m).

We all know that the better signals come from locations that have been carefully selected for either good ground reflecting properties or added effective antenna height (hilltop locations). The best overall antenna system is a system where one can work what one can hear, and where one hears well compared to neighboring hams. Separate receiving and transmitting antennas often provide such ideal conditions.

2.12 Feed Lines

2.12.1 THE ROLE OF THE FEED LINE

A feed line is the link between the antenna and the station, and it should efficiently transfer all the RF from the rig to the antenna. A feed line will only perform ideally when it is terminated in a resistive load having the same value as its characteristic impedance. In the real world, this is very seldom the case. Since it is normally terminated in a load with a complex impedance, in addition to acting as a transport vehicle for RF energy, the feed line will also act as a transformer, whereby the impedance (also the voltage and current) will be different at each point along the line. A feed line working under these circumstances is not "flat," but has standing waves. In some instances we will use lines with standing waves intentionally in order to transform impedances (such as the Christman matching system in Section 2.11.1.5) or to obtain voltages or currents with the desired phase.

2.12.2 THE TOTAL ANTENNA SYSTEM EFFICIENCY CONCEPT

Antennas and feed lines are really very similar. Boyer wrote two excellent articles entitled "Antenna-Transmission Line Analogy" (Ref 1314 and 1315) where the analogy between an antenna and a transmission line is well treated.

Very small antennas have been proven to be able to radiate the supplied power as efficiently as much larger ones (Section 2.4.1.1). Small antennas have two disadvantages, however. On one hand, since their radiation resistance is very low, the antenna efficiency will be lower than it would be if the radiation resistance were much higher. If the short antennas are to be loaded along the elements, the losses of the loading devices will have to be taken into account when calculating the antenna efficiency. On the other hand, if the short antenna (dipole or monopole) is not loaded, the feed-point impedance will have a large amount of capacitive reactance in addition to the resistive component.

One solution is to install a transformer at the antenna feed point to match the complex antenna impedance to the feed-line impedance. In this case, the feed line will no longer act as a transformer. Conversion will be done in the transformer at a given efficiency, and transforming extreme impedances inevitably results in poor transformation efficiencies. Transforming the impedance of a very short vertical with an impedance of $0.5 - j3000$ ohms to $50 + j0$ ohms is a very difficult task, and it cannot be done without a great deal of loss. In military applications where very short antennas are often required, one technique used to reduce circuit losses is the cooling of network components to near absolute zero (to achieve super conductivity of the metals involved).

One can also supply power to this feed point without inserting a transformer. In this case the feed line itself will act as a transformer. In the case of the above example, an extremely high SWR would be present on the feed line. This means that current and voltage will change periodically along the line and could reach very high values at certain points (antinodes). The feed line also uses materials with certain physical properties and limitations. The very high currents in the antinodes along the line will be responsible for extra conductivity related losses. The voltages associated with the voltage antinodes will be responsible for high dielectric losses. The transmission-line transformer is not a lossless component, and the losses will be determined by the quality of the materials used to make the feed line. We understand by now that for a transmission-line transformer, we need a low-loss feed line with good dielectric properties and high current-handling capabilities. A feeder which has such properties is an open-wire feeder. Air makes an excellent dielectric, and the conductivity can be made as good as required by using heavy gauge conductors. Good-quality open-wire feeders have always proven excellent as feed lines and transformers.

If we are not particularly interested in the transformation aspect of such a feed line, the line can be terminated in a low-loss antenna tuner. What is a quality antenna tuner? The same qualifications for feed lines apply here: one that can transform the impedances involved, at the required power levels, with minimal losses.

It can now be seen that the general representation of an antenna feed system consists of the following (Figure 2.143).
1) Antenna element, with loading elements if necessary.
2) Transformer at antenna.
3) Feed line.
4) Transformer at transmitter.

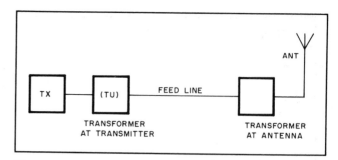

Figure 2.143—Basic elements that influence the efficiency of an antenna system. See text for discussion.

Note: In some cases, one of these elements can be omitted.

The efficiency of the antenna element with or without a loading element was dealt with in detail earlier in this chapter.

Transformers at the antenna terminals are not often used with horizontal wire antennas, mainly for mechanical reasons. With vertical antennas, it is very common to install matching networks at the antenna base (see Section 2.4.9). The efficiency of such networks (normally L-networks) will depend mainly on the Q factor of the coils involved.

The requirements for the feed line itself will depend on the mode in which it will operate. Coaxial lines are generally used when the SWR is less than 3:1. Higher SWR values can result in excessive losses when long runs are involved, and also in reduced power handling capability. Many of the popular low-band antennas have feed-point impedances which are reasonably low, and can result in an acceptable match to either a 50- or a 75-ohm coaxial cable. Quarter-wave matching transformers can further extend the working range of standard coaxial cables. Coaxial cables can also be paralleled to obtain half the nominal impedance. Coaxial cable feed lines are often preferred because they are physically easier to handle. As they show no external field (when properly terminated with an unbalanced load creating no antenna currents on the shield), they can be used under almost all circumstances. Sharp bending of coax should be avoided to prevent impedance irregularities and permanent displacement of the center conductor caused by cable dielectric heating and induced stresses. A minimum bending radius of five times the cable outside diameter is a good rule of thumb.

Like anything exposed to the elements, coaxial cables deteriorate with age. Under the influence of heat and ultraviolet light, some of the components of the outer sheath of the coaxial cable can decompose and migrate through the copper braid into the dielectric material, causing rapid degradation of the cable. Ordinary PVC jackets used on older coaxial cables (RG-8, RG-11) showed migration of the plasticizer into the polyethylene dielectric. Newer types of cable (RG-8A, RG-11A, RG-213A and so on) use non-contaminating sheaths which greatly extend the life of the cable.

It is always a good idea to check the attenuation of feed lines at regular intervals. This can easily be done by opening the feed line at one end, feeding some power into the line through an accurate SWR meter (such as a Bird wattmeter) at the other end, and measuring the SWR at the end of the line. A lossless line would show infinite SWR (Ref 1321). From the measured value the attenuation of the line can be deduced using the graph in Figure 2.144. It will often be difficult to do this test at low frequencies because the attenuation on the low bands is such that accurate

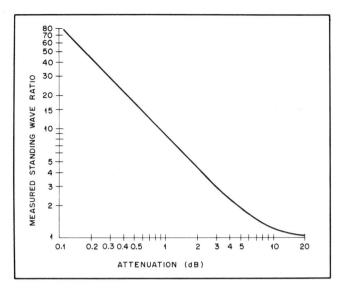

Figure 2.144—Cable loss vs measured SWR at the end of an open- or short-circuited cable. For best accuracy, the SWR should be in the 2:1 to 4:1 range.

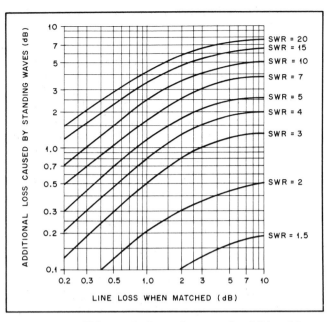

Figure 2.145—This graph shows how much additional loss occurs for a given SWR on a line with a known (nominal) flat-line attenuation.

measurements are difficult. For best measurement accuracy the loss of the cable to be measured should be in the order of 2 to 4 dB (SWR between 2:1 and 4:1). The test frequency can be chosen accordingly.

Open-wire feeders are great performers, but they are not very easy to work with. Extremely high efficiencies can be achieved. Elwell, N4UH has described the use and construction of home-made, low-loss open-wire transmission lines for long-distance transmission (Ref 1320). A combination of open-wire feeders and coaxial feed lines can also be very attractive. Quarter-wave stubs or Zepp matches are typical examples (see Figures 2.18, 2.132 and 2.133).

In many cases, the open-wire feeders are used under high SWR conditions (where the feeders do not introduce many additional losses) and are terminated in an antenna tuner. Figure 2.145 shows the additional losses due to standing waves on a transmission line. On the low bands, the extra losses caused by SWR are usually negligible (Ref 1319, 1322). A more important aspect of a line with high SWR is that the impedance at the transmitter end of the line can be such that a conjugate match does not exist. A conjugate match is a situation where all power is effectively coupled from the transmitter into the line, and where power reflected from the load (antenna) back to the transmitter due to SWR is reflected back towards the load again. A conjugate match is automatically achieved when we match the transmitter for maximum power transfer into the line. In transmitters or amplifiers using vacuum tubes, this is done by properly adjusting the common Pi or Pi-L network. Modern transceivers with fixed-impedance solid state amplifiers do not have this flexibility, and an external antenna tuner will be required in most cases if the SWR is higher than 1.5:1 or 2:1.

2.12.3 IMPEDANCE MATCHING ON FLAT LINES

Lengths of 75-ohm Hardline coaxial cable can often be obtained from local TV cable companies. If very long runs to low-band antennas are involved, the low attenuation of Hardline is an attractive asset. If one is concerned with providing a 50-ohm impedance, a transformer system must be used. Transformers using toroidal cores have been described (Ref 1307), as well as configurations using only

coaxial cable lengths. If 60-ohm coaxial cable is available (as in many European countries), a quarter-wave transformer will readily transform the 75 ohms to 50 ohms at the end of the Hardline. Carroll, K1XX, described the nonsynchronous matching transformer and compared it to a stub matching system (Ref 1318). While the toroidal transformer is fairly broadbanded, the stub and nonsynchronous transformers are single-band devices. Compared to the quarter-wave transformers, which need coaxial cable having an impedance equal to the geometric mean of the two impedances to be matched, the other two approaches require only cables of the same impedances as the values to be matched.

Quarter-Wave Sections Made of Paralleled Cables

As already explained in the section on arrays, quarter-wave transformer sections can also be made from paralleled lengths of coax. A 37.5-ohm section can be made of two paralleled quarter-wave lengths of 75-ohm cable. Make sure both physical lengths have identical electrical lengths (see Figure 2.71).

Stub Matching

Stub matching can be used for matching resistive or complex impedances to a given line impedance. The program "STUB MATCHING," listed in Chapter VII, calculates both the position of the stub on the line and the length of the stub, and whether the stub must be open or shorted at the end. This method of matching a (complex) impedance to a line can replace the L-networks which were described when dealing with feed systems for arrays. The approach saves the two L-network components, but necessitates extra cable to make the stub. Also, the stub may be located at a point along the feed line which is difficult to reach.

Replacing the Stub with a Discrete Component

Stub matching is often unattractive on the lower bands because of the lengths of cable required to make the stub. The program "STUB MATCHING" also displays the equivalent component value of the stub (in either μH or pF). Nothing prevents one from replacing the stub with an equivalent capacitor or inductor, which is then connected in parallel with the feed line at the point the stub would have been placed. The same program shows the voltage at the point the stub or discrete element is placed. In order to know the voltage requirement for a parallel capacitor, one must know the voltage at the load.

Consider the following example: The load is 50 ohms (resistive), the line impedance is 75 ohms, and the power at the antenna is 1500 W. Therefore, the RMS voltage at the antenna is:

$$V = \sqrt{PR} = \sqrt{1500 \times 50} = \sqrt{75,000} = 274 \text{ V}$$

Running the "STUB MATCHING" program, we find that a 75-ohm impedance point is located at a distance of 39.5° from the load. The required 75-ohm stub length to achieve this resistive impedance is 22.1° (equivalent to 228 pF for a design frequency of 3.775 MHz). The voltage at that point on the line is 335 Volts RMS (938 V pk-pk). In this example, the 22.1° length represents a stub length of only 3.21 m (126.4 inches), assuming a design frequency of 3.775 MHz and a cable velocity factor of 0.66 (solid polyethylene dielectric coax). In any case, the length of a stub will never be longer than ¼ λ (either open-circuited or short-circuited).

Matching with Series-Connected Discrete Components

A variation of the stub matching technique consists of replacing the stub by a series connected coil or capacitor. The values necessary can easily be calculated using two programs listed in Chapter VII.

Example: match a 50-ohm load to a 75-ohm line (same example as above).

The program "IMPEDANCE ITERATION" will list the impedances along the line in 1° increments, starting at 1° from the load. If we want to assess the current through the series element (which is especially important if the series element is a capacitor), we must enter real values for either current or voltage at the load when running the program. If, for instance, we have 200 W at the load (antenna), the current at the antenna is $I = \sqrt{(P/R)}$, or $I = \sqrt{(2000/75)} =$ 5.16 A. Somewhere along the line we will find an impedance where the real part is 50 ohms. Note the distance from the load. In our example this will be at 50.77° from the 50-ohm load. The impedance at that point is: $75 + j30.6$ ohms. All we need to do now is to connect an impedance of -30.6 ohms (capacitive reactance) in series with the line at that point. Also note that at this point the current is 6.32 A (see also Table 17). The program "SERIES IMPEDANCE NETWORK" can be used to calculate the required component value. In this example, the required capacitor has a value of 1369 pF for a frequency of 3.8 MHz (Figure 2.147). The required voltage rating (RMS) is calculated by multiplying the current through the capacitor by the capacitive reactance, which yields a value of 193.4 V (RMS) or 547 V pk-pk.

In the case of a complex load impedance, the procedure is identical, but instead of entering the resistive load impedance (50 ohms in the above example), we must enter the complex impedance.

The Non-Synchronous Transformer

The element lengths of the synchronous transformer have been verified using the program "IMPEDANCE ITERATION." In the example of a non-synchronous

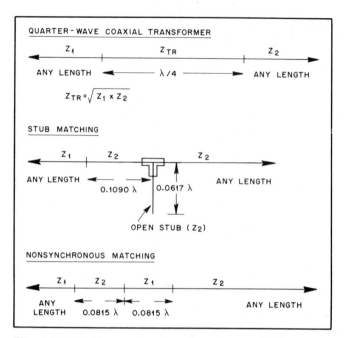

Figure 2.146—The quarter-wave transformer requires a cable having an impedance that is the geometric mean of the values to be matched. Stub and non-synchronous matching only require cables with the impedances of the lines to be matched. The stub itself of a classic stub-matching system can be replaced with a capacitor or inductor. Another matching system places a reactive element in series with the cable at a given point to achieve a perfect match. See text for details.

transformer transforming 50 to 75 ohms, the transformed impedance in the middle of the two matching sections is 57.7 $+ j20.5$ ohms. Figure 2.146 shows the configuration of the various matching methods described above.

2.12.4 WILKINSON POWER DIVIDERS

Atchley introduced the use of the Wilkinson power divider for supplying equal (in phase) outputs to the different elements in an array (Ref 939). Figure 2.147 shows a Wilkinson power divider. The power splitter (the T) is followed by two identical

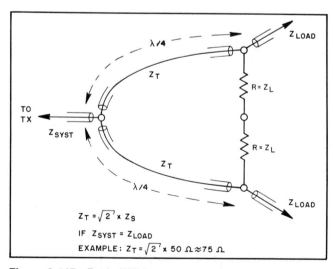

Figure 2.147—Basic Wilkinson power divider for two loads. The value of each resistor is equal to the load impedance. The impedance of the quarter-wave lines is such that after combination at the T, the nominal line impedance is obtained. For a 50-ohm system, 75-ohm quarter-wave lines will perform the transformation.

quarter-wavelength lines. A noninductive resistor is connected between the ends of the two quarter-wavelength lines. From there the feed lines run to the different loads. The forward power travels from the transmitter through the T into the two quarter-wave lines. At the end of the two lines, the split forward waves are still in phase and no power will be dissipated in the resistor. If the feed lines to the two loads (antennas) are perfectly matched, there will be no reflected wave traveling from the antenna back to the point where the resistor is connected, and consequently no power will be dissipated in the resistor.

If there is an imperfect match at the loads, there will be standing waves on the feed lines. In practically all cases the reflected waves in the separate feed lines will be out of phase and offset in magnitude. Consequently all power resulting from those returned waves will be dissipated in the resistor. This means that whatever the SWR may be on the lines to the antennas, the impedance will always be 50 ohms at the point where the resistor is connected. If the two quarter-wavelength lines are made of 75-ohm cable, the 50-ohm impedances will show up as 100 ohms at the T. Hence the power split is equal and the impedance at the T will be 50 ohms.

This is not to say that *any* SWR may be present on the lines between the Wilkinson resistor and the loads. The Wilkinson power dividers only perform equal power splitting when the loads are equal. Wilkinson power dividers are really intended for other purposes than feeding array elements, such as power sharing by two sources (2 power transistors, for instance), as a safety measure (should one transistor fail, the other will still see an essentially unchanged load).

Most lines terminate in a conjugate match. This may be at the end of the lines where there is proper matching to the transmitter, or somewhere along the line by some matching technique. At the point of the conjugate match, the reflected power is re-reflected towards the load. That is why in the case of a 3:1 SWR (reflected power equals 50 percent of forward power), the lost power is not 50 percent, but a value which depends on the nominal attenuation characteristics of the line.

In the case of the Wilkinson power divider, however, the discontinuity at the point where the resistor is connected is such that all of the reflected power will be dissipated in that resistor. That means that in the case of a 3:1 SWR, 50 percent of the forward power will be dissipated in the resistor. At the same time, however, the input to the divider will remain essentially constant, which means that if one tries to evaluate the system by SWR performance, the results will be highly misleading.

When used in the feed system of an antenna array, the Wilkinson power divider will not eliminate the effects of mutual coupling between array elements (see Section 2.11.1.4). In almost all arrays, the design objective is not equal power, but often equal element current amplitude. As the element feed-point impedances are most often complex and unequal (unless the phase shift is 0 or 180°), it must be emphasized that coaxial line lengths only supply phase shift equal to the line length in degrees under very specific circumstances (see Section 2.11.1.4).

2.12.5 THE NEED FOR LOW SWR

In the past, SWR was not understood by many radio amateurs. Reasons for low SWR were often false, and SWR was often used as the outstanding parameter telling us all about the performance of an antenna.

Maxwell, W2DU, published a series of articles on the subject of transmission lines. They are excellent reading material for anyone who has more than just a casual interest in antennas and transmission lines (Refs 1308-1311, 1325-1330 and 1332).

Everyone has heard comments like "My antenna really gets out because the SWR does not rise above 1.5:1 at the band edges." Low SWR is no indication at all of good antenna performance. The antenna with the best SWR is a dummy load. Antennas using dummy resistors as part of loading devices come next (Ref 663). It may be easily concluded from this that low SWR is no guarantee of radiation efficiency. The reason that SWR has been wrongly used as an important evaluation criterion for antennas is that it can be easily measured, while the important parameters such as efficiency and radiation characteristics are more difficult to measure.

Antennas with lossy loading devices, poor earth systems, high-resistance conductors and the like, will show flat SWR curves. Electrically short antennas should always have narrow bandwidths. If they do not, it means that they are inefficient.

The only really sound method of evaluating an antenna system is by on-the-air comparison. If you use a reference antenna, keep it well away from the antenna under evaluation. To find out if mutual coupling exists between the two antennas, feed RF into one antenna and alternately open- and short-circuit the other. If there is any detuning of the first antenna (the transmitter loading and SWR will change) one may conclude that there is mutual coupling occurring between the antennas which will disturb their performance. Instead of using a reference antenna, one may also use a reference station. Do not try to evaluate an antenna in one evening. It takes time to get a complete idea of how the antenna is working, because it must be evaluated under different circumstances (over different paths, with different propagation conditions, and so on).

2.13 Special Receiving Antennas

2.13.1 BEVERAGE ANTENNA

The Beverage antenna (named after Harold Beverage, W2BML) made history in 1921. In fact, a Beverage antenna was used in the first transatlantic tests on approximately 1.2 MHz. For many decades, the Beverage antenna wasn't used very much by hams, but in the last 15 years it has gained tremendous popularity with low-band DXers. The early articles on the Beverage antenna (Refs 1200-1204) are still excellent reading material for the ham who wants to familiarize himself with this unique antenna.

2.13.1.1 Principles

Figure 2.148 shows the basic configuration of the Beverage antenna (also called "wave antenna"). It consists of a long wire (typically 1 to 4 λ long) erected at low height above the ground.

The Beverage antenna has very interesting directional properties for an antenna so close to the ground, but it is relatively inefficient. This is the reason why the antenna is primarily used for reception only on the amateur low bands.

The Beverage antenna can be thought of as an open-wire transmission line with the ground as one conductor and the antenna wire as the other. In order to have a unidirectional pattern, the antenna has to be terminated at the far end in a resistor equal to the characteristic impedance of the antenna. If the Beverage antenna is to be used on VLF (where it was originally used), the velocity of propagation in the "two

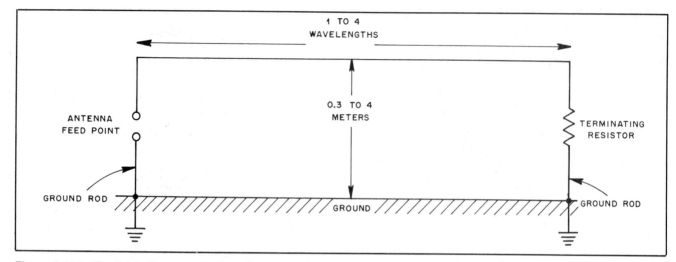

Figure 2.148—The basic Beverage antenna is a straight wire 1 to 4 λ long, constructed parallel to ground at a height of 1 to 14 feet (0.3 to 4 m). Length limitations are discussed in the text.

wires'' has to be different, so that the arriving wavefront (at zero wave angle for VLF signals) inclines onto the wire and induces an EMF in the wire. Therefore, the ground under the antenna must have rather poor conductivity for best performance.

On the amateur low bands, the situation is different, because the wave angle is not zero. It is typically 10 to 40° for DX signals on 160/80/40 meters. In this case the wave angle of the arriving signal itself is responsible for inducing voltage in the antenna wire, so that it is not essential that the antenna be installed over a poorly conducting ground. Some authors have mentioned that the highest useful frequency for the Beverage is 160 meters. This is not necessarily true, and many active users of this fine antenna can testify about its wonderful performance on 80 and even 40 meters! Arrays of Beverage antennas are also used on the HF bands for direction finding and over-the-horizon radar.

In any case, the tilted wave (tilted by the difference of velocity at VLF, and tilted due to the arriving wave angle on the HF bands) will induce signals in the wire. It may seem that the longer the Beverage antenna, the greater the induced signal. This is not the case, however. Gain increases with length, but beyond a certain length, gain actually begins to drop off. This length limitation varies with the velocity factor of the antenna, but is also dependent on the angle of the incoming signal. The drop in gain is caused by the currents in the wire increasingly lagging the tilted wave in space as the length of the wire is increased (due to the different velocity of propagation in space and in the wire). A point is eventually reached where the current in the wire is more than 90° out of phase with the space wave, and the wave begins to subtract from the signal on the wire, causing a reduction in gain.

The theoretical maximum length for a zero wave angle is:

$$L_{max} = \frac{\lambda \times Vf}{4\,(100 - Vf)}$$

where

λ = wavelength of operation
Vf = velocity factor of the antenna.

For non-zero wave angles, the above equation includes the wave angle factor as follows:

$$L_{max} = \frac{\lambda \times Vf}{4\,(100 - Vf \cos a)}$$

The maximum length can be determined this way because it is a function of the maximum gain of the antenna. Making the antenna longer will result in reduced output, but the horizontal wave angle can be further narrowed and the vertical angle further lowered with greater lengths (at the expense of signal strength).

Velocity factor is the ratio of velocity of propagation of the electromagnetic wave in the antenna wire to the velocity of propagation of electromagnetic energy in a vacuum. The velocity factor of a Beverage will vary typically from about 90% on 160 meters to 95% on 40 meters. These figures are for a height of 10 to 12 feet. At very low heights the velocity factor is much lower (approximately 85% at 3 feet). This is a major drawback of very low Beverage antennas.

The velocity of propagation of your Beverage antenna can be determined experimentally as follows.

1) Measure the physical length of the antenna, then calculate the theoretical wavelength (l_{qw}) and frequency (f_{qw}) on which the antenna is a quarter-wave long (assuming 100% velocity factor). Fill the figures in on the worksheet as in Table 34.

Table 34

Beverage Antenna Velocity of Propagation Worksheet

Physical antenna length: 200 meters
Calculated ¼ λ (L_{qw}): 4 × (300/L) = 600 meters
¼ λ frequency (F_{qw}): 300/600 = 0.5 MHz

Length	Open-End Freq	Shorted-End Freq	Velocity Factor (Dip freq / N × F_{qw})		
1 × ¼ λ	0.46	—	0.40/1 × 0.5 =	92
2 × ¼ λ	—	0.94	0.94/2 × 0.5 =	94
3 × ¼ λ	1.42	—	1.42/3 × 0.5 =	95
4 × ¼ λ	—	1.90	1.90/4 × 0.5 =	95
5 × ¼ λ	2.38	—	2.38/5 × 0.5 =	95
6 × ¼ λ	—	2.87	2.87/6 × 0.5 =	96
7 × ¼ λ	3.36	—	3.36/7 × 0.5 =	96
8 × ¼ λ	—	3.85	3.85/8 × 0.5 =	96
9 × ¼ λ	4.34	—	4.34/9 × 0.5 =	96
10 × ¼ λ	—	4.84	4.84/10 × 0.5 =	97
11 × ¼ λ	5.34	—	5.34/11 × 0.5 =	97
12 × ¼ λ	—	5.83	5.83/12 × 0.5 =	97

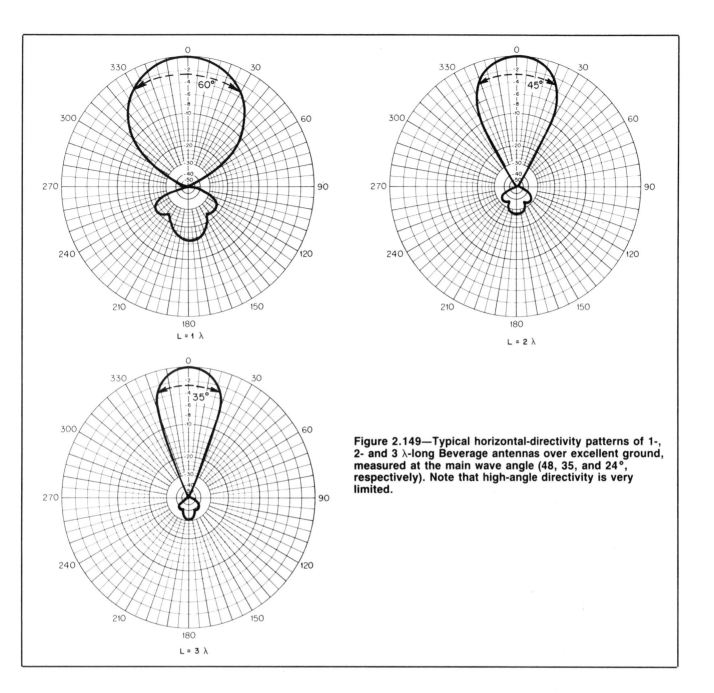

Figure 2.149—Typical horizontal-directivity patterns of 1-, 2- and 3 λ-long Beverage antennas over excellent ground, measured at the main wave angle (48, 35, and 24°, respectively). Note that high-angle directivity is very limited.

2) Open one end of the antenna and feed the antenna via a two-turn link from a dip oscillator. Tune through the spectrum starting at approximately 70% of the calculated quarter-wave frequency (approximately 350 kHz in the example case) and note the exact frequency of all the dips up to the maximum frequency of interest. Repeat the same procedure with the antenna end short-circuited to ground. Again note the dip frequencies.

Note that the velocity factor changes with frequency of operation. On 160 meters, the antenna in Table 34 shows a velocity factor of approximately 95%. On 80 meters the velocity factor is 96%.

Applying the maximum length formula, we find a maximum length of L_{max} = 480 meters for 80-meter operation and maximum length of 768 meters for 160 meters (for a zero wave angle).

If we consider elevation angles lower than 30° on 160 meters, the maximum length becomes 214 meters (Equation 2). For 80, (assuming a wave angle of 20°) the maximum length is 196 meters. The antenna under evaluation was 200 meters long, which is certainly a good compromise for use on both 160 and 80 meters.

Depending on the ground quality and the wave angle, Beverages as long as 2000 feet have been reported to work very well on 80 and 160 meters. See also Section 2.13.1.2.

2.13.1.2 Directional Characteristics and Gain

Figure 2.149 shows the horizontal directivity patterns for properly terminated Beverages of 1, 2 and 3 λ long. In past years, both the US and Canadian governments have done studies on Beverage antennas for use in direction finding and over-the-horizon radar. Some of this work has been described in the literature (Ref 1236). Tables 35, 36 and 37 give typical characteristics for a Beverage operating on 3.7 MHz. The data was scaled down from 2 MHz, and the gain figures are given for a 0° wave angle.

Careful study of the tables should show the reader that the gain starts dropping beyond a certain antenna length. Over poor and average (conductivity) earth, the horizontal beamwidth does not decrease continuously, but changes

Table 35

Typical Beverage Antenna Characteristics at 3.7 MHz

Case 1: Over ground with poor conductivity.
(Dielectric Constant: 8; Conductivity: 0.03 mS/m)

Parameter	Height	L = 100 m	L = 200 m	L = 300 m	L = 400 m
Hor Angle	0.3 m	57°	37°	53°	45°
Vert Angle	(1 ft)	36°	21°	44°	28°
Main Lobe Angle		28°	17°	33°	23°
Gain (dBi)		−8.0	−10.2	−8.4	−10.6
Hor Angle	1.0 m	61°	43°	34°	38°
Vert Angle	(3.3 ft)	39°	25°	19°	21°
Main Lobe Angle		31°	20°	16°	16°
Gain (dBi)		−6.9	−5.9	−7.4	−5.3
Hor Angle	2.0 m	63°	45°	38°	33°
Vert Angle	(6.6 ft)	41°	28°	22°	19°
Main Lobe Angle		34°	23°	18°	15°
Gain (dBi)		−6.1	−4.4	−4.4	−5.3
Hor Angle	3.0 m	63°	46°	37°	33°
Vert Angle	(10 ft)	46°	32°	23°	19°
Main Lobe Angle		36°	24°	19°	15°
Gain (dBi)		−5.6	−3.4	−3.0	−35

Table 36

Typical Beverage Antenna Characteristics at 3.7 MHz

Case 2: Over ground with average conductivity.
(Dielectric Constant: 12; Conductivity: 0.3 mS/m)

Parameter	Height	L = 100 m	L = 200 m	L = 300 m	L = 400 m
Hor Angle	0.3 m	58°	37°	49°	44°
Vert Angle	(1 ft)	36°	20°	36°	31°
Main Lobe Angle		27°	16°	60°	26°
Gain (dBi)		−8.6	−9.5	−12.0	−11.1
Hor Angle	1.0 m	63°	43°	34°	29°
Vert Angle	(3.3 ft)	43°	27°	20°	16°
Main Lobe Angle		32°	21°	16°	13°
Gain (dBi)		−7.5	−5.7	−6.0	−7.4
Hor Angle	2.0 m	63°	46°	36°	31°
Vert Angle	(6.6 ft)	47°	29°	24°	18°
Main Lobe Angle		35°	23°	18°	15°
Gain (dBi)		−6.6	−4.1	−3.4	−3.7
Hor Angle	3.0 m	63°	47°	38°	32°
Vert Angle	(10 ft)	51°	32°	23°	20°
Main Lobe Angle		35°	23°	18°	15°
Gain (dBi)		−5.7	−3.0	−2.1	−2.2

Table 37

Typical Beverage Antenna Characteristics at 3.7 MHz

Case 3: Over ground with good conductivity.
(Dielectric Constant: 26; Conductivity: 0.3 mS/m)

Parameter	Height	L = 100 m	L = 200 m	L = 300 m	L = 400 m
Hor Angle	0.3 m	63°	42°	32°	29°
Vert Angle	(1 ft)	40°	21°	16°	14°
Main Lobe Angle		24°	15°	11°	10°
Gain (dBi)		−13.8	−11.6	−12.3	−14.3
Hor Angle	1.0 m	64°	47°	39°	32°
Vert Angle	(3.3 ft)	56°	31°	21°	17°
Main Lobe Angle		36°	21°	15°	12°
Gain (dBi)		−12.3	−8.6	−7.7	−7.2
Hor Angle	2.0 m	61°	46°	39°	35°
Vert Angle	(6.6 ft)	49°	40°	31°	26°
Main Lobe Angle		46°	30°	23°	18°
Gain (dBi)		−7.5	−4.5	−4.2	−3.2
Hor Angle	3.0 m	63°	46°	39°	24°
Vert Angle	(10 ft)	49°	40°	31°	25°
Main Lobe Angle		47°	29°	23°	17°
Gain (dBi)		−7.7	−4.4	−4.4	−2.9

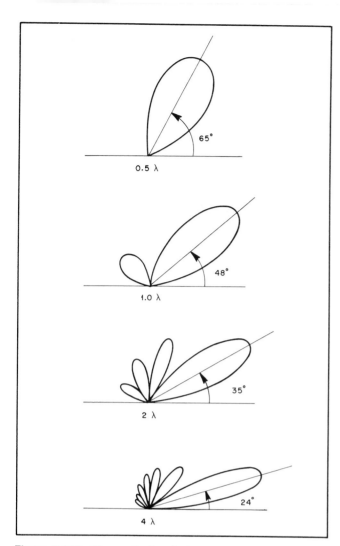

**Figure 2.150—The vertical radiation pattern shows
different lobes as the length of the antenna is increased.
The angle of the main lobe is lowered at the same time.**

radically with length. Over rich wet earth (good conductivity),
on the other hand, it is easier to predict performance at low
heights (1 foot or 0.3 m). However, these low heights are not
very practical for most amateurs, because of potential
interference from passing people and animals. Nevertheless,
over rich, moist earth, performance in the vertical plane is
excellent at low height.

You can see that at 3.5 MHz over poor or average soil, any
change in height from 1 to 3 meters has very little effect on
the horizontal beamwidth. Antenna height has greater effect
on the vertical beamwidth of short antennas (100 to 200
meters) than long ones (300 to 400 meters) with slightly
narrower beamwidth at lower heights.

The vertical angle of radiation on the nose of the main lobe
is slightly lower at 1 meter height, but there is no substantial
difference at heights ranging from 2 to 3 meters. Antennas
which are very long (400 meters or longer) favor a slightly
lower angle at greater height, but the difference is minor.

Short antennas (100 meters) show lower gain at lower
heights. On long antennas however, gain increases
substantially with greater heights (5 to 12 dB of difference
for a 400-meter Beverage). The same basic conclusions apply
for poor dry ground and rich wet soil, but height has greater
impact on the antennas installed over rich earth. In general,

these conclusions are the same at 1.8 MHz. We can expect
somewhat greater effects on 7 MHz.

From the tables, one might conclude that the Beverage has
only one vertical lobe, but this is not the case. Figure 2.150
shows the lobes for 80-meter Beverages at a height of 3 meters
and for lengths of 0.5, 1.0, 2.0 and 4.0 λ. The lowest quoted
angle is for installations over dry ground, the higher figure
if the antenna is installed over rich wet soil. We will see later
how the minor lobes (high-angle lobes and back lobes) can
be used to make an electrically steerable Beverage antenna
(Section 2.13.1.20), enabling us to get an almost infinite
rejection at certain wave angles.

Depending on the ground quality and the wave angle of
the incoming signal, Beverages as long as 2000 feet have
demonstrated excellent performance, even on 80 meters.
Worth, WB3GCG, has been successful in using eight
Beverages. The length of each Beverage can be switched to
500, 1000 or 2000 feet. Figure 2.151 shows a layout of such
a multi-length Beverage. The author's own experience is that
his 1000-foot Beverage substantially outperforms shorter ones.
This does not mean, however, that a Beverage as short as
1 λ cannot be a worthwhile investment.

2.13.1.3 Beverage Impedance

The characteristic impedance of the single-wire Beverage
antenna is a function of the antenna wire diameter and its
height above ground:

$$Z = 138 \log \left(\frac{4h}{d} \right)$$

where
   h = height of wire
   d = wire diameter (in the same units).

Table 38 is useful for estimating the terminating resistor
for a single-wire Beverage and for designing matching
transformers and networks. Note that the impedance does not
change drastically with height or wire size. Very low Beverages
do not have a very low impedance as is sometimes said.
Belrose (Ref 1236) reports impedances varying between
approximately 420 ohms and 550 ohms for a 360-foot
(110-meter) long Beverage at frequencies ranging from 2 to
10 MHz (height above ground = 3.7 feet or 1.1 meter).

The optimum terminating resistor value for a Beverage
antenna can also be determined experimentally. Couple a dip
meter to one end of the antenna via a two-turn link. Terminate
the other end with a 300-ohm resistor and tune the dip meter
from 1 to 7 MHz. Measure the depths of the resonant points
as you scan through the frequency range. Repeat the same
test with a 400-ohm and then a 500-ohm terminating resistor.
This process will allow you to find a resistor value for which
almost no dips will be found between 1 and 7 MHz. That will
be the resistor value for which the antenna is fully aperiodic
(nonresonant). The exact impedance can vary greatly with
ground conditions (season, humidity and so on). Misek,
W1WCR, described the use of wires under the Beverage to
stabilize ground conditions (Ref 1206).

2.13.1.4 Terminating the Single-Wire Beverage

A common way of terminating the single-wire Beverage is
to connect the proper terminating resistor (400 to 550 ohms)
between the end of the Beverage and the ground. This,
however, is not necessarily the best solution, especially on
frequencies higher than the very low ones, where the vertical

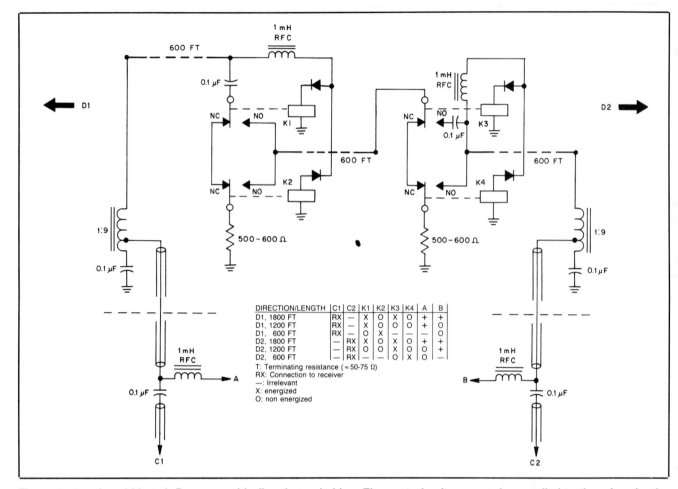

Figure 2.151—A multi-length Beverage with direction switching. The control voltages can be supplied to the relays by the circuit shown in the insert. As the two relays are never simultaneously energized, they can be fed by opposite-polarity voltages on the feed line.

DIRECTION/LENGTH	C1	C2	K1	K2	K3	K4	A	B
D1, 1800 FT	RX	—	X	O	X	O	+	+
D1, 1200 FT	RX	—	X	O	O	O	+	O
D1, 600 FT	RX	—	O	X	—	—	+	O
D2, 1800 FT	—	RX	X	O	X	O	+	+
D2, 1200 FT	—	RX	O	O	X	O	O	+
D2, 600 FT	—	RX	—	—	O	X	O	—

T: Terminating resistance (≈ 50-75 Ω)
RX: Connection to receiver
—: Irrelevant
X: energized
O: non energized

Table 38
Characteristic Impedance of Beverage Antennas

Height Above Ground	Characteristic Impedance (ohms)		
	1.3 mm OD Wire (16 AWG)	1.6 mm OD Wire (14 AWG)	2.0 mm OD Wire (12 AWG)
0.3 m (1 ft)	409	396	383
1.0 m (3.3 ft)	481	469	456
2.0 m (6.6 ft)	523	510	497
3.0 m (10 ft)	547	535	521
4.0 m (13 ft)	564	552	539

downlead that connects the Beverage to the terminating resistor becomes a significant part of a wavelength and thus picks up a lot of signal. This effect can greatly impair the front-to-back ratio of the antenna. For Beverages at relatively high heights (1 meter or higher) this is not the most suitable way of terminating the antenna.

Figure 2.152 shows how the directional characteristics of a Beverage can be degraded by the stray pickup of a downlead. The omnidirectional pickup from a 10-foot (3-m) downlead was superimposed on the directional characteristic of the 2 λ-long Beverage. Note that the directivity is not better than 15 dB in any direction.

Figure 2.153 shows the classic resistor termination system using the vertical downlead as well as alternative systems that eliminate vertical downlead pickup. The quarter-wave

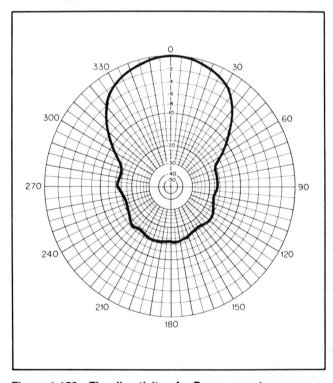

Figure 1.152—The directivity of a Beverage antenna can be degraded tremendously by stray pickup from vertical downleads acting as omnidirectional antennas at either end of the Beverage.

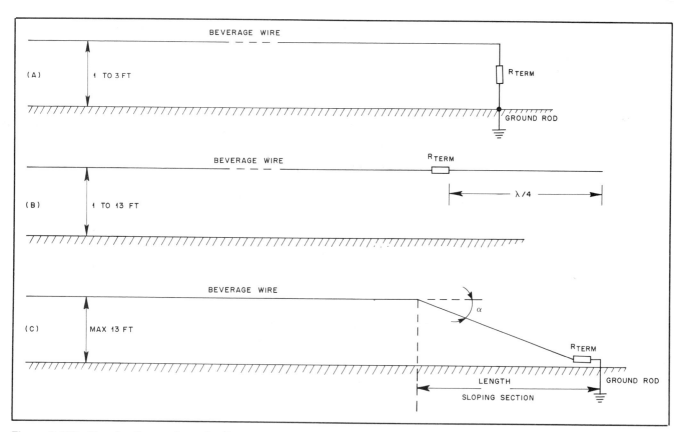

Figure 2.153—Terminating systems for Beverage antennas. Version A does nothing to eliminate stray pickup from the vertical downleads, and should only be used with very low antennas (maximum 3 feet or 1 meter high). Example B uses a quarter-wave terminating wire, while the sloping termination of version C is totally broadbanded and as such is the most favorable solution.

Table 39

Wave Angle Versus Slope Length for Beverage Antennas

Beverage Height	Wave Angle					
	10°	15°	20°	25°	30°	35°
0.3 m (1 ft)	1.7 m	1.2 m	0.9 m	0.7 m	0.6 m	0.5 m
1.0 m (3.3 ft)	5.8	3.9	2.9	2.4	2.0	1.7
2.0 m (6.6 ft)	11.5	7.7	5.8	4.7	4.0	3.5
3.0 m (10 ft)	17.3	11.6	8.8	7.1	6.0	5.2
	Slope Length in Meters					

termination is essentially a single-band termination. Traps can be included for multiband operation, or alternatively, parallel quarter-wavelength wires for different bands can be used. The disadvantage of this configuration is that it requires an extra quarter wavelength of real estate which does not contribute to the Beverage proper. The sloping termination has been extensively used by the author and found to work very well. The slope angle should be lower than the minimum expected arrival angle of the signal. Table 38 gives the length of the sloping wire as a function of the minimum wave angle and the Beverage height.

To obtain slope length in feet, multiply the above figures by 3.28 (1 meter = 3.28 feet). For a wave angle of 10°, the amount of real estate required for the sloping section is about ¼ λ (on 80 meters). The sloping wire section, however, is part of the antenna proper, and the sloping termination is fully broadbanded. The terminating resistor (400 to 550 ohms) is now connected between the end of the sloping wire and the ground system.

2.13.1.5 Ground Systems for Beverage Antennas

The ground system of a Beverage should consist of at least one 7- to 10-foot ground rod at each end of the antenna. If multiple shorter ground rods are used, they should be spaced approximately 5-7 feet apart for optimum performance. With wet rich ground, a ground rod system may be sufficient. One may include a number of quarter-wave (non-insulated) radial wires buried about 10 cm (4 inches) under the ground. Laying radial wire on the ground in directions different from the Beverage wire direction may result in pickup of signals from unwanted directions, and should therefore be avoided. Where rocky soil prevents the use of ground rods, a number of short radials can be buried (just below the surface) or laid on the ground; there will be a chance of stray pickup in the system, however. Stray pickup can also be reduced by running the radials only in the direction of the Beverage wire and at very low angles to the wire.

Where a sloping termination is used, the ground rod (7 to

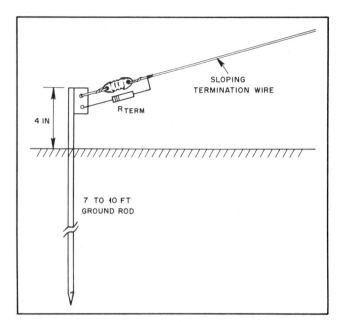

Figure 2.154—The sloping part of the Beverage antenna can be mechanically anchored at the 7- to 10-foot (2- to 3-m) long ground rod via an appropriate insulator. The terminating resistor must be connected between the end of the antenna and the ground rod itself.

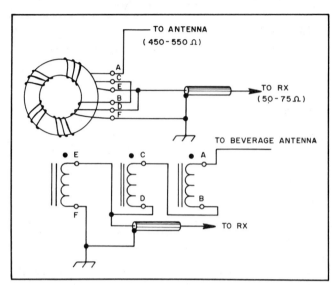

Figure 2.155—The transmission-line transformer consists of three parallel-wound wires spaced equally across a toroid core. The proper connecting scheme is shown. The enameled copper wire can be securely fixed to the core using electrical tape.

10 feet long) can be extended a few inches above ground to act as a mechanical termination post for the sloping wire section (Figure 2.154).

2.13.1.6 Feeding the Single-Wire Beverage

The easiest way to match the Beverage impedance (400 to 550 ohms) to the commonly used coaxial cable (50 or 75 ohms) is to use a wideband toroidal transformer. Such transformers are usually wound on magnetic-material cores. The magnetic material can be either ferrite or powdered iron. Ferrites attain much higher permeability (up to 10,000) than powdered iron materials (only up to 100), but are less stable at higher frequencies and saturate more easily. For wideband transformers which are not typically confronted with high power, such as in the Beverage antenna situation, ferrites are the most logical approach.

Several core sizes and core materials can be used for this job. As far as the size is concerned, the 0.5 inch cores (or even smaller ones) will do the job if the builder is not tempted to transmit on the Beverage. Larger size cores can be used as well, and give the added advantage that one can assess the SWR of the transformer by injecting low power (make sure not to saturate the core!) via a sensitive SWR bridge into the transformer primary and terminating the secondary with a resistor of adequate wattage. When a satisfactory match has been obtained, both the transformer and the terminating resistor can be installed on the Beverage and a new check can be made. Parallel-connected, high-wattage carbon resistors can be used for the terminating resistor. Do not try to use wirewound resistors; they are inductive at RF.

Alternatively, one may use a noise bridge to check the transformer. This approach does not require that you use a large core which is able to withstand the testing power (which may be substantial to get a usable SWR bridge reading on 160 meters).

The author has been using the high-permeability ferrite material very successfully. To note only one advantage, it is much easier to wind the cores when there are only a few turns! A 9:1 impedance transformer (3:1 turns ratio) will give a more than acceptable match for both 50 and 75 ohm lines. A transmission line transformer using a "trifilar" winding is well suited to this purpose. The wires can be twisted together at about two or three twists per inch. Figure 2.155 shows both the schematic and the winding information. Using Indiana General BBR7731 toroid cores, a 50-ohm to 450-ohm transformer would need only three trifilar turns across the core. Multiplying the number of turns by 1.414 would lower the low-frequency limit by a factor of 2.

Table 40 gives the winding information for some of the more common core materials and toroids ranging from 0.5- to 1.14-inch outer diameter. One section represents the total 50- or 75-ohm winding. The information is typically valid for a frequency range from 1.8 to 7 MHz. Transformers using high permeability materials and requiring few turns will extend much higher in operating frequency because of the reduced adjacent-turn capacitance. The turns data in Table 40 was derived by calculating the number of turns necessary to yield an impedance equal to three times the primary (50- or 75-ohm) impedance, and for a (minimum) design frequency of 1.8 MHz.

The AL value from Table 40 relates the required number of turns for a given core to achieve a given inductance. The relationship is:

$$N = 100 \sqrt{\frac{L}{AL}}$$

where
  N = number of turns
  L = required inductance in μH
  AL = the appropriate value taken from Table 40.

The numbers in the column labeled REF in Table 40 refer to Table 41, which lists some of the manufacturers and their part numbers. More complete data on toroid cores can be found in the *ARRL Handbook*.

Table 40

Winding Data for Beverage Antenna Matching Transformers

| Core Material | Core Dimensions | | | μ_i | AL Value | Turns Req'd for: | | Ref (Table 41) | Material Type |
	ID (in)	OD (in)	Height (in)			50 Ω	75 Ω		
Ferrite	—	0.500	—	10,000	—	3	4	1	
Ferrite	0.28	0.500	0.188	5000	2750	7	9	2	75,3E2A
Ferrite	0.52	0.825	0.250	5000	2950	7	9	3	75,3E2A
Ferrite	0.75	1.14	0.295	5000	3170	6	8	4	75,3E2A
Ferrite	0.28	0.500	0.188	125	68	44	57	5	61,Q1,4C4
Ferrite	0.52	0.825	0.250	125	73	42	55	6	61,Q1,4C4
Ferrite	0.75	1.14	0.295	125	79	41	53	7	61,Q1,4C4
Iron Powder	0.30	0.500	0.190	10	49	52	67	8	2
Iron Powder	0.495	0.795	0.250	10	55	48	63	9	2
Iron Powder	0.57	1.06	0.437	10	135	31	40	10	2

Table 41

Manufacturers' Part Numbers For Toroid Cores

Ref (Table 40)	Manufacturer	Core Number
1	Indiana General	BBR-7731
2	Amidon	FT-50-75
	Fair Rite	5975000301
	Ferroxcube	768T188/3E2A
3	Amidon	FT-82-75
	Fair Rite	5975000601
	Ferroxcube	846t250/3E2A
4	Amidon	FT-114-75
	Fair Rite	5975001001
	Ferroxcube	502T300/3E2A
5	Amidon	FT-50-61
	Fair Rite	5961000301
	Ferroxcube	768T188/4C4
6	Amidon	FT-82-61
	Fair Rite	5961000601
	Ferroxcube	846t250/4C4
7	Amidon	FT-114-61
	Fair Rite	5961001001
8	Amidon	T-50-2
9	Amidon	T-80-2
10	Amidon	T-106-2

2.13.1.7 Sloping Receiving-End Termination

The problems of stray pickup from vertical downleads, as addressed when discussing the Beverage termination, also exist at the "receiving" end of the Beverage. A sloping approach can be followed as earlier explained, and the same figures for angles, lengths and heights apply.

2.13.1.8 Simple Single-Wire Beverage Antenna

Figure 2.156 shows a sketch of a simple single-wire Beverage antenna, which consists of a single 10- to 13-foot support pole from which we slope two 80-meter (262-foot) long wires in one line towards the ground. The slope angle of the wires is only 2.2°, which will certainly allow excellent reception of very low-angle signals. We can use a 7- to 10-foot ground rod at both ends of the Beverage, letting the ends extend a few inches above ground, so that they may be used as end posts for the antenna. Copper-clad steel or bronze wire, as used for overhead open telephone lines, (preferably 1.6 mm in diameter, or 14 AWG) may be used where strength and very little stretch are important. Soft copper cannot be used for long unsuspended runs, as it stretches. The author has been using bronze wire for unsupported spans of over 100 meters (328 feet) with a sag of less than 1.5 feet on the wire. Use 6.6-feet (2 meters) as an average height for determining the antenna impedance (and terminating resistor value).

2.13.1.9 Bidirectional Beverage Antenna

When the Beverage antenna is not terminated, the

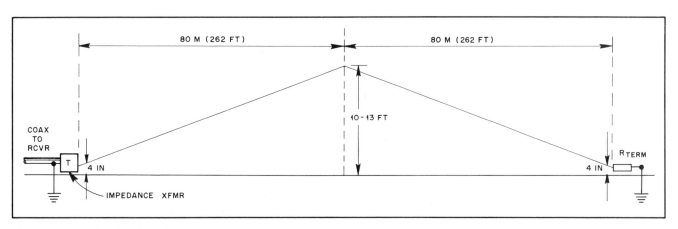

Figure 2.156—The simplest Beverage uses only one central support, while both ends are supported by the ground rods. The author has used this antenna with excellent results.

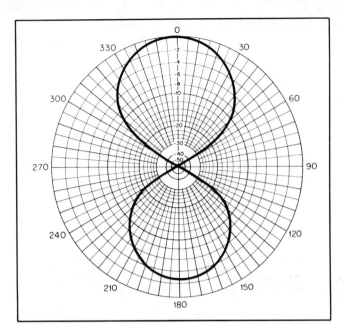

Figure 2.157—Directivity pattern of an unterminated Beverage antenna. Note the slight difference in relative gain between front and back. This is a result of extra losses encountered by the reflected wave.

directivity will be essentially bidirectional. Figure 2.157 shows the horizontal directivity pattern for a 1 λ long unterminated Beverage antenna. Notice the slight attenuation from the back direction because of the extra loss of the reflected wave in the wire.

A method of switching the Beverage from unidirectional to bidirectional is described in Figure 2.158. A relay at the far end of the antenna wire is fed through the antenna wire and the earth return via an RF choke and blocking capacitors (TV preamplifiers are fed in a similar manner via the coaxial cable).

Two directions can also be obtained from a single-wire Beverage by feeding coax to both ends of the antenna (with the appropriate matching network). In this case, one end is terminated in the shack with an appropriate impedance, while

the other is in use for reception. (See Ref 1210).

The "appropriate" terminating impedance can be determined as follows. First, determine the characteristic impedance of the Beverage by the method explained in section 2.13.1.3. Connect an impedance bridge or noise bridge across the high impedance secondary of the matching transformer. Adjust the terminating impedance at the end of the feed line (inside the shack) until a value is found which is the same as the Beverage impedance. In many cases, the impedance will be close to real, and a simple resistor with a value in the range of 50-75 ohms will provide the proper termination.

2.13.1.10 Two-Wire Switchable-Direction Antennas

Instead of erecting one wire, we can put up two wires at a distance of approximately 12 inches (or 30 cm), as in Figure 2.159. Signals arriving off the back of the antenna (direction B) will induce equal in-phase voltages in both wires. Because of the close spacing of the wires, there is no space diversity effect. At the end of the antenna, one wire is left open, while the other wire is short-circuited to ground. This provokes a 100% reflection of the wave, but with a 180° phase reversal. The signals received off the back of the antenna are now fed in a push-pull mode along the open-wire feeders towards the other end of the antenna. At this end a properly designed push-pull transformer (T1) transforms the RF from the push-pull mode (open wire feeder) to the unbalanced coaxial cable impedance. The cold end of the low-Z side of the transformer is connected to the ground system, as well as the center tap of the transformer secondary (via the secondary of transformer T2).

Signals arriving off the front of the antenna (direction A) also induce identical voltages into the parallel wires. At the receiving end, transformer T1 will not produce any output at the low-Z side provided a good balance is achieved in the transformer. The currents will, however produce output at the secondary of transformer T2 (single-ended transformer). Outputs from both directions are simultaneously available from outputs J1 and J2 of this system.

2.13.1.11 Sloping Two-Wire Beverage Terminations

In order to avoid stray pickup from the vertical downleads

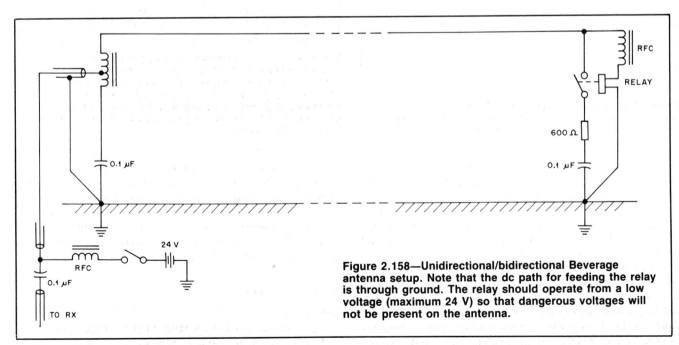

Figure 2.158—Unidirectional/bidirectional Beverage antenna setup. Note that the dc path for feeding the relay is through ground. The relay should operate from a low voltage (maximum 24 V) so that dangerous voltages will not be present on the antenna.

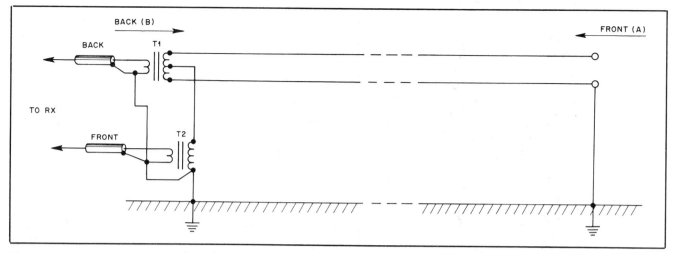

Figure 2.159—Schematic representation of the two-wire Beverage antenna, which allows reception from two directions. The two antenna wires should be side by side and parallel to the ground, although some users have reported satisfactory operation from wires suspended one above the other.

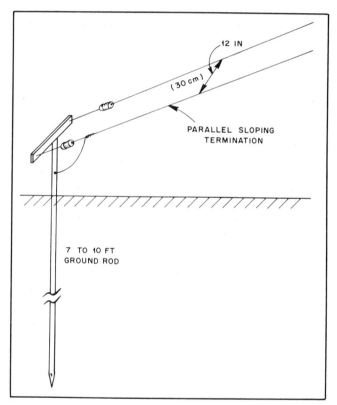

Figure 2.160—Sloping termination for a two-wire Beverage. One wire is directly connected to the ground rod, and the other wire is left floating.

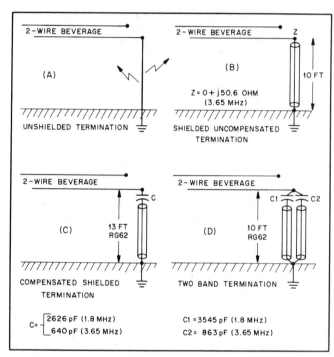

Figure 2.161—The shielded download shown at B does not represent a dead short to ground. The inductive reactance present will upset the required phase reversal at the end of the antenna. Compensating with a capacitor, as shown at C, will avoid this problem. A two-band shielded download with compensation is shown at D. See text for complete details.

of the earth connections, sloping terminations can be used as explained for the single-wire Beverage antenna. At the far end of the two-wire Beverage, one of the wires is directly connected to the ground rod while the other one is left open (Figure 2.160). At the receiving end, the terminating box containing the two transformers can be housed at ground level.

Where it is impossible to apply the sloping termination approach, there is an alternative ground download system that is virtually insensitive to RF pickup. Figure 2.161 shows how the single wire download is replaced by a coaxial cable. The outer shield of this cable is shorted to the inner conductor at ground level. Because of the shielding effect of the coaxial

cable, no RF signals will be present at the upper end of the cable. However, since the download is a transmission line (which is really also the case when a single wire is used), the impedance at the upper end of the cable will be the transformed impedance of the impedance at the bottom end.

The inductive reactance of the coaxial download (assuming a loss free cable and a perfect short at the bottom end) is given by:

$$Z = 2 Z_k \times \tan L$$

where

Z_k = characteristic impedance of the coaxial cable
L = length of the cable in degrees.

Table 42
Compensating Capacitors for Coaxial Downleads

Frequency (MHz)	Height (ft)	Length (degrees)	Top Line Impedance	Required Series Capacitor (pF)
1.825	6.6	5.0	16.3	5350
1.825	10.0	7.6	24.6	3545
1.825	13.0	10.2	33.2	2626
3.650	6.6	10.1	33.4	1307
3.650	10.0	15.3	50.6	863
3.650	13.0	20.3	68.2	640

The required capacitive reactance to tune the system is − Z.

Table 42 shows the relevant values for such compensated downlead structures for 160 and 80 meters and for cable lengths of 2 m (6.6 ft), 3 m (10 ft) and 4 m (13 ft). The values are valid only for RG-62 coaxial cable. This cable was chosen because it has a high velocity factor, resulting in a shorter physical length for a given electrical length.

A two-band system can be made by simply paralleling two single-band systems in a manner similar to paralleling two dipoles for different bands. One of the systems will always show an extremely low impedance on the band it has been designed for, so it will effectively short-circuit the impedance of the system designed for the other band.

The compensated coaxial cable download system can be adjusted in the workshop before installation in the field. The whole system can be connected in parallel with the input of a receiver, and the capacitor tuned for minimum signal at the desired frequency. The coaxial cable plus capacitor is then used as a parallel trap, effectively shorting the receiver input on the receiving frequency. An alternative method is to connect the system in parallel with a dummy load that is connected to the transceiver. The internal SWR meters of today's transceivers will indicate the highest SWR when the trap is tuned to resonance. Use a minimum amount of power to protect your final amplifier. See Figure 2.162 for alignment setup. In the field, the variable capacitor (for 160 meters, a four-gang broadcast variable, plus parallel fixed capacitors) used in the test setup can be replaced by a number of parallel-connected mica capacitors of appropriate value.

2.13.1.12 Designing the Transformers

The push-pull impedance of the open wire line is given by:

$$Z = 276 \log \frac{2s}{d}$$

where

S = spacing between conductors
d = diameter of wires (in the same units).

Table 43 gives the impedance for a range of spacings and wire diameters. The impedance and turns ratios for the transformer T1 are shown in Table 44. The impedance of the parallel wires over ground is given by:

$$Z = 69 \log \left[\frac{4h}{d} \sqrt{1 + \frac{(2H)^2}{s}} \right]$$

where

S = spacing between wires
d = diameter of wires
H = height of wires above ground (all in the same units).

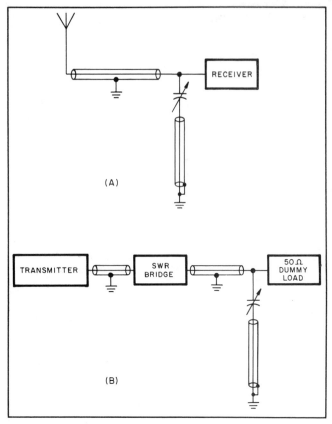

Figure 2.162—The compensated downlead can be connected in parallel with the input of the receiver as shown at A; the capacitor is then adjusted for minimum signal input on the operating frequency. Alternately, the download can be connected in parallel with a dummy load, as shown at B. The capacitor is then adjusted for *maximum* SWR on the line between the transmitter and dummy load/download combination.

Table 43
Impedance Of 2-Wire Beverage Antennas

Wire Spacing	For 1.3 mm wire (16 AWG)	For 1.6 mm wire (14 AWG)	For 2.0 mm wire (12 AWG)
25 cm (10 in)	713 ohms	688 ohms	661 ohms
30 cm (12 in)	735 ohms	710 ohms	683 ohms

Table 44
Winding Data For Impedance Transformers

Secondary Impedance (ohms)	50-Ohm Primary Z ratio	N ratio	75-Ohm Primary Z ratio	N ratio
661	13.2	3.6	8.8	3.0
693	13.9	3.7	9.4	3.0
688	13.8	3.7	9.2	3.0
710	14.2	3.8	9.5	3.1
713	14.3	3.8	9.5	3.1
735	14.7	3.8	9.8	3.1

Table 45 lists the range of antenna impedances for a spacing of 12 inches (30 cm) for three wire sizes and five wire heights. The antenna impedance differs only slightly for the three considered wire diameters. The transformation ratios

Table 45

Impedance of 2-Wire Beverage Antennas With 12-Inch Spacing Between Wires

Antenna Height	For 1.3 mm wire (16 AWG)	For 1.6 mm wire (14 AWG)	For 2.0 mm wire (12 AWG)
0.3 m (1 ft)	229 ohms	222 ohms	216 ohms
1.0 m (3.3 ft)	298 ohms	292 ohms	295 ohms
2.0 m (6.6 ft)	339 ohms	333 ohms	326 ohms
3.0 m (10 ft)	363 ohms	357 ohms	351 ohms
4.0 m (13.3 ft)	381 ohms	374 ohms	368 ohms

Table 46

Winding Data for Impedance Transformers

Secondary Impedance (ohms)	50-Ohm Primary		75-Ohm Primary	
	Z ratio	N ratio	Z ratio	N ratio
222	4.44	2.1	2.96	1.7
293	5.86	2.4	3.91	2.0
333	6.66	2.6	4.44	2.1
357	7.14	2.7	4.76	2.2
374	7.48	2.7	4.99	2.3

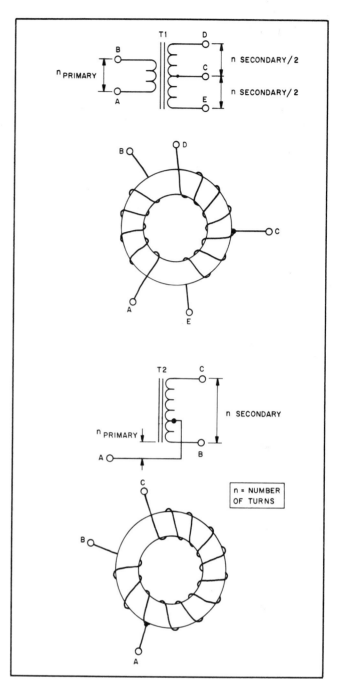

Figure 2.163—The windings of both T1 and T2 should be evenly spaced on the toroidal core. The enameled copper wire can be held on to the core with electrical tape.

(impedance and turns) for these impedances (for 14 AWG or 1.6 mm wire) versus 50 and 75 ohms are given in Table 46. For all practical purposes, the ratios are the same for other wire sizes.

T2 can be wound using the trifilar winding method, although a single winding with a tap also yields very good results. Figure 2.163 shows how transformers T1 and T2 can be wound. For a 50- and 75-ohm primary winding, the number of turns for cores from various suppliers is given in Table 40. Using the N-ratio from the Tables 44 (for T1) and 2.45 (for T2), the secondary turns can be calculated.

Example
1) For Transformer T1 (push-pull transformer).
Inputs:
• Wire size: AWG 14 (1.6 mm diameter)
• Wire spacing: 12 inches (30 cm)
• Coax impedance: 50 ohms
Calculations:
• Push-pull impedance = 710 ohms (see Table 43)
• Turns ratio (vs. 50-ohm primary impedance) = 3.8 (see Table 44)

If we use Indiana General BBR7731 cores, the primary should have three turns for 50-ohm coax (primary) impedance (see Table 40). The secondary should have $3 \times 3.8 = 11$ turns, with a center tap. The primary and secondary turns should be equally spaced around the core.

2) For transformer T2 (single-ended transformer).
Inputs:
• Antenna height: 10 feet (3 meters).
Calculations:
• Antenna impedance = 357 ohms (see Table 44.)
• Turns ratio (vs. 50-ohm primary impedance) = 2.7 (see Table 45.)
For the same BBR7731 cores with three turns for a 50-ohm primary, the secondary should be eight turns. The primary can be tapped at three turns from the cold end of the eight-turn secondary, or it can be wound across the cold end of

the secondary. Alternatively, three five-turn parallel windings can be wound in a trifilar fashion (transmission-line transformer), whereby we will remove 1.5 turns from the third winding (hot side) to obtain the proper matching ratio (see Figure 2.164 for a possible construction method).

2.13.1.13 Constructing the Transformers

After selecting the proper cores and calculating the number of turns for the different windings, the correct enameled wire size should be calculated. The optimum wire size just fills the inside of the toroid core without gaps. To determine the optimum wire diameter proceed as follows.

Measure the inside diameter of the core (d) and subtract 0.5 mm (0.025 inches). Calculate the inside circumference $(d - 0.5) \times 3.14$ mm or $(d - 0.025) \times 3.14$ inches and divide

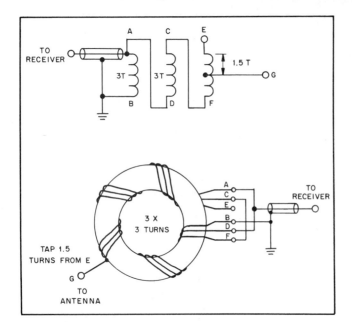

Figure 2.164—By tapping the third winding of the transmission-line transformer, a transformer with any transformation ratio between 4:1 and 9:1 can be made. The example shown is for a transformation ratio of 7:1.

the circumference by the total number of turns required for the entire transformer. This calculation gives the maximum possible wire diameter. If only a small number of turns are to be wound onto a relatively large core, the calculated wire diameter may be rather large, and using such thick wire may cause problems in achieving the proper close-winding on the core. In such a case, a smaller diameter wire must be used, and the turns should be equally spaced around the core. Conversely, when many turns are required (low-permeability material), several layers of wire may be required. The high-end frequency response of such transformers will be restricted due to large inter-winding capacitance. If trifilar windings are used, the three conductors can either be twisted together or laid parallel in a closely spaced manner. The group of three wires should be spaced equally around the core (see Figure 2.164). In all cases, using high-permeability material (μ = 1000 to 10,000) will greatly reduce your efforts in winding the transformers.

Example
BBR7731 cores measure 5/16 inches (7.9 mm) inner diameter. T1 needs a total of 13 windings, T2 needs 11.
T1: $(7.9 - 0.5) \times (\pi/13) = 1.78$ mm
T2: $(7.9 - 0.5) \times (\pi/11) = 2.11$ mm
It would not be possible to use such thick wire and achieve proper winding results on a small core. AWG 20 enameled wire (approximately 0.8 mm diameter) would be recommended on this core for both T1 and T2.

The author has been using aluminum and PVC-type diecast boxes of appropriate size to house the transformers. The PVC boxes are inexpensive and do not need feedthrough standoffs for the output to the Beverage antenna. A stainless steel screw with nuts and bolts mounted right through the plastic wall is all that is needed.

Do not economize on coax connectors. One excellent way of waterproofing coaxial connections (and any others) is to squeeze plenty of medical-grade petroleum jelly into both connector parts before mating. Some petroleum jelly can be applied to the box seams to waterproof the whole assembly once the cover has been put on. Petroleum jelly is an excellent electrical insulator (it has a very low dielectric constant—similar to Teflon and polyethylene). The same material is used by the author for protecting non-stainless steel antenna hardware. After many years of use in a humid and aggressive climate, the hardware still comes apart with no problems.

If the two-wire Beverage is constructed, one may save on coax cable by incorporating a relay in the box, and switching the coax line from direction A to direction B. The relay can be fed via a single coaxial cable, similar to the way shown in Figure 2.158. Both directions will not be simultaneously available at the receiver site (for electrical null steering purposes). Figure 2.165 shows possible layouts for transformer units for single-wire and two-wire Beverage antennas.

2.13.1.14 Testing the Transformers

The matching transformer for the single-wire Beverage, as well as the single-ended transformer (T2) for the two-wire Beverage, can easily be tested for SWR by terminating the secondary with a terminating resistor (of appropriate wattage) and feeding some RF into the antenna via a sensitive SWR bridge through the transformer to an appropriate terminating resistor. A more elegant way is to use a noise bridge. Using a noise bridge allows the use of small cores as very low power will be used when testing.

The SWR of the push-pull transformer (T1) can also be

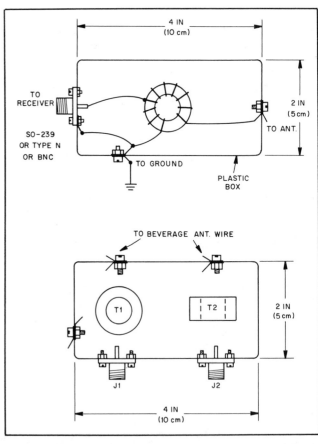

Figure 2.165—Suggested layouts for single- and two-wire receiving-end terminations. Plastic boxes are inexpensive and allow simple feedthrough systems to be used (screw and nut), while the toroidal transformers can be secured directly to the plastic material with silicone sealant.

Table 47
Typical Coaxial Cable Losses

Cable Type	Impedance (ohms)	Coaxial Cable Loss					
		1.8 MHz		3.8 MHz		7.0 MHz	
		dB per 100 m	dB per 100 feet	dB per 100 m	dB per 100 feet	dB per 100 m	dB per 100 feet
RG-8, RG-213, RG-214	50	0.75	0.23	1.20	0.36	1.80	0.55
RG-11	75	0.75	0.23	1.20	0.36	1.80	0.55
RG-58	50	1.65	0.50	2.50	0.58	3.90	1.20
RG-59	75	1.65	0.50	2.30	0.77	3.30	1.00
RG-8 (foam dielectric)	50	0.60	0.18	0.90	0.27	1.40	0.42
½-in Hardline	75	0.26	0.08	0.40	0.12	0.56	0.17
½-in Hardline	50	0.30	0.09	0.43	0.13	0.63	0.19
¼-in CATV drop*	75	1.20	0.36	1.80	0.55	2.80	0.85

* typical values

tested by connecting two resistors across the secondary to the center tap (each resistor should be equal to half of the impedance of the secondary, which is the impedance of the open-wire line).

The balance of the push-pull transformer can be tested by connecting the two secondary outputs together and feeding a small amount of RF from any source (RF generator or dip meter) to this connection. A perfectly balanced transformer should yield no output from this configuration. The physical symmetry of the transformer may be adjusted (slightly adjusting turn spacings on the toroidal core) while performing this test, until the lowest possible signal output is achieved. The balance can be assessed by temporarily disconnecting one of the secondary leads and measuring the signal-strength difference on the receiver. Better than 40 dB difference should be easily obtainable.

2.13.1.15 Feed Lines

Stray pickup from an improperly shielded feed-line system can upset all the directional characteristics of an otherwise properly operating Beverage antenna system. As the Beverage antennas will most likely be operated on relatively low frequencies, we need not use a feed line with the lowest possible loss, especially where all but the very longest feed line runs are being considered. It is still important, however, to use well-shielded coax in order to have a quiet feed system under all circumstances and on all frequencies. The author has been using double-shielded RG-214 (same size as RG-8 or RG-213, but with two densely woven copper shields) on his Beverage systems, which has provided a very quiet feed system. The large coax was used because one of the feed lines was 750 feet long. Smaller coax can be used, especially where runs are shorter. Table 47 shows the typical losses for common coaxial cables on 1.8, 3.5 and 7 MHz.

Often, 75-ohm CATV-type coax leftovers can be bought at reasonable prices from the local cable company. The flexible coax used for drop lines is good for anything but very long runs. Hardline is the ultimate choice for long runs, as it offers the lowest attenuation and best shielding characteristics.

It is advisable to bury the coaxial cables a few inches below the ground to further reduce stray pickup via the coax shield. The author uses 1.5-inch polyethylene water hose as a duct for the coax cables.

After installing the feed lines, try to receive signals with the coax connected to the receiver, with both the coax end open and then with it terminated in a resistor equal to the characteristic impedance of the cable. The receiver should be completely dead, as on the medium waves. If not, try grounding the coax shield at the receiver and/or the end of the line, until satisfactory performance is obtained. It is not advisable to suspend the feed line above ground or to hang it between trees.

After the feed lines have been tested for stray pickup, connect the termination box with the transformers, and connect the ground lead to the box. Without the Beverage wire(s) connected, the receiver should still be dead on all frequencies. This procedure will prove the performance of a good feed system with no reduction in directivity due to stray pickup.

2.13.1.16 Location of the Beverage

The author's experience with Beverage antennas has been over flat terrain consisting of rich, wet soil. As Beverage antennas receive vertically polarized signals, it is not recommended to run a Beverage antenna wire close to a large vertical transmitting antenna. Large vertical antennas reradiate strong signals and tend to upset the directivity pattern of the Beverage antenna if the antennas are less than ¼ λ apart. It is not necessary to have the receiving end close to the station. With a well-shielded, low-loss and well-matched feed line, the receiving end can be many wavelengths away from the shack.

Just as it is not recommended to put up a vertically polarized antenna between tall trees, it is not a good idea to run a Beverage antenna through the woods. Many hams have reported satisfactory performance from Beverage antennas strung between trees in the woods; the fact remains, however, that these antennas would probably perform much better if erected in a more appropriate environment. Beverage antennas for different directions may cross each other if the wires are kept separate by at least a foot and if the crossing angle is between 45 and 90°, to prevent coupling from one antenna to the other. Beverage antennas should also not be run in close proximity to parallel conductors such as fences, telephone lines, power lines (even if quiet) and the like.

2.13.1.17 Mechanical Construction of the Antenna

Almost any type of support will work for a Beverage antenna. The author has been using 13-foot (4 meter) lengths of 1¼ inch (3 cm) outer diameter steel water pipe for supports. About three feet (1 meter) of each pipe is buried in the ground.

Figure 2.166—A 10-foot-long (3-m) 1¼-inch steel pipe with a 12-inch (30-cm) crossbar at the top is used to support the two wires of the Beverage antenna on polyethylene electric-fence insulators on the author's antennas.

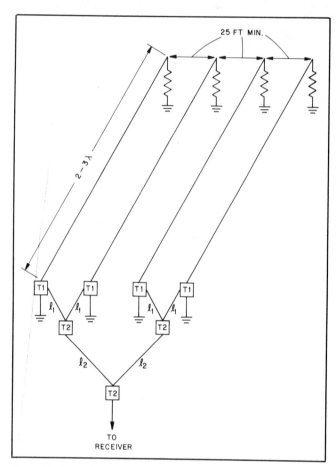

Figure 2.167—Arrays of Beverages can be close-spaced as shown here (25-foot or 7.5-m spacing recommended). The transformers designated T1 are receiving-end termination transformers; those designated T2 represent 3-dB power splitters.

A polyethylene insulator of the type commonly used for electric fences is mounted at the top of each pipe. For two-wire Beverages, two such insulators are spaced one foot (30 cm) on a metal crossbar on top of each pipe (Figure 2.166). The end supports are made from 2-inch OD steel pipe, installed in a small concrete pedestal for added strength and stability.

The author uses single-stranded bronze wire, 14 AWG (1.6 mm OD), which is pulled to approximately 100 lbs (45 kg) tension at one end of the total span. Copper-clad steel wire is also a good performer. If ice loading is to be expected, the wire should only be pulled to 30 lbs (14 kg). The sag on the wires will become objectionable for long runs, so that more supports will be required. Where ice loading is not a problem, supports are only needed every 260 to 330 feet (80 to 100 meters). This means that a 520- to 660-foot (160- to 200-meter) Beverage can be constructed with two end supports and only one intermediate support. If both ends are of the sloping type configuration (Section 2.10.1.11), no separate supports are needed, and the (extended) ground rods can act as mechanical ground posts for the antenna wire(s). Soft-drawn copper wire cannot be tensioned to any great degree without causing much stretching, and it is not suitable for long unsupported spans of wire. If one does not mind using many supports, a soft wire may be used for the antenna. In any case, do not wrap the antenna wire around trees or branches, as

the coils may severely degrade the performance of the antenna.

2.13.1.18 Arrays of Beverages

Although the use of arrays of Beverages is not known to the author except as a transmitting antenna (Ref 1236), arrays of Beverages could easily be implemented, as shown in Figure 2.167. The advantage for a receive-only antenna is not obvious, however, as the added gain will inevitably result in a more narrow pattern, which in turn would necessitate more Beverages to cover all directions.

Erecting arrays of Beverages for the sake of increased signal output does not seem to be useful either, as the signal produced by a single Beverage two or three wavelengths long is more than adequate on our noisy low-frequency bands. In order to establish a high-quality point-to-point link over distances up to 6000 miles (10,000 km), however, a Beverage array would make an exceptionally good low-noise receiving antenna. The outputs from the Beverages can be combined via Wilkinson power dividers as described in Section 2.14.2. When two beverages are involved, two 75-ohm quarter-wave transformers can be used to obtain 100-ohm impedances at the junction point. The Wilkinson resistor is $2 \times 50 = 100$ ohms. Where four antennas are involved, cascaded two-input Wilkinson dividers can be used as shown in Figure 2.168. Alternatively, the quarter-wave coaxial transformers can be replaced by a quarter-wave line made of lumped constants as shown in Figure 2.168 (Ref 1313). This solution is especially

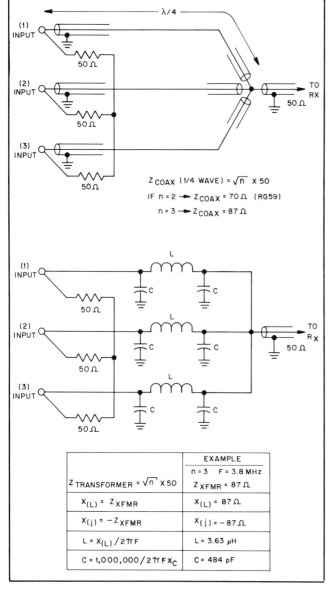

$$Z_{COAX} (1/4 \text{ WAVE}) = \sqrt{n} \times 50$$

IF $n = 2 \rightarrow Z_{COAX} = 70\,\Omega$ (RG59)

$n = 3 \rightarrow Z_{COAX} = 87\,\Omega$

	EXAMPLE
	$n = 3$ $F = 3.8\,MHz$
$Z_{TRANSFORMER} = \sqrt{n} \times 50$	$Z_{XFMR} = 87\,\Omega$
$X_{(L)} = Z_{XFMR}$	$X_{(L)} = 87\,\Omega$
$X_{(j)} = -Z_{XFMR}$	$X_{(j)} = -87\,\Omega$
$L = X_{(L)} / 2\pi F$	$L = 3.63\,\mu H$
$C = 1,000,000 / 2\pi F X_C$	$C = 484\,pF$

Figure 2.168—Quarter-wave coaxial transformers can be used in a Wilkinson power divider. Where coaxial cable with the right impedance is not available, the coaxial transformer can be replaced with a lumped-constant network as shown.

attractive where no coaxial cable with the correct characteristic impedance can be found for the construction of the quarter-wave transformer.

2.13.1.19 Beverage Performance

For the author, Beverage antennas have undoubtedly been the key to working the last 50 countries on 80 meters. Some Beverage users complain that the output from their antennas is too low and they need preamplifiers to boost the signals. If the antenna is properly constructed and has a proper matching transformer, this should not be the case. Beverages at a height of 10 feet (3 meters) should produce signals between -3 dBi and -10 dBi. This is only 1 to 1.5 S-units down from a large vertical. However, as the noise and QRM will be reduced to a much higher degree, the relative gain of a Beverage may be several S-units over a large, low-angle vertical. In every case (when conditions are good), the Beverages used by the author still produce atmospheric noise

which is substantially above the noise floor of the receiver. It has been the author's experience that in many cases, for distances between 3000 and 5000 miles (5000-8000 km) the absolute signal produced by the Beverage fed with 150 to 500 feet (45-150 meters) of RG-214 was only a few dB less than the signal produced by the 90-foot-high transmitting antenna. In some cases, the Beverages have even produced stronger absolute signals on DX paths as compared to a 90-foot (27-meter) vertical, although this is certainly not the general rule. In most of the cases mentioned it was possible to insert 10 or 20 dB of front-end attenuation on the receiver without degrading the readability of the signal. It goes without saying that in none of these cases was a preamplifier needed or desired. This does not mean that Beverages put up in less than ideal surroundings (in the woods or at very low heights) and fed via less efficient feed lines could not use a little "souping up." In that case, a preamp should be inserted at the receiving end of the antenna, not in the shack. Excellent preamplifiers for this purpose have been described in the literature (Ref 257, 267).

2.13.1.20 Electrical Null Steering

Electrical null steering is a technique used to obtain virtually infinite rejection of an unwanted signal source. This technique is most commonly used with small loop antennas to obtain a unidirectional radiation pattern. Signals from the sense antenna and the loop antenna are combined in the correct phase to achieve a cardioid pattern.

The article by Webb, W1ETC, on "Electrical Antenna Null Steering" (Ref 1235) is an excellent reference work for understanding the principles of this technique and its limitations. Misek, W1WCR, (Ref 1206) has described in detail the design and construction of a steerable-wave antenna.

The author has experimented quite extensively with null steering with Beverage antennas, using the basic setup shown in Figure 2.169. Control of phasing can be achieved most easily if the Beverage is an exact number of half wavelengths at the operating frequency, because only then will both the forward and rearward lobes be available in the shack with phase differences equal to a multiple of $180°$ (provided the coaxial cables feeding T1 and T2 are of identical electrical length). Figure 2.170 shows how the forward and rearward

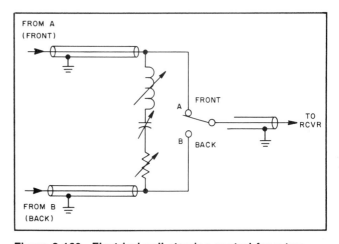

Figure 2.169—Electrical null steering control for a two-wire Beverage antenna. The outputs from directions A and B are combined via an RLC circuit that provides the correct phasing and amplitude control for null steering. Typical values for the components are: R = 500 ohms, C = 500 or 1000 pF and L = 2 to 10 μH.

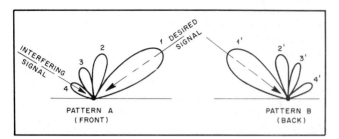

Figure 2.170—The interfering signal which falls in the minor lobe (lobe 4) of the front pattern is combined with the signal produced by lobe 1′ from the back lobe. Careful phase and amplitude control can result in total elimination of the interfering signal.

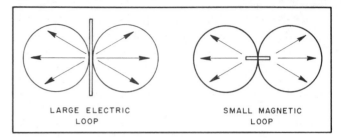

Figure 2.171—Horizontal radiation patterns of a large electric (1 λ circumference) and small (magnetic) loop antenna.

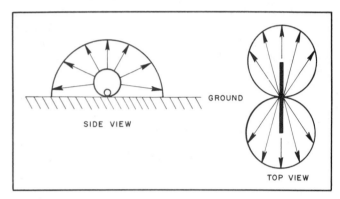

Figure 2.172—Vertical and horizontal radiation patterns of a small loop erected in a plane perpendicular to the ground (classic configuration).

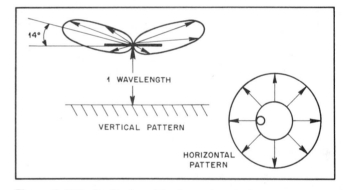

Figure 2.173—Vertical and horizontal radiation patterns of a small loop erected in a plane parallel to the ground.

radiation patterns of a Beverage antenna can be combined to null out a signal source at any angle. Assume we are receiving a desired signal which is right in the peak of the main lobe (1) of pattern B. At the same time, however, a much stronger interfering signal is being received in the rear lobe (4) of the same pattern. Although this lobe is much smaller (perhaps 20 dB down from the main lobe), the unwanted signal is still so strong that it makes reception of the desired signal impossible. Looking at pattern A (produced by the same antenna in the reverse direction), we now have the offending signal available (at great signal strength) in the forward lobe, 1′. If we now combine the signal produced by lobe 4 from the forward pattern (B) with the signal produced by lobe 1′ of the rearward pattern (A), and if these signals are equal in amplitude and 180° out of phase with each other, complete cancellation of the offending signal will result.

After many hours of experimentation on both 80 meters and the top end of the medium-wave broadcast band, the following observations were made:

• Extremely deep nulls (up to 50 dB or better) can be obtained on local (ground wave) broadcast stations in the medium-wave band. Because of the nature of the signals (AM), critical adjustment of both the amplitudes and phasing is possible.

• It becomes much more tricky to null out even a ground-wave SSB or CW signal on 80 meters because of the non-constant amplitude nature of the signals.

• Nulling out sky wave signals is generally impossible, because they often arrive via multiple paths of varying lengths.

• Nulling out sources of man-made noise can be accomplished quite easily, as these sources are usually vertically polarized and are generated in the vicinity of the receiving antenna.

2.13.2 SMALL LOOP ANTENNAS

In the early days of radio, small loop antennas were used extensively as receiving antennas. A small loop antenna is a magnetic antenna, which means that the antenna is excited by the magnetic rather than the electric component of a radio wave. Most other antennas such as dipoles, ground planes, rhombics, large loop antennas, and so on, are electric antennas, responding to the electric component of the wave.

Full-size loops (quads and delta loops) are not loop antennas in the strictest sense, but rather an array of close-spaced stacked dipoles. With large loops, the directivity is broadside to the loop plane. With small loops, the directivity is opposite this, in the plane of the loop (end fire). Figure 2.171 shows directivity patterns of both large and small loop antennas.

The windings of a loop antenna can best be compared to

the windings of a transformer. The antenna is then tuned to resonance with a tuning capacitor. The energy can then be coupled from the "transformer" by a link, or by an inductive or capacitive tap.

Most receiving-only designs use several turns for the loop. The radiation resistance and the loop efficiency are directly proportional to the loop diameter and the number of turns. Receiving-only loops have been described with dimensions ranging from one foot to five feet in diameter, using a variety of feed systems, and often employing built-in preamps (Refs 1219, 1226, and 1229). Such receiving-only loops have proven to be especially valuable for reception on 160 meters, where they are often extremely helpful in eliminating local sources of interference. Loop antennas can show a great deal of horizontal directivity, but when operated vertically (with the plane of the loop perpendicular to the ground) the loop has no vertical directivity at all. See Figures 2.172 and 2.173.

McCoy, W1ICP, described a small, single-turn loop in amateur literature (Ref 1227). The antenna was an 80 meter loop with a diameter of 12 feet, and was resonated by a series connection of three capacitors, with the feed line connected across the middle one (forming a capacitive voltage divider). Ohmic losses appeared to be the main problem in obtaining reasonable efficiency, in view of the very low radiation resistance. The military version is described as having gold-plated contact surfaces in order to reduce losses. The same design was further investigated by Wessendorpp, HB9AGK, (Ref 1228) who reported a consistent signal strength difference of 15 to 20 dB between the small loop and a half-wave dipole.

In recent years, Wuertz, DL2FA, Kaeferlein, DK5CZ, and Schwarzbeck, DL1BU, have experimented extensively with single-turn, transmission-type loops (Refs 1215-1217). Well-built commercial versions of these loops are manufactured by C. Kaeferlein, DK5CZ. The largest model has a diameter of 3.4 meters (11 feet) and is tunable from 3.5 to 7.2 MHz. The calculated gain in free space is −1.9 dBd on 3.5 MHz. The radiation resistance is only 50 milliohms, and the measured bandwidth is 18 kHz, but this is not a problem, because the antenna can be remotely tuned from the shack with a small motor. The narrow bandwidth adds a high degree of front-end selectivity, which can be an advantage in reducing intermodulation distortion. Although one cannot expect such a small loop antenna to be a competitive transmitting antenna for DX work on the low bands, it can be a worthwhile aid in obtaining better reception.

For man-made noise, the electric component of the radiated-wave is most often predominant in the near field. Because a loop only responds to the magnetic component of the signal, loops are much quieter receiving antennas than dipoles or monopoles. Man-made noise sources are almost always of local nature (ground-wave signals), and as such, the signal polarization and the phase are constant (assuming a stationary noise source). These are the necessary prerequisites for achieving a stable null on an interfering signal by orienting the loop in line with the noise source. A practical rejection of 20 dB or better is easily achievable.

When mounted vertically (the classic configuration), the height of the loop above ground does not influence the radiation pattern or the efficiency to any great degree. Poorly conducting ground will not influence the efficiency of a loop, as the magnetic field lines are parallel to the ground.

When mounted horizontally (plane of the loop parallel to ground), the horizontal directivity pattern becomes omnidirectional, and the vertical pattern shows a radiation angle which depends on the height of the antenna above ground (the radiation angles given for horizontal dipoles in Figure 2.3 can be used).

2.14 Summary

Antennas are a key factor in the effectiveness of a low-band station. Success depends on careful attention to the antenna system. The information in this chapter can help you improve your standings on the low bands. Special attention has been given to receiving antennas and the design and construction of reasonably sized (and some not-so-reasonably sized) yet effective transmitting antenna systems. The low bands are becoming a greater source of good DX which was only dreamed about just a few years ago, and the competition in this area has intensified accordingly. The best way to meet the competitive challenge afforded by the low bands is to consider your resources and apply the information in this chapter—as you are able—to your antenna system.

Chapter III

Transmitters

3.1 Power

It should be the objective of every sensible ham to build a well-balanced station. Success in DXing can only be achieved if the performance of the transmitter setup is well balanced with the performance of the receiving setup. It is true that you can only work what you can hear, but it is true also that you can only work the stations that can hear you. It is indeed frustrating when one can hear the DX very well but cannot make a QSO, and it must be frustrating for the station on the other end to hear a loud DX station calling without being able to raise it. We all know stations like that. Some characters just like to be loud. When they cannot hear the DX some even go as far as to make fictitious QSOs and "read the *Callbook*." Fortunately those are the rare exceptions.

A well-balanced station is the result of the combination of a good receiver, the necessary and reasonable amount of power and most of all the right transmitting and receiving antennas. It is of course handy to be able to run a lot of power for those occasions when it is necessary. In many countries in the world amateur licenses stipulate that the minimum amount of power necessary to maintain a good contact should be used, while there is of course a limitation of the maximum power.

There is only one mode of communication where we have real-time feedback of the quality of the communication link, and that is AMTOR (see Section 3.5). In CW as well as SSB we can only go by feeling and by the reports received, and therefore one is most of the time tempted to run "power." It is the author's experience that it is very difficult to work really long distance (over 10,000 km) on 80 meters without running some power, except for paths near the antipodes. It seems be nearly impossible to work over 250 countries on 80 meters without running an amplifier. It can be safely stated that just about all of the active 80-meter DXers run some form of power amplifier, and that most of them run between 800 and about 1500 W PEP output on SSB and about 700 W output on CW. This does not mean that it is impossible to work good DX with 100 W. Many good operators have worked well over 100 countries on 80 meters running a barefoot rig. This is especially true on CW. But when the kilowatt station with a good antenna is squeezing a 33 or 34 report out of a VKØ station, the low-power station will stand no chance to be heard. Fortunately most 80-meter buffs get involved gradually in the DX game. Together with building up a better receiving system (e.g. with Beverage antennas), the need for a little more power will become apparent. One word of warning, however: Low-band DX antennas by definition have a low angle of radiation. The field intensities in the neighborhood of the transmitting antenna can be quite high, and as such the risks for broadcast interference (BCI) are much higher than with a high-angle radiator.

3.2 Linear Amplifiers

Today, the newest technologies are utilized in receivers, transmitters and transceivers to a degree that makes competitive home construction of those pieces of equipment out of reach for but a few. Most of our high-power amplifiers still use vacuum tubes, however, and circuit integration as we know it for low-power devices has not yet come to the world of high-power amplifiers. At any major flea market it is possible to buy all the parts for a linear amplifier. Amateur Radio has come a long way in the past 25 years, from an era where the vast majority of amateur operators used all home-made equipment, to today where all but a few use state-of-the-art, high-tech (and fortunately also high-performance) equipment. Those among us who were in Amateur Radio 25 years or more ago will remember the immense degree of satisfaction we got from building our own equipment. There are at least two areas in Amateur Radio where the DXer can still get this kind of satisfaction: building his own amplifier and building his own antennas.

Those who say that homemade amplifiers are all running illegal power and that running excessive power is the only driving force behind home-brewing an amplifier have probably never built one themselves. The home builder will usually build more reserve into his design. He will have the option himself to spend a few more dollars on metal work and maybe on a larger power-supply transformer in order to have a better product that runs cool all the time and never lets him down. Maybe he will use two tubes instead of one,

Figure 3.1—This home-built amplifier makes use of surplus parts obtained at a hamfest.

and run those very conservatively so that the eventual cost-effectiveness of his own design will be better than for the commercial black box.

There have been excellent amplifier designs published in the Amateur Radio literature over the years. Very often the home builder will be driven by the availability of parts, especially final tubes. Zero-bias triodes have become very popular over the past 25 years for linear service. The popular 811 was followed by the 872, while the 3-500Z has been holding strong for almost 20 years. The latest ceramic 3CX800, 3CX1200 and 8877 seem to be logical choices if one is prepared to buy new tubes. Triodes can take quite a bit of beating. The only thing really to watch is grid dissipation. Excessive grid current and early tube failure can result if the amplifier is too lightly loaded.

Tetrodes such as the 4CX1000 and 4CX1500B can still be found at reasonable prices on the second hand market and are excellent transmitting tubes. They need far less drive than the triodes, but require careful amplifier design and knowledgeable operation because of the very sensitive screen grid.

Figure 3.1 shows an example of a home-built amplifier making use of surplus parts. An important part in the amplifier is the RF switching relay. A good state-of-the-art amplifier should be able to operate in QSK (full break-in) in CW and be fast enough to operate satisfactorily in AMTOR (Ref 335). This can be achieved with vacuum relays or by PIN-diode antenna switching (see also Section 3.5.).

3.3   Phone Operation

If you choose to play the DX game on phone (SSB), there are a few points that you should pay great attention to.

3.3.1   MICROPHONES

Never choose a microphone because it looks pretty. Most of the microphones that match (aesthetically) the popular transceivers have very poor audio. Most dynamic microphones have too many lows and too few highs. In some cases the response can be improved by "equalizing" the microphone output. Even if you have one of the specially designed communication microphones (e.g. Shure 444, Astatic D104 etc), it still may be necessary to apply some tailoring to match the microphone to your voice and the transmitter you are using. The most simple form of microphone equalization is a simple RC high-pass T-filter in the microphone lead. The author has successfully matched his voice to a Shure 444 microphone and a variety of transceivers by incorporating an RC filter consisting of a 1000 pF capacitor with a 50-kilohm resistor. The 3-dB cutoff frequency is given by:

$$F = \frac{1,000,000}{2\pi RC} = \text{approximately 3.2 kHz}$$

where

F = 3-dB cutoff frequency
π = 3.14159
R = parallel arm resistor in kilohms
C = series arm capacitor in nanofarads

The optimum value of the capacitor can be determined by cut-and-try methods, while R should be roughly equal to the output impedance of the microphone. The curve of a single-section RC filter is given in Figure 3.2. Heil, K9EID recognizes the problem of poor audio on our bands, and has tackled the

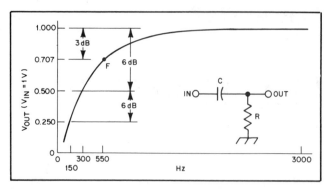

Figure 3.2—Attenuation characteristic of a single-element high-pass RC network. The roll-off for such a filter is 6 dB per octave (which means the output is halved each time the frequency is halved). Identical sections can be cascaded (2 sections would produce 12 dB per octave).

problem by designing a multistage op-amp equalizer which really can do wonders for bad microphones and awful voices (Ref 301 and 323). Both lows and highs can be independently adjusted (enhanced or attenuated). The center adjusting frequencies for lows and highs are 500 and 2200 Hz respectively.

In some cases the audio spectrum of a bad microphone can be drastically improved by changing the characteristics of the microphone resonant chamber. If the microphone has too many lows (which is usually the case), improvement can sometimes be obtained by filling the resonant chamber with absorbent foam material, or by closing any holes in the chamber (to dampen the membrane movement on the lower frequencies).

The most practical solution is to use a microphone designed for communications service. A typical communications microphone should have a flat peak response between 2000 and 3000 to 4000 Hz, a smooth roll-off of about 7 to 10 dB from 2000 to 500 Hz and have a much steeper roll-off below 500 Hz. Figure 3.3 shows the typical response curve for the Heil communications microphone elements. We should caution against overkill here too, however! We know that the higher voice frequencies carry the intelligence, while the lower frequencies carry the voice power. Therefore a good balance between the lows and highs is essential for maximum intelligibility combined with maximum power.

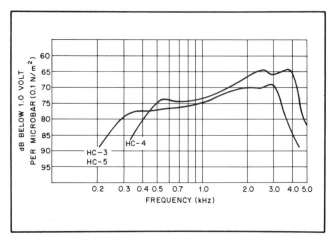

Figure 3.3—Typical response of Heil™ communication microphones with a 2000 ohm resistive load. Note the sharp cutoff below 300 and 500 Hz.

At this point it should also be mentioned that correct positioning of the carrier crystal on the slope of the filter in the sideband-generating section of the transmitter is at least as important as the choice of a correct microphone. Therefore you should test your equalized microphone system into a good-quality tape recorder before doing the on-the-air tests. Incorrectly positioned carrier crystals will also produce bad-sounding receive audio in a transceiver, as the filter is used in both the transmit and receive chain.

One way of checking to see if the USB and LSB carrier crystals have been set to a similar point on the filter slopes is to switch the rig to a dead band, turn the audio up, and switch from USB to LSB. The pitch of the noise will be a clear indication of the carrier position on the filter slope. The pitch should always be identical on both sidebands.

As important as the choice of the microphone is the use of the microphone. Communications microphones are made to be held close to the mouth when spoken into. Always keep the microphone at maximum two inches from your lips. A very easy way to control this is to use a headset/microphone combination. The BM-10 boom set from Heil contains a HC-5 cell in a very lightweight combination that makes DXing under the most difficult circumstances a real pleasure, even over very long periods. If you do not speak closely into the microphone, you will have to increase the microphone gain, which will bring the acoustic characteristics of the shack into the picture, and they are not always ideal. We often have high background noise levels because of the fans of our amplifiers. It is this background level, and the degree to which we practice close-talking into our microphone, which will determine the maximum level of clipping we can use in a system.

3.3.2 SPEECH PROCESSING

Speech processing should be applied to improve the intelligibility of the signal at the receiving station, not just to increase the ratio of average power to peak envelope power. This means that increased average power together with the introduction of lots of distortion may achieve little or nothing. Although audio clippers can achieve a high degree of average power ratio increase, the generation of in-band distortion products will raise the in-band equivalent noise power generated by harmonic and intermodulation distortion and in turn decrease the intelligibility (signal-to-noise ratio) at the receiving end.

RF clipping generates the same increase in the ratio of transmitted average power to PEP, but does not generate in-band distortion products. This basic difference eventually leads to a typical 8-dB improvement of intelligibility over AF clipping (Ref 322). All commercial manufacturers of ham equipment realized this long ago, and virtually all the current transceivers are equipped with RF clippers.

Adjusting the speech-processor level seems to be a difficult task with some modern transceivers. Each RF clipper should have at least two controls. One is the microphone level or level control before clipping (called PROCESSOR IN on some equipment). This gain adjustment will determine the amount of clipping. The second gain control (sometimes called PROCESSOR OUT) sets the level of the processed signal; in other words it acts as an RF-drive level control. These controls will have different names depending on the brand of transceiver.

We already said that the acoustics in the shack will be one of the factors determining the maximum allowable amount of speech clipping. By definition a speech-clipped audio signal has a low dynamic range. In order not to be objectionable the dynamic range should be kept on the order of 25 dB. This means that during speech pauses the transmitter output should be at least 25 dB down from the peak output power during speech. Let us assume we run 1400 W PEP output. A signal 25 dB down from 1400 W is just under 5 W PEP. Under no circumstances should our peak-reading wattmeter indicate more than 5 W peak (about 3 W average), or we will have objectionable background noise (Ref 305). The clipping level should be increased by increasing the PROCESSOR IN control, until we come to the point where the shack ambient noise produces 5 W PEP maximum or where the transceiver compression level indicator indicates maximum 20 dB or whatever the manual recommends as a maximum clipping level.

The PROCESSOR OUT control should only be used to obtain the correct amount of drive from the transceiver into the final or the correct amount of ALC. Never use the microphone gain or the PROCESSOR IN adjustment to adjust the drive to the final.

There is a way to completely eliminate the annoying background noise and still run a fair amount of RF clipping. Commercial amplifiers such as the ALPHA 77DX use an *electronic bias switch* (EBS). Using an electronic bias switch in the linear amplifier one can adjust the sensitivity of the

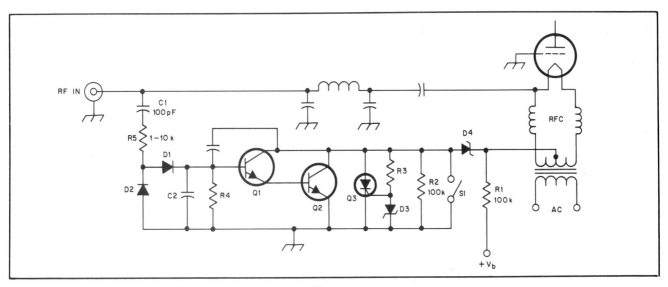

Figure 3.4—Typical EBS circuit for a grounded-grid amplifier.

bias switch in such a way that it does not switch on with the background noise but is turned on only when a given threshold level is exceeded. This way, we can achieve a very impressive dynamic range. The electronic bias switch is a semiconductor switch that switches the final tube(s) from normal transmitting condition to cutoff at the rate of the modulating signal (Ref 316 and 320). It acts as a Schmitt trigger, which means that above a certain RF drive level the switch is on and will be off for all levels below this threshold.

A well-engineered EBS circuit has a means to adjust the threshold level. In our previous example we would like to set this threshold at approximately 0.5 W PEP driver output, assuming a 10-dB-gain amplifier. The electronic bias switch has the great advantage of reducing the average power dissipation of the final tube(s). This is also the case in CW where the final tube(s) will be cut off during every key-up period.

Figure 3.4 shows a basic EBS schematic for a grounded grid amplifier. This circuit uses a voltage-doubling RF rectifier in order to achieve enough sensitivity, together with the two NPN transistors which are connected as a Darlington pair (very high gain). Typically the input transistor can be a 2N3439 or 2N3440 and the second one a 2N3902. These are all 400 volt devices. The thyristor/Zener circuit across the output transistor is the familiar crowbar protection circuit which serves to short the EBS circuit if a given voltage is reached. With R1 equal to R2, the voltage across the output transistor is normally Vb/2. D3 is chosen (operating voltage higher than Vb/2) so that it will only conduct if the collector voltage of Q2 exceeds the D3 Zener voltage. When D3 conducts, it will apply a positive voltage to the gate of Q3 and make it conduct. This is to prevent high voltage appearing on the line if for any reason R2 should open up. The sensitivity of the circuit can be adjusted by changing the value of R5. C3 is the integrating capacitor that with R6 determines the switching speed of the EBS. A MOV or Tranzorb™ semiconductor spike-protection device can be connected across the output of the switch (between the collector and the emitter of the output transistor) for added device protection.

The EBS circuit for a grounded-cathode amplifier uses two PNP transistors as a Darlington pair or an integrated pair in one package (Figure 3.5). There is no need for the crowbar protection circuit. The bias voltage should be at least equal to the full cutoff voltage for the tube in question. D3 prevents the bias voltage from going too low (excessive plate idling current). The bias-set potentiometer is a 4-W wirewound type. Values are typical only and may need changing for particular tubes. This circuit has been successfully used with a 4CX1000 amplifier for many years.

Figure 3.6 shows an ideal CW keying waveform at the top, and below that the same output waveform as output from an amplifier using an EBS. Notice the very steep rise and fall from zero to a voltage level B. If A/B = 5 and the full power (level A) output is 1000 W, the output for level B is 1000/ (5 × 5) = 40 W. If the drive level for 1000 W out is 100 W, the drive level for 40 W is 4 W (if the amplifier response is linear). This is an acceptable sensitivity for the EBS circuit for CW operation (dynamic range is: 10 × log (1000/40) = 14 dB).

For SSB such a sensitivity adjustment would be incorrect. The EBS circuit would have to be adjusted so that the transistor would switch at a lower drive level. Figure 3.7 shows a typical SSB waveform with and without EBS, in both cases with approximately 15 to 20 dB of speech processing.

Ratio A/B must be approximately 16:1 in order to achieve

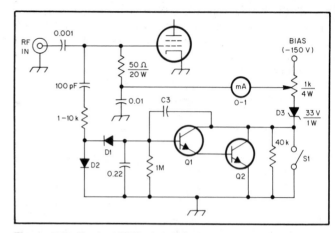

Figure 3.5—Typical EBS circuit for a grounded-cathode amplifier. This particular schematic shows a passive-grid amplifier.

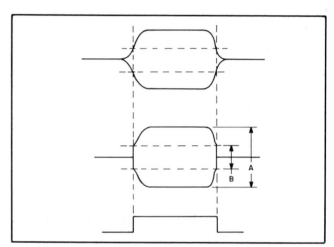

Figure 3.6—CW waveform with and without EBS. The bottom trace shows the switching action of the EBS transistor.

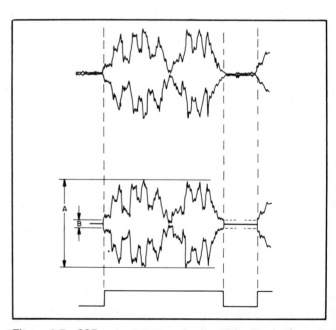

Figure 3.7—SSB output pattern from an amplifier with and without EBS. Note that the background noise noticeable on the top trace is completely eliminated with the EBS in action. Bottom trace again shows the EBS transistors switching.

a 25-dB dynamic range [25 dB = $10 \times \log (16 \times 16)$]. This means that if full output power is achieved with 100 W (PEP) of drive, the EBS circuit should trip with 0.4 W (PEP) of drive. This represents a drive voltage of approximately 4.5 V (peak-to-peak) across a 50-ohm line. The bottom trace shows the envelope pattern for a properly adjusted EBS circuit and speech processor. Too much sensitivity of the EBS circuit or too much processing would show up in rippled line on speech pauses, such as pattern A. When the adjustment is marginal, the EBS would switch on and off randomly on background noise, which would show up as an intermittent rippled line on the scope and as a crackling distorted noise on the air.

Always adjust the speech processor first with the amplifier on but with the EBS circuits bypassed (S1 shorted). When the correct settings of the transceiver are found to achieve at least 25 dB dynamic range, then the EBS can be switched on and the sensitivity adjusted as described above. When the EBS is properly adjusted for 15 to 20 dB of speech clipping, it is likely that with the processor switched off, the EBS circuit will switch continuously between speech syllables, which may cause a crackling sound on the transmitted audio. In that case one can switch the EBS off altogether or increase the detector time constant by changing the value of C2 in Figure 3.5 from 220 nF to 2.2 μF. A toggle switch on the amplifier front panel can allow selection of either time constant. The processor is not normally switched out altogether but the level is rather reduced to between 5 to 10 dB, in which case the EBS circuit still functions correctly and no switching effect can be heard with the shorter time constant.

3.4 CW Operation

The most important feature for a CW transmitter is the ability to work full break-in (QSK). This means that you can hear received audio between transmitted dots and dashes. Anyone who is serious about CW must have a transceiver with full QSK capabilities, or operate a separate transmitter and receiver. Before choosing a transceiver, it is interesting to get a copy of a professional review (Ref 400-416) of the radio, so that the keying of the transceiver using high-speed QSK can be analyzed.

Another equally important characteristic is the speed of the keyed antenna relay line (used to switch the antenna relay in an amplifier). The fastest system uses a solid-state keying line, but this requires that the user pay attention to correct polarity, voltage and current. For example, the early models of the Kenwood TS-930S used solid-state line keying, and the built-in timing of the unit made it possible to control an amplifier using vacuum-relay switching in full-QSK mode, without any signs of hot switching (switching the antenna relay with transmitted RF applied to it). With the TS-940S, which uses a relay output in the linear-keying line, severe hot switching occurred.

Replacing the built-in relay with a solid-state relay can solve the problem. Figure 3.8 shows monitor scope displays of hot switching amplifiers. With some equipment it will be necessary to key the amplifier first (in time sequence) and then the exciter. A PIN diode switching system is faster than any type of mechanical relay and can bring relief. PIN diode antenna-switching systems are usually driven by a timing unit creating the correct timing relationship to switch the diodes (Ref 318 and 326).

Keying waveform shapes can be very different from one transmitter to another. The shape should not be too soft, and

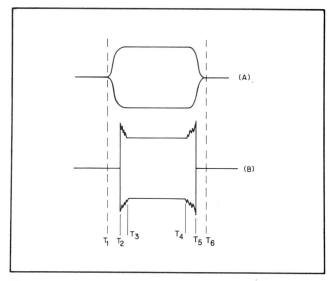

Figure 3.8—Top pattern shows a perfectly shaped CW pattern. The bottom pattern shows both make and break hot-switching. Where the relay should have closed before T1, it only closed at T3 and by almost closing started arcing at T2. At T4 the relay opens, and keeps drawing arcs until T5; it should only have opened after T6. Needless to say that such switching characteristics wreak havoc on the bands and will result in an early death of the relay and the amplifier tubes!

neither be too hard; hard keying can cause terrible key clicks. Figure 3.9 shows different keying waveforms, as well as the delays between key closure and output, for a few popular transceivers. Notice the large difference from one transceiver to another. Some radios exhibit very short dots especially in full QSK. The shaping itself seems adequate with most radios.

3.5 AMTOR

The author had his first exposure to RTTY back in 1962, when he made the first two-way RTTY QSO in Belgium with ON4HW. In 1981 he made it back to the green keys with a brand new fully solid-state system. What an improvement! Getting letter-perfect copy on regular (Baudot code) RTTY on a DX link on 80 meters is not often possible, however. To achieve this the signal-to-noise ratio has to be really excellent. The solution to the perfect-copy problem came when Peter Martinez, G3PLX adapted the commercial TOR (Teleprinting Over Radio) system and AMTOR was born.

AMTOR is an error-detecting handshaking RTTY system, as described under CCIR recommendations 476 and 625. There have been some excellent articles on AMTOR in Amateur Radio literature (Ref 326-333). In AMTOR, bursts of three letters are transmitted after which the transmitting station listens for an acknowledgement from the receiving station. If the receiving station has not received the group of three letters correctly, it will ask for a repeat and the last burst will be repeated. If the three-letter group was received correctly, another group of three letters will be transmitted.

How does the receiving station know whether or not the received code was correct? The received characters are tested using a *parity check*. AMTOR does not use the old five-bit Baudot code (used in regular RTTY), but a newly developed seven-bit code, without a start or stop pulse. This means that

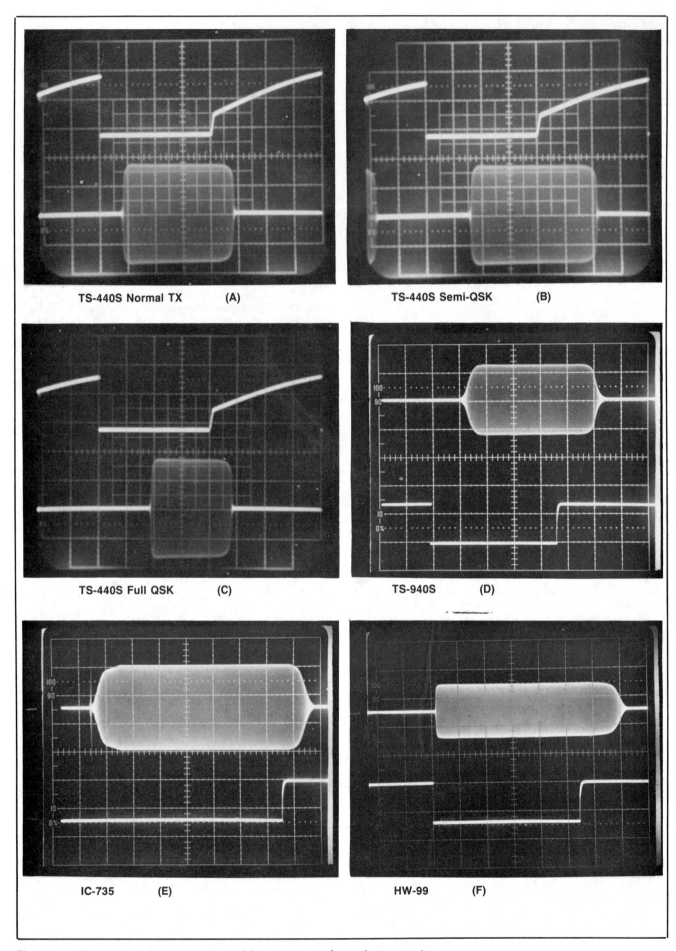

TS-440S Normal TX (A)

TS-440S Semi-QSK (B)

TS-440S Full QSK (C)

TS-940S (D)

IC-735 (E)

HW-99 (F)

Figure 3.9—Keying waveforms as obtained from a range of popular transceivers.

III-6   Chapter III

the system works in a synchronous mode. Out of the theoretically possible 128 combinations of a seven-bit code, only those characters were selected which yield a 4:3 on/off ratio (four high bits for every three low bits). This reduces the number of available combinations to 35. Testing the received information is done by checking for the 4:3 ratio for the three consecutive characters. This is known as parity check. The chance that the string of pulses is distorted by QRM and/or atmospherics without changing the 4:3 ratio three times in a row is almost nonexistent.

If the 4:3 ratio is valid after reception, an acknowledgement of receipt will be sent back to the transmitting station, while a repeat request will be sent if the parity test fails. The repeat request will be repeated as long as the three-letter group is not received correctly. This is the most essential feature of AMTOR. If the reception is poor, the traffic speed will slow down, and maybe even stop (and resume when the QRM has gone), but at no time will the receiving station print any garbage! A few of the outstanding characteristics of AMTOR are:

1) Requests for repeat are made visible on an LED or on the computer screen at both ends of the link. For the first time we have a situation in Amateur Radio where we have real-time information about the quality of the reception at the other end of the link. It is as if we had an R-meter (readability) at the other station in our shack! This allows us at all times to use the minimum required power to establish and maintain a perfect link. All we have to do is to adjust the power so that the repeat requests are limited to a minimum.

2) The AMTOR system is built around the selective calling concept. This means that each station has a unique identifier, and will only respond to signals addressed to it. Using this system, a great number of stations can remain on standby on the same frequency while reception will only take place by the addressed station.

3) The receiving station can break in on the transmitting station at any time.

Because of the handshaking nature of AMTOR, some special requirements apply for the radio equipment used. The transmission speed of three characters in one block (one burst) is 100 bauds (100 elements per second). The total time for one block is 0.45 second. The time difference between the time required for the transmission of the three characters (0.21 sec) and the total block time is used for:

1) Switching the receiver and transmitter from transmit to receive and vice-versa.

2) Taking into account the propagation delay of radio waves. The one-way delay for a 10,000 km link is 33 ms (velocity of propagation is 300 km per second).

This means that the radio system must be able to switch between transmit and receive very quickly (less than 0.02 second is typically preferred). This also means that the total range of an AMTOR link is limited to just over 20,000 km, which means that genuine long paths cannot be covered.

The transmission speed of 100 bauds during the block (or burst), together with the idle time between blocks, yields an equivalent transmission speed of 60 WPM or 45 bauds, when there are no repeat requests.

The requirements for fast transmit/receive switching are similar to those required for full break-in operation in CW. In the first years of AMTOR most transceivers needed slight modifications in order to be fast enough. By now all major amateur-equipment manufacturers have learned about AMTOR and taken the necessary steps to speed up the system response time. Solid-state antenna switching in the transceivers has also made AMTOR operation silent. If high power is required, vacuum antenna relay or PIN-diode switching can be used. High-power PIN diodes are now available that will easily handle a kilowatt or more (Ref 326 and 329).

Operating AMTOR on 80-meter DX has been a real thrill. Seeing perfect copy on the screen from a signal halfway around the globe on 80 gives a new dimension to 80-meter DXing. It is my feeling that AMTOR is for Amateur Radio today what SSB was back around 1960. In another 10 years there will be little or no regular Baudot RTTY left, in my opinion.

In AMTOR you have to be able to be on frequency plus or minus 10 Hz. That's why you need a digital readout with 10-Hz accuracy. Frequencies are still specified by giving the MARK frequency. If you use AFSK on your radio to run AMTOR, or regular Baudot RTTY for that sake, on LSB, and you are using the high tones (2125 and 2295), don't forget that your digital readout reads the frequency of your suppressed carrier, and that your mark tone is 2125 Hz below that frequency. So if you make a schedule on 3590 kHz, set your dial at 3592.125.

Some transceivers have provision for FSK. An example is the Kenwood TS-930S, but here the readout (in FSK) gives the SPACE frequency. So for a contact on 3590 kHz, set the dial on 3589.83. It sounds a little complicated but that's the way it is! Rumors have been going around that frequency specification would eventually be changed to specifying the frequency between mark and space, but that is certainly not practiced as yet.

The internationally recognized AMTOR frequencies on 80 meters are 3580 to 3590 kHz. Calling frequencies are 3588, 3589 and 3590 kHz. On 40 the international AMTOR sub-band is 7030 to 7035 kHz. I have had many QSOs "across the pond" and even into the west coast on AMTOR, and it is amazing when you see how far you can turn the power down before the traffic slows down. Outputs of 10 W have at times yielded 100 percent traffic speed for paths across the North Atlantic! Newland, AD7I, wrote a very comprehensive introduction to AMTOR operation (Ref 336).

3.6 Monitoring Systems

It is essential that the station operator have some means of monitoring the quality of his transmission. All modern transceivers have a built-in audio monitor system which allows the operator to check the transmitted signal. It should not be a mere audio output, but should be a detected SSB signal which makes it possible to evaluate the adjustment of the speech processor. This feature allows the operator to check the audio quality and is very useful for checking for RF pickup into the audio circuits.

A monitor scope should be mandatory in any amateur station. With a monitor scope you can:

1) Monitor your output waveform (envelope)

2) Check and monitor linearity of your amplifier (trapezoid pattern)

3) Monitor the keying shape on CW

4) Observe any trace of hot-switching on QSK (CW or AMTOR)

5) Check the tone of the CW signal (ripple on the power supply)

6) Correctly adjust the speech processor

7) Adjust the sensitivity and time constant of the EBS circuit for both CW and SSB

8) Display a cross-pattern as a reception aid for RTTY and AMTOR

The author has been using a monitor scope for 25 years now, and without this simple tool he would feel distinctly uncomfortable when he is on the air.

3.7 Areas of Improvement

Some hams think that the new generation of transceivers should have more output than what seems to be the standard today (100 W). The problem with this idea is that with more power many of the standard amplifiers could be grossly over driven, and the quality of the transmitted signal would be very poor. The author on the contrary thinks that the equipment designers should aim their efforts toward reducing the distortion products of the new generation of transmitters. In addition the transmitters should be designed in such a way that it is virtually impossible to transmit a poor-quality signal.

The author also feels the bandwidth of the transmitted signal could be significantly reduced. Where 20 years ago a bandwidth of 2.1 kHz (at −6 dB) was sufficient for good quality (e.g. Collins mechanical filters), today most transceivers have a 2.7-kHz bandwidth. The audio quality may be more pleasing, but this can hardly be an acceptable reason for increasing the signal bandwidth on our crowded ham bands. A few sources (e.g. International Radio Inc., in Port St Lucie, FL) are supplying kits for popular transceivers (e.g. the Kenwood TS940S) consisting of 2.1-kHz wide second (8.8 MHz) and third IF (455 kHz) filters which not only dramatically improve the receiver performance but also reduce the bandwidth of the transmitted signal. Using those narrow-band filters requires more critical adjustment of the carrier position on the filter slope as a function of the operator's voice and the microphone characteristics.

Chapter IV

Receivers

4.1 Receiver Specifications

Until about 10 years ago, receiver performance was most frequently and almost exclusively measured by sensitivity and selectivity. In the fifties and early sixties a triple-conversion superheterodyne receiver was a status symbol. It was not until the mid sixties that strong-signal handling came up as an important parameter (Ref 250). Today we consider the following topics to be most important for a communication receiver (not in order of importance):

1) Sensitivity
2) Intermodulation distortion
3) Gain compression
4) Dynamic range
5) Cross modulation
6) Reciprocal mixing
7) Selectivity
8) Stability
9) Frequency display accuracy

The above parameters will be discussed in detail and their importance will be highlighted, especially in view of low-band DXing. Figure 4.1 shows the voltage and power relationships involved in the discussion and evaluation of receiver parameters.

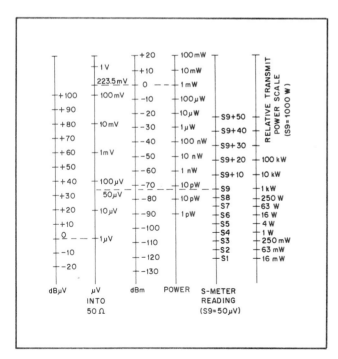

Figure 4.1—This table shows the relationship between receiver input voltages, standard S-meter readings and transmitter output power.

4.2 Sensitivity

Sensitivity is the ability of a receiver to detect weak signals. The most important concept related to sensitivity performance is the concept of signal-to-noise ratio. Good reception of a weak signal implies that the signal is substantially stronger than the noise. It is accepted as a standard that comfortable SSB reception requires a 10-dB signal-to-noise ratio. CW reception requires a much lower S/N ratio and any CW operator can deal with a 0-dB S/N ratio quite well. Experienced operators can dig CW signals out of the noise at −10 dB S/N ratio. This proves again the inherent advantage of CW over SSB for weak-signal communications.

The noise present at the receiver output terminals is generated in different ways.

4.2.1 THERMAL NOISE

Receiver noise is produced by the movement of electrons in any substance (such as resistors, transistors and FETs) that has a temperature above absolute zero (−273 ° C or 0 K). Electrons move in a random fashion colliding with relatively immobile ions that make up the bulk of the material. The final result of this effect is that in most substances there is no net current in any particular direction on a long-term average, but rather a series of random pulses. These pulses produce what is called thermal-agitation noise, or simply *thermal noise*.

The Boltzmann equation expresses the noise power in a system. The equation is written as:

$$p = kTB$$

where p is the thermal noise power, k is Boltzmann's constant $(1.38 \times 10^{-23}$ joules/kelvin), T is absolute temperature in kelvins and B is the bandwidth in hertz. Notice that the power is directly proportional to temperature, and that at 0 K the thermal noise power is zero.

Expressing equivalent noise voltage, the equation is rewritten as:

$$E = \sqrt{4kTBR}$$

where R is the system impedance (usually 50 ohms).

For example, at an ambient temperature of 27 degrees C (300 kelvins), in a 50-ohm system with a receiver bandwidth of 3 kHz, the thermal noise is −139 decibels below 1 milliwatt (dBm), which is equivalent to 32 dB below 1 μV or −32 dBμV (Ref 223). This would be the theoretical maximum sensitivity of the receiver under the given bandwidth and temperature conditions. (See also Section 4.7).

4.2.2 RECEIVER NOISE

No receiver is noiseless. The internally generated noise is often evaluated by two measurements, called *noise figure* and

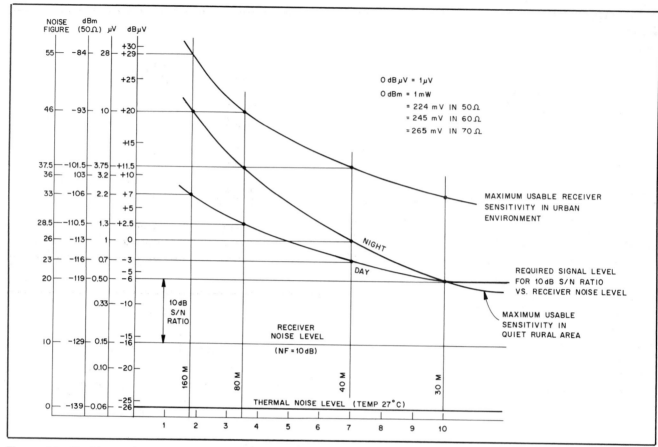

Figure 4.2—Usable receiver sensitivity on the low bands. This example is for a receiver with a noise floor of −129 dBm.

noise factor. Noise factor is by definition the ratio of the total output noise power to the input noise power when the termination is at the standard temperature of 290 K (17°C). Being a ratio it is independent of bandwidth, temperature and impedance. The noise figure is the logarithmic expression of the noise factor:

$$NF = 10 \log F$$

where F is the noise factor.

4.2.3 ATMOSPHERIC NOISE

Figure 4.2 shows the maximum usable receiver sensitivity for (a) an urban environment, (b) a quiet rural environment during the day and (c) a quiet rural environment at night. The curved lines correspond to the limits imposed by the atmospheric noise. The figures apply for a receiver with 3-kHz bandwidth. For a 300 Hz bandwidth (CW) all noises (thermal, receiver and atmospheric) drop by a factor of the square root of ten or 3.2 times. The noise levels shown are typical for a receiving system consisting of an efficient half-wave dipole or quarter-wave vertical. Less-efficient antennas will produce less noise and will therefore require a more sensitive receiver (ref 201, 202, 205, 223 and 247).

A typical present-day receiver has the following sensitivity characteristics (specified for a 3-kHz bandwidth):

noise figure: 10 dB
noise floor: −129 dBm
required signal for 10 dB S/N ratio: −119 dBm or 0.25 μV

The minimum required receiver sensitivity for the low bands under typical circumstances is shown in Table 1. To have a 10-dB S/N ratio, the signal has to be 10 dB stronger than the listed minimum sensitivity. Atmospheric noise on 80 meters is so great that most receivers have some "surplus" sensitivity. You may notice that the S-meter will be riding quite high on noise (maybe up to S7 in an urban environment) at all times. This is not necessarily a problem, but with higher input signal levels, the chances are greater that an (imperfect) receiver will generate internal distortion products. Better receivers have an input attenuator, and a good system will be adjustable (in steps) from 0 to at least 30 dB of attenuation.

When using a separate receiving antenna such as the Beverage antenna, the "extra" sensitivity may come in quite handy, as some of those antennas are very inefficient and much less susceptible to noise (atmospheric and man-made) because of their directive characteristics. This means that the noise (and desired signal) input from these antennas is lower and the extra receiver sensitivity is useful.

The author has had many occasions to use his input attenuator. In almost all cases 10 or 20 dB of additional front-end attenuation did not change the readability and signal-to-noise ratio at all. Even with well-designed Beverage antennas with reasonably loss-free feeders, attenuation can still be useful.

4.3 Intermodulation Distortion

Intermodulation distortion (IMD) is an effect caused by two strong signals that drive the front end of the receiver beyond

Table 1
Minimum Required Receiver Sensitivity

	Quiet Rural Day	Quiet Rural Night	Urban	Freq (MHz)
Acceptable Noise Figure	33 dB	46 dB	55 dB	1.8
Min. Sensitivity	2.2 μV	10 μV	28 μV	
Acceptable Noise Figure	28 dB	37.5 dB	46 dB	3.5
Min. Sensitivity	1.3 μV	3.75 μV	10 μV	
Acceptable Noise Figure	23 dB	26 dB	37.5 dB	7.0
Min. Sensitivity	0.7 μV	1 μV	11.5 μV	
Noise Figure	10 dB	10 dB	10 dB	Typical Receiver
Sensitivity	0.15 μV	0.15 μV	0.15 μV	

its linear range so that spurious signals called *intermodulation-distortion products* are produced. Third-order IMD is the most common and annoying front-end overload effect. Third-order IMD products increase in amplitude three times as fast as the pair of equal parent signals (Ref 210, 211, 213, 226, 239, 247, 255, 274, 281).

Figure 4.3 shows the IMD spectrum for an example where the parent signals are spaced 1 kHz apart. The vertical scale in Figure 4.4 is the relative output of the receiver front end in dB, referenced to an arbitrary zero level. The horizontal axis shows the input level of the two equal parent signals, expressed in dBm. Point A sits right on the receiver noise floor. Increasing the power of the parent signals results in an increase of the fundamental output signal at a one to one ratio. Between -129 dBm and -44 dBm, no IMD products are generated that are equal to or stronger than the receiver noise floor. At -44 dBm the third-order IMD products have risen to exactly the receiver noise floor level.

Point B is called the two-tone IMD point. It is usually expressed in dBm. Further increasing the power of the parent input signals will continue to raise the power of the third-order IMD products three times faster than that of the parent signals. At some point, the fundamental and third-order response lines will flatten because of "gain compression." Extensions of both response lines cross at a point called the third-order intercept point. The level can be read from the input scale in dBm.

The intercept point (Ip) can be calculated from the IMD point as follows:

$$Ip = \frac{2 \text{ MDS (noise floor)} + 3 \text{ IMD DR}}{2}$$

where MDS is the minimum discernable signal and IMD DR is the IMD dynamic range.

Inversely, the two-tone IMD point can be derived mathematically from the intercept point as follows:

$$P(IMD) = \frac{1}{3} \times ((2 \times Ip) + Nf)$$

An example (for a receiver having a -3 dBm intercept point and -129 dBm noise floor) is:

$$P(IMD) = \frac{1}{3} \times ((2 \times (-3)) + -129) = -45 \text{ dBm}$$

What does this figure mean? It means that signals below

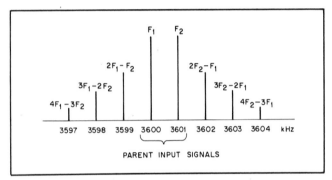

Figure 4.3—Third, fifth and seventh order intermodulation products generated by parent input signals on 3600 and 3601 kHz.

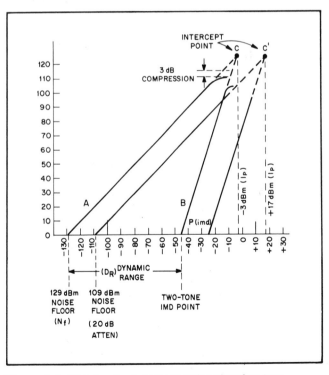

Figure 4.4—Third order intercept point showing two examples, with and without 20-dB front-end attenuation. The intercept point increases by the same amount as attenuation is introduced.

45 dBm will not create audible IMD products, while stronger signals will. This means that signals at around S9 + 30 dB will start generating audible IMD products! In Europe this is an everyday situation on the 7-MHz band where 30 to 50 mV signals are common.

A look at the receiver evaluation figures (Section 4.13) will show that some designs did not perform as well as anticipated (for example, the Signal One CX7 at -33 dB intercept and -126 dBm noise floor yields an IMD point of only -64 dBm, which is equivalent to about S9 + 10 dB!)

When evaluating third-order intercept points, we must always look at receiver noise floor levels at the same time. When we raise the noise floor from -129 dBm to -109 dBm (for example by inserting 20 dB of attenuation into the receiver input line), both response lines and the intercept point will shift 20 dB to the right (see Figure 4.4). This means that the intercept point has been improved by 20 dB! Any (average) receiver with a $+5$ dBm intercept point can be raised to $+25$ dBm by merely inserting 20 dB of attenuation into the input. Remember that this can frequently be done with present-day receivers as they often have a large "surplus" sensitivity (see Section 4.2.3).

The frequency separation of the two parent input signals can greatly influence the intermodulation results. The worst case applies when there is no selectivity in the front end to attenuate one of the signals. This happens when both input signals are within the passband of the first IF filter and the intermodulation products are produced in the second mixer. Most present-day receivers have a rather wide first IF so that they can accommodate narrow-band FM and AM without requiring filter changes.

Measurements at 2-kHz spacing using a 500-Hz second IF filter (CW filter) are often used to find the worst-case IMD performance. Measurements at 20- and 100-kHz spacing are also used for assessing receiver-intermodulation performance. With this much spacing, the first IF filter often improves the picture considerably, while in some receivers with high-Q tuned input circuits the front-end tuned input circuits will also add to the selectivity and further improve the IMD performance. The 100-kHz spacing is typically used for measuring receivers where the local oscillator (LO) noise limits measurement accuracy at 20 kHz and closer spacings (see Section 4.7).

4.4 Gain Compression or Receiver Blocking

Gain compression occurs when a strong signal drives an amplifier stage (for example a receiver front end) so hard that it cannot produce any more output. The stage is driven beyond its linear operating region and is saturated. Gain compression can be recognized by a decrease in the background-noise level when saturation occurs (Ref 223, 239, 281). Gain compression can be caused by other amateur stations nearby; such as in a multi-operator contest environment. Outboard front-end filters are the answer to this problem. (See Section 4.12.)

4.5 Dynamic Range

The lower limit of the *dynamic range* of a receiver is the power level of the weakest detectable signal (receiver noise floor). The upper limit is the power level of the signals at which IMD becomes noticeable (intermodulation products are equal to the receiver noise-floor level). Refer to Figure 4.4

for a graphical representation of dynamic range. Dynamic range can be calculated as follows:

$$DR = P(IMD) - Nf$$

where DR is the dynamic range in dB, P(IMD) is the two-tone IMD point in dBm and Nf is the receiver noise floor in dBm.

If the intercept point is known instead of the two-tone IMD point we can use the following equation:

$$DR = \tfrac{2}{3} \times (Ip - Nf)$$

where Ip is the intercept point in dBm.

The dynamic range of a receiver is important because it allows us to directly compare the strong-signal handling performance of receivers (Ref 234, 239, 255).

4.6 Cross Modulation

Cross modulation occurs when modulation from an undesired signal is partially transferred to a desired signal in the passband of the receiver. Cross modulation starts at the 3-dB compression point on the fundamental response curve as shown in Figure 4.4. Cross modulation is independent of the strength of the desired signal and proportional to the square of the undesired signal amplitude, so a front-end attenuator can be very helpful in reducing the effects of cross modulation. Introducing 10 dB of attenuation will reduce cross modulation by 20 dB. This exclusive relationship can also help to distinguish cross modulation from other IMD phenomena (Ref 223, 247).

4.7 Reciprocal Mixing

Reciprocal mixing is a large-signal effect caused by noise sidebands of the local oscillator feeding the input mixer. Oscillators are mostly thought of as single-signal sources, but this is never so in reality. All oscillators have sidebands to a certain extent. One example of the sidebands produced by an oscillator is shown in Figure 4.5. The detrimental effect of these noise sidebands remained largely unnoticed until recently, when voltage-controlled oscillators (VCOs) were introduced in state-of-the art receivers.

VCOs are much more prone to creating noise sidebands than LC oscillators. The wide-range phase-locked loops in VCOs are responsible for the poor noise spectrum (Ref 209). Figure 4.6 shows the relationship in the usual superheterodyne receiver between the input signal, the IF and the local oscillator for both the ideal situation of a noiseless LO and for a real-world case where the LO has important noise sidebands.

Reciprocal mixing introduces off-channel signals into the IF at levels proportional to the frequency separation between the desired signal and the unwanted signal. This effectively reduces the selectivity of the receiver. In other words, if the static response of the IF filters is specified down to -80 dB, the noise in the LO must be down at least the same amount in the same bandwidth in order not to degrade the effective selectivity of the filter.

According to the thermal-noise equation (see Section 4.2.1), the noise power is -174 dBm at room temperature for a bandwidth of 1 Hz. The noise in an SSB bandwidth of X Hz can be scaled to a 1-Hz bandwidth using the factor (10 log X).

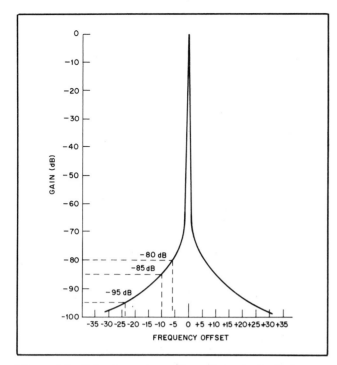

Figure 4.5—Output spectrum of a voltage-controlled oscillator. The oscillator sideband performance (referred to 1-Hz bandwidth) is 85 + 34 = 119 dBc (if the measurement was done at a 3-kHz bandwidth).

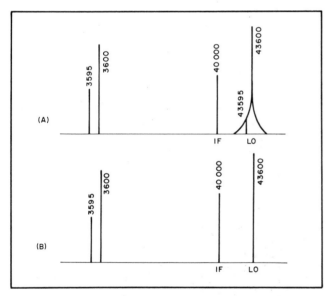

Figure 4.6—An LO with noise sidebands can produce reciprocal mixing products inside the bandwidth of the IF filter. At A, the undesired signal at 3595 kHz mixes with sideband energy from the LO at 43595 kHz to produce an output signal at the IF of 40000 kHz. The LO at B has no sideband energy, so the unwanted signal produces a mixing product at 40005 kHz, outside the IF passband.

This equation yields a factor of 34.8 dB for a 3-kHz bandwidth, 34.3 dB for 2.7 kHz and 33.2 dB for 2.1 kHz. Continuing with the example where the static response of the IF filter is − 80 dB and the filter has a 3-kHz bandwidth, the noise of the LO should be no more than 80 + 34 = 114 dBm referenced to a 1-Hz bandwidth. The carrier noise referenced to a 1-Hz bandwidth is usually called dBc.

4.7.1 MEASURING RECIPROCAL MIXING

If we specify the offset between two signals and the bandwidth of the IF filter, and then gradually raise the strength of one signal, we will find that at some signal strength the signal-to-noise ratio of the other signal will be degraded by 3 dB. (Ref 281, 274, 247).

4.7.1.1 Conversion to dBc

If, with a filter of 2.7 kHz, it takes an input level of − 60 dBm at a spacing of 10 kHz to reduce the desired signal 3 dB, and given a receiver noise floor of − 135 dBm, the level with respect to the noise floor is: 135 − 60 = 75 dB. Referred to a bandwidth of 2.1 kHz we have to add our conversion factor of 33 dB, which gives an oscillator noise sideband performance of 75 + 33 = 108 dBc.

4.8 Selectivity

Selectivity is the ability of a receiver to separate (select) a desired signal from unwanted signals. The ideal selectivity for SSB reception can vary, depending on the interference on adjacent frequencies.

4.8.1 SSB BANDWIDTH

On a quiet band with a reasonably strong desired signal, the best audio and signal-to-noise ratio can be obtained with selectivities on the order of 2.7 kHz at 6 dB. Under adverse conditions selectivities as narrow as 1 kHz can be used for SSB, but the carrier positioning on the filter slope becomes very critical for optimum readability.

4.8.2 PASSBAND TUNING

Passband tuning (IF shift) allows the position of the passband on the slope to be altered without requiring that the receiver be retuned. The bandwidth of the passband filter remains constant, however. In some cases interfering signals can be moved outside the passband of the receiver by adjusting the passband tuning. In better receivers, passband tuning has been replaced by a filter with a continuously variable bandwidth.

4.8.3 CONTINUOUSLY VARIABLE IF BANDWIDTH

A continuously variable IF bandwidth, where the filter can be independently narrowed down from both sides (low pass and high pass) is ideal. The better state-of-the-art receivers have this function, and it becomes very useful on our crowded low bands.

4.8.3.1 Shape Factor

The filter *shape factor* is expressed as the ratio of the bandwidth at 60 dB to the bandwidth at 6 dB. Good filters should have a shape factor of 1.5 or better. In recent years it has been common to see transceivers equipped with rather wide IF filters (typically 2.7 kHz at 6 dB) having mediocre skirt selectivity. For the average operator this may be an acceptable situation, although the serious DXer and contest operator may want to go a step farther.

Several sources (e.g. International Radio, Fox Tango and Sherwood Engineering) offer modification kits for modern transceivers, where the wider (2.7-kHz) IF filters can be replaced with sharper 2.1-kHz filters. A combination of two matched 2.1-kHz-wide filters in the 8.8-MHz and 455-kHz IF strips of the Kenwood TS930 or TS940 yields a shape factor (6/60 dB) of 1.25, which is quite spectacular. The paired filters for CW give a -6 dB bandwidth of 400 Hz and a -60 dB bandwidth of less than 700 Hz.

4.8.4 CW/RTTY BANDWIDTH

On CW, 6-dB IF filters with bandwidths between 500 Hz and 250 Hz are commonly used. Similar filters can be used on RTTY and AMTOR.

4.8.5 STATIC AND DYNAMIC SELECTIVITY

Figure 4.7 shows the typical *static selectivity* curve of a filter system with independent slope tuning (e.g. TS-930S). The static selectivity curve is the transfer curve of the filter with no reciprocal mixing. The *dynamic selectivity* of the receiver front end is shown in Figure 4.8. The dynamic selectivity is the combination of the static selectivity and the effects of reciprocal mixing. Note that the static selectivity can be deteriorated by the effect of reciprocal mixing with noise from the local oscillator.

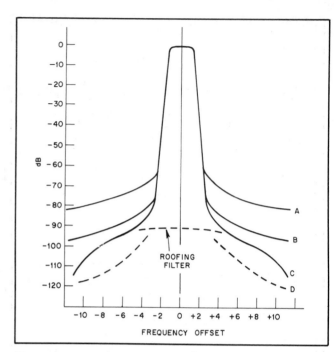

Figure 4.8—The total dynamic front-end filter response is the combination of the main selectivity filter (second IF) and the roofing filter (first IF). Curve (a) is the selectivity curve with a LO with 80 dB noise suppression (at 10-kHz spacing), curve (b) is for 95 dB suppression and curve (c) for an LO with 115 dB suppression. Dotted curve (d) represents the noise level from the LO that yields curve (c). In (c) the selectivity curve is not influenced by the LO noise (up to ±10 kHz from the center frequency), but is made up by a combination of the main selectivity filter and the first IF roofing filter.

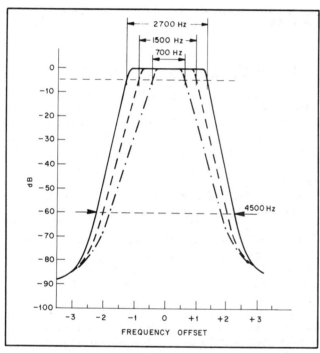

Figure 4.7—Static selectivity curve of a receiver using continuously variable bandwidth. This result is obtained by using selective filters in the first (or second) and second (or third) IF, and by shifting the two superimposed filters slightly through a change in mixing frequency. Note that the shape factor worsens as the bandwidth is reduced. It is not ideal to use this method to achieve CW bandwidth. The shape factor may deteriorate to 4 or more, while a good stand-alone CW filter can yield a shape factor of less than 2.

If the amplitudes of the reciprocal mixing products are greater than the stop-band attenuation of the filter, the ultimate stop-band characteristics of the filter will deteriorate. Good frequency-synthesizer designs can yield 95 dB (-129 dBc), while good crystal oscillators can achieve over 110 dB (-144 dBc) at a 10-kHz offset. This means it is useless to use an excellent filter with a 100-dB stopband characteristic if the reciprocal mixing figure is only 75 dB.

4.8.6 FILTER POSITION

The filter providing the bulk of the operational selectivity

can theoretically be inserted anywhere in a receiver between the RF input and audio output. When considering parameters other than selectivity, however, it is clear that the filter should be as close as possible to the antenna terminals of the receiver. In Section 4.3 we saw that front-end selectivity can help reduce IMD products.

Audio filters can also be used to improve the signal-to-noise ratio caused by wideband noise introduced in the receiver IF. If audio filtering is relied on for the signal selectivity proper, however, strong signals in the passband of the wider IF filter can reduce the gain of the receiver (if the AGC is IF-derived as in almost all receivers) and hence reduce the post-filter dynamic range. This can only be overcome with audio-derived AGC.

4.8.7 NOTCH FILTER

Another useful feature is a *notch filter*. As its name implies, a notch filter is used to reduce the amplitude of signals in a narrow stop band. A good receiver needs a good notch filter to help the low-band operator "notch out" strong adjacent signals. Ideally, the notch filter should be incorporated in the receiver chain ahead of the AGC detector (see Section 4.8.6).

Very sharp notch filters can only be achieved at low frequencies. Triple-conversion or quadruple-conversion receivers often use very low last IFs (for example, the TS930S and 940S use a 100-kHz last IF). At this frequency a reasonably sharp notch filter with a notch depth of better than 60 dB can be built.

Even sharper notch filters can be realized at audio frequencies. Figure 4.9 shows the notch depths that can be

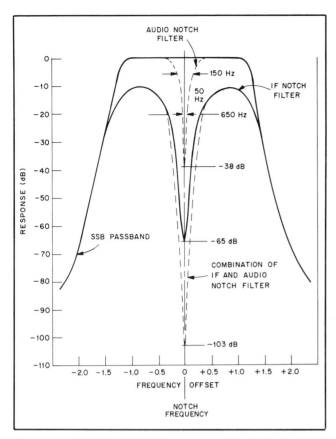

Figure 4.9—Notch filter frequency response. The 100-kHz IF filter has a very deep notch but relatively wide shoulders. The Datong audio filter provides a very sharp notch with narrow shoulders, but the notch is shallower. The combination of both yields a remarkable notch depth of over 100 dB!

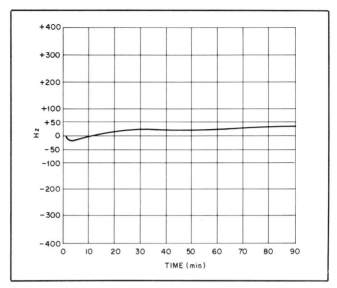

Figure 4.10—Typical stability curve for a modern transceiver.

reached with IF and AF notch filters, and shows the effect of using the IF and the AF notch filter simultaneously. The curves are representative for the combination of a TS930S IF notch and the Datong (TM) FL2 or FL3 audio notch filter. (See also Section 4.11.)

4.9 Stability

State-of-the-art fully synthesized receivers have the stability of the reference source. All present-day receivers have achieved a level of stability which is adequate for all types of amateur traffic. Figure 4.10 shows the drift curve of a modern transceiver.

4.10 Frequency Readout

A frequency readout displaying frequency to the nearest 100 Hz is adequate for amateur SSB and most CW operation, but for fixed channel AMTOR operation 10-Hz resolution is mandatory. On CW the display should show the carrier frequency and not the receive frequency (which is 500 to 800 Hz from the actual carrier frequency). Most older receivers and transceivers actually display the receive frequency, and this can cause confusion when arranging a schedule on CW. On FSK (RTTY and AMTOR), it would be ideal if the display showed the MARK frequency, although the author does not know any transceiver that does this (most show the center frequency, halfway between MARK and SPACE).

4.11 Outboard Audio Filters

Audio filters can never replace IF filters (see Section 4.8.6). They can be welcome additions, however, especially on CW. Introducing some AF filtering reduces any remaining wide-band IF noise, and can improve the S/N ratio. Removing some of the higher-pitched hiss can also be quite advantageous, especially when long operating times are involved, such as in a contest (Ref 237).

A wide variety of audio filters have been described in Amateur Radio literature, using either LC networks (Ref 236, 246, 261, 265, 278, 283, 284 and 285) or op-amp systems (Ref 200 and 264). Tong, G4GMQ has developed a very effective auto-tune AF notch-filter system, which he incorporated in the Datong™ FL1 (Ref 270) and FL3 filters. The FL2 filter does not have the auto-notch facility; this filter has been reviewed by Schwarzbeck (Ref 212).

The FL3 filter is probably the most complete audio filter available. On SSB one or both slopes can be adjusted independently, and the auto-notch facility performs extremely well. Within a fraction of a second, the filter will notch out a strong signal that has come into the passband. When used in addition to a good IF notch filter which has the advantage of acting prior to the AGC detector, signals of S9 + can be completely eliminated (Ref Section 4.8.7.).

4.12 Outboard Front-End Filters

Most of our present-day amateur receivers and receiver sections in transceivers are general coverage (100 kHz to 30 MHz). They make wide use of half-octave front-end filters, which do not provide any narrow front-end selectivity. Older amateur-band only receivers used either tracked-tuned filters or narrow bandpass filters, which provide a much higher degree of front-end protection, especially in highly RF-polluted areas. Instead of providing automatic antenna tuners in modern transceivers, I believe that the same space could more advantageously be taken up by some sharply tuned input filters which could be switched into the receiver when needed.

Excellent articles are available that describe selective front-end receiving filters (Ref 219, 221, 251 and 266). Martin (Ref

219) and Hayward (Ref 221) describe tunable preselector filters which are very suitable for low-band applications in highly polluted areas. Sherwood Engineering of 1268 S Ogden St, Denver CO 80210 now also offers front-end crystal filters, which are the ultimate solution for multi-op contest stations and for protection against megawatt broadcast stations in the 7-MHz band. The bandwidth of the six-pole 50-ohm filters is 50 kHz on 20 meters, 25 kHz on 40 meters, 12.5 kHz on 80 meters and 5 kHz on 160 meters. The shape factor (6/60 dB) is 2.5/1. The customer can specify the design frequency of the filter. Eight-pole filters with 2/1 shape factor and a bandwidth of 12.5 kHz on are also available for 20, 40 and 80 meters.

4.13 Receiver Evaluations

It is important that every avid low-band DXer understand the parameters which make a receiver good for the low bands. It is not possible for most of us to perform the tests ourselves, however. The test methods have been very well defined in the amateur literature (Ref 210, 211, 234 and 255), and Schwarzbeck, DL1BU and Hart, G3SJX have been publishing a series of excellent equipment evaluations in *CQDL* and *Radio Communication* (Ref 400-417). More receiver evaluations were made available by Craig (N6ND), Sherwood (WBØJGP), Waxweiler (DJ7VD), and Vercruyssen (ON5DO). Evaluation data for several commercial receivers is shown in Table 2.

Where the source only mentioned the noise floor (Nf) and the dynamic range (DR), the following formula was used to calculate the intercept point (Ip):

Ip = Nf + 3/2 × DR

Where only the Intercept Point was given (Ip), the dynamic

Table 2
Tabulated Receiver Data

Type	Noise Floor – dBm	Local Oscill – dBc	at kHz	Dynamic Range dB	at kHz	dB	at kHz	Intercept Point dBm	at kHz	dBm	at kHz	Source	Lit Ref
Kenwood													
R820S	125	123	10	74	20	74	4	– 14	20	– 14	4	WBØJGP	276
R820S	133			78	20			– 16	20			N6ND	275
R820								– 19	20			DJ7VD	211
R820	133			81	20			– 11	20			DL1BU	213
R820		148	20									ON5DO	
TS520	139			63	20	63	3	– 44	20	– 67	3	WBØJGP	276
TS120	132			68	20			– 31	20			N6ND	275
TS120	134			82	20			– 11	20			DL1BU	213
TS120	133			79	20			– 14	20			ON5DO	
TS120V								– 18	20			DJ7VD	211
TS130	130			79	20			– 12	20			ON5DO	
TS820S	137	125	10	79	20	78	3	– 17	20	– 20	3	WBØJGP	276
TS820S	133			67	20			– 32	20			N6ND	275
TS820S								– 18	20			DJ7VD	211
TS820S	132			76	20			– 18	20			DL1BU	213
TS820S	133	134	20	76	20			– 18	20			ON5DO	
TS180S	139	120	10	70	20	68	3	– 34	20	– 37	3	WBØJGP	276
TS180S	134			74	20			– 23	20			N6ND	275
TS180S								– 12	20			DJ7VD	211
TS180S	134			69	20			– 30	20			DL1BU	213
TS180S				74	20			– 26	20			ON5DO	
TS830S	136	113	2	84	20	70	3	– 10	20	– 31	3	WBØJGP	276
TS830S	129	114	2	84	20	81	2	– 3	20	– 7	2	WBØJGP(1)	276
TS830S	134			88	20			– 2	20			N6ND	275
TS830S	134			85	20			– 6	20			DL1BU	213
TS830S	134			105	200			+ 23	200			DL1BU	213
TS830S	135	132		85	20			– 8	20			ON5DO	
TS430S	136	102	10	78	20	69	5	– 19	20	– 32	5	WBØJGP	276
TS430S	134			94	100			+ 7	100			N6ND	275
TS430S	134	115	10	77	20	62	5	– 18	20	– 41	5	G3SJX	417
TS430S	134	115	10	96	40			+ 10	40			G3SJX	417
TS430S	135	132	20	89	20			+ 5	20			ON5DO	
TS930S	135	115	10	86	20	73	3	– 6	20	– 25	3	WBØJGP	276
TS930S	131			93	100			+ 8	100			N6ND	275
TS930S	131	122	10	100	200	73	3	+ 19	200	– 24	3	DL1BU	409
TS930S	133	129	20	96	20			+ 11	20			ON5DO	
TS940S	134	127	20	99	20			+ 14	20			ON5DO	
TS940S	135			91	100			+ 2	100			N6ND	

(1) with YK88 filter

Table 2 continued on next page

Table 2 continued . . .

Type	Noise Floor – dBm	Local Oscill – dBc	at kHz	Dynamic Range dB	at kHz	dB	at kHz	Intercept Point dBm	at kHz	dBm	at kHz	Source	Lit Ref
Yaesu													
FT101E	141			60	20	59	3	– 51	20	– 52	3	WBØJGP	276
FT101S	132			75	20			– 19	20			N6ND	275
FT101B	134			53	20			– 54	20			N6ND	275
FT101EE	130			64	20			– 34	20			N6ND	275
FT901DM	135	109	2	87	20	80	2.5	– 4	20	– 19	2.5	WBØJGP	276
FT901DM	132			81	20			– 10	20			N6ND	275
FT901D								– 6	20			DJ7VD	211
FT901		123	10	81	20							DL1BU	402
FT901	130			86	20			– 6	20			ON5DO	
FT902DM	134			76	20			– 20	20			N6ND	275
FT902	134			76	20			– 20	20			ON5DO	
FT757 *	134	109	10	86	20	56	3	– 5	20	– 50	3	WBØJGP	276
FT757 *	134	118	10	88	20	55	5	– 2	20	– 51	5	G3SJX	416
FT757 *	133			91	20			+ 3	20			N6ND	
FT757 #	120			88	20			+ 12	20			N6ND	
FT-ONE	131			89	100			+ 2	100			N6ND	275
FT-ONE	131	109	10	94	200			+ 10	200			DL1BU	406
FT102 *	130			87	20			+ 1	20			N6ND	275
FT102 #	118			89	20			+ 16	20			N6ND	275
FT102 *	133	137	10	88	25			– 1	25			G3SJX	411
FT102 #	120	137	10	90	25			+ 15	25			G3SJX	411
FT102 *	137			89	20			– 4	20			DL1BU	213
FT102 #	116			87	20			+ 15	20			DL1BU	213
FT980	135			95	20			+ 7	20			N6ND	275
FT980	134	110	10	96	50			+ 10	50			G3SJX	414
FT77	136	124	15	95	50			+ 7	50			G3SJX	413
FT7								– 15	20			DJ7VD	211
FT107	129			85	20			– 1	20			DL1BU	213
FT107	133			93	20			+ 6	20			N6ND	
FT707	133			85	20			– 5	20			DL1BU	213
FT707	131			85	20			– 3	20			N6ND	
FT707	130	130	20	82	20			– 6	20			ON5DO	
ICOM													
IC720A	137	125	10	93	50	78	3	+ 2	50	– 20	3	WBØJGP	276
IC720	133			93	100			+ 6	100			N6ND	275
IC720	130			90	20			+ 5	20			ON5DO	
IC720A	130	130	20	87	20			+ 1	20			ON5DO	
IC730 *	140	118	10	92	50	74	3	– 2	50	– 29	3	WBØJGP	276
IC730 *	134			93	100			+ 5	100			N6ND	275
IC730 #	131			100	100			+ 19	100			N6ND	275
IC730 *	137	135	10	95	20	73	3	+ 3	20	– 30	3	DL1BU	407
IC730 #	130	135	10	94	20	72	20	+ 12	20	– 22	3	DL1BU	407
IC730 *	135	135	20	100	20			+ 20	20			ON5DO	
IC701	125			80	20			– 5	20			DL1BU	213
R70 *	134			94	100			+ 7	100			N6ND	275
R70 #	130			95	100			+ 12	100			N6ND	275
IC701	129	125	10	81	50	73	4	– 7	50	– 19	4	WBØJGP	276
IC701								– 5	20			DJ7VD	211
IC701		125	20	80	20			– 5	20			DL1BU	405
IC740 *	134			90	100			+ 1	100			N6ND	275
IC740 #	130			95	100			+ 12	100			N6ND	275
IC740 *	135	130	10	93	25			+ 4	25			G3SJX	412
IC740 #	128	130	10	95	25			+ 14	25			G3SJX	412
IC745 *	133			94	100			+ 8	100			N6ND	
IC745 #	126			96	100			+ 18	100			N6ND	
IC745 *	133	130	20	96	20			+ 11	20			ON5DO	
IC751 *	133	127	10	84	20	64	2	– 7	50	– 22	2	WBØJGP	276
IC751 *	130			93	100			+ 9	20			N6ND	
IC751 #	125			93	100			+ 14	20			N6ND	
IC751 *	130			99	20			+ 19	20			ON5DO	
IC757	130	126		80	20			0	20			ON5DO	

Table 2 continued on next page

Table 2 continued . . .

Type	Noise Floor −dBm	Local Oscill −dBc	at kHz	Dynamic Range dB	at kHz	dB	at kHz	Intercept Point dBm	at kHz	dBm	at kHz	Source	Lit Ref
Ten Tec													
Corsair	128	131	10	90	20			+8	20			G3SJX	415
Corsair	131 *			86	20			−2	20			N6ND	275
Corsair	121 #			88	20			+11	20			N6ND	275
Corsair	131	132	5	93	20	79	2.5	+8	20	−12	2.5	WBØJGP	276
Omni A	125			90	20			+10	20			N6ND	275
Omni B	136	130	10	87	20	74	2	−5	20	−25	2	WBØJGP	276
Omni D	124			86	20			+5	20			DL1BU	213
Collins													
R390A	137	130	2	81	20	79	2	−15	20	−18	2	WBØJGP	276
R390A								−4	20			DJ7VD	211
75S3B	146	120	4	88	20	74	2	−15	20	−18	2	WBØJGP(2)	276
75S3C	132			82	20			−9	20			N6ND	
75S3	145			75	20	63	3	−32	20	−50	3	WBØJGP(3)	276
KWM380	127	99	10	94	50	64	2	+14	50	−31	2	WBØJGP	276
KWM380	126			97	20			+19	20			N6ND	275
KWM380	124			98	100			+23	100			DL1BU	213

(2): Round Emblem (early model)
(3): Wing Emblem (late model)

Type	Noise Floor −dBm	Local Oscill −dBc	at kHz	Dynamic Range dB	at kHz	dB	at kHz	Intercept Point dBm	at kHz	dBm	at kHz	Source	Lit Ref
Drake													
R7 *	140	114	10	97	100	75	2	+5	100	−27	2	WBØJGP	276
R7 #	135	114	10	97	100	75	2	+10	100	−22	2	WBØJGP	276
R7 *	131			93	20			+8	20			N6ND	275
R7 #	126			96	20			+18	20			N6ND	275
R7 *	126			93	20			+13	20			DL1BU	213
R7 #	120			98	20			+27	20			DL1BU	213
TR5	127			84	20			−1	20			N6ND	275
TR7	134	116	10	99	100	75	2	+14	10	−21	2	WBØJGP	276
TR7	130			96	20			+14	20			N6ND	275
TR7								+15	20			DJ7VD	211
TR7	127			98	20			+20	20			DL1BU	213
TR4C	124	130	10	74	20	68	2	−13	20	−22	2	WBØJGP	276
R4C	139	130	10	85	20	58	2	−11	20	−51	2	WBØJGP	276
R4C	134			70	20			−29	20			N6ND	275
R4C	133			80	20			−13	20			DL1BU	213
R4C (4)					20			+1	20			DJ7VD	211
R4C-mod	139	130	10	85	20	85	2	−11	20	−11	2	WBØJGP	276
R4C-mod	133			75	20			−20	20			N6ND	275

(4) With Narrow Japanese first IF filter.

Type	Noise Floor −dBm	Local Oscill −dBc	at kHz	Dynamic Range dB	at kHz	dB	at kHz	Intercept Point dBm	at kHz	dBm	at kHz	Source	Lit Ref
Heath													
SB303	134			66	20	64	4	−35	20	−38	4	WBØJGP	276
SB100					20			+3	20			DJ7VD	211
Atlas													
350XL	131	125	4	81	20	81	2	−9	20	−9	20	WBØJGP	276
350XL	129			83	20			−4	20			N6ND	275
210	120			76	20	76	2	−12	20	−12	20	WBØJGP	276
210	125			80	20			+2	20			N6ND	275
Signal One													
CX7A	126			62	20			−33	20			N6ND	275
CX11	124			99	200			+24	20			DL1BU	213
JRC													
NRD515	138	118	10	95	20	77	2	+4	20	−22	2	WBØJGP	276
NRD93	141	133	10	94	20	63	2	0	20	−46	2	WBØJGP	276
Telefunken													
E1500	131			103	20			+23	20			DL1BU	213
E863kw2	138			70	20			−33	20			DL1BU	213

* : with preamplifier
# : without preamplifier

range (DR) was calculated as follows:

$$DR = \frac{2}{3} \times (Ip - Nf)$$

The measurements by DJ7VD do not mention the receiver noise floor, and therefore the dynamic ranges are not calculated.

Dynamic range and intercept point are given for wide and narrow spacing. With wide spacing one of the parent signals is outside the passband of the first IF filter (roofing filter). 20-kHz spacing is typically used for wide spacing. Where more than 20 kHz is noted in the table for wide spacing, it normally means that the LO noise did affect the measurement at 20 kHz. With the narrow spacing measurement both parent signals normally pass through the roofing filter, which accounts for the much poorer performance under these circumstances.

As a rule, different measurements by different authors correlate quite closely. There are some exceptions, however. Different authors tested different units of the same receiver model, which could also account for some spread in the results.

4.14 Graphical Representation

Hart, G3SJX uses an interesting graphical representation of the main receiver parameters. Two examples are shown in Figure 4.11 and Figure 4.12. The following information can be found on the graphs:

- Receiver noise floor
- Dynamic filter response
- Local-oscillator noise output
- Front-end blocking level in dBm
- Second mixer blocking in dBm
- Two-tone (spurious-free) dynamic range as a function of parent signal spacing

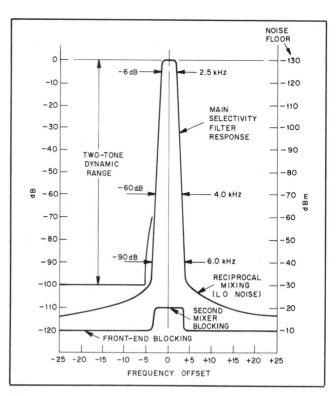

Figure 4.12—Merit graph for a "dream receiver." Note that the first IF filter (roofing filter) has a bandwidth which is similar to the bandwidth of the main selectivity filter.

Parent signal spacing

The performance of a run-of-the-mill present-day receiver is shown in Figure 4.11. The graph in Figure 4.12 shows what a really good receiver would look like. This receiver would show a steep IF filter response (1.5 shape factor), where the ultimate rejection would be over 120 dB, and where the dynamic broadening of the filter passband would not show up before at least −100 dB. To perform this well, the receiver would need an excellent local oscillator with a noise sideband performance of greater than 134 dBc. The better receiver would have narrow first IF filters to match the mode to be used (3 kHz for SSB and 500 Hz for CW), in order to have a two-tone spurious-free dynamic range that would be at least 100 dB both on close spacing (5 kHz) and wide spacing (50 kHz).

The figures for our ideal receiver read:

- Spurious free dynamic range: 100 dB
- Noise floor: −130 dBm
- Third-order intercept point: +20 dBm
- IMD point level: −30 dBm (equivalent to over 10 mV or nearly S9 + 60 dB)
- LO sideband noise performance: better than 135 dBc

4.15 In Practice

After you understand what makes a receiver good or bad for low-band DXing and study all the available equipment reviews, remember that what really counts is how the radio operates at your location, in your environment, with your antennas, how it satisfies your expectations, and how it compares to the receiver you have been using. The easiest test is still to try the receiver when the band is really crowded, when signals are at their strongest. When you listen closely where it is relatively calm, you may hear weak crud that

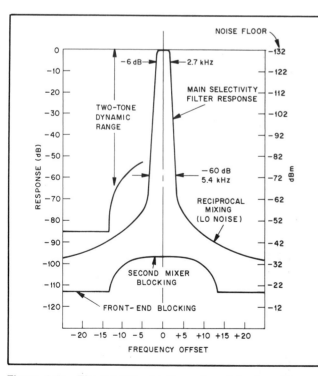

Figure 4.11—The receiver merit graph as introduced by G3SJX. This example is for an average quality receiver with no outstanding features.

sounds like intermodulation or noise mixing products. If you insert 10 dB or 20 dB of attenuation in the antenna input line, and the crud is still there, there is a good chance that the signal is really there. As the attenuation raises the intercept point by the same amount in dB as the attenuation figure, it is likely that raising the intercept point by 10 or 20 dB would have stopped intermodulation.

4.16   Areas for Improvement

The really devoted DXer, and especially the low-band buff, would certainly welcome further improvements to our present-day receivers. Some of the author's suggestions:

1) A tunable ham-band only preselector to improve front-end selectivity. The operator should be able to switch the preselector in and out of the circuit.

2) A switchable selection of varying-bandwidth first IF filters. Three selectivities should be provided as options: wide for AM, medium for SSB and narrow for CW. The filters should have characteristics approaching those of the present-day main selectivity filters.

3) Main selectivity IF filters with a stop-band attenuation of over 100 dB.

4) Improvement of the LO noise performance to 135 dBc or better.

5) Built-in IF and AF quality notch filters.

Instead of spending more money on bells and whistles like more memories, more sophisticated readouts etc, new development efforts should be channeled towards the needs of better basic performance, as specified above. If the conscious ham tells his supplier about his real wishes, he will contribute to achieving this goal. Development of modern amateur radio equipment is largely market driven. If the marketers keep telling the designers they want more bells and whistles, that is what the user will get. If users tell the manufacturers they want better basic performance often enough, maybe the designers will get the right message and we will see more progress toward better receiver performance.

Chapter V

Transceivers

5.1 Transceivers vs Separates

The question of whether transceivers are better than the combination of a separate receiver and transmitter has been a hotly debated topic in amateur circles. Today there is no longer any point in disputing this issue. Amateur equipment designers and manufacturers have realized that a transceiver should not simply be a less expensive combination of a transmitter and a receiver. As a result, transceivers have evolved into sophisticated pieces of equipment that offer much more than the combination of individual receiver and transmitter ever could. Some of the manufacturers still offer separate receivers, but stand-alone transmitters have disappeared from most product lines.

For a very long time I have been advocating the separate setup, or at least a setup with a separate receiver, as I always felt totally lost on CW not being able to listen to my own signal. When I can listen to my signal, I am always sure of being on the correct frequency on CW. The newer and better transceivers ensure that you are right on frequency no matter what your preference for CW receive pitch.

As far as the transmit and receive specifications of the transceiver are concerned, the specifications detailed in Chapter III (transmitters) and IV (receivers) apply to transceivers as well. There are some specific transceiver aspects that need to be highlighted however, and these are covered below.

5.2 Frequency Readout

Both on transmit and on receive, the digital frequency display should show you:
- the carrier frequency on CW
- the suppressed carrier frequency on SSB
- the mark frequency in FSK

A display with 100-Hz resolution is sufficient for SSB operation, but in AMTOR 10-Hz resolution is mandatory, and 10-Hz resolution is very helpful for CW skeds.

Older and simpler transceivers indicate the zero-beat frequency on CW and on SSB. On SSB you zero-beat your signal with someone you are working, but on CW if you zero-beat the received signal you will not hear it! The receiver is usually set some 400 to 800 Hz off the zero-beat frequency, and this produces the beat note you hear. If the frequency display is showing you actual receive frequency, it is actually off by whatever separation is producing the beat note. Some transceivers indicate the carrier frequency on CW provided you listen at 800 Hz exactly. If you like to listen to a note of 450 Hz, the reading will be 350 Hz off. The better fully synthesized transceivers indicate the carrier frequency no matter what pitch is chosen; changing the BFO frequency automatically corrects the display.

5.3 RIT and XIT

All modern transceivers have two VFOs built in. Two VFOs are needed in order to be able to work split-frequency when chasing the latest DXpedition. Most of our QSOs are made using only one transceiver mode, however. Receiver Incremental Tuning (RIT) gives you a means of shifting the receive frequency slightly without changing the transmit frequency. Chapter VI details the author's opinions on RIT, so it will suffice to say here that if a receiver has RIT it should also have Transmitter Incremental Tuning (XIT). XIT can be used as a handy addition to RIT; for example, suppose you are in a QSO, and suddenly you hear a station very close to the frequency, causing QRM to your QSO. With the RIT you check quickly and find that the QRM is caused by a station calling CQ 1.5 kHz below you. You leave the RIT set on the offending station, switch off the RIT and continue listening to your QSO. When the QRM ceases, you switch the XIT in (which has the same offset as the RIT), and ask the station that caused all the QRM to QSY a little.

5.4 Transmit/Receive Switching

Transmit/receive switching characteristics are especially important for QSK (full break-in) CW and for AMTOR operation.

5.4.1 INTERNAL ANTENNA SWITCHING

Internal antenna switching is most often done by PIN diodes in modern transceivers. This method is much quieter than mechanical systems (especially in QSK CW and AMTOR), and it can be quite a bit faster too, provided the internal switch timing is properly designed.

5.4.2 RECEIVE/TRANSMIT SWITCHING TIMES

Even a transceiver designed for full QSK CW operation may not have fast enough transmit/receive switching for AMTOR. For AMTOR the receiver should be at full sensitivity within 20 ms after the PTT line has gone open, and the transmitter should be at full output within 20 ms after the PTT line has been closed. Many older transceivers did not meet this requirement, but could usually be speeded-up by fairly simple modifications. The designers of the latest radios have apparently incorporated the switching time requirement in their design input list, and the latest transceivers normally fulfill the requirement.

5.4.3 AMPLIFIER SWITCHING LINE

The amplifier keying line should follow the receive/transmit switching times as close as possible. The fastest systems use a transistor for switching, as any mechanical relay will inevitably introduce additional delay times. Figure 5.1 shows

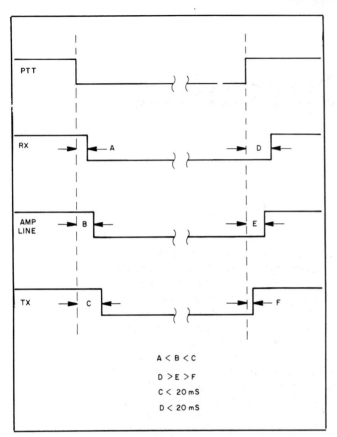

A < B < C
D > E > F
C < 20 mS
D < 20 mS

Figure 5-1—This switching diagram shows the correct PTT sequencing for a transmitter, receiver and amplifier. For QSK operation the sequencing is especially critical to prevent hot-switching the amplifier.

the timing relationships involved. Keying transistors can be damaged more easily than relays, so care should be taken to observe correct polarity, voltage and current ratings when connecting equipment using transistor keying. Early TS930S transceivers used a transistor-keyed line, which was fast enough to key a linear with vacuum antenna relay switching without any signs of arcing. The newer TS940S uses a reed relay, and is too slow for the same application. The experienced amateur can easily dig into the transceiver, however, and provide a transistor switching output.

5.4.4 SEPARATE RECEIVING ANTENNA INPUT

It is also advantageous to have a separate receiving antenna input, as in many cases we will use a separate antenna (such as a Beverage) for receiving on the low bands.

5.5 Bells and Whistles

Bells and whistles are by definition those gadgets that make operating on the air easier, but do not constitute an essential characteristic of a good transceiver. Having a whole range of memory frequencies that you can scan is an example of such a luxury. You should not be tempted to buy a new radio for the bells and whistles without having first checked the essential characteristics that make a good receiver and transmitter.

5.6 Areas for Improvement

As part of a poll, the top 80 meter DXers were asked where they see possible areas for improvement of our present-day transceivers. The following topics were raised:

• Availability of a built-in electronic keyer

The author had one transceiver with a built-in keyer and never used it. Once a CW operator gets used to a certain keyer, he often likes to stay with it. Every keyer feels different, and many operators seem to keep their electronic keyers for a long time. I have had three keyers in 25 years of operating: a W9TO keyer (using vacuum tube flip-flops), a home-made TTL keyer and now an Accu-Memory II keyer.

• Full dual VFOs using two separate tuning knobs (a la Signal One)

There is something to be said for this approach. It might reduce the chances of using the wrong VFO in split-frequency pileups.

• Higher power output from transceivers

Many of those using zero-bias triodes in their final amplifiers would like to see 200-watt transceivers. High-mu triodes such as the 8877 and 3CX800 require less drive than the older 3-500Z and 3-1000Z, however, and there are still excellent tetrodes around that need very little drive power (See Section 3.2).

• Lower intermodulation distortion products from the power amplifier, and built-in circuits that prevent the operator from overdriving the rig and causing splatter

When you select a transceiver, remember the same guidelines we spoke about in the Transmitters and Receivers chapters. Also remember that if you get a chance to actually operate with a transceiver, you can tell more from a short period of on-the-air time than from quite a lot of studying the specifications.

Chapter VI

Low-Band DX Operating

6.1 Frequencies

Probably the most important operating skill one can acquire is to learn where (and when) to find the DX. The 80-meter band is not allocated uniformly in all continents and countries. The information in Table 1 should help you locate the frequency ranges in which to look for DX in any particular area of the world.

Table 1

Worldwide 80-Meter Allocations

Area/Country	CW	Phone	Phone DX
Africa (most ctr)	3500-3600	3600-3800	3775-3800
Argentina/Chile	3500-3600	3600-3800	3775-3800
Australia	3500-3600	3600-3700	3690-3700
		3795-3800	3795-3800
Canada	3500-3725	3725-4000	3750-3810
Europe (not USSR)	3500-3600	3600-3800	3775-3800
Far East	3500-3600		3775-3800
Greece	3500-3600	3500-3600	3590-3600
India	3500-3550	3650-3700	3690-3700
		3890-3900	3890-3900
Italy		3613-3627	
		3647-3667	
Japan	3500-3550	3550-3775	3793-3803
New Zealand	3500-3600	3600-4000	3775-3825
South America	3500-3600	3600-3800	3750-3800
USA	3500-3750	3750-4000	3750-3800
USSR	3500-3600	3600-3650	3640-3650
		3600-3800	3750-3800

* During the major DX contests only.

The DX window for CW is the same all over the world: 3500 to 3510 kHz, with the largest concentration of DX activity taking place in the bottom 5 kHz. A secondary window exists between 3525 and 3530 kHz, which is the lower limit for General and Advanced Class amateurs in the US.

The universal DX window for RTTY is 3580 to 3590 kHz, with 3588 and 3589 as AMTOR calling frequencies. The JA RTTY window is 3770-3775 kHz.

Until a few years ago, the SSB DX window was 3790 to 3800 kHz, almost exclusively, for Europe, Africa, South America, the Middle and Far East. It took many long years of effort before the IARU (International Amateur Radio Union) Region 1 officially recognized this window as reserved exclusively for intercontinental QSOs. Since the FCC decided to expand SSB privileges in the US, first to 3775 and later to 3750 kHz for Extra Class amateurs, the window has

expanded from below 3750 to 3800 during openings to the US, although the top 10 kHz is still the focal area. DXpeditions very often use 3503 to 3505 kHz and 3795 to 3800 kHz as their primary operating frequencies.

Many amateurs are unaware that 80 meters is a shared band in many parts of the world. In the US, 80 meters sounds like a VHF band compared to what it sounds like in Europe. Because of the many commercial stations on the band, the 10-kHz DX window can often hold only 2 QSOs in between the extremely strong commercial stations in the local evening hours. Those of you fortunate enough to live in a region where 80 meters is an exclusive band, please be aware of this, and bear with those who must continuously fight the commercial QRM.

In the middle of the day, the DX segments can be used for local work, although one should be aware that local QSOs could cause great QRM to a DXer (at, say, 500 miles) who is already in the grayline zone, and who could just enjoy peak propagation conditions at his QTH. Situations like this occur almost daily in the winter when northern Scandinavian stations can work the Pacific and the West Coast of the US at 1300 to 1400 UTC, while western Europe is in bright daylight and does not hear the DX at all. Western Europeans can hear the Scandinavians quite well, and consequently the Scandinavians can hear western Europe—certainly well enough to get QRMed by other hams there. The DXer must be aware of these situations so as not to interfere with his counterparts in other areas.

The frequency allocations on 160 meters vary widely all over the world. Table 2 shows the 160-meter frequency allocations (as of mid-1986). The information was collected by the IARU from its member societies. There are no details included concerning operating modes. Lindholm, W1XX, has reported in detail on the existing band plan and possible future alterations (Ref 507). An excellent operating aid for the 160-meter DXer is a publication by N7CKD entitled "World Top-Band Frequency Allocations." It contains all 160-meter frequency allocations available, and is updated regularly. Copies can be obtained from: D. G. Peterson, N7CKD, 4248 'A' Street SE, Space 609, Auburn, WA 98002. Prices are: $3.50 in North America, $5.00 overseas.

Table 3 lists non-amateur stations on the 1800 to 2000 kHz band as of late 1985 (tnx K4PI). The 1800-1850 kHz window is generally accepted worldwide as the DX window on 160 meters. 1907.5 kHz through 1912.5 kHz is the Japanese 160-meter DX window. 1850-1855 kHz is widely used as the North American DX transmit window, while 1825-1850 kHz serves mainly as the European DX transmit window. 1837 kHz is a popular frequency in South America on SSB, and 1835

Table 2

Worldwide 160-Meter Allocations

Continent/Country	Frequencies	Continent/Country	Frequencies
Africa		Portugal	1830-1850
Djibouti	1810-1850	San Marino	1810-1850
Kenya	1830-1850	Spain	1830-1850
Lesotho	1800-2000	Sweden	1830-1845
Nigeria	1800-2000	Switzerland	1810-1850
Senegal	1810-1850	UK	1810-2000
South Africa	1810-1850	USSR	1830-1930
Asia		**North America**	
Bahrein	1800-2000	Antigua/Barbuda	1800-2000
Cyprus	1800-2000	Bahamas	1800-1825,
Hong Kong	1800-2000		1975-2000
Indonesia	1800-2000	Belize	1800-2000
Japan	1907.5-1912.5	Bermuda	1800-1825,
Korea	1810-1825		1875-1900
Malaysia	1800-2000	Canada	1800-2000
Oman	1800-2000	Costa Rica	1800-2000
Pakistan	1800-2000	El Salvador	1800-2000
Singapore	1800-2000	Grenada	1800-2000
Sri Lanka	1850-2000	Honduras	1800-2000
Syria	1830-1850	Mexico	1800-1850
Europe		Montserrat	1800-2000
Andorra	1810-1875	Neth Antilles	1800-2000
Austria	1810-1850	Nicaragua	1800-2000
Belgium	1830-1850	Trinadad/Tobago	1800-2000
Czechoslovakia	1825-1850	USA	1800-2000
Denmark	1830-1850	**South America**	
Faroe Islands	1830-1850	Argentina	1800-1850
FRG	1815-1835,	Brazil	1800-1850
	1850-1890	Colombia	1800-2000
Finland	1820-1845,	Guatemala	1800-2000
	1915-1955	Paraguay	1850-2000
France	1830-1850	Peru	1800-2000
GDR	1810-1950	Suriname	1800-2000
Gibraltar	1800-2000	**Oceania**	
Ireland	1825-2000	Australia	1800-1866
Luxembourg	1830-1850	French Polynesia	1800-2000
Malta	1810-2000	New Zealand	1803-1857
Netherlands	1825-1835	Papua New Guinea	1800-1866,
Norway	1802-1850		1874-2000
Poland	1750-1800,	Solomon Islands	1800-2000
	1810-1830,	Vanuatu	1800-2000
	1850-1930	Western Samoa	1800-2000

Table 3

Non-Amateur Stations in the 1.8 to 2 MHz Band as of Late 1985 (tnx K4PI)

1801: Beacon
1803: Beacon
1804-1806: RTTY
1810: Beacon
1814-1815: Beacon
1816: Barrier
1817-1820: Beacon
1825-1826: Carriers
1830: DHJ beacon
1831: OSN beacon
1834: TL31 beacon
1835: USB stn
1837: ZA01/OY12 beacons
1851-1852: RTTY
1855-1756: RTTY
1857-1862: RTTY
1865: MPG beacon (UK)
1870: JD18 beacon
1871: Carrier
1873: Carrier
1877: Carrier
1880: Carrier
1884: Carrier
1885: Carrier
1888: Beacon
1890-1905: Beacons
1909: Carrier
1915: Carrier
1922: Carrier
1927: Carrier
1932: Carrier
1935-1936: RTTY
1945: Carrier
1947-1950: RTTY
1957: RTTY
1965: Beacon
1969-1971: Carriers
1973-1977: Beacons
1979: Carrier
1981-1983: Beacons
1985: Carrier
1988: Carrier
1994: RTTY

kHz and 1845 kHz are popular on the African continent. 1824 kHz is often used by Pacific stations. For timely updates and current happenings, a 160-meter DX information net operates every Saturday on 14.337 MHz at 1400 UTC.

6.2 Zero Beat Operation

It is common practice to zero beat on phone. The RIT (Receiver Incremental Tuning) on present-day transceivers has created a problem where stations in QSO drift apart and use RIT to compensate instead of making sure that they stay on the same frequency. Fortunately, modern equipment is less prone to frequency-drift than older rigs, so this is not as much of a problem as it could be.

As an example of where this is a problem, let us assume station A does not have a stable VFO. If station A and station B start a QSO zero beat (station A and station B on exactly the same frequency), there are three sequences of events that a monitoring station might observe:

1) Neither station uses RIT: One station always follows the other. The QSO may wander all over, but at least there will be no sudden frequency jumps when passing the microphone, and the QSO will be on one drifting frequency.

2) One station uses RIT, the other does not: If we are still listening on the same frequency that the QSO began on, there will be a frequency jump at the start of transmission of one of the stations, but not for the other station. The QSO will still drift.

3) Both stations use RIT: Again, if we are listening on the original frequency, there will be a frequency jump at the start

of transmission for both stations, and the two stations may drift away from one another. The QSO will take up more space on the band, and it will be very annoying to listen to. Should RIT be used in such a case? Decide for yourself!

There are some instances where RIT is a welcome feature:

1) Some operators like to listen to SSB signals that sound very high-pitched, like "Donald Duck." That means that they tune in too high on LSB. To the other operator, their transmission will sound too low-pitched, because they are no longer zero beat. Tuning in a station using RIT will allow one to listen to the voice pitch he prefers, while staying zero beat with the other station(s) on frequency.

2) When trying to beat a pileup, it can be advantageous to sound a little high in frequency. Adjusting the RIT slightly in such a case will yield that result.

3) Let us assume our transceiver is designed for working CW at an 800-Hz beat note, and it is only when listening at this note that the transmit frequency will be exactly the same as the receiving frequency. One can use RIT to offset the transmit frequency (by, say, 300 Hz—to bring the note down to 500 Hz), and still transmit on the receiving frequency. So you can see that RIT can be a useful feature without creating unnecessary QRM at the same time.

As previously stated, most DX QSOs on 80 meters are on only one frequency. There is no need to waste space on the band by working a station slightly off your frequency. It can, however, sometimes be necessary to work split-frequency, such as when someone causes deliberate QRM, when working rare DX stations or DXpeditions, or when working into areas where a different band plan exists.

6.3 Split-Frequency Operation

According to the band plan in the country of the DX station, split-frequency operation may be unavoidable. For instance, if a station in the US wants to work a station in the USSR on SSB, the stations must work split, because the USSR amateur cannot transmit on SSB above 3650 kHz, and SSB privileges in the US do not go below 3750 kHz. When you encounter such a situation, always make it a point to indicate your receiving frequency accurately, and make it a single frequency, or, if the pileup is too big, make it a reasonable range (10 kHz is usually sufficient). There is really no need to take more of the frequency spectrum than is absolutely necessary. Some stations in the USSR have received permission to transmit up to 3800 kHz, but only during the major world-wide contest weekends; the normal restrictions apply at all other times.

Sometimes we are forced to work split in the midst of deliberate QRM. In such a case, announce the split frequency very briefly during the jammer's transmission so that he cannot copy your new listening frequency.

A very good reason for split operation is to work a DXpedition or, for the DXpeditioner, to work the rest of the world (see Section 6.5).

The split-frequency technique is highly recommended for the rare DX station working the low bands. It is the most effective way of making as many QSOs as possible during the short low-band openings, because the marginal conditions often encountered are conducive to great chaos if stations are calling the DX on his frequency. It also gives a fair chance to the stations that have the best propagation to the DX station. With list operations this is not necessarily so, and stations having peak propagation can bite off their finger-nails while the MC is passing along stations who barely make contact and have to fight to get a 3×3 report.

A few general rules apply for split-frequency operation:

1) If possible, the DX station should operate from a part of the band where the stations from the area he is working into cannot operate. Examples: Middle-East stations should transmit on a frequency below 3750 kHz when working North America, and a station in the Pacific working Europe should transmit above 3800 kHz and listen below 3800 kHz. It is not reasonable, however, for a European to transmit inside the US phone band (3780 kHz, for example) and listen on 3810 kHz. If this is done, two windows inside the US subband are occupied for one QSO, and the potential for QRM and confusion is increased. The inverse situation would be equally undesirable.

2) The DX station should indicate his listening frequency at least every minute—it only takes a second to do so, and it goes a long way towards keeping order.

3) If the DX station is working by call area, he should impose enough authority to reject those calling from areas other than those specified.

4) It is a good idea for the DX station to check with a strong station in another part of the world to make sure the frequency is clear. This can be done periodically, especially if there is a sudden unexplained drop in QSO rate.

6.4 Zero Beating on CW

This subject has been covered in Sections 4.10, 5.2 and 6.2. Most of the older transceivers were designed so that you are transmitting on the same frequency as the station you are working only if the beat note is some specific frequency, 800 Hz for instance. This beat-note frequency is usually specified in the operating manual. This means that one does not zero beat on CW (nobody listens to a zero-Hz beat note!). Because many hams do not care for the specified 800- or 1000-Hz beat note, they just listen to what pleases them (450 Hz is the author's preference). As a result of this, those operators are always off frequency by 500 Hz or so on CW. This is not a problem if the receiving station uses a 2-kHz filter, but it is a real problem if he uses a 300- or 500-Hz filter. Again, think of all the wasted space on the band. This is the reason that (until quite recently) the author has advocated the use of a separate receiver and transmitter on CW. Then, at least one could really listen to one's own frequency! The better transceivers now have the provision for operating right on frequency on CW. A transceiver should at least have an adjustable beat note. (The CW monitor note should shift accordingly.) The only precaution here is to tune in the station you want to work at exactly the same beat note as your CW monitor note. That's all there is to it. This way, one can get easily within 50 Hz of the other station and still listen to the preferred beat note.

There is a lot of personal preference involved in choosing the beat note itself. It is generally accepted that it is very tiring to listen to a beat note over 700 Hz for extended periods of time. Also, the ability of the normal ear to discriminate signals very close in frequency is best at lower frequencies. For example, listen to a station with a beat note of 1000 Hz. Assume a second station of very similar signal strength and keying characteristics starts transmitting 50 Hz off frequency (at a 950-Hz or 1050-Hz beat note). Separating these two signals with IF or audio filters would be very difficult. Let us assume we have to rely on the "filters" in our ears to do the discrimination. The relative frequency difference is: $(1050/1000) \times 100\% = 5\%$. If you were using a 400-Hz beat note, the offender would have been at 450 Hz (or 350 Hz), which is a 13% relative frequency difference. This is much more easily discernible to the ear.

6.5 DXpeditions

DXpeditions usually operate split frequency, both on CW and SSB. Gus Browning, W4BPD, was one of the first to do so (in the early 1960s). The advantage of split-frequency operation on the low bands is much more outstanding than on the higher bands, because the openings are much shorter and signals can be much weaker than on the higher bands. Working split makes it easier for calling stations to hear the DX on his frequency. Otherwise, the strong pileup of callers will inevitably cover up the DX station, resulting in a very low QSO rate.

Frequently we hear DXpeditions spreading the pileups over a wide portion of the band, which is not generally advantageous for the QSO rate, and very inconsiderate towards the other users of the band. It is also not unheard of for two DXpeditions to be on at the same time, both listening in the same part of the band. The net result of this is maximum confusion and frustration on the part of everyone involved. There will inevitably be many "not in log" QSOs where people ended up in the wrong log.

A better system is to use just a few exact frequencies on which the DXpedition will listen. With modern equipment with digital readouts to 10 Hz and an abundance of memories, this approach seems very reasonable (Ref 501). On 80 meters, the typical DXpedition frequencies are 3501 to 3505 for CW, listening 2 to 3 kHz up, and sometimes 3525 (the bottom end of the General and Advanced Class subband in the US), listening up 2 or 3 kHz. The most common SSB frequencies are 3795 to 3800 kHz.

One of the problems that DXpeditions encounter on the low bands is difficulty discerning the part of the world to which propagation is peaking at a given time. Very often the DXpedition will get callers from some nearby area all of the time. In this case, it is useful for the operation to have a couple of reliable sources in other areas, so that the DXpeditioners will be able to assess the propagation situation accurately and direct operations accordingly. The operators of a recent DXpedition to an island in the Pacific had made clear their intentions to look for European stations. They were very conscientious in doing this. One day they were heard working only European stations on 40 meters while the band was marginal. The next day, they were S9 in Europe, but were only working US stations. That day they could have easily worked Europe on 80 meters as well, but there was no way for them to know it. It is the author's opinion that the only way to avoid such situations is to set up some "pilot stations" in different areas of the world, which the DXpedition can call at regular times on a given band during the operation in order to assess the band conditions accurately.

Twenty years ago it was a rarity to have a DXpedition show up on 80 meters. 80 meters was thought by most to be only for local QSOs—even some of the DXpeditioners did not seem to know better. Today, 80 meters is, for most expeditions, just another band, and during the lower parts of the sunspot cycle it will definitely bring in a lot more DX than 21 and 28 MHz! The 5 Band DXCC, 5 Band WAS and 5 Band WAZ awards have greatly promoted low-band DXing, together

with the single-band scores and record listings in the DX contests.

6.6 List Operation

List operation, which occurs almost daily on the HF bands, stems from net operations such as the Pacific DX net, the P29JS/VK9NS net, and others. In these nets, a "master of ceremonies" (MC) will check in both the DX and the non-DX stations, usually by area. After completing the check-in procedure, the MC directs the non-DX stations (one at a time, in turn) to call and work the DX station. In most cases the non-DX station has indeed worked the DX station, but there was no competition, no challenge, no know-how involved. Some even call the MC on the telephone to get on his list. What satisfaction can one derive from such a QSO? Yes, it gives the QRP operator a better chance to work the DX station, and the only thing you have to do is copy your report—the MC will QSP your call. And if the DX station is a DXpedition, there is a good chance that he will give everyone a 59 report, so it becomes even simpler—just like shooting fish in a barrel, in the author's opinion.

In the late 1970s, list operations run by organized nets suddenly started showing up in great numbers all over the bands, run by "voluntary" MCs. This list system soon spread to 80-meter phone. Fortunately, lists have never made it on CW. This is yet another reason why real DXers love CW (Ref 505). Many active 80-meter DXers dislike the list system, but most have learned to live with it.

The list system cannot be used if the DX station refuses to take part in it. Fortunately, we have seen such operations, and they have all proven that DXpeditions can work much better without lists. I have witnessed stations asking Carl, WB4ZNH, operating as 3C1BG, if they could run a list for him. Carl was insulted by the proposition, so he asked the station to announce on his transmitting frequency (he was working split, of çourse) that he would not work anyone whose call sign was passed along by another station.

If the DX station is involved in a list operation, it generally means he cannot cope with the situation. An ability to cope is part of "the game" for rare DX stations. There should definitely be no excuse for such things to happen to DXpeditions. If you are not a good enough operator to handle the situation yourself, you should not go on a DXpedition. DXpeditioners often complain that the 80-meter DXers don't listen well enough, and sometimes the DXpedition has difficulty getting an operation going on the low bands. This would be an excuse for operating with lists. If the DXpeditions announced their operating schedules (bands, times) more regularly (every 5 or 10 minutes at least), and stuck to the schedule, QSYs to the low bands would work out better.

Some time ago, a station on a DXpedition in the Caribbean asked the author to make a list of approximately 100 (!) European stations for him, which he would then work the next morning. This was flatly refused with the comment that it was ridiculous to ask this, as he was S9 plus in Europe for hours every day, and he could probably work two stations per minute if he worked split-frequency. He was offered the frequency so that he could find another European station to "work" for him. An HB9 station took a long list for the next hour or more. The confusion the next morning was worse than anything I've ever heard before. Half of those on the list were not there, and more wanted to get on the list.

Don't ask a DX station to make a list for him.

If the DX station chooses to work from a list, here are the "10 Commandments" of list operation that the DX station and the MC should obey:

1) The MC station should have absolute Q5 copy of the DX station.

2) The lists should be taken at the time of operation. Only short lists should be taken—ideally they should contain no more than 10 stations. The MC should try to be as objective as possible when picking calls in the pileup.

3) The MC should make use of a second station far enough away to cover different areas. The second station could also take short lists on a different frequency.

4) The MC should never pick up stations that continually break out of turn, or keep calling when no list is being taken. Tail-ending is a good way of getting one's call in, provided it really is tail-ending. It is extremely frustrating to hear so-called tail-enders calling right when the DX station is giving the report—and a second later give a Q5 report to the DX station.

5) The MC should never make mention of deliberate jamming on the frequency. If there is deliberate jamming and many comments, then shouldn't he suspect that he is doing something wrong after all?

6) The MC should listen for other DX when taking a list (sometimes DX likes to work other DX). The MC should be aware of propagation conditions to the DX station as well as the grayline conditions at the DX station QTH. When taking the lists, the MC should use selective calling, always giving priority to stations which are near their sunset or sunrise and are about to lose propagation to the DX station. In other words, the MC should be very knowledgeable about low-band DXing.

7) The MC should never relay a report.

8) A calling station should be given no more than two or three tries by the MC, in order to speed up the operation.

9) It is up to the MC, but the author strongly suggests that the MC check the exchange of reports and make sure that the correct reports are confirmed at both ends to ensure that a valid QSO took place. He should make sure that the report is confirmed at both ends. If no exchange can be made, he should advise the DX station that no QSO took place, and if anyone has relayed a report, the MC might advise the DX station to change the report and try another exchange.

10) The list system should only be used as a last resort.

There are also a few rules for the "mere participant" in the list game:

1) The QSO should consist of a fully exchanged and confirmed report. The caller should confirm the report with the DX station so that both the MC and the DX station can make sure a valid QSO was made.

2) The caller should not repeat the DX station's call sign. The exchange length should be kept to a minimum.

3) The caller should not get on the list if he cannot copy the DX station reasonably well. If he does not come back when the DX station turns it over to him, and if this situation repeats itself, he is just making a fool of himself.

4) If the caller cannot hear the MC, but hears the DX very well, he can try to ask the DX station to ask the MC to put him on the list. (This happened to the author when trying to work a station in Africa when the MC was in Germany and skip prevented getting on the list in the normal way).

In almost all cases, list operation can be avoided by working split frequency (see Section 6.3).

6.7 Getting the Rare Ones

Working the first 100 countries on 80 meters is fairly easy—well-equipped stations have done it in one contest weekend. Anyone with a good station should be able to do it easily within a year. A growing number of stations have achieved DXCC on 160 meters. The major DX contests (CQ-WW, ARRL DX, WAE, All-Asian, etc) are excellent opportunities to increase low-band scores. Almost all DXpeditions now include a fair amount of low-band DXing in their operating scheme. The best way to keep yourself informed about what is happening on the bands is to subscribe to one of the many DX bulletins or news sheets. Some of the major ones are listed in Table 4.

Even under the best of circumstances, the news related in the bulletins is always a few days old. The DX information nets attempt to fill this gap. The French DX information net

Table 4
DX Bulletins and News Sheets

USA/Canada:	Europe/DX:
The DX Bulletin c/o Chod Harris, WB2CHO PO Box 50 Fulton, CA 95439-0050	Down Under DXers PO Box 31, Winmalee NSW 2777, Australia
The DXers Magazine c/o Gus Browning, W4BPD PO Drawer DX Cordova, SC 29039	DX Info c/o W. Bedrich, Y39XO Gorschstr 7, DDR-1100 Berlin GDR
Inside DX c/o Arthur Hubert, N2AU 436 N Geneva St Ithaca, NY 14850	DX News RSGB Lambda House, Cranborne Rd Potters Bar Herts EN6 3JE England
Kansas City DX Club c/o Mike Crabtree, AB0X 7871 Webster Kansas City, KS 66109	DX NL c/o W. Geyrhalter, DL3RK PO Box 1328 D-8950 Kaufbeuren FRG
Long Island DX Bulletin c/o J. H. McCoy, W2IYX PO Box 173 Huntington, NY 11743-0876	DX Press John Fung-Loy Strausslaan 4 NL 2551 NM Deb Haag, Holland
Long Skip c/o J. Sklepkowycz, VE3IPR 300 Deloraine Ave Toronto, ON N4W 3K4 Canada	GACW Carlos Diehl 1854 Longchamps Buenos Aires, Argentina
NCDXF PO Box 2368 Stanford, CA 94301	HIDXA PO Box 90 Norfolk Island 2899 Australia
QRZ DX c/o Bob Winn, W5KNE PO Box 834072 Richardson, TX 75083	How's DX c/o K. McLachlan, VK3AH Box 39 Mooroolbark Victoria 31138, Australia
Radiosporting PO Box 282 Pine Brook, NJ 07058	Japan DX News PO Box 42 2025 Urawa Saitama 336 Japan
Totem Tabloid c/o Jack Bock, K7ZR 7317 S Jewett Rd, Clinton, WA 98236	Les Nouvelles DX c/o J. M. Duthilleul, F6AJA 515 Rue du Petit Hem Bouvignies 59870 Marchiennes, France
Westlink Report 28221 Stanley Ct Canyon Country, CA 91351	

on 14.170 MHz at 1700 UTC is an excellent example of such a DX information net. Local DX nets on VHF/UHF can be very rewarding if the members of the local DX community make it a habit to announce the hot news on the repeater. This works very well in areas with active DXers, as after having an initial QSO on 80 meters with a good DX station, an announcement on the DX repeater brings in many callers within just a few minutes.

RTTY, AMTOR and packet-radio mailboxes can be excellent tools for getting the latest info on DX to any user at any time of the day. Anyone can leave a message in the mailbox, and a user can look through the messages for late-breaking DX news. With AMTOR and packet radio, this can be done with 100% copy at all times. A user can also copy the information on a printer for hard copy. Since there are home computers in so many shacks these days, it is the author's belief that the use of mailboxes for this purpose will become commonplace in the next few years. If well-managed, such information systems could soon make present-day bulletins obsolete. It may, however, be necessary to have closed mailboxes, just as there are closed repeaters.

6.8   Awards

There are few low-band-only DX awards. ARRL (225 Main Street, Newington, CT 06111, USA) issues 160- and 80-meter WAC (Worked All Continents) awards, and a 160-meter DXCC, but no 80-meter version. *CQ* magazine issues single-band WAZ awards (for any band). Applications for the WAZ award go to: Leo Haijsman, W4KA, 1044 SE 43 Street, Cape Coral, FL 33904. In addition, there are 5-band awards which are very challenging: 5 Band WAS (Worked All States), 5 band DXCC (worked 100 countries on each of 5 bands), both issued by ARRL, and 5 band WAZ (worked all 40 *CQ* zones on each of the 5 bands, 10 through 80 meters), issued by *CQ* (also via W4KA).

The achievement awards issued by the sponsors of the major DX contests that have single-band categories are also highly valued by low-band DX enthusiasts. Continental and world records are being broken regularly, depending on sunspots and activity. Figure 6.1 shows a collection of 3 five-band awards collected by the author. Collecting awards is not necessarily an essential part of low-band DXing. Collecting the QSL cards for the new countries is, however, essential. Unfortunately, there are too many bootleggers on the bands (and too many unconfirmed exchanges that optimists would like to count as QSOs). These factors have made written confirmation essential—unless of course the operator never wishes to claim country or zone totals at all. Many other achievements can be the result of a goal one has set out to reach. The ultimate low-band DXing achievement would be

Figure 6.1—The author's 5 band WAS, 5 band WAZ and 5 band DXCC awards.

to get on the DXCC Honor Roll (within 9 countries of the current total) with 80-meter-only QSOs. At present, there is no special recognition for this.

6.9   80-meter DXer Survey

During the summer of 1985, a survey was made of over 100 of the leading 80-meter DXers worldwide. One interesting side note about this survey is that about the same time, Rosen, K2RR, made a similar survey amongst the leading low-band DXers (according to him), in the preparation of an article (Ref 675, 676). It was amazing to find out that many of Rosen's choices as outstanding low-band DXers were missing from the author's list and vice versa. The survey results are shown in Table 5. CFD is the all time DXCC confirmed countries (including deleted ones). WKD is the number of countries worked according to the present list (316 at the time of writing), while CFD1 is the number of confirmed countries according the same criteria. The CW and SSB columns show the percentage of time worked on each mode.

The author did a similar survey about eight years ago, and one of the most striking differences is that much bigger and better antennas are being used. The scores have skyrocketed accordingly. The use of Beverage antennas has also become very common among the top low-band DXers. Those not using a Beverage antenna often said "No room for a Beverage." Japanese-made equipment has also become very common, and one particular brand seems to be leading the pack as far as the choice of many low-band DXers.

6.10   The 80-meter DXer

There are a few kinds of people who really do want to work DX on the low bands:

The Listener: This is the guy you never hear except when a rare one shows up. He is an excellent operator, and hates lists. He never brags about his accomplishments, and he makes his way right to the top.

The Socializing DXer: This fellow has his daily QSOs, year in, year out, with his friends near the antipodes. Being able to keep these contacts going all year around is more of a satisfaction to him than getting the rare one, but he does not mind adding a new one to his total.

The Arduous, Always-hunting DXer: He sits day and night on a DX frequency. He does not have the time for a social chat—all he wants to do is call CQ DX. He loves running lists, as this gives him more of an ego trip than working a new one.

The CW-only DXer: This fellow has given up the poor manners and frequency monopolizing that sometimes goes on in the phone DX windows. He likes to run his own show, without interference from outside, but suffers from the fact that not all the good DX is available on CW. He knows CW has the advantage over SSB when dealing with weak signals under adverse conditions.

But, after all, it's good that not all 80-meter DXers are alike. That would be a boring affair. The one thing they all have in common is the drive to achieve what is difficult and challenging. In their endeavor to achieve this common goal, wonderful friendships have been established. One of the most touching examples the author has witnessed was the spontaneous donation by many dozens of 80-meter DXers of flowers and wishes for a speedy recovery to Bob, ZL2BT, after he had an accident in early 1985. One thing you can say about most 80-meter DXers: they're a nice bunch!

Table 5

80-Meter DXer Survey Results

CALL	CFD	WKD	CFD1	ZONE	CW	SSB	XCVR	RCVR	ANTENNAS	RX ANTENNAS
ON4UN	320	304	304	40	40	60	TS930S, 940S	Same	3/8-wave vertical	Beverages
W6NLZ		306	297	40	5	95	TS830S, 930S, 940S, CX11	Same	4-el KLM @120 ft	Same
K4MSK	312	294	294	40	10	90	IC-751	Same	Lazy-H, ½-wave vert, slopers	Beverage
ZL2BT	307			39	10	90	TS930S	Same	Quad, phased array, etc all @130 ft	Same
K2LWR	302	290	290	40	50	50	T4XB	R4C	3 × ¼-wave vert, 4 × ¼-wave vert	Same
EA8AK	296	287	287	40	50	50	TR7, T4XC, S-line	R4C	Top-loaded vert, dipoles, slopers	Beverage, quad loop
W4DR	295	287	287	40	35	65	TS940S	R4C	4-el W1CF array	6 × 500-ft Beverages
W8AH	289	269	268	40	40	60	TS830S, 930S, 940S	IC720	Phased 18HTS verts	Same
OH1XX	276	275	272	40	30	70	TS830S	JR599	77-ft vert, 160-m delta loop	Same
W9ZR	275	271	271	40	50	50	TS830S, TR7	R4C	Slopers @100 ft	500-ft Beverages
VE1ZZ		277	269	40	75	25	FT101	HQ170	4-el W1CF array	5 Beverages
W1NH	273	288	263	40	100	0	None	HQ170	4 verts, 4 slopers	5 × 100-ft Beverages
K4MQG		267	264	40	20	80	FT102, SB101	Same	Slopers, half-slopers	Same
K2FV	270	271	265	40	10	90	TS180S, IC745	Same	Phased dipoles, ½-slopers, ½-square, delta loop	
G6LX	269	289	281	40	75	25	TS930S	Same	Loop, 84-ft vert, slopers w/refl	(No room for Beverage)
K5UR	261	254	247	40	5	95	T4XC	R4C	Half-slopers	7 × Beverages
OH3YI	259	259	255	40	15	85	T4XC	R4C	Inv-V @120 ft	7-MHz ant
W0ZV		256	255					None	½-sloper, vert, 2-el wire Yagi @125-ft	Beverage
OH1RY		236	231	40	1	99	FT102, 757	Same	3-el full-size Yagi, sloper	3 Beverages
CT1FL	254	256	250	40	0	100	TR4C, IC720, T4XB	R4C	2 × ½-wave slopers	Same
ON5NT	252	252	251	40	40	60	TS830S	Same	Inv-V, delta loop @60 ft	Same
W6RJ	243	238			30	70	TS940S	Same	3-el KLM @90 ft	Same
K6NA	241	240	235	39	40	60	TS940S, TR7	R7	Dipole @135 ft, Inv-V @140 ft	
F5VU	240	243	240	40	0	100	FT102, TR7	Same	Inv-V, Sloper @¼ wave	Same
AA6AA	238	245	237	40	50	50	TS930S	Same	3-el KL @75 ft	Same
JA6BSM	235	238	233	40	30	70	TS830S	Same	Sloper @66 ft, vert	Long wires
DJ4AX	235	236	230		5	95	T4XC	R4C	2-el wire Yagi @165 ft, slopers	Same
K6SSS		233	228	40	40	60	TS830S	Same	50-ft vert	2-m loop
F6DZU	226	228	224	40	0	100	TS830S	Same	Dipole @66 ft	Same
G3KMA	226	227	223	38	30	70	TR7	Same	Inv-V @60 ft	Same
SM7CRW	223	229	219	40	0	100	S-line	75A4, R4C	Slopers	Beverage
W6KUT	222		218	40	75	25	TS930S	Same	Phased verts	Beverages, loop
UB5WE	216	224	214	—	90	10	Homebrew	Homebrew	¼-wave vert	Loop
ZS5LB	215	215	212	40	70	30	TS830S, 430S	Same	¼-wave vert, long wires	Beverages
K4PI	215	220	210	37	40	60	FT107M	Same	Inv-L(70 ft vert), half-slopers, loop, etc 1- to 2-wave-length	Beverages
N0XA	202	215	201	39	50	50	TS930S	Same	2-el KLM @100 ft, 3 × ¼-wave vert	Long wires
W0SD		225	200	40	30	70	TS830S	Same	110-ft vert w/120 radials	Beverages
G2PU		200	200		0	100	IC740, FT200B	Drake2B, GalRS30	Delta loops, ¼-wave vert	Loop
W7IVX	190	220	190	40	5	95	TS930S	Same	2-el KLM @110 ft	Same
KQ5G		262		40	1	99	TS930S	75A4	3-el KLM @150 ft, 4-el vert array	Same
W5YU		230		40	0	100	TS930S, FT901,101	Same	Rhombic @100 ft, slopers @100 ft	Same

Chapter VII

Computer Programs

This chapter contains printouts of most of the programs used or referred to in the previous chapters. The listings are in APPLESOFT BASIC.

All programs were originally developed by the author in APPLESOFT BASIC, and some programs have been compiled for faster execution. The author uses a 3.5-MHz accelerator board in his Apple 2e along with a 512-kbyte RAM board which is used as a RAMdisk. This combination results in super-fast execution of all programs.

All of the programs have been translated into other operating systems by Bill Jorden, K7KI. Software for the following systems is available at this time:

DOS 3.3 80 column for Apple 2e or 2c
DOS 3.3 40 column for Apple 2, 2+, 2e or 2c
MS DOS for IBM or IBM compatibles
CP/M for Kaypro or similar computers
Apple MacIntosh
CP/M for Commodore 128 (80 column)
Commodore 64 40-column

The disk contains all programs which are referred to in this book plus a number of other very useful programs for the serious antenna experimenter and low-band DXer.

The programs on the disk are:

1. Introduction (how to use the programs)
2. Mutual impedance calculation
3. Element driving impedance calculation
4. Voltage along feedlines iteration
5. Impedance along feedline iteration
6. Feed line transformer
7. Shunt-input L-network iteration
8. Series-input L-network iteration
9. L-network design
10. Stub matching
11. Shunt impedance network
12. Series impedance network
13. PI-network line stretcher
14. T-network line stretcher
15. Feedline T junction (paralleling complex impedances)
16. Coil calculation (air-wound and toroidal cores)
17. SWR calculation

18. SWR iteration
19. LC circuit transformation (parallel to series and vice versa)
20. Sunrise/sunset time calculation (*)
21. Listing sunrise sunset times in 500+ locations (*)
22. Sunrise/sunset calendar
23. Great-circle directions and distances (*)
24. Listing great-circle distances and directions to 500+ locations (*)
25. Gray-line program (*)
26. Wave angle of horizontal antennas
27. Design program for lumped-constant loaded-vertical antennas
28. Design program for top-loaded vertical antennas
29. Radiation pattern calculation for vertical arrays
30. Influence of element taper on resonant frequency (also Yagi design)

The programs indicated by (*) are not listed in this chapter, because they are very complex and they make use of a large data base (which is included on the disk) containing the coordinates of over 500 locations worldwide.

Although part of the software is listed in this chapter, the author retains the copyright to all the programs.

All registered customers of the software will be informed once per year of software improvements and changes, which will be made available to registered customers at a minimal cost covering the mailing and diskette cost only.

Disks can be obtained from:

John Devoldere, ON4UN
Poelstraat 215
B9220 Merelbeke Belgium

B. W. Jorden, K7KI
6861 Kenana Place
Tucson, AZ 85704 USA

ARRL
225 Main Street
Newington, CT 06111 USA

And from radio shops and book stores selling ARRL publications.

```
10   REM name: MUTUAL IMPEDANCE
20   REM   by: John Devoldere, ON4UN
30   ONERR  GOTO 50
40   GOTO 60
50   HOME : VTAB 13: POKE 36,32: PRINT "FATA
     L ENTRY": PRINT  CHR$ (7): FOR A = 1 TO
     5000: NEXT
60   HOME : PRINT  CHR$ (13) + CHR$ (4);"PR
     #3": PRINT : POKE 36,24: PRINT "MUTUAL
      IMPEDANCE CALCULATION";: POKE 36,71: PRINT
     "by ON4UN": PRINT "--------------------
     -----------------------------------
     -----------------------"
70   PRINT "THIS PROGRAMS ALLOWS THE CALCULA
     TION OF THE MUTUAL IMPEDANCES BETWEEN
     ELEMENTS  OF AN ARRAY. THE INPUTS ARE
     THE SELF IMPEDANCES OF THE ELEMENTS, A
     ND THE DRIVING";
80   PRINT "POINT IMPEDANCE OF ONE ELEMENT O
     F A PAIR, THE OTHER BEING FULLY COUPLE
     D. WITH   QUARTER WAVE ELEMENTS COUPLI
     NG MEANS GROUNDING THE ELEMENT.": PRINT
     "-------------------------------------
     ------------------------------------
     ----": POKE 34,8
90   VTAB 22: PRINT "----------------------
     -----------------------------------
     -------------------": POKE 35,21: HOME

100  VTAB 9: INPUT "SELF IMPED. ELEM NR 1
     REAL PART > ";A$:B =  VAL (A$): IF B =
     0 THEN  PRINT  CHR$ (7): GOTO 100
110  VTAB 10: INPUT "SELF IMPED. ELEM NR 1
      IMAG PART > ";B$:C =  VAL (B$): IF C =
     0 AND B$ <  > "0" THEN  PRINT  CHR$ (7
     ): GOTO 110
120  VTAB 11: INPUT "SELF IMPED. ELEM NR 2
      REAL PART > ";C$:D =  VAL (C$): IF D =
     0 THEN  PRINT  CHR$ (7): GOTO 120
130  VTAB 12: INPUT "SELF IMPED. ELEM NR 2
      IMAG PART > ";D$:E =  VAL (D$): IF E =
     0 AND D$ <  > "0" THEN  PRINT  CHR$ (7
     ): GOTO 130
140  VTAB 13: INPUT "REAL PART DRIVE Z NR 1
     ANT, NR 2 GROUNDED > ";E$:F =  VAL (E
     $): IF F = 0 THEN  PRINT  CHR$ (7): GOTO
     140
150  VTAB 14: INPUT "IMAG PART DRIVE Z NR 1
     ANT, NR 2 GROUNDED > ";F$:G =  VAL (F
     $): IF G = 0 AND F$ <  > "0" THEN  PRINT
     CHR$ (7): GOTO 150
160  H = B - F:I = C - G:J = (D * H) - (E *
     I):K = (D * I) + (H * E):L = (( SQR (J
      ^ 2 + K ^ 2) - J) / 2) ^ .5:M = K / (
     2 * L):N =  INT (M * 100 + .5) / 100:O
     =  INT (L * 100 + .5) / 100:P =  -  INT
     (M * 100 + .5) / 100:Q =  -  INT (L *
     100 + .5) / 100: IF O > 0 THEN G$ = "
     +j "
170  IF O < 0 THEN G$ = " -j "
180  IF Q > 0 THEN H$ = " +j "
190  IF Q < 0 THEN H$ = " -j "
200  VTAB 15:O =  ABS (O):Q =  ABS (Q): PRINT
     "MUTUAL IMPEDANCE = ";N;G$;O;" ohm or"
     : PRINT "MUTUAL IMPEDANCE = ";P;H$;Q;"
     ohm"
210  PRINT : PRINT "YOU MUST CONSULT PUBLIS
     HED TABLES TO MAKE SURE YOU CHOSE THE
     CORRECT SIGN. THE   SOFTWARE MANUAL SHO
     WS MUTUAL IMPEDANCE FOR HALF-WAVE DIPO
     LES. FOR QUARTER WAVE  VERTICALS THE V
     ALUES MUST BE DIVIDED BY A FACTOR 2.":
     VTAB 23
220  PRINT "             MORE    >>>ANY KEY<<<
                   EXIT    >>>E<<< ";: VTAB
     23: POKE 36,39: GET I$: IF I$ = "E" OR
     I$ = "e" THEN  HOME : PRINT  CHR$ (13)
      + CHR$ (4);"RUN MENU"
230  POKE 35,23: VTAB 22: PRINT : POKE 36,0
     : CALL  - 868: POKE 35,21: HOME : GOTO
     100
```

```
10   REM name: DRIVING IMPEDANCE
20   REM  by: John Devoldere, ON4UN
30   ONERR  GOTO 50
40   F =  ATN (1) * 4: GOTO 60
50   VTAB 13: POKE 36,34: PRINT  CHR$ (7): PRINT
     "FATAL ERROR": FOR G = 1 TO 3000: NEXT

60   POKE 34,0: HOME : PRINT  CHR$ (13) +  CHR$
     (4);"PR#3": PRINT : POKE 36,20: PRINT
     "VERTICAL ARRAY FEED IMPEDANCE CALCULA
     TION.";: POKE 36,71: PRINT "by ON4UN":
      PRINT "------------------------------
     ----------------------------------------
     -----------"
70   PRINT "THIS PROGRAM ALLOWS THE CALCULAT
     ION OF THE DRIVING IMPEDANCES OF ARRAY
     S MADE OF MAXIMUM 4 VERTICAL ELEMENTS.
      THE REQUIRED INPUTS ARE THE ELEMENT S
     ELF IMPEDANCE"
80   PRINT "(USUALLY 36+j0 OHM FOR QUARTER W
     AVE VERTICALS), THE FEED CURRENT, THE
     PHASE     DELAY IN THE FEED CURRENT (T
     HE FIRST ELEMENT IS USUALLY TAKEN WITH
      A 0 DEGREE   PHASE DELAY), AND THE MU
     TUAL IMPEDANCES BETWEEN THE ELEMENTS."

90   PRINT "IMPEDANCES ARE ENTERED AS COMPLE
     X VALUES (a+jb).": PRINT "-------------
     ----------------------------------------
     ----------------------------": VTAB 2
     3: PRINT "-----------------------------
     --------------": POKE 35,21: POKE 34,11

100  VTAB 12: INPUT "ELEMENT SELF IMPEDANCE
      RESISTIVE PART > ";A$:A =  VAL (A$): IF
     A = 0 THEN  PRINT  CHR$ (7): GOTO 100
110  VTAB 13: INPUT "ELEMENT SELF IMPEDANCE
      REACTIVE PART  > ";B$:B =  VAL (B$): IF
     B = 0 AND B$ < > "0" THEN  PRINT  CHR$
     (7): GOTO 110
120  VTAB 15: INPUT "NUMBER OF ANTENNAS (MA
     X 4) > ";C$:C =  VAL (C$): IF C = 0 THEN
      PRINT  CHR$ (7): GOTO 120
130  IF C > 4 THEN  PRINT  CHR$ (7): GOTO 1
     20
140  HOME : FOR D = 1 TO C: HOME : VTAB 12:
      PRINT : PRINT "ANTENNA NR ";D: PRINT
     "------------"
150  VTAB 15: INPUT "CURRENT     > ";E$(D):
     A(D) =  VAL (E$(D)): IF A(D) = H THEN
      PRINT  CHR$ (7): GOTO 150
160  VTAB 16: INPUT "PHASE (deg) > ";D$(D):
     B(D) =  VAL (D$(D)): IF B(D) = 0 AND D
     $(D) < > "0" THEN  PRINT  CHR$ (7): GOTO
     160
170  FOR E = D + 1 TO C: IF E > C GOTO 200
180  VTAB 17: PRINT "MUTUAL IMPED. VS. ANT
     NR ";E;: INPUT " ,REAL PART > ";F$(D,E
     );:C(D,E) =  VAL (F$(D,E)): IF C(D,E) =
     0 AND F$(D,E) < > "0" THEN  PRINT  CHR$
     (7): GOTO 180
190  VTAB 18: PRINT "MUTUAL IMPED. VS. ANT
     NR ";E;: INPUT " ,IMAG PART > ";G$(D,E
     );:D(D,E) =  VAL (G$(D,E)): IF D(D,E) =
     0 AND G$(D,E) < > "0" THEN  PRINT  CHR$
     (7): GOTO 190
200  NEXT E: NEXT D: FOR D = 1 TO C:C(D,D) =
     A:D(D,D) = B: NEXT D: POKE 34,0: HOME
     : POKE 36,20: PRINT "VERTICAL ARRAY FE
     ED IMPEDANCE CALCULATION.";: POKE 36,7
     1: PRINT "by ON4UN": PRINT "----------
     ----------------------------------------
     -------------------------"
210  PRINT "                            ANT 1
                ANT 2         ANT 3        ANT 4
     ": PRINT "
     X     R      X     R      X     R
          X": PRINT "-----------------------
     ----------------------------------------
     ------------------"
220  PRINT "SELFIMPEDANCE";;: POKE 36,22: PRINT
     C(1,1);;: POKE 36,29: PRINT D(1,1);;: POKE
     36,36: PRINT C(2,2);;: POKE 36,43: PRINT
     D(2,2);;: POKE 36,50: PRINT C(3,3);;: POKE
     36,57: PRINT D(3,3);;: POKE 36,64: PRINT
     C(4,4);;: POKE 36,71: PRINT D(4,4)
230  PRINT "MUTUAL IMP ANT 1";;: POKE 36,36:
      PRINT C(1,2);;: POKE 36,43: PRINT D(1,
     2);;: POKE 36,50: PRINT C(1,3);;: POKE 3
     6,57: PRINT D(1,3);;: POKE 36,64: PRINT
     C(1,4);;: POKE 36,71: PRINT D(1,4): PRINT
     "MUTUAL IMP ANT 2";;: POKE 36,50: PRINT
     C(2,3);;: POKE 36,57: PRINT D(2,3);;: POKE
     36,64: PRINT C(2,4);;: POKE 36,71: PRINT
     D(2,4)
240  PRINT "MUTUAL IMP ANT 3";;: POKE 36,64:
      PRINT C(3,4);;: POKE 36,71: PRINT D(3,
     4): PRINT "ANTENNA CURRENT";;: POKE 36,
     25: PRINT A(1);;: POKE 36,39: PRINT A(2
     );;: POKE 36,53: PRINT A(3);;: POKE 36,6
     7: PRINT A(4): PRINT "ANTENNA PHASE  "
     ;;: POKE 36,25: PRINT B(1);;: POKE 36,39
     : PRINT B(2);;: POKE 36,53: PRINT B(3);
     ;: POKE 36,67: PRINT B(4)
250  PRINT "-------------------------------
     ----------------------------------------
     ----------": POKE 34,12: POKE 35,21: HOME
     : VTAB 24: PRINT "                    IF
      NOT OK ENTER >>N<<, ELSE ANY OTHER KE
     Y > ";: POKE 36,65: GET A$: PRINT : IF
     A$ = "N" THEN  GOTO 30
260  HOME : VTAB 24: PRINT "        ENTER  >>>
     E<<< TO EXIT      ---        ANY O
     THER KEY TO CONTINUE";;:C(4,3) = C(3,4)
     :D(4,3) = D(3,4):C(4,2) = C(2,4):D(4,2
     ) = D(2,4):C(4,1) = C(1,4):D(4,1) = D(
     1,4):C(3,2) = C(2,3):D(3,2) = D(2,3):C
     (3,1) = C(1,3):D(3,1) = D(1,3)
270  C(2,1) = C(1,2):D(2,1) = D(1,2): FOR G =
     1 TO C:E(G) = A(G) *  COS (B(G) * F /
     180):F(G) = A(G) *  SIN (B(G) * F / 18
     0): NEXT G: FOR G = 1 TO C:I = E(G) ^
     2 + F(G) ^ 2:J = ((E(G) * E(1)) + (F(1
     ) * F(G))) / I:K = ((F(1) * E(G)) - (E
     (1) * F(G))) / I:L = ((E(G) * E(2)) +
     (F(2) * F(G))) / I:M = ((F(2) * E(G)) -
     (E(2) * F(G))) / I
280  N = ((E(G) * E(3)) + (F(3) * F(G))) / I
     :O = ((F(3) * E(G)) - (E(3) * F(G))) /
     I:P = ((E(G) * E(4)) + (F(4) * F(G))) /
     I:Q = ((F(4) * E(G)) - (E(4) * F(G))) /
     I:G(G) = (J * C(G,1)) - (K * D(G,1)) +
     (L * C(G,2)) - (M * D(G,2)) + (N * C(G
     ,3)) - (O * D(G,3)) + (P * C(G,4)) - (
     Q * D(G,4))
290  H(G) = (J * D(G,1)) + (K * C(G,1)) + (L
     * D(G,2)) + (M * C(G,2)) + (N * D(G,3
     )) + (O * C(G,3)) + (P * D(G,4)) + (Q *
     C(G,4)):G(G) =  INT (100 * G(G) + .5) /
     100:H(G) =  INT (100 * H(G) + .5) / 10
     0: NEXT G: HOME : POKE 36,28: PRINT "E
     LEMENT FEED IMPEDANCES": POKE 36,28: PRINT
     "====================="
300  POKE 36,21: PRINT "ELEMENT NR    RESI
     STIVE     REACTIVE": POKE 36,21: PRINT
     "----------------------------------------
     ": FOR D = 1 TO C: POKE 36,25: PRINT D
     ;;: POKE 36,38: PRINT  INT (100 * G(D) +
     .5) / 100;;: POKE 36,52: PRINT  INT (10
     0 * H(D) + .5) / 100: NEXT D: VTAB 24:
      POKE 36,74: GET H$: IF H$ = "E" OR H$
     = "e" THEN  HOME : PRINT  CHR$ (13) +
     CHR$ (4);"RUN MENU"
310  HOME : CLEAR : GOTO 30
```

```
10   REM name: FEEDLINE VOLTAGE
20   REM by: John Devoldere, ON4UN
30   ONERR  GOTO 50
40   GOTO 60
50   VTAB 14: POKE 36,34: PRINT "FATAL ERROR
     ": PRINT  CHR$ (7): FOR I = 1 TO 5000:
     NEXT : GOTO 30
60   J =  ATN (1) * 4: PRINT  CHR$ (13) +  CHR$
     (4);"PR#3": HOME : PRINT : POKE 36,27:
     PRINT "FEEDLINE VOLTAGE PROGRAM.";: POKE
     36,71: PRINT "by ON4UN": PRINT "------
     -------------------------------------
     ----------------------------------"
70   PRINT "THIS PROGRAM WILL CALCULATE THE
     VOLTAGE (AMPLITUDE AND ANGLE) ON A FEE
     DLINE, IN 1 DEGREE INCREMENTS STARTING
     AT THE LOAD (ANTENNA). REQUIRED INPUT
     S ARE LOAD"
80   PRINT "IMPEDANCE (AMPLITUDE AND ANGLE)
     AND LINE CHARACTERISTIC IMPEDANCE. LOW
     ER SCAN   LIMIT AND INCREMENT CAN BE U
     SER DEFINED FOR BETTER RESOLUTION.": PRINT
     "-------------------------------------
     -------------------------------------
     ----"
90   VTAB 22: PRINT "------------------------
     -------------------------------------
     ------------------": POKE 35,21
100  POKE 34,8: HOME :K = 0:L = 1
110  VTAB 23: PRINT "            RESULTS TO S
     CREEN     >>>S<<<         TO PRINTER   >
     >>P<<<   > ";: GET A$: IF A$ < > "S" AND
     A$ < > "s" AND A$ < > "P" AND A$ < >
     "p" THEN  PRINT  CHR$ (7): GOTO 110
120  POKE 35,23: VTAB 22: PRINT : POKE 36,0
     : CALL  - 868: POKE 35,21: HOME : IF A
     $ = "P" OR A$ = "p" THEN  POKE 35,23: HOME
     : VTAB 23: PRINT "--------------------
     -------------------------------------
     ------------------": PRINT "
     THE PRINT-OUT WILL BE IN 1 DEGREE ST
     EPS FROM 0 TO 360 DEGREES.";: POKE 35,
     21
130  VTAB 10: PRINT : INPUT "CABLE IMPEDANC
     E Zk > ";B$:M =  VAL (B$): IF M < = 0
     THEN  PRINT  CHR$ (7): GOTO 130
140  VTAB 13: INPUT "NUMBER ANTENNAS (1-4)
     > ";C$:N =  VAL (C$): IF N = < 0 OR N
     > 4 THEN  PRINT  CHR$ (7): GOTO 140
150  FOR K = 1 TO N: VTAB 15: PRINT "ANTENN
     A NR ";K: PRINT "============"
160  VTAB 17: CALL  - 958: INPUT "IMPEDANCE
     RESISTIVE PART Z > ";D$(K):A(K) =  VAL
     (D$(K)): IF A(K) = 0 THEN  PRINT  CHR$
     (7): GOTO 160
170  VTAB 18: INPUT "IMPEDANCE REACTIVE PAR
     T Z > ";E$(K):B(K) =  VAL (E$(K)): IF
     B(K) = 0 AND E$(K) < > "0" THEN  PRINT
     CHR$ (7): GOTO 170
180  VTAB 19: INPUT "ANTENNA CURRENT I > ";
     F$(K):C(K) =  VAL (F$(K)): IF C(K) = <
     0 THEN  PRINT  CHR$ (7): GOTO 180
190  VTAB 20: INPUT "PHASE ANGLE > ";G$(K):
     D(K) =  VAL (G$(K)): IF D(K) = 0 AND G
     $(K) < > "0" THEN  PRINT  CHR$ (7);: GOTO
     190
200  NEXT K: DEF  FN E(O) =  -  ATN (O /  SQR
     ( - O * O + 1)) + 1.5708: IF A$ = "P" OR
     A$ = "p" THEN  PRINT  CHR$ (13) +  CHR$
     (4);"PR#1"
210  IF A$ = "S" OR A$ = "s" THEN  PRINT  CHR$
     (13) +  CHR$ (4);"PR#3"
220  PRINT : POKE 36,27: PRINT "FEEDLINE VO
     LTAGE ITERATION.";: POKE 36,71: PRINT
     "by ON4UN": PRINT "--------------------
     -------------------------------------
     --------------------": PRINT "CABLE
     IMPEDANCE = ";M
230  PRINT "ANTENNA NR = ";: POKE 36,14: PRINT
     "1";: IF N > 1 THEN  POKE 36,23: PRINT
     "2";: IF N > 2 THEN  POKE 36,32: PRINT
     "3";: IF N > 3 THEN  POKE 36,41: PRINT
     "4";
240  PRINT : PRINT "------------ ";: POKE 3
     6,14: PRINT "------";: IF N > 1 THEN  POKE
     36,23: PRINT "------";: IF N > 2 THEN
     POKE 36,32: PRINT "------";: IF N > 3
     THEN  POKE 36,41: PRINT "------";
250  PRINT : PRINT "RESIST. PRT= ";: POKE 3
     6,14: PRINT A(1);: IF N > 1 THEN  POKE
     36,23: PRINT A(2);: IF N > 2 THEN  POKE
     36,32: PRINT A(3);: IF N > 3 THEN  POKE
     36,41: PRINT A(4);
260  PRINT : PRINT "REACT. PART= ";: POKE 3
     6,14: PRINT B(1);: IF N > 1 THEN  POKE
     36,23: PRINT B(2);: IF N > 2 THEN  POKE
     36,32: PRINT B(3);: IF N > 3 THEN  POKE
     36,41: PRINT B(4);
270  PRINT : PRINT "PHASE ANGLE= ";: POKE 3
     6,14: PRINT D(1);: IF N > 1 THEN  POKE
     36,23: PRINT D(2);: IF N > 2 THEN  POKE
     36,32: PRINT D(3);: IF N > 3 THEN  POKE
     36,41: PRINT D(4);
280  PRINT : PRINT "ANTEN. CURR. ";: POKE 3
     6,14: PRINT C(1);: IF N > 1 THEN  POKE
     36,23: PRINT C(2);: IF N > 2 THEN  POKE
     36,32: PRINT C(3);: IF N > 3 THEN  POKE
     36,41: PRINT C(4);
290  PRINT : PRINT "------------------------
     -------------------------------------
     ------------------": PRINT "DIST
     ANTENNA 1";: IF N > 1 THEN  PRINT "
         ANTENNA 2";: IF N > 2 THEN  PRINT
     "       ANTENNA 3";: IF N > 3 THEN  PRINT
     "       ANTENNA 4";
300  PRINT : PRINT "DEG    VOLT    ANGLE";
     : IF N > 1 THEN  PRINT "  VOLT    ANG
     LE";: IF N > 2 THEN  PRINT "  VOLT
     ANGLE";: IF N > 3 THEN  PRINT "  VOL
     T    ANGLE";
310  PRINT : PRINT "----   ----------------";
     : IF N > 1 THEN  PRINT "   -----------
     --";: IF N > 2 THEN  PRINT "   -------
     -------";: IF N > 3 THEN  PRINT "   ---
     -----------";
320  IF A$ = "P" OR A$ = "p" THEN  PRINT : GOTO
     340
330  PRINT : VTAB 23: PRINT "---------------
     -------------------------------------
     ------------------------": VTAB 24:
     PRINT "          NEW ITERATION   >>>
     N<<<          EXIT   >>>E<<<";: POKE
     35,22: POKE 34,14
340  HOME
350  I = I + L: IF I = 361 THEN  HOME : PRINT
     CHR$ (13) +  CHR$ (4);"RUN MENU"
360  PRINT  INT (I * 100 + .5) / 100;: FOR
     K = 1 TO N: IF A$ = "P" GOTO 400
370  IF  PEEK ( - 16384) = 238 OR  PEEK ( -
     16384) = 206 THEN  HOME : GOTO 440
380  IF  PEEK ( - 16384) = 197 OR  PEEK ( -
     16384) = 229 THEN  GET H$: HOME : PRINT
     CHR$ (13) +  CHR$ (4);"RUN MENU"
390  POKE - 16368,0
400  A =  COS (I * J / 180):B =  SIN (I * J /
     180):C = A(K) * A:C = C * C(K):D = B(K
     ) * A:E = M * B:F = D + E:F = F * C(K)
     :G = ((F * F) + (C * C)) ^ .5:H =  FN
     E(C / G):P = H * 180 / J: IF F < 0 THEN
     P =  - P
410  P = P + D(K): IF Q <  - 180 THEN Q = Q +
     360
420  IF Q > 180 THEN Q = Q - 360
430  POKE 36,((K * 16) - 8): PRINT  INT (10
     0 * G) / 100;: POKE 36,(K * 16): PRINT
     INT (100 * Q) / 100;: NEXT K: PRINT :
     GOTO 350
```

```
440  GET H$: HOME : IF H$ = "E" OR H$ = "e"
     THEN PRINT CHR$ (13) + CHR$ (4);"R
     UN MENU"
450  VTAB 15: INPUT "LOWER LIMIT > ";F$:I =
     VAL (F$): IF I = 0 AND F$ < > "0" THEN
     PRINT CHR$ (7): GOTO 450
460  VTAB 16: INPUT "NEW INCREMENT (> 0.01)
     > ";I$:L = VAL (I$): IF L = 0 AND I
     $ < > "0" THEN PRINT CHR$ (7): GOTO
     460
470  IF L < .01 THEN PRINT CHR$ (7): GOTO
     460
480  I = I - L: HOME : GOTO 350
```

Computer Programs   VII-5

FEEDLINE VOLTAGE ITERATION.

CABLE IMPEDANCE = 50

ANTENNA NR =	1	2	3
RESIST. PRT=	21.4	51.4	0
REACT. PART=	-15	15	0
PHASE ANGLE=	0	-90	0
ANTEN. CURR.	1	1	0

DIST	ANTENNA 1		ANTENNA 2	
DEG	VOLT	ANGLE	VOLT	ANGLE
0	26.13	-35.03	53.54	-73.74
1	25.63	-33.44	53.78	-72.84
2	25.15	-31.78	54.02	-71.96
3	24.68	-30.05	54.26	-71.08
4	24.23	-28.27	54.49	-70.21
5	23.8	-26.41	54.72	-69.35
6	23.38	-24.49	54.94	-68.5
7	22.98	-22.5	55.16	-67.65
8	22.61	-20.44	55.37	-66.81
9	22.26	-18.31	55.58	-65.97
10	21.93	-16.12	55.78	-65.14
11	21.63	-13.87	55.98	-64.32
12	21.36	-11.55	56.17	-63.5
13	21.12	-9.18	56.36	-62.69
14	20.9	-6.76	56.54	-61.89
15	20.72	-4.29	56.72	-61.09
16	20.58	-1.78	56.89	-60.29
17	20.46	.76	57.05	-59.5
18	20.38	3.33	57.2	-58.71
19	20.34	5.91	57.35	-57.93
20	20.33	8.5	57.49	-57.15
21	20.35	11.08	57.63	-56.37
22	20.41	13.66	57.76	-55.6
23	20.51	16.21	57.88	-54.83
24	20.64	18.74	57.99	-54.07
25	20.8	21.23	58.1	-53.3
26	21	23.68	58.2	-52.54
27	21.22	26.08	58.29	-51.79
28	21.48	28.43	58.37	-51.03
29	21.77	30.71	58.45	-50.28
30	22.08	32.94	58.52	-49.53
31	22.42	35.1	58.58	-48.78
32	22.78	37.2	58.63	-48.03
33	23.16	39.22	58.67	-47.28
34	23.57	41.18	58.71	-46.53
35	23.99	43.07	58.74	-45.79
36	24.44	44.9	58.76	-45.05
37	24.9	46.66	58.77	-44.3
38	25.37	48.35	58.78	-43.56
39	25.86	49.98	58.78	-42.81
40	26.36	51.55	58.77	-42.07
41	26.87	53.06	58.75	-41.33
42	27.39	54.51	58.72	-40.58
43	27.92	55.91	58.68	-39.84
44	28.46	57.26	58.64	-39.09
45	29	58.55	58.59	-38.34
46	29.55	59.8	58.53	-37.59
47	30.11	61	58.47	-36.84
48	30.66	62.16	58.39	-36.09
49	31.22	63.28	58.31	-35.33
50	31.79	64.36	58.22	-34.58
51	32.35	65.4	58.12	-33.82
52	32.91	66.4	58.02	-33.06
53	33.48	67.37	57.91	-32.29
54	34.04	68.31	57.79	-31.52
55	34.6	69.22	57.66	-30.75
56	35.16	70.1	57.53	-29.98
57	35.71	70.95	57.39	-29.2
58	36.27	71.78	57.24	-28.42
59	36.82	72.58	57.09	-27.63
60	37.36	73.36	56.93	-26.84
61	37.9	74.11	56.76	-26.04
62	38.44	74.84	56.59	-25.24
63	38.97	75.56	56.41	-24.44
64	39.49	76.25	56.22	-23.63
65	40.01	76.93	56.03	-22.81
66	40.52	77.59	55.83	-21.99
67	41.02	78.24	55.63	-21.16
68	41.52	78.86	55.43	-20.33
69	42	79.48	55.21	-19.49
70	42.48	80.08	55	-18.65
71	42.96	80.66	54.77	-17.79
72	43.42	81.24	54.55	-16.93
73	43.87	81.8	54.32	-16.07
74	44.32	82.35	54.08	-15.19
75	44.75	82.89	53.84	-14.31
76	45.18	83.42	53.6	-13.42
77	45.59	83.94	53.36	-12.52
78	46	84.45	53.11	-11.61
79	46.39	84.95	52.86	-10.7
80	46.78	85.44	52.6	-9.77
81	47.15	85.92	52.35	-8.84
82	47.51	86.4	52.09	-7.9
83	47.87	86.87	51.83	-6.95
84	48.21	87.34	51.57	-5.98
85	48.53	87.79	51.31	-5.01
86	48.85	88.24	51.05	-4.03
87	49.15	88.69	50.78	-3.04
88	49.45	89.13	50.52	-2.04
89	49.73	89.56	50.26	-1.03
90	50	90	50	0
91	50.25	90.42	49.73	1.03
92	50.49	90.84	49.47	2.07
93	50.72	91.26	49.22	3.13
94	50.94	91.67	48.96	4.19
95	51.15	92.08	48.7	5.27
96	51.34	92.49	48.45	6.36
97	51.52	92.9	48.2	7.46
98	51.68	93.3	47.96	8.57
99	51.83	93.7	47.72	9.7
100	51.97	94.09	47.48	10.83
101	52.1	94.49	47.24	11.98
102	52.21	94.88	47.01	13.13
103	52.31	95.27	46.79	14.3
104	52.39	95.67	46.57	15.48
105	52.47	96.05	46.36	16.67
106	52.52	96.44	46.15	17.87
107	52.57	96.83	45.95	19.08
108	52.6	97.22	45.76	20.3
109	52.62	97.6	45.57	21.54
110	52.62	97.99	45.39	22.78
111	52.61	98.38	45.22	24.03
112	52.59	98.76	45.06	25.29
113	52.55	99.15	44.9	26.56
114	52.5	99.54	44.75	27.84
115	52.44	99.93	44.62	29.13
116	52.36	100.32	44.49	30.42
117	52.27	100.71	44.37	31.72
118	52.16	101.1	44.26	33.03
119	52.04	101.49	44.16	34.35
120	51.91	101.89	44.07	35.67
121	51.77	102.29	43.99	36.99
122	51.61	102.69	43.91	38.32
123	51.44	103.09	43.85	39.66
124	51.25	103.5	43.81	41
125	51.05	103.91	43.77	42.34
126	50.84	104.32	43.74	43.68
127	50.62	104.73	43.72	45.02
128	50.38	105.15	43.71	46.37
129	50.13	105.58	43.72	47.71
130	49.87	106	43.73	49.05
131	49.6	106.44	43.76	50.4
132	49.31	106.87	43.79	51.74
133	49.02	107.32	43.84	53.08
134	48.71	107.76	43.9	54.41
135	48.38	108.22	43.97	55.74
136	48.05	108.68	44.04	57.07
137	47.71	109.15	44.13	58.39
138	47.35	109.62	44.23	59.71
139	46.98	110.1	44.34	61.02
140	46.6	110.59	44.46	62.32
141	46.21	111.08	44.58	63.62
142	45.81	111.59	44.72	64.91
143	45.4	112.1	44.86	66.19
144	44.98	112.63	45.02	67.46
145	44.55	113.16	45.18	68.72
146	44.11	113.71	45.35	69.98
147	43.67	114.26	45.52	71.22
148	43.21	114.83	45.71	72.46
149	42.74	115.41	45.9	73.68
150	42.26	116	46.1	74.9
151	41.78	116.61	46.31	76.1
152	41.29	117.23	46.52	77.29
153	40.79	117.86	46.73	78.48
154	40.28	118.51	46.96	79.65
155	39.77	119.18	47.18	80.81
156	39.25	119.86	47.42	81.95
157	38.72	120.57	47.65	83.09
158	38.19	121.29	47.9	84.22
159	37.65	122.04	48.14	85.33
160	37.11	122.8	48.39	86.43
161	36.56	123.59	48.64	87.53
162	36.01	124.4	48.89	88.61
163	35.46	125.24	49.15	89.68
164	34.9	126.1	49.41	90.73
165	34.34	127	49.67	91.78
166	33.78	127.92	49.93	92.82
167	33.22	128.87	50.19	93.84
168	32.65	129.86	50.45	94.86
169	32.09	130.88	50.72	95.86
170	31.53	131.94	50.98	96.85
171	30.97	133.03	51.24	97.84
172	30.41	134.17	51.5	98.81
173	29.85	135.35	51.76	99.78
174	29.3	136.57	52.02	100.73
175	28.75	137.84	52.28	101.67
176	28.21	139.16	52.54	102.61
177	27.68	140.53	52.79	103.54
178	27.15	141.95	53.04	104.45
179	26.63	143.43	53.29	105.36
180	26.13	144.97	53.54	106.26
181	25.63	146.56	53.78	107.16
182	25.15	148.22	54.02	108.04
183	24.68	149.95	54.26	108.92
184	24.23	151.73	54.49	109.79
185	23.8	153.59	54.72	110.65
186	23.38	155.51	54.94	111.5
187	22.98	157.5	55.16	112.35
188	22.61	159.56	55.37	113.19
189	22.26	161.69	55.58	114.03
190	21.93	163.88	55.78	114.86
191	21.63	166.13	55.98	115.68
192	21.36	168.45	56.17	116.5
193	21.12	170.82	56.36	117.31
194	20.9	173.24	56.54	118.11
195	20.72	175.71	56.72	118.91
196	20.58	178.22	56.89	119.71
197	20.46	-179.24	57.05	120.5
198	20.38	-176.67	57.2	121.29
199	20.34	-174.09	57.35	122.07
200	20.33	-171.5	57.49	122.85
201	20.35	-168.92	57.63	123.63
202	20.41	-166.34	57.76	124.4
203	20.51	-163.79	57.88	125.17
204	20.64	-161.26	57.99	125.93
205	20.8	-158.77	58.1	126.7
206	21	-156.32	58.2	127.46
207	21.22	-153.92	58.29	128.21
208	21.48	-151.58	58.37	128.97
209	21.77	-149.29	58.45	129.72
210	22.08	-147.06	58.52	130.47
211	22.42	-144.9	58.58	131.22
212	22.78	-142.81	58.63	131.97
213	23.16	-140.78	58.67	132.72
214	23.57	-138.82	58.71	133.46
215	23.99	-136.93	58.74	134.21
216	24.44	-135.1	58.76	134.95
217	24.9	-133.34	58.77	135.7
218	25.37	-131.65	58.78	136.44
219	25.86	-130.02	58.78	137.19
220	26.36	-128.45	58.77	137.93
221	26.87	-126.94	58.75	138.67
222	27.39	-125.49	58.72	139.42
223	27.92	-124.09	58.68	140.16
224	28.46	-122.74	58.64	140.91
225	29	-121.45	58.59	141.66
226	29.55	-120.2	58.53	142.41
227	30.11	-119	58.47	143.16
228	30.66	-117.84	58.39	143.91
229	31.22	-116.72	58.31	144.67
230	31.79	-115.64	58.22	145.42
231	32.35	-114.6	58.12	146.18
232	32.91	-113.6	58.02	146.94
233	33.48	-112.63	57.91	147.71
234	34.04	-111.69	57.79	148.48
235	34.6	-110.78	57.66	149.25
236	35.16	-109.9	57.53	150.02
237	35.71	-109.05	57.39	150.8
238	36.27	-108.22	57.24	151.58
239	36.82	-107.42	57.09	152.37
240	37.36	-106.65	56.93	153.16
241	37.9	-105.89	56.76	153.96
242	38.44	-105.16	56.59	154.76
243	38.97	-104.44	56.41	155.56
244	39.49	-103.75	56.22	156.37
245	40.01	-103.07	56.03	157.19
246	40.52	-102.41	55.83	158.01
247	41.02	-101.77	55.63	158.83
248	41.52	-101.14	55.43	159.67
249	42	-100.52	55.21	160.51
250	42.48	-99.92	55	161.35
251	42.96	-99.34	54.77	162.21
252	43.42	-98.76	54.55	163.07
253	43.87	-98.2	54.32	163.93
254	44.32	-97.65	54.08	164.81
255	44.75	-97.11	53.84	165.69
256	45.18	-96.58	53.6	166.58
257	45.59	-96.07	53.36	167.48
258	46	-95.56	53.11	168.39
259	46.39	-95.05	52.86	169.3
260	46.78	-94.56	52.6	170.23
261	47.15	-94.08	52.35	171.16
262	47.51	-93.6	52.09	172.1
263	47.87	-93.13	51.83	173.05
264	48.21	-92.66	51.57	174.02
265	48.53	-92.21	51.31	174.99
266	48.85	-91.76	51.05	175.97
267	49.15	-91.31	50.78	176.96
268	49.45	-90.87	50.52	177.96
269	49.73	-90.44	50.26	178.97
270	50	-90.01	50	179.99
271	50.25	-89.58	49.73	-178.97
272	50.49	-89.16	49.47	-177.93
273	50.72	-88.74	49.22	-176.87
274	50.94	-88.33	48.96	-175.81
275	51.15	-87.92	48.7	-174.73
276	51.34	-87.51	48.45	-173.64
277	51.52	-87.1	48.2	-172.54
278	51.68	-86.7	47.96	-171.43
279	51.83	-86.3	47.72	-170.3
280	51.97	-85.91	47.48	-169.17
281	52.1	-85.51	47.24	-168.02
282	52.21	-85.12	47.01	-166.87
283	52.31	-84.73	46.79	-165.7
284	52.39	-84.34	46.57	-164.52
285	52.47	-83.95	46.36	-163.33
286	52.52	-83.56	46.15	-162.13
287	52.57	-83.17	45.95	-160.92
288	52.6	-82.78	45.76	-159.7
289	52.62	-82.4	45.57	-158.46
290	52.62	-82.01	45.39	-157.22
291	52.61	-81.62	45.22	-155.97
292	52.59	-81.24	45.06	-154.71
293	52.55	-80.85	44.9	-153.44
294	52.5	-80.46	44.75	-152.16
295	52.44	-80.07	44.62	-150.87

296	52.36	−79.68	44.49	−149.58	318	47.35	−70.38	44.23	−120.29	340	37.11	−57.2	48.39	−93.57
297	52.27	−79.29	44.37	−148.28	319	46.98	−69.9	44.34	−118.98	341	36.56	−56.41	48.64	−92.47
298	52.16	−78.9	44.26	−146.97	320	46.6	−69.41	44.46	−117.68	342	36.01	−55.6	48.89	−91.39
299	52.04	−78.51	44.16	−145.65	321	46.21	−68.92	44.58	−116.38	343	35.46	−54.76	49.15	−90.32
300	51.91	−78.11	44.07	−144.33	322	45.81	−68.41	44.72	−115.09	344	34.9	−53.9	49.41	−89.27
301	51.77	−77.71	43.99	−143.01	323	45.4	−67.9	44.86	−113.81	345	34.34	−53	49.67	−88.22
302	51.61	−77.31	43.91	−141.68	324	44.98	−67.37	45.02	−112.54	346	33.78	−52.08	49.93	−87.18
303	51.44	−76.91	43.85	−140.34	325	44.55	−66.84	45.18	−111.28	347	33.22	−51.13	50.19	−86.16
304	51.25	−76.5	43.81	−139	326	44.11	−66.29	45.35	−110.02	348	32.65	−50.14	50.45	−85.14
305	51.05	−76.1	43.77	−137.66	327	43.67	−65.74	45.52	−108.78	349	32.09	−49.12	50.72	−84.14
306	50.84	−75.68	43.74	−136.32	328	43.21	−65.17	45.71	−107.54	350	31.53	−48.06	50.98	−83.14
307	50.62	−75.27	43.72	−134.98	329	42.74	−64.59	45.9	−106.32	351	30.97	−46.97	51.24	−82.16
308	50.38	−74.85	43.71	−133.63	330	42.26	−64	46.1	−105.1	352	30.41	−45.83	51.5	−81.19
309	50.13	−74.42	43.72	−132.29	331	41.78	−63.39	46.31	−103.9	353	29.85	−44.65	51.76	−80.22
310	49.87	−74	43.73	−130.95	332	41.29	−62.77	46.52	−102.71	354	29.3	−43.43	52.02	−79.27
311	49.6	−73.56	43.76	−129.6	333	40.79	−62.14	46.73	−101.53	355	28.75	−42.16	52.28	−78.32
312	49.31	−73.13	43.79	−128.26	334	40.28	−61.49	46.96	−100.35	356	28.21	−40.84	52.54	−77.39
313	49.02	−72.68	43.84	−126.92	335	39.77	−60.82	47.18	−99.19	357	27.68	−39.47	52.79	−76.46
314	48.71	−72.24	43.9	−125.59	336	39.25	−60.14	47.42	−98.05	358	27.15	−38.05	53.04	−75.55
315	48.38	−71.78	43.97	−124.26	337	38.72	−59.43	47.65	−96.91	359	26.63	−36.57	53.29	−74.64
316	48.05	−71.32	44.04	−122.93	338	38.19	−58.71	47.9	−95.78	360	26.13	−35.03	53.54	−73.74
317	47.71	−70.86	44.13	−121.61	339	37.65	−57.96	48.14	−94.67					

```
10   REM name: RC/RL TRANSFORMATION
20   REM by: John Devoldere, ON4UN
30   ONERR  GOTO 50
40   GOTO 60
50   VTAB 14: POKE 36,34: PRINT "FATAL ERROR
     ": PRINT  CHR$ (7): FOR A = 1 TO 5000:
     NEXT : GOTO 30
60   CLEAR : PRINT  CHR$ (13) + CHR$ (4);"P
     R#3": POKE 34,0: HOME : PRINT : POKE 3
     6,3: PRINT "CONVERSION PARALLEL -> SER
     IAL / SERIAL -> PARALLEL RL/RC CIRCUIT
     ";: POKE 36,70: PRINT "by  ON4UN": PRINT
     "----------------------------------------
     -----------------------------------------
     ----"
70   PRINT "THIS PROGRAM CALCULATES THE EQUI
     VALENT PARELLEL RC OR RL CIRCUIT FOR A
         GIVEN    SERIAL RC OR RL CIRCUIT, AND
         THE EQUIVALENT SERIAL RC OR RL CIRCUI
     T FOR A GIVEN PARALLEL RC OR RL CIRCUI
     T."
80   PRINT "ONE CAN ALSO FIRST CALCULATE THE
         REACTIVE IMPEDANCE OF A COIL OR CAPAC
     ITOR GIVENTHE OPERATING FREQUENCY.": PRINT
     "-----------------------------------------
     -----------------------------------------
     ----": VTAB 22
90   PRINT "-----------------------------------
     -----------------------------------------
     ---------": POKE 35,21: POKE 34,9
100  CLEAR : VTAB 8: PRINT
110  VTAB 10: PRINT "DO YOU WANT TO CALCULA
     TE THE IMPEDANCE OF A CAPACITOR OR COI
     L (Y/N)? ";: GET A$: PRINT : VTAB 10: CALL
      - 868: PRINT : VTAB 11: IF A$ = "N" OR
     A$ = "n" THEN  HOME : GOTO 250
120  IF A$ = "Y" OR A$ = "y" GOTO 140
130  PRINT  CHR$ (7): GOTO 110
140  VTAB 12: INPUT "OPERATING FREQUENCY (M
     Hz) > ";B$:B =  VAL (B$): IF B = 0 THEN
     PRINT  CHR$ (7): GOTO 140
150  VTAB 13: PRINT "IS THE REACTIVE COMPON
     ENT A CAPACITOR OR INDUCTOR (C/L) > ";
     : GET A$: IF A$ = "C" GOTO 180
160  IF A$ = "L" GOTO 200
170  PRINT  CHR$ (7): GOTO 150
180  PRINT : VTAB 14: INPUT "ENTER CAPACITO
     R VALUE IN pF > ";C$:C =  VAL (C$): IF
     C < = 0 THEN  PRINT  CHR$ (7): GOTO 1
     80
190  D = 1000000 / (2 * 3.14159 * B * C):D =
      INT (D * 100 + .5) / 100:D =  - D: HOME
     : GOTO 220
200  PRINT : VTAB 14: INPUT "ENTER INDUCTOR
      VALUE IN uH > ";D$:E =  VAL (D$): PRINT
     : IF E < = 0 THEN  PRINT  CHR$ (7): GOTO
     200
210  D = 2 * 3.14159 * B * E: HOME :D =  INT
     (D * 100 + .5) / 100
220  PRINT "FREQ.: ";B;" MHz";: IF A$ = "C"
     OR A$ = "c" THEN  POKE 36,24: PRINT "
     CAPAC. VALUE = ";C;" pF";
230  IF A$ = "L" OR A$ = "l" THEN  POKE 36,
     24: PRINT "COIL VALUE = ";E;" uH";
240  POKE 36,54: PRINT "REACTANCE = ";D;" o
     hm"
250  VTAB 12: PRINT "SERIES TO PARALLEL (S)
      OR PARALLEL TO SERIES (P) CONVERSION?
     > ";: GET A$: IF A$ = "P" OR A$ = "p"
     GOTO 430
260  IF A$ = "S" OR A$ = "s" GOTO 280
270  PRINT  CHR$ (7): GOTO 250
280  PRINT : VTAB 12: CALL  - 868: PRINT "S
     ERIAL TO PARALLEL RL/RC CIRCUIT CONVER
     SION.": PRINT "======================="
     ===================="
290  VTAB 14: INPUT "ENTER RESISTANCE VALUE
      (ohm) > ";E$:F =  VAL (E$): IF F = 0 AND
     E$ < > "0" THEN  PRINT  CHR$ (7): GOTO
     290
300  VTAB 15: INPUT "ENTER REACTANCE OF C(-
     ) OR L(+) IN ohm > ";F$:G =  VAL (F$):
     IF G = 0 AND F$ < > "0" THEN  PRINT
     CHR$ (7): GOTO 300
310  IF G = 0 AND F = 0 THEN  PRINT  CHR$ (
     7): GOTO 300
320  IF G = 0 THEN H = 0:I = F: GOTO 350
330  IF F = 0 THEN I = 9999999:H = G: GOTO
     350
340  I = F + ((G ^ 2) / F):H = G + ((F ^ 2) /
     G):I =  INT (I * 1000 + .5) / 1000:H =
     INT (H * 1000 + .5) / 1000:G$ =  STR$
     (I)
350  IF I = 9999999 THEN G$ = ">>>>>"
360  VTAB 17: PRINT "EQUIVALENT PARALLEL NE
     TWORK:": PRINT "-----------------------
     ------": VTAB 19: IF H > 0 THEN C$ = "
     COIL"
370  IF H < 0 THEN C$ = "CAPACITOR"
380  PRINT "VALUE OF PARALLEL RESISTOR = ";
     G$;" ohm": PRINT "REACTANCE OF ";C$;"
     = ";H;" ohm";: IF B = 0 GOTO 420
390  IF H > 0 THEN J = H / (2 * 3.14159 * B
     ):D =  INT (100 * J + .5) / 100:H$ = "
     uH":I$ = "        INDUCTOR VALUE = "
400  IF H < 0 THEN K =  - 1000000 / (2 * 3.
     14159 * H * B):D =  INT (K * 100 + .5)
     / 100:H$ = " pF":I$ = "       CAPACITO
     R VALUE = "
410  PRINT I$;D;H$;
420  GOTO 550
430  PRINT : VTAB 12: CALL  - 868: PRINT "P
     ARALLEL TO SERIAL RL/RC CIRCUIT CONVER
     SION.": PRINT "======================="
     ====================="
440  VTAB 14: INPUT "ENTER RESISTANCE VALUE
      (ohm) > ";G$:I =  VAL (G$): IF I = 0 AND
     G$ < > "0" THEN  PRINT  CHR$ (7): GOTO
     440
450  IF I = 0 THEN  PRINT  CHR$ (7): GOTO 4
     40
460  VTAB 15: INPUT "ENTER REACTANCE OF C(-
     ) OR L(+) IN ohm > ";J$:H =  VAL (J$):
     IF H = 0 AND J$ < > "0" THEN  PRINT
     CHR$ (7): GOTO 460
470  IF H = 0 THEN G = 0:F = I: GOTO 490
480  F = (I * (H ^ 2)) / ((I ^ 2) + (H ^ 2))
     :G = ((I ^ 2) * H) / ((I ^ 2) + (H ^ 2
     )):F =  INT (F * 1000 + .5) / 1000:G =
     INT (G * 1000 + .5) / 1000
490  VTAB 17: PRINT "EQUIVALENT SERIES NETW
     ORK:": PRINT "-----------------------
     --": VTAB 19: IF G > 0 THEN C$ = "COIL
     "
500  IF G < 0 THEN C$ = "CAPACITOR"
510  PRINT "VALUE OF SERIES RESISTOR = ";F;
     " ohm": PRINT "REACTANCE OF ";C$;" = "
     ;G;" ohm";: IF B = 0 GOTO 550
520  IF G > 0 THEN J = G / (2 * 3.14159 * B
     ):D =  INT (100 * J + .5) / 100:H$ = "
     uH":I$ = "        INDUCTOR VALUE = "
530  IF G < 0 THEN K =  - 1000000 / (2 * 3.
     14159 * G * B):D =  INT (K * 100 + .5)
     / 100:H$ = " pF":I$ = "       CAPACITO
     R VALUE = "
540  PRINT I$;D;H$;
550  POKE 35,23: VTAB 22: PRINT :L = 1: POKE
     36,0: PRINT "          ENTER >>N<< F
     OR NEW RUN        ENTER >>E<< FOR EXIT"
     ;: VTAB 23: POKE 36,38: GET D$: POKE 3
     5,23: VTAB 22: PRINT : POKE 36,0: CALL
      - 868: POKE 35,20: IF D$ = "E" OR D$ =
     "e" THEN  HOME : PRINT  CHR$ (13) + CHR$
     (4);"RUN MENU"
560  HOME : GOTO 100
```

```
10   REM name: SHUNT INPUT L NETWORK ITERATI
     ON
20   REM by: John Devoldere, ON4UN
30   ONERR  GOTO 50
40   GOTO 60
50   VTAB 14: POKE 36,34: PRINT "FATAL ERROR
     ": PRINT  CHR$ (7): FOR A = 1 TO 5000:
     NEXT : GOTO 30
60   CLEAR : HOME : PRINT  CHR$ (13) + CHR$
     (4);"PR#3":B =  ATN (1) * 4: PRINT : POKE
     36,20: PRINT "SHUNT INPUT L-NETWORK IT
     ERATION.";: POKE 36,71: PRINT "by ON4U
     N": PRINT "----------------------------
     ----------------------------------------
     ---------------"
70   PRINT "THIS PROGRAM ALLOWS YOU TO SELEC
     T THE INPUT IMPEDANCE OF A SHUNT-INPUT
             L NETWORK, GIVEN THE OUTPUT
     PARAMETERS AND THE REQUIRED INPUT VOLT
     AGE MAGNITUDE.";
80   PRINT "THE METHOD IS ITERATIVE AND THE
     VALUES WILL BE DISPLAYED FOR INPUT IMP
     EDANCE     INCREMENTS OF 1 OHM.": PRINT
     "THE LOWER LIMIT AS WELL AS THE INCREM
     ENTS CAN BE CHANGED BY THE USER FOR
            IMPROVED RESOLUTION."
90   PRINT "-----------------------------------
     --------------------------------------
     ---------": VTAB 23: PRINT "----------
     --------------------------------------
     ---------------------------"
100  VTAB 14: INPUT "TARGET INPUT VOLTAGE M
     AGNITUDE > ";A$:C =  VAL (A$): IF C =
     0 THEN  PRINT  CHR$ (7): GOTO 100
110  IF C < 0 THEN  PRINT  CHR$ (7): GOTO 1
     00
120  VTAB 15: INPUT "TARGET INPUT VOLTAGE A
     NGLE      > ";B$:D =  VAL (B$): IF D =
     0 AND B$ <  > "0" THEN  PRINT  CHR$ (7
     ): GOTO 120
130  VTAB 17: INPUT "LOAD IMPEDANCE REAL PA
     RT > ";C$:E =  VAL (C$): IF E = 0 THEN
     PRINT  CHR$ (7): GOTO 130
140  IF E < 0 THEN F =  INT (E)
150  IF E > 0 THEN F =  INT (E)
160  IF E > 0 THEN G = 1
170  IF E < 0 THEN G =  - 1
180  VTAB 18: INPUT "LOAD IMPEDANCE IMAG PA
     RT > ";D$:H =  VAL (D$): IF H = 0 AND
     D$ <  > "0" THEN  PRINT  CHR$ (7): GOTO
     180
190  I =  SQR (E ^ 2 + H ^ 2):J =  ATN (H /
     E):J = J * 180 / B: IF E < K AND H > 0
     THEN J = J + 180
200  IF E < K AND H < 0 THEN J = J - 180
210  VTAB 20: INPUT "LOAD VOLTAGE MAGNITUDE
     > ";E$:L =  VAL (E$): IF L = 0 THEN  PRINT
     CHR$ (7): GOTO 210
220  IF L < 0 THEN  PRINT  CHR$ (7): GOTO 2
     10
230  IF L > C THEN  PRINT  CHR$ (7): VTAB 2
     4: PRINT "THIS TRANSFORMATION REQUIRES
     A SERIES INPUT L NETWORK. PRESS RETUR
     N.";: GET F$: HOME : PRINT  CHR$ (13) +
     CHR$ (4);"RUN MENU"
240  VTAB 21: INPUT "LOAD VOLTAGE ANGLE
     > ";G$:M =  VAL (G$): IF M = 0 AND G$
     <  > "0" THEN  PRINT  CHR$ (7): GOTO
     240
250  N = L *  COS (M * B / 180):O = L *  SIN
     (M * B / 180):P = ((N * E) + (O * H)) /
     (E ^ 2 + H ^ 2):Q = ((O * E) - (N * H)
     ) / (E ^ 2 + H ^ 2):R =  SQR (P ^ 2 +
     Q ^ 2):S =  ATN (Q / P):S = S * 180 /
     B: IF P = 0 THEN T = 90: GOTO 270
260  T =  ATN (Q / P):T = T * 180 / B
270  IF P < K AND Q > 0 THEN T = T + 180
280  IF P < K AND Q < 0 THEN T = T - 180
290  HOME : POKE 36,24: PRINT "SHUNT INPUT
     L-NETWORK DESIGN";: POKE 36,71: PRINT
     "by ON4UN": PRINT "-------------------
     ----------------------------------------
     ---------------------": PRINT "
             REAL PART     IMAG. PART
        ABSOL. VALUE        ANGLE"
300  PRINT "     ---------     -----------      ----
     -": PRINT "IMPEDANCE (ohm)=  ";: POKE
     36,21: PRINT E;: POKE 36,36: PRINT H;:
     POKE 36,50: PRINT  INT (I * 10000 + .
     5) / 10000;: POKE 36,65: PRINT  INT (J
     * 10000 + .5) / 10000
310  PRINT "CURRENT (Amp) = ";: POKE 36,21
     : PRINT  INT (10000 * P + .5) / 10000;
     : POKE 36,36: PRINT  INT (10000 * Q +
     .5) / 10000;: POKE 36,50: PRINT  INT (
     R * 10000 + .5) / 10000;: POKE 36,65: PRINT
     INT (T * 10000 + .5) / 10000
320  PRINT "VOLTAGE (Volt) = ";: POKE 36,21
     : PRINT  INT (10000 * N + .5) / 10000;
     : POKE 36,36: PRINT  INT (10000 * O +
     .5) / 10000;: POKE 36,50: PRINT  INT (
     L * 10000 + .5) / 10000;: POKE 36,65: PRINT
     INT (M * 10000 + .5) / 10000: PRINT "
     ----------------------------------------
     ----------------------------------------
     ---"
330  PRINT "TARGET INPUT VOLTAGE =>  MAGNIT
     UDE = ";C;" Volt. ANGLE = ";D;" deg.":
     PRINT "Z-in";: POKE 36,6: PRINT "X-se
     r";: POKE 36,14: PRINT "X-par";: POKE
     36,23: PRINT "V-in";: POKE 36,32: PRINT
     "angle";: POKE 36,41: PRINT "X-ser";: POKE
     36,50: PRINT "X-par";: POKE 36,59: PRINT
     "V-in";: POKE 36,68: PRINT "angle"
340  PRINT "----";: POKE 36,6: PRINT "-----
     ";: POKE 36,14: PRINT "-----";: POKE 3
     6,23: PRINT "----";: POKE 36,32: PRINT
     "-----";: POKE 36,41: PRINT "-----";: POKE
     36,50: PRINT "-----";: POKE 36,59: PRINT
     "----";: POKE 36,68: PRINT "-----": PRINT
     : VTAB 23: PRINT "--------------------
     ----------------------------------------
     --------------------"
350  VTAB 24: PRINT "  CONTROL SCROLLING >>
     >CTRL-S<<<          NEW ITERATION >>>N<<<
           EXIT >>>E<<<";: POKE 35,22: POKE
     34,11: HOME
360  U = F
370  U = U + G: IF  PEEK ( - 16384) = 206 OR
     PEEK ( - 16384) = 238 THEN  HOME : GOTO
     480
380  IF  PEEK ( - 16384) = 197 OR  PEEK ( -
     16384) = 229 THEN  GET F$: HOME : PRINT
     CHR$ (13) + CHR$ (4);"RUN MENU"
390  POKE - 16368,0:V =  - H +  SQR (E * (
     U - E)):W =  - H -  SQR (E * (U - E)):
     X =  - (E ^ 2 + (V + H) ^ 2) / (V + H)
     :Y =  - (E ^ 2 + (W + H) ^ 2) / (W + H
     ):Z = N - V * Q:A1 = O + V * P:B1 =  SQR
     (Z ^ 2 + A1 ^ 2):C1 =  ATN (A1 / Z):C1
     = C1 * (180 / B): IF Z < 0 AND A1 > 0
     THEN C1 = C1 + 180
400  IF Z < 0 AND A1 < 0 THEN C1 = C1 - 180
410  D1 = Z / U:E1 = A1 / U:F1 =  SQR (D1 ^
     2 + E1 ^ 2):G1 =  ATN (E1 / D1):G1 = G
     1 * (180 / B): IF D1 < 0 AND E1 > 0 THEN
     G1 = G1 + 180
420  IF D1 < 0 AND E1 < 0 THEN G1 = G1 - 18
     0
```

```
430   PRINT  INT (U * 100 + .5) / 100;:: POKE
      36,6: PRINT  INT (V * 100 + .5) / 100;
      : POKE 36,14: PRINT  INT (X * 100 + .5
      ) / 100;:: POKE 36,23: PRINT  INT (B1 *
      100 + .5) / 100;:: POKE 36,32: PRINT  INT
      (100 * C1 + .5) / 100;::Z = N - W * Q:A
      1 = O + W * P:B1 = SQR (Z ^ 2 + A1 ^
      2):C1 = ATN (A1 / Z):C1 = C1 * 180 /
      B: IF Z < 0 AND A1 > 0 THEN C1 = C1 +
      180
440   IF Z < 0 AND A1 < 0 THEN C1 = C1 - 180

450 D1 = Z / U:E1 = A1 / U:F1 = SQR (D1 ^
      2 + E1 ^ 2):G1 = ATN (E1 / D1):G1 = G
      1 * (180 / B): IF D1 < 0 AND E1 > 0 THEN
      G1 = G1 + 180
460   IF D1 < 0 AND E1 < 0 THEN G1 = G1 - 18
      0
470   POKE 36,41: PRINT  INT (W * 100 + .5) /
      100;:: POKE 36,50: PRINT  INT (Y * 100 +
      .5) / 100;:: POKE 36,59: PRINT  INT (B1
      * 100 + .5) / 100;:: POKE 36,68: PRINT
      INT (100 * C1 + .5) / 100: GOTO 370

480   GET F$: HOME
490   VTAB 12: VTAB 12: INPUT "NEW LOWER LIM
      IT > ";H$: VTAB 14: CALL  - 868:F = VAL
      (H$): IF F = 0 AND H$ < > "0" THEN  PRINT
      CHR$ (7): GOTO 490
500   IF E > 0 AND F < = E THEN  PRINT CHR$
      (7);:: PRINT "LOWER LIMIT MUST BE LARGE
      R THAN :";E: GOTO 490
510   IF E < 0 AND F > = E THEN  PRINT  CHR$
      (7);:: PRINT "LOWER LIMIT MUST BE SMALL
      ER THAN :";E: GOTO 490
520   PRINT
530   VTAB 14: INPUT "NEW INCREMENT (MUST BE
      LARGER THAN 0.01) > ";I$:G = VAL (I$
      ): IF E < 0 THEN G =  - G
540   IF G = 0 AND I$ < > "0" THEN  PRINT CHR$
      (7): GOTO 530
550   IF  ABS (G) < .01 THEN  PRINT  CHR$ (7
      ): GOTO 530
560 F = F - G: HOME : GOTO 360
```

```
10   REM name: SERIES INPUT L NETWORK ITERAT
     ION
20   REM by: John Devoldere, ON4UN
30   ONERR  GOTO 50
40   GOTO 60
50   VTAB 13: POKE 36,33: PRINT "FATAL ERROR
     ": PRINT  CHR$ (7): FOR A = 1 TO 5000:
     NEXT : GOTO 30
60   CLEAR : HOME : PRINT  CHR$ (13) + CHR$
     (4);"PR#3":B =  ATN (1) * 4: PRINT : POKE
     36,20: PRINT "SERIES INPUT L-NETWORK I
     TERATION.";: POKE 36,71: PRINT "by ON4
     UN": PRINT "-------------------------
     ----------------"
70   PRINT "THIS PROGRAM ALLOWS YOU TO SELEC
     T THE INPUT IMPEDANCE OF A SERIES-INPU
     T        L NETWORK, GIVEN THE OUTPUT
     PARAMETERS AND THE REQUIRED INPUT VOLT
     AGE MAGNITUDE.";
80   PRINT "THE METHOD IS ITERATIVE AND THE
     VALUES WILL BE DISPLAYED FOR INPUT IMP
     EDANCE   INCREMENTS OF 1 OHM.": PRINT
     "THE LOWER LIMIT AS WELL AS THE INCREM
     ENTS CAN BE CHANGED BY THE USER FOR
     IMPROVED RESOLUTION."
90   PRINT "-------------------------------
     ---------": VTAB 23: PRINT "----------
     -------------------------------
     ----------------------------"
100  VTAB 14: INPUT "TARGET INPUT VOLTAGE M
     AGNITUDE > ";A$:C =  VAL (A$): IF C =
     0 AND A$ <  > "0" THEN  PRINT  CHR$ (7
     ): GOTO 100
110  IF C = 0 THEN  PRINT  CHR$ (7): GOTO 1
     00
120  IF C < 0 THEN  PRINT  CHR$ (7): GOTO 1
     00
130  VTAB 15: INPUT "TARGET INPUT VOLTAGE A
     NGLE    > ";B$:D =  VAL (B$): IF D =
     0 AND B$ <  > "0" THEN  PRINT  CHR$ (7
     ): GOTO 130
140  VTAB 17: INPUT "LOAD IMPEDANCE REAL PA
     RT > ";C$:E =  VAL (C$): IF E = 0 AND
     C$ <  > "0" THEN  PRINT  CHR$ (7): GOTO
     140
150  IF E = 0 THEN  PRINT  CHR$ (7): GOTO 1
     40
160  F =  INT (E): IF F > 0 THEN G =  - 1
170  IF F < 0 THEN G = 1
180  IF F > 0 AND F < 2 THEN G =  - .1
190  IF F < 0 AND F > 2 THEN G = .1
200  VTAB 18: INPUT "LOAD IMPEDANCE IMAG PA
     RT > ";D$:H =  VAL (D$): IF H = 0 AND
     D$ <  > "0" THEN  PRINT  CHR$ (7): GOTO
     200
210  I =  SQR (E ^ 2 + H ^ 2):J =  ATN (H /
     E):J = J * 180 / B: IF E < K AND H > 0
     THEN J = J + 180
220  IF E < K AND H < 0 THEN J = J - 180
230  VTAB 20: INPUT "LOAD VOLTAGE MAGNITUDE
     > ";E$:L =  VAL (E$): IF L < 0 THEN  PRINT
     CHR$ (7): GOTO 230
240  IF L = 0 AND E$ <  > "0" THEN  PRINT  CHR$
     (7): GOTO 230
250  IF L = 0 THEN  PRINT  CHR$ (7): GOTO 2
     30
260  IF  SGN (C) <  > SGN (L) THEN  PRINT
     CHR$ (7);: PRINT "SIGN OR LOAD AND IN
     PUT VOLTAGE MUST BE THE SAME": GOTO 23
     0
270  IF L < C THEN  PRINT  CHR$ (7): PRINT
     "FOR THIS TRANSFORMATION YOU NEED A SH
     UNT INPUT L NETWORK": VTAB 24: PRINT "
                       HIT ANY KEY TO GO
     TO MENU
     ";: GET F$: HOME : PRINT  CHR$ (13) +
     CHR$ (4);"RUN MENU"
280  VTAB 21: CALL  - 868: INPUT "LOAD VOLT
     AGE ANGLE   > ";G$:M =  VAL (G$): IF
     M = 0 AND G$ <  > "0" THEN  PRINT  CHR$
     (7): GOTO 280
290  N = L *  COS (M * B / 180):O = L *  SIN
     (M * B / 180):P = ((N * E) + (O * H)) /
     (E ^ 2 + H ^ 2):Q = ((O * E) - (N * H)
     ) / (E ^ 2 + H ^ 2):R =  SQR (P ^ 2 +
     Q ^ 2):S =  ATN (Q / P):S = S * 180 /
     3.14159:T =  ATN (Q / P):T = T * 180 /
     B: IF P < K AND Q > 0 THEN T = T + 180
300  IF P < K AND Q < 0 THEN T = T - 180
310  HOME : POKE 36,24: PRINT "SERIES INPUT
     L-NETWORK DESIGN";: POKE 36,71: PRINT
     "by ON4UN": PRINT "-------------------
     ---------------------------------------
     ----------------------": PRINT "
                     REAL PART    IMAG. PART
          ABSOL. VALUE       ANGLE"
320  PRINT "  ---------    ------------    ----
     -": PRINT "IMPEDANCE (ohm)= ";: POKE
     36,21: PRINT E;: POKE 36,36: PRINT H;:
     POKE 36,50: PRINT  INT (I * 10000 + .
     5) / 10000;: POKE 36,65: PRINT  INT (J
     * 10000 + .5) / 10000
330  PRINT "CURRENT (Amp)  = ";: POKE 36,21
     : PRINT  INT (10000 * P + .5) / 10000;
     : POKE 36,36: PRINT  INT (10000 * Q +
     .5) / 10000;: POKE 36,50: PRINT  INT (
     R * 10000 + .5) / 10000;: POKE 36,65: PRINT
     INT (T * 10000 + .5) / 10000
340  PRINT "VOLTAGE (Volt) = ";: POKE 36,21
     : PRINT  INT (10000 * N + .5) / 10000;
     : POKE 36,36: PRINT  INT (10000 * O +
     .5) / 10000;: POKE 36,50: PRINT  INT (
     L * 10000 + .5) / 10000;: POKE 36,65: PRINT
     INT (M * 10000 + .5) / 10000: PRINT "
     ---------------------------------------
     ---------------------------------------
     ---"
350  PRINT "TARGET INPUT VOLTAGE =>  MAGNIT
     UDE = ";C;" Volt. ANGLE = ";D;" deg.":
     PRINT "Z-in";: POKE 36,6: PRINT "X-se
     r";: POKE 36,14: PRINT "X-par";: POKE
     36,23: PRINT "V-in";: POKE 36,32: PRINT
     "angle";: POKE 36,41: PRINT "X-ser";: POKE
     36,50: PRINT "X-par";: POKE 36,59: PRINT
     "V-in";: POKE 36,68: PRINT "angle"
360  PRINT "----";: POKE 36,6: PRINT "-----
     ";: POKE 36,14: PRINT "-----";: POKE 3
     6,23: PRINT "----";: POKE 36,32: PRINT
     "-----";: POKE 36,41: PRINT "-----";: POKE
     36,50: PRINT "-----";: POKE 36,59: PRINT
     "-----";: POKE 36,68: PRINT "-----": PRINT
     : VTAB 23: PRINT "--------------------
     ---------------------------------------
     ----------------------"
370  VTAB 24: PRINT "  CONTROL SCROLLING >>
     >CTRL-S<<<        NEW ITERATION >>>N<<<
     EXIT    >>>E<<<";: POKE 35,22: POKE
     34,11: HOME
380  U = F
390  U = U + G: IF E > 0 AND U = < 0 THEN  VTAB
     24: CALL  - 868: POKE 36,28: PRINT "HI
     T ANY KEY TO CONTINUE ";: GET F$: HOME
     : GOTO 540
400  IF E < 0 AND U = > 0 THEN  POKE 36,28
     : PRINT "HIT ANY KEY TO CONTINUE ";: GET
     F$: HOME : GOTO 540
410  IF  PEEK ( - 16384) = 206 OR  PEEK ( -
     16384) = 238 THEN  HOME : GOTO 520
420  IF  PEEK ( - 16384) = 197 OR  PEEK ( -
     16384) = 229 THEN  GET F$: HOME : PRINT
     CHR$ (13) +  CHR$ (4);"RUN MENU"
```

```
430  POKE  - 16368,0:V = (( - U * H) + SQR
     (U * E * (E ^ 2 + H ^ 2 - U * E))) / (
     U - E):W = (( - U * H) - SQR (U * E *
     (E ^ 2 + H ^ 2 - U * E))) / (U - E):X =
     ( - V * (E ^ 2 + H * (V + H))) / (E ^
     2 + (V + H) ^ 2):Y = ( - W * (E ^ 2 +
     H * (W + H))) / (E ^ 2 + (W + H) ^ 2):
     Z = (O * V / V ^ 2) + P:A1 = ( - (N *
     V) / V ^ 2) + Q:B1 = Z * U:C1 = A1 * U
     :D1 = SQR (B1 ^ 2 + C1 ^ 2): IF B1 =
     0 THEN E1 = 90: GOTO 450
440  E1 = ATN (C1 / B1):E1 = E1 * 180 / B
450  IF B1 < 0 AND C1 > 0 THEN E1 = E1 + 18
     0
460  IF B1 < 0 AND C1 < 0 THEN E1 = E1 - 18
     0
470  PRINT  INT (U * 100 + .5) / 100;: POKE
     36,6: PRINT  INT (X * 100 + .5) / 100;
     : POKE 36,14: PRINT  INT (V * 100 + .5
     ) / 100;: POKE 36,23: PRINT  INT (D1 *
     100 + .5) / 100;: POKE 36,32: PRINT  INT
     (100 * E1 + .5) / 100;:Z = (O * W / W ^
     2) + P:A1 = ( - (N * W) / W ^ 2) + Q:B
     1 = Z * U:C1 = A1 * U:D1 = SQR (B1 ^
     2 + C1 ^ 2): IF B1 = 0 THEN E1 = 90: GOTO
     490
480  E1 = ATN (C1 / B1):E1 = E1 * 180 / B
490  IF B1 < 0 AND C1 > 0 THEN E1 = E1 + 18
     0
500  IF B1 < 0 AND C1 < 0 THEN E1 = E1 - 18
     0
510  POKE 36,41: PRINT  INT (Y * 100 + .5) /
     100;: POKE 36,50: PRINT  INT (W * 100 +
     .5) / 100;: POKE 36,59: PRINT  INT (D1
     * 100 + .5) / 100;: POKE 36,68: PRINT
     INT (100 * E1 + .5) / 100: GOTO 390
520  GET F$: HOME
530  VTAB 12
540  VTAB 24: PRINT "   CONTROL SCROLLING >
     >>CTRL-S<<<      NEW ITERATION >>>N<<<
          EXIT >>>E<<<";: HOME
550  VTAB 12: INPUT "NEW LOWER LIMIT > ";H$
     : IF H$ = "E" THEN  PRINT  CHR$ (13) +
     CHR$ (4);"RUN MENU"
560  F = VAL (H$): IF F = 0 AND H$ < > "0"
     THEN  PRINT  CHR$ (7): GOTO 530
570  IF  SGN (F) < >  SGN (E) THEN  PRINT
     CHR$ (7);: PRINT "SIGN LOAD AND INPUT
     IMPEDANCE MUST BE THE SAME": GOTO 550
580  VTAB 13: CALL  - 868: IF E > 0 AND F >
     = E THEN  PRINT  CHR$ (7);: PRINT "LO
     WER LIMIT MUST BE LESS THAN ";E;" ohm"
     : GOTO 550
590  IF E < 0 AND F < = E THEN  PRINT  CHR$
     (7);: PRINT "LOWER LIMIT MUST BE LESS
     THAN ";E;" ohm": GOTO 550
600  VTAB 13: INPUT "NEW INCREMENT > ";I$:G
     = VAL (I$): IF G < .01 THEN  PRINT  CHR$
     (7);: PRINT "INCREMENT MUST BE LARGER
     THAN 0.01": GOTO 600
610  IF E < 0 GOTO 630
620  G =  - G
630  F = F - G: HOME : GOTO 380
```

```
10   REM name: L-NETWORK
20   REM by: John Devoldere, ON4UN
30   POKE 34,0: ONERR  GOTO 50
40   GOTO 60
50   PRINT  CHR$ (7): HOME : VTAB 14: POKE 3
     6,34: PRINT "FATAL ERROR": FOR A = 1 TO
     5000: NEXT : GOTO 30
60   CLEAR : HOME : PRINT  CHR$ (13) + CHR$
     (4);"PR#3":B =  ATN (1) * 4: PRINT "
                        L NETWORK DESI
     GN";: POKE 36,71: PRINT "by ON4UN": PRINT
     "-----------------------------------------
     -----------------------------------------
     ----"
70   PRINT "THIS PROGRAM ALLOWS YOU TO DESIG
     N AN L-NETWORK GIVEN THE OUTPUT IMPEDA
     NCE        (a+bj) AND THE INPUT IMPEDAN
     CE (resistive). ADDITIONALLY THE OUTPU
     T VOLTAGE MAY"
80   PRINT "BE SPECIFIED, IN WHICH CASE THE
     INPUT VOLTAGE WILL BE CALCULATED AS WE
     LL AS THE INPUT AND OUTPUT CURRENT.": PRINT
     "THE COMPUTATION ALWAYS YIELDS AT LEAS
     T TWO SOLUTIONS. ALL SOLUTIONS WILL BE
              SHOWN."
90   PRINT "-------------------------------------
     ------------------------------------
     ----------": VTAB 23: PRINT "----------
     -------------------------------------
     ----------------------------": POKE
     35,22: POKE 34,10: HOME
100  VTAB 12: INPUT "DESIGN FREQUENCY (IN M
     Hz) > ";A$:C =  VAL (A$): IF C =  < 0 THEN
     PRINT  CHR$ (7): GOTO 100
110  VTAB 14: INPUT "INPUT IMPEDANCE > ";B$
     :D =  VAL (B$): IF D = 0 THEN  PRINT  CHR$
     (7): GOTO 110
120  VTAB 16: INPUT "LOAD IMPEDANCE REAL PA
     RT > ";C$:E =  VAL (C$): IF  SGN (D) <
     >  SGN (E) THEN  PRINT  CHR$ (7);: PRINT
     "SIGN OF INPUT AND OUTPUT IMPEDANCE MU
     ST BE THE SAME": GOTO 120
130  CALL  - 868: IF E = 0 THEN  PRINT  CHR$
     (7): GOTO 120
140  IF D < E AND E < 0 GOTO 180
150  IF E > D THEN  GOTO 300
160  IF E < D AND D < 0 GOTO 300
170  IF E = D THEN  PRINT  CHR$ (7): PRINT
     "REAL PART IMPEDANCES ARE IDENTICAL! U
     SE >>SERIES IMPEDANCE<< OR >>PARALLEL
     IMPE-DANCE<< PROGRAMS.  HIT ANY KEY TO
     CONTINUE.": GET D$: PRINT  CHR$ (13) +
     CHR$ (4);"RUN MENU"
180  VTAB 17: CALL  - 868: INPUT "LOAD IMPE
     DANCE IMAG PART > ";E$:F =  VAL (E$): IF
     F = 0 AND E$ <  > "0" THEN  PRINT  CHR$
     (7): GOTO 180
190  G =  SQR (E ^ 2 + F ^ 2):H =  ATN (F /
     E):H = H * 180 / B: IF E < I AND F > 0
     THEN H = H + 180
200  IF E < I AND F < 0 THEN H = H - 180
210  VTAB 18: INPUT "LOAD VOLTAGE MAGNITUDE
     > ";F$:J =  VAL (F$): IF J =  < 0 THEN
     PRINT  CHR$ (7): GOTO 210
220  VTAB 19: INPUT "LOAD VOLTAGE ANGLE
     > ";G$:K =  VAL (G$): IF K = 0 AND G$
     <  > "0" THEN  PRINT  CHR$ (7): GOTO
     220
230  POKE 34,3: HOME :L = J *  COS (K * B /
     180):M = J *  SIN (K * B / 180):N = ((
     L * E) + (M * F)) / (E ^ 2 + F ^ 2):O =
     ((M * E) - (L * F)) / (E ^ 2 + F ^ 2):
     P =  SQR (N ^ 2 + O ^ 2): IF N = 0 THEN
     Q = 90: GOTO 250
240  Q =  ATN (O / N):Q = Q * 180 / B: IF N =
     0 THEN R = 90: GOTO 260
250  R =  ATN (O / N):R = R * 180 / B
260  IF N < I AND O > 0 THEN R = R + 180
270  IF N < I AND O < 0 THEN R = R - 180
280  IF N < I AND O = 0 THEN R = 180
```

```
290  PRINT :S =  - F +  SQR (E * (D - E)):T
     =  - F -  SQR (E * (D - E)):U =  - (E
     ^ 2 + (S + F) ^ 2) / (S + F):V =  - (
     E ^ 2 + (T + F) ^ 2) / (T + F):W = T: GOSUB
     790: POKE 34,0: HOME : POKE 36,10: PRINT
     "THE NETWORK HAS THE SHUNT ELEMENT ACR
     OSS THE RESISTIVE INPUT.": GOSUB 520: GOSUB
     550:T = S:V = U:W = S: GOSUB 790: GOSUB
     550
300  IF E < D AND (E ^ 2 + F ^ 2 - D * E) >
     = I AND F <  > 0 THEN  GOSUB 500: GOTO
     450
310  IF E = D THEN  PRINT  CHR$ (7): PRINT
     "REAL PART IMPEDANCES ARE IDENTICAL!":
     PRINT "TUNE OUT REACTANCE WITH COIL O
     R CAPACITOR. USE PROGRAM FOR DESIGNING
     SERIES OR PARALLEL IMPEDANCE NETWORKS.
     ": GET D$: HOME : PRINT  CHR$ (13) +  CHR$
     (4);"RUN MENU"
320  IF E < D AND E > 0 THEN  GOSUB 510: POKE
     36,65: GET D$: GOTO 470
330  IF E > D AND E < 0 THEN  GOSUB 510: POKE
     36,65: GET D$: GOTO 470
340  VTAB 17: CALL  - 868: INPUT "LOAD IMPE
     DANCE IMAG PART > ";E$:F =  VAL (E$): IF
     F = I AND E$ <  > "0" THEN  PRINT  CHR$
     (7);: GOTO 340
350  G =  SQR (E ^ 2 + F ^ 2):H =  ATN (F /
     E):H = H * 180 / B: IF E < I AND F > 0
     THEN H = H + 180
360  IF E < I AND F < 0 THEN H = H - 180
370  VTAB 18: INPUT "LOAD VOLTAGE MAGNITUDE
     > ";F$:J =  VAL (F$): IF J <  = 0 THEN
     PRINT  CHR$ (7);: GOTO 370
380  VTAB 19: INPUT "LOAD VOLTAGE ANGLE
     > ";G$:K =  VAL (G$): IF K = 0 AND G$
     <  > "0" THEN  PRINT  CHR$ (7);: GOTO
     380
390  POKE 34,3: HOME :L = J *  COS (K * B /
     180):M = J *  SIN (K * B / 180):N = ((
     L * E) + (M * F)) / (E ^ 2 + F ^ 2):O =
     ((M * E) - (L * F)) / (E ^ 2 + F ^ 2):
     P =  SQR (N ^ 2 + O ^ 2):Q =  ATN (O /
     N):Q = Q * 180 / B: IF N = 0 THEN X =
     90: GOTO 410
400  R =  ATN (O / N):R = R * 180 / B
410  IF N < I AND O > 0 THEN R = R + 180
420  IF N < I AND O < 0 THEN R = R - 180
430  IF N < I AND O = 0 THEN R = 180
440  PRINT
450  U = (( - D * F) +  SQR (D * E * (E ^ 2 +
     F ^ 2 - D * E))) / (D - E):V = (( - D *
     F) -  SQR (D * E * (E ^ 2 + F ^ 2 - D *
     E))) / (D - E):S = ( - U * (E ^ 2 + F *
     (U + F))) / (E ^ 2 + (U + F) ^ 2):T = (
     - V * (E ^ 2 + F * (V + F))) / (E ^
     2 + (V + F) ^ 2):Y = V: GOSUB 780: POKE
     34,0: HOME : POKE 36,5: PRINT "THE NET
     WORK HAS THE SERIES ELEMENT CONNECTED
     TO THE RESITIVE INPUT.": GOSUB 520
460  GOSUB 550:T = S:V = U:Y = U: GOSUB 780
     : GOSUB 550: VTAB 24: PRINT "
         MORE CALCULATIONS  >>C<<
           EXIT  >>E<<";: VTAB 24: POKE 36,67
     : GET D$
470  IF D$ = "E" OR D$ = "e" GOTO 490
480  GOTO 30
490  HOME : PRINT  CHR$ (13) +  CHR$ (4);"R
     UN MENU"
500  VTAB 24: CALL  - 958: VTAB 24: CALL  -
     958: POKE 36,0: PRINT "THERE ARE TWO M
     ORE SOLUTIONS. HIT ANY KEY TO CONTINUE
     .";: VTAB 24: POKE 36,55: GET D$: HOME

510  VTAB 24: POKE 36,0: CALL  - 958: PRINT
     "           MORE CALCULATIONS  >>C<<
                EXIT  >>E<<";: RETURN
```

```
520  PRINT "-------------------------------
     ------------------------------------
     -----------": PRINT "OUTPUT
          REAL PART   IMAG. PART    ABSOL. VA
     LUE       ANGLE": PRINT "------
          ----------   ----------    -----
     -------     -----"
530  PRINT "IMPEDANCE (ohm)=  ";: POKE 36,2
     1: PRINT E;: POKE 36,36: PRINT F;: POKE
     36,50: PRINT  INT (G * 10000 + .5) / 1
     0000;: POKE 36,65: PRINT  INT (H * 100
     00 + .5) / 10000: PRINT "CURRENT (Amp)
        = ";: POKE 36,21: PRINT  INT (10000 *
     N + .5) / 10000;: POKE 36,36: PRINT  INT
     (10000 * O + .5) / 10000;: POKE 36,50:
      PRINT  INT (P * 10000 + .5) / 10000;:
      POKE 36,65: PRINT  INT (R * 10000 + .
     5) / 10000
540  PRINT "VOLTAGE (Volt) = ";: POKE 36,21
     : PRINT  INT (10000 * L + .5) / 10000;
     : POKE 36,36: PRINT  INT (10000 * M +
     .5) / 10000;: POKE 36,50: PRINT  INT (
     J * 10000 + .5) / 10000;: POKE 36,65: PRINT
      INT (K * 10000 + .5) / 10000: RETURN

550  PRINT "-------------------------------
     ------------------------------------
     -----------": PRINT "IMPEDANCE SERIES A
     RM = "; INT (100 * T + .5) / 100;" ohm
     ";: IF T > 0 THEN Z = T / (2 * B * C)
560  IF T < 0 THEN Z =  - 1000000 / (2 * B *
     T * C)
570  IF T > 0 THEN  POKE 36,40: PRINT "==>>
      INDUCTANCE = "; INT (Z * 100 + .5) /
     100;" uH"
580  IF T < 0 THEN  POKE 36,40: PRINT "==>>
      CAPACITANCE= "; INT (Z * 100 + .5) /
     100;" pF"
590  IF T = 0 THEN  PRINT
600  PRINT "IMPEDANCE PARALLEL ARM = "; INT
     (100 * V + .5) / 100;" ohm";: IF V > 0
     THEN A1 = V / (2 * B * C)
610  IF V < 0 THEN A1 =  - 1000000 / (2 * B
     * V * C)
620  IF V > 0 THEN  POKE 36,40: PRINT "==>>
      INDUCTANCE = "; INT (A1 * 100 + .5) /
     100;" uH"

630  IF V < 0 THEN  POKE 36,40: PRINT "==>>
      CAPACITANCE= "; INT (A1 * 100 + .5) /
     100;" pF"
640  IF V = 0 THEN  PRINT
650  B1 =  SQR (C1 ^ 2 + D1 ^ 2): IF C1 = 0 THEN
     E1 = 90: GOTO 670
660  E1 =  ATN (D1 / C1):E1 = E1 * 180 / B
670  IF C1 < 0 AND D1 > 0 THEN E1 = E1 + 18
     0
680  IF C1 < 0 AND D1 < 0 THEN E1 = E1 - 18
     0
690  IF C1 < 0 AND D1 = 0 THEN E1 = 180
700  F1 =  SQR (G1 ^ 2 + H1 ^ 2): IF G1 = 0 THEN
     I1 = 90: GOTO 720
710  I1 =  ATN (H1 / G1):I1 = I1 * 180 / B
720  IF G1 < 0 AND H1 > 0 THEN I1 = I1 + 18
     0
730  IF G1 < 0 AND H1 < 0 THEN I1 = I1 - 18
     0
740  IF G1 < 0 AND H1 = 0 THEN I1 = 180
750  PRINT "                    REAL PART
          IMAG. PART    ABSOL. VALUE       ANG
     LE": PRINT "                    -----
     ----   ----------    ------------
     -----"
760  PRINT "VOLTAGE (Volt) = ";: POKE 36,21
     : PRINT  INT (10000 * C1 + .5) / 10000
     ;: POKE 36,36: PRINT  INT (10000 * D1 +
     .5) / 10000;: POKE 36,50: PRINT  INT (
     B1 * 10000 + .5) / 10000;: POKE 36,65:
      PRINT  INT (E1 * 10000 + .5) / 10000
770  PRINT "CURRENT (Amp)  = ";: POKE 36,21
     : PRINT  INT (10000 * G1 + .5) / 10000
     ;: POKE 36,36: PRINT  INT (10000 * H1 +
     .5) / 10000;: POKE 36,50: PRINT  INT (
     F1 * 10000 + .5) / 10000;: POKE 36,65:
      PRINT  INT (I1 * 10000 + .5) / 10000:
      RETURN
780  G1 = ((M * Y) / Y ^ 2) + N:H1 = O - (L *
     Y) / Y ^ 2:C1 = G1 * D:D1 = H1 * D: RETURN

790  C1 = L - W * O:D1 = M + W * N:G1 = C1 /
     D:H1 = D1 / D: RETURN
```

```
10   REM name: SHUNT IMPEDANCE NETWORK
20   REM by: John Devoldere, ON4UN
30   ONERR  GOTO 50
40   GOTO 60
50   VTAB 13: POKE 36,34: PRINT "FATAL ERROR
     ": PRINT  CHR$ (7): FOR A = 1 TO 5000:
     NEXT : GOTO 30
60   CLEAR : HOME : PRINT  CHR$ (13) + CHR$
     (4);"PR#3":B =  ATN (1) * 4: PRINT : POKE
     36,27: PRINT "PARALLEL IMPEDANCE NETWO
     RK.";: POKE 36,71: PRINT "by ON4UN": PRINT
     "--------------------------------------
     --------------------------------------
     ----"
70   PRINT "THIS PROGRAM ALLOWS YOU TO ADD A
      PARALLEL IMPEDANCE (INDUCTANCE OR CAP
     ACITANCE) AS A NETWORK. INPUTS ARE LOA
     D RESISTANCE (a+jb), AND LOAD VOLTAGE
     (magnitude    and angle)."
80   PRINT "OUTPUTS ARE INPUT IMPEDANCE, INP
     UT VOLTAGE AND CURRENT (ALL IN a+jb FO
     RM OR AS  MAGNITUDES PLUS ANGLE).": PRINT
     "--------------------------------------
     --------------------------------------
     ----": VTAB 23
90   PRINT "--------------------------------
     --------------------------------------
     ----------"
100  VTAB 11: INPUT "DESIGN FREQUENCY (IN M
     Hz) > ";A$:D =  VAL (A$): IF D = < 0 THEN
      PRINT  CHR$ (7): GOTO 100
110  VTAB 13: INPUT "LOAD IMPEDANCE REAL PA
     RT > ";B$:E =  VAL (B$): IF E = 0 THEN
      PRINT  CHR$ (7): GOTO 110
120  VTAB 14: INPUT "LOAD IMPEDANCE IMAG PA
     RT > ";C$:F =  VAL (C$): IF F = 0 AND
     C$ < > "0" THEN  PRINT  CHR$ (7): GOTO
     120
130  G =  SQR (E ^ 2 + F ^ 2):H =  ATN (F /
     E):H = H * 180 / B: IF E < 0 AND F > 0
     THEN H = H + 180
140  IF E < 0 AND F < 0 THEN H = H - 180
150  VTAB 16: INPUT "LOAD VOLTAGE MAGNITUDE
     > ";D$:I =  VAL (D$): IF I = < 0 THEN
      PRINT  CHR$ (7): GOTO 150
160  VTAB 17: INPUT "LOAD VOLTAGE ANGLE
     > ";E$:J =  VAL (E$): IF J = 0 AND E$
     < > "0" THEN  PRINT  CHR$ (7): GOTO
     160
170  K = I *  COS (J * B / 180):M = I *  SIN
     (J * B / 180):N = ((I * E) + (M * F)) /
     (E ^ 2 + F ^ 2):P = ((M * E) - (K * F)
     ) / (E ^ 2 + F ^ 2):Q =  SQR (N ^ 2 +
     P ^ 2):R =  ATN (P / N):R = R * 180 /
     B: IF N < O AND P > 0 THEN R = R + 180
180  IF N < O AND P < 0 THEN R = R - 180
190  PRINT : HOME : POKE 36,24: PRINT "PARA
     LLEL IMPEDANCE NETWORK.";: POKE 36,71:
     PRINT "by ON4UN": PRINT "-------------
     --------------------------------------
     ----------------------------": PRINT
     "DESIGN FREQUENCY = ";D;" MHz": PRINT
200  PRINT "OUTPUT              REAL PART
        IMAG. PART    ABSOL. VALUE      ANGL
     E": PRINT "------              ------
     ---   ----------    -----------
     -----": PRINT "IMPEDANCE (ohm)=   ";: POKE
     36,21: PRINT E;: POKE 36,36: PRINT F;:
     POKE 36,50: PRINT  INT (G * 10000 + .
     5) / 10000;: POKE 36,65: PRINT  INT (H
     * 10000 + .5) / 10000
210  PRINT "CURRENT (Amp)  = ";: POKE 36,21
     : PRINT  INT (10000 * N + .5) / 10000;
     : POKE 36,36: PRINT  INT (10000 * P +
     .5) / 10000;: POKE 36,50: PRINT  INT (
     Q * 10000 + .5) / 10000;: POKE 36,65: PRINT
     INT (R * 10000 + .5) / 10000
```

```
220  PRINT "VOLTAGE (Volt) = ";: POKE 36,21
     : PRINT  INT (10000 * K + .5) / 10000;
     : POKE 36,36: PRINT  INT (10000 * M +
     .5) / 10000;: POKE 36,50: PRINT  INT (
     I * 10000 + .5) / 10000;: POKE 36,65: PRINT
      INT (J * 10000 + .5) / 10000: PRINT "
     --------------------------------------
     --------------------------------------
     ---": PRINT
230  S = (F + E ^ 2 / F):T =  INT (100 * S +
     .5) / 100: PRINT "REQUIRED IMPEDANCE T
     O TUNE OUT REACTANCE = "; - T;" ohm": POKE
     34,12: VTAB 23: PRINT "--------------
     --------------------------------------
     --------------------------"
240  PRINT "   NEW INPUTS    >>N<<
     MORE CALCULATIONS  >>C<<          EXIT
       >>E<<";: POKE 35,21:S =  - S
250  HOME
260  VTAB 13: PRINT "DO YOU WANT OTHER VALU
     E? (Y/N) > ";: GET F$: IF F$ < > "Y" AND
     F$ < > "y" AND F$ < > "N" AND F$ < >
     "n" THEN  PRINT  CHR$ (7): GOTO 260
270  HOME : IF F$ < > "Y" OR F$ < > "y" GOTO
     290
280  INPUT "ENTER PARALLEL REACTANCE VALUE
     (+ FOR IND., - FOR CAP.) > ";G$:S =  VAL
     (G$): IF S = 0 THEN  PRINT  CHR$ (7): VTAB
     13: GOTO 280
290  POKE 34,12:U = K:V = M:W = (F / S) + 1
     :X =  - E / S:Y = (N * W) - (P * X):Z =
     (N * X) + (P * W):A1 =  SQR (Y ^ 2 + Z
     ^ 2): IF Y = 0 THEN B1 = 90: GOTO 310
300  B1 =  ATN (Z / Y):B1 = B1 * 180 / B
310  IF Y < 0 AND Z > 0 THEN B1 = B1 + 180
320  IF Y < 0 AND Z > 0 THEN B1 = B1 - 180
330  C1 = ((U * Y) + (V * Z)) / (Y ^ 2 + Z ^
     2):H = ((V * Y) - (U * Z)) / (Y ^ 2 +
     Z ^ 2):D1 =  SQR (C1 ^ 2 + H ^ 2):E1 =
     ATN (H / C1):E1 = E1 * 180 / B: IF C1
     < 0 AND H > 0 THEN E1 = E1 + 180
340  IF C1 < 0 AND H < 0 THEN E1 = E1 - 180
350  F1 = I:G1 = J: IF S > 0 THEN L = S / (2
     * B * D)
360  IF S < O THEN C =  - 1000000 / (2 * B *
     D * S)
370  IF S = O GOTO 400
380  IF S > 0 THEN  PRINT "INDUCTANCE = "; INT
     (L * 100 + .5) / 100;" uH"
390  IF S < 0 THEN  PRINT "CAPACITANCE = ";
     INT (C * 100 + .5) / 100;" pF"
400  PRINT : PRINT "INPUT                RE
     AL PART    IMAG. PART    ABSOL. VALUE
         ANGLE": PRINT "-----
     ---------   ----------    -----------
          -----"
410  PRINT "IMPEDANCE      = ";: POKE 36,21
     : PRINT  INT (10000 * C1 + .5) / 10000
     ;: POKE 36,36: PRINT  INT (10000 * H +
     .5) / 10000;: POKE 36,50: PRINT  INT (
     D1 * 10000 + .5) / 10000;: POKE 36,65:
     PRINT  INT (E1 * 10000 + .5) / 10000
420  PRINT "CURRENT (Amp)  = ";: POKE 36,21
     : PRINT  INT (10000 * Y + .5) / 10000;
     : POKE 36,36: PRINT  INT (10000 * Z +
     .5) / 10000;: POKE 36,50: PRINT  INT (
     A1 * 10000 + .5) / 10000;: POKE 36,65:
     PRINT  INT (B1 * 10000 + .5) / 10000
```

```
430  PRINT "VOLTAGE (Volt) = ";: POKE 36,21
     : PRINT  INT (10000 * U + .5) / 10000;
     : POKE 36,36: PRINT  INT (10000 * V +
     .5) / 10000;: POKE 36,50: PRINT  INT (
     F1 * 10000 + .5) / 10000;: POKE 36,65:
      PRINT  INT (G1 * 10000 + .5) / 10000:
      VTAB 24: GET F$: IF F$ = "E" OR F$ =
     "e" THEN  HOME : PRINT  CHR$ (13) + CHR$
     (4);"RUN MENU"
```

```
440  IF F$ = "N" OR F$ = "n" THEN  HOME : GOTO
     30
450  HOME : GOTO 250
```

```
10   REM name: SERIES IMPEDANCE NETWORK
20   REM by: John Devoldere, ON4UN
30   ONERR  GOTO 50
40   GOTO 60
50   VTAB 14: POKE 36,34: PRINT "FATAL ERROR
     ": PRINT  CHR$ (7): FOR A = 1 TO 5000:
     NEXT : GOTO 30
60   CLEAR : HOME : PRINT  CHR$ (13) + CHR$
     (4);"PR#3":B =  ATN (1) * 4: PRINT : POKE
     36,29: PRINT "SERIES IMPEDANCE NETWORK
     .";: POKE 36,71: PRINT "by ON4UN": PRINT
     "----------------------------------------
     ----------------------------------------
     ----"
70   PRINT "THIS PROGRAM ALLOWS YOU TO ADD A
      SERIES IMPEDANCE (INDUCTANCE OR CAPAC
     ITANCE)   AS A NETWORK. INPUTS ARE LOA
     D RESISTANCE (a+jb), AND LOAD VOLTAGE
     (magnitude     and angle)."
80   PRINT "OUTPUTS ARE INPUT IMPEDANCE, INP
     UT VOLTAGE AND CURRENT (ALL IN a+jb FO
     RM OR AS  MAGNITUDES PLUS ANGLE).": PRINT
     "----------------------------------------
     ----------------------------------------
     ----": VTAB 23
90   PRINT "----------------------------------------
     ----------------------------------------
     ---------"
100  VTAB 11: INPUT "DESIGN FREQUENCY (IN M
     Hz) > ";A$:D =  VAL (A$): IF D <  = 0 THEN
      PRINT  CHR$ (7): GOTO 100
110  VTAB 13: INPUT "LOAD IMPEDANCE REAL PA
     RT > ";B$:E =  VAL (B$): IF E = 0 THEN
      PRINT  CHR$ (7): GOTO 110
120  VTAB 14: INPUT "LOAD IMPEDANCE IMAG PA
     RT > ";C$:F =  VAL (C$): IF F = 0 AND
     C$ <  > "0" THEN  PRINT  CHR$ (7): GOTO
     120
130  G =  SQR (E ^ 2 + F ^ 2):H =  ATN (F /
     E):H = H * 180 / B: IF E < 0 AND F > 0
     THEN H = H + 180
140  IF E < 0 AND F < 0 THEN H = H - 180
150  VTAB 16: INPUT "LOAD VOLTAGE MAGNITUDE
     > ";D$:I =  VAL (D$): IF I = < 0 THEN
      PRINT  CHR$ (7): GOTO 150
160  VTAB 17: INPUT "LOAD VOLTAGE ANGLE
     > ";E$:J =  VAL (E$): IF J = 0 AND E$
     <  > "0" THEN  PRINT  CHR$ (7): GOTO
     160
170  K = I *  COS (J * B / 180):M = I *  SIN
     (J * B / 180):N = ((K * E) + (M * F)) /
     (E ^ 2 + F ^ 2):P = ((M * E) - (K * F)
     ) / (E ^ 2 + F ^ 2):Q =  SQR (N ^ 2 +
     P ^ 2):R =  ATN (P / N):R = R * 180 /
     B: IF N < O AND P > 0 THEN R = R + 180
180  IF N < O AND P < 0 THEN R = R - 180
190  PRINT : HOME : POKE 36,26: PRINT "SERI
     ES IMPEDANCE NETWORK.";: POKE 36,71: PRINT
     "by ON4UN": PRINT "--------------------
     -----------------------": PRINT "DESIGN
      FREQUENCY = ";D;" MHz": PRINT : PRINT
     "OUTPUT              REAL PART     IMAG
     . PART    ABSOL. VALUE        ANGLE"
200  PRINT "------            ----------    ---------
           ---------    ----
     -": PRINT "IMPEDANCE (ohm) = ";: POKE
     36,21: PRINT E;: POKE 36,36: PRINT F;:
     POKE 36,50: PRINT  INT (G * 10000 + .
     5) / 10000;: POKE 36,65: PRINT  INT (H
     * 10000 + .5) / 10000
210  PRINT "CURRENT (Amp)   = ";: POKE 36,21
     : PRINT  INT (10000 * N + .5) / 10000;
     : POKE 36,36: PRINT  INT (10000 * P +
     .5) / 10000;: POKE 36,50: PRINT  INT (
     Q * 10000 + .5) / 10000;: POKE 36,65: PRINT
      INT (R * 10000 + .5) / 10000
```

```
220  PRINT "VOLTAGE (Volt) = ";: POKE 36,21
     : PRINT  INT (10000 * K + .5) / 10000;
     : POKE 36,36: PRINT  INT (10000 * M +
     .5) / 10000;: POKE 36,50: PRINT  INT (
     I * 10000 + .5) / 10000;: POKE 36,65: PRINT
      INT (J * 10000 + .5) / 10000: PRINT "
     ----------------------------------------
     ----------------------------------------
     ---": PRINT
230  PRINT "REQUIRED IMPEDANCE TO TUNE OUT
     REACTANCE = ";  - F;" ohm": POKE 34,12:
     VTAB 23: PRINT "--------------------
     --------------------": PRINT "     NEW
     INPUTS  >>N<<         MORE CALCULATI
     ONS  >>C<<          EXIT  >>E<<";: POKE
     35,21
240  HOME :S =  - F
250  VTAB 13: PRINT "DO YOU WANT OTHER VALU
     E? (Y/N) > ";: GET F$: IF F$ <  > "Y" AND
     F$ <  > "y" AND F$ <  > "N" AND F$ <  >
     "n" THEN  PRINT  CHR$ (7): GOTO 250
260  HOME : IF F$ <  > "Y" OR F$ <  > "y" GOTO
     280
270  INPUT "ENTER SERIES REACTANCE VALUE (+
      FOR IND., - FOR CAP) > ";S
280  POKE 34,12:T =  - S * P:U = S * N:V =
     K + T:W = M + U:X =  SQR (V ^ 2 + W ^
     2): IF V = 0 THEN Y = 90: GOTO 300
290  Y =  ATN (W / V):Y = Y * 180 / B
300  IF V < 0 AND W > 0 THEN Y = Y + 180
310  IF V < 0 AND W < 0 THEN Y = Y - 180
320  E = E:Z = F + S:A1 =  SQR (E ^ 2 + Z ^
     2):B1 =  ATN (Z / E):B1 = B1 * 180 / B
     : IF E < 0 AND Z > 0 THEN B1 = B1 + 18
     0
330  IF E < 0 AND Z < 0 THEN B1 = B1 - 180
340  C1 = ((V * E) + (W * Z)) / (E ^ 2 + Z ^
     2):D1 = ((W * E) - (V * Z)) / (E ^ 2 +
     Z ^ 2):E1 =  SQR (C1 ^ 2 + D1 ^ 2): IF
     C1 = 0 THEN F1 = 90: GOTO 360
350  F1 =  ATN (D1 / C1):F1 = F1 * 180 / B
360  IF C1 < 0 AND D1 > 0 THEN F1 = F1 + 18
     0
370  IF C1 < 0 AND D1 < 0 THEN F1 = F1 - 18
     0
380  IF S > 0 THEN L = S / (2 * B * D)
390  IF S < O THEN C =  - 1000000 / (2 * B *
     D * S)
400  IF S = O GOTO 430
410  IF S > 0 THEN  PRINT "INDUCTANCE = "; INT
     (L * 100 + .5) / 100;" uH"
420  IF S < 0 THEN  PRINT "CAPACITANCE = ";
     INT (C * 100 + .5) / 100;" pF"
430  PRINT : PRINT "INPUT              RE
     AL PART    IMAG. PART    ABSOL. VALUE
        ANGLE": PRINT "-----
     ---------    ----------    ----------
     -----"
440  PRINT "IMPEDANCE       = ";: POKE 36,21
     : PRINT  INT (10000 * E + .5) / 10000;
     : POKE 36,36: PRINT  INT (10000 * Z +
     .5) / 10000;: POKE 36,50: PRINT  INT (
     A1 * 10000 + .5) / 10000;: POKE 36,65:
     PRINT  INT (B1 * 10000 + .5) / 10000
450  PRINT "CURRENT (Amp)   = ";: POKE 36,21
     : PRINT  INT (10000 * C1 + .5) / 10000
     ;: POKE 36,36: PRINT  INT (10000 * D1 +
     .5) / 10000;: POKE 36,50: PRINT  INT (
     E1 * 10000 + .5) / 10000;: POKE 36,65:
     PRINT  INT (F1 * 10000 + .5) / 10000
```

```
460    PRINT "VOLTAGE (Volt) = ";: POKE 36,21
       : PRINT  INT (10000 * V + .5) / 10000;
       : POKE 36,36: PRINT  INT (10000 * W +
       .5) / 10000;: POKE 36,50: PRINT  INT (
       X * 10000 + .5) / 10000;: POKE 36,65: PRINT
        INT (Y * 10000 + .5) / 10000: VTAB 24
       : GET F$: IF F$ = "E" OR F$ = "e" THEN
        HOME : PRINT  CHR$ (13) +  CHR$ (4);"
       RUN MENU"

470    IF F$ = "N" OR F$ = "n" THEN  HOME : GOTO
       30
480    HOME : GOTO 240
```

```
10   REM name: PI FILTER LINE STRETCHER
20   REM by: John Devoldere, ON4UN
30   ONERR  GOTO 50
40   GOTO 60
50   VTAB 13: POKE 36,34: PRINT "FATAL ERROR
     ": PRINT  CHR$ (7): FOR C = 1 TO 5000:
     NEXT : GOTO 30
60   CLEAR : HOME :E =  ATN (1) * 4: POKE 34
     ,0: PRINT  CHR$ (13) +  CHR$ (4);"PR#3
     ": PRINT : POKE 36,22: PRINT "REVERSIB
     LE PI FILTER - LINE STRETCHER";: POKE
     36,71: PRINT "by ON4UN": PRINT "------
     -----------------------------------------
     -----------------------------------"
70   PRINT "THIS PROGRAM ALLOWS YOU TO CALCU
     LATE THE SYMMETRICAL PI-FILTER WHICH I
     S EXCLUSI-LY USED FOR ADDING A PHASE D
     ELAY WITH A GIVEN CHARACTERISTIC IMPED
     ANCE.": PRINT "----------------------
     --------------------------------------
     -------------------": VTAB 22
80   PRINT "-------------------------------
     --------------------------------------
     ---------": POKE 35,21: POKE 34,6: HOME
90   VTAB 7: INPUT "DESIGN FREQUENCY (MHz)
     > ";C$:F =  VAL (C$): IF F < = 0 THEN
      PRINT  CHR$ (7): GOTO 90
100  VTAB 8: INPUT "CHARACTERISTIC IMPEDANC
     E > ";D$:G =  VAL (D$): IF G = < 0 THEN
      PRINT  CHR$ (7): GOTO 100
110  PRINT
120  VTAB 9: PRINT : INPUT "OUTPUT PHASE AN
     GLE        > ";A$:A =  VAL (A$): IF A =
     0 AND A$ < > "0" THEN  PRINT  CHR$ (7
     ): GOTO 120
130  VTAB 10: PRINT : CALL  - 958:H = A: GOSUB
     290:A = H
140  VTAB 11: PRINT : INPUT "INPUT PHASE AN
     GLE        > ";B$:B =  VAL (B$): IF B =
     0 AND B$ < > "0" THEN  PRINT  CHR$ (7
     ): GOTO 140
150  IF A = B THEN  PRINT  CHR$ (7): GOTO 1
     40
160  H = B: GOSUB 290:B = H:D = B - A: IF  INT
     (D + .5) = 180 OR  INT (D + .5) = - 1
     80 THEN  PRINT  CHR$ (7): VTAB 21: PRINT
     "THE PHASE DIFFERENCE IS 180 DEGREES.
     YOU MUST CASCADE TWO FILTERS.";: GOTO
     120
170  IF D > 180 OR D <  - 180 THEN  PRINT  CHR$
     (7): VTAB 20: PRINT "REARRANGE YOUR PH
     ASE ANGLE INPUT/OUTPUT (DIFF. = ";D;"
     DEG).";: GOTO 120
180  IF D > 135 OR D <  - 135 THEN  PRINT  CHR$
     (7): VTAB 21: PRINT "THE PHASE ANGLE D
     IFFERENCE IS QUITE LARGE (";D;" DEG),
     AND BW. WILL BE SMALL.";
190  VTAB 13:I = G *  SIN (D * E / 180):J =
      - (G *  SIN (D * 3.14159 / 180)) / (1
      -  COS (D * E / 180)): PRINT : PRINT
     "SERIES ARM IMPEDANCE = "; INT (I * 10
     0 + .5) / 100;" ohm": IF I > 0 THEN K =
     I / (2 * E * F)
200  IF I < 0 THEN K = 1000000 / (2 * E * F
     * I)
210  L =  INT (K * 100 + .5) / 100: IF K > 0
     THEN  PRINT "SERIES ARM INDUCTANCE =
     ";L;" uH"
220  IF K < 0 THEN  PRINT "SERIES ARM CAPAC
     ITANCE= ";  - L;" pF"
230  PRINT : PRINT "PARALLEL ARMS IMPED. =
     "; INT (J * 100 + .5) / 100;" ohm": IF
     J > 0 THEN M = J / (2 * E * F)
240  IF J < 0 THEN M = 1000000 / (2 * E * F
     * J)
250  M =  INT (M * 100 + .5) / 100: IF M > 0
     THEN  PRINT "PARAL. ARMS INDUCTANCE =
     ";M;" uH"
260  IF M < 0 THEN  PRINT "PARAL. ARMS CAPA
     CITANCE= ";  - M;" pF"
270  VTAB 23: PRINT "                  EXIT >
     >>E<<<                 MORE  >>>ANY
     KEY<<<";: POKE 36,38: GET E$: IF E$ =
     "E" OR E$ = "e" THEN  HOME : PRINT  CHR$
     (13) +  CHR$ (4);"RUN MENU"
280  POKE 35,23: VTAB 22: PRINT : POKE 36,0
     : CALL  - 868: POKE 35,21: HOME : GOTO
     90
290  IF H >  = - 360 AND H < = 360 THEN  RETURN
300  IF A = H THEN F$ = "INPUT"
310  IF H = B THEN F$ = "OUTPUT"
320  IF H >  = 360 THEN H = H - 360: GOTO 3
     20
330  IF H <  = - 360 THEN H = H + 360: GOTO
     330
340  VTAB 19: PRINT : CALL  - 868: VTAB 20:
      PRINT F$;" PHASE ANGLE CONVERTED TO "
     ;H;" DEG.";: IF F$ = "INPUT" THEN  VTAB
     10: POKE 36,42: PRINT "===>> ";H
350  IF F$ = "OUTPUT" THEN  VTAB 12: POKE 3
     6,42: PRINT "===>> ";H
360  RETURN
```

```
10   REM name: T FILTER LINE STRETCHER
20   REM by: John Devoldere, ON4UN
30   ONERR  GOTO 50
40   GOTO 60
50   VTAB 14: POKE 36,34: PRINT "FATAL ERROR
     ": PRINT  CHR$ (7): FOR C = 1 TO 5000:
     NEXT : GOTO 30
60   CLEAR : HOME :E =  ATN (1) * 4: POKE 34
     ,0: PRINT  CHR$ (13) + CHR$ (4);"PR#3
     ": PRINT : POKE 36,22: PRINT "REVERSIB
     LE T FILTER - LINE STRETCHER"; POKE 3
     6,71: PRINT "by ON4UN": PRINT "-------
     -----------------------------------
     ----------------------------------"
70   PRINT "THIS PROGRAM ALLOWS YOU TO CALCU
     LATE THE SYMMETRICAL T-FILTER WHICH IS
     EXCLUSI- VELY USED FOR ADDING A PHASE
     DELAY WITH A GIVEN CHARACTERISTIC IMP
     EDANCE.": PRINT "--------------------
     -------------------------------------
     ---------------------": VTAB 22
80   PRINT "--------------------------------
     -------------------------------------
     ---------": POKE 35,21: POKE 34,6: HOME
90   VTAB 7: INPUT "DESIGN FREQUENCY (MHz)
     > ";C$:F =  VAL (C$): IF F < = 0 THEN
     PRINT  CHR$ (7): GOTO 90
100  VTAB 8: INPUT "CHARACTERISTIC IMPEDANC
     E > ";D$:G =  VAL (D$): IF G = < 0 THEN
     PRINT  CHR$ (7): GOTO 100
110  PRINT
120  VTAB 9: PRINT : INPUT "OUTPUT PHASE AN
     GLE      > ";A$:A =  VAL (A$): IF A =
     0 AND A$ < > "0" THEN  PRINT  CHR$ (7
     ): GOTO 120
130  VTAB 19: PRINT : CALL  - 958:H = A: GOSUB
     290:A = H
140  VTAB 11: PRINT : INPUT "INPUT PHASE AN
     GLE      > ";B$:B =  VAL (B$): IF B =
     0 AND B$ < > "0" THEN  PRINT  CHR$ (7
     ): GOTO 140
150  IF A = B THEN  PRINT  CHR$ (7): GOTO 1
     40
160  H = B: GOSUB 290:B = H:D = B - A: IF  INT
     (D + .5) = 180 OR  INT (D + .5) = - 1
     80 THEN  PRINT  CHR$ (7);;: VTAB 21: PRINT
     "THE PHASE DIFFERENCE IS 180 DEGREES,
     YOU MUST CASCADE TWO FILTERS.";: GOTO
     120
170  IF D > 180 OR D <  - 180 THEN  PRINT  CHR$
     (7): VTAB 20: PRINT "REARRANGE YOUR PH
     ASE ANGLE INPUT/OUTPUT (DIFF. = ";D;"
     DEG).";: GOTO 120
180  IF D >`135 OR D <  - 135 THEN  PRINT  CHR$
     (7): VTAB 21: PRINT "THE PHASE ANGLE D
     IFFERENCE IS QUITE LARGE (";D;" DEG),
     AND BW. WILL BE SMALL.";
190  VTAB 13:I =  - G *  SIN (D * E / 180):
     J = G * (1 -  COS (D * E / 180)) /  SIN
     (D * E / 180): PRINT : PRINT "PARALLEL
     ARM IMPED. = "; INT (I * 100 + .5) /
     100;" ohm": IF I > 0 THEN K = I / (2 *
     E * F)
200  IF I < 0 THEN K = 1000000 / (2 * E * F
     * I)
210  L =  INT (K * 100 + .5) / 100: IF K > 0
     THEN  PRINT "PARALL.ARM INDUCTANCE =
     ";L;" uH"
220  IF K < 0 THEN  PRINT "PARALL.ARM CAPAC
     ITANCE= "; - L;" pF"
230  PRINT : PRINT "SERIES ARMS IMPED.  =
     "; INT (J * 100 + .5) / 100;" ohm": IF
     J > 0 THEN M = J / (2 * E * F)
240  IF J < 0 THEN M = 1000000 / (2 * E * F
     * J)
250  N =  INT (M * 100 + .5) / 100: IF M > 0
     THEN  PRINT "SERIES ARMS INDUCTANCE =
     ";N;" uH"
260  IF M < 0 THEN  PRINT "SERIES ARMS CAPA
     CITANCE= "; - N;" pF"
270  VTAB 23: PRINT "              EXIT >
     >>E<<<              MORE  >>>ANY
     KEY<<<";: POKE 36,39: GET E$: IF E$ =
     "E" OR E$ = "e" THEN  HOME : PRINT  CHR$
     (13) +  CHR$ (4);"RUN MENU"
280  POKE 35,23: VTAB 22: PRINT : POKE 36,0
     : CALL  - 868: POKE 35,21: HOME : GOTO
     90
290  IF H > = - 360 AND H < = 360 THEN  RETURN
300  IF A = H THEN F$ = "INPUT"
310  IF H = B THEN F$ = "OUTPUT"
320  IF H > = 360 THEN H = H - 360: GOTO 3
     20
330  IF H < = - 360 THEN H = H + 360: GOTO
     330
340  VTAB 19: PRINT : CALL  - 868: VTAB 20:
     PRINT F$;" PHASE ANGLE CONVERTED TO "
     ;H;" DEG.";: IF F$ = "INPUT" THEN  VTAB
     10: POKE 36,42: PRINT "===> ";H
350  IF F$ = "OUTPUT" THEN  VTAB 12: POKE 3
     6,42: PRINT "===>  ";H
360  RETURN
```

```
10  REM name: T JUNCTION
20  REM by: John Devoldere, ON4UN
30  ONERR  GOTO 50
40  GOTO 60
50  VTAB 14: POKE 36,34: PRINT "FATAL ERROR
    ": PRINT  CHR$ (7): FOR A = 1 TO 5000:
     NEXT : GOTO 30
60  CLEAR : PRINT  CHR$ (13) +  CHR$ (4);"P
    R#3": POKE 34,0: HOME : PRINT : POKE 3
    6,24: PRINT "FEEDLINE T-JUNCTION IMPED
    ANCE";: POKE 36,71: PRINT "by ON4UN": PRINT
    "---------------------------------
    -------------------------------------
    ----"
70  PRINT "THIS PROGRAM CALCULATES THE COMP
    LEX IMPEDANCE (a + jb) RESULTING FROM
    CONNEC-   TING A NUMBER OF FEEDLINES I
    N PARALLEL, EACH FEEDLINE REPRESENTING
     A COMPLEX    IMPEDANCE AT THE JUNCTIO
    N POINT."
80  PRINT "--------------------------------
    ----------------------------------
    ---------": VTAB 23: PRINT "----------
    -------------------------------------
    -----------------------------": POKE
    34,8: POKE 35,21
90  HOME
100 VTAB 8: INPUT "NUMBER OF IMPEDANCES TO
     BE PARALLELED > ";A$:B =  VAL (A$): IF
    B =  < 0 THEN  PRINT  CHR$ (7): GOTO 1
    00
110 FOR A = 1 TO B: VTAB 11: CALL  - 958: PRINT
    "IMPEDANCE ";A: PRINT "------------"
120 VTAB 13: PRINT "REAL PART IMPEDANCE NR
    ";A;"     > ";: INPUT "";B$(A):A(A) =
    VAL (B$(A)): IF A(A) = 0 AND B$(A) <
    > "0" THEN  PRINT  CHR$ (7): GOTO 120
130 VTAB 14: PRINT "REACTIVE PART IMPEDANC
    E NR ";A;" > ";: INPUT "";C$(A):B(A) =
    VAL (C$(A)): IF B(A) = 0 AND C$(A) <
    > "0" THEN  PRINT  CHR$ (7): GOTO 130
140 IF B(A) = 0 AND A(A) = 0 THEN  PRINT  CHR$
    (7): GOTO 120
150 PRINT : NEXT A: FOR A = 1 TO B:C(A) =
    A(A) / (A(A) ^ 2 + B(A) ^ 2):D(A) = -
    B(A) / (A(A) ^ 2 + B(A) ^ 2): NEXT A: FOR
    A = 1 TO B:E(A) = E(A - 1) + C(A):F(A)
     = F(A - 1) + D(A): NEXT A:C = E(B) /
    (E(B) ^ 2 + F(B) ^ 2):D = - F(B) / (E
    (B) ^ 2 + F(B) ^ 2):C =  INT (C * 1000
    0 + .5) / 10000:D =  INT (D * 10000 +
    .5) / 10000: VTAB 17
160 PRINT "RESULTING IMPEDANCE: REAL PART
    = ";C;" ohm": PRINT "------------------
    --   IMAG PART = ";D;" ohm": VTAB 24: PRINT
    "              MORE  >>ANY KEY<<
                  EXIT  >>E<<";: VTAB 24:
    POKE 36,39: GET D$: IF D$ = "E" OR D$
    = "e" THEN  HOME : PRINT  CHR$ (13) +
    CHR$ (4);"RUN MENU"
170 HOME : GOTO 90
```

```
10   REM name: COIL CALCULATION
20   REM by: John Devoldere, ON4UN
30   ONERR  GOTO 50
40   GOTO 60
50   VTAB 14: POKE 36,34: PRINT "FATAL ERROR
     ": PRINT  CHR$ (7): FOR A = 1 TO 5000:
     NEXT : GOTO 30
60   CLEAR : PRINT  CHR$ (13) + CHR$ (4);"P
     R#3": POKE 34,0: HOME : PRINT : POKE 3
     6,30: PRINT "COIL CALCULATION";: POKE
     36,71: PRINT "by ON4UN": PRINT "------
     ------------------------------------
     -----------------------------------"
70   PRINT "THIS PROGRAM CALCULATES THE COIL
      PARAMETERS GIVEN A REQUIRED INDUCTANC
     E OR THE  COIL INDUCTANCE GIVEN THE CO
     IL PARAMETERS FOR BOTH AIR WOUND AND T
     OROIDAL IN-    DUCTANCES."
80   PRINT "------------------------------
     ------------------------------------
     ---------": VTAB 23: PRINT "----------
     ------------------------------------
     ------------------------------": POKE
     34,9: POKE 35,21:B = 1:A$ = "INCHES": HOME
90   VTAB 8: PRINT : PRINT "INCHES OR CENTIM
     ETERS (I/C) ? > ";: GET B$: IF B$ = "C
     " OR B$ = "c" THEN B = 1 / 2.54:A$ = "
     CM."
100  IF B$ < > "C" AND B$ < > "c" AND B$ <
      > "I" AND B$ < > "i" THEN  PRINT CHR$
      (7);: GOTO 90
110  VTAB 7: PRINT : PRINT "ALL DIMENSIONS
     ARE IN ";A$: PRINT "------------------
     ------------------------------------
     ----------------": HOME
120  VTAB 10: PRINT "AIR WOUND COIL OR TORO
     IDAL CORE? (A/T) > ";: GET C$: IF C$ =
     "T" OR C$ = "t" THEN  PRINT : GOTO 260
130  PRINT : PRINT : PRINT "COMPUTE INDUCTA
     NCE (I) OR COIL PARAMETERS (C) > ";: GET
     C$: IF C$ = "C" OR C$ = "c" GOTO 210
140  PRINT : PRINT
150  VTAB 15: PRINT "COIL DIAMETER IN ";A$;
     : INPUT " > ";D$:C =  VAL (D$): IF C <
      = 0 THEN  PRINT  CHR$ (7): GOTO 150
160  C = C * B
170  VTAB 16: PRINT "COIL LENGTH IN ";A$;: INPUT
     " > ";E$:D =  VAL (E$): IF D <  = 0 THEN
     PRINT  CHR$ (7): GOTO 170
180  D = D * B
190  VTAB 17: INPUT "NUMBER OF TURNS > ";F$
     :E =  VAL (F$): IF E <  = 0 THEN  PRINT
      CHR$ (7): GOTO 190

200  A = ((C ^ 2) * (E ^ 2)) / ((18 * C) + (
     40 * D)): VTAB 18: POKE 36,28: PRINT "
     INDUCTANCE = "; INT (A * 100 + .5) / 1
     00;" uH": GOTO 350
210  PRINT
220  VTAB 15: INPUT "RQD. INDUCTANCE (uH)>
     ";E$:D =  VAL (E$): IF D =  < 0 THEN  PRINT
     CHR$ (7): GOTO 220
230  VTAB 16: PRINT "COIL DIAMETER IN ";A$;
     : INPUT " > ";D$:C =  VAL (D$): IF C =
     < 0 THEN  PRINT  CHR$ (7): GOTO 230
240  C = C * B: VTAB 17: PRINT "COIL LENGTH
     IN ";A$;: INPUT " > ";G$:F =  VAL (G$)
     : IF 0.4 * C > F THEN  PRINT  CHR$ (7)
     : VTAB 22: POKE 36,7: PRINT "For good
     Q factor the coil shoud be approximate
     ly square in form.";
250  F = F * B:E =  SQR (D * (18 * C + (40 *
     F))) / C: VTAB 19: POKE 36,22: PRINT "
     REQUIRED NUMBER OF TUNRS = "; INT (E *
     10 + .5) / 10: GOTO 350
260  VTAB 11: PRINT "COMPUTE INDUCTANCE (I)
      OR COIL PARAMETERS (C) > ";: GET C$: IF
     C$ = "C" OR C$ = "c" GOTO 310
270  PRINT
280  VTAB 13: INPUT "AL FACTOR (uH per 100
     turns) > ";H$:G =  VAL (H$): IF G <  =
     0 THEN  PRINT  CHR$ (7): GOTO 280
290  VTAB 14: INPUT "NUMBER OF TURNS > ";F$
     :E =  VAL (F$): IF E <  = 0 THEN  PRINT
     CHR$ (7): GOTO 290
300  A = ((E ^ 2) * G) / 10000: VTAB 18: POKE
     36,28: PRINT "INDUCTANCE = "; INT (A *
     100 + .5) / 100;" uH": GOTO 350
310  PRINT
320  VTAB 13: INPUT "RQD. INDUCTANCE (uH)>
     ";E$:D =  VAL (E$): IF D =  < 0 THEN  PRINT
     CHR$ (7): GOTO 320
330  VTAB 14: INPUT "AL-FACTOR (uH per 100
     turns) > ";H$:G =  VAL (H$): IF G <  =
     0 THEN  PRINT  CHR$ (7): GOTO 330
340  E = 100 *  SQR (D / G): VTAB 18: POKE 3
     6,22: PRINT "REQUIRED NUMBER OF TUNRS
     = "; INT (E * 10 + .5) / 10
350  VTAB 24: PRINT "          MORE CALCUL
     ATIONS >>C<<                  EXIT
     >>E<<";: VTAB 24: POKE 36,78: GET C$: IF
     C$ = "E" OR C$ = "e" THEN  HOME : PRINT
      CHR$ (13) + CHR$ (4);"RUN MENU"
360  HOME : POKE 34,9: HOME : GOTO 120
```

```
10   REM name: SWR RATIO
20   REM by: John Devoldere, ON4UN
30   ONERR  GOTO 50
40   GOTO 60
50   VTAB 14: POKE 36,34: PRINT "FATAL ERROR
     ": PRINT  CHR$ (7): FOR A = 1 TO 5000:
     NEXT : GOTO 30
60   CLEAR : PRINT  CHR$ (13) +  CHR$ (4);"P
     R#3": POKE 34,0: HOME : PRINT : POKE 3
     6,32: PRINT "S.W.R. CALCULATION";: POKE
     36,70: PRINT "by  ON4UN": PRINT "-----
     ------------------------------------
     ------------------------------------"
70   PRINT "THIS PROGRAM ALLOWS YOU TO CALCU
     LATE THE SWR GIVEN A TRANSMISSION LINE
      CHARACTE-RISTIC IMPEDANCE (Zo) AND TH
     E LOAD IMPEDANCE (R + j X).": PRINT "-
     ------------------------------------
     --": VTAB 22
80   PRINT "-------------------------------
     ------------------------------------
     ---------": POKE 34,6
90   VTAB 8: PRINT : INPUT "CABLE IMPEDANCE
     Zo > ";A$:B =  VAL (A$): IF B < = 0 THEN
      PRINT  CHR$ (7): GOTO 90
100  VTAB 11: PRINT "LOAD IMPEDANCE": PRINT
     "--------------"
110  VTAB 13: INPUT "RESISTIVE PART Z > ";B
     $:C =  VAL (B$): IF C = 0 AND B$ <  >
     "0" THEN  PRINT  CHR$ (7): GOTO 110
120  VTAB 14: INPUT "REACTIVE PART Z > ";C
     $:D =  VAL (C$): IF D = 0 AND C$ <  >
     "0" THEN  PRINT  CHR$ (7): GOTO 120
130  E =  SQR (C ^ 2 + D ^ 2):F =  ATN (D /
     C):F = F * 180 / 3.14159: IF C < 0 AND
     D > 0 THEN F = F + 180
140  IF C < 0 AND D < 0 THEN F = F - 180
150  G =  SQR ((C + B) ^ 2 + D ^ 2):H =  SQR
     ((C - B) ^ 2 + D ^ 2):I = (G + H) / (G
      - H):I =  INT (I * 100 + .5) / 100:I =
      ABS (I): VTAB 16: POKE 36,32: PRINT "
     S.W.R. = ";I: POKE 36,32: PRINT "=====
     ========": IF J = 1 GOTO 170
160  VTAB 22: PRINT "----------------------
     ------------------------------------
     -------------------": VTAB 23:J = 1: PRINT
     "         ENTER >>N<< FOR NEW RUN
              ENTER >>E<< FOR EXIT";
170  VTAB 23: POKE 36,38: GET D$: POKE 35,2
     3: VTAB 22: PRINT : CALL  - 868: POKE
     35,21: IF D$ = "E" OR D$ = "e" THEN  HOME
     : PRINT  CHR$ (13) +  CHR$ (4);"RUN ME
     NU"
180  HOME : GOTO 90
```

```
10   REM name: SWR ITERATION
20   REM by: John Devoldere, ON4UN
30   ONERR  GOTO 50
40   GOTO 60
50   VTAB 14: POKE 36,34: PRINT "FATAL ERROR
     ": PRINT  CHR$ (7): FOR A = 1 TO 5000:
     NEXT : GOTO 30
60   CLEAR : PRINT  CHR$ (13) +  CHR$ (4);"P
     R#3": POKE 34,0: HOME :B = 1: PRINT : POKE
     36,28: PRINT "S.W.R. ITERATION PROGRAM
     ";: POKE 36,71: PRINT "by ON4UN": PRINT
     "------------------------------------
     --------------------------------------
     ----"
70   PRINT "THIS PROGRAM ALLOWS YOU TO CALCU
     LATE THE SWR VALUES FOR A RANGE OF CHA
     RACTERIS- TIC SYSTEM IMPEDANCES AND FO
     R GIVEN COMPLEX (R + j X) LOAD IMPEDAN
     CES.": PRINT "-------------------------
     ------------------------": VTAB 23
80   PRINT "------------------------------------
     --------------------------------------
     ---------": POKE 35,21
90   VTAB 8: PRINT : INPUT "MINIMUM SYSTEM Z
     o > ";A$:C =  VAL (A$): IF C = 0 AND A
     $ <  > "0" THEN  PRINT  CHR$ (7): GOTO
     90
100  VTAB 10: INPUT "MAXIMUM SYSTEM Zo > ";
     B$:D =  VAL (B$): IF D = 0 OR D < C THEN
      PRINT  CHR$ (7): GOTO 100
110  VTAB 12: INPUT "NUMBER OF LOADS TO BE
     EVALUATED (MAX 5) > ";C$:E =  VAL (C$)
     : IF E < 1 OR E > 5 THEN  PRINT  CHR$
     (7): GOTO 110
120  FOR A = 0 TO E - 1: VTAB 14: CALL  - 9
     58: PRINT "IMPEDANCE LOAD ";A + 1: PRINT
     "-----------------": PRINT
130  VTAB 16: INPUT "RESISTIVE PART Z > ";D
     $:A(A) =  VAL (D$): IF A(A) = 0 AND D$
     <  > "0" THEN  PRINT  CHR$ (7): GOTO
     130
140  VTAB 17: INPUT "REACTIVE PART  Z > ";E
     $:B(A) =  VAL (E$): IF B(A) = 0 AND E$
     <  > "0" THEN  PRINT  CHR$ (7): GOTO
     140
150  NEXT : PRINT : HOME : POKE 36,28: PRINT
     "S.W.R. COMPUTATION.";: POKE 36,71: PRINT
     "by ON4UN": PRINT "--------------------
     --------------------------------------
     -------------------": PRINT "SYSTEM
        LOAD 1          LOAD 2          LOAD 3
              LOAD 4          LOAD 5"
160  PRINT "IMPED.";: POKE 36,75: PRINT "<-
     R": POKE 36,75: PRINT "<- X": FOR A =
     0 TO E - 1: VTAB 4: POKE 36,(A * 15) +
     8: PRINT A(A);: VTAB 5: POKE 36,(A * 1
     5) + 8: PRINT B(A);: NEXT : PRINT : PRINT
     "------------------------------------
     --------------------------------------
     ----": POKE 34,6: POKE 35,22: VTAB 23
170  PRINT "------------------------------------
     --------------------------------------
     ----------": HOME : VTAB 24: PRINT "
     ENTER >>N<< FOR NEW LIMITS/INCREMENTS
               ENTER >>E<< FOR EXIT";: HOME
180  F = C - B
190  F = F + B: IF  INT (10000 * F + .5) / 1
     0000 = 0 GOTO 190
200  IF  PEEK ( - 16384) = 206 THEN  GOTO 2
     70
210  IF  PEEK ( - 16384) = 197 THEN  HOME :
     GET F$: PRINT  CHR$ (13) +  CHR$ (4);
     "RUN MENU"
220  POKE  - 16368,0: POKE 36,1: PRINT  INT
     (100 * F + .5) / 100;: FOR G = 0 TO E -
     1:H =  SQR ((F + A(G)) ^ 2 + B(G) ^ 2)
     :I =  SQR ((F - A(G)) ^ 2 + B(G) ^ 2):
     J = (H + I) / (H - I):J =  ABS (J):J =
     INT (J * 100 + .5) / 100: POKE 36,(G *
     15) + 8: PRINT J;: NEXT G: PRINT : IF
     F =  > D GOTO 240
230  GOTO 190
240  VTAB 24: CALL  - 868: PRINT "
     ENTER >>N<< FOR NEW RUN          ENTER
     >>E<< FOR EXIT";: PRINT : VTAB 24: POKE
     36,38: GET G$: HOME : IF G$ = "N" THEN
     GOTO 30
250  IF G$ = "E" THEN  HOME : PRINT  CHR$ (
     13) +  CHR$ (4);"RUN MENU"
260  VTAB 4
270  GET F$
280  VTAB 20: CALL  - 958: INPUT "NEW LOWER
     LIMIT > ";A$:C =  VAL (A$): IF C = 0 AND
     H$ <  > "0" THEN  PRINT  CHR$ (7): GOTO
     280
290  VTAB 21: CALL  - 958: INPUT "NEW INCRE
     MENT (not smaller than 0.01) > ";I$:B =
     VAL (I$): IF B = 0 AND I$ <  > "0" THEN
     PRINT  CHR$ (7);: GOTO 290
300  IF B < .01 THEN  PRINT  CHR$ (7);: GOTO
     290
310  HOME : GOTO 180
```

```
10   REM   name: COAX TRANSFORMER
20   REM by: John Devoldere, ON4UN
30   PRINT : VTAB 13: POKE 36,33: PRINT "FAT
     AL ENTRY": PRINT  CHR$ (7): FOR G = 1 TO
     5000: NEXT : GOTO 10
40   CLEAR :H =  ATN (1) * 4: PRINT  CHR$ (1
     3) +  CHR$ (4);"PR#3": POKE 34,0: HOME
     : PRINT "                          COA
     XIAL FEEDLINE TRANSFORMER.";: POKE 36,
     71: PRINT "by ON4UN": PRINT "---------
     -------------------------------------
     --------------------------------"
50   PRINT "THIS PROGRAM ALLOWS YOU TO CALCU
     LATE THE TRANSFORMATION RESULTS OF A F
     EEDLINE    OF A GIVEN LENGTH, GIVEN THE
     LOAD IMPEDANCE AND EITHER THE LOAD CU·
     RRENT          (ABSOLUTE VALUE PLUS ANG
     LE) OR LOAD VOLTAGE (ABSOLUTE VALUE PL
     US ANGLE)"
60   PRINT "-----------------------------------
     -------------------------------------
     ---------": VTAB 21: PRINT "-----------
     -------------------------------------
     ----------------------------": POKE
     35,20
70   VTAB 7: INPUT "CABLE IMPEDANCE Zk > ";A
     $:I =  VAL (A$): IF I = < 0 THEN  PRINT
     CHR$ (7): GOTO 70
80   VTAB 9: PRINT "LOAD IMPEDANCE": PRINT "
     --------------"
90   VTAB 11: INPUT "RESISTIVE PART Z > ";B$
     :K =  VAL (B$): IF K = 0 THEN  PRINT  CHR$
     (7): GOTO 90
100  VTAB 12: INPUT "REACTIVE PART  Z > ";C
     $:P =  VAL (C$): IF P = 0 AND C$ < >
     "0" THEN  PRINT  CHR$ (7): GOTO 100
110  Q =  SQR (K ^ 2 + P ^ 2):R =  ATN (P /
     K):R = R * 180 / H: IF K < 0 AND P > 0
     THEN R = R + 180
120  IF K < 0 AND P < 0 THEN R = R - 180
130  VTAB 14: PRINT "LOAD VOLTAGE": PRINT "
     ------------": PRINT "ENTER 0 IF LOAD
     CURRENT WILL BE INPUTTED"
140  VTAB 17: INPUT "ABSOLUTE VALUE > ";D$:
     S =  VAL (D$): IF S = 0 AND D$ < > "0
     " THEN  PRINT  CHR$ (7);: GOTO 140
150  IF S < 0 THEN  PRINT  CHR$ (7);: GOTO
     140
160  IF S = 0 GOTO 190
170  VTAB 18: INPUT "ANGLE           > ";E$:
     T =  VAL (E$): IF T = 0 AND E$ < > "0
     " THEN  PRINT  CHR$ (7);: GOTO 170
180  E = S *  COS (T * H / 180):F = S *  SIN
     (T * H / 180): PRINT : IF S < > 0 THEN
     HOME : GOTO 230
190  VTAB 14: CALL  - 958: PRINT "LOAD CURR
     ENT": PRINT "------------"
200  VTAB 16: INPUT "ABSOLUTE VALUE > ";F$:
     U =  VAL (F$): IF U < = 0 THEN  PRINT
     CHR$ (7): GOTO 200
210  VTAB 17: INPUT "ANGLE           > ";G$:
     V =  VAL (G$): IF V = 0 AND G$ < > "0
     " THEN  PRINT  CHR$ (7): GOTO 210
220  HOME :G = U *  COS (V * H / 180):J = U
     *  SIN (V * H / 180): GOTO 270
230  G = ((E * K) + (P * F)) / (K ^ 2 + P ^
     2):J = ((F * K) - (P * E)) / (K ^ 2 +
     P ^ 2):U =  SQR (G ^ 2 + J ^ 2): IF G =
     0 THEN V = 90: GOTO 260
240  V =  ATN (J / G):V = V * 180 / H: IF G <
     0 AND J > 0 THEN V = V + 180
250  IF G < 0 AND J < 0 THEN V = V - 180
260  GOTO 280
270  E = ((G * K) - (J * P)):F = ((G * P) +
     (J * K))
280  S =  SQR (E ^ 2 + F ^ 2): IF E = 0 THEN
     T = 90: GOTO 310
290  T =  ATN (F / E):T = T * 180 / H: IF E <
     O AND F > O THEN T = T + 180
300  IF E < O AND F < O THEN T = T - 180
310  W =  SQR ((K + I) ^ 2 + P ^ 2):X =  SQR
     ((K - I) ^ 2 + P ^ 2):Y = (W + X) / (W
     - X):Y =  INT (Y * 100 + .5) / 100:Y =
     ABS (Y): PRINT : POKE 35,23: POKE 36,
     28: PRINT "FEEDLINE TRANSFORMER";: POKE
     36,71: PRINT "by ON4UN": PRINT "------
     -------------------------------------
     -------------------------------------"
320  PRINT "Zk = ";I;" ohm";: POKE 36,21: PRINT
     "REAL PART";: POKE 36,36: PRINT "IMAG
     PART";: POKE 36,50: PRINT "MAGNITUDE";
     : POKE 36,65: PRINT "ANGLE": PRINT "SW
     R= ";Y;: POKE 36,21: PRINT "----------
     ";: POKE 36,36: PRINT "---------";: POKE
     36,50: PRINT "---------";: POKE 36,65:
     PRINT "-----"
330  PRINT "IMPEDANCE (ohm) = ";: POKE 36,2
     1: PRINT K;: POKE 36,36: PRINT P;: POKE
     36,50: PRINT  INT (Q * 10000 + .5) / 1
     0000;: POKE 36,65: PRINT  INT (R * 100
     00 + .5) / 10000: PRINT "CURRENT (Amp)
     = ";: POKE 36,21: PRINT  INT (10000 *
     G + .5) / 10000;: POKE 36,36: PRINT  INT
     (10000 * J + .5) / 10000;: POKE 36,50:
     PRINT  INT (U * 10000 + .5) / 10000;:
     POKE 36,65: PRINT  INT (V * 10000 + .
     5) / 10000
340  PRINT "VOLTAGE (Volt) = ";: POKE 36,21
     : PRINT  INT (10000 * E + .5) / 10000;
     : POKE 36,36: PRINT  INT (10000 * F +
     .5) / 10000;: POKE 36,50: PRINT  INT (
     S * 10000 + .5) / 10000;: POKE 36,65: PRINT
     INT (T * 10000 + .5) / 10000: PRINT :
     PRINT "-----------------------------
     -------------------------------------
     -----------": PRINT
350  POKE 36,26: PRINT "DISTANCE TO LOAD =
     ": PRINT : POKE 36,21: PRINT "REAL PAR
     T";: POKE 36,36: PRINT "IMAG PART";: POKE
     36,50: PRINT "MAGNITUDE";: POKE 36,65:
     PRINT "ANGLE": POKE 36,21: PRINT "---
     -------";: POKE 36,36: PRINT "--------
     -";: POKE 36,50: PRINT "---------";: POKE
     36,65: PRINT "-----": PRINT "IMPEDANCE
     (ohm) = ": PRINT "CURRENT (Amp)    = "
360  PRINT "VOLTAGE (Volt)   = ": VTAB 21: PRINT
     "-----------------------------------
     -------------------------------------
     ----": PRINT "    ENTER DEGREES   OR
     >>>N<<< FOR NEW RUN    OR    >>>E<<< FOR
     EXIT": POKE 34,15: POKE 35,19: POKE 3
     2,19: POKE 33,60: PRINT
370  VTAB 23: INPUT "";H$: HOME : IF H$ = "
     N" OR H$ = "n" THEN  GOTO 10
380  IF H$ = "E" OR H$ = "e" THEN  HOME : PRINT
     CHR$ (13) +  CHR$ (4);"RUN MENU"
390  L =  VAL (H$): IF H$ < > "0" AND L = 0
     THEN  PRINT  CHR$ (7): GOTO 370
400  PRINT : VTAB 12: POKE 36,7: PRINT "
     ": VTAB 12: POKE 36,7: PRINT
     L;" deg":L = L * H / 180:A =  COS (L):
     D = A:B = I *  SIN (L):C =  SIN (L) /
     I:M = A * K:N = A * P:Z = M:A1 = N + B
     :Q = D - (P * C):B1 = K * C:C1 = ((Z *
     Q) + (A1 * B1)) / (Q ^ 2 + B1 ^ 2):D1 =
     ((A1 * Q) - (Z * B1)) / (Q ^ 2 + B1 ^
     2):E1 =  SQR (D1 ^ 2 + C1 ^ 2): IF C1 =
     0 AND D1 > 0 THEN F1 = 90: GOTO 440
410  IF C1 = 0 AND D1 < 0 THEN F1 =  - 90: GOTO
     440
420  F1 =  ATN (D1 / C1):F1 = F1 * 180 / H: IF
     C1 < 0 AND D1 > 0 THEN F1 = F1 + 180
430  IF C1 < 0 AND D1 < 0 THEN F1 = F1 - 18
     0
```

```
440 G1 = (G * Z) - (J * A1):H1 = (G * A1) +
    (J * Z):I1 = ((G1 * C1) + (H1 * D1)) /
    (C1 ^ 2 + D1 ^ 2):J1 = ((H1 * C1) - (G
    1 * D1)) / (C1 ^ 2 + D1 ^ 2):K1 = SQR
    (I1 ^ 2 + J1 ^ 2): IF I1 = 0 AND J1 >
    0 THEN L1 = 90: GOTO 490
450 IF I1 = 0 AND J1 < 0 THEN L1 = - 90: GOTO
    490
460 L1 = ATN (J1 / I1):L1 = L1 * 180 / H: IF
    I1 < 0 AND J1 > 0 THEN L1 = L1 + 180
470 IF I1 < 0 AND J1 < 0 THEN L1 = L1 - 18
    0
480 IF I1 < 0 AND J1 = 0 THEN L1 = 180
490 M1 = SQR (G1 ^ 2 + H1 ^ 2): IF G1 = 0 AND
    H1 < 0 THEN N1 = - 90: GOTO 540
500 IF G1 = 0 AND H1 > 0 THEN N1 = 90: GOTO
    540
510 N1 = ATN (H1 / G1):N1 = N1 * 180 / H: IF
    G1 < 0 AND H1 > 0 THEN N1 = N1 + 180
520 IF G1 < 0 AND H1 < 0 THEN N1 = N1 - 18
    0
530 IF G1 < 0 AND H1 = 0 THEN N1 = 180
540 C1 = INT (10000 * C1 + .5) / 10000:D1 =
    INT (10000 * D1 + .5) / 10000:E1 = INT
    (10000 * E1 + .5) / 10000:F1 = INT (1
    0000 * F1 + .5) / 10000:G1 = INT (100
    00 * G1 + .5) / 10000:H1 = INT (10000
    * H1 + .5) / 10000:I1 = INT (10000 *
    I1 + .5) / 10000:J1 = INT (10000 * J1
    + .5) / 10000:M1 = INT (10000 * M1 +
    .5) / 10000:N1 = INT (10000 * N1 + .5
    ) / 10000
550 K1 = INT (10000 * K1 + .5) / 10000:L1 =
    INT (10000 * L1 + .5) / 10000:I$ = STR$
    (F1):J$ = STR$ (L1):K$ = STR$ (N1): IF
    I$ = "180" THEN I$ = "180 or -180"
560 IF J$ = "180" THEN J$ = "180 or -180"
570 IF K$ = "180" THEN K$ = "180 or -180"
580 VTAB 15: PRINT : POKE 36,3: PRINT C1;:
    POKE 36,18: PRINT D1;: POKE 36,32: PRINT
    E1;: POKE 36,47: PRINT I$: POKE 36,3: PRINT
    I1;: POKE 36,18: PRINT J1;: POKE 36,32
    : PRINT K1;: POKE 36,47: PRINT J$: POKE
    36,3: PRINT G1;: POKE 36,18: PRINT H1;
    : POKE 36,32: PRINT M1;: POKE 36,47: PRINT
    K$: GOTO 370
```

```
10   REM name: IMPEDANCE ITERATION
20   REM by: John Devoldere, ON4UN
30   ONERR  GOTO 50
40   GOTO 60
50   VTAB 14: POKE 36,34: PRINT "FATAL ERROR
     ": PRINT  CHR$ (7): FOR G = 1 TO 5000:
     NEXT : GOTO 30
60   H =  ATN (1) * 4: PRINT  CHR$ (13) + CHR$
     (4);"PR#3": HOME : PRINT : POKE 36,27:
     PRINT "IMPEDANCE ALONG FEEDLINES";: POKE
     36,71: PRINT "by ON4UN": PRINT "------
     -----------------------------------------
     -----------------------------------"
70   PRINT "THIS PROGRAM CALCULATES THE IMPE
     DANCE, VOILTAGE AND CURRENT ALONG A FE
     EDLINE,    INITIALLY IN 1 DEGREE INCREM
     ENTS. REQUIRED INPUTS ARE THE LINE IMP
     EDANCE, THE"
80   PRINT "LOAD IMPEDANCE AND THE LOAD CURR
     ENT OR VOLTAGE.   LIMITS AND INCREMENTS
     CAN BE    ADJUSTED FOR BETTER RESULUTI
     ON": PRINT "-------------------------
     -----------------------------------------
     ----------------"
90   VTAB 22: PRINT "-----------------------
     -----------------------------------------
     -----------------": POKE 35,21
100  POKE 34,8: HOME :I = 0:K = 1
110  VTAB 23: PRINT "            RESULTS TO S
     CREEN    >>>S<<<      TO PRINTER    >>
     >P<<<    > ";: GET A$: IF A$ <  > "S" AND
     A$ <  > "s" AND A$ <  > "P" AND A$ <  >
     "p" THEN  PRINT  CHR$ (7): GOTO 110
120  POKE 35,23: VTAB 22: PRINT : POKE 36,0
     : CALL  - 868: POKE 35,21: HOME
130  VTAB 8: PRINT : INPUT "CABLE IMPEDANCE
     Zk > ";B$:P =  VAL (B$): IF P =  < 0 THEN
     PRINT  CHR$ (7): GOTO 130
140  VTAB 11: PRINT "LOAD IMPEDANCE": PRINT
     "--------------"
150  VTAB 13: INPUT "RESISTIVE PART Z > ";D
     $:Q =  VAL (D$): IF Q = 0 THEN  PRINT
     CHR$ (7): GOTO 150
160  VTAB 14: INPUT "REACTIVE PART  Z > ";E
     $:R =  VAL (E$): IF R = 0 AND E$ <  >
     "0" THEN  PRINT  CHR$ (7): GOTO 160
170  S =  SQR (Q ^ 2 + R ^ 2):T =  ATN (R /
     Q):T = T * 180 / H: IF Q < 0 AND R > 0
     THEN T = T + 180
180  IF Q < 0 AND R < 0 THEN T = T - 180
190  VTAB 16: PRINT "LOAD VOLTAGE": PRINT "
     ------------": PRINT "ENTER 0 IF LOAD
     CURRENT WILL BE INPUTTED"
200  VTAB 19: INPUT "ABSOLUTE VALUE > ";F$:
     U =  VAL (F$): IF U = 0 AND F$ <  > "0
     " THEN  PRINT  CHR$ (7);: GOTO 200
210  IF U < 0 THEN  PRINT  CHR$ (7);: GOTO
     200
220  IF U = 0 GOTO 250
230  VTAB 20: INPUT "ANGLE        > ";G$:
     V =  VAL (G$): IF V = 0 AND G$ <  > "0
     " THEN  PRINT  CHR$ (7);: GOTO 230
240  E = U *  COS (V * H / 180):F = U *  SIN
     (V * H / 180): PRINT : IF U <  > 0 THEN
     HOME : GOTO 290
250  VTAB 16: CALL  - 958: PRINT "LOAD CURR
     ENT": PRINT "------------"
260  VTAB 18: INPUT "ABSOLUTE VALUE > ";H$:
     W =  VAL (H$): IF W =  < 0 THEN  PRINT
     CHR$ (7): GOTO 260
270  VTAB 19: INPUT "ANGLE        > ";I$:
     X =  VAL (I$): IF X = 0 AND I$ <  > "0
     " THEN  PRINT  CHR$ (7): GOTO 270
280  HOME : POKE 34,0:G = W *  COS (X * H /
     180):J = W *  SIN (X * H / 180): GOTO
     330
290  G = ((E * Q) + (R * F)) / (Q ^ 2 + R ^
     2):J = ((F * Q) - (R * E)) / (Q ^ 2 +
     R ^ 2):W =  SQR (G ^ 2 + J ^ 2): IF G =
     0 THEN W = 90: GOTO 320
300  X =  ATN (J / G):X = X * 180 / H: IF G <
     0 AND J > 0 THEN X = X + 180
310  IF G < 0 AND J < 0 THEN X = X - 180
320  GOTO 340
330  E = ((G * Q) - (J * R)):F = ((G * R) +
     (J * Q))
340  U =  SQR (E ^ 2 + F ^ 2): IF E = 0 THEN
     V = 90: GOTO 370
350  V =  ATN (F / E):V = V * 180 / H: IF E <
     O AND F > O THEN V = V + 180
360  IF E < O AND F < O THEN V = V - 180
370  Y =  SQR ((Q + P) ^ 2 + R ^ 2):Z =  SQR
     ((Q - P) ^ 2 + R ^ 2):A1 = (Y + Z) / (
     Y - Z):A1 =  INT (A1 * 100 + .5) / 100
     :A1 =  ABS (A1): IF A$ <  > "P" AND A$
     <  > "p" THEN  POKE 34,0: HOME : GOTO
     400
380  POKE 34,8: POKE 35,23: HOME : VTAB 15:
     POKE 36,5: PRINT "PRINT-OUT WILL BE F
     ROM  0 TO 360 DEGREES IN 1 DEGREE INCR
     EMENTS": VTAB 22: PRINT "-------------
     -----------------------------------------
     ------------------------------": PRINT "
     >>>S<<< TO S
     TOP PRINTING";: POKE 35,12
390  PRINT  CHR$ (13) + CHR$ (4);"PR#1"
400  PRINT : POKE 36,28: PRINT "FEEDLINE TR
     ANSFORMER";: POKE 36,71: PRINT "by ON4
     UN": PRINT "-------------------------
     -----------------------------------------
     --------------": PRINT "Zk = ";P;" oh
     m";: POKE 36,21: PRINT "REAL PART";: POKE
     36,36: PRINT "IMAG PART";: POKE 36,50:
     PRINT "MAGNITUDE";: POKE 36,65: PRINT
     "ANGLE"
410  PRINT "SWR= ";A1;: POKE 36,21: PRINT "
     ----------";: POKE 36,36: PRINT "-----
     ----";: POKE 36,50: PRINT "---------";
     : POKE 36,65: PRINT "-----": PRINT "IM
     PEDANCE (ohm) = ";: POKE 36,21: PRINT
     Q;: POKE 36,36: PRINT R;: POKE 36,50: PRINT
     INT (S * 10000 + .5) / 10000;: POKE 3
     6,65: PRINT  INT (T * 10000 + .5) / 10
     000
420  PRINT "CURRENT (Amp)  = ";: POKE 36,21
     : PRINT  INT (10000 * G + .5) / 10000;
     : POKE 36,36: PRINT  INT (10000 * J +
     .5) / 10000;: POKE 36,50: PRINT  INT (
     W * 10000 + .5) / 10000;: POKE 36,65: PRINT
     INT (X * 10000 + .5) / 10000
430  PRINT "VOLTAGE (Volt) = ";: POKE 36,21
     : PRINT  INT (10000 * E + .5) / 10000;
     : POKE 36,36: PRINT  INT (10000 * F +
     .5) / 10000;: POKE 36,50: PRINT  INT (
     U * 10000 + .5) / 10000;: POKE 36,65: PRINT
     INT (V * 10000 + .5) / 10000: PRINT "
     -----------------------------------------
     ------------------------------------
     ---": PRINT : POKE 34,9: IF A$ = "P" OR
     A$ = "p" GOTO 450
440  VTAB 23: PRINT "         NEW RUN >>>R<<<
            NEW ITERATION >>>N<<<          E
     XIT >>>E<<<";: POKE 35,21
450  HOME : PRINT "LENGTH";: POKE 36,13: PRINT
     "IMPEDANCE";: POKE 36,33: PRINT "CURRE
     NT";: POKE 36,53: PRINT "VOLTAGE": POKE
     36,1: PRINT "DEG.";: POKE 36,10: PRINT
     "RESIS.";: POKE 36,20: PRINT "REACT.";
     : POKE 36,30: PRINT "AMPL.";: POKE 36,
     40: PRINT "ANGL.";: POKE 36,50: PRINT
     "AMPL.";: POKE 36,60: PRINT "ANGL.": POKE
     36,1: PRINT "----";: POKE 36,10: PRINT
     "------";: POKE 36,20: PRINT "------";
460  POKE 36,30: PRINT "-----";: POKE 36,40
     : PRINT "-----";: POKE 36,50: PRINT "-
     ----";: POKE 36,60: PRINT "-----": POKE
     34,12:I =  INT (I + .5)
```

```
470 I = I + K: IF I > 360 AND A$ = "P" THEN
    PRINT CHR$ (13) + CHR$ (4);"RUN MEN
    U"
480 IF I > 360 THEN I = 1:K = 1
490 I = INT (I * 100 + .5) / 100: POKE 36,
    1: PRINT I;: IF A$ = "P" OR A$ = "p" GOTO
    530
500 IF PEEK ( - 16384) = 206 OR PEEK ( -
    16384) = 238 THEN HOME : GOTO 690
510 IF PEEK ( - 16384) = 197 OR PEEK ( -
    16384) = 229 THEN GET J$: HOME : PRINT
    CHR$ (13) + CHR$ (4);"RUN MENU"
520 IF PEEK ( - 16384) = 210 OR PEEK ( -
    16384) = 242 THEN HOME : GET C$: GOTO
    30
530 IF A$ < > "P" AND A$ < > "p" GOTO 56
    0
540 IF PEEK ( - 16384) = 211 OR PEEK ( -
    16384) = 243 THEN GET C$: GOTO 30
550 POKE - 16368,0
560 L = I * H / 180:A = COS (L):D = A:B =
    P * SIN (L):C = SIN (L) / P:M = A *
    Q:N = A * R:B1 = M:C1 = N + B:S = D -
    (R * C):D1 = Q * C:E1 = ((B1 * S) + (C
    1 * D1)) / (S ^ 2 + D1 ^ 2):F1 = ((C1 *
    S) - (B1 * D1)) / (S ^ 2 + D1 ^ 2):G1 =
    (G * B1) - (J * C1):H1 = (G * C1) + (J
    * B1):I1 = ((G1 * E1) + (H1 * F1)) /
    (E1 ^ 2 + F1 ^ 2):J1 = ((H1 * E1) - (G
    1 * F1)) / (E1 ^ 2 + F1 ^ 2)
570 K1 = SQR (I1 ^ 2 + J1 ^ 2): IF I1 = 0 THEN
    L1 = 90: GOTO 610
580 L1 = ATN (J1 / I1):L1 = L1 * 180 / H: IF
    I1 < 0 AND J1 > 0 THEN L1 = L1 + 180
590 IF I1 < 0 AND J1 < 0 THEN L1 = L1 - 18
    0
600 IF I1 < 0 AND J1 = 0 THEN L1 = 180
610 M1 = SQR (G1 ^ 2 + H1 ^ 2): IF G1 = 0 THEN
    N1 = 90: GOTO 640
620 IF G1 = 0 THEN N1 = 90: GOTO 680
630 N1 = ATN (H1 / G1):N1 = N1 * 180 / H
640 IF G1 < 0 AND H1 > 0 THEN N1 = N1 + 18
    0
650 IF G1 < 0 AND H1 < 0 THEN N1 = N1 - 18
    0
660 IF G1 < 0 AND H1 = 0 THEN N1 = 180
670 L = VAL (L$)
680 E1 = INT (1000 * E1 + .5) / 1000:F1 =
    INT (1000 * F1 + .5) / 1000:M1 = INT
    (1000 * M1 + .5) / 1000:N1 = INT (100
    0 * N1 + .5) / 1000:K1 = INT (1000 *
    K1 + .5) / 1000:L1 = INT (1000 * L1 +
    .5) / 1000: POKE 36,10: PRINT E1;: POKE
    36,20: PRINT F1;: POKE 36,30: PRINT K1
    ;: POKE 36,40: PRINT L1;: POKE 36,50: PRINT
    M1;: POKE 36,60: PRINT N1: GOTO 470
690 GET J$: HOME : IF J$ = "E" OR J$ = "e"
    THEN PRINT CHR$ (13) + CHR$ (4);"R
    UN MENU"
700 VTAB 15: INPUT "LOWER LIMIT > ";K$:I =
    VAL (K$): IF I = 0 AND K$ < > "0" THEN
    PRINT CHR$ (7): GOTO 700
710 VTAB 16: INPUT "NEW INCREMENT (> 0.01)
    > ";M$:K = VAL (M$): IF K = 0 AND M
    $ < > "0" THEN PRINT CHR$ (7): GOTO
    710
720 IF K < .01 THEN PRINT CHR$ (7): GOTO
    710
730 I = I - K: HOME : GOTO 470
```

```
10   REM name: SUNRISE CALENDAR
20   REM  by: JOHN DEVOLDERE, ON4UN
30   ONERR  GOTO 50
40   GOTO 60
50   VTAB 14: POKE 36,34: PRINT "FATAL ERROR
     ": PRINT  CHR$ (7): FOR A = 1 TO 5000:
     NEXT : GOTO 30
60   PRINT  CHR$ (13) + CHR$ (4);"PR#3": POKE
     34,0: HOME : CLEAR : PRINT : POKE 36,2
     9: PRINT "SUNRISE CALENDAR.";: POKE 36
     ,70: PRINT "by  ON4UN": PRINT "-------
     ----------------------------------------
     ------------------------------------"
70   PRINT "THIS PROGRAM WILL PRINT A LISTIN
     G OF THE SUNRISE AND SUNSET TIMES (IN
     UTC) FOR  A GIVEN QTH WITH 1 DAY INCRE
     MENTS OVER THE ENTIRE YEAR.": PRINT "-
     ----------------------------------------
     ----------------------------------------
     --": VTAB 22
80   PRINT "----------------------------------
     ----------------------------------------
     ---------": POKE 35,21: POKE 34,6: HOME
     : VTAB 7: PRINT "QTH COORDINATES": PRINT
     "---------------": INPUT "COUNTRY NAME
     > ";B$: INPUT "CITY NAME > ";C$: INPUT
     "CALL > ";E$
90   VTAB 13: INPUT "LATITUDE IN DEG.CENTIDE
     G NORTH > ";F$:B =  VAL (F$): IF B = 0
     AND F$ <  > "0" THEN  PRINT  CHR$ (7)
     : GOTO 90
100  IF B > 90 OR B <  - 90 THEN  PRINT  CHR$
     (7): GOTO 90
110  VTAB 14: INPUT "LONGITUDE IN DEG.CENTI
     DEG WEST > ";G$:C =  VAL (G$): IF C <
     - 180 OR C > 180 THEN  PRINT  CHR$ (7
     ): GOTO 110
120  IF C = 0 AND G$ <  > "0" THEN  PRINT  CHR$
     (7): GOTO 110
130  HOME : VTAB 7: PRINT "TIMING INPUT": PRINT
     "-------------": IF C = 0 AND G$ <  > "
     0" THEN  PRINT  CHR$ (7): GOTO 110
140  PRINT "YEAR PRINT-OUT? (Y/N) > ";: GET
     H$: PRINT : IF H$ = "Y" THEN E = 1:F =
     365:G = 1: GOTO 240
150  VTAB 10: INPUT "STARTING DATE (MONTH,D
     AY) > ";I$,J$:H =  VAL (I$): IF H = 0 OR
     H > 12 THEN  PRINT  CHR$ (7): GOTO 150
160  E =  VAL (J$): IF E = 0 OR E > 31 THEN
     PRINT  CHR$ (7): GOTO 150
170  I = H:D = E: GOSUB 750:E = D
180  VTAB 11: INPUT "ENDING DATE (MONTH,DAY
     ) > ";K$,L$:J =  VAL (K$): IF J = 0 OR
     J > 12 THEN  PRINT  CHR$ (7): GOTO 180
190  F =  VAL (L$): IF F = 0 OR F > 31 THEN
     PRINT  CHR$ (7): GOTO 180
200  I = J:D = F: GOSUB 750:F = D: IF F < E THEN
     PRINT  CHR$ (7);: GOTO 180
210  PRINT "CALENDAR INCREMENT IS 1 DAY ? (
     Y/N) ";: GET H$: IF H$ = "Y" THEN G =
     1: GOTO 240
220  PRINT
230  VTAB 13: INPUT "ENTER INCREMENT (IN DA
     YS) > ";M$:G =  VAL (M$): IF G =  < 0 THEN
     PRINT  CHR$ (7);: GOTO 230
240  HOME : VTAB 7: PRINT "PRINTER INITIALI
     SATION.": PRINT "---------------------
     --"
250  VTAB 9: INPUT "PAPER LENGTH (11 OR 12
     INCH) > ";A$:L =  VAL (A$): IF L <  >
     11 AND L <  > 12 THEN  PRINT  CHR$ (7)
     ;: GOTO 250
260  VTAB 10: INPUT "LINES PER INCH (6 OR 8
     ) > ";A$:M =  VAL (A$): IF M <  > 6 AND
     M <  > 8 THEN  PRINT  CHR$ (7);: GOTO
     260
270  PRINT : PRINT : PRINT : PRINT : PRINT
     CHR$ (7);: PRINT  CHR$ (7): PRINT : POKE
     36,3: PRINT "INITIALIZE YOUR PRINTING
     IN ACCORDANCE WITH THE GIVEN FORMATTIN
     G INPUTS.": VTAB 23: PRINT "
                      HIT ANY KEY TO CONTIN
     UE   ";: GET H$: HOME : IF L = 11 AND M
     = 6 THEN N = 56
280  IF L = 12 AND M = 6 THEN N = 62
290  IF L = 11 AND M = 8 THEN N = 76
300  IF L = 12 AND M = 8 THEN N = 84
310  D$ =  CHR$ (13) + CHR$ (4): PRINT D$;"
     PR#1": PRINT "COUNTRY: ";B$: PRINT "CI
     TY : ";C$: PRINT "CALL : ";E$: PRINT "
     LATITUDE NORTH : ";B: PRINT "LONGITUDE
     WEST : ";C: GOSUB 330:O = 4: FOR D =
     E TO F STEP G:O = O + 1: IF O / N =  INT
     (O / N) THEN  PRINT  CHR$ (13) + CHR$
     (4);"PR#1    ": GOSUB 340: GOSUB 330
320  GOSUB 390: GOSUB 420: NEXT : PRINT  CHR$
     (13) + CHR$ (4);"PR#1": PRINT : PRINT
     : PRINT : PRINT  CHR$ (13) + CHR$ (4)
     ;"RUN MENU"
330  PRINT  CHR$ (13) + CHR$ (4);"PR#1": PRINT
     "MONTH/DAY";: POKE 36,15: PRINT "SUNRI
     SE";: POKE 36,27: PRINT "SUNSET": PRINT
     "---------";: POKE 36,15: PRINT "-----
     --";: POKE 36,27: PRINT "------";: PRINT
     CHR$ (13) + CHR$ (4);"PR#3": RETURN
340  IF M = 6 THEN  FOR K = 1 TO 7: PRINT :
     NEXT : RETURN
350  IF M = 8 THEN  FOR K = 1 TO 9: PRINT :
     NEXT : RETURN
360  IF B > P THEN Q = 0
370  IF B < P THEN Q = 180
380  RETURN
390  FOR R = 1 TO  LEN (N$): IF  MID$ (N$,R
     ,1) = "/" THEN 410
400  NEXT
410  N$ =  LEFT$ (N$,R - 1): RETURN
420  S = 3.1415927:T =  - .97599592:U = .217
     78881:V = .39777961:W = .9174811:X =  -
     .014834754:Y = C * S / 180:Z = B * S /
     180:I = (2 * S * D + Y) / 365.24219 -
     .052708:L = I - 1.351248:A1 =  - .033
     43 *  COS (I):C1 = .99944 *  SIN (I) /
     A1:D1 = ( COS (I) - .03343) / A1:E1 =
     T * D1 + U * C1:F1 = U * D1 - T * C1:G
     1 = V * E1:B1 = X - G1 *  SIN (Z)
430  H1 = ( COS (Z)) ^ 2 * (1 - G1 * G1) - B
     1 * B1: IF H1 < = 0 THEN O$ = "NO.SR"
     :P$ = "NO.SS": GOTO 450
440  I1 =  ATN (B1 /  SQR (H1)) - S / 2:J1 =
     ATN (( COS (L) * W * E1 -  SIN (L) *
     F1) / ( SIN (L) * W * E1 +  COS (L) *
     F1)): GOSUB 480:O$ =  STR$ (K1):I1 =  -
     I1: GOSUB 480:P$ =  STR$ (K1)
450  IF A = 1 GOTO 470
460  PRINT  CHR$ (13) + CHR$ (4);"PR#1": GOSUB
     620: PRINT Q$;
470  R$ = O$: GOSUB 510: POKE 36,15: PRINT R
     $;:R$ = P$: GOSUB 510: POKE 36,27: PRINT
     R$;: PRINT  CHR$ (13) + CHR$ (4);"PR#
     3": RETURN
480  L1 = J1 + I1 + Y + S: IF L1 < 0 THEN L1
     = L1 + S + S
490  L1 =  INT (L1 * 720 / S + .5): IF L1 >
     1439 THEN L1 = L1 - 1440
500  K1 = .4 *  INT (L1 / 60) + L1 / 100: RETURN
510  IF  LEN (R$) = 5 THEN R$ = R$
520  IF  LEN (R$) = 4 AND  MID$ (R$,2,1) =
     "." THEN R$ = "0" + R$: GOTO 610
530  IF  LEN (R$) = 4 AND  MID$ (R$,3,1) =
     "." THEN R$ = R$ + "0": GOTO 610
540  IF  LEN (R$) = 3 AND  MID$ (R$,2,1) =
     "." THEN R$ = "0" + R$ + "0": GOTO 610
```

```
550  IF  LEN (R$) = 3 AND  LEFT$ (R$,1) = "
     ." THEN R$ = "00" + R$: GOTO 610
560  IF  LEN (R$) = 2 AND  LEFT$ (R$,1) = "
     ." THEN R$ = "00" + R$ + "0": GOTO 610

570  IF  LEN (R$) = 2 AND  LEFT$ (R$,1) < >
     "." THEN R$ = R$ + ".00": GOTO 610
580  IF  LEN (R$) = 1 THEN R$ = "0" + R$ +
     ".00": GOTO 610
590  IF  LEN (R$) = 1 THEN R$ = "0" + R$ +
     ".00": GOTO 610
600  IF  LEN (R$) = 0 THEN R$ = "00.00": GOTO
     610
610  RETURN
620 M1 = D: IF D < 32 THEN S$ = "JAN":N1 =
     D: GOTO 740
630  IF D < 60 THEN S$ = "FEB":N1 = D - 31:
     GOTO 740
640  IF D < 91 THEN S$ = "MAR":N1 = D - 59:
     GOTO 740
650  IF D < 121 THEN S$ = "APR":N1 = D - 90
     : GOTO 740
660  IF D < 152 THEN S$ = "MAY":N1 = D - 12
     0: GOTO 740
670  IF D < 182 THEN S$ = "JUN":N1 = D - 15
     1: GOTO 740
680  IF D < 213 THEN S$ = "JUL":N1 = D - 18
     1: GOTO 740

690  IF D < 244 THEN S$ = "AUG":N1 = D - 21
     2: GOTO 740
700  IF D < 274 THEN S$ = "SEP":N1 = D - 24
     3: GOTO 740
710  IF D < 305 THEN S$ = "OCT":N1 = D - 27
     3: GOTO 740
720  IF D < 335 THEN S$ = "NOV":N1 = D - 30
     4: GOTO 740
730  IF D < 366 THEN S$ = "DEC":N1 = D - 33
     4: GOTO 740
740 D$ =  STR$ (N1):Q$ = S$ + "/" + D$: RETURN

750  IF I = 1 THEN D = D
760  IF I = 2 THEN D = D + 31
770  IF I = 3 THEN D = D + 59
780  IF I = 4 THEN D = D + 90
790  IF I = 5 THEN D = D + 120
800  IF I = 6 THEN D = D + 151
810  IF I = 7 THEN D = D + 181
820  IF I = 8 THEN D = D + 212
830  IF I = 9 THEN D = D + 243
840  IF I = 10 THEN D = D + 273
850  IF I = 11 THEN D = D + 304
860  IF I = 12 THEN D = D + 334
870  RETURN
```

DESIGN FREQUENCY : 1.825 Mhz   TOTAL LOSS RESISTANCE : 12 Ohm
LOADING COIL Q-FACTOR : 300   ELECTRICAL LENGTH CAPACITY HAT : 20 DEG.
DIAMETER ANTENNA = 10 INCHES (.573 DEG)

LENGTH deg/ft	HAT pF	HAT inch	R-rad Ohm	Surg-Z Ohm	X(L) Ohm	L uH	R Ohm	Q-fact —	BW kHz	Eff %	Eff -DB	Z OHM
70/98.92	139	155.5	32.43	228	0	0	0	7	259	72	1.4	44
68/96.06	140	156.7	30.1	226	7	.6	.02	8	243	71	1.5	42
66/93.18	141	157.9	27.93	224	15	1.3	.05	8	227	69	1.6	40
64/90.32	142	159.1	25.9	222	23	2	.07	9	213	68	1.7	38
62/87.43	144	161.4	24	221	31	2.7	.1	9	199	66	1.8	36
60/84.58	145	162.2	22.22	219	38	3.3	.12	10	186	64	1.9	34
58/81.69	146	163.4	20.55	217	46	4	.15	10	174	62	2	33
56/78.84	148	165.7	18.99	214	53	4.6	.17	11	163	60	2.2	31
54/75.98	149	166.9	17.52	212	60	5.2	.2	12	152	58	2.3	30
52/73.1	151	169.3	16.15	210	68	5.9	.22	13	142	56	2.4	28
50/70.24	153	171.3	14.85	208	75	6.5	.25	14	132	54	2.6	27
48/67.39	154	172.4	13.64	205	82	7.1	.27	15	123	52	2.8	26
46/64.5	156	174.8	12.5	203	90	7.8	.3	16	115	50	3	25
44/61.65	158	176.8	11.42	200	97	8.4	.32	17	107	48	3.2	24
42/58.79	161	180.3	10.41	197	104	9	.34	18	99	45	3.4	23
40/55.94	163	182.7	9.46	194	112	9.7	.37	20	92	43	3.6	22
38/53.08	166	185.8	8.57	191	119	10.3	.39	21	85	40	3.9	21
36/50.23	168	188.2	7.73	188	126	10.9	.42	23	79	38	4.2	20
34/47.38	172	192.5	6.94	184	133	11.5	.44	25	73	35	4.5	19
32/44.52	175	196.1	6.21	181	141	12.2	.47	27	67	33	4.8	19
30/41.67	179	200.4	5.51	177	148	12.9	.49	30	61	30	5.1	18
28/38.81	183	205.1	4.86	173	155	13.5	.51	32	56	27	5.5	17
26/35.96	188	210.6	4.26	168	162	14.1	.54	35	52	25	6	17
24/33.1	193	216.1	3.69	164	169	14.7	.56	39	47	22	6.4	16
22/30.25	200	224	3.16	158	175	15.2	.58	42	43	20	7	16
20/27.43	207	231.9	2.68	153	182	15.8	.6	47	39	17	7.6	15
18/24.57	216	241.7	2.22	146	186	16.2	.62	51	35	14	8.3	15
16/21.72	227	254.3	1.81	139	191	16.6	.63	57	32	12	9	14
14/18.9	241	270.1	1.43	131	194	16.9	.64	63	28	10	9.9	14
12/16.04	259	290.2	1.09	122	195	17	.65	70	26	7	11	14
10/13.22	285	319.3	.79	111	192	16.7	.64	78	23	5	12.3	13
8 /10.37	323	361.8	.53	98	184	16	.61	86	21	4	13.9	13
6 /7.51	392	439	.31	80	164	14.3	.54	94	19	2	16.2	13

DESIGN FREQUENCY : 3.775 Mhz   TOTAL LOSS RESISTANCE : 10 Ohm
LOADING COIL Q-FACTOR : 300   DIAMETER ANTENNA = 4 INCHES (.46 deg.)

LENGTH deg/ft	COIL deg	COIL ft	R-rad Ohm	SURGE-Z Ohm	X(L) Ohm	L uH	R Ohm	Q-fact —	BW kHz	Eff %	Eff -dB	Z Ohm
90/61.88	0	0	36.71	256	0	0	0	6.9	541	78	1.05	47
85/58.4	0	0	30.82	253	22	.9	.07	8.1	461	75	1.23	41
85/58.4	5	3.41	30.85	253	22	.9	.07	8.1	461	75	1.23	41
85/58.4	10	6.86	30.92	253	22	.9	.07	8.1	462	75	1.23	41
85/58.4	15	10.3	31.04	253	23	.9	.07	8.1	464	75	1.23	41
85/58.4	20	13.71	31.2	253	23	.9	.07	8	466	75	1.22	41
85/58.4	25	17.16	31.41	253	24	1	.08	8	469	75	1.21	41
85/58.4	30	20.6	31.67	253	26	1	.08	7.9	473	75	1.21	42
85/58.4	35	24.05	31.96	253	27	1.1	.09	7.8	478	76	1.2	42
85/58.4	40	27.46	32.29	253	29	1.2	.09	7.8	483	76	1.19	42
85/58.4	45	30.91	32.66	253	32	1.3	.1	7.7	488	76	1.18	43
85/58.4	50	34.35	33.05	253	36	1.5	.12	7.6	495	76	1.16	43
85/58.4	55	37.8	33.48	253	42	1.7	.14	7.5	501	76	1.15	44
85/58.4	60	41.21	33.93	253	49	2	.16	7.4	508	76	1.14	44
85/58.4	65	44.65	34.41	253	61	2.5	.2	7.3	516	77	1.13	45
85/58.4	70	48.1	34.9	253	80	3.3	.26	7.1	524	77	1.12	45
85/58.4	75	51.54	35.4	253	120	5	.4	7	534	77	1.12	46
85/58.4	80	54.95	35.92	253	239	10	.79	6.8	547	76	1.15	47
85/58.4	85	58.4	36.43	253	CAP	TOP	HAT	6.9	543	78	1.06	46
80/54.92	0	0	25.85	249	43	1.8	.14	9.5	394	71	1.44	36
80/54.92	5	3.41	25.9	249	44	1.8	.14	9.5	394	71	1.44	36
80/54.92	10	6.86	26.04	249	44	1.8	.14	9.5	397	71	1.43	36
80/54.92	15	10.3	26.28	249	45	1.8	.15	9.4	400	72	1.42	36
80/54.92	20	13.71	26.6	249	47	1.9	.15	9.3	405	72	1.41	37
80/54.92	25	17.16	27.01	249	49	2	.16	9.1	411	72	1.39	37
80/54.92	30	20.6	27.5	249	52	2.1	.17	8.9	419	73	1.37	38
80/54.92	35	24.02	28.07	249	56	2.3	.18	8.8	428	73	1.35	38
80/54.92	40	27.46	28.71	249	62	2.6	.2	8.6	438	73	1.32	39
80/54.92	45	30.91	29.42	249	69	2.9	.23	8.3	449	74	1.3	40
80/54.92	50	34.32	30.19	249	79	3.3	.26	8.1	461	74	1.28	40
80/54.92	55	37.76	31.01	249	93	3.9	.31	7.9	474	75	1.25	41
80/54.92	60	41.21	31.88	249	114	4.8	.38	7.7	489	75	1.23	42
80/54.92	65	44.62	32.78	249	151	6.3	.5	7.4	504	75	1.21	43
80/54.92	70	48.06	33.71	249	225	9.4	.75	7.2	522	75	1.21	44
80/54.92	75	51.51	34.66	249	447	18.8	1.49	6.8	548	75	1.25	46
80/54.92	80	54.92	35.61	249	CAP	TOP	HAT	6.9	540	78	1.08	46
75/51.44	0	0	21.61	245	65	2.7	.21	11.2	336	67	1.68	32
75/51.44	5	3.41	21.68	245	66	2.7	.22	11.1	337	67	1.68	32
75/51.44	10	6.86	21.89	245	67	2.8	.22	11	340	68	1.67	32
75/51.44	15	10.27	22.23	245	69	2.9	.23	10.9	346	68	1.65	32
75/51.44	20	13.71	22.71	245	71	2.9	.23	10.6	353	68	1.62	33
75/51.44	25	17.13	23.31	245	75	3.1	.25	10.3	363	69	1.59	34
75/51.44	30	20.57	24.03	245	81	3.4	.27	10	374	70	1.55	34
75/51.44	35	24.02	24.86	245	88	3.7	.29	9.7	387	70	1.51	35
75/51.44	40	27.43	25.8	245	98	4.1	.32	9.3	402	71	1.47	36
75/51.44	45	30.87	26.83	245	111	4.6	.37	9	419	72	1.42	37
75/51.44	50	34.28	27.93	245	131	5.5	.43	8.6	437	72	1.38	38
75/51.44	55	37.73	29.11	245	161	6.7	.53	8.2	456	73	1.35	40
75/51.44	60	41.14	30.35	245	212	8.9	.7	7.8	478	73	1.32	41
75/51.44	65	44.59	31.63	245	315	13.2	1.05	7.4	503	74	1.31	43
75/51.44	70	48.03	32.93	245	628	26.4	2.09	6.9	539	73	1.36	45
75/51.44	75	51.44	34.25	245	CAP	TOP	HAT	7.1	527	77	1.12	44

70/47.97	0	0	18	241	87	3.6	.29	13.1	286	63	1.97	28
70/47.97	5	3.41	18.09	241	88	3.7	.29	13.1	287	63	1.96	28
70/47.97	10	6.82	18.36	241	89	3.7	.29	12.9	292	64	1.94	29
70/47.97	15	10.27	18.8	241	92	3.8	.3	12.6	299	64	1.9	29
70/47.97	20	13.68	19.42	241	97	4	.32	12.2	309	65	1.86	30
70/47.97	25	17.13	20.21	241	103	4.3	.34	11.7	321	66	1.8	31
70/47.97	30	20.54	21.14	241	112	4.7	.37	11.1	337	67	1.74	32
70/47.97	35	23.98	22.22	241	124	5.2	.41	10.6	354	68	1.67	33
70/47.97	40	27.4	23.43	241	140	5.9	.46	10	374	69	1.61	34
70/47.97	45	30.84	24.75	241	164	6.9	.54	9.5	396	70	1.55	35
70/47.97	50	34.25	26.16	241	202	8.5	.67	8.9	420	71	1.49	37
70/47.97	55	37.7	27.66	241	265	11.1	.88	8.4	447	71	1.45	39
70/47.97	60	41.11	29.21	241	394	16.6	1.31	7.8	478	72	1.43	41
70/47.97	65	44.55	30.81	241	783	33	2.61	7.2	523	70	1.49	43
70/47.97	70	47.97	32.42	241	CAP	TOP	HAT	7.4	507	76	1.17	42
65/44.49	0	0	14.89	237	110	4.6	.36	15.5	243	58	2.3	25
65/44.49	5	3.41	15.01	237	111	4.6	.37	15.4	244	59	2.29	25
65/44.49	10	6.82	15.34	237	113	4.7	.37	15	250	59	2.25	26
65/44.49	15	10.27	15.89	237	118	4.9	.39	14.5	259	60	2.19	26
65/44.49	20	13.68	16.64	237	124	5.2	.41	13.8	271	61	2.11	27
65/44.49	25	17.09	17.6	237	134	5.6	.44	13.1	287	62	2.03	28
65/44.49	30	20.54	18.73	237	147	6.1	.49	12.3	306	64	1.94	29
65/44.49	35	23.95	20.04	237	166	6.9	.55	11.5	327	65	1.84	31
65/44.49	40	27.36	21.49	237	194	8.1	.64	10.7	352	66	1.75	32
65/44.49	45	30.81	23.06	237	237	9.9	.79	9.9	380	68	1.67	34
65/44.49	50	34.22	24.74	237	311	13.1	1.03	9.1	410	69	1.61	36
65/44.49	55	37.66	26.5	237	461	19.4	1.53	8.4	446	69	1.57	38
65/44.49	60	41.08	28.32	237	916	38.6	3.05	7.5	499	68	1.65	41
65/44.49	65	44.49	30.15	237	CAP	TOP	HAT	7.8	480	75	1.25	40
60/41.01	0	0	12.23	232	133	5.6	.44	18.2	206	53	2.68	23
60/41.01	5	3.41	12.37	232	135	5.6	.45	18	208	54	2.66	23
60/41.01	10	6.82	12.76	232	138	5.8	.46	17.5	215	54	2.6	23
60/41.01	15	10.24	13.4	232	144	6	.48	16.7	225	56	2.51	24
60/41.01	20	13.65	14.28	232	154	6.4	.51	15.6	240	57	2.4	25
60/41.01	25	17.09	15.4	232	168	7	.56	14.5	259	59	2.27	26
60/41.01	30	20.51	16.72	232	189	7.9	.63	13.3	282	61	2.14	27
60/41.01	35	23.92	18.22	232	220	9.2	.73	12.2	308	62	2.02	29
60/41.01	40	27.33	19.88	232	267	11.2	.89	11.1	338	64	1.9	31
60/41.01	45	30.77	21.68	232	350	14.7	1.16	10.1	371	66	1.81	33
60/41.01	50	34.19	23.58	232	517	21.7	1.72	9.1	411	66	1.76	35
60/41.01	55	37.6	25.54	232	1026	43.2	3.42	8	471	65	1.84	39
60/41.01	60	41.01	27.53	232	CAP	TOP	HAT	8.4	448	73	1.35	38
55/37.57	0	0	9.94	226	158	6.6	.52	21.5	174	48	3.14	20
55/37.57	5	3.41	10.09	226	159	6.7	.53	21.2	177	48	3.11	21
55/37.57	10	6.82	10.54	226	164	6.9	.54	20.3	185	50	3.01	21
55/37.57	15	10.24	11.27	226	173	7.2	.57	19	197	51	2.88	22
55/37.57	20	13.65	12.28	226	188	7.9	.62	17.5	215	53	2.71	23
55/37.57	25	17.06	13.53	226	209	8.8	.69	15.8	237	55	2.53	24
55/37.57	30	20.47	15.02	226	241	10.1	.8	14.2	264	58	2.36	26
55/37.57	35	23.88	16.69	226	292	12.3	.97	12.7	295	60	2.2	28
55/37.57	40	27.3	18.53	226	380	16	1.26	11.4	330	62	2.07	30
55/37.57	45	30.71	20.5	226	561	23.6	1.87	10.1	373	63	1.99	32
55/37.57	50	34.12	22.54	226	1111	46.8	3.7	8.6	438	62	2.07	36
55/37.57	55	37.57	24.63	226	CAP	TOP	HAT	9.1	411	71	1.48	35
50/34.09	0	0	7.98	221	185	7.7	.61	25.7	146	42	3.68	19
50/34.09	5	3.38	8.14	221	187	7.8	.62	25.2	149	43	3.63	19
50/34.09	10	6.79	8.64	221	194	8.1	.64	23.8	158	44	3.49	19
50/34.09	15	10.2	9.45	221	208	8.7	.69	21.7	173	46	3.29	20
50/34.09	20	13.62	10.57	221	229	9.6	.76	19.5	193	49	3.05	21
50/34.09	25	17.03	11.95	221	262	11	.87	17.2	219	52	2.81	23
50/34.09	30	20.44	13.57	221	315	13.2	1.05	15.1	249	55	2.59	25
50/34.09	35	23.85	15.38	221	408	17.2	1.36	13.1	286	57	2.41	27
50/34.09	40	27.26	17.35	221	600	25.2	2	11.4	330	59	2.29	29
50/34.09	45	30.68	19.42	221	1185	49.9	3.95	9.4	399	58	2.36	33
50/34.09	50	34.09	21.54	221	CAP	TOP	HAT	10.2	368	68	1.66	32

45/30.61	0	0	6.3	214	214	9	.71	30.5	123	37	4.32	17
45/30.61	5	3.38	6.48	214	217	9.1	.72	29.7	127	37	4.24	17
45/30.61	10	6.79	7.02	214	227	9.5	.75	27.5	137	39	4.04	18
45/30.61	15	10.2	7.91	214	247	10.4	.82	24.4	154	42	3.75	19
45/30.61	20	13.58	9.12	214	279	11.7	.93	21.2	177	45	3.43	20
45/30.61	25	16.99	10.6	214	332	13.9	1.1	18.2	206	48	3.11	22
45/30.61	30	20.41	12.32	214	428	18	1.42	15.5	242	51	2.85	24
45/30.61	35	23.82	14.23	214	625	26.3	2.08	13.1	287	54	2.67	26
45/30.61	40	27.2	16.26	214	1232	51.9	4.1	10.5	359	53	2.72	30
45/30.61	45	30.61	18.35	214	CAP	TOP	HAT	11.6	323	64	1.89	28
40/27.17	0	0	4.85	207	246	10.3	.82	36.4	103	30	5.09	16
40/27.17	5	3.38	5.05	207	251	10.5	.83	35.1	107	31	4.98	16
40/27.17	10	6.79	5.64	207	267	11.2	.89	31.6	119	34	4.67	17
40/27.17	15	10.17	6.59	207	296	12.4	.98	27.3	138	37	4.26	18
40/27.17	20	13.58	7.87	207	348	14.6	1.16	22.8	164	41	3.84	19
40/27.17	25	16.96	9.44	207	444	18.7	1.48	18.9	199	45	3.46	21
40/27.17	30	20.37	11.22	207	644	27.1	2.14	15.4	243	48	3.19	23
40/27.17	35	23.75	13.15	207	1264	53.2	4.21	11.9	316	48	3.19	27
40/27.17	40	27.17	15.16	207	CAP	TOP	HAT	13.6	276	60	2.2	25
35/23.69	0	0	3.65	199	284	11.9	.94	43.3	87	25	6.02	15
35/23.69	5	3.38	3.86	199	291	12.2	.97	41.1	91	26	5.85	15
35/23.69	10	6.76	4.48	199	315	13.2	1.05	35.9	104	28	5.4	16
35/23.69	15	10.14	5.48	199	363	15.3	1.21	29.7	127	32	4.84	17
35/23.69	20	13.52	6.82	199	455	19.1	1.51	23.8	158	37	4.3	18
35/23.69	25	16.93	8.42	199	655	27.6	2.18	18.7	201	40	3.89	21
35/23.69	30	20.31	10.2	199	1277	53.8	4.25	13.7	274	41	3.8	24
35/23.69	35	23.69	12.07	199	CAP	TOP	HAT	16.4	229	54	2.62	22
30/20.24	0	0	2.62	190	329	13.8	1.09	51	73	19	7.18	14
30/20.24	5	3.35	2.85	190	340	14.3	1.13	47.7	79	20	6.91	14
30/20.24	10	6.73	3.5	190	380	16	1.26	39.8	94	23	6.25	15
30/20.24	15	10.1	4.54	190	465	19.6	1.55	31.1	121	28	5.49	16
30/20.24	20	13.48	5.9	190	658	27.7	2.19	23.4	160	32	4.87	18
30/20.24	25	16.86	7.48	190	1271	53.5	4.23	16.2	232	34	4.63	22
30/20.24	30	20.24	9.17	190	CAP	TOP	HAT	20.6	182	47	3.21	19
25/16.8	0	0	1.79	179	383	16.1	1.27	58.3	64	13	8.61	13
25/16.8	5	3.35	2.03	179	403	16.9	1.34	53	71	15	8.19	13
25/16.8	10	6.69	2.7	179	474	19.9	1.58	41.7	90	18	7.23	14
25/16.8	15	10.07	3.76	179	653	27.5	2.17	30.1	125	23	6.27	16
25/16.8	20	13.42	5.08	179	1242	52.3	4.14	19.3	194	26	5.78	19
25/16.8	25	16.8	6.55	179	CAP	TOP	HAT	27.2	138	39	4.03	17
20/13.35	0	0	1.14	166	456	19.2	1.52	62.4	60	9	10.46	13
20/13.35	5	3.31	1.37	166	493	20.7	1.64	54.9	68	10	9.75	13
20/13.35	10	6.66	2.06	166	644	27.1	2.14	39.4	95	14	8.38	14
20/13.35	15	10.01	3.08	166	1191	50.2	3.97	23.5	160	18	7.43	17
20/13.35	20	13.35	4.28	166	CAP	TOP	HAT	38.6	97	30	5.23	14
15/9.91	0	0	.62	149	556	23.4	1.85	60	62	5	12.97	12
15/9.91	5	3.28	.87	149	642	27	2.14	49.4	76	6	11.73	13
15/9.91	10	6.59	1.54	149	1112	46.8	3.7	28.4	132	10	9.95	15
15/9.91	15	9.91	2.45	149	CAP	TOP	HAT	60.5	62	19	7.05	12
10/6.46	0	0	.28	124	703	29.6	2.34	47.3	79	2	16.54	13
10/6.46	5	3.22	.52	124	994	41.9	3.31	32.3	116	3	14.25	14
10/6.46	10	6.46	1.09	124	CAP	TOP	HAT	112.7	33	9	10.04	11
5 /3.05	0	0	.07	83	948	39.9	3.16	25.6	146	0	22.77	13
5 /3.05	5	3.05	.26	83	CAP	TOP	HAT	307.4	12	2	15.81	10

DESIGN FREQUENCY : 1.825 Mhz   TOTAL LOSS RESISTANCE : 15 Ohm
LOADING COIL Q-FACTOR : 300   DIAMETER ANTENNA = 10 INCHES (.556 deg.)

LENGTH deg/ft	COIL deg	COIL ft	R-rad Ohm	SURGE-Z Ohm	X(L) Ohm	L uH	R Ohm	Q-fact –	BW kHz	Eff %	Eff -dB	Z Ohm
90/127.7	0	0	36.71	245	0	0	0	6.6	273	70	1.49	52
85/120.5	0	0	30.82	241	21	1.8	.07	7.7	233	67	1.73	46
85/120.5	5	7.09	30.85	241	21	1.8	.07	7.7	234	67	1.73	46
85/120.5	10	14.17	30.92	241	21	1.8	.07	7.7	234	67	1.73	46
85/120.5	15	21.26	31.04	241	21	1.8	.07	7.7	235	67	1.72	46
85/120.5	20	28.35	31.2	241	22	1.9	.07	7.7	236	67	1.72	46
85/120.5	25	35.43	31.41	241	23	2	.07	7.6	238	67	1.71	46
85/120.5	30	42.52	31.67	241	24	2	.08	7.5	240	67	1.7	47
85/120.5	35	49.61	31.96	241	26	2.2	.08	7.5	242	67	1.68	47
85/120.5	40	56.69	32.29	241	28	2.4	.09	7.4	245	68	1.67	47
85/120.5	45	63.81	32.66	241	31	2.7	.1	7.3	248	68	1.66	48
85/120.5	50	70.9	33.05	241	34	2.9	.11	7.2	251	68	1.64	48
85/120.5	55	77.99	33.48	241	40	3.4	.13	7.1	254	68	1.62	49
85/120.5	60	85.07	33.93	241	47	4	.15	7	258	69	1.61	49
85/120.5	65	92.16	34.41	241	58	5	.19	6.9	262	69	1.59	50
85/120.5	70	99.25	34.9	241	77	6.7	.25	6.8	266	69	1.58	50
85/120.5	75	106.3	35.4	241	114	9.9	.38	6.7	271	69	1.57	51
85/120.5	80	113.4	35.92	241	228	19.8	.76	6.5	277	69	1.58	52
85/120.5	85	120.5	36.43	241	CAP	TOP	HAT	6.6	275	70	1.5	51
80/113.3	0	0	25.85	238	41	3.5	.13	9.1	199	63	2.01	41
80/113.3	5	7.05	25.9	238	42	3.6	.14	9.1	199	63	2	41
80/113.3	10	14.14	26.04	238	42	3.6	.14	9	200	63	1.99	41
80/113.3	15	21.23	26.28	238	43	3.7	.14	9	202	63	1.98	41
80/113.3	20	28.31	26.6	238	45	3.9	.15	8.8	205	63	1.96	42
80/113.3	25	35.4	27.01	238	47	4	.15	8.7	208	64	1.94	42
80/113.3	30	42.49	27.5	238	50	4.3	.16	8.6	212	64	1.91	43
80/113.3	35	49.57	28.07	238	54	4.7	.18	8.4	216	64	1.88	43
80/113.3	40	56.66	28.71	238	59	5.1	.19	8.2	221	65	1.85	44
80/113.3	45	63.75	29.42	238	66	5.7	.22	8	227	65	1.82	45
80/113.3	50	70.83	30.19	238	75	6.5	.25	7.8	233	66	1.78	45
80/113.3	55	77.92	31.01	238	89	7.7	.29	7.6	240	66	1.75	46
80/113.3	60	85.01	31.88	238	109	9.5	.36	7.3	247	67	1.71	47
80/113.3	65	92.09	32.78	238	144	12.5	.48	7.1	255	67	1.68	48
80/113.3	70	99.18	33.71	238	215	18.7	.71	6.9	263	68	1.67	49
80/113.3	75	106.3	34.66	238	428	37.3	1.42	6.5	276	67	1.69	51
80/113.3	80	113.3	35.61	238	CAP	TOP	HAT	6.6	273	70	1.53	51
75/106.1	0	0	21.61	234	62	5.4	.2	10.7	170	58	2.32	37
75/106.1	5	7.05	21.68	234	63	5.4	.21	10.6	170	58	2.31	37
75/106.1	10	14.14	21.89	234	64	5.5	.21	10.5	172	59	2.3	37
75/106.1	15	21.23	22.23	234	65	5.6	.21	10.4	175	59	2.27	37
75/106.1	20	28.28	22.71	234	68	5.9	.22	10.2	178	59	2.23	38
75/106.1	25	35.37	23.31	234	72	6.2	.24	9.9	183	60	2.19	39
75/106.1	30	42.45	24.03	234	77	6.7	.25	9.6	189	61	2.14	39
75/106.1	35	49.54	24.86	234	84	7.3	.28	9.3	196	61	2.09	40
75/106.1	40	56.59	25.8	234	93	8.1	.31	8.9	203	62	2.03	41
75/106.1	45	63.68	26.83	234	106	9.2	.35	8.6	211	63	1.97	42
75/106.1	50	70.77	27.93	234	125	10.9	.41	8.2	221	64	1.91	43
75/106.1	55	77.85	29.11	234	154	13.4	.51	7.8	231	65	1.86	45
75/106.1	60	84.91	30.35	234	202	17.6	.67	7.5	241	65	1.81	46
75/106.1	65	91.99	31.63	234	301	26.2	1	7.1	254	66	1.78	48
75/106.1	70	99.08	32.93	234	599	52.2	1.99	6.6	272	65	1.81	50
75/106.1	75	106.1	34.25	234	CAP	TOP	HAT	6.8	267	69	1.58	49

70/98.98	0	0	18	230	83	7.2	.27	12.5	144	54	2.67	33
70/98.98	5	7.05	18.09	230	84	7.3	.28	12.5	145	54	2.66	33
70/98.98	10	14.14	18.36	230	85	7.4	.28	12.3	147	54	2.63	34
70/98.98	15	21.19	18.8	230	88	7.6	.29	12	151	55	2.59	34
70/98.98	20	28.28	19.42	230	92	8	.3	11.6	156	55	2.53	35
70/98.98	25	35.33	20.21	230	98	8.5	.32	11.2	162	56	2.46	36
70/98.98	30	42.42	21.14	230	107	9.3	.35	10.6	170	57	2.37	36
70/98.98	35	49.48	22.22	230	118	10.2	.39	10.1	179	59	2.29	38
70/98.98	40	56.56	23.43	230	134	11.6	.44	9.6	189	60	2.2	39
70/98.98	45	63.62	24.75	230	157	13.6	.52	9.1	200	61	2.12	40
70/98.98	50	70.7	26.16	230	192	16.7	.64	8.5	212	62	2.04	42
70/98.98	55	77.76	27.66	230	253	22	.84	8	226	63	1.97	44
70/98.98	60	84.84	29.21	230	376	32.7	1.25	7.5	241	64	1.93	45
70/98.98	65	91.9	30.81	230	747	65.1	2.49	6.9	264	63	1.96	48
70/98.98	70	98.98	32.42	230	CAP	TOP	HAT	7	257	68	1.66	47
65/91.8	0	0	14.89	225	104	9	.34	14.7	123	49	3.08	30
65/91.8	5	7.05	15.01	225	105	9.1	.35	14.6	124	49	3.06	30
65/91.8	10	14.11	15.34	225	108	9.4	.36	14.3	127	49	3.02	31
65/91.8	15	21.16	15.89	225	112	9.7	.37	13.8	131	50	2.94	31
65/91.8	20	28.22	16.64	225	118	10.2	.39	13.2	138	51	2.85	32
65/91.8	25	35.3	17.6	225	127	11	.42	12.4	146	53	2.74	33
65/91.8	30	42.36	18.73	225	140	12.2	.46	11.7	155	54	2.62	34
65/91.8	35	49.41	20.04	225	158	13.7	.52	10.9	166	56	2.5	36
65/91.8	40	56.46	21.49	225	184	16	.61	10.1	179	57	2.38	37
65/91.8	45	63.55	23.06	225	225	19.6	.75	9.4	193	59	2.27	39
65/91.8	50	70.6	24.74	225	295	25.7	.98	8.7	208	60	2.17	41
65/91.8	55	77.66	26.5	225	438	38.1	1.46	8	226	61	2.1	43
65/91.8	60	84.71	28.32	225	870	75.8	2.9	7.2	253	61	2.13	46
65/91.8	65	91.8	30.15	225	CAP	TOP	HAT	7.4	244	66	1.76	45
60/84.61	0	0	12.23	220	127	11	.42	17.3	105	44	3.55	28
60/84.61	5	7.02	12.37	220	128	11.1	.42	17.1	106	44	3.52	28
60/84.61	10	14.07	12.76	220	131	11.4	.43	16.6	109	45	3.45	28
60/84.61	15	21.13	13.4	220	137	11.9	.45	15.8	114	46	3.33	29
60/84.61	20	28.18	14.28	220	146	12.7	.48	14.8	122	48	3.19	30
60/84.61	25	35.24	15.4	220	160	13.9	.53	13.8	132	49	3.03	31
60/84.61	30	42.29	16.72	220	179	15.6	.59	12.7	143	51	2.87	32
60/84.61	35	49.34	18.22	220	208	18.1	.69	11.6	156	53	2.7	34
60/84.61	40	56.4	19.88	220	254	22.1	.84	10.6	171	55	2.55	36
60/84.61	45	63.45	21.68	220	331	28.8	1.1	9.6	189	57	2.42	38
60/84.61	50	70.51	23.58	220	490	42.7	1.63	8.7	209	58	2.32	40
60/84.61	55	77.56	25.54	220	973	84.8	3.24	7.6	238	58	2.35	44
60/84.61	60	84.61	27.53	220	CAP	TOP	HAT	7.9	228	64	1.89	43
55/77.46	0	0	9.94	215	150	13	.5	20.5	88	39	4.08	25
55/77.46	5	7.02	10.09	215	152	13.2	.5	20.2	89	39	4.04	26
55/77.46	10	14.07	10.54	215	156	13.6	.52	19.4	93	40	3.94	26
55/77.46	15	21.1	11.27	215	165	14.3	.55	18.1	100	42	3.77	27
55/77.46	20	28.15	12.28	215	178	15.5	.59	16.7	109	44	3.56	28
55/77.46	25	35.2	13.53	215	199	17.3	.66	15.1	120	46	3.34	29
55/77.46	30	42.22	15.02	215	229	19.9	.76	13.6	133	48	3.12	31
55/77.46	35	49.28	16.69	215	278	24.2	.92	12.2	149	51	2.91	33
55/77.46	40	56.33	18.53	215	362	31.5	1.2	10.8	167	53	2.73	35
55/77.46	45	63.35	20.5	215	534	46.5	1.78	9.6	189	54	2.6	37
55/77.46	50	70.41	22.54	215	1057	92.1	3.52	8.2	221	54	2.61	41
55/77.46	55	77.46	24.63	215	CAP	TOP	HAT	8.7	209	62	2.07	40
50/70.28	0	0	7.98	209	175	15.2	.58	24.4	74	33	4.71	24
50/70.28	5	7.02	8.14	209	177	15.4	.59	23.9	76	34	4.65	24
50/70.28	10	14.04	8.64	209	184	16	.61	22.5	80	35	4.49	24
50/70.28	15	21.06	9.45	209	196	17	.65	20.6	88	37	4.24	25
50/70.28	20	28.12	10.57	209	216	18.8	.72	18.5	98	40	3.96	26
50/70.28	25	35.14	11.95	209	248	21.6	.82	16.3	111	43	3.67	28
50/70.28	30	42.16	13.57	209	298	25.9	.99	14.3	127	45	3.39	30
50/70.28	35	49.18	15.38	209	386	33.6	1.28	12.5	145	48	3.14	32
50/70.28	40	56.23	17.35	209	567	49.4	1.89	10.8	168	50	2.96	34
50/70.28	45	63.25	19.42	209	1121	97.7	3.73	9	202	50	2.94	38
50/70.28	50	70.28	21.54	209	CAP	TOP	HAT	9.6	188	58	2.3	37

45/63.12	0	0	6.3	203	203	17.7	.67	29.1	62	28	5.43	22
45/63.12	5	6.99	6.48	203	206	17.9	.68	28.3	64	29	5.34	22
45/63.12	10	14.01	7.02	203	216	18.8	.72	26.2	69	30	5.11	23
45/63.12	15	21.03	7.91	203	234	20.4	.78	23.3	78	33	4.77	24
45/63.12	20	28.05	9.12	203	264	23	.88	20.2	89	36	4.38	25
45/63.12	25	35.07	10.6	203	315	27.4	1.05	17.4	104	39	4.01	27
45/63.12	30	42.06	12.32	203	406	35.4	1.35	14.8	122	42	3.67	29
45/63.12	35	49.08	14.23	203	593	51.7	1.97	12.5	145	45	3.41	31
45/63.12	40	56.1	16.26	203	1169	102	3.89	10	181	46	3.35	35
45/63.12	45	63.12	18.35	203	CAP	TOP	HAT	11	165	55	2.6	33
40/55.97	0	0	4.85	196	233	20.3	.77	34.8	52	23	6.28	21
40/55.97	5	6.99	5.05	196	238	20.7	.79	33.5	54	24	6.16	21
40/55.97	10	13.98	5.64	196	252	21.9	.84	30.2	60	26	5.81	21
40/55.97	15	20.96	6.59	196	280	24.4	.93	26	70	29	5.34	23
40/55.97	20	27.99	7.87	196	330	28.7	1.1	21.8	83	32	4.84	24
40/55.97	25	34.97	9.44	196	420	36.6	1.4	18	100	36	4.38	26
40/55.97	30	41.96	11.22	196	610	53.1	2.03	14.7	123	39	4.01	28
40/55.97	35	48.98	13.15	196	1197	104	3.99	11.4	159	40	3.88	32
40/55.97	40	55.97	15.16	196	CAP	TOP	HAT	12.9	141	50	2.99	30
35/48.82	0	0	3.65	188	268	23.3	.89	41.4	44	18	7.29	20
35/48.82	5	6.96	3.86	188	275	23.9	.91	39.4	46	19	7.1	20
35/48.82	10	13.94	4.48	188	298	25.9	.99	34.3	53	21	6.6	20
35/48.82	15	20.9	5.48	188	343	29.9	1.14	28.3	64	25	5.96	22
35/48.82	20	27.89	6.82	188	430	37.4	1.43	22.7	80	29	5.33	23
35/48.82	25	34.88	8.42	188	618	53.8	2.06	17.9	101	33	4.81	25
35/48.82	30	41.83	10.2	188	1206	105	4.02	13.2	138	34	4.57	29
35/48.82	35	48.82	12.07	188	CAP	TOP	HAT	15.5	117	44	3.51	27
30/41.7	0	0	2.62	179	310	27	1.03	48.9	37	14	8.51	19
30/41.7	5	6.92	2.85	179	320	27.9	1.06	45.7	39	15	8.22	19
30/41.7	10	13.88	3.5	179	358	31.2	1.19	38.1	47	17	7.5	20
30/41.7	15	20.83	4.54	179	438	38.1	1.46	29.7	61	21	6.65	21
30/41.7	20	27.79	5.9	179	620	54	2.06	22.4	81	25	5.9	23
30/41.7	25	34.74	7.48	179	1197	104	3.99	15.5	116	28	5.49	26
30/41.7	30	41.7	9.17	179	CAP	TOP	HAT	19.4	93	37	4.21	24
25/34.55	0	0	1.79	168	360	31.3	1.2	56	32	9	10	18
25/34.55	5	6.89	2.03	168	378	32.9	1.26	51	35	11	9.55	18
25/34.55	10	13.81	2.7	168	445	38.8	1.48	40.1	45	14	8.51	19
25/34.55	15	20.73	3.76	168	612	53.3	2.04	28.9	63	18	7.43	21
25/34.55	20	27.66	5.08	168	1165	102	3.88	18.7	97	21	6.74	24
25/34.55	25	34.55	6.55	168	CAP	TOP	HAT	25.6	71	30	5.17	22
20/27.43	0	0	1.14	154	423	36.8	1.41	60.3	30	6	11.88	18
20/27.43	5	6.86	1.37	154	457	39.8	1.52	53.1	34	7	11.14	18
20/27.43	10	13.71	2.06	154	598	52.1	1.99	38	48	10	9.66	19
20/27.43	15	20.57	3.08	154	1105	96.3	3.68	22.7	80	14	8.49	22
20/27.43	20	27.43	4.28	154	CAP	TOP	HAT	35.8	50	22	6.53	19
15/20.34	0	0	.62	137	511	44.5	1.7	58.7	31	3	14.4	17
15/20.34	5	6.76	.87	137	590	51.4	1.96	48.3	37	4	13.1	18
15/20.34	10	13.55	1.54	137	1022	89.1	3.4	27.7	65	7	11.11	20
15/20.34	15	20.34	2.45	137	CAP	TOP	HAT	55.6	32	14	8.52	17
10/13.25	0	0	.28	113	640	55.8	2.13	46.8	38	1	17.94	17
10/13.25	5	6.63	.52	113	906	79	3.02	31.9	57	2	15.52	19
10/13.25	10	13.25	1.09	113	CAP	TOP	HAT	102.7	17	6	11.66	16
5 /6.1	0	0	.07	71	811	70.7	2.7	25.6	71	0	24.05	18
5 /6.1	5	6.1	.26	71	CAP	TOP	HAT	262.9	6	1	17.53	15

```
10   REM name: DESIGN LOADED VERTICALS
20   REM by: John Devoldere, ON4UN
30   ONERR  GOTO 50
40   GOTO 60
50   VTAB 14: POKE 36,34: PRINT "FATAL ERROR
     ": PRINT  CHR$ (7): FOR H = 1 TO 5000:
     NEXT : GOTO 30
60   PRINT  CHR$ (13) +  CHR$ (4);"PR#3": HOME
     : CLEAR : GOSUB 440: POKE 35,22: HOME
     : PRINT "PRINTER OR SCREEN? (P/S) > ";
     : GET D$: HOME :I = 1:E$ = "CM.":Pl =
     1: PRINT "DIMENSIONS IN CENTIMETERS OR
     INCHES? (C/I) > ";: GET F$: IF F$ = "
     I" OR F$ = "i" THEN I = 2.54:E$ = "INC
     HES":Pl = 1 / .3048
70   HOME
80   VTAB 4
90   INPUT "ENTER DESIGN FREQUENCY (MHz) > "
     ;A$:A =  VAL (A$): IF A = < 0 THEN  PRINT
     CHR$ (7): GOTO 80
100  IF A < .1 THEN  PRINT  CHR$ (7);: PRINT
     "LOWER FREQ. LIMIT IS 100 KHZ ": GOTO
     80
110  IF A > 30 THEN  PRINT  CHR$ (7);: PRINT
     "UPPER FREQ.LIMIT IS 30 MHZ": GOTO 80
120  VTAB 5: INPUT "ENTER RESISTANCE GROUND
     -SYSTEM PLUS RADIATOR IN OHM >";B$:B =
     VAL (B$): IF B < 0 THEN  PRINT  CHR$
     (7): GOTO 120
130  IF B = 0 AND B$ < > "0" THEN  PRINT  CHR$
     (7): GOTO 120
140  IF B > 50 THEN  PRINT  CHR$ (7);: PRINT
     "TRY A BETTER GROIUND SYSTEM!": GOTO 1
     20
150  VTAB 5: PRINT : INPUT "ENTER LOADING C
     OIL Q-FACTOR > ";G$:G =  VAL (G$): IF
     G = < 0 THEN  PRINT  CHR$ (7): GOTO 1
     50
160  IF G < 25 THEN  PRINT  CHR$ (7);: PRINT
     "TRY A BETTER Q!": GOTO 150
170  VTAB 6: PRINT : PRINT "ENTER DIAMETER
     VERTICAL IN ";E$;: INPUT " > ";C$:C =
     VAL (C$): IF C = < 0 THEN  PRINT  CHR$
     (7): GOTO 170
180  IF C < .1 OR C > 200 / I THEN  PRINT  CHR$
     (7);: PRINT "CHECK YOUR DIAMETER INPUT
     !": GOTO 170
190  C = C * I:D = (360 * A * C) / (300 * 10
     0): HOME :E = 3.14159: IF D$ < > "P" AND
     D$ < > "p" GOTO 210
200  PRINT  CHR$ (13) +  CHR$ (4);"PR#1": PRINT
     : POKE 36,23: PRINT "VERTICAL ANTENNA
     DESIGN PROGRAM.";: POKE 36,71: PRINT "
     by ON4UN": PRINT "--------------------
     ---------------------------
     ---------------------"
210  PRINT "DESIGN FREQUENCY : ";A;: PRINT
     " Mhz";: POKE 36,38: PRINT "TOTAL LOSS
     RESISTANCE : ";B;" Ohm": PRINT "LOADI
     NG COIL Q-FACTOR : ";G;:Ql =  INT (100
     * C / I + .5) / 100: POKE 36,38: PRINT
     "DIAMETER ANTENNA = ";Ql;" ";E$;" (";  INT
     (1000 * D) / 1000;" deg.)"
220  PRINT "----------------------------
     -------------------------------
     ----------": PRINT "LENGTH    COIL  COI
     L    R-rad SURGE-Z X(L)    L     R    Q-fa
     ct  BW   Eff  Eff    Z"
230  IF F$ = "I" THEN  PRINT "deg/ft   deg
     ft       Ohm   Ohm     Ohm  uH  Ohm
     -    kHz   %    -dB  Ohm": GOTO 25
     0
240  PRINT "deg/m   deg       m       Ohm   O
     hm     Ohm  uH  Ohm     -    kHz   %
     -dB  Ohm"
250  PRINT "-----    ----  ----     -----  -
     ---   ---  ---  ---
     ---   ---": PRINT : POKE 34,9: VTAB 1
     0: FOR H = 90 TO 5 STEP  - 5:J = (300 *
     H) / (A * 360):M = 100 * J / C:N = 1 -
     (1 / (4.671922895 *  LOG (2 * M) - 8))
     :O = ((1 -  SIN ((90 - H) * E / 180)) /
     ( COS ((90 - H) * E / 180))) * (180 /
     E):P = ( SIN (H * E / 180)) * (180 / E
     )
260  S = (300 * O) / (360 * A):U = (300 * P)
     / (360 * A):V = 1450 * ((S ^ 2) / (30
     0 / A) ^ 2):V =  INT (100 * V) / 100:W
     = 1450 * ((U ^ 2) / (30^ / A) ^ 2):W =
     INT (100 * W) / 100:Y = W - V:Al = 90
     / H: FOR K = 0 TO H STEP 5:Bl = (300 *
     N * K) / (A * 360):Bl =  INT (Bl * 100
     ) / 100: IF K = 0 THEN F = V: GOTO 280
270  F = ((1 -  COS (Al * K * E / 180)) * Y)
     + V
280  GOSUB 320: NEXT : PRINT : NEXT : IF D$
     = "P" THEN  PRINT  CHR$ (13) +  CHR$
     (4);"PR#3": GOSUB 440
290  VTAB 24: POKE 36,0: PRINT "
     MORE RUNS    >>N<<
     EXIT    >>E<<";: POKE 36,39: GET H$: IF
     H$ = "E" OR H$ = "e" THEN  HOME : PRINT
     CHR$ (13) +  CHR$ (4);"RUN
     MENU"
300  IF D$ = "P" OR D$ = "p" THEN  PRINT  CHR$
     (13) +  CHR$ (4);"PR#3": GOTO 30
310  POKE 34,3: HOME : GOTO 90
320  Cl = J * N:Dl =  INT (100 * Cl) / 100:F
     l =  INT (1000 * N) / 10:Z = 60 * ( LOG
     (H / D) - 1):Z =  INT (Z):T = 1 /  TAN
     (H * E / 180):Gl = (300 * H) / (A * 36
     0): IF  SIN (E / 2 * (H - K) / H) = 0 THEN
     X = 999: GOTO 340
330  X = Z * T:Hl = X / ( SIN (E / 2 * (H -
     K) / H)):X =  INT (Hl):Il = ( SIN (E /
     2 * (H - C) / H))
340  R =  INT (100 * X / G) / 100: IF X = 99
     9 THEN R = 0
350  Kl = Z / (F + R):Q =  INT (Kl * 10) / 1
     0:Ll = A / Kl:Ll =  INT (1000 * Ll):L =
     X / (2 * E * A):L =  INT (10 * L) / 10
     : IF F = 0 THEN  END
360  Ml = F / (F + R + B + Jl):El =  INT (10
     0 * Ml) / 100:Nl = 4.3429 *  LOG (Ml):
     Nl = - INT (Nl * 100) / 100:Ol =  INT
     (F + R + B + .5):F =  INT ((100 * F)) /
     100: IF L > = 100 THEN L =  INT (L +
     .5)
370  A$ =  STR$ (X):B$ =  STR$ (L):C$ =  STR$
     (R): IF X = 999 THEN A$ = "CAP":B$ = "
     TOP":C$ = "HAT"
380  IF H = 90 AND K < > 0 GOTO 430
390  Dl = Dl * Pl:Dl =  INT (100 * Dl + .5) /
     100:Bl = Bl * Pl:Bl =  INT (100 * Bl +
     .5) / 100: IF Bl > = 100 THEN Bl =  INT
     (10 * Bl + .5) / 10
400  IF Dl > = 100 THEN Dl =  INT (10 * Dl
     + .5) / 10
410  IF Dl > = 1000 THEN Dl =  INT (Dl + .
     5)
420  POKE 36,0: PRINT H;: POKE 36,2: PRINT
     "/";: POKE 36,3: PRINT Dl;: POKE 36,10
     : PRINT K;: POKE 36,15: PRINT Bl;: POKE
     36,23: PRINT F;: POKE 36,30: PRINT Z;:
     POKE 36,37: PRINT A$;: POKE 36,42: PRINT
     B$;: POKE 36,47: PRINT C$;: POKE 36,54
     : PRINT Q;: POKE 36,60: PRINT Ll;: POKE
     36,66: PRINT 100 * El;: POKE 36,70: PRINT
     Nl;: POKE 36,77: PRINT Ol
```

```
430  RETURN
440  PRINT : POKE 36,23: PRINT "VERTICAL AN
     TENNA DESIGN PROGRAM.";: POKE 36,71: PRINT
     "by ON4UN": PRINT "--------------------
     -------------------------------------
     ----------------------": POKE 34,3: VTAB
     23: PRINT "-------------------------
     -------------------------------------
     --------------": RETURN
```

```
10    REM name: HORIZONTAL ANTENNAS
20    REM by: John Devoldere, ON4UN
30    ONERR  GOTO 50
40    GOTO 60
50    VTAB 14: POKE 36,34: PRINT "FATAL ERROR
      ": PRINT  CHR$ (7): FOR C = 1 TO 5000:
      NEXT : GOTO 30
60    PRINT  CHR$ (13) +  CHR$ (4);"PR#3": POKE
      34,0: HOME : PRINT : POKE 36,25: PRINT
      "WAVE ANGLE HORIZONTAL ANTENNAS";: POKE
      36,70: PRINT "by  ON4UN": PRINT "-----
      -------------------------------------
      ------------------------------------"
70    PRINT "THIS PROGRAM ALLOWS YOU TO CALCU
      LATE THE REQUIRED HEIGHT OF A HORIZONT
      ALLY       POLARIZED ANTENNA ON A FLAT
      OR SLOPING TERRAIN AS A FUNCTION OF TH
      E DESIRED WAVEANGLE.": PRINT "IT CAN A
      LSO CALCULATE THE WAVE ANGLE FOR A GIV
      EN ANTENNA HEIGHT."
80    PRINT "-----------------------------
      -----------,-------------------------
      ----------": VTAB 22: PRINT "----------
      -------------------------------------
      -----------------------------": POKE
      35,21: POKE 34,8:E = 3.14159
90    IF G = 1 GOTO 130
100   VTAB 10: PRINT "DIMENSIONS IN FEET OR
      METERS ? (F/M) > ";: GET C$: PRINT : IF
      C$ = "M" GOTO 120
110   I = 1:D$ = " ft.": GOTO 130
120   I = .3048:D$ = " m."
130   VTAB 12: PRINT "DOES THE TERRAIN HAVE
      A SLOPE IN THE DIRECTION YOU WANT TO E
      VALUATE ? (Y/N) > ";: GET C$: PRINT : IF
      C$ = "N" THEN A = 0: GOTO 150
140   VTAB 14: INPUT "ENTER THE SLOPE ANGLE
      IN DEGREES (- SIGN IS DOWNHILL SLOPE)
      > ";A$:A =  VAL (A$): IF A = 0 AND A$ <
      > "0" THEN  PRINT  CHR$ (7): GOTO 140

150   VTAB 16: PRINT "CALCULATE THE NECESSAR
      Y ANTENNE HEIGHT FOR A GIVEN WAVE ANGL
      E (1)": POKE 36,18: PRINT "OR THE WAVE
      ANGLE FOR A GIVEN ANTENNA HEIGHT (2) >
      ";: GET C$: PRINT : IF C$ = "2" GOTO
      240
160   IF C$ <  > "1" THEN  PRINT  CHR$ (7);:
      GOTO 150

170   HOME : PRINT "THE SLOPE ANGLE IS ";A;"
      DEG."
180   VTAB 11: INPUT "REQUIRED WAVE ANGLE (D
      EGREES) > ";B$:B =  VAL (B$)
190   IF B = < 0 THEN  PRINT  CHR$ (7): GOTO
      180
200   IF A = > B THEN  PRINT  CHR$ (7): PRINT
      "WAVE ANGLE CONFLICTS WITH POSITIVE TE
      RRAIN SLOPE!": GOTO 180
210   VTAB 13: CALL  - 868: VTAB 13: INPUT "
      FREQUENCY OF OPERATION (MHz) > ";E$:F =
      VAL (E$): IF F < = 0 THEN  PRINT  CHR$
      (7): GOTO 190
220   J = B * E / 180:K = A * E / 180:H = 245
      .5 / (F *  COS (K) *  SIN (J - K)): VTAB
      15: PRINT "REQUIRED ANTENNA HEIGHT = "
      ; INT (H);" ft.": PRINT "
            = "; INT (10 * H * .3048 +
      .5) / 10;" m.":D = H / ( TAN (J - K)):
      VTAB 18: PRINT "POINT OF REFLECTION I
      S AT "; INT (D);" ft FROM THE ANTENNA.
      "
230   PRINT "                          "; INT
      (10 * D * .3048 + .5) / 10;" m FROM TH
      E ANTENNA.": GOTO 300
240   HOME : PRINT "THE SLOPE ANGLE IS ";A;"
      DEG."
250   VTAB 11: PRINT "ENTER ANTENNA HEIGHT I
      N ";D$;: INPUT " > ";F$:H =  VAL (F$):
      IF H = < 0 THEN  PRINT  CHR$ (7): GOTO
      250
260   H = H / I: VTAB 13: INPUT "FREQUENCY OF
      OPERATION (MHz) > ";E$:F =  VAL (E$):
      IF F < = 0 THEN  PRINT  CHR$ (7): GOTO
      190
270   L = 246 / (H * F *  COS (K)): IF L > 1 THEN
      M = 90: GOTO 290
280   N =  ATN (L /  SQR ( - L * L + 1)) + K:
      M = N * 180 / E
290   VTAB 17: PRINT "WAVE ANGLE = "; INT (M
      );" deg."
300   POKE 35,23: IF G = 1 GOTO 320
310   VTAB 23:G = 1: POKE 36,0: PRINT "
            ENTER >>N<< FOR NEW RUN          E
      NTER >>E<< FOR EXIT";
320   VTAB 23: POKE 36,38: GET G$: POKE 35,2
      0: IF G$ = "E" THEN  HOME : PRINT  CHR$
      (13) +  CHR$ (4);"RUN MENU"
330   HOME : GOTO 90
```

```
10    REM DESIGN T/B LOADED VERTICALS
20    REM by: John Devoldere, ON4UN
30    ONERR  GOTO 50
40    GOTO 60
50    VTAB 14: POKE 36,34: PRINT "FATAL ERROR
      ": PRINT  CHR$ (7): FOR I = 1 TO 5000:
       NEXT : GOTO 30
60    PRINT  CHR$ (13) +  CHR$ (4);"PR#3": HOME
      : CLEAR : GOSUB 380: POKE 35,22: HOME
      : PRINT "PRINTER OR SCREEN? (P/S) > ";
      : GET A$: HOME :W = 1:B$ = "CM.":N1 =
      1: PRINT "DIMENSIONS IN CENTIMETERS OR
       INCHES? (C/I) > ";: GET C$: IF C$ = "
      I" OR C$ = "i" THEN W = 2.54:B$ = "INC
      HES":N1 = 1 / .3048
70    HOME
80    VTAB 4: INPUT "ENTER FREQUENCY > (MHz)
      > ";D$:G =  VAL (D$): IF G = < 0 THEN
       PRINT  CHR$ (7): GOTO 80
90    IF G < .1 THEN  PRINT  CHR$ (7);: PRINT
      "LOWER FREQUENCY LIMIT IS 100 KHZ": GOTO
      80
100   VTAB 5: INPUT "ENTER RESISTANCE GROUND
      -SYSTEM PLUS RADIATOR IN OHM > ";E$:H =
      VAL (E$): IF H = 0 AND E$ < > "0" THEN
       PRINT  CHR$ (7): GOTO 100
110   IF H < 0 THEN  PRINT  CHR$ (7): GOTO 1
      00
120   IF H > 50 THEN  PRINT  CHR$ (7);: PRINT
      "TRY A BETTER GROUND SYSTEM!": GOTO 10
      0
130   VTAB 6: INPUT "ENTER ASSUMED LOADING C
      OIL Q-FACTOR > ";F$:K =  VAL (F$): IF
      K < = 0 THEN  PRINT  CHR$ (7): GOTO 1
      30
140   IF K < 25E THEN  PRINT  CHR$ (7);: PRINT
      "TRY A BETTER Q!": GOTO 130
150   VTAB 7: INPUT "ENTER CAPACITY HAT IN E
      QUIV LENGTH DEGREES > ";G$:M =  VAL (G
      $): IF M = < 0 THEN  PRINT  CHR$ (7):
       GOTO 150
160   IF M > 45 THEN  PRINT  CHR$ (7);: PRINT
      "THE MAX LIMIT IS 45 DEGREES": GOTO 15
      0
170   VTAB 8: PRINT "ENTER DIAMETER ANTENNA
      IN ";B$;: INPUT " > ";H$:N =  VAL (H$)
      : IF N < = 0 THEN  PRINT  CHR$ (7): GOTO
      170
180   IF N < .1 OR N > 100 / W THEN  PRINT  CHR$
      (7);: PRINT "CHECK ANTENNA DIAMETER!":
       GOTO 170
190   N = N * W:I = (360 * G * N) / (300 * .9
      7 * 100):I =  INT (1000 * I) / 1000: HOME
      :O = 3.14159: IF A$ < > "P" AND A$ <
       > "p" GOTO 210
200   PRINT  CHR$ (13) +  CHR$ (4);"PR#1": POKE
      36,18: PRINT "TOP LOADED VERTICAL· ANTE
      NNA DESIGN PROGRAM.";: POKE 36,71: PRINT
      "by ON4UN": PRINT "--------------------
      ------------------------------------
      ------------------------"
210   PRINT "DESIGN FREQUENCY : ";G;: PRINT
      " Mhz";: POKE 36,38: PRINT "TOTAL LOSS
      RESISTANCE : ";H;" Ohm": PRINT "LOADI
      NG COIL Q-FACTOR : ";K;: POKE 36,38: PRINT
      "ELECTRICAL LENGTH CAPACITY HAT : ";M;
      " DEG.":O1 = N / W: PRINT "DIAMETER AN
      TENNA = ";O1;" ";B$;" (";I;" DEG)"
220   PRINT "----------------------------
      --------------": PRINT "LENGTH    HAT    HA
      T    R-rad  Surg-Z  X(L)    L     R    Q-fact
        BW   Eff  Eff     Z"
230   IF C$ = "I" THEN  PRINT "deg/ft     pF
       inch     Ohm      Ohm      Ohm     uH   Ohm
        -      kHz      %     -DB     OHM": GOTO 250
240   PRINT "deg/m      pF     cm          Ohm    O
      hm   Ohm      uH   Ohm      -      kHz      %     -D
      B   OHM"
250   PRINT "------    ----   ----   ----- -
      --  ----  ----   ---   ---   ---- ---- -
      --- ---": POKE 34,10:N = N / W: IF M =
      0 THEN P = 1000000: GOTO 270
260   P = 1 /  TAN (M * O / 180)
270   FOR J = (90 - M) TO 6 STEP  - 2:U = (3
      00 * J) / (G * 360):B = (90 - J) - M:A
      =  SIN ((90 - M) * O / 180) -  SIN ((
      90 - M - J) * O / 180):C = A * 180 / O
      :D = C /  COS ((90 - M - J) * O / 180)
      : GOSUB 310: NEXT J: IF A$ = "P" OR A$
      = "p" THEN  PRINT  CHR$ (13) +  CHR$
      (4);"PR#3": GOSUB 380
280   VTAB 24: PRINT "                    MORE RU
      NS   >>N<<              EXIT    >>E<
      <";: POKE 36,38: GET I$: IF I$ = "E" OR
      I$ = "e" THEN  HOME : PRINT  CHR$ (13)
       +  CHR$ (4);"RUN              MENU"
290   IF A$ = "P" OR A$ = "p" THEN  PRINT  CHR$
      (13) +  CHR$ (4);"PR#3": GOTO 30
300   GOTO 30
310   S = J / I:V = 1 - (1 / (4.671922895 *  LOG
      (2 * S) - 8)):E = (300 * D) / (360 * G
      ):F = 1450 * ((E ^ 2) / (300 / G) ^ 2)
      :F =  INT (100 * F) / 100:Y = U * V:A1
      =  INT (100 * Y) / 100:Z = 60 * ( LOG
      (J / I) - 1): IF M = 0 GOTO 330
320   B1 = Z * P:C1 = 1000000 / (2 * O * G *
      B1):C1 =  INT (C1 + .5):D1 =  INT (.5 +
      2.8448 * C1)
330   F1 = Z * P:G1 = 1000000 / (2 * O * G *
      F1):Z = 1 /  TAN ((J + M)
      * O / 180):X = Z * T:X =  INT (X):R =
      INT (100 * X / K) / 100:I1 = Z / (F +
      R):Q =  INT (I1 + .5):J1 = G / I1:J1 =
      INT (1000 * J1):L = X / (2 * O * G):L
      =  INT (10 * L) / 10: IF L > = 100 THEN
      L =  INT (L + .5)
340   K1 = F / (F + R + H):E1 =  INT (100 * K
      1) / 100:L1 = 4.3429 *  LOG (K1):L1 =
      -  INT (L1 * 10 + .5) / 10:M1 =  INT
      (H + R + F + H1 + .5):A1 = A1 * N1:A1 =
      INT (100 * A1 + .5) / 100:D1 = D1 / W
      :D1 =  INT (10 * D1 + .5) / 10: IF A1 >
      = 100 THEN A1 =  INT (10 * A1) / 10
350   IF C1 > = 1000 THEN C1 =  INT (C1)
360   IF D1 > = 10000 THEN D1 =  INT (D1)
370   POKE 36,0: PRINT J;: POKE 36,2: PRINT
      "/";: POKE 36,3: PRINT A1;: POKE 36,10
      : PRINT C1;: POKE 36,16: PRINT D1;: POKE
      36,23: PRINT F;: POKE 36,30: PRINT Z;:
       POKE 36,36: PRINT X;: POKE 36,41: PRINT
      L;: POKE 36,46: PRINT R;: POKE 36,52: PRINT
      Q;: POKE 36,58: PRINT J1;: POKE 36,63:
       PRINT 100 * E1;: POKE 36,68: PRINT L1
      ;: POKE 36,74: PRINT M1: RETURN
380   PRINT : POKE 36,18: PRINT "TOP LOADED
      VERTICAL ANTENNA DESIGN PROGRAM.";: POKE
      36,71: PRINT "by ON4UN": PRINT "------
      ------------------------------------
      --------------------------------": POKE
      34,3: VTAB 23
390   PRINT "----------------------------
      ------------------------------------
      ----------": RETURN
```

```
10   REM name: ARRAY
20   REM by: John Devoldere, ON4UN
30   ONERR  GOTO 50
40   GOTO 60
50   VTAB 14: POKE 36,34: PRINT "FATAL ERROR
     ": PRINT  CHR$ (7): FOR I = 1 TO 5000:
     NEXT : GOTO 30
60   PRINT  CHR$ (13) +  CHR$ (4);"PR#3": CLEAR
     : HOME : PRINT : POKE 36,28: PRINT "VE
     RTICAL ANTENNA ARRAYS";: POKE 36,71: PRINT
     "by ON4UN": PRINT "--------------------
     ----------------------------------------
     -----------------------": POKE 34,3
70   VTAB 23: PRINT "-----------------------
     ----------------------------------------
     -------------------": POKE 35,22: HOME
     : PRINT : PRINT "THIS PROGRAM ONLY RUN
     S WITH A PRINTER CONNECTED TO THE COMP
     UTER. TURN THE          PRINTER ON.": PRINT
80   VTAB 8: INPUT "ENTER THE NUMBER OF ANTE
     NNAS IN THE ARRAY (MAX 10) > ";A$:A =
     VAL (A$): IF A = 0 THEN  PRINT  CHR$
     (7): GOTO 80
90   IF A > 10 THEN  PRINT  CHR$ (7): GOTO 8
     0
100  HOME : PRINT "ONE OF THE ANTENNAS MUST
     BE CHOOSEN AS REFERENCE POINT IN THE
     ARRAY.": PRINT "LOCATION AND EXCITATIO
     N DATA FOR THE OTHER ELEMENTS MUST BE
     SPECIFIED WITH": PRINT "RESPECT TO THE
     REFERENCE ANTENNA."
110  PRINT "THE ELEMENT DIRECTION IS THE DI
     RECTION OF THE LINE GOING FROM THE REF
     ERENCE": PRINT "ANTENNA TO THE ELEMENT
     UNDER CONSIDERATION. THE DISTANCE AND
     ANTENNA LENGTH": PRINT "ARE EXPRESSED
     IN DEGREES (1 WAVEL. = 360 DEG). THE
     ELEMENT EXCITATION IS"
120  PRINT "SPECIFIED IN ANTENNA CURRENT AM
     PLITUDE AND PHASE (CAN BE + OR - WITH
     RESPECT": PRINT "TO THE REFERENCE ANTE
     NNA).": PRINT "THE AZIMUTH, PHASE AND
     SPACING MUST BE 0, AND THE RELATIVE DR
     IVE CURRENT 1 FOR": PRINT "THE REFEREN
     CE ANTENNA.": VTAB 24
130  POKE 36,26: PRINT "PRESS ENTER TO CONT
     INUE. ";: GET A$: HOME : VTAB 24: CALL
     - 868:B = 3.14159: DIM A(10,5): DIM B
     (36,10): FOR D = 1 TO A: HOME : VTAB 1
     0: PRINT "INPUT, FOR ANTENNA No. ";D: PRINT
     "------------------------"
140  VTAB 12: INPUT "AZIMUTH, DEGREES > ";A
     $(D,1):A(D,1) =  VAL (A$(D,1)): IF A(D
     ,1) = 0 AND A$(D,1) <  > "0" THEN  PRINT
     CHR$ (7): GOTO 140
150  VTAB 13: INPUT "SPACING, DEGREES > ";A
     $(D,2):A(D,2) =  VAL (A$(D,2)): IF A(D
     ,2) = 0 AND A$(D,2) <  > "0" THEN  PRINT
     CHR$ (7): GOTO 150
160  VTAB 14: INPUT "PHASE,   DEGREES > ";A
     $(D,3):A(D,3) =  VAL (A$(D,3)): IF A(D
     ,3) = 0 AND A$(D,3) <  > "0" THEN  PRINT
     CHR$ (7): GOTO 160
170  VTAB 15: INPUT "RELATIVE CURRENT INPUT
     , DIMENSIONLESS > ";A$(D,4):A(D,4) =  VAL
     (A$(D,4)): IF A(D,4) = 0 AND A$(D,4) <
     > "0" THEN  PRINT  CHR$ (7): GOTO 170
180  VTAB 16: INPUT "ELECTRICAL HEIGHT, DEG
     REES > ";A$(D,5):A(D,5) =  VAL (A$(D,5
     )): IF A(D,5) = 0 AND A$(D,5) <  > "0"
     THEN  PRINT  CHR$ (7): GOTO 180
190  NEXT
200  GOSUB 280: GOSUB 290: PRINT :E = 10: PRINT
     CHR$ (13) +  CHR$ (4);"PR#1": GOSUB 5
     50: PRINT : PRINT : PRINT : PRINT  TAB(
     13)"RELATIVE FIELD STRENGTH CALCULATIO
     N RESULTS": PRINT  TAB( 13)"==========
     ================================": PRINT
     : PRINT  CHR$ (13) +  CHR$ (4);"PR#3":
     PRINT : VTAB 14: POKE 36,35: PRINT "I
     AM WORKING": PRINT  CHR$ (13) +  CHR$
     (4);"PR#1": FOR F = 0 TO 9:G = F * 10:
     D = 0
210  H = 0:I = 0: FOR J = 1 TO A: GOSUB 370:
     NEXT J:L =  SQR ((H ^ 2) + (I ^ 2)):B
     (D / 10,F) = L: IF D = 360 THEN  NEXT
     F
220  IF F = 9 GOTO 380
230  D = D + E: IF D > 360 THEN D = 360
240  GOTO 210
250  VTAB 22: PRINT : VTAB 23: PRINT "-----
     ----------------------------------------
     ----------------------------------------":
     VTAB 24: PRINT "   COMPLETE RERUN >>0
     <<      REVISE DATA AND RERUN >>1<<
     EXIT >>2<< ";: GET C$:M =  VAL (C
     $): IF M = 2 THEN  HOME : PRINT  CHR$
     (13) +  CHR$ (4);"RUN MENU"
260  IF M = 1 THEN 200
270  RUN
280  HOME : GOSUB 550: RETURN
290  VTAB 17: PRINT "DATA OK? (Y/N) > ";: GET
     C$: IF C$ = "N" GOTO 320
300  GOTO 310
310  PRINT : HOME : PRINT  CHR$ (13) +  CHR$
     (4);"PR#1": PRINT : POKE 36,22: PRINT
     "ARRAY CALCULATION.";: POKE 36,61: PRINT
     "by ON4UN": PRINT "--------------------
     ----------------------------------------
     -----------": RETURN
320  GOSUB 330: GOSUB 280: GOTO 290
330  GOSUB 280: PRINT : VTAB 17: PRINT "CHA
     NGE INPUTS": PRINT "-------------"
340  VTAB 19: INPUT "ELEMENT NUMBER ·> ";D$:
     N =  VAL (D$): IF N <  = 0 OR N > A GOTO
     340
350  VTAB 20: INPUT "COLUMN  NUMBER > ";E$:
     O =  VAL (E$): IF O <  = 0 OR O > 5 GOTO
     350
360  VTAB 21: INPUT "CORRECT VALUE  > ";F$:
     P =  VAL (F$):A(N,O) = P: RETURN
370  C = .0174553:Q = A(J,1) * C:T = D * C:U
     = A(J,3) * C:V = A(J,5) * C:W = G * C
     :X =  COS (V *  SIN (W)) -  COS (V):Y =
     COS (W) * (1 -  COS (V)):Z = X / Y:Al
     = Z * A(J,4):Bl = A(J,2) *  COS (
     (Q - T)) + U:N = Al *  COS (Bl):O = Al
     *  SIN (Bl):H = H + N:I = I + O: RETURN
380  POKE 36,19: PRINT "RELATIVE FIELD STRE
     NGTH VALUES": PRINT : PRINT "AZIM  ---
     ------------------ELEVATION ANGLE------
     ------------------": PRINT "DEG    0
     10    20    30    40    50    60    7
     0    80    90": PRINT "----------------
     -----------"
390  FOR R = 0 TO 36: PRINT R * 10;: FOR S =
     0 TO 9: IF B(R,S) > Cl THEN Cl = B(R,S
     )
400  IF  INT (B(R,S)) <  INT (B(R,S)) + .00
     1 THEN B(R,S) = B(R,S) + .001
410  Dl =  INT (100 * B(R,S)) / 100:B$ =  STR$
     (Dl): IF Dl = 0 THEN B$ = "0.00": GOTO
     450
420  IF Dl < 1 THEN B$ = "0" + B$
430  IF  LEN (B$) = 3 THEN B$ = B$ + "0"
440  IF  LEN (B$) = 1 THEN B$ = B$ + ".00"
```

```
450  POKE 36,(6 + (S * 6)): PRINT B$;: NEXT
     : PRINT : NEXT : FOR El = 1 TO 18: PRINT
     : NEXT : POKE 36,23: PRINT "dB VALUES
     V.S. MAIN LOBE": PRINT : PRINT "AZIM
     --------------------ELEVATION ANGLE---
     ------------------": PRINT "DEG   0
         10    20    30    40    50    60
         70    80    90"
460  PRINT "-------------------------------
     -----------------------------------": PRINT
     : FOR R = 0 TO 36: PRINT R * 10;: FOR
     S = 0 TO 9:F1 = B(R,S): IF F1 = 0 THEN
     B$ = "INFIN": GOTO 540
470  G1 = 8.685889638 *  LOG (F1 / C1):G1 =
     INT (10 * G1) / 10:G1 =  - G1:B$ =  STR$
     (G1): IF G1 = 0 THEN B$ = "  0.0": GOTO
     540
480  IF  LEN (B$) = 4 THEN B$ = " " + B$
490  IF  LEN (B$) = 3 AND  MID$ (B$,2,1) =
     "." THEN B$ = "  " + B$
500  IF  LEN (B$) = 3 THEN B$ = B$ + ".0"
510  IF  LEN (B$) = 2 AND  LEFT$ (B$,1) = "
     ." THEN B$ = "  0" + B$
520  IF  LEN (B$) = 2 THEN B$ = " " + B$ +
     ".0"
530  IF  LEN (B$) = 1 THEN B$ = "  " + B$ +
     ".0"
540  POKE 36,(6 + (S * 6)): PRINT B$;: NEXT
     : PRINT : NEXT : PRINT : PRINT : PRINT
     : PRINT : PRINT : PRINT  CHR$ (13) +  CHR$
     (4);"PR#3": HOME : GOTO 250
550  POKE 36,4: PRINT " EL.";: POKE 36,34: PRINT
     "REL.";: POKE 36,42: PRINT "REL.CURR."
     ;: POKE 36,52: PRINT "ELECT.": POKE 36
     ,5: PRINT "#";: POKE 36,11: PRINT "AZI
     MUTH";: POKE 36,22: PRINT "SPACING";: POKE
     36,33: PRINT "PHASE";: POKE 36,43: PRINT
     "INPUT";: POKE 36,52: PRINT "HEIGHT": PRINT
     "   -------------------------------
     --------------------"
560  FOR K = 1 TO A: POKE 36,5: PRINT K;: POKE
     36,13: PRINT A(K,1);: POKE 36,24: PRINT
     A(K,2);: POKE 36,34: PRINT A(K,3);: POKE
     36,44: PRINT A(K,4);: POKE 36,53: PRINT
     A(K,5);: IF K = 1 THEN  POKE 36,60: PRINT
     "<= REFER.";
570  PRINT : NEXT : RETURN
```

EL. #	AZIMUTH	SPACING	REL. PHASE	REL.CURR. INPUT	ELECT. HEIGHT	
1	0	0	0	1	90	<= REFER.
2	0	90	-90	1	90	

RELATIVE FIELD STRENGTH CALCULATION RESULTS

RELATIVE FIELD STRENGTH VALUES

AZIM DEG	0	10	20	30	40	50	60	70	80	90
0	2.00	1.95	1.82	1.63	1.39	1.11	0.83	0.55	0.27	0.00
10	2.00	1.95	1.82	1.63	1.39	1.11	0.83	0.55	0.27	0.00
20	1.99	1.95	1.82	1.63	1.38	1.11	0.83	0.55	0.27	0.00
30	1.98	1.94	1.81	1.62	1.38	1.11	0.83	0.55	0.27	0.00
40	1.96	1.92	1.79	1.60	1.36	1.09	0.82	0.54	0.27	0.00
50	1.92	1.88	1.75	1.57	1.33	1.07	0.80	0.53	0.26	0.00
60	1.84	1.80	1.69	1.50	1.28	1.03	0.77	0.51	0.25	0.00
70	1.73	1.70	1.59	1.42	1.20	0.97	0.72	0.48	0.23	0.00
80	1.59	1.55	1.45	1.30	1.10	0.89	0.66	0.44	0.21	0.00
90	1.41	1.38	1.29	1.15	0.98	0.79	0.59	0.39	0.19	0.00
100	1.20	1.18	1.10	0.98	0.84	0.67	0.50	0.33	0.16	0.00
110	0.98	0.96	0.90	0.80	0.68	0.55	0.41	0.27	0.13	0.00
120	0.76	0.74	0.70	0.62	0.53	0.42	0.32	0.21	0.10	0.00
130	0.55	0.54	0.50	0.45	0.38	0.31	0.23	0.15	0.07	0.00
140	0.36	0.35	0.33	0.29	0.25	0.20	0.15	0.10	0.05	0.00
150	0.21	0.20	0.19	0.17	0.14	0.11	0.08	0.05	0.02	0.00
160	0.09	0.09	0.08	0.07	0.06	0.05	0.04	0.02	0.01	0.00
170	0.02	0.02	0.02	0.02	0.01	0.01	0.01	0.00	0.00	0.00
180	0.00	0.00	0.00	0.00	0.00	0.00	0.00	0.00	0.00	0.00
190	0.02	0.02	0.02	0.02	0.01	0.01	0.01	0.00	0.00	0.00
200	0.09	0.09	0.08	0.07	0.06	0.05	0.04	0.02	0.01	0.00
210	0.21	0.20	0.19	0.17	0.14	0.11	0.08	0.05	0.02	0.00
220	0.36	0.35	0.33	0.29	0.25	0.20	0.15	0.10	0.05	0.00
230	0.55	0.54	0.50	0.45	0.38	0.31	0.23	0.15	0.07	0.00
240	0.76	0.74	0.70	0.62	0.53	0.42	0.32	0.21	0.10	0.00
250	0.98	0.96	0.90	0.80	0.68	0.55	0.41	0.27	0.13	0.00
260	1.21	1.18	1.10	0.98	0.84	0.67	0.50	0.33	0.16	0.00
270	1.41	1.38	1.29	1.15	0.98	0.79	0.59	0.39	0.19	0.00
280	1.59	1.55	1.45	1.30	1.10	0.89	0.66	0.44	0.21	0.00
290	1.74	1.70	1.59	1.42	1.20	0.97	0.72	0.48	0.23	0.00
300	1.84	1.80	1.69	1.50	1.28	1.03	0.77	0.51	0.25	0.00
310	1.92	1.88	1.75	1.57	1.33	1.07	0.80	0.53	0.26	0.00
320	1.96	1.92	1.79	1.60	1.36	1.09	0.82	0.54	0.27	0.00
330	1.98	1.94	1.81	1.62	1.38	1.11	0.83	0.55	0.27	0.00
340	1.99	1.95	1.82	1.63	1.38	1.11	0.83	0.55	0.27	0.00
350	2.00	1.95	1.82	1.63	1.39	1.11	0.83	0.55	0.27	0.00
360	2.00	1.95	1.82	1.63	1.39	1.11	0.83	0.55	0.27	0.00

dB VALUES V.S. MAIN LOBE

AZIM DEG	0	10	20	30	ELEVATION ANGLE 40	50	60	70	80	90
0	0.0	0.2	0.8	1.8	3.2	5.1	7.6	11.2	17.3	64.0
10	0.0	0.2	0.8	1.8	3.2	5.1	7.6	11.2	17.3	66.1
20	0.1	0.2	0.8	1.8	3.2	5.1	7.6	11.2	17.3	66.1
30	0.1	0.3	0.9	1.9	3.3	5.1	7.7	11.3	17.3	66.1
40	0.2	0.4	1.0	2.0	3.4	5.2	7.8	11.3	17.4	66.1
50	0.4	0.6	1.2	2.2	3.6	5.4	8.0	11.5	17.6	66.1
60	0.7	0.9	1.5	2.5	3.9	5.8	8.3	11.9	18.0	66.1
70	1.3	1.5	2.0	3.0	4.4	6.3	8.8	12.4	18.5	66.1
80	2.0	2.2	2.8	3.8	5.2	7.1	9.6	13.2	19.2	66.1
90	3.1	3.3	3.8	4.8	6.2	8.1	10.6	14.2	20.3	66.1
100	4.4	4.6	5.2	6.2	7.6	9.5	12.0	15.6	21.6	66.1
110	6.2	6.4	6.9	7.9	9.3	11.2	13.7	17.3	23.4	66.1
120	8.4	8.6	9.2	10.1	11.5	13.4	16.0	19.5	25.6	66.1
130	11.2	11.4	12.0	13.0	14.4	16.2	18.8	22.3	28.3	66.1
140	14.8	15.0	15.6	16.6	18.0	19.8	22.4	25.9	31.9	66.1
150	19.6	19.8	20.4	21.4	22.8	24.6	27.1	30.7	36.6	66.1
160	26.5	26.7	27.3	28.2	29.6	31.5	34.0	37.4	43.2	66.1
170	38.3	38.5	39.1	40.0	41.3	43.1	45.4	48.6	53.6	66.1
180	63.4	63.4	63.6	63.8	64.1	64.5	64.8	65.2	65.7	66.1
190	38.2	38.4	39.0	39.9	41.3	43.0	45.4	48.5	53.5	66.1
200	26.5	26.7	27.2	28.2	29.6	31.4	33.9	37.4	43.2	66.1
210	19.6	19.8	20.4	21.3	22.7	24.6	27.1	30.6	36.6	66.1
220	14.8	15.0	15.6	16.5	17.9	19.8	22.3	25.9	31.9	66.1
230	11.2	11.4	12.0	12.9	14.3	16.2	18.7	22.3	28.3	66.1
240	8.4	8.6	9.2	10.1	11.5	13.4	15.9	19.5	25.6	66.1
250	6.2	6.4	6.9	7.9	9.3	11.2	13.7	17.3	23.4	66.1
260	4.4	4.6	5.2	6.2	7.6	9.5	12.0	15.6	21.6	66.1
270	3.1	3.2	3.8	4.8	6.2	8.1	10.6	14.2	20.3	66.1
280	2.0	2.2	2.8	3.8	5.2	7.1	9.6	13.2	19.2	66.1
290	1.3	1.5	2.0	3.0	4.4	6.3	8.8	12.4	18.5	66.1
300	0.7	0.9	1.5	2.5	3.9	5.8	8.3	11.9	18.0	66.1
310	0.4	0.6	1.2	2.2	3.6	5.4	8.0	11.5	17.6	66.1
320	0.2	0.4	1.0	2.0	3.4	5.2	7.8	11.3	17.4	66.1
330	0.1	0.3	0.9	1.9	3.3	5.1	7.7	11.3	17.3	66.1
340	0.1	0.2	0.8	1.8	3.2	5.1	7.6	11.2	17.3	66.1
350	0.0	0.2	0.8	1.8	3.2	5.1	7.6	11.2	17.3	66.1
360	0.0	0.2	0.8	1.8	3.2	5.1	7.6	11.2	17.3	66.1

```
10   REM name: ELEMENT TAPER
20   REM by: John Devoldere, ON4UN
30   ONERR  GOTO 50
40   GOTO 60
50   VTAB 14: POKE 36,34: PRINT "FATAL ERROR
     ": PRINT  CHR$ (7): FOR A = 1 TO 5000:
     NEXT : GOTO 30
60   GOSUB 800
70   HOME : CLEAR : DIM A(15,2),B(10),C(10),
     E(10),F(10),G(10),H(10),D(10): PRINT "
     YAGI DESIGN OR VERTICAL DESIGN ? (Y/V)
     OR >E< TO EXIT > ";: GET I$: IF I$ =
     "E" OR I$ = "e" THEN  HOME : PRINT  CHR$
     (13) +  CHR$ (4);"RUN MENU"
80   GOSUB 770: IF I$ = "Y" OR I$ = "y" THEN
     GOSUB 630
90   VTAB 19: INPUT "ENTER NUMBER OF SECTION
     S (MAX 10) > ";B$:B =  VAL (B$):B =  INT
     (B): IF B < = 1 OR B > 10 THEN  PRINT
     CHR$ (7): GOTO 90
100  C$ = ""
110  VTAB 20: PRINT "DIMENSIONS IN INCHES O
     R CM (I/C) > ";: GET C$:D = 1: IF C$ =
     "C" OR C$ = "c" THEN D = 1 / 2.54:E$ =
     " CM.": GOTO 140
120  IF C$ = "I" OR C$ = "i" THEN D = 1:E$ =
     " INCHES": GOTO 140
130  PRINT  CHR$ (7): GOTO 110
140  HOME : HOME : PRINT "SECTION 1 IS BOTT
     OM SECTION (LARGEST DIAMETER). ": PRINT
     "-----------------------------------
     ------------------------------------
     ----"
150  VTAB 12: IF I$ = "Y" OR I$ = "y" THEN
     PRINT "BOOM DIAMETER IN ";E$;" > ";: INPUT
     "";J$:L =  VAL (J$): IF L < = 0 THEN
     PRINT  CHR$ (7): GOTO 150
160  M = (L / 2) * .0625 / D:N = 9.4 / (C *
     D): FOR A = 1 TO B: VTAB 13: PRINT "SE
     CTION NR ";A: PRINT "--------------"
170  VTAB 15: PRINT "SECTION LENGTH IN ";E$;
     " > ";: INPUT "";F$(A):I(A) =  VAL (F$
     (A)): IF I(A) < = 0 THEN  PRINT  CHR$
     (7): GOTO 170
180  VTAB 16: PRINT "SECTION DIAMETER IN";E
     $;" > ";: INPUT "";D$(A): VTAB 17: CALL
     - 868:J(A) =  VAL (D$(A)): IF J(A) <
     = 0 THEN  PRINT  CHR$ (7):: GOTO 180
190  IF A = 1 GOTO 210
200  IF J(A) > = J(A - 1) THEN  PRINT  CHR$
     (7):: PRINT "SECTIONS MUST BE ENTERED
     IN ORDER OF DECREASING DIAMTER": GOTO
     180
210  NEXT A
220  HOME : VTAB 10: PRINT "DESIGN FREQUENC
     Y = ";C;" MHZ.": IF I$ < > "Y" AND I$
     < > "y" THEN  PRINT : GOTO 260
230  IF K$ < > "Y" AND K$ < > "y" GOTO 26
     0
240  PRINT "REFL. LENGTH = ";O;:: POKE 36,26
     : PRINT "DRIV. EL LENGTH = ";P;:: IF Q =
     0 THEN  PRINT : GOTO 260
250  POKE 36,52: PRINT "LENGTH DIRECTOR(S)
     =";Q
260  GOSUB 470: VTAB 12: PRINT : IF G$ = "M
     " OR G$ = "m" THEN G$ = "": GOTO 280
270  VTAB 17: PRINT "OK? (Y/N) > ": GET G$:
     VTAB 17: CALL  - 868: IF G$ < > "N" AND
     G$ < > "n" GOTO 350
280  VTAB 17: INPUT "ENTER NUMBER OF SECTIO
     N TO BE CORRECTED > ";H$:A =  VAL (H$)
     : IF A = < 0 THEN  PRINT  CHR$ (7): GOTO
     280
290  IF A > B THEN  PRINT  CHR$ (7): GOTO 2
     80
300  VTAB 18: INPUT "ENTER NEW SECTION LENG
     TH > ";F$(A):I(A) =  VAL (F$(A)): IF I
     (A) < = 0 THEN  PRINT  CHR$ (7): GOTO
     300
310  IF A = 1 THEN R = 999: GOTO 330
320  R = J(A - 1)
330  VTAB 19: INPUT "ENTER NEW SECTION DIAM
     . > ";D$(A):J(A) =  VAL (D$(A)): IF J
     (A) < = 0 OR J(A) > = R THEN  PRINT
     CHR$ (7): GOTO 330
340  GOTO 220
350  FOR A = 1 TO B:D(A) = J(A) * D:B(A) =
     I(A) * D: NEXT A:E = 0:F = ( ATN (1) *
     4) / 180: FOR A = 1 TO B:E = E + B(A):
     NEXT A:A(G,2) = 0:A(1,1) = 0: FOR A = 1
     TO B:A(A,2) = B(A) * F * 90 / E + A(
     A - 1,2):A(A + 1,1) = A(A,2): NEXT A: FOR
     A = 1 TO B:E(A) = ( SIN (2 * A(A,2)) -
     SIN (2 * A(A,1))) / (2 * A(A,2) - 2 *
     A(A,1)): NEXT A:H =  LOG (((984 / C) *
     12) / .4375) /  LOG (10): FOR A = 1 TO
     B
360  F(A) = 2 * 984 * 12 / (C * D(A)):F(A) =
     LOG (F(A)) /  LOG (10): NEXT A: FOR A
     = 1 TO B:G(A) = (43.03 * F(A) - 32) /
     (43.03 * H - 32): NEXT A: FOR A = 1 TO
     B:C(A) = B(A) * ((G(A) + 1 / G(A)) / 2
     + (G(A) - 1 / G(A)) * E(A) / 2): NEXT
     A:I = 0: FOR A = 1 TO B:I = I + C(A): NEXT
     :E = E / D:E =  INT (100 * E + .5) / 1
     00: PRINT "ACTUAL LENGTH = ";E;E$:J =
     I:I = I / D:S =  INT (100 * I + .5) /
     100
370  PRINT "EQUIVALENT LENGTH = ";S;E$: GOSUB
     460:K = 100 * T * 300 / (2.54 * J * 4)
     :K =  INT (K * 1000 + .5) / 1000: IF I
     $ = "Y" OR I$ = "y" GOTO 390
380  PRINT "RESONANT FREQUENCY = ";K;" Mhz.
     ": GOTO 400
390  U = (J / 6) / (984 / C):U =  INT (10000
     0 * U + .5) / 100000: PRINT "ELECTRICA
     L LENGTH OF ELEMENT = ";U;" WAVELENGTH
     "
400  IF I$ = "Y" OR I$ = "y" THEN  PRINT "A
     DD ";  INT (100 * (M + N) + .5) / 100;E
     $;" TO THE OUTER SECTIONS FOR ELEM. TO
     BOOM CLAMP COMPENSATION"
410  VTAB 23: PRINT " >P<=PRINT RES.  >F<=
     CHANGE FREQ.  >M<=MODIF.DIM.  >N<=NE
     W RUN  >E<=EXIT";: POKE 36,78: GET G$
     : IF G$ = "M" OR G$ = "m" THEN  VTAB 2
     3: POKE 36,0: CALL  - 868: POKE 35,21:
     GOTO 220
420  POKE 35,23: IF G$ = "P" OR G$ = "p" THEN
     HOME : PRINT  CHR$ (13) +  CHR$ (4);"
     PR#1": GOSUB 520: GOSUB 470: GOSUB 480
     : PRINT  CHR$ (13) +  CHR$ (4);"PR#3":
     GOSUB 800: GOTO 220
430  IF G$ = "E" OR G$ = "e" THEN  HOME : PRINT
     CHR$ (13) +  CHR$ (4);"RUN MENU"
440  IF G$ = "F" OR G$ = "f" THEN  VTAB 23:
     POKE 36,0: CALL  - 868: POKE 35,21: GOSUB
     770: GOTO 220
450  VTAB 23: POKE 36,0: CALL  - 868: POKE
     35,21: GOTO 70
460  T = (1 - 1 / (4.671922895 *  LOG (J / .
     875) - 8)): RETURN
470  VTAB 12: PRINT "SECT. ";: FOR A = 1 TO
     B: PRINT "  ";A;"    ";: NEXT : PRINT
     : VTAB 13: PRINT "------ ";: FOR A = 1
     TO B: PRINT "------ ";: NEXT : PRINT
     : VTAB 14: PRINT "LENGTH";: FOR A = 1 TO
     B: POKE 36,(A * 7): PRINT I(A);: NEXT
     A: PRINT : VTAB 15: PRINT "DIAM.";: FOR
     A = 1 TO B: POKE 36,(A * 7): PRINT J(A
     );: NEXT A: RETURN
480  PRINT : PRINT : PRINT "ACTUAL LENGTH =
     ";E;E$: PRINT "EQUIVALENT LENGTH = ";
     S;E$: IF I$ = "Y" OR I$ = "y" GOTO 500
490  PRINT "RESONANT FREQUENCY = ";K;" Mhz.
     ": GOTO 510
```

```
500  PRINT "ELECTRICAL LENGTH OF ELEMENT =
     ";U;" WAVELENGTH": IF I$ = "Y" OR I$ =
     "y" THEN  PRINT "ADD "; INT (100 * (M +
     N) + .5) / 100;E$" TO THE OUTER SECTIO
     NS FOR ELEM. TO BOOM CLAMP COMPENSATIO
     N."
510  PRINT : PRINT : PRINT : PRINT : RETURN

520  IF I$ = "Y" AND I$ = "y" THEN  PRINT "
     YAGI ELEMENT DESIGN. ALL LENGTHS ARE H
     ALF ELEMENT LENGTHS.": PRINT "--------
     -------------": GOTO 540
530  PRINT "QUARTER WAVE VERTICAL ANTENNA D
     ESIGN.": PRINT "-----------------------
     ----------------": IF K$ < > "Y" AND K
     $ < > "y" GOTO 580
540  IF I$ < > "Y" AND I$ < > "y" GOTO 58
     0
550  IF K$ < > "Y" AND K$ < > "y" GOTO 58
     0
560  PRINT "THE YAGI HAS ";V;" ELEMENTS.": GOSUB
     740: IF C$ = "I" OR C$ = "i" THEN  PRINT
     "SPACING BETWEEN ELEMENTS = ";W;" INCH
     ES.": GOTO 580
570  PRINT "SPACING BETWEEN ELEMENTS = ";X;
     " CM."
580  PRINT "DESIGN FREQUENCY = ";C;" MHZ.":
     IF I$ < > "Y" OR I$ < > "y" GOTO 60
     0
590  PRINT "BOOM DIAMETER = ";L;E$
600  PRINT : IF C$ = "I" OR C$ = "i" THEN  PRINT
     "ALL DIMENSIONS ARE IN INCHES": GOTO 6
     20
610  PRINT "ALL DIMENSIONS ARE IN CENTIMETE
     RS": PRINT
620  RETURN
630  HOME : PRINT "DO YOU WANT YAGI DESIGN
     INFORMATION ? (Y/N) > ";: GET K$: IF K
     $ < > "N" AND K$ < > "n" GOTO 650
640  PRINT : RETURN
650  HOME : PRINT "ENTER TOTAL NUMBER OF YA
     GI ELEMENTS (2 - 6) > ";: GET L$:V =  VAL
     (L$): IF V < 2 OR V > 6 THEN  PRINT  CHR$
     (7);: GOTO 650
660  IF V = 2 OR V = 3 OR V = 6 THEN X = .1
     5 * 300 / C
670  IF V = 4 THEN X = .25 * 300 / C
680  IF V = 5 THEN X = .1875 * 300 / C
690  X = X * 100:W = X / 2.54:X =  INT (X *
     100 + .5) / 100:W =  INT (W * 100 + .5
     ) / 100: HOME : PRINT "ALL ";V;" ELEME
     NTS MUST BE EQUALLY SPACED AT ";X;" CM
     . OR ";W;" INCHES FROM ONE": PRINT "AN
     OTHER ON THE BOOM.": IF V = 2 THEN O =
     .49366:P = .47050

700  IF V = 3 THEN O = .49801:P = .48963:Q =
     .469
710  IF V = 4 THEN O = .49185:P = .479:Q =
     .46319
720  IF V = 5 THEN O = .49994:P = .4804:Q =
     .45232
730  IF V = 6 THEN O = .49528:P = .48028:Q =
     .44811
740  PRINT : PRINT "TARGET ELEMENT LENGTHS
     IN WAVELENGTHS.": PRINT "-------------
     -------------------------": PRINT "REF
     LECTOR LENGTH = ";O;" WAVELENGTHS.": PRINT
     "DRIV. EL. LENGTH = ";P;" WAVELENGTHS.
     ": IF V < 3 THEN  GOTO 760
750  PRINT "DIRECTOR LENGTH  = ";Q;" WAVELE
     NGTHS."
760  PRINT : RETURN
770  VTAB 10: PRINT : CALL  - 868: INPUT "E
     NTER DESIGN FREQUENCY (MHz) > ";A$:C =
     VAL (A$): IF C = < 0 THEN  PRINT  CHR$
     (7): GOTO 770
780  IF C < .1 OR C > 30 THEN  PRINT  CHR$
     (7);: PRINT "FREQ. LIMITS ARE 100 KHz
     and 30 MHz": GOTO 770
790  RETURN
800  PRINT  CHR$ (13) +  CHR$ (4);"PR#3": PRINT
     : POKE 36,24: PRINT "TAPERED ELEMENT L
     ENGTH CALCULATION";: POKE 36,71: PRINT
     "by ON4UN": PRINT "-------------------
     --------------------------------------
     ----------------------"
810  PRINT "THIS PROGRAMS CALCULATES THE RE
     SONANT FREQUENCY OF QUARTER WAVE VERTI
     CALS OR THEELECTRICAL LENGTH OF THE EL
     EMENTS OF A YAGI AS A FUNCTION OF VARY
     ING ELEMENT    DIAMETER, DEFINED IN SE
     CTIONS OF GIVEN LENGTH AND DIAMETER."
820  PRINT "THE EQUIVALENT LENGTH IS REFERE
     D TO AN UNTAPERED ELEMENT WITH  A 7/8
     INCH (2.2225CM) DIAMETER. FOR YAGI DES
     IGN REFER TO Ham Radio, Dec 80, pg 30.
     ": PRINT "----------------------------
     --------------------------------------
     ---------------": POKE 34,9
830  VTAB 22: PRINT "----------------------
     --------------------------------------
     --------------------": POKE 35,21: RETURN
```

```
10   REM name: STUB MATCHING
20   REM by: John Devoldere, ON4UN
30   ONERR GOTO 50
40   GOTO 60
50   VTAB 14: POKE 36,34: PRINT "FATAL ERROR
     ": PRINT CHR$ (7): FOR G = 1 TO 5000:
     NEXT : GOTO 30
60   H = ATN (1) * 4: PRINT CHR$ (13) + CHR$
     (4);"PR#3": HOME : PRINT : POKE 36,33:
     PRINT "STUB MATCHING";: POKE 36,71: PRINT
     "by ON4UN": PRINT "--------------------
     ------------------------------------------
     -----------------------"
70   PRINT "CALCULATES THE POSITION OF THE S
     TUB AS WELL AS THE LENGTH OF THE STUB.
     THE PRO- GRAM IS ITERATIVE, AND DISPL
     AYS THE WHOLE RANGE OF REAL IMPEDANCES
     WHICH CAN"
80   PRINT "BE ACHIEVED USING STUB MATCHING.
     POSITION AND LENGTHS ARE IN ELECTRICA
     L DEGREES.THE STUB CAN BE REPLACED WIT
     H A COIL OR CAPACITOR WITH LISTED VALU
     E.": PRINT "--------------------------
     ------------------------------------------
     ----------------"
90   VTAB 22: PRINT "------------------------
     ------------------------": POKE 35,21
100  POKE 34,8:I = 0:K = 1
110  VTAB 23: PRINT "              RESULTS TO S
     CREEN    >>>S<<<        TO PRINTER   >>
     >P<<<    > ";: GET A$: IF A$ < > "S" AND
     A$ < > "s" AND A$ < > "P" AND A$ < >
     "p" THEN PRINT CHR$ (7): GOTO 110
120  VTAB 8: PRINT : INPUT "DESIGN FREQUENC
     Y (IN MHz) > ";B$:P = VAL (B$): IF P =
     < 0 THEN PRINT CHR$ (7): GOTO 120
130  VTAB 10: INPUT "CABLE IMPEDANCE Zk > "
     ;D$:Q = VAL (D$): IF Q = < 0 THEN PRINT
     CHR$ (7): GOTO 130
140  VTAB 11: PRINT "LOAD IMPEDANCE": PRINT
     "--------------"
150  VTAB 13: INPUT "RESISTIVE PART Z > ";E
     $:R = VAL (E$): IF R = 0 THEN PRINT
     CHR$ (7): GOTO 150
160  VTAB 14: INPUT "REACTIVE PART  Z > ";F
     $:S = VAL (F$): IF S = 0 AND F$ < >
     "0" THEN PRINT CHR$ (7): GOTO 160
170  T = SQR (R ^ 2 + S ^ 2):U = ATN (S /
     R):U = U * 180 / H: IF R < 0 AND S > 0
     THEN U = U + 180
180  IF R < 0 AND S < 0 THEN U = U - 180
190  VTAB 16: PRINT "LOAD VOLTAGE": PRINT "
     ------------": PRINT "ENTER 0 IF LOAD
     CURRENT WILL BE INPUTTED"
200  VTAB 19: INPUT "ABSOLUTE VALUE > ";G$:
     V = VAL (G$): IF V = 0 AND G$ < > "0
     " THEN PRINT CHR$ (7);: GOTO 200
210  IF V < 0 THEN PRINT CHR$ (7);: GOTO
     200
220  IF V = 0 GOTO 250
230  VTAB 20: INPUT "ANGLE          > ";H$:
     X = VAL (H$): IF X = 0 AND H$ < > "0
     " THEN PRINT CHR$ (7);: GOTO 230
240  E = V * COS (X * H / 180):F = V * SIN
     (X * H / 180): PRINT : IF V < > 0 THEN
     HOME : GOTO 290
250  VTAB 16: CALL - 958: PRINT "LOAD CURR
     ENT": PRINT "------------"
260  VTAB 18: INPUT "ABSOLUTE VALUE > ";I$:
     Y = VAL (I$): IF Y < = 0 THEN PRINT
     CHR$ (7): GOTO 260
270  VTAB 19: INPUT "ANGLE          > ";J$:
     Al = VAL (J$): IF Al = 0 AND J$ < >
     "0" THEN PRINT CHR$ (7): GOTO 270
280  HOME : POKE 34,0:G = Y * COS (Al * H /
     180):J = Y * SIN (Al * H / 180): GOTO
     330
290  G = ((E * R) + (S * F)) / (R ^ 2 + S ^
     2):J = ((F * R) - (S * E)) / (R ^ 2 +
     S ^ 2):Y = SQR (G ^ 2 + J ^ 2): IF G =
     0 THEN Al = 90: GOTO 320
300  Al = ATN (J / G):Al = Al * 180 / H: IF
     G < 0 AND J > 0 THEN Al = Al + 180
310  IF G < 0 AND J < 0 THEN Al = Al - 180
320  GOTO 340
330  E = ((G * R) - (J * S)):F = ((G * S) +
     (J * R))
340  V = SQR (E ^ 2 + F ^ 2): IF E = 0 THEN
     X = 90: GOTO 370
350  X = ATN (F / E):X = X * 180 / H: IF E <
     O AND F > O THEN X = X + 180
360  IF E < O AND F < O THEN X = X - 180
370  Bl = SQR ((R + Q) ^ 2 + S ^ 2):Dl = SQR
     ((R - Q) ^ 2 + S ^ 2):El = (Bl + Dl) /
     (Bl - Dl):El = INT (El * 100 + .5) /
     100:El = ABS (El): POKE 34,0: IF A$ <
     > "P" AND A$ < > "p" THEN POKE 34,0
     : HOME : GOTO 400
380  POKE 34,8: POKE 35,23: HOME : VTAB 15:
     POKE 36,5: PRINT "PRINT-OUT WILL BE I
     N 1 DEGREE INCREMENTS FROM 0 TO 360 DE
     GREES.": VTAB 22: PRINT "-------------
     ------------------------------------------
     ------------------------": PRINT "
     >>>S<<< T
     O STOP PRINTING";: POKE 35,12
390  PRINT CHR$ (13) + CHR$ (4);"PR#1"
400  PRINT : PRINT "Des. Freq.= ";P;" MHz";
     : POKE 36,33: PRINT "STUB MATCHING";: POKE
     36,71: PRINT "by ON4UN": PRINT "------
     ------------------------------------------
     ------------------------------------"
410  PRINT "Zk = ";Q;" ohm";: POKE 36,21: PRINT
     "REAL PART";: POKE 36,36: PRINT "IMAG
     PART";: POKE 36,50: PRINT "MAGNITUDE";
     : POKE 36,65: PRINT "ANGLE": PRINT "SW
     R= ";El;: POKE 36,21: PRINT "---------
     -";: POKE 36,36: PRINT "---------";: POKE
     36,50: PRINT "---------";: POKE 36,65:
     PRINT "-----"
420  PRINT "IMPEDANCE (ohm) = ";: POKE 36,2
     1: PRINT R;: POKE 36,36: PRINT S;: POKE
     36,50: PRINT INT (T * 10000 + .5) / 1
     0000;: POKE 36,65: PRINT INT (U * 100
     00 + .5) / 10000: PRINT "CURRENT (Amp)
     = ";: POKE 36,21: PRINT INT (10000 *
     G + .5) / 10000;: POKE 36,36: PRINT INT
     (10000 * J + .5) / 10000;: POKE 36,50:
     PRINT INT (Y * 10000 + .5) / 10000;:
     POKE 36,65: PRINT INT (Al * 10000 +
     .5) / 10000
430  PRINT "VOLTAGE (Volt) = ";: POKE 36,21
     : PRINT INT (10000 * E + .5) / 10000;
     : POKE 36,36: PRINT INT (10000 * F +
     .5) / 10000;: POKE 36,50: PRINT INT (
     V * 10000 + .5) / 10000;: POKE 36,65: PRINT
     INT (X * 10000 + .5) / 10000: PRINT "
     ------------------------------------------
     ------------------------------------------
     ---": PRINT : POKE 34,9: IF A$ = "P" OR
     A$ = "p" GOTO 450
440  VTAB 23: PRINT "          NEW RUN >>>R<<
     <        NEW ITERATION >>>N<<<       EX
     IT >>>E<<<          ";: POKE 35,21
450  HOME : PRINT "POSITION";: POKE 36,10: PRINT
     "IMPEDANCE";: POKE 36,28: PRINT "VOLTA
     GE";: POKE 36,41: PRINT "------------
     STUB------------": POKE 36,73: PRINT
     "IMPED": POKE 36,1: PRINT "STUB";: POKE
     36,8: PRINT "RESIS.";: POKE 36,16: PRINT
     "REACT.";: POKE 36,25: PRINT "AMPL.";:
     POKE 36,33: PRINT "ANGL.";: POKE 36,4
     1: PRINT "IMPED.";: POKE 36,50: PRINT
     "VALUE";: POKE 36,58: PRINT "LENGTH";
```

```
460  POKE 36,66: PRINT "TYPE";: POKE 36,74:
     PRINT "ohm": POKE 36,1: PRINT "----";
     : POKE 36,8: PRINT "------";: POKE 36,
     16: PRINT "------";: POKE 36,25: PRINT
     "-----";: POKE 36,33: PRINT "-----";: POKE
     36,41: PRINT "-----";: POKE 36,50: PRINT
     "-----";: POKE 36,58: PRINT "------";:
     POKE 36,66: PRINT "----";: POKE 36,74
     : PRINT "---": POKE 34,12:I = INT (I +
     .5)
470  I = I + K: IF I > 180 AND A$ = "P" THEN
     PRINT CHR$ (13) + CHR$ (4): PRINT CHR$
     (13) + CHR$ (4);"RUN MENU"
480  IF I > 360 THEN I = 1:K = 1
490  I = INT (I * 100 + .5) / 100: POKE 36,
     1: PRINT I;: IF A$ = "P" OR A$ = "p" GOTO
     530
500  IF PEEK ( - 16384) = 206 OR PEEK ( -
     16384) = 238 THEN HOME : GOTO 790
510  IF PEEK ( - 16384) = 210 OR PEEK ( -
     16384) = 242 THEN HOME : GET C$: GOTO
     30
520  IF PEEK ( - 16384) = 197 OR PEEK ( -
     16384) = 229 THEN GET M$: HOME : PRINT
     CHR$ (13) + CHR$ (4);"RUN MENU"
530  IF A$ < > "P" AND A$ < > "p" GOTO 55
     0
540  IF PEEK ( - 16384) = 211 OR PEEK ( -
     16384) = 243 THEN GET C$: GOTO 30
550  POKE - 16368,0:L = I * H / 180:A = COS
     (L):D = A:B = Q * SIN (L):C = SIN (L
     ) / Q:M = A * R:N = A * S:F1 = M:G1 =
     N + B:T = D - (S * C):H1 = R * C:I1 =
     ((F1 * T) + (G1 * H1)) / (T ^ 2 + H1 ^
     2):J1 = ((G1 * T) - (F1 * H1)) / (T ^
     2 + H1 ^ 2):K1 = (G * F1) - (J * G1):L
     1 = (G * G1) + (J * F1):M1 = ((K1 * I1
     ) + (L1 * J1)) / (I1 ^ 2 + J1 ^ 2)
560  N1 = ((L1 * I1) - (K1 * J1)) / (I1 ^ 2 +
     J1 ^ 2):P1 = SQR (M1 ^ 2 + N1 ^ 2): IF
     M1 = 0 THEN Q1 = 90: GOTO 600
570  Q1 = ATN (N1 / M1):Q1 = Q1 * 180 / H: IF
     M1 < 0 AND N1 > 0 THEN Q1 = Q1 + 180
580  IF M1 < 0 AND N1 < 0 THEN Q1 = Q1 - 18
     0
590  IF M1 < 0 AND N1 = 0 THEN Q1 = 180
600  R1 = SQR (K1 ^ 2 + L1 ^ 2): IF K1 = 0 THEN
     S1 = 90: GOTO 630
610  IF K1 = 0 THEN S1 = 90: GOTO 670
620  S1 = ATN (L1 / K1):S1 = S1 * 180 / H
630  IF K1 < 0 AND L1 > 0 THEN S1 = S1 + 18
     0
640  IF K1 < 0 AND L1 < 0 THEN S1 = S1 - 18
     0
650  IF K1 < 0 AND L1 = 0 THEN S1 = 180
660  L = VAL (L$)
670  T1 = INT (100 * I1 + .5) / 100:U1 = INT
     (10 * J1 + .5) / 10:V1 = INT (100 * R
     1 + .5) / 100:W1 = INT (10 * S1 + .5)
     / 10:Z = INT (100 * Z + .5) / 100:Q1
     = INT (1000 * Q1 + .5) / 1000: POKE
     36,8: PRINT T1;: POKE 36,16: PRINT U1;
     : POKE 36,25: PRINT V1;: POKE 36,33: PRINT
     W1;: GOSUB 840: IF ABS (Z) > 10000 THEN
     N$ = STR$ ( INT (Z)): GOTO 780
680  IF ABS (Z) < = 100 THEN N$ = STR$ (
     INT (Z * 10 + .5) / 10)
690  IF ABS (Z) > = 100 THEN N$ = STR$ (
     INT (Z))
700  IF INT (1000 * ABS (X1)) = 0 THEN N$
     = " "
710  POKE 36,41: PRINT N$;: IF Z < 0 GOTO 7
     50

720  IF ABS (L) < 100 THEN POKE 36,49: PRINT
     INT (L * 10 + .5) / 10;" uH";
730  IF ABS (L) > = 100 THEN POKE 36,49:
     PRINT INT (L);" uH";
740  GOTO 760
750  POKE 36,49: PRINT INT (C1);" pF";
760  O$ = STR$ (W): IF INT (1000 * ABS (X
     1)) = 0 THEN O$ = " "
770  POKE 36,59: PRINT O$;: POKE 36,66: PRINT
     P$;
780  POKE 36,74: PRINT INT (Y1 * 10 + .5) /
     10: GOTO 470
790  GET M$: HOME : IF M$ = "E" THEN PRINT
     CHR$ (13) + CHR$ (4);"RUN MENU"
800  VTAB 15: INPUT "LOWER LIMIT > ";K$:I =
     VAL (K$): IF I = 0 AND K$ < > "0" THEN
     PRINT CHR$ (7): GOTO 800
810  VTAB 16: INPUT "NEW INCREMENT (> 0.01)
     > ";Q$:K = VAL (Q$): IF K = 0 AND Q
     $ < > "0" THEN PRINT CHR$ (7): GOTO
     810
820  IF K < .01 THEN PRINT CHR$ (7): GOTO
     810
830  I = I - K: HOME : GOTO 470
840  Z1 = I1:X1 = J1:A2 = R1 * COS (S1 * H /
     180):B2 = R1 * SIN (S1 * H / 180):C2 =
     ((A2 * Z1) + (B2 * X1)) / (Z1 ^ 2 + X1
     ^ 2): IF INT (1000 * ABS (X1)) = 0 THEN
     L = 0:C1 = 0:Z = 0:Y1 = I1:W = 0:P$ =
     "": RETURN
850  D2 = ((B2 * Z1) - (A2 * X1)) / (Z1 ^ 2 +
     X1 ^ 2):E2 = ATN (D2 / C2):E2 = E2 *
     180 / H: IF C2 < O1 AND D2 > 0 THEN E2
     = E2 + 180
860  IF C2 < O1 AND D2 < 0 THEN E2 = E2 - 1
     80
870  Z = (X1 + Z1 ^ 2 / X1):F2 = INT (100 *
     Z + .5) / 100:Z = - Z:G2 = A2:H2 = B2
     :I2 = (X1 / Z) + 1:J2 = - Z1 / Z:K2 =
     (C2 * I2) - (D2 * J2):L2 = (C2 * J2) +
     (D2 * I2):M2 = SQR (K2 ^ 2 + L2 ^ 2):
     IF K2 = 0 THEN N2 = 90: GOTO 890
880  N2 = ATN (L2 / K2):N2 = N2 * 180 / H
890  IF K2 < 0 AND L2 > 0 THEN N2 = N2 + 18
     0
900  IF K2 < 0 AND L2 < 0 THEN N2 = N2 - 18
     0
910  Y1 = ((G2 * K2) + (H2 * L2)) / (K2 ^ 2 +
     L2 ^ 2):O2 = ((H2 * K2) - (G2 * L2)) /
     (K2 ^ 2 + L2 ^ 2):P2 = SQR (Y1 ^ 2 +
     O2 ^ 2):Q2 = ATN (O2 / Y1):Q2 = Q2 *
     180 / H: IF Y1 < 0 AND O2 > 0 THEN Q2 =
     Q2 + 180
920  IF Y1 < 0 AND O2 < 0 THEN Q2 = Q2 - 18
     0
930  GOTO 940
940  IF Z > 0 THEN L = Z / (2 * H * P)
950  IF Z < 0 THEN C1 = - 1000000 / (2 * H
     * P * Z)
960  GOSUB 970: RETURN
970  IF Z < 0 THEN P$ = "OPEN": GOTO 990
980  P$ = "SHORT":W = ATN (Z / Q):W = W * 1
     80 / H: GOTO 1000
990  W = - ATN (Z / Q) + 1.5708:W = W * 18
     0 / H:W = 180 - W
1000 W = INT (W * 10 + .5) / 10: RETURN
```

Chapter VIII

Literature Review

The literature review lists over 500 reference works, cataloged by subject. Copies may be obtained directly from the magazines listed at the following addresses:

CQ Magazine: 76 N. Broadway, Hicksville, NY 11082

CQ DL: DARC, Postfach 11 55, 3507 Baunatal 1, West Germany

Ham Radio Magazine: Greenville, NH 03048-0498

QST: ARRL Hq, 225 Main St, Newington, CT 06111

Radio Communication: RSGB Hq, Lambda House, Cranborne Rd, Potters Bar, Herts EN6 3JE, England, or directly from the author for $2.00 per article copy.

1. Propagation

Ref 100 K. J. Hortenbach, et al, "Propagation of Short Waves Over Long Distances: Predictions and Observations," *Telecommunications Journal*, Jun 1979, p 320

Ref 101 M. Wilson, AA2Z, ed., *The ARRL Handbook for the Radio Amateur* (Newington, CT: ARRL, 1986)

Ref 102 John Devoldere, ON4UN, *80-Meter DX-ing*

Ref 103 George Jacobs, W3ASK, et al, *The Shortwave Propagation Handbook*

Ref 104 Peter Saveskie, W4LGF, *Radio Propagation Handbook*

Ref 105 William Orr, W6SAI, *Radio Handbook*

Ref 106 Gerald L. Hall, K1TD, ed., *The ARRL Antenna Book*, (Newington, CT: ARRL, 1982)

Ref 107 Wayne Overbeck, N6NB, et al, *Computer Programs for Amateur Radio*

Ref 108 Dale Hoppe, K6UA, et al, "The 'Grayline' Method of DXing," *CQ*, Sep 1975, p 27

Ref 109 Rod Linkous, W7OM, "Navigating to 80 Meter DX," *CQ*, Jan 1978, p 16

Ref 110 Yuri Blanarovich, VE3BMV, "Electromagnetic Wave Propagation By Conduction," *CQ*, Jun 1980, p 44

Ref 111 Guenter Schwarzbeck, DL1BU, "Bedeuting des Vertikalen Abstralwinkels von KW-Antennen," *CQ DL*, Mar 1985, p 130

Ref 112 Guenter Schwarzbeck, DL1BU, "Bedeutung des Vertikalen Abstrahlwinkels von KW-Antennen (Part 2)," *CQ DL* Apr 1985, p 184

Ref 113 Henry Elwell, N4UH, "Calculator-aided Propagation Predictions," *Ham Radio*, Apr 1979, p 26

Ref 114 Donald C. Mead, K4DE, "How to Determine True North for Antenna Orientation," *Ham Radio*, Oct 1980, p 38

Ref 115 Henry Elwell, N4UH, "Antenna Geometry for Optimum Performance," *Ham Radio*, May 1982, p 60

Ref 116 Stan Gibilisco, W1GV/4, "Radiation of Radio Signals," *Ham Radio*, Jun 1982, p 26

Ref 117 Garth Stonehocker, KØRYW, "Forecasting by Computer," *Ham Radio*, Aug 1982, p 80

Ref 118 Bradley Wells, KR7L, "Fundamentals of Grayline Propagation," *Ham Radio*, Aug 1984, p 77

Ref 119 Van Brollini, NS6N, et al, "DXing by Computer," *Ham Radio*, Aug 1984, p 81

Ref 120 Calvin R. Graf, W5LFM, et al, "High-Frequency Atmospheric Noise, Part 2," *QST*, Feb 1972, p 16

Ref 121 Jim Kennedy, K6MIO, et al, "D-Layer Absorption During a Solar Eclipse," *QST*, Jul 1972, p 40

Ref 122 Edward P. Tilton, W1HDQ, "The DXer's Crystal Ball," *QST*, Jun 1975, p 23

Ref 123 Edward P. Tilton, W1HDQ, "The DXer's Crystal Ball, Part II," *QST*, Aug 1975, p 40

Ref 124 Paul Argo, et al, "Radio Propagation and Solar Activity," *QST*, Feb 1977, p 24

Ref 125 Kenneth Johnston, W7LIX, et al, "An Eclipse Study on 80 Meters," *QST*, Jul 1979, p 14

Ref 126 V. Kanevsky, UL7GW, "Ionospheric Ducting at HF," *QST*, Sep 1979, p 20

Ref 127 Robert B. Rose, K6GKU, "MINIMUF: Simplified MUF-Prediction Program for Microcomputers," *QST*, Dec 1982, p 36

Ref 128 Tom Frenaye, K1KI, "The KI Edge," *QST*, Jun 1984, p 54

Ref 129 Richard Miller, VE3CIE, "Radio Aurora," *QST*, Jan 1985, p 14

Ref 130 Pat Hawker, G3VA, "Technical Topics: Transequatorial Supermode Theories," *Radio Communication*, Feb 1972, p 94

Ref 131 Pat Hawker, G3VA, "Technical Topics: Whispering Galleries," *Radio Communication*, May 1972, p 306

Ref 132 Pat Hawker, G3VA, "Technical Topics: Low Angles for Chordal Hops and TEP," *Radio Communication*, Nov 1972, p 746

Ref 133 A. P. A. Ashton, G3XAP, "160M DX from Suburban Sites," *Radio Communication*, Dec 1973, p 842

Ref 134 Pat Hawker, G3VA, "Technical Topics: Path Deviations, One-Way Propagation, HF Tropo and LDEs," *Radio Communication*, Oct 1974, p 686

Ref 135 Pat Hawker, G3VA, "Fading and the Ionosphere," *Radio Communication*, Mar 1978, p 217

Ref 136 Pat Hawker, G3VA, "Technical Topics: When Long-Path is Better," *Radio Communication*, Sep 1979, p 831

Ref 137 V. Kanevsky, UL7GW, "DX QSOs," *Radio Communication*, Sep 1979, p 835

Ref 138 Pat Hawker, G3VA, "Technical Topics: Chordal Hop and Ionospheric Focussing," *Radio Communication*, Apr 1984, p 315

2. Receivers

Ref 200 M. Wilson, AA2Z, ed., *The ARRL Handbook for the Radio Amateur* (Newington, CT: ARRL, 1986)

Ref 201 ON4EG, "Sensibilite des Recepteurs," *CQ-QSO*, Jan 1985

Ref 202 ON4EG, "Sensibilite des Recepteurs," *CQ-QSO* Feb 1985

Ref 203 Michael Martin, DJ7JV, "Emfangereingangsteil mit Grossem Dynamik Bereich," DL/QTC Jun 1975

Ref 204 M. Wilson, AA2Z, ed., *The ARRL Handbook for the Radio Amateur* (Newington, CT: ARRL, 1986)

Ref 205 John Devoldere, ON4UN *80-Meter DX-ing*

Ref 206 William Orr, W6SAI, *Radio Handbook*

Ref 207 Robert Sternowsky, "Using Preselectors to Improve HF Performance," *Communications International*, May 1980, p 34

Ref 208 John Devoldere, ON4UN, "Improved Performance from the Drake R-4B and T4X-B," *CQ*, Mar 1976, p 37

Ref 209 Michael Martin, DJ7VY, "Rauscharmer Oszillator fur Empfaenger mit grossem Dynamikbereich," *CQ DL*, Dec 1976, p 418

Ref 210 Wes Hayward, W7ZOI, "Der Dynamische Bereich eines Empfaengers," *CQ DL*, Mar 1977, p 93

Ref 211 Richard Waxweller, DJ7VD, "Hochfrequenz-Zweitongenerator," *CQ DL*, Sep 1980, p 412

Ref 212 Guenter Schwarzbeck, DL1BU, "Testbericht: NF-Filter Datong FL2," *CQ DL*, Feb 1981, p 56

Ref 213 Guenter Schwarzbeck, DL1BU, "Grosssignalverhalten von Kurzwellenempfaengern," *CQ DL*, Mar 1981, p 117

Ref 214 Walter Flor, OE1LO, "KW-Eingangsteile: Eingangsfilter," *CQ DL*, Aug 1981, p 373

Ref 215 Walter Flor, OE1LO, "IM-feste Verstaerker fuer den KW-bereich," *CQ DL*, Oct 1981, p 473

Ref 216 Walter Flor, OE1LO, "KW-Eingangsteile: Extrem IM-feste selektive Vorverstaerker," *CQ DL*, Aug 1982, p 376

Ref 217 Guenter Schwarzbeck, DL1BU, "Geraeteeigenschaften: Besonderheiten zwischen Testbericht und Praxis," *CQ DL*, Sep 1982, p 424

Ref 218 Erich Vogelsang, DJ2IM, "Grundrmauschen und Dynamiekbereich bei Kurzwellenempfaengern," *CQ DL*, Sep 1982, p. 432

Ref 219 Michael Martin, DJ7YV, "Intermodulationsfster Preselector fur 1.5 - 30 MHz," *CQ DL*, Jul 1984, p 320

Ref 220 Ray Moore, "Designing Communication Receivers for Good Strong-Signal Performance," *Ham Radio*, Feb 1973, p 6

Ref 221 Wes Hayward, W7ZOI, "Bandpass Filters for Receiver Preselectors," *Ham Radio*, Feb 1975, p 18

Ref 222 Ulrich Rohde, DJ2LR, "High Dynamic Range Receiver Input Stages," *Ham Radio*, Oct 1975, p 26

Ref 223 James Fisk, W1DTY, "Receiver Noise Figure Sensitivity and Dynamic Range—What The Numbers Mean," *Ham Radio*, Oct 1975, p. 8

Ref 224 Marvin Gonsior, W6FR, "Improved Selectivity for Collins S-line Receivers," *Ham Radio*, Jun 1976, p 36

Ref 225 Howard Berlin, K3NEZ, "Increased Flexibility for MFJ CW Filters," *Ham Radio*, Dec 1976, p 58

Ref 226 Ulrich Rohde, DJ2LR, "I-F Amplifier Design," *Ham Radio*, Mar 1977, p 10

Ref 227 Alex Burwasser, WB4ZNV, "Reducing Intermodulation Distortion in High-Frequency Receivers," *Ham Radio*, Mar 1977, p. 26

Ref 228 Wayne C. Ryder, W6URM, "General Coverage Communications Receiver," *Ham Radio*, Nov 1977, p 10

Ref 229 R. Sherwood, WB0JGP, et al, "Receivers—Some Problems and Cures," *Ham Radio*, Dec 1977, p 10

Ref 230 R. Sherwood, WB0JGP, et al, "New Product Detector for R-4C," *Ham Radio*, Oct 1978, p 94

Ref 231 R. Sherwood, WB0JGP, et al, "Audio Amplifier for the Drake R-4C," *Ham Radio*, Apr 1979, p 48

Ref 233 James M. Rohler, N0DE, "Biquad Bandpass Filter," *Ham Radio*, Jun 1979, p 70

Ref 234 Sidney Kaiser, WB6CTW, "Measuring Receiver Dynamic Range," *Ham Radio*, Nov 1979, p 56

Ref 235 Ulrich Rohde, DJ2LR, "Recent Developments in Circuits and Techniques for High Frequency Communications Receivers," *Ham Radio*, Apr 1980, p 20

Ref 236 Edward Wetherhold, W3NQN, "High Performance CW Filter," *Ham Radio*, Apr 1981, p 18

Ref 237 D. A. Tong, G4GMQ, "Add-On Selectivity for Communication Receivers," *Ham Radio*, Nov 1981, p 41

Ref 238 Ulrich Rohde, DJ2LR, "Communication Receivers for the Year 2000: Part 1," *Ham Radio*, Nov 1981, p 12

Ref 239 Jan K. Moller, K6FM, "Understanding Performance Data of High-Frequency Receivers," *Ham Radio*, Nov 1981, p 30

Ref 240 Ulrich Rohde, DJ2LR, "Communication Receivers for the Year 2000, Part 2," *Ham Radio*, Dec 1981, p 6

Ref 241 Ulrich Rohde, DJ2LR, "Performance Capability of Active Mixers, Part 1," *Ham Radio*, Mar 1982, p 30

Ref 242 Ulrich Rohde, DJ2LR, "Performance Capability of Active Mixers, Part 2," *Ham Radio*, Apr 1982, p 38

Ref 243 R. W. Johnson, W6MUR, "Bridged T-Filters for Amateur Use," *Ham Radio*, Oct 1982, p 51

Ref 244 Cornell Drentea, WB3JZO, "Designing a Modern Receiver," *Ham Radio*, Nov 1983, p 3

Ref 245 Edward Wetherhold, W3NQN, "Elliptic Lowpass Audio Filter Design," *Ham Radio*, Jan 1984, p 20

Ref 246 J. A. Dyer, G4OBU, "High Frequency Receiver Performance," *Ham Radio*, Feb 1984, p 33

Ref 247 E. A. Andrade, W0DAN, "Recent Trends in Receiver Front-End Design," *QST*, Jun 1962, p 17

Ref 248 William K. Squires, W2PUL, "A New Approach to Receiver Front-End Design," *QST*, Sep 1963, p 31

Ref 249 Byron Goodman, W1DX, "Some Thoughts on Home Receiver Design," *QST*, May 1965, p 11

Ref 250 E. H. Conklin, K6KA, "Front-End Receiving Filters," *QST*, Aug 1967, p 14

Ref 251 Doug DeMaw, W1CER, "Rejecting Interference from Broadcast Stations," *QST*, Dec 1967, p 35

Ref 252 Rudolf Fisher, DL6WD, "An Engineer's Solid-State Ham-Band Receiver," *QST*, Mar 1970, p 11

Ref 253 Douglas A. Blakeslee, W1KLK, "An Experimental Receiver for 75 Meter DX Work," *QST*, Feb 1972, p 41

Ref 254 Wes Hayward, W7ZOI, "Defining and Measuring Receiver Dynamic Range," *QST*, Jul 1975, p 15

Ref 255 Doug DeMaw, W1FB, "His Eminence, the Receiver," *QST*, Jun 1976, p 27

Ref 256 Wes Hayward, W7ZOI, "CER-Verters," *QST*, Jun 1976, p 31

Ref 257 Doug DeMaw, W1FB, "Build this 'Quickie' Preamp," *QST*, Apr 1977, p 43

Ref 258 Wes Hayward, W7ZOI, "More Thoughts on Receiver Performance Specification," *QST*, Nov 1979, p 48

Ref 259 Ulrich Rohde, DJ2LR, "Increasing Receiver Dynamic Range," *QST*, May 1980, p 16

Ref 260 Edward Wetherhold, W3NQN, "Modern Design of a CW Filter Using 88- and 44-mH Surplus Inductors," *QST*, Dec 1980, p 14

Ref 261 Doug DeMaw, et al, "Modern Receiver Mixers for High Dynamic Range," *QST*, Jan 1981, p 19

Ref 262 Wes Hayward, W7ZOI, "A Progressive Communications Receiver," *QST*, Nov 1981, p 11

Ref 263 Robert E. Lee, K2TWK, "Build an Audio Filter with Pizzazz," *QST*, Feb 1982, p 18

Ref 264 Harold Mitchell, NØARQ, "88-mH Inductors—A Trap," *QST*, Jan 1983, p 38

Ref 265 Gerald B. Hull, AK4L/VE1CER, "Filter Systems for Multi-transmitter Amateur Stations," *QST*, Jul 1983, p 28

Ref 266 John K. Webb, W1ETC, "High-Pass Filters for Receiving Applications," *QST*, Oct 1983, p 17

Ref 267 Doug DeMaw, W1FB, "Receiver Preamps and How to Use Them," *QST*, Apr 1984, p 19

Ref 268 Pat Hawker, G3VA, "Trends in H.F. Receiver Front-ends," *Radio Communication*, Sep 1963, p 161

Ref 269 D. A. Tong, G4GMQ, "Audio Filters as an Aid to Reception," *Radio Communication*, Feb 1978, p 114

Ref 270 John Bazley, G3HCT, "The Datong Multi-Mode Filter FL-2," *Radio Communication*, Aug 1980, p 783

Ref 271 Pat Hawker, G3VA, "Technical Topics: More Thoughts On 'Ideal' HF Receivers," *Radio Communication*, Oct 1982, p 861

Ref 272 Edward Wetherhold, W3NQN, "Simplified Elliptic Lowpass Filter Design Using Surplus 88-mH Inductors," *Radio Communication*, Apr 1983, p 318

Ref 273 P. E. Chadwick, G3RZP, "Dynamic Range, Inter-modulation and Phase Noise," *Radio Communication*, Mar 1984, p 223

Ref 274 Pat Hawker, G3VA, "Technical Topics: Comparing Receiver Front-Ends," *Radio Communication*, May 1984, p 400

Ref 275 Pat Hawker, G3VA, "Technical Topics: Receivers: Numbers Right or Wrong?," *Radio Communication*, Aug 1984, p 677

Ref 276 Pat Hawker, G3VA, "Technical Topics: Receivers of Top Performance," *Radio Communication*, Oct 1984, p 858

Ref 277 Edward Wetherhold, W3NQN, "A CW Filter for the Radio Amateur Newcomer," *Radio Communication*, Jan 1985, p 26

Ref 278 Pat Hawker, G3VA, "Technical Topics: Whither Experimentation?," *Radio Communication*, Mar 1985, p 189

Ref 279 Ian White, G3SEK, "Modern VHF/UHF Front-End Design, Part 1," *Radio Communication*, Apr 1985, p 264

Ref 280 Ian White, G3SEK, "Modern VHF/UHF Front-End Design, Part 2," *Radio Communication*, May 1985, p 367

Ref 281 Ian White, G3SEK, "Modern VHF/UHF Front-End Design, Part 3," *Radio Communication*, Jun 1985, p 445

Ref 282 Pat Hawker, G3VA, "Technical Topics: Weak Signal Reception," *Radio Communication*, Jul 1985, p 540

Ref 283 D. H. G. Fritsch, GØCKZ, "Active Elliptic Audio Filter Design Using Op-Amps (Part 1)," *Radio Communication*, Feb 1986, p 98

3. Transmitters

Ref 300 M. Wilson, AA2Z, ed., *The ARRL Handbook for the Radio Amateur* (Newington, CT: ARRL, 1986)

Ref 301 Bob Heil, K9EID, "Equalise That Microphone," *Radiosporting*, Apr 1985, p 27

Ref 302 M. Wilson, AA2Z, ed., *The ARRL Handbook for the Radio Amateur* (Newington, CT: ARRL, 1986)

Ref 303 John Devoldere, ON4UN, *80-Meter DX-ing*

Ref 304 William Orr, W6SAI, *Radio Handbook*

Ref 305 John Devoldere, ON4UN, "Improved Performance from the Drake R-4B and T4X-B," *CQ*, Mar 1976, p 37

Ref 306 John Schultz, W4FA, "An Optimum Speech Filter," *CQ*, Oct 1978, p 22

Ref 307 L. McCoy, W1ICP, "The Design Electronics QSK-1500," *CQ*, Apr 1985, p 40

Ref 308 Guenter Schwarzbeck, DL1BU, "Geraeteeigenschaften: Besonderheiten zwischen Testbericht und Praxis," *CQ DL*, Sep 1982, p 424

Ref 309 Leslie Moxon, G6XN, "Performance of RF Speech Clippers," *Ham Radio*, Nov 1972, p 26

Ref 310 Charles Bird, K6HTM, "RF Speech Clipper for SSB," *Ham Radio*, Feb 1973, p 18

Ref 311 Henry Elwell, W2MB, "RF Speech Processor," *Ham Radio*, Sep 1973, p 18

Ref 312 Barry Kirkwood, ZL1BN, "Principles of Speech Processing," *Ham Radio*, Feb 1975, p 28

Ref 313 Timothy Carr, W6IVI, "Speech Processor for the Heath SB-102," *Ham Radio*, Jun 1975, p 38

Ref 314 Jim Fisk, W1DTY, "New Audio Speech Processing Technique," *Ham Radio*, Jun 1976, p 30

Ref 315 Frank C. Getz, K3PDW, "Logarithmic Speech Processor," *Ham Radio*, Aug 1977, p 48

Ref 316 Michael James, W1CBY, "Electronic Bias Switching for the Henry 2K4 and 3KA linear amplifiers," *Ham Radio*

Ref 317 Wesley D. Stewart, N7WS, "Split-Band Speech Processor," *Ham Radio*, Sep 1979, p 12

Ref 318 J. R. Sheller, KN8Z, "High Power RF Switching With Pin Diodes," *Ham Radio*, Jan 1985, p 82

Ref 319 William Sabin, WØIYH, "R.F. Clippers for S.S.B.," *QST*, Jul 1967, p 13

Ref 320 J. A. Bryant, W4UX, "Electronic Bias Switching for RF Power Amplifiers," *QST*, May 1974, p 36

Ref 321 Robert Myers, W1FBY, "Quasi-Logarithmic Analog Amplitude Limiter," *QST*, Aug 1974, p 22

Ref 322 Hal Collins, W6JES, "SSB Speech Processing Revisited," *QST*, Aug 1976, p 38

Ref 323 Bob Heil, K9EID, "Equalize Your Microphone and Be Heard!," *QST*, Jul 1982, p 11

Ref 324 R. C. V. Macario, G4ADL, et al, "An Assured Speech Processor," *Radio Communication*, Apr 1978, p 310

Ref 325 H. Leerning, G3LLL, "Improving the FT-101," *Radio Communication*, Jun 1979, p 516

Ref 326 L. McCoy, W1ICP, "The Design Electronics QSK-1500," *CQ*, Apr 1985, p 40

Ref 327 Alfred Trossen, DL6YP, "Die AMTOR-II einheit nach G3PLX," *CQ DL*, Jul 1983, p 316

Ref 328 Alfred Trossen, DL6YP, "Die AMTOR-II einheit nach G3PLX," *CQ DL*, Aug 1983, p 368

Ref 329 J. R. Sheller, KN8Z, "High Power RF Switching With Pin Diodes," *Ham Radio*, Jan 1985, p 82

Ref 330 Peter Martinez, G3PLX, "AMTOR, an Improved Error-Free RTTY System," *QST*, Jun 1981, p 25

Ref 331 Paul Newland, AD7I, "Z-AMTOR: An Advanced AMTOR Code Converter," *QST*, Feb 1984, p 25

Ref 332 Peter Martinez, G3PLX, "AMTOR, an Improved Radio Teleprinter System Using a Microprocessor," *Radio Communication*, Aug 1979, p 714

Ref 333 Peter Martinez, G3PLX, "AMTOR the Easy Way," *Radio Communication*, Jun 1980, p 610

Ref 334 Jon Towle, WB1DNL, "QSK 1500 High-Power RF Switch," *QST*, Sep 1985, p 39

Ref 335 Dr. J. R. Sheller, KN8Z, "What Does 'QSK' Really Mean?," *QST*, Jul 1985, p 31

Ref 336 Paul Newland, AD7I, "A User's Guide to AMTOR Operation," *QST*, Oct 1985, p 31

4. Equipment Review

Ref 400 Guenter Schwarzbeck, DL1BU, "Testbericht: Transceiver TS820," *CQ DL*, Apr 1977, p 130

Ref 401 Guenter Schwarzbeck, DL1BU, "Testbericht und Beschreibung TS-520S," *CQ DL*, Feb 1978, p 50

Ref 402 Guenter Schwarzbeck, DL1BU, "Testbericht un Messdaten FT-901 DM (receiver section)," *CQ DL*, Oct 1978, p 438

Ref 403 Guenter Schwarzbeck, DL1BU, "Testbericht und Messdaten FT-901 DM (transmitter section)," *CQ DL*, Nov 1978, p 500

Ref 404 Guenter Schwarzbeck, DL1BU, "KW-Empfaenger Drake R-4C mit Zusatzfiltern," *CQ DL*, Feb 1979, p 56

Ref 405 Guenter Schwarzbeck, DL1BU, "KW Transceiver Icom IC-701," *CQ DL*, Feb 1979, p 65

Ref 406 Guenter Schwarzbeck, DL1BU, "Testbericht: Vorausbericht FT-ONE," *CQ DL*, Jan 1982, p 11

Ref 407 Guenter Schwarzbeck, DL1BU, "Testbericht und Messwerte IC-730," *CQ DL*, Mar 1982, p 117

Ref 408 Guenter Schwarzbeck, DL1BU, "Testbericht und Messwerte FT-102," *CQ DL*, Aug 1982, p 387

Ref 409 Guenter Schwarzbeck, DL1BU, "Testbericht und Messwerte TS930S," *CQ DL*, Oct 1982, p 484

Ref 410 Peter Hart, G3SJX, "The Trio TS-830 HF Transceiver," *Radio Communication*, Jul 1982, p 576

Ref 411 Peter Hart, G3SJX, "The Yaesu Musen FT102 HF Transceiver," *Radio Communication*, Jan 1983, p 32

Ref 412 Peter Hart, G3SJX, "The Icom IC740 HF Transceiver," *Radio Communication*, Nov 1983, p 985

Ref 413 Peter Hart, G3SJX, "The Yaesu FT77 HF Transceiver," *Radio Communication*, Jun 1984, p 482

Ref 414 Peter Hart, G3SJX, "The Yaesu Musen FT980 HF Transceiver," *Radio Communication*, Sep 1984, p 761

Ref 415 Peter Hart, G3SJX, "The Ten-Tec Corsair HF Transceiver," *Radio Communication*, Nov 1984, p 957

Ref 416 Peter Hart, G3SJX, "The Yaesu Musen FT757GX HF Transceiver," *Radio Communication*, May 1985, p 351

Ref 417 Peter Hart, G3SJX, "The Trio TS430S HF Transceiver," *Radio Communication*, Jun 1985, p 441

5. Operating

Ref 500 M. Wilson, AA2Z, ed., *The ARRL Handbook for the Radio Amateur* (Newington, CT: ARRL, 1986)

Ref 501 Erik, SMØAGD, "Split Channel Operation," *Radio-sporting*, Apr 1985, p 10

Ref 502 John Devoldere, ON4UN, *80-Meter DX-ing*

Ref 503 Wayne Overbeck, N6NB, *Computer Programs for Amateur Radio*

Ref 504 Rod Linkous, W7OM, "Navigating to 80 Meter DX," *CQ*, Jan 1978, p 16

Ref 505 Larry Brockman, "The DX-list Net—What a Mess," *CQ*, May 1979, p 48

Ref 506 Wolfgang Roberts, DL7RT, "Wie werde ich DX-er?," *CQ DL*, Oct 1981, p 493

Ref 507 John Lindholm, W1XX, "Is 160 Your Top Band?," *QST*, Aug 1985, p 45

Ref 508 V. Kanevsky, UL7GW, "DX QSOs," *Radio Communication*, Sep 1979, p 835

6. Antennas

6.1 GENERAL

Ref 600 M. Wilson, AA2Z, ed., *The ARRL Handbook for the Radio Amateur* (Newington, CT: ARRL, 1986)

Ref 601 J. J. Wiseman, "How Long is a Piece of Wire," *Electronics and Wireless World*, Apr 1985, p 24

Ref 602 William Orr, W6SAI, et al, *Antenna Handbook*

Ref 603 Gerald Hall, K1TD, et al, *The ARRL Antenna Compendium* (Newington, CT: ARRL, 1985)

Ref 604 Keith Henney, *Radio Engineering Handbook*, 5th Edition

Ref 605 Howard W. Sams, *Reference Data for Radio Engineers*, 5th Edition

Ref 606 John Kraus, W8JK, *Antennas*

Ref 607 Joseph Boyer, W6UYH, "The Multi-Band Trap Antenna, Part I," *CQ*, Feb 1977, p 26

Ref 608 Joseph Boyer, W6UYH, "The Multi-Band Trap Antenna, Part II," *CQ*, Mar 1977, p 51

Ref 609 Bill Salerno, W2ONV, "The W2ONV Delta/Slope Antenna," *CQ*, Aug 1978, p 52

Ref 610 Cornelio Nouel, KG5B, "Exploring the Vagaries of Traps," *CQ*, Aug 1984, p 32

Ref 611 K. H. Kleine, DL3CI, "Der Verkuerzte Dipol," *CQ DL*, Jun 1977, p 230

Ref 612 Hans Wuertz, DL2FA, "Bis zu Einer S-Stufe mehr auf 80 Meter," *CQ DL*, Dec 1977, p 475

Ref 613 Hans Wuertz, DL2FA, "DX-Antennen mit spiegelnden Flaechen," *CQ DL*, Aug 1979, p 353

Ref 614 Hans Wuertz, DL2FA, "DX-Antennen mit spiegelnden Flaechen," *CQ DL*, Jan 1980, p 18

Ref 615 Willi Nitschke, DJ5DW, et al, Richtungskarakteristik, Fusspunktwiederstand etc von Einelementantennen," *CQ DL*, Nov 1982, p 535

Ref 616 Guenter Schwarzbeck, DL1BU, "Bedeuting des Vertikalen Abstralwinkels von KW-Antennen," *CQ DL*, Mar 1985, p 130

Ref 617 Guenter Schwarzbeck, DL1BU, "Bedeutung des Vertikalen Abstrahlwinkels von KW-antennas (part 2)," *CQ DL*, Apr 1985, p 184

Ref 618 E. Vogelsang, DJ2IM, "Vertikaldiagramme typische Kurzwellenantenne," *CQ DL*, Jun 1985, p 300

Ref 619 John Schultz, W2EEY, "Stub-Switched Vertical Antennas," *Ham Radio*, Jul 1969, p 50

Ref 620 Malcolm P. Keown, W5RUB, "Simple Antennas for 80 and 40 Meters," *Ham Radio*, Dec 1972, p 16

Ref 621 Earl Whyman, W2HB, "Standing-Wave Ratios," *Ham Radio*, Jul 1973, p 26

Ref 622 Robert Baird, W7CSD, "Nonresonant Antenna-Impedance Measurements," *Ham Radio*, Apr 1974, p 46

Ref 623 H. Glenn Bogel, WA9RQY, "Vertical Radiation Patterns," *Ham Radio*, May 1974, p 58

Ref 624 Robert Leo, W7LR, "Optimum Height for Horizontal Antennas," *Ham Radio*, Jun 1974, p 40

Ref 625 Bob Fitz, K4JC, "High Performance 80-Meter Antenna," *Ham Radio*, May 1977, p 56

Ref 626 Everett S. Brown, K4EF, "New Multiband Longwire Antenna Design," *Ham Radio*, May 1977, p 10

Ref 627 William A. Wildenhein, W8YFB, "Solution to the Low-Band Antenna Problem," *Ham Radio*, Jan 1978, p 46

Ref 628 John Becker, K9MM, "Lightning Protection," *Ham Radio*, Dec 1978, p 18

Ref 629 James Lawson, W2PV, "Part V Yagi Antenna Design: Ground or Earth Effects," *Ham Radio*, Oct 1980, p 29

Ref 630 Henry G. Elwell, N4UH, "Antenna Geometry for Optimum Performance," *Ham Radio*, May 1982, p 60

Ref 631 Randy Rhea, N4HI, "Dipole Antenna over Sloping Ground," *Ham Radio*, May 1982, p 18

Ref 632 Bradley Wells, KR7L, "Lightning and Electrical Transient Protection," *Ham Radio*, Dec 1983, p 73

Ref 633 R. C. Marshall, G3SBA, "An End-Fed Multiband 8JK," *Ham Radio*, May 1984, p 81

Ref 634 David Atkins, W6VX, "Capacitively Loaded High-Performance Dipole," *Ham Radio*, May 1984, p 33

Ref 635 David Courtier-Dutton, G3FPQ, "Some Notes on a 7-MHz Linear Loaded Quad," *QST*, Feb 1972, p 14

Ref 636 John Kaufmann, WA1CQW, et al, "A Convenient Stub-Tuning System for Quad Antennas," *QST*, May 1975, p 18

Ref 637 Hardy Lankskov, W7KAR, "Pattern Factors for Elevated Horizontal Antennas Over Real Earth," *QST*, Nov 1975, p 19

Ref 638 Robert Dome, W2WAM, "Impedance of Short Horizontal Dipoles," *QST*, Jan 1976, p 32

Ref 639 Donald Belcher, WA4JVE, et al, "Loops vs Dipole Analysis and Discussion," *QST*, Aug 1976, p 34

Ref 640 Roger Sparks, W7WKB, "Build this C-T Quad Beam for Reduced Size," *QST*, Apr 1977, p 29

Ref 641 Ronald K. Gorski, W9KYZ, "Efficient Short Radiators," *QST*, Apr 1977, p 37

Ref 642 Byron Goodman, W1DX, "My Feedline Tunes My Antenna," *QST*, Apr 1977, p 40

Ref 643 Doug DeMaw, W1FB, "The Gentlemen's Band: 160 Meters," *QST*, Oct 1977, p 33

Ref 644 David S. Hollander, N7RK, "A Big Signal from a Small Lot," *QST*, Apr 1979, p 32

Ref 645 Dana Atchley, W1CF, "Putting the Quarter-Wave Sloper to Work on 160," *QST*, Jul 1979, p 19

Ref 646 Stan Gibilisco, W1GV, "The Imperfect Antenna System and How it Works," *QST*, Jul 1979, p 24

Ref 647 John Belrose, VE2CV, "The Half Sloper," *QST*, May 1980, p. 31

Ref 648 Larry May, KE6H, "Antenna Modeling Program for the TRS 80," *QST*, Feb 1981, p 15

Ref 649 Colin Dickman, ZS6U, "The ZS6U Minishack Special," *QST*, Apr 1981, p 32

Ref 650 Doug DeMaw, W1FB, "More Thoughts on the 'Confounded' Half Sloper," *QST*, Oct 1981, p 31

Ref 651 John S. Belrose, VE2CV, "The Effect of Supporting Structures on Simple Wire Antennas," *QST*, Dec 1982, p 32

Ref 652 Gerald Hall, K1TD, "A Simple Approach to Antenna Impedances," *QST*, Mar 1983, p 16

Ref 653 Jerry Hall, K1TD, "The Search for a Simple Broadband 80-Meter Dipole," *QST*, Apr 1983, p 22

Ref 654 Charles L. Hutchinson, K8CH, "Getting the Most out of Your Antenna," *QST*, Jul 1983, p 34

Ref 655 Doug DeMaw, W1FB, "Building and Using 30-Meter Antennas," *QST*, Oct 1983, p 27

Ref 656 James Rautio, AJ3K, "The Effect of Real Ground on Antennas, Part 1," *QST*, Feb 1984, p 15

Ref 657 James Rautio, AJ3K, "The Effect of Real Ground on Antennas, Part 2," *QST*, Apr 1984, p 34

Ref 658 James Rautio, AJ3K, "The Effect of Real Ground on Antennas, Part 3," *QST*, Jun 1984, p 30

Ref 659 Doug DeMaw, W1FB, "Trap for Shunt-Fed Towers," *QST*, Jun 1984, p 40

Ref 660 James Rautio, AJ3K, "The Effects of Real Ground on Antennas, Part 4," *QST*, Aug 1984, p 31

Ref 661 James Rautio, AJ3K, "The Effect of Real Ground on Antennas, Part 5," *QST*, Nov 1984, p 35

Ref 662 Robert C. Sommer, N4UU, "Optimizing Coaxial-Cable Traps," *QST*, Dec 1984, p 37

Ref 663 Bob Schetgen, KU7G, ed., "Technical Correspondence," *QST*, Apr 1985, p 51

Ref 664 Pat Hawker, G3VA, "Technical Topics: Low Angle Operation," *Radio Communication*, Apr 1971, p 262

Ref 665 Pat Hawker, G3VA, "Technical Topics: Low-Angle Radiation and Sloping-Ground Sites," *Radio Communication*, May 1972, p 306

Ref 666 Pat Hawker, G3VA, "Technical Topics: All-Band Terminated Long-Wire," *Radio Communication*, Nov 1972, p 745

Ref 667 A.P.A. Ashton, G3XAP, "160M DX from Suburban Sites," *Radio Communication*, Dec 1973, p 842

Ref 668 L. A. Moxon, G6XN, "Gains and Losses in HF Aerials, Part 1," *Radio Communication*, Dec 1973, p 834

Ref 669 L. A. Moxon, G6XN, "Gains and Losses in HF Aerials, Part 2," *Radio Communication*, Jan 1974, p 16

Ref 670 Pat Hawker, G3VA, "Technical Topics: Thoughts on Inverted-Vs," *Radio Communication*, Sep 1976, p 676

Ref 671 A. P. A. Ashton, G3XAP, "The G3XAP Directional Antenna for the Lower Frequencies," *Radio Communication*, Nov 1977, p 858

Ref 672 S. J. M. Whitfield, G3IMW, "3.5 MHz DX Antennas for a Town Garden," *Radio Communication*, Aug 1980, p 772

Ref 673 Pat Hawker, G3VA, "Technical Topics: Low Profile 1.8 and 3.5 MHz Antennas," *Radio Communication*, Aug 1980, p 792

Ref 674 Pat Hawker, G3VA, "Technical Topics: Half Delta Loop, Sloping One-Mast Yagi," *Radio Communication*, Oct 1983, p 892

Ref 675 R. Rosen, K2RR, "Secrets of Successful Low Band Operation, Part 1," *Ham Radio*, May 1986, p 16

Ref 676 R. Rosen, K2RR, "Secrets of Successful Low Band Operation, Part 2," *Ham Radio*, Jun 1986

Ref 677 J. Dietrich, WAØRDX, "Loops and Dipoles: A Comparative Analysis," *QST*, Sep 1985, p 24

6.2 VERTICALS

Ref 701 Paul Lee, K6TS, *Vertical Antenna Handbook*

Ref 702 Wait & Pope, "Input Resistance of LF Unipole Aerials," *Wireless Engineer*, May 1955, p 131

Ref 703 J. J. Wiseman, "How Long is a Piece of Wire," *Electronics and Wireless World*, Apr 1985, p 24

Ref 704 Carl C. Drumller, W5JJ, "Using Your Tower as an Antenna," *CQ*, Dec 1977, p 75

Ref 705 Karl T. Thurber, W8FX, "HF Verticals, Plain And Simple," *CQ*, Sep 1980, p 22

Ref 706 John E. Magnusson, WØAGD, "Improving Antenna Performance," *CQ*, Jun 1981, p 32

Ref 707 Larry Strain, N7DF, "What Looks Like a Birdcage for a 2000 Pound Canary? A 3.5 to 30 MHz Discage Antenna, That's What" *CQ*, Apr 1984, p 18

Ref 708 Karl Hille, DL1VU, "Optimierte T-Antenne," *CQ DL*, Jun 1978, p 246

Ref 709 Rolf Schick, DL3AO, "Loop, Dipol und Vertikalanten-nen, Vergleiche und Erfahrungen," *CQ DL*, Mar 1979, p 115

Ref 710 Guenter Schwarzbeck, DL1BU, "DX Antennen fuer 80 und 160 Meter," *CQ DL*, Apr 1979, p 150

Ref 711 Hans Wurtz, DL2FA, "DX-Antennen mit spiegelenden Flaechen," *CQ DL*, Aug 1979, p 353

Ref 712 Hans Wurtz, DL2FA, "DX-Antennen mit spiegelenden Flaechen," *CQ DL*, Sep 1979, p 400

Ref 713 Hans Wurtz, DL2FA, "DX-Antennen mit spiegelenden Flaechen," *CQ DL*, Jan 1980, p 18

Ref 714 Hans Wurtz, DL2FA, "DX-Antennen mit spiegelenden Flaechen," *CQ DL*, Jun 1980, p 272

Ref 715 Hans Wurtz, DL2FA, "DX-Antennen mit spiegelenden Flaechen," *CQ DL*, Jul 1980, p 311

Ref 716 Hans Wurtz, DL2FA, "DX-Antennen mit spiegelenden Flaechen," *CQ DL*, Feb 1981, p 61

Ref 717 Hans Wurtz, DL2FA, "DX-Antennen mit spiegelenden Flaechen," *CQ DL*, Jul 1981, p 330

Ref 718 Guenter Schwarzbeck, DL1BU, "Groundplane- und Vertikalantennenf," *CQ DL*, Sep 1981, p 420

Ref 719 Hans Wurtz, DL2FA, "DX-Antennen mit spiegelenden Flaechen," *CQ DL*, Apr 1983, p 170

Ref 720 Hans Wurtz, DL2FA, "DX-Antennen mit spiegelenden Flaechen," *CQ DL*, May 1983, p 224

Ref 721 Hans Wurtz, DL2FA, "DX-Antennen mit spiegelenden Flaechen," *CQ DL*, Jun 1983, p 278

Ref 722 Hans Adolf Rohrbacher, DJ2NN, "Basic-Programm zu Berechnungh von Vertikalen Antennen," *CQ DL*, Jun 1983, p 275

Ref 723 Hans Wurtz, DL2FA, "DX-Antennen mit spiegelenden Flaechen," *CQ DL*, Jul 1983, p 326

Ref 724 John Schultz, W2EEY, "Stub-Switched Vertical Antennas," *Ham Radio*, Jul 1969, p 50

Ref 725 John True, W4OQ, "The Vertical Radiator," *Ham Radio*, Apr 1973, p 16

Ref 726 John True, W4OQ, "Vertical-Tower Antenna System," *Ham Radio*, May 1973, p 56

Ref 727 George Smith, W4AEO, "80- and 40-Meter Log-Periodic Antennas," *Ham Radio*, Sep 1973, p 44

Ref 728 Robert Leo, W7LR, "Vertical Antenna Characteristics," *Ham Radio*, Mar 1974, p 34

Ref 729 Robert Leo, W7LR, "Vertical Antenna Radiation Patterns," *Ham Radio*, Apr 1974, p 50

Ref 730 Raymond Griese, K6FD, "Improving Vertical Antennas," *Ham Radio*, Dec 1974, p 54

Ref 731 Harry Hyder, W7IV, "Large Vertical Antennas," *Ham Radio*, May 1975, p 8

Ref 732 John True, W4OQ, "Shunt-Fed Vertical Antennas," *Ham Radio*, May 1975, p 34

Ref 733 H. H. Hunter, W8TYX, "Short Vertical for 7 MHz," *Ham Radio*, Jun 1977, p 60

Ref 734 Laidacker M. Seaberg, W0NCU, "Multiband Vertical Antenna System," *Ham Radio*, May 1978, p 28

Ref 735 Joseph D. Liga, K2INA, "80-Meter Ground-Plane Antennas," *Ham Radio*, May 1978, p 48

Ref 736 John M. Haerle, WB5IIR, "Folded Umbrella Antenna," *Ham Radio*, May 1979, p 38

Ref 737 Paul A. Scholz, W6PYK, "Vertical Antenna for 40 and 75 Meters," *Ham Radio*, Sep 1979, p 44

Ref 738 Ed Marriner, W6XM, "Base-Loaded Vertical for 160 Meters," *Ham Radio*, Aug 1980, p 64

Ref 739 John S. Belrose, VE2CV, "The Half-Wave Vertical," *Ham Radio*, Sep 1981, p 36

Ref 740 Stan Gibilisco, W1GV/4, "Efficiency of Short Antennas," *Ham Radio*, Sep 1982, p 18

Ref 741 John S. Belrose, VE2CV, "Top-Loaded Folded Umbrella Vertical Antenna," *Ham Radio*, Sep 1982, p 12

Ref 742 W. J. Byron, W7DHD, "Short Vertical Antennas for the Low Bands, Part 1," *Ham Radio*, May 1983, p 36

Ref 743 Forrest Gehrke, K2BT, "Vertical Phased Arrays, Part 1," *Ham Radio*, May 1983, p 18

Ref 744 John Belrose, VE2CV, "The Grounded Monopole with Elevated Feed," *Ham Radio*, May 1983, p 87

Ref 745 Forrest Gehrke, K2BT, "Vertical Phased Arrays, Part 2," *Ham Radio*, Jun 1983, p 24

Ref 746 W. J. Byron, W7DHD, "Short Vertical Antennas for the Low Bands, Part 2," *Ham Radio*, Jun 1983, p 17

Ref 747 Forrest Gehrke, K2BT, "Vertical Phased Arrays, Part 3," *Ham Radio*, Jul 1983, p 26

Ref 748 Forrest Gehrke, K2BT, "Vertical Phased Arrays, Part 4," *Ham Radio*, Oct 1983, p 34

Ref 749 Forrest Gehrke, K2BT, "Vertical Phased Arrays, Part 5," *Ham Radio*, Dec 1983, p 59

Ref 750 Marc Bacon, WB9VWA, "Verticals Over REAL Ground," *Ham Radio*, Jan 1984, p 35

Ref 751 Robert Leo, W7LR, "Remote Controlled 40, 80, and 160 Meter Vertical," *Ham Radio*, May 1984, p 38

Ref 752 Harry Hyder, W7IV, "Build a Simple Wire Plow," *Ham Radio*, May 1984, p 107

Ref 753 Gene Hubbell, W9ERU, "Feeding Grounded Towers as Radiators," *QST*, Jun 1960, p 33

Ref 754 Eugene E. Baldwin, W0RUG, "Some Notes on the Care and Feeding of Grounded Verticals," *QST*, Oct 1963, p 45

Ref 755 N. H. Davidson, K5JVF, "Flagpole Without a Flag," *QST*, Nov 1964, p 36

Ref 756 Jerry Sevick, W2FMI, "The Ground-Image Vertical Antenna," *QST*, Jul 1971, p 16

Ref 757 Jerry Sevick, W2FMI, "The W2FMI 20-Meter Vertical Beam," *QST*, Jun 1972, p 14

Ref 758 Jerry Sevick, W2FMI, "The W2FMI Ground-Mounted Short Vertical Antenna," *QST*, Mar 1973, p 13

Ref 759 Jerry Sevick, W2FMI, "A High Performance 20, 40 and 80 Meter Vertical System," *QST*, Dec 1973, p 30

Ref 760 Jerry Sevick, W2FMI, "The Constant Impedance Trap Vertical," *QST*, Mar 1974, p 29

Ref 761 Barry A. Boothe, W9UCW, "The Minooka Special," *QST*, Dec 1974, p 15

Ref 762 Zilli Richartz, HB9ADQ, "A Stacked Multiband Vertical for 80-10 Meters," *QST*, Feb 1975, p 44

Ref 763 John S. Belrose, VE2CV, "The HF Discone Antenna," *QST*, Jul 1975, p 11

Ref 764 Earl Cunningham, W5RTQ, "Shunt Feeding Towers for Operating on the Low Amateur Frequencies," *QST*, Oct 1975, p 22

Ref 765 Dennis Kozakoff, W4AZW, "Designing Small Vertical Antennas," *QST*, Aug 1976, p 24

Ref 766 Ronald Gorski, W9KYZ, "Efficient Short Radiators," *QST*, Apr 1977, p 37

Ref 767 Richard Lodwig, W2KK, "The Inverted-L Antenna," *QST*, Apr 1977, p 32

Ref 768 Asa Collins, K6VV, "A Multiband Vertical Radiator," *QST*, Apr 1977, p 22

Ref 769 Walter Schultz, K3OQF, "Slant-Wire Feed for Grounded Towers," *QST*, May 1977, p 23

Ref 770 Yardley Beers, WØJF, "Optimizing Vertical Antenna Performance," *QST*, Oct 1977, p 15

Ref 771 Walter Schultz, K3OQF, "Designing a Vertical Antenna," *QST*, Sep 1978, p 19

Ref 772 John S. Belrose, VE2CV, "A Kite Supported 160M (or 80M) Antenna for Portable Application," *QST*, Mar 1981, p 40

Ref 773 Wayne Sandford, K3EQ, "A Modest 45 Foot Tall DX Vertical for 160, 80, 40 and 30 Meters," *QST*, Sep 1981, p 27

Ref 774 Doug DeMaw, W1FB, "Shunt Fed Towers, Some Practical Aspects," *QST*, Oct 1982, p 21

Ref 775 John F. Lindholm, W1XX, "The Inverted L Revisited," *QST*, Jan 1983, p 20

Ref 776 Carl Eichenauer, W2QIP, "A Top Fed Vertical Antenna for 1.8 MHz—Plus 3," *QST*, Sep 1983, p 25

Ref 777 Robert Snyder, KE2S, "Modified Butternut Vertical for 80-Meter Operation," *QST*, Apr 1985, p 50

Ref 778 Doug DeMaw, W1FB, "A Remotely Switched Inverted-L Antenna," *QST*, May 1985, p 37

Ref 779 Pat Hawker, G3VA, "Technical Topics: Low Angle Operation," *Radio Communication*, Apr 1971, p 262

Ref 780 Pat Hawker, G3VA, "Technical Topics: Improving the T Antenna," *Radio Communication*, Sep 1978, p 770

Ref 781 J. Bazley, G3HCT, "A 7 MHz Vertical Antenna," *Radio Communication*, Jan 1979, p 26

Ref 782 P.J. Horwood, G3FRB, "Feed Impedance of Loaded λ/4 Vertical Antennas and the Effects of Earth Systems," *Radio Communication*, Oct 1981, p 911

Ref 783 Pat Hawker, G3VA, "Technical Topics: The Inverted Groundplane Family," *Radio Communication*, May 1983, p 424

Ref 784 Pat Hawker, G3VA, "Technical Topics: More on Groundplanes," *Radio Communication*, Sep 1983, p 798

Ref 785 Pat Hawker, G3VA, "Technical Topics: Sloping One-Mast Yagi," *Radio Communication*, Oct 1983, p 892

Ref 786 V. C. Lear, G3TKN, "Gamma Matching Towers and Masts at Lower Frequencies," *Radio Communication*, Mar 1986, p 176

Ref 787 B. Wermager, KØEOU, "A Truly Broadband Antenna for 80/75 Meters," *QST*, Apr 1986, p 23

Ref 788 Pat Hawker, G3VA, "Technical Topics: Elements of Non-Uniform Cross Section," *Radio Communication*, Jan 1986, p 36

6.3 GROUND SYSTEMS

Ref 800 Jager, "Effect of Earth's Surface on Antenna Patterns in the Short Wave Range," *Int. Elek.* Rundshau 24 1970, p 101

Ref 801 G. H. Brown, et al, "Ground Systems as a Factor in Antenna Efficiency," *I.R.E. Proceedings*, Jun 1937, p 753

Ref 802 Abbott, "Design Of Optimum Buried RF Ground Systems," *I.R.E. Proceedings*, Jul 1952, p 846

Ref 803 Monteath, "The Effect of Ground Constants of an Earth System on Vertical Aerials," *I.R.E. Proceedings*, Jan 1958, p 292

Ref 804 Caid, "Earth Resistivity and Geological Structure," *Electrical Engineering*, Nov 1935, p 1153

Ref 805 Wait Hill, "Calculated Pattern of a Vertical Antenna With a Finite Radial-Wire Ground System" *Radio Science*, Jan 1973, p 81

Ref 806 John E. Magnusson, WØAGD, "Improving Antenna Performance," *CQ*, Jun 1981, p 32

Ref 807 Arch Doty, K8CFU, "Improving Vertical Antenna Efficiency—A Study of Radial Wire Ground Systems," *CQ*, Apr 1984, p 24

Ref 808 Robert Leo, W7LR, "Vertical Antenna Ground System," *Ham Radio*, May 1974, p 30

Ref 809 Robert Sherwood, WBØJGP, "Ground Screen, Alternative to Radials," *Ham Radio*, May 1977, p 22

Ref 810 Alan M. Christman, WD8CBJ, "Ground Systems for Vertical Antennas," *Ham Radio*, Aug 1979, p 31

Ref 811 H. Vance Mosser, K3ZAP, "Installing Radials for Vertical Antennas," *Ham Radio*, Oct 1980, p 56

Ref 812 See Ref 811

Ref 813 Bradley Wells, KR7L, "Installing Effective Ground Systems," *Ham Radio*, Sep 1983, p 67

Ref 814 Marc Bacon, WB9VWA, "Verticals Over REAL Ground," *Ham Radio*, Jan 1984, p 35

Ref 815 Harry Hyder, W7IV, "Build a Simple Wire Plow," *Ham Radio*, May 1984, p 107

Ref 816 John Stanley, K4ERO/HC1, "Optimum Ground System for Vertical Antennas," *QST*, Dec 1976, p 13

Ref 817 Roger Hoestenbach, W5EGS, "Improving Earth-Ground Characteristics," *QST*, Dec 1976, p 16

Ref 818 Jerry Sevick, W2FMI, "Short Ground Radial Systems for Short Verticals," *QST*, Apr 1978, p 30

Ref 819 Jerry Sevick, W2FMI, "Measuring Soil Conductivity," *QST*, Mar 1981, p 38

Ref 820 Archibald C. Doty, K8CFU, et al, "Efficient Ground Systems for Vertical Antennas," *QST*, Feb 1983, p 20

Ref 821 Brian Edward, N2MF, "Radial Systems for Ground-Mounted Vertical Antennas," *QST*, Jun 1985, p 28

Ref 822 Pat Hawker, G3VA, "Technical Topics: Vertical Polarization and Large Earth Screens," *Radio Communication*, Dec 1978, p 1023

Ref 823 P. J. Horwood, G3FRB, "Feed Impedance of Loaded ¼ Wave Vertical Antenna Systems," *Radio Communication*, Oct 1981, p. 911

Ref 824 J. A. Frey, W3ESU, "The Minipoise," *CQ*, Aug 1985, p 30

6.4 ARRAYS

Ref 900 Bill Guimont, W7KW, "Liftoff on 80 Meters," *CQ*, Oct 1979, p 38

Ref 901 Guenter Schwarzbeck, DL1BU, "HB9CV Antenna," *CQ DL*, Jan 1983, p 10

Ref 902 Rudolf Fisher, DL6WD, "Das Monster, eine 2-Element Delta-Loop fuer 3.5 MHz," *CQ DL*, Jul 1983, p 331

Ref 903 G. E. Smith, W4AEO, "Log-Periodic Antennas for 40 Meters," *Ham Radio*, May 1973, p 16

Ref 904 G. E. Smith, W4AEO, "80- and 40-Meter Log-Periodic Antennas," *Ham Radio*, Sep 1973, p 44

Ref 905 G. E. Smith, W4AEO, "Log-Periodic Antenna Design," *Ham Radio*, May 1975, p 14

Ref 906 Jerry Swank, W8HXR, "Phased Vertical Array," *Ham Radio*, May 1975, p 24

Ref 907 Henry Keen, W5TRS, "Electrically-Steered Phased Array," *Ham Radio*, May 1975, p 52

Ref 908 Gary Jordan, WA6TKT, "Understanding the ZL Special Antenna," *Ham Radio*, May 1976, p 38

Ref 909 William Tucker, W4FXE, "Fine Tuning the Phased Vertical Array," *Ham Radio*, May 1977, p 46

Ref 910 Paul Kiesel, K7CW, "Seven-Element 40-Meter Quad," *Ham Radio*, Aug 1978, p 30

Ref 911 Eugene B. Fuller, W2LU, "Sloping 80-meter Array," *Ham Radio*, May 1979, p 70

Ref 912 Harold F. Tolles, W7ITB, "Scaling Antenna Elements," *Ham Radio*, Jul 1979, p 58

Ref 913 P. A. Scholz, W6PYK, et al, "Log-Periodic Antenna Design," *Ham Radio*, Dec 1979, p 34

Ref 914 James Lawson, W2PV, "Yagi Antenna Design: Experiments Confirm Computer Analysis," *Ham Radio*, Feb 1980, p 19

Ref 915 James Lawson, W2PV, "Yagi Antenna Design: Multi-Element Simplistic Beams," *Ham Radio*, Jun 1980, p 33

Ref 916 Paul Scholtz, W6PYK, et al, "Log Periodic Fixed-Wire Beams for 75-Meter DX," *Ham Radio*, Mar 1980, p 40

Ref 917 George E. Smith, W4AEO, "Log Periodic Fixed-Wire Beams for 40 Meters," *Ham Radio*, Apr 1980, p 26

Ref 918 Ed Marriner, W6XM, "Phased Vertical Antenna for 21 MHz," *Ham Radio*, Jun 1980, p 42

Ref 919 William M. Kelsey, N8ET, "Three-Element Switchable Quad for 40 Meters," *Ham Radio*, Oct 1980, p 26

Ref 920 Patrick McGuire, WB5HGR, "Pattern Calculation for Phased Vertical Arrays," *Ham Radio*, May 1981, p 40

Ref 921 Forrest Gehrke, K2BT, "Vertical Phased Arrays, Part 1," *Ham Radio*, May 1983, p 18

Ref 922 Forrest Gehrke, K2BT, "Vertical Phased Arrays, Part 2," *Ham Radio*, Jun 1983, p 24

Ref 923 Forrest Gehrke, K2BT, "Vertical Phased Arrays, Part 3," *Ham Radio*, Jul 1983, p 26

Ref 924 Forrest Gehrke, K2BT, "Vertical Phased Arrays, Part 4," *Ham Radio*, Oct 1983, p 34

Ref 925 Forrest Gehrke, K2BT, "Vertical Phased Arrays, Part 5," *Ham Radio*, Dec 1983, p 59

Ref 926 R. C. Marshall, G3SBA, "An End Fed Multiband 8JK," *Ham Radio*, May 1984, p 81

Ref 927 Forrest Gehrke, K2BT, "Vertical Phased Arrays, Part 6," *Ham Radio*, May 1984, p 45

Ref 928 R. R. Schellenbach, W1JF, "The End Fed 8JK, A Switchable Vertical Array," *Ham Radio*, May 1985, p 53

Ref 929 Al Christman, KB8I, "Feeding Phased Arrays, an Alternate Method," *Ham Radio*, May 1985, p 58

Ref 930 Dana Atchley, W1HKK, "A Switchable Four Element 80-Meter Phased Array," *QST*, Mar 1965, p 48

Ref 931 James Lawson, W2PV, "A 75/80-Meter Vertical Antenna Square Array," *QST*, Mar 1971, p 18

Ref 932 James Lawson, W2PV, "Simple Arrays of Vertical Antenna Elements," *QST*, May 1971, p 22

Ref 933 Garry Elliott, KH6HCM/W7UXP, "Phased Verticals for 40-Meters," *QST*, Apr 1972, p 18

Ref 934 Jerry Sevick, W2FMI, "The W2FMI 20-meter Vertical Beam," *QST*, Jun 1972, p 14

Ref 935 Robert Myers, W1FBY, et al, "Phased Verticals in a 40-Meter Beam Switching Array," *QST*, Aug 1972, p 36

Ref 936 Robert Jones, KH6AD, "A 7-MHz Parasitic Array," *QST*, Nov 1973, p 39

Ref 937 J. G. Botts, K4EQJ, "A Four-Element Vertical Beam for 40/15 Meters," *QST*, Jun 1975, p 30

Ref 938 Jarda Dvoracek, OK1ATP, "160-Meter DX with a Two-Element-Beam," *QST*, Oct 1975, p 20

Ref 939 Dana Atchley, W1CF, et al, "360°-Steerable Vertical Phased Arrays," *QST*, Apr 1976, p 27

Ref 940 Richard Fenwick, K5RR, et al, "Broadband, Steerable Phased Arrays," *QST*, Apr 1977, p 18

Ref 941 Dana Atchley, W1CF, "Updating Phased Array Technology," *QST*, Aug 1978, p 22

Ref 942 Bob Hickman, WB6ZZJ, "The Poly Tower Phased Array," *QST*, Jan 1981, p 30

Ref 943 W.B. Bachelor, AC3K, "Combined Vertical Directivity," *QST*, Feb 1981, p 19

Ref 944 Walter J. Schultz, K3OQF, "Vertical Array Analysis," *QST*, Feb 1981, p 22

Ref 945 Edward Peter Swynar, VE3CUI, "40 meters with a Phased Delta Loop," *QST*, May 1984, p 20

Ref 946 Riki Kline, 4X4NJ, "Build a 4X Array for 160 Meters," *QST*, Feb 1985, p 21

Ref 947 Trygve Tondering, OZ1TD, "Phased Verticals," *Radio Communication*, May 1972, p 294

Ref 948 Pat Hawker, G3VA, "Technical Topics: The Half Square Aerial," *Radio Communication*, Jun 1974, p 380

Ref 949 J.L. Lawson, W2PV, "Yagi Antenna Design," *Ham Radio*, Jan 1980, p 22

Ref 950 J.L. Lawson, W2PV, "Yagi Antenna Design," *Ham Radio*, Feb 1980, p 19

Ref 951 J.L. Lawson, W2PV, "Yagi Antenna Design," *Ham Radio*, May 1980, p 18

Ref 952 J.L. Lawson, W2PV, "Yagi Antenna Design," *Ham Radio*, Jun 1980, p 33

Ref 953 J.L. Lawson, W2PV, "Yagi Antenna Design," *Ham Radio*, Jul 1980, p 18

Ref 954 J.L. Lawson, W2PV, "Yagi Antenna Design," *Ham Radio*, Sep 1980, p 37

Ref 954 J.L. Lawson, W2PV, "Yagi Antenna Design," *Ham Radio*, Oct 1980, p 29

Ref 955 J.L. Lawson, W2PV, "Yagi Antenna Design," *Ham Radio*, Nov 1980, p 22

Ref 956 J.L. Lawson, W2PV, "Yagi Antenna Design," *Ham Radio*, Dec 1980, p 30

Ref 957 J.L. Lawson, W2PV, *Yagi Antenna Design,* (Newington, CT: ARRL, 1986)

6.5 BROADBAND AERIALS

Ref 1000 Larry Strain, N7DF, "A 3.5 to 30 MHz Discage Antenna," *CQ*, Apr 1984, p 18

Ref 1001 F.J. Bauer, W6FPO, "Low SWR Dipole Pairs for 1.8 through 3.5 MHz," *Ham Radio*, Oct 1972, p 42

Ref 1002 M. Walter Maxwell, W2DU, "A Revealing Analysis of the Coaxial Dipole Antenna," *Ham Radio*, Aug 1976, p 46

Ref 1003 Terry Conboy, N6RY, "Broadband 80-meter Antennas," *Ham Radio*, May 1979, p 44

Ref 1004 Mason Logan, K4MT, "Stagger Tuned Dipoles Increase Bandwidth," *Ham Radio*, May 1983, p 22

Ref 1005 C.C. Whysall, "The Double Bazooka," *QST*, Jul 1968, p 38

Ref 1006 John S. Belrose, VE2CV, "The Discone HF Antenna," *QST*, Jul 1975, p 11

Ref 1007 Allen Harbach, WA4DRU, "Broadband 80 Meter Antenna," *QST*, Dec 1980, p 36

Ref 1008 Jerry Hall, K1TD, "The Search for a Simple Broadband 80-meter Dipole," *QST*, Apr 1983, p 22

Ref 1009 John Grebenkemper, KA3BLO, "Multiband Trap and Parallel HF Dipoles, a Comparison," *QST*, May 1985, p 26

Ref 1010 N.H. Sedgwick, G8WV, "Broadband Cage Aerials," *Radio Communication*, May 1965, p 287

Ref 1011 Pat Hawker, G3VA, "Technical Topics: Broadband Bazooka Dipole," *Radio Communication*, Aug 1976, p 601

6.6 LOOP ANTENNAS

Ref 1100 William Orr, W6SAI, *All About Cubical Quads*

Ref 1101 Bill Salerno, W2ONV, "The W2ONV Delta/Sloper Antenna," *CQ*, Aug 1978, p 86

Ref 1102 Roy A. Neste, WØWFO, "Dissecting Loop Antennas To Find Out What Makes Them Tick," *CQ*, Aug 1984, p 36

Ref 1103 Rolf Schick, DL3AO, "Loop, Dipol und Vertikalantennen, Vergleiche und Erfahrungen," *CQ DL*, Mar 1979, p 115

Ref 1104 Guenter Schwarzbeck, DL1BU, "DX Antennen fuer 80 und 160 Meter," *CQ DL*, Apr 1979, p 150

Ref 1105 Gunter Steppert, DK8NG, "Zweielement Delta Loop mit einem Mast," *CQ DL*, Aug 1980, p 370

Ref 1106 Hans Wurtz, DL2FA, "DX-Antennen mit spiegelenden Flaechen," *CQ DL*, Apr 1981, p 162

Ref 1107 Hans Wurtz, DL2FA, "DX-Antennen mit spiegelenden Flaechenans," *CQ DL*, Dec 1981, p 583

Ref 1108 Dieter Pelz, DF3IK et al, "Rahmenantenne -- keine Wunderantenne," *CQ DL*, Sep 1982, p 435

Ref 1109 Willi Nitschke, DJ5DW, et al, "Richtkarakteristik, Fusspunktwiderstand etc von Einelementantennen," *CQ DL*, Dec 1982, p 580

Ref 1110 Hans Wurtz, DL2FA, "DX-Antennen mit spiegelenden Flaechen," *CQ DL*, Feb 1983, p 64

Ref 1111 Rudolf Fisher, DL6WD, "Das Monster, eine 2-Element Delta-Loop fuer 3,5 MHz," *CQ DL*, Jul 1983, p 331

Ref 1112 John True, W4OQ, "Low Frequency Loop Antennas," *Ham Radio*, Dec 1976, p 18

Ref 1113 Paul Kiesel, K7CW, "7-Element 40-Meter Quad," *Ham Radio*, Aug 1978, p 30

Ref 1114 Glenn Williman, N2GW, "Delta Loop Array," *Ham Radio*, Sep 1978, p 16

Ref 1115 Frank J. Witt, W1DTV, "Top Loaded Delta Loop Antenna," *Ham Radio*, Dec 1978, p 57

Ref 1116 George Badger, W6TC, "Compact Loop Antenna for 40 and 80-Meter DX," *Ham Radio*, Oct 1979, p 24

Ref 1117 William M. Kesley, N8ET, "Three Element Switchable Quad for 40-Meters," *Ham Radio*, Oct 1980, p 26

Ref 1118 Jerrold Swank, W8HXR, "Two Delta Loops fed in Phase," *Ham Radio*, Aug 1981, p 50

Ref 1119 Hasan Schiers, NØAN, "The Half Square Antenna," *Ham Radio*, Dec 1981, p 48

Ref 1120 John S. Belrose, VE2CV, "The Half Delta-Loop," *Ham Radio*, May 1982, p 37

Ref 1121 V.C. Lear, G3TKN, "Reduced Size, Full Performance Corner Fed Delta Loop," *Ham Radio*, Jan 1985 p 67

Ref 1122 Lewis Mc Coy, W1ICP, "The Army Loop in Ham Communication," *QST*, Mar 1968, p 17

Ref 1123 J. Wessendorp, HB9AGK, "Loop Measurements," *QST*, Nov 1968, p 46

Ref 1124 F.N. Van Zant, W2EGH, "160, 75 and 40 Meter Inverted Dipole Delta Loop," *QST*, Jan 1973, p 37

Ref 1125 Ben Venster, K3DC, "The Half Square Antenna," *QST*, Mar 1974, p 11

Ref 1126 John Kaufmann, WA1CQW et al, "A Convenient Stub Tuning System for Quad Antennas," *QST*, May 1975, p 18

Ref 1127 Robert Edlund, W5DS, "The W5DS Hula-Hoop Loop," *QST*, Oct 1975, p 16

Ref 1128 Donald Belcherm, WA4JVE et al, "Loops vs Dipole Analysis and Discussion," *QST*, Aug 1976, p 34

Ref 1129 Roger Sparks, W7WKB, "Build this C-T Quad Beam for Reduced Size," *QST*, Apr 1977, p 29

Ref 1130 John S. Belrose, VE2CV, "The Half-Delta Loop: a Critical Analysis and Practical Deployment," *QST*, Sep 1982, p 28

Ref 1131 Richard Gray, W9JJV, "The Two Band Delta Loop Antenna," *QST*, Mar 1983, p 36

Ref 1132 Edward Peter Swynar, VE3CUI, "40 Meters with a Phased Delta Loop," *QST*, May 1984, p 20

Ref 1133 Doug DeMaw, W1FB et al, "The Full-Wave Delta Loop at Low Height," *QST*, Oct 1984, p 24

Ref 1134 Pat Hawker, G3VA, "Technical Topics: Another Look at Transmitting Loops," *Radio Communication*, Jun 1971, p 392

Ref 1135 Pat Hawker, G3VA, "Technical Topics: Vertically Polarized Loop Elements," *Radio Communication*, Jun 1973, p 404

Ref 1136 Laury Mayhead, G3AQC, "Loop Aerials Close to Ground," *Radio Communication*, May 1974, p 298

Ref 1137 Pat Hawker, G3VA, "Technical Topics: The Half Square Aerial," *Radio Communication*, Jun 1974, p 380

Ref 1138 Pat Hawker, G3VA, "Miniaturized Quad Elements," *Radio Communication*, Mar 1976, p 206

Ref 1139 Pat Hawker, G3VA, "Technical Topics: Radiation Resistance of Medium Loops," *Radio Communication*, Feb 1979, p 131

Ref 1140 F. Rasvall, SM5AGM, "The Gain of the Quad," *Radio Communication*, Aug 1980, p 784

Ref 1141 Pat Hawker, G3VA, "Technical Topics: Polygonal Loop Antennas," *Radio Communication*, Feb 1981, p 141

Ref 1142 B. Myers, K1GQ, "The W2PV 80-Meter Quad," *Ham Radio*, May 1986 p 56

6.7 RECEIVING ANTENNAS

Ref 1200 I. Herliz, "Analysis of Action of Wave Antennas," *A.I.E.E. Transactions* 1942, p 260 vol 42

Ref 1201 "Diversity Receiving System of RCA Communications for Radio Telegraphy," *A.I.E.E. Transactions,* Feb 1923, p 215 vol 42

Ref 1202 Peterson Beverage, "The Wave Antenna, a New Type of Highly Directive Antenna," *Proceedings of the I.R.E.*

Ref 1203 Dean Baily, "Receiving System for Long-Wave Transatlantic Radio Telephone," *Proceedings of the I.R.E.* Dec 1928

Ref 1204 "Antennas for Reception of Standard Broadcast Signals," *FCC Report*, Apr 1958

Ref 1205 M. Wilson, AA2Z, ed., *The ARRL Handbook for the Radio Amateur* (Newington, CT: ARRL, 1986)

Ref 1206 Victor Misek, W1WCR, *The Beverage Antenna Handbook*

Ref 1207 M. Wilson, AA2Z, ed., *The ARRL Handbook for the Radio Amateur* (Newington, CT: ARRL, 1986)

Ref 1208 John Devoldere, ON4UN, *80-Meter DX-ing*

Ref 1209 William Orr, W6SAI, *Radio Handbook*

Ref 1210 Bob Clarke, N1RC, "Six Antennas from Three Wires," *73*, Oct 1983, p 10

Ref 1211 Davis, Harold, W8MTI, "The Wave Antenna," *CQ* May 1978, p 24

Ref 1212 Ulrich Rohde, DJ2LR, "Active Antennas," *CQ* Dec 1982, p 20

Ref 1213 Karl Hille, 9A1VU, "Vom Trafo zum Kurz-wellenempgaenger," *CQ DL*, Mar 1977, p 99

Ref 1214 Dieter Pelz, DF3IK et al, "Rahmenantenne - keine Wunderantenne-," *CQ DL*, Sep 1982, p 435

Ref 1215 Hans Wurtz, DL2FA, "Magnetische Antennen," *CQ DL*, Feb 1983, p 64

Ref 1216 Hans Wurtz, DL2FA, "Magnetische Antennen," *CQ DL*, Apr 1983, p 170

Ref 1217 Hans Wurtz, DL2FA, "Elektrisch Magnetische Beam Antennen (EMBA)," *CQ DL*, Jul 1983, p 326

Ref 1218 Guenter Shwarzenbeck, D11BU, "Rhamen- und Ringantennen," *CQ DL*, May 1984, p 226

Ref 1219 Charles Bird, K6HTM, "160-Meter Loop for Receiving," *Ham Radio*, May 1974, p 46

Ref 1220 Ken Cornell, W2IMB, "Loop Antenna Receiving Aid," *Ham Radio*, May 1975, p 66

Ref 1221 John True, W4OQ, "Loop Antennas," *Ham Radio*, Dec 1976

Ref 1222 Henry Keen, W5TRS, "Selective Receiving Antennas: a Progress Report," *Ham Radio*, May 1978, p 20

Ref 1223 Byrd H. Brunemeier, KG6RT, "40-Meter Beverage Antenna," *Ham Radio*, Jul 1979, p 40

Ref 1224 David Atkins, W6VX, "Capacitively Loaded Dipole," *Ham Radio*, May 1984, p 33

Ref 1225 H.H. Beverage, "A Wave Antenna for 200 Meter Reception," *QST*, Nov 1922, p 7

Ref 1226 John Isaacs, W6PZV, "Transmitter Hunting on 75 Meters," *QST*, Jun 1958, p 38

Ref 1227 Lewis McCoy, W1ICP, "The Army Loop in Ham Communication," *QST*, Mar 1968, p 17

Ref 1228 J. Wessendorp, HB9AGK, "Loop Measurements," *QST*, Nov 1968, p 46

Ref 1229 Katashi Nose, KH6IJ, "A 160 Meter Receiving Loop," *QST*, Apr 1975, p 40

Ref 1230 Tony Dorbuck, W1YNC, "Radio Direction Finding Techniques," *QST*, Aug 1975, p 30

Ref 1231 Robert Edlund, W5DS, "The W5DS Hula-Hoop Loop," *QST*, Oct 1975, p 16

Ref 1232 Doug DeMaw, W1FB, "Build this 'Quickie' Preamp," *QST*, Apr 1977, p 43

Ref 1233 Barry Boothe, W9UCW, "Weak Signal Reception on 160—Some Antenna Notes," *QST*, Jun 1977, p 35

Ref 1234 Doug DeMaw, W1FB, "Low-Noise Receiving Antennas," *QST*, Dec 1977, p 36

Ref 1235 Doug DeMaw, W1FB, "Maverick Trackdown," *QST*, Jul 1980, p 22

Ref 1236 John Belrose, VE2CE, "Beverage Antennas for Amateur Communications," *QST*, Sep 1981, p 51

Ref 1237 H.H. Beverage, "H.H. Beverage on Beverage Antennas," *QST*, Dec 1981, p 55

Ref 1238 Doug DeMaw, W1FB et al, "The Classic Beverage Antenna Revisited," *QST*, Jan 1982, p 11

Ref 1239 John Webb, W1ETC, "Electrical Null Steering," *QST*, Oct 1982, p 28

Ref 1240 John F. Belrose, VE2CV et al, "The Beverage Antenna for Amateur Communications," *QST*, Jan 1983, p 22

Ref 1241 Doug DeMaw, W1FB, "Receiver Preamps and How to Use Them," *QST*, Apr 1984, p 19

Ref 1242 Pat Hawker, G3VA, "Technical Topics: Beverage Aerials," *Radio Communication*, Oct 1970, p 684

Ref 1243 Pat Hawker, G3VA, "Technical Topics: All Band Terminated Longwire," *Radio Communication*, Nov 1972, p 745

Ref 1244 Pat Hawker, G3VA, "Technical Topics: A 1.8 MHz Active Frame Aerial," *Radio Communication*, Aug 1976, p 601

Ref 1245 Pat Hawker, G3VA, "Technical Topics: Low-Noise 1.8/3.5 MHz Receiving Antennas," *Radio Communication*, Apr 1978, p 325

Ref 1246 Pat Hawker, G3VA, "Technical Topics: Radiation Resistance of Medium Loops," *Radio Communication*, Feb 1979, p 131

Ref 1247 J.A. Lambert, G3FNZ, "A Directional Active Loop Receiving Antenna System," *Radio Communication*, Nov 1982, p 944

Ref 1248 R.C. Fenwick, K5RR, "A Loop Array for 160 Meters," *CQ*, Apr 1986, p 25

6.8 TRANSMISSION

Ref 1300 Wilkinson, "A N-way Hybrid Power Divider," *I.R.E. Transactions on Microwave*, Jan 1960

Ref 1301 M. Wilson, AA2Z, ed., *The ARRL Handbook for the Radio Amateur* (Newington, CT: ARRL, 1986)

Ref 1302 Pat Hawker, G3VA, *Amateur Radio Techniques*

Ref 1303 Keith Henney, *Radio Engineering Handbook, 5th edition*

Ref 1304 Howard W. Sams, *Reference Data for Radio Engineers, 5th Edition*

Ref 1305 John Devoldere, ON4UN, *80-Meter DX-ing*

Ref 1306 William Orr, W6SAI, *Radio Handbook*

Ref 1307 Gerald L. Hall, K1TD, ed., *The ARRL Antenna Book* (Newington, CT: ARRL, 1982)

Ref 1308 Walter Maxwell, W2DU, "Niedriges SWR aus falschem Grund (teil 1)," *CQ DL*, Jan 1976, p 3

Ref 1309 Walter Maxwell, W2DU, "Niedriges SWR aus falschem Grund (teil 2)," *CQ DL*, Feb 1976, p 47

Ref 1310 Walter Maxwell, W2DU, "Niedriges SWR aus falschem Grund (teil 3)," *CQ DL*, Jun 1976, p 202

Ref 1310 Walter Maxwell, W2DU, "Niedriges SWR aus falschem Grund (teil 4)," *CQ DL*, Aug 1976, p 238

Ref 1311 Walter Maxwell, W2DU, "Niedriges SWR aus falschem Grund (teil 5)," *CQ DL*, Sep 1976, p 272

Ref 1312 Jim Fisk, W1HR, "The Smith Chart," *Ham Radio*, Nov 1970, p 16

Ref 1313 Richard Taylor, W1DAX, "N-Way Power Dividers and 3-dB Hybrids," *Ham Radio*, Aug 1972, p 30

Ref 1314 Joseph Boyer, W6UYH, "Antenna-Transmission Line Analogy," *Ham Radio*, Apr 1977, p 52

Ref 1315 Joseph Boyer, W6UYH, "Antenna-Transmission Line Analog, Part 2," *Ham Radio*, May 1977, p 29

Ref 1316 J. Reisert, W1JR, "Simple and Efficient Broadband Balun," *Ham Radio*, Sep 1978, p 12

Ref 1317 Jack M. Schulman, W6EBY, "T-Network Impedance Matching to Coaxial Feedlines," *Ham Radio*, Sep 1978, p 22

Ref 1318 Charlie J. Carroll, K1XX, "Matching 75-Ohm CATV Hardline to 50-Ohm Systems," *Ham Radio*, Sep 1978, p 31

Ref 1319 John Battle, N4OE, "What is Your SWR?," *Ham Radio*, Nov 1979, p 48

Ref 1320 Henry Elwell, N4UH, "Long Transmission Lines for Optimum Antenna Location," *Ham Radio*, Oct 1980, p 12

Ref 1321 John W. Frank, WB9TQG, "Measuring Coax Cable Loss with an SWR Meter," *Ham Radio*, May 1981, p 34

Ref 1322 Stan Gibilisco, W1GV/4, "How Important is Low SWR?," *Ham Radio*, Aug 1981, p 33

Ref 1323 Lewis T. Fitch, W4VRV, "Matching 75-Ohm Hardline to 50-Ohm Systems," *Ham Radio*, Oct 1982, p 43

Ref 1324 L. A. Cholewski, K6CRT, "Some Amateur Applications of the Smith Chart," *QST*, Jan 1960, p 28

Ref 1325 Walter Maxwell, W2DU, "Another Look at Reflections, Part 1," *QST*, Apr 1973, p 35

Ref 1326 Walter Maxwell, W2DU, "Another Look at Reflections, Part 2," *QST*, Jun 1973, p 20

Ref 1327 Walter Maxwell, W2DU, "Another Look at Reflections, Part 3," *QST*, Aug 1973, p 36

Ref 1328 Walter Maxwell, W2DU, "Another Look at Reflections, Part 4," *QST*, Oct 1973, p 22

Ref 1329 Walter Maxwell, W2DU, "Another Look at Reflections, Part 5," *QST*, Apr 1974, p 26

Ref 1330 Walter Maxwell, W2DU, "Another Look at Reflections, Part 6," *QST*, Dec 1974, p 11

Ref 1331 Gerald Hall, K1PLP, "Transmission-Line Losses," *QST*, Dec 1975, p 48

Ref 1332 Walter Maxwell, W2DU, "Another Look at Reflections, Part 7," *QST*, Aug 1976, p 16

Ref 1333 Charles Brainard, WA1ZRS, "Coaxial Cable, The Neglected Link," *QST*, Apr 1981, p 28

Ref 1335 Crawford MacKeand, WA3ZKZ, "The Smith Chart in BASIC," *QST*, Nov 1984, p 28

Ref 1336 R. C. Hills, G3HRH, "Some Reflections on Standing Waves," *Radio Communication*, Jan 1964, p 15

Ref 1337 Pat Hawker, G3VA, "Technical Topics: Another Look at SWR," *Radio Communication*, Jun 1974, p 377

Ref 1338 Garside, G3MYT, "More on the Smith Chart," *Radio Communication*, Dec 1977, p 934

Ref 1339 Pat Hawker, G3VA, "Technical Topics: SWR-How Important?," *Radio Communication*, Jan 1982, p 41

Ref 1340 Kenneth Parker, G3PKR, "Reflected Power Does Not Mean Lost Power," *Radio Communication*, Jul 1982, p 581

Ref 1341 Pat Hawker, G3VA, "Technical Topics: Reflected Power is Real Power," *Radio Communication*, Jun 1983, p 517

Ref 1342 H. Ashcroft, G4CCM, "Critical Study of the SWR Meter," *Radio Communication*, Mar 1985, p 186

6.9 MATCHING

Ref 1400 M. Wilson, AA2Z, ed., *The ARRL Handbook for the Radio Amateur* (Newington, CT: ARRL, 1986)

Ref 1401 Harold Tolles, W7ITB, "Gamma-Match Design," *Ham Radio*, May 1973, p 46

Ref 1402 Robert Baird, W7CSD, "Antenna Matching Systems," *Ham Radio*, Jul 1973, p 58

Ref 1403 Earl Whyman, W2HB, "Standing-Wave Ratios," *Ham Radio*, Jul 1973, p 26

Ref 1404 Robert Leo, W7LR, "Designing L-networks," *Ham Radio*, Feb 1974, p 26

Ref 1405 G. E. Smith, W4AEO, "Log-Periodic Feed Systems," *Ham Radio*, Oct 1974, p 30

Ref 1406 John True, W4OQ, "Shunt-Fed Vertical Antennas," *Ham Radio*, May 1975, p 34

Ref 1407 I. L. McNally, K6WX, et al, "Impedance Matching by Graphical Solution," *Ham Radio*, Mar 1978, p 82

Ref 1408 Jim Fisk, W1HR, "Transmission-Line Calculations with the Smith Chart," *Ham Radio*, Mar 1978, p 92

Ref 1409 Jack M. Schulman, W6EBY, "T-Network Impedance Matching to Coaxial Feedlines," *Ham Radio*, Sep 1978, p 22

Ref 1410 Ernie Franke, WA2EWT, "Appreciating the L Matching Network," *Ham Radio*, Sep 1980, p.27

Ref 1411 Robert Leo, W7LR, "Remote-Controlled 40, 80, and 160-Meter Vertical," *Ham Radio*, May 1984, p 38

Ref 1412 James Sanford, WB4GCS, "Easy Antenna Matching," *Ham Radio*, May 1984, p 67

Ref 1413 Chris Bowick, WD4C, "Impedance Matching: A Brief Review," *Ham Radio*, Jun 1984, p 49

Ref 1414 Richard Nelson, WBØIKN, "Basic Gamma Matching," *Ham Radio*, Jan 1985, p 29

Ref 1415 L. A. Cholewski, K6CRT, "Some Amateur Applications of the Smith Chart," *QST*, Jan 1960, p 28

Ref 1416 Gene Hubbell, W9ERU, "Feeding Grounded Towers as Radiators," *QST*, Jun 1960, p 33

Ref 1417 J. D. Gooch, W9YRV, et al, "The Hairpin Match," *QST*, Apr 1962, p 11

Ref 1418 Eugene E. Baldwin, WØRUG, "Some Notes on the Care and Feeding of Grounded Verticals," *QST*, Oct 1963, p 45

Ref 1419 N. H. Davidson, K5JVF, "Flagpole Without a Flag," *QST*, Nov 1964, p 36

Ref 1420 Robert Leo, K7KOK, "An Impedance Matching Method," *QST*, Dec 1968, p 24

Ref 1421 D. J. Healey, W3PG, "An Examination of the Gamma Match," *QST*, Apr 1969, p 11

Ref 1422 Donald Belcher, WA4JVE, "RF Matching Techniques, Design and Example," *QST*, Oct 1972, p 24

Ref 1423 James McAlister, WA5EKA, "Simplified Impedance Matching and the Mac Chart," *QST*, Dec 1972, p 33

Ref 1424 John Kaufmann, WA1CQW, et al, "A Convenient Stub Tuning System for Quad Antennas," *QST*, May 1975, p 18

Ref 1425 Earl Cunningham, W5RTQ, "Shunt Feeding Towers for Operating on the Low Amateur Frequencies," *QST*, Oct 1975, p 22

Ref 1426 Doug DeMaw, W1CER, "Another Method of Shunt-Feeding Your Tower," *QST*, Oct 1975, p 25

Ref 1427 Jerry Sevick, W2FMI, "Simple Broadband Matching Networks," *QST*, Jan 1976, p 20

Ref 1428 Walter Schulz, K3OQF, "Slant-Wire Feed for Grounded Towers," *QST*, May 1977, p 23

Ref 1429 Bob Pattison, N6RP, "A Graphical Look at the L Network," *QST*, Mar 1979, p 24

Ref 1430 Tony Dorbuck, K1FM, "Matching-Network Design," *QST*, Mar 1979, p 26

Ref 1431 Herbert Drake Jr., N6QE, "A Remotely Controlled Antenna-Matching Network," *QST*, Jan 1980, p 32

Ref 1432 Doug DeMaw, W1FB, "Ultimate Transmatch Improved," *QST*, Jul 1980, p 39

Ref 1433 Colin Dickman, ZS6U, "The ZS6U Minishack Special," *QST*, Apr 1981, p 32

Ref 1434 Claude L. Frantz, F5FC/DJØOT, "A New, More Versatile Transmatch," *QST*, Jul 1982, p 31

Ref 1435 Doug DeMaw, W1FB, "A 'Multipedance' Broadband Transformer," *QST*, Aug 1982, p 39

Ref 1436 Don Johnson, W6AAQ, "Mobile Antenna Matching —Automatically!," *QST*, Oct 1982, p 15

Ref 1437 Doug DeMaw, W1FB, "Shunt-Fed Towers: Some Practical Aspects," *QST*, Oct 1982, p 21

Ref 1438 Crawford MacKaend, WA3ZKZ, "The Smith Chart in BASIC," *QST*, Nov 1984, p 28

Ref 1439 J. A. Ewen, G3HGM, "Design of L-Networks for Matching Antennas to Transmitters," *Radio Communication*, Aug 1984, p 663

Ref 1440 H. Ashcroft, G4CCM, "Critical Study of the SWR Meter," *Radio Communication*, Mar 1985, p 186

Ref 1441 C. Huether, KM1H, "Build a High-Performance, Shunt-Fed, 160 Meter Vertical Antenna," *CQ,* Dec 1986, p 38

6.10 BALUNS

Ref 1500 J. Schultz, W4FA, "A Selection of Baluns from Palomar Engineers," *CQ*, Apr 1985, p 32

Ref 1501 William Orr, W6SAI, "Broadband Antenna Baluns," *Ham Radio*, Jun 1968, p 6

Ref 1502 J. Reisert, W1JR, "Simple and Efficient Broadband Balun," *Ham Radio*, Sep 1978, p 12

Ref 1503 John J. Nagle, K4KJ, "High Performance Broadband Balun," *Ham Radio*, Feb 1980, p 28

Ref 1504 George Badger, W6TC, "A New Class of Coaxial-Line Transformers," *Ham Radio*, Feb 1980, p 12

Ref 1505 George Badger, W6TC, "Coaxial-Line Transformers," *Ham Radio*, Mar 1980, p 18

Ref 1506 John Nagle, K4KJ, "The Half-Wave Balun: Theory and Application," *Ham Radio*, Sep 1980, p 32

Ref 1507 Roy N. Lehner, WA2SON, "A Coreless Balun," *Ham Radio*, May 1981, p 62

Ref 1508 John Nagle, K4KJ, "Testing Baluns," *Ham Radio*, Aug 1983, p 30

Ref 1509 Lewis McCoy, W1ICP, "Is a Balun Required?," *QST*, Dec 1968, p 28

Ref 1510 R. H. Turrin, W2IMU, "Application of Broadband Balun Transformers," *QST*, Apr 1969, p 42

Ref 1511 Bruce Eggers, WA9NEW, "An Analysis of the Balun," *QST*, Apr 1980, p 19

Ref 1512 William Fanckboner, W9INN, "Using Baluns in Transmatches with High-Impedance Lines," *QST*, Apr 1981, p 51

Ref 1513 Doug DeMaw, W1FB, "A 'Multipedance' Broadband Transformer," *QST*, Aug 1982, p 39

Ref 1514 R. G. Titterington, G3ORY, "The Ferrite-Cored Balun Transformer," *Radio Communication*, Mar 1982, p 216

6.11 ANTENNA MEASURING

Ref 1600 M. Wilson, AA2Z, ed., *The ARRL Handbook for the Radio Amateur* (Newington, CT: ARRL, 1986)

Ref 1601 John Schultz, W4FA, "The MFJ-202B R.F. Noise Bridge," *CQ*, Aug 1984, p 50

Ref 1602 Michael Martin, DJ7YV, "Die HF-Stromzange," *CQ DL*, Dec 1983, p 581

Ref 1603 Reginald Brearley, VE2AYU, "Phase-Angle Meter," *Ham Radio*, Apr 1973, p 28

Ref 1604 Robert Baird, W7CSD, "Nonresonant Antenna-Impedance Measurements," *Ham Radio*, Apr 1974, p 46

Appendix A

Low-Band DXing Addendum

A.1 Calculating Feed Systems for Arrays—Loss-Free Feed Lines Compared to Real Feed Lines

A.1.1 DESIGN SOFTWARE

The author's antenna design software, used to develop feed systems for low-band arrays, was written for theoretical loss-free cables. These conditions are often approached on the low bands (80 and 160 meters). Typically, RG-213 cable has 0.39 dB loss per 100 feet at 3.75 MHz and about 0.28 dB per 100 feet at 1.8 MHz when the line is "flat." The attenuation can increase significantly with high SWR, however. Attenuation and SWR also cause the magnitudes of current and voltage to be different and influence the phase angle—this can be seen in the examples.

The software programs dealing with feed lines have been rewritten to include attenuation as a feed-line parameter. Originally feed lines were only specified by their impedance; the new programs allow the user to specify the cables by characteristic impedance, attenuation, velocity factor (Vf) or dielectric constant of the insulating material (the last two factors are interrelated).

The new UNIVERSAL FEED LINE PROGRAM calculates the exact attenuation of the feed line at any frequency of interest if the user can supply attenuation data at a lower and a higher frequency. For example, if attenuation is known at 1 and 10 MHz, the program will calculate the exact attenuation at 3.75 MHz.

The program can now be used without need for interpretation or further conversion in two different modes: 1. Looking from the transmitter (or receiver) towards the load (antenna) for calculating the impedance (and voltage and current) at the end of a feed line, given the antenna impedance (and current). 2. Looking from the load (antenna) down towards the transmitter (or receiver) for calculating the antenna impedance if the impedance at the end of the feed line has been measured with an appropriate impedance bridge or noise bridge.

Without these two distinct modes of operation, the user must be very careful in dealing with conjugate impedance. For example, if the impedance on a line, looking towards the load (antenna) is $a + jb$ ohms and the impedance looking toward the generator (receiver, transmitter) from the same point on the line is $a - jb$ ohms, one impedance is the conjugate of the other. When the program is started, the user is asked if he wants to look toward the load or toward the generator; the answer to this question is very important but once it is answered the conjugate impedance problem is solved.

In addition to specifying cable length in degrees (one degree equals one wavelength divided by 360), one can also specify the length in metric (centimeters) or imperial units (inches). Conversion is done on screen between inches and centimeters, and degrees and radians.

One very interesting part of the program is the power balance. This gives the user the following information:
- power into the load
- power into the feed line
- power lost in the feed line
- power lost due to flat feed line (nominal attenuation)
- power lost due to SWR on the feed line (additional attenuation

The levels are expressed in dB or in watts (the result in watts depends on the load current and the resistive component of the load impedance).

Figure A.1 shows a printout of a program run for an example of 200 feet of RG-213 feeding a load of $8 - j12$ ohms at 3.75 MHz (assuming a loss of 0.39 dB per 100 feet). Figure A.2 shows a program run for loss-free cable.

A.1.2 IMPLICATIONS FOR ARRAY FEED SYSTEMS

To assess the influence of cable loss on the design approaches for arrays as described earlier in the book, we will evaluate two of the more popular configurations in each case with the four different design methods: the Gehrke, the Christman, the Collins and the Lewallen method. The cable used in the exercise is RG-213 or RG-8 (where indicated), with a loss of 0.39 and 0.29 dB per 100 feet respectively (at 3.75 MHz).

A.1.2.1 Two-Element, ¼-Wave-Spaced, Fed 90 Degrees Out of Phase (Producing the Classic Cardioid Pattern)

Gehrke Method

The impedance, voltage and current values at the end of the feed lines are shown in Table 1 for both the loss-free and the real case.

```
(1)                     UNIVERSAL FEEDLINE PROGRAM                          by ON4UN
-------------------------------------------------------------------------------------
Zcable: 50 ohm              VELOCITY FACTOR: .66                    FREQ:3.75 MHz
WAVELENGTH= 80.00 METER                    WAVELENGTH IN CABLE = 52.8 METER
CABLE=60.96 M        OR 2400 INCH          OR 415.64 DEG        OR 7.25 RADS
TOTAL ATTENUATION = .78 dB           or .0898 NEPERS
-------------------------------------------------------------------------------------
                         REAL PART       IMAG PART       MAGNITUDE       ANGLE
                         ---------       ---------       ---------       -----
IMPEDANCE (ohm)=          8               -12             14.4222        -56.3099   A
CURRENT (Amp)   =         1               0               1              0          N
VOLTAGE (Volt)  =         8               -12             14.4222        -56.3099   T
-------------------------------------------------------------------------------------
IMPEDANCE (ohm)=         20.45            40.39           45.2731         63.1472   E
CURRENT (Amp)   =        .7738            .1946           .7979           14.1199   N
VOLTAGE (Volt)  =        7.9614           35.2331         36.1214         77.2671   D
-------------------------------------------------------------------------------------
POWER INTO COAX   =      13.02 W               POWER INTO LOAD = 8 W
TOTAL SYSTEM LOSS=        5.02 W   = -2.11 dB                           EFFICIENCY:
FLAT COAX LOSS    =       2.14 W   = -0.78 dB                           -----------
SWR COAX LOSS     =       2.88 W   = -1.33 dB                             61.45%
INPUT SWR= 4.21/1                               SWR AT LOAD = 6.61/1
-------------------------------------------------------------------------------------
0=Exit  1=Rerun  CHANGE>>>  2=Zant  3=Iant  4=Zk  5=V.fact  6=Att/Fq  7=Lgth
```

Figure A.1 — Screen dump of UNIVERSAL FEED LINE PROGRAM using a "real" cable feeding a load with a high SWR.

```
(1)                     UNIVERSAL FEEDLINE PROGRAM                          by ON4UN
-------------------------------------------------------------------------------------
Zcable: 50 ohm              VELOCITY FACTOR: .66                    FREQ:3.75 MHz
WAVELENGTH= 80.00 METER                    WAVELENGTH IN CABLE = 52.8 METER
CABLE=60.96 M        OR 2400 INCH          OR 415.64 DEG        OR 7.25 RADS
TOTAL ATTENUATION =   0 dB          or    0 NEPERS
-------------------------------------------------------------------------------------
                         REAL PART       IMAG PART       MAGNITUDE       ANGLE
                         ---------       ---------       ---------       -----
IMPEDANCE (ohm)=          8               -12             14.4222        -56.3099   A
CURRENT (Amp)   =         1               0               1              0          N
VOLTAGE (Volt)  =         8               -12             14.4222        -56.3099   T
-------------------------------------------------------------------------------------
IMPEDANCE (ohm)=         13.36            42.93           44.9594         72.7171   E
CURRENT (Amp)   =        .7625            .1321           .7739            9.8262   N
VOLTAGE (Volt)  =        4.5155           34.50           34.7945         82.5433   D
-------------------------------------------------------------------------------------
POWER INTO COAX   =         8 W                POWER INTO LOAD = 8 W
TOTAL SYSTEM LOSS=          0 W  =     0 dB                             EFFICIENCY:
FLAT COAX LOSS    =         0 W  =     0 dB                             -----------
SWR COAX LOSS     =         0 W  =     0 dB                              100.00%
INPUT SWR= 6.61/1                               SWR AT LOAD = 6.61/1
-------------------------------------------------------------------------------------
0=Exit  1=Rerun  CHANGE>>>  2=Zant  3=Iant  4=Zk  5=V.fact  6=Att/Fq  7=Lgth
```

Figure A.2 — Screen dump for the loss-free situation (otherwise information is identical to those used in Figure A.1).

Table 1
Element Data for the Gehrke Feed System

Element	*Loss-Free*	*Real Cable*
1	Z = 40.8 + *j*43.6 ohms E = 43.3 V ∠80.1° I = 0.72 A ∠34.12°	Z = 41.6 + *j*42.5 ohms E = 43.6 ∠80.5° I = 0.73 A ∠34.8°
2	Z = 53.9 − *j*14.9 ohms E = 54.6 V ∠−17.2° I = 0.97 A ∠−1.81°	Z = 53.0 − *j*14.4 ohms E = 55.4 V ∠−17.1° I = 0.99 A ∠−2.08°

The resultant worksheet is shown in Figure A.3. It can be seen that the values in the worksheet in Figure A.3 are only slightly different from the values in the worksheet in Figure 2.87.

Christman Method

The FEED LINE VOLTAGE computer program has also been rewritten to take cable loss into account. This program iterates through the cable length in one-degree steps.

The loss-free approach yielded two points with identical voltage: at 84 degrees on feed line one and at 161 degrees on

```
|                                                                                                      |
|         (2 El 1/4 wave spacing    |            CABLE VELOCITY FACTOR: 0.66                       |
| ARRAY: (ENDFIRE, CARDIOID          |            MIN FEEDER LENGTH: 71.6 DEG                       |
|         (90 DEG PHASE              |            F = 3.75 MHz                                      |
|------------------------------------|------------------------------------------------------------------|
|A|              | ELEM 1.          | ELEM.2            | ELEM.3            | ELEM.4            |
|N|--------------|------------------|-------------------|-------------------|-------------------|
|T|              |Z(1,2)= 15-j15    |Z(2,3)=            |Z(3,4)=            |                   |
|E|              |Z(1,3)=           |Z(2.4)=            |                   |                   |
|N|              |Z(1,4)=           |                   |                   |                   |
|N|--------------|------------------|-------------------|-------------------|-------------------|
|A|Z (ohm)      =| 21.4 - j 15      | 51.4 + j15        |                   |                   |
|S|E (V, deg)=  | 26.13 / -35.03   | 53.5 / -73.73     |                   |                   |
| |I (A, deg)=  | 1 / 0            | 1 / -90           |                   |                   |
|=|==============|==================|===================|===================|===================|
| |CABLES -->    |50 OHM, 71.6 deg  |50 ohm, 71.6 deg   |                   |                   |
| |              |                  |                   |                   |                   |
|N|Z(series)     |                  |                   |                   |                   |
|E|Z(parallel)   |   SWR = 2.59/1   |   SWR=1.34/1      |                   |                   |
|T|Value. ser    |                  |                   |                   |                   |
|W|Value. par.   |                  |                   |                   |                   |
|O|     Z(ohm)=  | 41.6+j42.5       |   53.9-j14.4      |                   |                   |
|R|   E(E,deg)=  | 43.6 / +80.5     |   55.4 / -17.1    |                   |                   |
|K|   I(A,deg)=  | 0.73 / +34.8     |   0.999/ -2.08    |                   |                   |
|1|              |                  |                   |                   |                   |
|=|==============|==================|===================|===================|===================|
| |              | SHUNT INPU L NETW| SHUNT INPUT L NETW| SHUNT INPUT L NETW| SHUNT IN L NETW   |
| |              | --------(1)------| --------(2)-------| -------(3)--------| ------(4)---------|
|N|Z(series)     | -116             | +30.6             | +44.8             | -15.8             |
|E|Z(parallel)   | +96.7            | -96.7             | -126.4            | +126.4            |
|T|Value. ser    | 367 pF           | 1.3 uH            | 1.89 uH           | 2689 pF           |
|W|Value. par.   | 4.11 uH          | 438 pF            | 336 pF            | 5.37 uH           |
|O|     Z(ohm)=  | 170              | 170               | 70.8              | 70.8              |
|R|   E(E,deg)=  | 61.6 / -25.5     | 61.6 / +95.2      | 61.3 / +27.1      | 61.3 / -31.4      |
|K|   I(A,deg)=  | 0.36 / -25.2     | 0.36 / +95.2      | 0.87 / +27.1      | 0.87 /-31.4       |
|2|              |                  |                   |                   |                   |
|=|==============|==================|===================|===================|===================|
| |              | IN(1) --> OUT(3) | IN(3) --> OUT(1)  | IN(4) --> OUT(1)  | IN(1) --> OUT(1)  |
| |              | --(5)---|---(6)---| --(7)---|---(8)--| --(9)--|---(10)--| --(11)--|--(12)- |
|N|Z(series)     |-56 (PI) |-35.0 (T)|+135 (PI)|+84  (T)|-17 (PI)|-8.8 (T) |+7.4 (PI)|+3.7 (T)|
|E|Z(parallel)   |+143     |+56.2    |-343     |-135    |+3299   |+17.5    |-1350    |-7.30   |
|T|Value. ser    |754 pF   |1213 pF  |5.73 uH  |3.57 uH |2429 pF |4845 pF  |0.31 uH  |0.15uH  |
|W|Value. par.   |6.1 uH   |2.4 uH   |124 pF   |314 pF  |140 uH  |0.74 uH  |31 pF    |5832 pF |
|O|     Z(ohm)=  |70.8     |70.8     |170      |170     |170     |170      |70.8     |70.8    |
|R|   E(E,deg)=  |         |         |         |        |        |         |         |        |
|K|   I(A,deg)=  |         |         |         |        |        |         |         |        |
|3|              |         |         |         |        |        |         |         |        |
|=|==============|==================|===================|===================|===================|
| |              | IN(3) --> OUT(2) | IN(2) --> OUT(3)  | IN(4) --> OUT(2)  | IN(2) --> OUT(4)  |
| |              | --(13)--|--(14)--| --(15)--|--(16)--| --(17)-|--(18)---| --(19)--|--(20)- |
|N|Z(series)     |-158 (PI)|-116 (T)|+66  (PI)|+48  (T)|-137(PI)|-338  (T)|+57  (PI)|+141 (T)|
|E|Z(parallel)   |+252     |+158    |-105     |-66     |+86     |+136     |-35.6    |-56.8   |
|T|Value. ser    |269 pF   |369 pFH |2.79 uH  |2.03 uH |311 pF  |126 pF   |2.4 uH   |6.0 uH  |
|W|Value. par.   |10.7 uH  |6.7 uH  |405 pF   |646 pF  |3.6 uH  |5.8 uH   |1191 pF  |746 pF  |
|O|     Z(ohm)=  |170      |170     |70.8     |70.8    |170     |170      |70.8     |70.8    |
|R|   E(E,deg)=  |         |        |         |        |        |         |         |        |
|K|   I(A,deg)=  |         |        |         |        |        |         |         |        |
|3|              |         |        |         |        |        |         |         |        |
```

Figure A.3 — Worksheet for the two-element end-fire array (¼-wave spacing, fed 90 degrees out of phase) according to the Gehrke method and using real cable (RG-213).

feed line two. The exercise with real coax yields identical voltage points at 93 degrees and 164 degrees; this is a marked difference of 152 centimeters (52 inches) and 44 centimeters (17.3 inches) from the original cable length. The new worksheet is shown in Figure A.4.

An interesting analysis technique is to assume the cable lengths as dictated by the loss-free approach, and then calculate the element drive currents (magnitude and phase). For example, assume a voltage of 51.2 V $/90.0°$ (see worksheet in Figure A.4) at the junction of the two feed lines, and (incorrect) line lengths of 84 degrees for element one and 161 degrees for element two. The resulting element currents are: I = 1.03 A $/3.6°$ (as opposed to the required 1 A $/0°$) and I = 0.98 A $/-86.9°$ (as opposed to the required 1 A $/-90°$). These element currents can easily be calculated by the new

program UNIVERSAL FEED LINE PROGRAM in operating mode two.

Using this element current information, the influence of front to back was evaluated using ANNIE. The results are rather startling: The F/B changes only 0.1 dB (22.5 to 22.4 dB, the better value being for the "incorrect" feed system!). The figures were calculated in a situation over real (good) ground, at an elevation angle of 25 degrees (this is the peak wave angle).

Collins Method

Using the Collins feed method, the impedance, current and voltage at the end of the quarter-wave lines are shown in Table 2.

Here again we can calculate the influence of the real cables

ARRAY:	(2 El 1/4 wave spacing (ENDFIRE, CARDIOID (90 DEG PHASE	CABLE VELOCITY FACTOR: 0.66 MIN FEEDER LENGTH: 71.6 DEG F = 3.75 Mhz		
A N		ELEM 1.	ELEM.2	ELEM.3	ELEM.4
I T E N N		Z(1,2)= 15-J15 Z(1,3)= Z(1,4)=	Z(2,3)= Z(2,4)=	Z(3,4)=	
A S	Z (ohm) = E (V, deg)= I (A, deg)=	21.4-J15 26.13 $/-35.03$ 1 $/0$	51.4 + J15 53.4 $/-73.7$ 1 $/-90$		
	CABLES	50 ohm, 93 deg	50 ohm, 164 deg		
N E T W O R K 1	Z(series) Z(parallel) Value. ser Value. par. Z(ohm)= E(E,deg)= I(A,deg)=	SWR = 2.59/1 86.8 + j 49.8 51.2 $/+90.9$ 0.511 $/+61.1$	SWR = 1.34/1 44.42 + j 11.77 51.3 $/+90.2$ 1.11 $/+75.3$		
N E T W O R K 2	PARALLELLING BOTH IMPEDANCES Z(series) Z(parallel) Value. ser Value. par. Z(ohm)= E(E,deg)= I(A,deg)=	29.9 + j 10.6 48.4 $/+90.5$ 1.52 $/+71.00$			
N E T W O R K 3	Z(series) Z(parallel) Value. ser Value. par. Z(ohm)= E(E,deg)= I(A,deg)=	SHUNT INPUT L NETW ------(1)------ 13.9 -61.0 0.59 UH 696 pF 50 + j0 59.0 $/+110.3$ 1.18 $/+110.3$	SHUNT INPUT L NETW ------(2)------ -35.1 61.00 1208 pF 2.59 uH 50 + j0 59.0 $/+31.6$ 1.18 $/+31.6$	SERIES REACTANCE ------(3)------- -10.6 – 4004 pF – 29.9 + j0 45.60 $/+71.00$ 1.53 $/+71.00$	PARALLEL REACTANCE ------(4)------- -94.9 – 447 pF – 33.6 +j0 48.4 $/+90.5$ 1.44 $/+90.5$
N E T W O R K 4	Z(series) Z(parallel) Value. ser Value. par. Z(ohm)= E(E,deg)= I(A,deg)=			QUARTER WAVE TRANSF ------(5)------- Z COAX = 50 ohm 50 + j0	QUARTER WAVE TRF. ------(6)------- Z COAX = 37 ohm (=2 x 75 ohm in parallel 50 + j0

Figure A.4 — Worksheet for the Christman feed method for the two-element end-fire array fed with RG-213.

Table 2
Element Data for the Collins Feed System

Element	*Loss-Free*	*Real Cable*
1	Z = 87.3 +*j*54.9 ohms E = 50.0 V /90.0° I = 0.52 A /54.97°	Z = 78.0 +*j*51.7 ohms E = 50.4 V /89.7° I = 0.54 A /56.2°
2	Z = 44.8 +*j*13.1 ohms E = 50.0 V /0.00° I = 1.07 A /16.27°	Z = 45.1 −*j*12.6 ohms E = 51.0 V /0.33° I = 1.09 A /15.98°

on the array performance. The net difference in F/B between the theoretical loss-free case and the practical case (using RG-213 cable) is less than 0.1 dB.

Lewallen Method

As the same quarter wave feed lines apply to the Lewallen methods as well, it can be seen that the deviation from the original figures is also marginal for this feed system.

A.1.2.2 Four-Square Array With ¼-Wave Spacing
Gehrke Method

Gehrke reports a "non trivial" error when using the lossless approach on the ¼-wave-spaced diamond array[1]. Figure A.5 shows the original worksheet (Figure 2.99 in the book)

[1]Gehrke, Forrest, K2BT, "Real Coax: Impedance and Phase Relationships," *Ham Radio*, April 1987, p 8.

ARRAY: (4 SQUARE ARRAY (1/4 WAVE SPACING (QUADRATURE FED		CABLE VELOCITY FACTOR: 0.66 MIN FEEDER LENGTH: 100 DEG F = 3.80 MHz			
		ELEM 1.	ELEM.2	ELEM.3	ELEM.4
ANTENNA		Z(1,2)= 15-j15 Z(1,3)= 15-j15 Z(1,4)= 3-j17.5	Z(2,3)= 3-j17.5 Z(2,4)= 15-j15	Z(3,4)= 15-j15	
AS	Z (ohm) =	3.4 -j12.5	39.4-j17.5	39.4-j17.5	63.4+j47.5
	E (V, deg)=	12.95 / -74.29	43.11 / -113.95	43.11 / -113.95	79.22 / -143.16
	I (A, deg)=	1 / 0	1 / -90	1 / -90	1 / -180
	CABLES -->	50 ohm, 100 deg (A)	50 ohm, 100 deg (B)	50 ohm, 100 deg (C)	50 ohm, 100 deg (D)
NETWORK 1	Z(series)				
	Z(parallel)	SWR = 15.6/1	SWR = 1.58/1	SWR = 1.58/1	SWR = 2.34/1
	Value. ser				
	Value. par.				
	Z(ohm)=	345.5 + j285.9	62.01 + j21.39	62.01 + j21.39	23.63 - j11.15
	E(E,deg)=	51.49 / +90.57	53.5 / +7.14	53.5 / +7.14	44.07/ -73.91
	I(A,deg)=	0.115 / +50.97	0.81 / -11.88	0.81 / -11.88	1.68 / -48.66
		SHUNT IN L NETW. (1)	(B)+(C) IN PARALL. (2)	SHUNT IN L NETW. (3)	SHUNT IN L NETW. (4)
NETWORK 2	Z(series)	-1073		+32.9	+57.6
	Z(parallel)	+939		-66	-58.4
	Value. ser	40 PF		1.40 uH	2.44 uH
	Value. par.	40 uH		646 pF	726 pF
	Z(ohm)=	2141+ j0	31.0 + j10.70	92.4 +j0	114.8 + j0
	E(E,deg)=	98.7 / -15.4	53.5 / +7.14	87.3 / +42.70	87.8 / +14.40
	I(A,deg)=	0.0461 / -15.4	1.62 / -11.88	0.945 / +42.70	0.765 / +14.40
		PI NETWORK (7)			PI NETWORK (8)
NETWORK 3	Z(series)	+1817			+54.4
	Z(parallel)	-3854			-455
	Value. ser	77.1 uH			2.3 uH
	Value. par.	11 pF			93.0 pF
	Z(ohm)=	2141 + j0			114.8 + j0
	E(E,deg)=	98.7 / +42.70			87.8 / +42.70
	I(A,deg)=	0.0461 / +42.70			0.765 / +42.70
			(3)+(7)+(8) PARAL. (9)		
NETWORK 4	Z(series)				
	Z(parallel)				
	Value. ser				
	Value. par.				
	Z(ohm)=		50 + j0		
	E(E,deg)=		87.80 / +42.70		
	I(A,deg)=		1.76 / +42.70		

Figure A.5 — Worksheet for the Gehrke feed method for the four-element quarter-wave-spaced diamond array fed with RG-213.

redone with real cables (RG-213).

We can see that there is not much difference between the old and new solutions (at least with good RG-213 cable). It is interesting to note that the voltage and current values at the input of the network are just slightly higher (2%) in magnitude (due to loss), while the phase angle is within one degree of the original value. This solution assumes that all the networks (L and PI) are loss-free; this is not actually the case. Again, the influence will be rather negligible if good quality components are used. In any event, the fine tuning must be done with the real system.

Christman Method

As with the example of the two-element array, it appears that the influence of cable attenuation is quite marked on the line lengths producing identical voltage points. On elements two, three and four (page II-81 of the book), line lengths of 109, 109 and 147 degrees produced equal voltages (54.5 V $\underline{/13.61°}$) in the loss-free case. With RG-213 at 3.75 MHz the required line lengths become 102, 102 and 144 degrees producing a voltage of 54.0 V $\underline{/8.39°}$. Line length difference compared to the loss-free case is 103 centimeters (40.4 inches) and 70 centimeters (28.9 inches) respectively. Another marked difference appears in the impedance at the end of the 120-degree-long feed line to element one; the impedance changes from 40.55 $-j166.36$ ohms to 54.36 $-j158.35$ ohms. The new worksheet is shown in Figure A.6.

Collins and Lewallen Methods

The quarter-wave feed lines must be made of foam RG-8

ARRAY:	(4 SQUARE ARRAY (1/4 WAVE SPACING (QUADRATURE FED	CABLE VELOCITY FACTOR: 0.66 MIN FEEDER LENGTH: 100 DEG F = 3.80 MHz		
A N T E N N A	ELEM 1.	ELEM.2	ELEM.3	ELEM.4
	Z(1,2)= 15-j15 Z(1,3)= 15-j15 Z(1,4)= 3-j17.5	Z(2,3)= 3-j17.5 Z(2,4)= 15-j15	Z(3,4)= 15-j15	
A S I Z(ohm) = E (V,deg)= I (A,deg)=	3.4 -j12.5 12.95 $\underline{/-74.29}$ 1 $\underline{/0}$	39.4-j17.5 43.11 $\underline{/-113.95}$ 1 $\underline{/-90}$	39.4-j17.5 43.11 $\underline{/-113.95}$ 1 $\underline{/-90}$	63.4+j47.5 79.22 $\underline{/-143.16}$ 1 $\underline{/-180}$
CABLES -->	50 ohm, 120 deg	50 ohm, 102 deg ------(A)-------	50 ohm, 102 deg ------(B)-------	50 ohm, 144 deg ------(C)-------
N E T W O R K 1 Z(series) Z(parallel) Value. ser Value. par. Z(ohm)= E(E,deg)= I(A,deg)=	SWR = 15.6/1 45.36 - j158.35 49.70 $\underline{/+92.40}$ 0.29 $\underline{/+163.4}$	SWR = 1.58/1 63.85 + j20.65 54.0 $\underline{/+8.56}$ 0.80 $\underline{/-9.36}$	SWR = 1.58/1 63.85 + j20.65 54.0 $\underline{/+8.56}$ 0.80 $\underline{/-9.36}$	SWR = 2.34/1 27.54 + j20.17 54.0 $\underline{/+8.39}$ 1.58 $\underline{/-27.9}$
N E T W O R K 2 Z(series) Z(parallel) Value. ser Value. par. Z(ohm)= E(E,deg)= I(A,deg)=	SHUNT IN L NETW. ------(1)------- +368 -224 15.6 uH 189 pF 864 + j0 64.3 $\underline{/-121.1}$ 0.0745 $\underline{/-121.1}$	SHUNT IN L NETW. ------(2)------- -51.4 +224 825 pF 9.5 uH 864 + j0 64.3 $\underline{/+88.0}$ 0.0745 $\underline{/+88.0}$		
N E T W O R K 3 Z(series) Z(parallel) Value. ser Value. par. Z(ohm)= E(E,deg)= I(A,deg)=	PI STRETCHER ------(3)------- +666 -407 28.2 uH 104 pF 864 + j0 54.0 $\underline{/+8.5}$	T STRETCHER ------(4)------- +1836 -666 78 uH 64 pF 864 + j0 54.0 $\underline{/+8.5}$	PI STRETCHER ------(5)------- -850 +1039 50 pF 44 uH 864 + j0 54.0 $\underline{/+8.5}$	T STRETCHER ------(6)------- -719 +850 59 pF 36 uH 864 + j0 54.0 $\underline{/+8.5}$
N E T W O R K 4 Z(series) Z(parallel) Value. ser Value. par. Z(ohm)= E(E,deg)= I(A,deg)=	PARALLEL IMPED parallelling (A)+ (B)+(C)+(3) or (4) or (5) or (6) 15.07 + j7.51 54.0 $\underline{/+8.5}$ 3.20 $\underline{/-18.00}$	SHUNT IN L NETW. ------(7)------- +15.43 -32.84 0.66 uH 1292 pF 50 + j0 88.03 $\underline{/+38.7}$ 1.76 $\underline{/+38.7}$	SHUNT IN L NETW. ------(8)------- -30.45 32.84 1394 pF 1.39 uH 50 + j0 88.03 $\underline{/-74.7}$ 1.76 $\underline{/-74.7}$	SER Z PAR Z --(9)---|--(10)- -7.51 | - |-37.8 |5631pF |1124pF - | 15.07+j0 |18.81+j0 48.3/-18 |54.5/8 3.2/-18 |2.9/8

Figure A.6 — Worksheet for the Christman feed method for the four-element diamond array fed with RG-213.

in order to reach the center of the diamond. Let us assume the loss is 0.3 dB per 100 feet at 3.75 MHz and the velocity factor is 0.80. The resulting element information is shown in Table 3.

As with the two-element array, the differences are minimal, but as expected the differences are more obvious on the 270-degree-long line. Collins recommends the use of a variable length "phase corrector" (as shown in Figure 2.102) to compensate for these slight differences, as well as differences in individual antenna-element parameters.

Conclusion

The loss-free approach is reasonably accurate for designing feed systems for arrays according to all four methods described, provided good-quality low-loss cable is used. Better results can be obtained with the new design programs which include loss as a cable parameter, however. The new design software will yield accurate results under all circumstances for frequencies from 1.8 MHz to several GHz.

A.2 Calculating Antenna Impedance From Measurements at the End of a Lossy Feed Line

The UNIVERSAL FEED LINE program has been specifically organized to deal with this situation. First, the user does not need to know the exact line length to the antenna. The line length can be calculated from a simple measurement. First, an antenna noise bridge is nulled with a 500 to 1000-ohm

Table 3
Element Data for the Collins and Lewallen Feed Systems

Element	Loss-Free	Real Cable
1	Z = 50.6 +j186.2 ohms E = 50.0 V /90.0° I = 0.26 A /15.21°	Z = 60.5 +j180.1 ohms E = 50.1 V /89.7° I = 0.26 A /19.4°
2 and 3	Z = 53.0 +j23.5 ohms E = 50.0 V /0.00° I = 0.86 A /−23.95°	Z = 53.1 −j22.8 ohms E = 50.6 V /0.29° I = 0.88 A /−23.5°
4	Z = 25.3 +j28.9 ohms E = 50.0 V /90.00° I = 1.58 A /126.8°	Z = 27.2 −j18.1 ohms E = 52.9 V /92.31° I = 1.62 A /126.0°

resistor. The feed line is then disconnected at the antenna and the feed line is connected to the noise bridge in parallel with the resistor used to null the bridge. A receiver is then used to tune and determine the frequencies where the bridge is in balance (minimal noise output).

The approximate length of the cable is usually known. After the program asks for approximate length, it will tell you the approximate lowest frequency where the open cable will balance the noise bridge. This makes it easier to look for the first "dip" frequency. The higher dips will be multiples of the lower one. Let's show how it works with a practical example:

```
(2)                    UNIVERSAL FEEDLINE PROGRAM              by ON4UN
------------------------------------------------------------------------
Zcable: 50 ohm          VELOCITY FACTOR: .66           FREQ:3.75 MHz
WAVELENGTH= 80.00 METER             WAVELENGTH IN CABLE = 52.8 METER
CABLE=60.85 M      OR 2395.6 INCH      OR 414.87 DEG      OR 7.24 RADS
TOTAL ATTENUATION = .73 dB      or .0841 NEPERS
------------------------------------------------------------------------
                 REAL PART     IMAG PART     MAGNITUDE      ANGLE
                 ---------     ---------     ---------      -----
IMPEDANCE (ohm)=    64           -23          68.0074     -19.7672   E
CURRENT (Amp)  =     1            0            1            0        N
VOLTAGE (Volt) =    64           -23          68.0074     -19.7672   D
------------------------------------------------------------------------
IMPEDANCE (ohm)=   56.38         29.56        63.6575      27.6695   A
CURRENT (Amp)  =    .1395        -0.953        .9633      -81.7163   N
VOLTAGE (Volt) =   36.1951      -49.9041      61.6482     -54.0468   T
------------------------------------------------------------------------
POWER INTO COAX  =    64.00 W         POWER INTO LOAD = 52.87 W
TOTAL SYSTEM LOSS=    11.13 W = -0.83 dB                  EFFICIENCY:
FLAT COAX LOSS   =     9.68 W = -0.73 dB                  ----------
SWR COAX LOSS    =     1.45 W = -0.10 dB                     82.61%
INPUT SWR= 1.60/1                  SWR AT LOAD = 1.75/1
------------------------------------------------------------------------
0=Exit  1=Rerun  CHANGE>>>  2=Zend  3=Iend  4=Zk  5=V.fact  6=Att/Fq  7=Lgth
```

Figure A.7 — Screen dump showing the UNIVERSAL FEED LINE PROGRAM in operating mode two, as indicated by the (2) in the top left corner of the screen.

The cable length is approximately 200 feet. The user first has to choose the mode of operation: option two (looking toward the generator) must be selected. Assume we have measured the impedance at the end of the approximately 200 feet of RG-213 cable (with an impedance bridge or a suitable noise bridge) and found it to be $(64 - j23)$ ohms. Assume also that the operating frequency is 3.75 MHz.

The program asks us to enter the line-end impedance $(64 - j23)$ ohms and the line-end current (enter the reference value 1 A $\underline{/0}°$). Now the feed-line parameters must be entered. We need the characteristic impedance (50 ohms for RG-213) and velocity factor (0.66 for RG-213) or dielectric constant (2.3 for solid PE). Next is the nominal cable attenuation. Let's assume we know the attenuation for RG-213 is 0.21 dB per 100 feet at 1 MHz and 0.51 dB at 10 MHz. We need the value at 3.75 MHz. The program will automatically calculate the value for the design frequency. The only thing left now is to specify the cable length. Remember we did not know exactly, so we told the computer it was approximately 200 feet. The computer told us the first cable resonant length (half wave) would be at approximately 1.6 MHz. We found a series of resonant frequencies at 1610, 3230, 4862, 6493 and 8118 kHz. The average difference between the resonant frequencies is

$(8118 - 1610) \div 5 = 1627$ kHz. Now we can enter this frequency (in MHz) into the computer, and the computer will tell us that the line length is exactly 60.85 meters (199.7 feet).

Figure A.7 shows a screen dump of the text example. The program prompt line allows you to change one parameter at a time without having to re-enter all input data.

The power balance is relative. If we want real power we can enter the current. For example, if we enter 5 A current the power into the coax would be $5 \times 5 \times 64 = 1600$ W.

A.3 New Design Programs

The following design programs, listed in Chapter VII of the book, are being rewritten to include loss and phase factor data:

- Voltage Along Feed Line Iteration
- Impedance Along Feed Line Iteration
- Feed Line Transformer (now called Universal Feed Line Transformer)
- Stub Matching

These programs will be made available upon request (and at cost) to owners of the original software.

Index

Notes

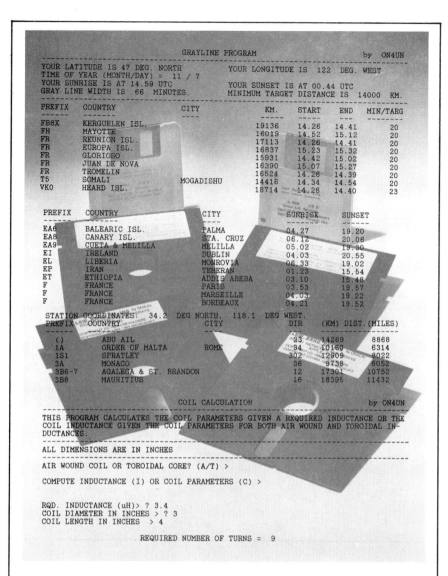

Please use this form to give us your comments on this book and what you'd like to see in future editions.

Name _____ Call sign _____

Address _____ Daytime Phone ( ) _____

City _____ State/Province _____ ZIP/Postal Code _____

From _____

_____

_____

Editor, Low-Band DXing, 2nd Printing
American Radio Relay League
225 Main Street
Newington, CT USA 06111
USA

please fold and tape